The Battle for Leningrad, 1941–1944

The Battle for Leningrad, 1941–1944

David M. Glantz

University Press of Kansas

Published by the University Press of Kansas (Lawrence, Kansas 66049), which was
organized by the Kansas Board of Regents and is operated and funded by Emporia
State University, Fort Hays State University, Kansas State University, Pittsburg State
University, the University of Kansas, and Wichita State University

Library of Congress Cataloging-in-Publication Data

Glantz, David M.
    The battle for Leningrad : 1941–1944 / David M. Glantz.
        p. cm.—(Modern war studies)
    Includes bibliographical references and index.
    ISBN 0-7006-1208-4 (cloth : alk. paper)
    1. Saint Petersburg (Russia)—History—Siege, 1941–1944
I. Title. II. Series.
D764.3.L4 G59 2002
940.54'21721—dc21   2002006749

British Library Cataloguing in Publication Data is available.

Printed in the United States of America

10 9 8 7 6 5 4 3 2

The paper used in this publication meets the minimum requirements of the
American National Standard for Permanence of Paper for Printed Library Materials
Z39.48-1984.

Contents

Part II. Blockade

Part III. Victory

Tables, Maps, and Illustrations

ILLUSTRATIONS

Following page 86:
Adolf Hitler
I. V. Stalin
Colonel General Franz Halder
Field Marshal Ritter von Leeb
Colonel General Erich Hoepner
Colonel General Erich von Manstein
Army General G. K. Zhukov
Marshal of the Soviet Union B. M. Shaposhnikov
Lieutenant General A. M. Vasilevsky
Lieutenant General N. F. Vatutin
Marshal of the Soviet Union K. E. Voroshilov
Colonel General F. I. Kuznetsov
Lieutenant General P. P. Sobennikov
Lieutenant General V. I. Morozov
Major General M. E. Berzarin
Lieutenant General M. M. Popov
A. A. Zhdanov
Red Army T-26 light tank
Red Army T-28 medium tank
Red Army T-35 heavy tank
Red Army BT-7 tank
Red Army T-34 medium tank
Red Army KV-1 heavy tank
Red Army soldiers on parade (1939)
Soviet propaganda poster, "The beginning. . . ."
German infantry advancing during the border battles
Advancing German artillery
Red Army infantry deploying to the front (June 1941)
Red Army poster (1941), "Under the banner of Lenin—Onward to
    victory!"
Red Army poster (1941), "The Motherland calls!"
Dead Red Army soldiers
Red Army troops deploying past the Kirov factory

Following page 148:
Red Army anitaircraft positions along the Neva River
Workers from the Kirov factory erect a barricade
A Leningrad workers battalion heads for the front
Leningrad's first civilian victims

German artillery shells exploding in Leningrad's streets
Red Army infantry marching along the Neva River
Trucks on the "Road of Life"
The evacuation of Soviet industry to the east
Women working in a Soviet arms factory

Following page 232:
Army General K. A. Meretskov
Army General L. A. Govorov and A. A. Zhdanov
Red Army snipers on the Leningrad Front
Red Army wounded receiving assistance
Tanks repaired at the Kirov factory head to the front
German prisoners march down Nevsky Prospect
German "Bertha" siege gun
A Russian "highway"
A building in Leningrad damaged by German artillery
A women's volunteer unit marching through Leningrad
Soviet poster, "Fight to the death!"
Soviet poster, "Soldiers of the Red Army, save us!"
A Red Army antiaircraft gun firing on German aircraft
Soviet poster, "Death to the child killers!"
KV heavy tanks being built at Leningrad's Kirov factory
Civilians evacuating Leningrad by way of Lake Ladoga

Following page 304:
Army General L. A. Govorov and A. A. Zhdanov
The Volkhov Front's Military Council
Lieutenant General I. I. Fediuninsky
Major General N. P. Simoniak
Katiushas firing during the artillery preparation
Red Army officers at a forward observation post
Soldiers of the 86th Rifle Division storm Preobrazhenskaia Hill
German field fortifications and obstacles
Red Army soldiers and tanks in their jumping-off positions
A German heavy gun captured by Red Army forces
Leningrad Front troops assault a German pillbox
Leningrad and Volkhov Front forces link up
A German fuel train blown up by partisans
A Red Army armored train after the cracking of the Leningrad
    blockade
A Red Army woman antiaircraft artillery observer

Following page 366:
K. A. Meretskov, F. P. Ozerov, and G. E. Degtiarev
A. I. Eremenko, L. M. Sandalov, A. P. Pigurov, and V. N. Bogatkin
The 59th Army's Military Council
The Leningrad Front's armor on the attack
The 42d Army's 123d Rifle Corps assaults German defenses
Major General N. P. Simoniak
Troops of the 2d Shock and 42d Armies link up
Leningrad Front soldiers burn a German road sign
Leningrad Front submachine gunners
German destruction of the main hall in the Catherine Palace

Following page 458:
Red Army heavy artillery pounded Finnish defensive positions
A captured Finnish strong point in the Mannerheim Line
Red Army infantry and artillery cross a river on the Karelian Isthmus
Red Army troops passing a destroyed Finnish artillery piece
Red Army aircraft on a bombing mission over the Karelian Isthmus
N. M. Shvernik awards L. A. Govorov
Soldiers of the Leningrad Front celebrate the capture of Vyborg
Red Army troops erect signs along the restored Soviet-Finnish border

No chapter in the Soviet Union's prolonged brutal struggle with Nazi Germany during the Second World War is fraught with greater drama, sacrifice, and sheer human suffering than the titanic three-year battle for the city of Leningrad. Born in war, an enduring crucible of revolution, and Russia's window on the West for both tsar and commissar, Tsar Peter's city has been an enduring symbol of the greatness and often ominous and even threatening potential of the Russian Empire and, later, the Bolshevik Soviet Union, to Russia's enemies. It is therefore understandable that when Adolph Hitler made the Soviet Union a principal objective in Germany's drive for living space (*Lebensraum*), the city of Peter and Lenin became one of the focal points of his ruthless ambition. It could not be otherwise given the city's momentous symbolic, strategic, and ideological significance.

Thousands of books authored by Russian and Western historians and journalists alike have documented the dramatic course of Leningrad's wartime ordeal. Most have described and memorialized the monumental suffering of Leningrad's population during the blockade. The vivid and often poignant descriptions of the human anguish and agony associated with the siege have elevated a few of these works, such as Harrison E. Salisbury's *900 Days* and Dmitrii Pavlov's *Leningrad 1941: The Blockade,* to the status of genuine classics. The personal memoirs of thousands of civilians who endured the ordeal, some accurate and others apocryphal, embellish the gruesome panorama of life during the blockade. While disputes still rage over the full extent of the population's suffering in terms of human loss, no doubt lingers over the nature and magnitude of that suffering or the tortured existence of Leningrad's population during their nearly three-year ordeal.

To this day, however, even the best of these works provide only partial context for this immense tale of human suffering and endurance. As is the case with Red Army military operations during the war as a whole, the military dimensions of the Battle for Leningrad remain appallingly obscure. Though hundreds of Soviet military historians have written numerous tomes on the Red Army's struggle for Leningrad, political and ideological fetters have forced these authors to obfuscate or simply ignore much of the combat that actually took place in the region. Vanity, the Soviet Union's penchant for secrecy in the interest of national security, the preservation of political and military repu-

xiv   The Battle for Leningrad

tations, and the simple desire to avoid political or military embarrassment have combined to produce these yawning gaps in the historical record. These blank pages of history encompass some of the most desperate and heated periods of fighting during the long siege.

As is the case with the war as a whole, the human dimension of the Red Army's titanic military struggle likewise remains tragically obscure. As is the case with other sectors of the front, tens if not hundreds of generals, political commissars, and senior commanders and staff officers who participated in Red Army operations in and around Leningrad during the blockade have described their experiences in memoirs or memoir articles. However, while accurate in general terms, virtually all of these memoirs are seriously flawed by political and ideological constraints prevalent during the periods in which they were written. While a few unexpurgated versions of these heavily censored memoirs have appeared since the fall of the Soviet Union in 1991, they too bear the marks of the censor, and their authors no longer survive to correct them.

Tragically for the historical record, unlike their German counterparts, few Red Army soldiers recorded their wartime experiences, simply because regulations forbade them to do so. Prohibited from keeping diaries in wartime, since war's end simple fear of censure and lack of access to the print media presses have precluded common soldiers from revealing their experiences. Since the fall of the Soviet Union in 1991, a few veteran soldiers have finally overcome their fears and inhibitions and have prepared short memoirs. However, these works are few, and the veterans who wrote them lacked archival access and most had fallen victim to the ravages of old age.

Nor do histories written from the German perspective adequately fill these considerable historical gaps. Mesmerized by the imposing and seemingly unbroken mosaic of titanic battles of almost unprecedented proportions that characterized combat on their Eastern Front, German participants and historians scarcely had either the desire, time, or capacity for detecting and noting the intricacies of the Red Army's military efforts. This applied, in particular, to Red Army operations that failed, the category into which most of the missing 40 percent of the war's forgotten battles fall.

Today, recent Russian archival releases finally permit us to begin correcting the operational record of the Battle for Leningrad and of the war in general.* For the first time, we can compare the extensive archival documentation of German army groups, armies, and subordinate forces, which has long existed, with the new Russian documentation and, by doing so, begin to fill in the historical record.

---

*While by no means complete, the Russian Federation has released many of the *Stavka*'s (Soviet Supreme High Command's) wartime directives and associated orders and transcripts of conversations between it and the Red Army's operating *fronts*.

Sadly, given the near total absence of soldiers' memoirs, this volume is primarily a history of military operations. Rather than replicating the already superb accounts written about the unparalleled human suffering engendered by the siege, it simply seeks to establish a sounder and more accurate description of the military operations that provided essential context for all else that occurred at Leningrad. Further, it represents a modest beginning in what will undoubtedly be a long process of restoring to public view what actually occurred during the Leningraders' 900 days of unsurpassed trial under fire. This book is dedicated to the 1.6–2 million soldiers and civilians who perished during the battle and siege, the 2.4 million soldiers who became casualties, the 1.6 million civilians who escaped or survived the siege, and the countless millions of people scarred by the Battle for Leningrad.

Dramatis Personae

Akimov, Lieutenant General S. D.: Deputy Commander, Northwestern Front (June–August 1941); Acting Commander, 5th Airborne Corps (June–July 1941); and Commander, 48th Army (August 1941).

Antoniuk, Lieutenant General M. A.: Commander, Petrozavodsk Operational Group, 7th Separate Army (June–September 1941), 48th Army (September 1941), and 60th Army (July 1942).

Cherepanov, Lieutenant General A. I.: Chief Inspector in the Northwestern Direction High Command (July–September 1941); Commander, 23d Army (September 1941–July 1944); Assistant and Deputy Chairman, Union Control Commission, Bulgaria (November 1944–1945).

Dukhanov, Lieutenant General M. P.: Commander, 10th Rifle Division (September 1941); Chief of Staff, Neva Operational Group (October 1941); Deputy Commander and Commander, Neva Operational Group (October 1941–October 1942); Commander, 67th Army (October 1942–December 1943); Deputy Commander, 8th Army (March 1944–May 1945).

Fediuninsky, Colonel General I. I.: Commander, 15th Rifle Corps, 5th Army (June–August 1941), 32d Army (August–September 1941), 42d Army (September–October 1941), Leningrad Front (October 1941), 54th Army (October 1941–April 1942), 5th Army (April–October 1942); Deputy Commander, Volkhov Front (October 1942–May 1943), Briansk Front (May–July 1943); Commander, 11th Army (July–December 1943), 2d Shock Army (December 1943–May 1945).

Galanin, Major General I. V.: Commander, 12th Army (August–October 1941), 59th Army (November 1941–April 1942); Deputy Commander, Western Front (May–August 1942), Voronezh Front (August–September 1942); Commander, 24th Army (October 1942–April 1943), 70th Army (April–September 1943), 4th Guards Army (September 1943–January 1944), 53d Army (January–February 1944), 4th Guards Army (February–November 1944).

Govorov, Marshal of the Soviet Union L. A.: Chief, Dzerzhinsky Artillery Academy (May–July 1941); Chief of Artillery, Western Direction and Reserve

Front (July–August 1941); Deputy Commander, Mozhaisk Defense Line and Chief of Artillery, Western Front (August–October 1941); Commander, 5th Army (October 1941–April 1942), Leningrad Group of Forces (April–June 1942), Leningrad Front (June 1942–May 1945).

Gusev, Colonel General N. I.: Commander, 25th Cavalry Division (July 1941–January 1942), 13th Cavalry Corps (January–June 1942), 4th Army (June 1942–November 1943), 20th, 47th, and 48th Armies (November 1943–May 1945).

Iakovlev, Lieutenant General V. F.: Chief of Rear Services, Southwestern Front, and Deputy Chief, Red Army General Staff (June–September 1941); Commander, 4th Army (September–November 1941), 52d Army (January 1942–July 1943); Deputy Commander, Steppe Front (August–October 1943); Commander, Belorussian and Stavropol' Military Districts (1943–1946).

Ivanov, Lieutenant General F. S.: 2d Deputy Commander, Kiev Special Military District (June 1941); Commander, 8th Army (June–August 1941), 42d Army (August–September 1941), Leningrad garrison and internal defense (September–December 1941). Assigned to the Leningrad Front Military Council (15 December) and the NKO's Main Cadre Directorate (18 January 1942). Arrested on 22 January 1942; imprisoned until 8 January 1946; freed on 15 January 1946; retired in 1952.

Khozin, Lieutenant General M. S.: Chief of Rear Services, Front of Reserve Armies, and Deputy Chief, Red Army General Staff (June–September 1941); Chief of Staff, Leningrad Front (September–October 1941); Commander, 54th Army (September–October 1941), Leningrad Front (October 1941–June 1942), 33d Army (June–December 1942), 20th Army (December 1942–February 1943), and Special Group Khozin (February–March 1943); Deputy Commander, Western Front (March 1943–March 1944); Commander, Volga Military District (March 1944–May 1945).

Klykov, Lieutenant General N. K.: Commander, 32d Army (July–August 1941), 52d Army (August 1941–January 1942), 2d Shock Army (January–April, July–December 1942); Deputy Commander, Volkhov Front (December 1942–June 1943), Moscow Military District (June 1943–June 1944), North Caucasus Military District (1944–1945).

Korovnikov, Lieutenant General I. T.: Commander, Northwestern Front operational group and Novgorod Army Group of Forces operational group (June 1941–January 1942), 2d Shock Army operational group (January–April 1942), 59th Army (April 1942–May 1945).

Kulik, Marshal of the Soviet Union G. I.: Deputy People's Commissar of Defense and Chief, Red Army Main Artillery Directorate (1939–1941); Commander, 54th Army (August–September 1941). Relieved of command and assigned to the NKO (September 1941–April 1943). Com-

mander, 4th Guards Army (April–September 1943); Deputy Chief, NKO
Directorate for the Formation and Manning of the Soviet Army (January
1944–May 1945).

Kurochkin, Colonel General P. A.: Commander, 20th Army (July–August
1941), and 43d Army (August 1941); *Stavka* representative, Northwestern Front, Commander, Northwestern Front, and Deputy Commander,
Northwestern Front (August 1941–October 1942, June–November 1943);
Commander, 11th Army (November 1942–March 1943), 34th Army
(March–June 1943); Deputy Commander, 1st Ukrainian Front (December 1943–February 1944); Commander, 2d Belorussian Front (February–April 1944), 60th Army (April 1944–May 1945).

Kuznetsov, Lieutenant General A. A.: 2d Secretary, Leningrad Communist
Party Regional and City Council (1938–1945); Member, Baltic Fleet Military Council (1938–1946), Northern Front Military Council (June–August
1941), Leningrad Front Military Council (September 1941–December
1942, March 1943–May 1945), 2d Shock Army Military Council (December 1942–March 1943).

Kuznetsov, Colonel General F. I.: Commander, Baltic Special Military Dis-
trict and Northwestern Front (June–October 1941); Commander, 21st
Army and Central Front, Chief of Staff, 28th Army, Commander, 51st
Army, Deputy Commander, Western Front, and Commander, 61st Army
(October 1941–April 1942); Chief, General Staff Academy, and Deputy
Commander, Volkhov and Karelian Fronts (April 1942–February 1945);
Commander, Ural Military District (February 1945–1948).

Lazarov, Major General I. G.: Commander, 10th Mechanized Corps (June–
September 1941), 55th Army (September–November 1941).

Maslennikov, Colonel General I. I.: (NKVD officer); Commander, 29th Army
(July–December 1941), 39th Army, North Caucasus Front's Northern
Group of Forces, North Caucasus Front (December 1941–May 1943);
Deputy Commander, Volkhov, Southwestern, and 3d Ukrainian Fronts
(May–December 1943); Commander, 42d Army (December 1943–March
1944); Deputy Commander, Leningrad Front (March–April 1944); Com-
mander, 3d Baltic Front (April 1944–1945).

Mekhlis, L. Z.: Chief, Red Army's Main Political Directorate and Deputy
People's Commissar of Defense (1941–1942); *Stavka* representative,
Volkhov Front (January 1942), Crimean Front (February–May 1942);
Member, 6th Army Military Council, Voronezh Front Military Council,
Volkhov Front Military Council, Briansk Front Military Council, 2d Baltic
Front Military Council, Western Front Military Council, 2d Belorussian
Front Military Council, 4th Ukrainian Front Military Council (1942–1944).

Meretskov, Army General K. A.: Deputy People's Commissar of Defense
(January–September 1941); *Stavka* representative, Northwestern and

Karelian Fronts (August–September 1941). Arrested, imprisoned, but ex-
onerated (September–October 1941). Commander, 7th Separate Army
(October–November 1941), 4th Army (November–December 1941),
Volkhov Front (December 1941–May 1942, June 1942–February 1944);
Commander, 33d Army (May–June 1942), Karelian Front (February–
August 1945), 1st Far Eastern Front (August–September 1945).

Piadyshev, Lieutenant General K. P.: 1st Deputy Commander, Northern
Front (June–July 1941); Commander, Luga Operational Group (6 July–
August 1941). Arrested (23 July), sentenced to 10 years' imprisonment,
died in prison in 1943. Rehabilitated posthumously in 1968.

Popov, Lieutenant General M. M.: Commander, Northern and Leningrad
Fronts (June–September 1941), 61st and 40th Armies (November 1941–
October 1942); Deputy Commander, Stalingrad and Southwestern Fronts,
and Commander, 5th Shock and 5th Tank Armies (October 1942–January
1943); Commander, Mobile Group Popov (February–March 1943), Reserve Front and Steppe Military District (April–May 1943), Briansk Front
(June–October 1943), Baltic and 2d Baltic Fronts (October 1943–April
1944); Chief of Staff, Leningrad and 2d Baltic Fronts (April 1944–July
1945).

Roginsky, Lieutenant General S. V.: Commander, 111th (24th Guards) Rifle
Division (July 1941–April 1942), 6th Guards Rifle Corps (April–June
1942), 4th Guards Rifle Corps (September–October 1942); Deputy Commander, 59th, 8th, and 2d Shock Armies (June–September 1942, October 1942–March 1943); Commander, 54th Army (March 1943–December
1944), 67th Army (February–May 1945).

Romanovsky, Lieutenant General V. Z.: Commander, Arkhangel'sk Military
District (1941–1942); Deputy Commander and Commander, 1st Shock
Army (May-December 1942). Commander, 2d Shock Army (December
1942–December 1943); Deputy Commander, 4th Ukrainian Front (De-
cember 1943–March 1944); Commander, 42d Army (March 1944), 67th
Army (March 1944–March 1945, 19th Army (March–May 1945).

Shcherbakov, Major General V. I.: Commander, 50th Rifle Corps (June–
August 1941), 8th, 42d, and 11th Armies (August–September 1941);
Deputy Commander, 23d Army (September 1941–March 1942); Com-
mander, 14th Army (March 1942–May 1945).

Shevaldin, Lieutenant General T. I.: Commandant, Krasnogvardeisk Fortified Region (August 1941); Commander, 8th Army (September–November 1941).

Simoniak, Lieutenant General N. P.: Commander, 8th Separate Rifle Brigade
(June 1941–March 1942), 136th (63d Guards) Rifle Division (March 1942–
April 1943), 30th Guards Rifle Corps (April 1943–October 1944), 3d Shock
Army (October 1944–March 1945), 67th Army (March–May 1945).

Sobennikov, Lieutenant General P. P.: Commander, 8th Army (March–June 1941), Northwestern Front (July–August 1941), 43d Army (September–October 1941); Deputy Commander, 3d Army (1942–May 1945).

Sokolov, Lieutenant General G. G.: (NKVD officer); Commander, 2d Shock Army (December 1941–January 1942).

Stalin, Marshal of the Soviet Union I. V.: First Secretary, Communist Party of the Soviet Union (1941–1945); Chairman, State Defense Committee (GKO) (1941–1945); Chairman, *Stavka VGK* (1941–1945); People's Commissar of Defense (1941–1945); Supreme High Commander, Soviet Armed Forces (1941–1945); Generalissimo (1945).

Starikov, Lieutenant General F. N.: Chief, Luga Operational Group's Eastern Sector (July–August 1941); Commander, 19th Rifle Corps (August–September 1941), 23d Army, Siniavino Operational Group (December 1941–January 1942); Deputy Commander, 8th Army and Volkhov Operational Group (January–April 1942); Commander, 8th Army (April 1942–May 1945).

Sukhomlin, Lieutenant General A. V.: Chief of Staff, Northwestern Front and 54th Army (June 1941–January 1942); Commander, 8th Army (January–April 1942), 54th Army (April 1942–March 1943); Deputy Commander, Volkhov Front (March–September 1943); Commander, 10th Guards Army (September 1943–February 1944); 1st Deputy Chief, Frunze Academy (February 1944–May 1945).

Sviridov, Lieutenant General V. P.: Chief of Artillery, Northern Front, and Chief of Artillery and Deputy Commander, Leningrad Front (June–November 1941); Commander, 55th Army (November 1941–December 1943), 67th Army (December 1943–March 1944), 42d Army (March 1944–May 1945).

Timoshenko, Marshal of the Soviet Union S. K.: People's Commissar of Defense (May 1940–June 1941); Deputy People's Commissar of Defense (July–September 1941); Commander, Western Direction and Western Front (July–September 1941), Southwestern Direction and Southwestern Front (September 1941–June 1942), Stalingrad Front (July–October 1942), Northwestern Front (October 1942–March 1943); *Stavka* representative, Leningrad and Volkhov Fronts (March–June 1943), North Caucasus Front and Black Sea Fleet (June–November 1943), 2d and 3d Baltic Fronts (February–June 1944), 2d, 3d, and 4th Ukrainian Fronts (August 1944–May 1945).

Tributs, Admiral V. F.: Commander, Baltic Fleet (1939–1947).

Vatutin, Army General N. F.: 1st Deputy Chief, Red Army General Staff (1941); Chief of Staff, Northwestern Front (June–August 1941); Deputy Chief, Red Army General Staff (May–July 1942); Commander, Voronezh Front (July–October 1942, March–October 1943), Southwestern Front

(October 1942–March 1943), 1st Ukrainian Front (March 1943–March 1944). Killed by partisans in March 1944.

Vlasov, Lieutenant General A. A.: Commander, 99th Rifle Division and 4th Mechanized Corps (June–July 1941), 37th Army (July–October 1941), 20th Army (October 1941–February 1942); Deputy Commander, Volkhov Front (February–April 1942); Commander, 2d Shock Army (April–July 1942). Captured by the Germans in July 1942.

Voronov, Chief Marshal of Artillery N. N.: Deputy People's Commissar of Defense (1941); Chief, Red Army Main Directorate for Air Defense (1941); Chief of Artillery, Red Army, and Deputy Commissar of Defense (July 1941–March 1943); *Stavka* representative, Leningrad Front (October–November 1941); Commander, Red Army artillery (March 1943–1946).

Voroshilov, Marshal of the Soviet Union K. E.: Member, State Defense Committee (GKO) and *Stavka* (1941–1944); Commander, Northwestern Direction Main Command (July–August 1941), Leningrad Front (September 1941); *Stavka* representative, Volkhov Front (February–March 1942), Leningrad and Volkhov Fronts (December 1942–January 1943), Separate Coastal Army (December 1943).

Zhdanov, A. A.: Secretary, Communist Party Central Committee and Leningrad Regional and City Party Committees (1934–44); Permanent Advisor, *Stavka* VGK (June 1941); Member, Northwestern Direction Command Military Council (June–August 1941), Leningrad Front Military Council (September 1941–July 1945), Red Army's Main Political Directorate's Military-Political Propaganda Council.

Zhukov, Marshal of the Soviet Union G. K.: Chief of Staff, Red Army, and Deputy People's Commissar of Defense (January–June 1941); Member, *Stavka* VGK (1941–1945); 1st Deputy People's Commissar of Defense and Supreme High Commander (August 1942–1945); *Stavka* VGK representative, Southwestern Front (June 1941); Commander, Reserve Front (July–September 1941), Leningrad Front (September–October 1941), Western Front (October 1941–August 1942), Western Direction Main Command (February–May 1942); *Stavka VGK* representative, Reserve Front (October 1941), Western and Kalinin Fronts (November–December 1942), Leningrad and Volkhov Fronts (January 1943), Northwestern Front (February–March 1943), Voronezh and Steppe Fronts (April 1943), North Caucasus Front (April–May 1943), Voronezh, Central, and Western Fronts (May–June 1943), Southwestern Front (June 1943), Briansk, Central, and Western Fronts (June–July 1943), Steppe and Voronezh Fronts (August–September 1943), Central and Voronezh Fronts (September–December 1943), 1st and 2d Ukrainian Fronts (January–March 1944); Commander, 1st Ukrainian Front (March–May 1944);

Stavka VGK representative, 1st and 2d Belorussian and 1st Ukrainian Fronts (June–August 1944), 3d Ukrainian Front (September 1944), 1st and 2d Belorussian and 1st Ukrainian Fronts (September–November 1944); Commander, 1st Belorussian Front (November 1944–May 1945).

GERMAN

Busch, Colonel General Ernst: Commander, Sixteenth Army (June 1941–October 1943), Army Group Center (October 1943–June 1944).

Halder, Colonel General Franz: Chief, Army General Staff (OKH) (1941–September 1942).

Hoepner, Colonel General Erich: Commander, Fourth Panzer Group (June 1941–January 1942).

Keitel, Colonel General Wilhelm: Chief, German Armed Forces (OKW) (1941–1945).

Kuechler, Colonel General Georg von: Commander, Eighteenth Army (June–January 1942); Commander, Army Group North (January 1942–February 1944).

Leeb, Field Marshal Ritter von: Commander, Army Group North (June 1941–January 1942).

Lindemann, Colonel General Georg: Commander, L Army Corps (June 1941–January 1942), Eighteenth Army (January 1942–February 1944).

Manstein, Field Marshal Erich von: Commander, LVI Motorized Corps (March–September 1941), Eleventh Army (September 1941–December 1942), Army Group Don (December 1942–February 1943), Army Group South (February 1943–March 1944).

Model, Field Marshal Walter: Commander, Ninth Army (June 1941–February 1944), Army Group North (February–March 1944), Army Group South and North Ukraine (March–June 1944), Army Group Center (June–August 1944), Western Theater (August 1944–April 1945). Killed in action in the Ruhr region in April 1945.

Reinhardt, Colonel General Hans: Commander, XXXXI Motorized Corps (June–October 1941), Third Panzer Group and Third Panzer Army (October 1941–August 1944), Army Group Center (August 1944–January 1945).

Schmidt, Colonel General Rudolf: Commander, XXXIX Motorized Corps (June–November 1941), Second Army and Army Group Schmidt (November 1941–January 1942), Second Panzer Army (January 1942–July 1943).

Zeitzler, Colonel General Kurt: Chief of Staff, Army Group "D" (1941–1942); Chief, Army General Staff (OKH) (September 1942–July 1944).

PART I
BARBAROSSA

CHAPTER 1

The City of Peter and Lenin

Lenin's namesake city, the former city of Petrograd and St. Petersburg, was, by history and reputation, an enticing target for Adolph Hitler when he began planning his invasion of the Soviet Union in summer 1940. This could not be otherwise given the city's long and illustrious history. From its founding in 1703 as St. Petersburg, the city's history reflected its strategic importance as the northwestern gateway to Russia, an important political, economic, and cultural center, and an enduring symbol of revolution. Consequently, along with Moscow, the capital of old Muscovy as well as the new Bolshevik State, and Kiev, the ancient capital of Kievan Rus and modern Ukraine, Leningrad, the cradle of revolution, occupied an honored place among the initial strategic objectives Hitler assigned his *Wehrmacht* in his crusade against Russian Bolshevism.

FOUNDING

Tsar Peter 1 (The Great), the father of the modern Russian Empire, founded St. Petersburg, Leningrad's imperial ancestor, in 1703 during the Great Northern War with King Charles XII of Sweden. Peter founded his new city on primordial Russian land adjacent to the old Varangian trade routes to Byzantium, which had belonged to the feudal principalities of Novgorod in the ninth and tenth centuries and Izhorsk in the thirteenth century. The land upon which Peter constructed his city had become part of Russia (former Muscovy) in 1478 along with the remainder of Novgorod, when Tsar Ivan III (The Great) defeated his powerful neighbor Lithuania and forced Novgorod to submit to Russian rule. Soon after, in 1494 Ivan ended German influence in the region, when he expelled the Hanseatic merchants, the heirs of the former Teutonic Knights, from the region.[1]

After 200 years of incessant wars, Peter I completed the consolidation of the Russian state that his illustrious predecessors had begun. While struggling to gain supremacy in the Baltic region, on 11 October 1702, Peter's forces stormed the Swedish fort at Noteborg near the old Russian town of Oreshek at the junction of the Neva River and Lake Ladoga and renamed the fortress Shlissel'burg ("key city"). In May of the following year, Peter's armies captured the small Swedish fort at Nyenschantz at the junction of the Neva and Okhta rivers and renamed it St. Petersburg. Below the walls of the old fort, he built the Fortress of St. Petersburg (later renamed Petropavlovsk Fortress) on Zaiachii Island. The same year, Peter built a port, a trade exchange, trading posts, and a palace on Lake Berzovyi, which later was renamed Lake Petrogradskii. Peter completed construction of these new military installations in the winter of 1703–1704 when he built Kronshlot (renamed Kronshtadt after 1723) Fortress on Kotlin Island and, still later, the Admiralty Fortress on the left bank of the Neva River.

Peter constructed these military facilities and the extensive new port, trading posts, and palaces that grew up around them in a strategically vital geographical location at the mouth of the Neva River and on 42 islands in the river's delta. Once fully developed, the city encompassed an area of 570 square kilometers (220 square miles), bordered on the north by the Pargolovo highlands, on the south by the Pulkova, Duderhof, and Ligovo highlands, and on the east by the Koltushi highlands. The city's coastal climate, which was characterized by mild winters and frequent thaws, contrasted sharply with that of the remainder of Russia. The city's average temperature is 7.9°C (46.22°F) in January and 17.7°C (63.9°F) in July. Then as now, the adjacent Neva River is generally frozen for four months each year.[2]

The founding of the city signaled the completion of a century-long struggle between Russian princes and tsars and their German (Teutonic), Lithuanian, Swedish, and Polish counterparts for permanent Russian access to the Baltic Sea. Peter's strenuous building effort underscored his intent to gain and maintain access to the Baltic as Russia's strategically vital "Window on the West." At the same time, however, the city's location on marshland required that, over a period of many months, thousands of wooden piles be driven deep into the earth to create a stable foundation for the city. Peasants forcibly recruited from their squires all across Russia accomplished most of this arduous and often dangerous work. Tens of thousands of lives were lost to epidemics during the city's hasty construction. Thus a tradition of suffering was established that the city's population would replicate in the twentieth century.

DEVELOPMENT

After its founding, the conscious decision reached by Peter and many of his imperial successors to make the city the seat of Russian imperial power, complete with many of the trappings of a modern Western city, only burnished St. Petersburg's reputation, strategic value, and prestige. Even though the city remained a relatively crude backwater during Peter's lifetime, under his descendants, Elizabeth (1741–1762) and Catherine II (the Great) (1762–

1796), St. Petersburg became a beautiful shining city, worthy of the title "Capital of the Russian Empire." The period of the two empresses' rule represented the golden age of Russian nobility, a legendary age of Russian opulence and glitter, and a spectacular age for the city of St. Petersburg. Throughout this half-century, the city developed rapidly according to a distinct plan, and its development came to symbolize the dramatic achievements of Russia's population and the development of Russian imperial power as a whole.

The city served as the capital of the Russian Empire from 1712, when Peter the Great boldly moved his court to the partially completed city as a symbol of Russia's resolve to retain its "Window to the West," until 1728. That year, however, Peter's grandson, Peter II, who disliked the city's rough frontier nature and coarseness, moved the imperial court back to Moscow. After Peter II's death in 1732 at age 15, his more illustrious successor, Empress Anna, the daughter of Peter the Great's brother Ivan V, who had ruled prior to Peter the Great, succeeded Peter II to the throne. She promptly echoed her famous uncle's intent by moving the imperial capital back to St. Petersburg. There it remained until 1918.

By the mid-eighteenth century, Peter and his imperial successors had transformed St. Petersburg into Russia's most important political, administrative, cultural, and military center and a main outpost on the country's northwestern border. Characterized by its brilliant court, extensive military establishment and bureaucracy, and imposing shipbuilding and ordnance industries, St. Petersburg became Russia's most important political, administrative, cultural, and military center. Symbolizing the city's military importance, the famous Putilov Ordnance Works were founded in the city in 1801, beginning the city's great reputation as a center of the arms production industry. The city's growth from a population of 425,000 in 1825 to 1,534,000 in 1905 reflected its growing importance.[3]

Throughout its history, St. Petersburg developed a distinct symbolism and mystique of its own, which endured even after tsarist times. For more than 200 years, the city represented a bulwark of autocracy, nobility, and later, the bourgeoisie (middle class), which burgeoned in late nineteenth-century Russia. At the same time, it was an advanced center of Russian scientific activity and culture and the focal point of progressive thought and social and revolutionary movements, in part due to its proximity to the West and its population's contact with Western thought.

Understandably then, a certain creative tension emerged between Peter's, Elizabeth's, and Catherine's fledgling city and Moscow, the old capital of the Muscovite state, which had been Ivan the Terrible's seat of power. St. Petersburg clearly came to signify a Europeanized Russia and a "Window to the West," while Moscow represented "Old Mother Russia" and Russia's massive Slavic heartland, which was still geographically, intellectually, and culturally remote from the rest of modern Europe. Accordingly, while Peter I lived, St. Petersburg "stood for the tutelary light of the West against the Byzantine dark of Moscow."[4] Thereafter, both in terms of population and prestige, St. Petersburg tended to eclipse Moscow, whose population reached 306,000 in 1830 and 1,092,000 in 1905.[5] Despite its disadvantages, throughout the nineteenth century, Moscow gradually recouped its influence and power by becoming a major manufacturing and commercial center, particularly for the textile industry, and, through Moscow University, a vibrant center of intellectual activity.

Given its vastly increased stature and prestige, St. Petersburg inevitably emerged as a focal point for Russia's international and internal struggles. As its sole military outpost along the Baltic Sea, St. Petersburg played a major role in Russia's Great Northern War (1700–1721) with Sweden as an operational base for its ground forces and the fledgling Baltic Fleet. During the Crimean War (1853–1856) over two centuries later, the Kronshtadt Fortress with its associated defensive installations and the Baltic Fleet prevented an Anglo-French squadron from reaching St. Petersburg (1855) and attacking Kronshtadt. The fortress and fleet limited the British and French forces to blockading the coast and bombarding Russian coastal cities along the Gulf of Finland. Quite naturally, however, the war produced subtle changes, prompting St. Petersburg to become more Russian in mood and composition.

While he recognized Leningrad's importance as a prestigious political, economic, and cultural center, Hitler also viewed Leningrad as a citadel of revolution and the birthplace of his arch enemy, Bolshevism. In the distant and recent past, specifically in 1820, 1825, the period 1905–1907, February 1918, August 1918, October 1918, and 1921, the city had been the site of vigorous and often violent revolutionary outbursts. Throughout this period, St. Petersburg's nobility, bourgeoisie, and, later, its proletariat formed the vanguard of the Russian social and political revolutionary movement.

Russian Guards officers were exposed to Western revolutionary ideas during the War of Liberation against Napoleon (1813–1814), during which Russian armies marched through Central Europe and helped liberate Paris. When they returned to Russia after the war, in the period 1816–1817, these officers founded the Union of Salvation, a secret revolutionary political society in St. Petersburg whose goal was to promote representative government and liberate the serfs. The Union was reestablished in 1818 as the Union of Welfare, a secret organization that harbored distinctly anti-foreign overtones. During this period, on 16 October 1820, the soldiers of the tsar's Semenovsky Regiment revolted against what they viewed as the arbitrary and unwarranted policies of Tsar Alexander II, who, in their view, failed to act vigorously enough to embrace revolutionary reform. The ensuing Decembrist movement, an organization rooted in the earlier revolutionary "unions," fostered a popular revolt on Senate Square on 14 (26) December 1825, which loyal tsarist troops bloodily suppressed.[6]

Throughout the latter half of the nineteenth century, such "democratic" and revolutionary leaders as V. G. Belinsky, N. G. Chernyshevsky, N. A. Dobroliubov, and D. I. Pisarev gravitated to the city. Through their writings and speeches, these figures only enhanced St. Petersburg's image as a center of revolutionary thought and ferment. Shortly before the turn of the twentieth century, in 1895, V. I. Lenin formed his Union for the Struggle of the Working Class in St. Petersburg, an organization which began to introduce the principles of Marxist socialism to the city's workers' movement. Subsequently, the city was the site of many of the most important events of the Revolution of 1905 to 1907, including the Kronshtadt mutiny of 8 November 1904 and Bloody Sunday on 9 January 1905, when tsarist troops fired on and killed many demonstrators.

When the First World War broke out in 1914, the Russian government renamed St. Petersburg "Petrograd" to eradicate its association with all things German. The ensuing war, with its numerous operational catastrophes, immense human costs, and appalling economic consequences for the Russian people, ravaged the Russian Army and had a shockingly demoralizing effect on the Russian government and people. Stirred to action by war's ill effects, the bourgeois-democratic revolution of February (March) 1917 and the socialist revolution of October (November) radiated from their focal point in St. Petersburg. In the wake of the February Revolution, in August the city's workers successfully resisted a counterrevolutionary coup attempt led by General L. G. Kornilov and, in so doing, elevated the workers' soviets (councils) to new preeminence in the revolutionary movement.

The historic meeting of the Russian Bolshevik Party Central Committee, where Lenin's resolution concerning armed uprising was adopted, took place in Petrograd on 10 (23) October 1917.[7] On 12 (25) October, the Petrograd Soviet organized the Petrograd Military-Revolutionary Committee as the headquarters for Lenin's planned revolutionary uprising. The Red Guards, the revolutionary force of revolutionary workers, soldiers, and sailors, under Bolshevik leadership, seized key governmental installations and strategic control of the city on 25 October (7 November), in accordance with Lenin's plan. The Red Guards stormed the Winter Palace on 26 October (8 November) and arrested members of Alexander Kerensky's Provisional Government.[8]

The same day, the 2d All-Russian Congress of Soviets convened in the city. The Congress immediately issued decrees transferring all power to the soviets, promulgated Lenin's decrees on peace, land, and bread, and created the world's first workers' and peasants' government—the Soviet of People's Commissars, under Lenin's leadership. Within days, on 31 October (13 November), the revolutionary soldiers and workers had defeated

Kerensky's and Krasnov's counterrevolutionary forces at Pulkovo Heights, two days after they suppressed Junkers (military students) loyal to the former Provisional Government.

Petrograd remained the focal point of Bolshevik power as the party extended its control over the entire country. In early 1918, while the former tsarist army was demobilizing and the Red Guard was being transformed into a new Red Army, the Germans began an advance on Petrograd, Minsk, Kiev (18 February), and Odessa (28 February).[9] Since the Red Guards and fledgling Red Army were in no state to halt the German advance, Lenin's Bolshevik government had no choice but to assent to the unequal Treaty of Brest-Litovsk (3 March 1918). The harsh treaty stripped the Soviet state of much of Russia's former western territories and established its new western border along the Narva River and southward through Pskov.

With the security of its western border in doubt and insurrection looming from virtually every direction, on 9 March 1918, the Bolsheviks moved the country's capital from Petrograd to Moscow, where it remained thereafter. The city then became a focal point of civil war and a priority target for the White armies as they sought to overthrow Bolshevik rule. Twice during 1919 (from May through August and in October and November), the White forces of General N. Iudenich's Northwestern Army attempted to seize Petrograd in conjunction with General Denikin's and Admiral Kolchak's White armies, which were advancing against Moscow from the south and east. Both of Iudenich's offensives failed, in part due to stiff but crude resistance by the Red Army and Petrograd's worker militia and also because of flagging Allied support. About 170,000 Leningraders saw service in the Red Army during the Civil War. On 5 December 1919, the 7th All-Russian Congress of Soviets awarded Leningrad's "proletariat" collectively with the Order of the Red Banner for its steadfast resistance and service to the revolution.[10]

Nor did Leningrad's revolutionary traditions cease in Bolshevik (Communist) times. After several harsh years of increasingly draconian political repression accompanied by outbreaks of famine incurred by Lenin's severe policy of war communism, the sailors of the Kronshtadt naval base revolted in protest in February and March 1921. Although forces led by War Commissar Leon Trotsky managed to suppress the uprising brutally, the sailors' actions prompted Lenin to introduce his more lenient New Economic Policy (NEP) at the 10th Party Congress in March 1921. After Lenin was felled by a stroke in 1921, at the request of the city's workers, the 2d Congress of Soviets of the USSR changed Petrograd's name to Leningrad on 26 January 1924.

Leningrad continued its perceived notoriety as a revolutionary city during the 1930s while Stalin was busily consolidating his power. S. M. Kirov, the charismatic Leningrad Party first secretary since 1924, became a potential rival to Stalin by virtue of his popularity within the Party, his advocacy of a moderate policy of economic reform, and his opposition to Stalin's early program of repression. Ostensibly a distraught Trotskyite student murdered Kirov on 1 December 1934. Actually, however, Stalin orchestrated Kirov's murder to rid himself of a rival and establish justification for his subsequent wholesale purge of potential opponents within the Party's apparatus.[11] Many appreciated Leningrad's close identification with Kirov's "liberal socialism" and believed that Stalin's subsequent harsh treatment of the city during and after the Second World War reflected his hatred for Kirov and his fear of the city's liberal influence.

Leningrad's association with war continued during the initial phases of the Second World War. In the wake of the Molotov-Ribbentrop Nonaggression Pact between Hitler and Stalin in 1939, the Soviet Union provoked war with Finland, ostensibly to improve the defenses along its northwestern borders. During the ensuing Soviet-Finnish War (1939–1940), usually referred to as the Winter War, the Leningrad Military District became the controlling headquarters and operational and logistical base for Red Army operations against Finland. The Red Army's parlous performance during the war, and particularly during its first phase, encouraged Hitler to undertake Operation Barbarossa. From the very beginning of his planning for a summer 1940 invasion, Leningrad, by then a city with a population of 2,544,000 souls, became one of Hitler's priority wartime objectives (see Maps 1 and 2).

Hitler reasoned that the destruction of the Soviet state and, with it, the force of international Bolshevism required the capture of Leningrad and, if necessary, its obliteration from the earth. This was the ugly judgment that Hitler's *Wehrmacht* sought to inflict upon the city of Peter and Lenin.

MILITARY ORGANIZATION

Given its long and illustrious military past and its current political, economic, cultural, and strategic importance, Leningrad was an appropriate target for Hitler's wrath. Overall responsibility for the city's defense rested with the Soviet government and central military and administrative organs. Obviously, this included I. V. Stalin, Chief of State and First Secretary of the Communist Party; Marshal of the Soviet Union S. K. Timoshenko, the USSR's Commissar of Defense; and Army General G. K. Zhukov, Chief of the Red Army's General Staff. Regional and local representatives of these organs were directly responsible for the city's defense. Administratively, this included officials of the Leningrad region *(oblast')*, administrations and councils *(sovet)* in districts *(raion)*, cities *(gorod)*, and towns within the Leningrad region, and the mayors of those cities and towns. Politically, A. A. Zhdanov, Stalin's close associate, a member of the Politburo, and arguably Stalin's heir apparent, headed

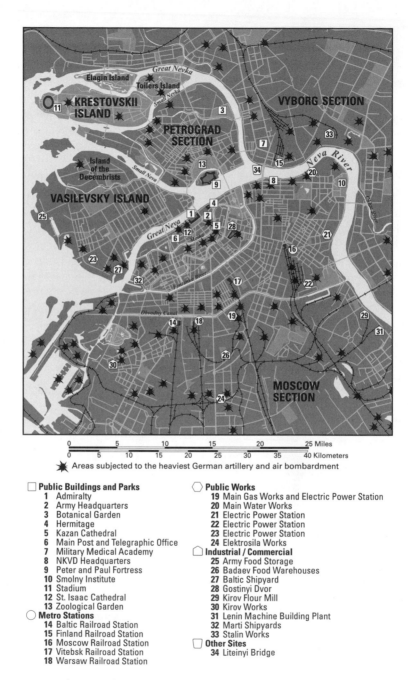

Areas subjected to the heaviest German artillery and air bombardment

□ Public Buildings and Parks	◇ Public Works
1 Admiralty	**19** Main Gas Works and Electric Power Station
2 Army Headquarters	**20** Main Water Works
3 Botanical Garden	**21** Electric Power Station
4 Hermitage	**22** Electric Power Station
5 Kazan Cathedral	**23** Electric Power Station
6 Main Post and Telegraphic Office	**24** Elektrosila Works
7 Military Medical Academy	◠ Industrial / Commercial
8 NKVD Headquarters	**25** Army Food Storage
9 Peter and Paul Fortress	**26** Badaev Food Warehouses
10 Smolny Institute	**27** Baltic Shipyard
11 Stadium	**28** Gostinyi Dvor
12 St. Isaac Cathedral	**29** Kirov Flour Mill
13 Zoological Garden	**30** Kirov Works
◯ Metro Stations	**31** Lenin Machine Building Plant
14 Baltic Railroad Station	**32** Marti Shipyards
15 Finland Railroad Station	**33** Stalin Works
16 Moscow Railroad Station	□ Other Sites
17 Vitebsk Railroad Station	**34** Liteinyi Bridge
18 Warsaw Railroad Station	

Map 1. The City of Leningrad, June 1941

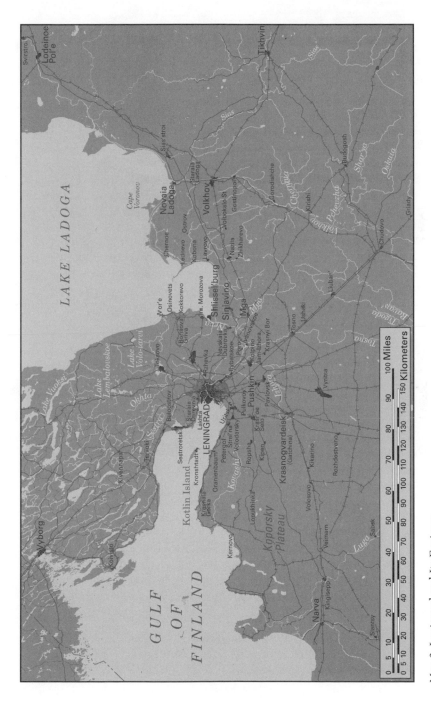

Map 2. Leningrad and Its Environs

the Leningrad Communist Party as its first secretary. Together with A. A. Kuznetsov, secretary of the Leningrad Regional Party Committee, Zhdanov headed a hierarchy of regional, district, and city Party committees that effectively dominated all matters, whether political or military, that took place in or affected Leningrad.[12] As is the case in any totalitarian structure, tight organization, strict centralization of authority, and pervasive Party discipline permitted the Party to mobilize virtually all of the city's resources to accomplish any given task.

Militarily, the People's Commissariat of Defense (*Narodnyi komissariat oborony*—NKO), which Stalin and the Communist Party Politburo and Central Committee supervised closely, established all state defense policy and approved general and specific force readiness measures. The Red Army General Staff, headed by Army General G. K. Zhukov, which drafted Soviet mobilization, deployment, and war plans, had a key role in implementing these plans but could act only with the NKO's approval. Finally, the Military Council (*Voennyi sovet*) in each military district, which consisted of the military district's commander, commissar, and chief of staff, were responsible for maintaining the readiness of district forces and fulfilling General Staff plans, but only when specifically ordered to do so by the NKO.

By definition, on the eve of war the Leningrad Military District (LMD) was the "premier operational-strategic territorial formation of the Soviet Union deployed at Leningrad and in the surrounding region (*oblast'*)."[13] As was the case with other military districts on the Soviet Union's frontiers, in wartime the LMD was to become an operating *front*, in this case, the Northern Front. As such, under strict NKO supervision, the Northern Front was responsible for implementing mobilization and deployment plans and for conducting military operations in accordance with the General Staff's mobilization and war plans and other higher-level directives.

The LMD had a long and illustrious history as one of the Red Army's premier military districts. The first Soviet military district, it was formed as the Petrograd Military District on 6 September 1918, and was renamed the Leningrad Military District on 1 February 1924, to accord with the renaming of the city. During the 1920s and 1930s, the LMD was at the forefront in the development of advanced military concepts and tested these concepts in frequent maneuvers. Among the numerous military innovations introduced and field-tested in the military district were air and chemical defense in 1926, air assault and air landings in 1930, and the twin tactical and operational concepts of deep battle (*glubokii boi*) and the deep operation (*glubokaia operatsiia*) in 1935 and 1936. The LMD's roster of distinguished commanders included:

A. I. Egorov (April–September 1921)
V. M. Gittis (September 1921–October 1925)

B. M. Shaposhnikov (October 1925–May 1927, September 1935–June 1937

A. I. Kork (May 1927–June 1931)

M. N. Tukhachevsky (May 1928–June 1931)

I. P. Belov (June 1931–September 1935)

P. E. Dybenko (June 1937–April 1938)

M. S. Khozin (April 1938–January 1939)

K. A. Meretskov (January 1939–January 1940)

S. K. Timoshenko (January–June 1940)

M. P. Kirponos (June 1940–January 1941)

M. M. Popov (January–June 1941)

The LMD planned, organized, and conducted Red Army military operations during the infamous and difficult Soviet-Finnish War of 1939 and 1940. Its headquarters planned and directed military operations during the war's first phase, from 30 November 1939 through 9 February 1940, but with appallingly poor results. During this period, district forces failed to penetrate the Finnish Mannerheim Defense Line, which traversed the Karelian Isthmus, and saw several of its attacking divisions annihilated by Finnish forces north of Lakes Ladoga and Onega. On 7 January 1940, a thoroughly embarrassed Stalin removed responsibility for conducting military operations in the region away from the LMD, assigning it instead to the newly formed Northwestern Front, which was commanded by S. K. Timoshenko, the former commander of the Kiev Military District. Timoshenko employed the LMD staff as the nucleus for his new *front*.

The Northwestern Front subsequently directed military operations during the war's second phase, from 10 February through war's end in early March 1940, and after the war ended, the *front* was disbanded on 26 March 1940. Although the Red Army's forces did not cover themselves with glory during the short Winter War, Timoshenko's forces finally managed to penetrate the Mannerheim Defense Line and force the Finns to sue for peace. The peace terms included Soviet annexation of much of the Karelian Isthmus, a sizable chunk of territory between and north of Lakes Ladoga and Onega in central Karelia, and the naval base of Hango ("Hanko," in Russian) on the southern coast of Finland.[14]

After war's end, Stalin elevated Timoshenko to the rank of Marshal of the Soviet Union and, as a reward for his performance in the Russo-Finnish War, appointed him as Soviet People's Commissar of Defense. Quite naturally, after the Red Army's embarrassingly poor performance in the Winter War, the first task Stalin assigned to Timoshenko was to reform the Red Army so that it could cope with the rigors and challenges of future war. While Timoshenko was attempting to reform the Red Army as a whole after the Finnish debacle, the Leningrad Military District focused on implementing its portion of the so-called Timoshenko reforms. It did so during the second half of 1940 and 1941 by forming and deploying new mechanized and aviation formations equipped with new generations of advanced military weaponry, primarily armor and aircraft. In addition, the military district created the Northern Air Defense (*Protivo-vozdushnaia*—PVO) Zone in February 1941, in an attempt to improve the district's air defense, and also began constructing an extensive network of fortified regions and positions along important prospective defense lines protecting the approaches to Leningrad.

The Leningrad Military District commander on the eve of Operation Barbarossa was Lieutenant General M. M. Popov, who had been appointed to command on 14 January 1941. A veteran of the Russian Civil War and a graduate of the Vystrel Infantry Course (1925) and the Frunze Academy (1936), Popov had most recently served as chief of staff and then commander of the Far Eastern Military District's elite 1st Red Banner Army.[15] Popov's commissar (member of the Military Council) was Corps Commissar N. N. Klement'ev, and his chief of staff was Major General D. N. Nikishev.

On the eve of war, the Leningrad Military District encompassed the Leningrad and Murmansk regions and the Karelo-Finnish Soviet Socialist Republic (SSR). The military district's forces included the 7th, 14th, and 23d Armies, the 19th, 42d, and 50th Rifle Corps, the 5th and 10th Mechanized Corps, the 1st Fighter Aviation Corps, and the 2d PVO Corps and 7th Fighter Aviation Corps PVO (assigned to the Northern PVO Zone) (see Appendixes). A total of 15 rifle divisions, 1 rifle brigade, 4 tank and 2 motorized divisions, and 8 fortified regions formed the nucleus of the military district's ground forces. On 22 June 1941, Popov's military district numbered 404,470 men (including 49,227 in schools), 7,901 guns and mortars, 1,857 tanks (1,543 of which were operational), and 1,342 aircraft (1,222 of which were operational).[16]

The NKO assigned the Northern PVO Zone responsibility for protecting the northern Soviet Union, including the Leningrad, Murmansk, and adjacent regions, against enemy air attack. The zone included the 2d PVO Corps and the Vyborg, Murmansk, Pskov, Luga, and Petrozavodsk PVO Brigade Regions. On 22 June the 2d PVO Corps and the 7th Fighter Aviation Corps were responsible for air defense in the immediate vicinity of Leningrad. The 2d PVO Corps, commanded by Major General M. M. Protsvetkin, which consisted of the 115th, 169th, 189th, 192d, 194th, and 351st Antiaircraft Artillery Regiments, numbered 950 antiaircraft guns, 230 antiaircraft machine guns, 300 searchlights, 360 aerial obstacle balloons, 302 VNOS (early warning) posts, and 8 radio-location sites. The Baltic Fleet's PVO division with 191 guns was also operationally subordinate to the 2d PVO Corps. The 7th Fighter Aviation Corps, commanded by Colonel S. P. Danilov, consisted of the 3d and 54th Fighter Aviation Divisions (PVO) and was equipped with 300 fighter aircraft.

The 2d PVO Corps defended Leningrad by establishing a series of air defense zones, which radiated outward from the city's center. The corps' antiaircraft artillery forces defended a zone extending 35 kilometers (21.7 miles) from the city's center, and aircraft from the 7th Fighter Aviation Corps defended a zone of air cover in a belt extending 20–60 kilometers (12.4–37.3 miles) from the city. Finally, a system of air observation and VNOS posts was deployed 120–140 kilometers (74.6–87 miles) from the city's center. The 2d PVO Corps provided centralized control and direction for all of these air defense forces.

However, Leningrad's air defenses suffered from several serious short-comings on the eve of war. Airfields were in short supply, and once war began, the rapid German advance disrupted the VNOS system's target acquisition effort, forcing the defenders to rely on radio-location procedures that were essentially unreliable. To help compensate for this deficiency, the Soviet command placed eight PVO antiaircraft gun batteries on barges in the Gulf of Finland to increase the depth of its artillery antiaircraft defenses. To further improve its air defenses, Leningrad Party organizations also supplemented the overall PVO effort by forming local air defense (*Mestnaia protivo-vozduzhnaia oborona*—MPVO) forces. These forces consisted of from 10 to 12 self-defense groups with from 600 to 800 men and women each, totaling approximately 300,000 persons, who were responsible for observation, security, and defense of separate city blocks and individual buildings within those blocks.[17]

The Red Banner Baltic Fleet, whose long history dated back to its creation by Peter the Great in 1701, was responsible for defending the Soviet naval bases in the Baltic region and at Leningrad and along the Baltic coast against naval, air, and ground attack. The fleet was also tasked with operating in close coordination with and providing support to Red Army ground forces operating in adjacent land theaters. Its commander throughout the entire war was Vice Admiral V. F. Tributs, an experienced naval officer who was promoted to full admiral in May 1943.

On the eve of war, the Baltic Fleet consisted of a surface ship squadron, a light ship detachment, three submarine brigades, two torpedo boat brigades, a wide array of cutters, its own air force, coastal defense regions and sectors, and rear service installations and facilities. The fleet's forces were stationed at four major naval bases located at Tallin in Estonia, Hango on the southern coast of Finland, Kronshtadt in the Gulf of Finland west of Leningrad, and Libau near Riga, Latvia. Its more than 300 ships included 2 battleships, 2 cruisers, 2 destroyer leaders, 18 destroyers, 68 submarines, 2 cannon (gun) ships, 7 destroyer escorts, 4 armored cutters, 55 torpedo boats, 34 minesweep-ers, 4 mine and net layers, 34 submarine hunters, and numerous coastal cutters. The Baltic Fleet's air forces numbered 656 aircraft, including 172 bombers, and naval coastal defense artillery fielded 424 45mm to 356mm guns.[18]

While the bulk of the Baltic Fleet supported the Baltic Special Military District from its bases at Tallin and Libau, the fleet's bases at Kronshtadt and Hango supported the Leningrad Military District. The Leningrad Military Naval Base at Kronshtadt was responsible for defending the sea approaches to Leningrad and the city itself. The base had been founded as the Petrograd Naval Base in March 1919, but was abolished shortly after the end of the Russian Civil War. On 6 November 1939, a Soviet Naval Fleet (*Voenno-morskoi flot*—VMF) order reestablished the base primarily because of the deteriorating international situation and employed it as the Baltic Fleet's premier base during the Soviet-Finnish War. After war's end, on 5 July 1940, the VMF deactivated the base but reactivated it once again in October 1941 as the Baltic Fleet's principal base, with the mission of assisting in the defense of Leningrad.[19] The Kronshtadt base's primary wartime missions were to conduct counter-battery fire and serve as a transshipment point for forces between Leningrad and the town of Lomonosov in the Oranienbaum bridgehead southwest of Leningrad.

The existence of the Hango Naval Base dated back to the period from 1809 through 1917, when the Russian Empire controlled Hango. However, in 1917, during the turbulent period of revolution and civil war, the town and base reverted to Finnish control. In turn, by virtue of their defeat in the Russo-Finnish War, the Finns returned the port to Soviet control in March 1940 on the basis of a 30-year lease, and the Soviet Union immediately converted the region into a fortified naval base. On 22 June the nucleus of the naval base's defense force consisted of the 8th Separate Rifle Brigade and border-guards and engineer-construction units. These forces were supported by 95 batteries of coastal and antiaircraft artillery, consisting of 37mm to 305mm guns, an aviation group of 20 aircraft, and a naval security detachment of 7 armed cutter-hunters and 16 auxiliary ships for a total of 25,000 men.[20]

Supplementing and subordinate to the Baltic Fleet, the Ladoga Naval Flotilla was an operational-tactical naval formation formed on 25 October 1939. The flotilla's wartime mission was to defend the shores of Lake Ladoga with a division of 7 training ships, a division of 35 training cutters, and an artillery training battalion with 3 102mm and 8 76mm guns. After war began, on 25 June 1941, the VMF Commissariat reorganized the flotilla into divisions of cutters, boats, minesweepers, security cutters, cutter-minesweepers, and coastal boats and units. Subsequently, the flotilla's commanders were:

Captain 2d Rank S. V. Zemlianichenko (June–July 1941)
Vice-Admiral P. A. Trainin (July 1941)
Captain 1st Rank V. P. Bogolepov (July–August 1941)

Captain 1st Rank (Vice Admiral on 16 September) B. V. Khoroshkhin
(August–October 1941)
Captain 1st Rank (Vice Admiral from January 1944) V. S. Cherikov (Oc-
tober 1941–November 1944)[21]

DEFENSE PLANNING

If and when war occurred, the Leningrad Military District was to become
the Red Army's Northern Front. In cooperation with the Northern and Baltic Fleets, the military district's wartime mission was to defend the USSR's
state borders with Finland from the Rybachii Gulf to the Gulf of Finland,
the Estonian coast, and the naval base on the Hango Peninsula in accordance
with the State Defense Plan (DP-1941).[22] The development of the Soviet State
Defense Plan was an arduous process that had begun within the NKO and
General Staff in mid-1940 and was still incomplete as war approached. Although Defense Commissar Timoshenko and Chief of the General Staff
Zhukov were instrumental in the plan's development, it also had to be coordinated carefully with the military districts' commanders, their staffs, and the
chief of combat, combat support, and logistical services.

By early May 1941, the General Staff had completed a draft plan for the
defense of the Soviet Union's western borders, "The 1941 Plan for Defending
the State Borders," and sent it, along with directives from the People's Commissariat of Defense, to the five western border military districts. Popov received
his directive on 14 May 1941. Titled Directive No. 503913/ob/cc, it ordered
Popov to prepare and submit his new defense plan to the commissariat:

> To protect mobilization and the final concentration and deployment
> of the Leningrad Military District's forces, you and the district's chief of
> staff and chief of the Operations Section will develop [the following] by
> 25 May 1941:
> a. A detailed plan for defense of the coast from the Barents Sea to
>   Iokan'go, including the state border from the Barents Sea to the Gulf
>   of Finland and the coast of Estonia SSR from the Narva Gulf to the
>   Gulf of Matsala.
> b. A detailed plan for air defense with primary attention to a reliable
>   defense of the city of Leningrad.[23]

From the very start, however, the planning process was severely flawed.
Prepared during a turbulent period of rapid changes in the international climate, which confounded military district and General Staff planning, the basic

plan incorporated several false planning assumptions. The most serious of these was that the *Wehrmacht* would require 10–15 days to deploy for an invasion and, during that period, would be unable to conceal its offensive preparations. By excluding the possibility that the Germans would achieve surprise, Soviet planners assumed the forces in its border military district would have time to mobilize, deploy, and repel any German offensive, while other forces in military districts in the depths of the country were mobilizing and deploying. This false assumption was particularly damaging to the Leningrad Military District, whose force mobilization and deployment was supposed to be protected by the Baltic Special Military District, which defended the Soviet Union's border along and south of the Baltic Sea coast. Worse still, the border military districts were not able to complete their plans before the Germans began Operation Barbarossa on 22 June. This meant that, on that fateful date, the General Staff's comprehensive DP-1941 was also far from complete.[24]

Once drafted by Popov and his staff on 25 May 1941, the Leningrad Military District's Defense Plan, "Notes on the Protection of the State Borders in the Territory of the Leningrad Military District," began by enunciating the district's principal missions (see the Appendixes for the complete plan):

DEFENSE MISSIONS

1. To prevent both enemy ground and air invasion of the district's territory.

2. A firm defense of fortified regions and field fortifications along the line of the state borders:

  a. To provide for a reliable defense of Leningrad along the Vyborg and Keksholm axes, considering this to be the primary mission of the Leningrad Military District's forces.

  b. To prevent the enemy from penetrating the defensive front and reaching Lake Ladoga.

  c. To protect the Kirov railroad's uninterrupted operation and to prevent the enemy from reaching it, at all cost.

  d. Together with the Northern Fleet, to retain control of the Riabachii and Srednii Peninsulas, to protect the port of Murmansk reliably, and to prevent enemy naval amphibious landings on the coast of the Kola Peninsula from Iokan'go to the state border with Finland.

3. Beginning on the ninth day of mobilization, accept transfer of the Estonian SSR coast from the Gulf of Narva to the Gulf of Matsalulakht [sic] from the Baltic Special Military District and, together with the Baltic Fleet, defend it, while preventing enemy amphibious assault forces from landing on it.

4. Assist the Red Banner Baltic Fleet in closing off the entrance into the Gulf of Finland to enemy naval forces by defending the northern coast of the Estonian SSR and the Hango Peninsula.

5. Determine in timely fashion the nature of enemy forces concentrations and groupings by all types of intelligence means available to the district.

6. Gain air superiority by active air operations, and destroy and disrupt the concentration and deployment of enemy forces by powerful strikes, primarily against railroad centers, bridges, staging areas, and force groupings.

7. Prevent enemy airborne assaults and diversionary activity on the district's territory.

8. If conditions are favorable, all defending forces and army and district reserves will be prepared to deliver decisive blows against the enemy in accordance with the High Command's orders.[25]

Popov's plan proposed the formation of five "covering regions," each of which was manned by the forces of a single army. Individually, each covering region was responsible for defending a key projected enemy attack axis, and, collectively, the five regions defended the entire military district. The 14th Army, commanded by Lieutenant General V. A. Frolov, was responsible for defending Covering Region No. 1, which protected the city of Murmansk, the ground approaches to the city, and the territory of Leningrad region from the Kola Peninsula southward, halfway to the northern shore of Lake Onega. Frolov had at his disposal the 42d Rifle Corps' 104th and 122d Rifle Divisions, the separate 14th and 52d Rifle Divisions and the 23d (Murmansk) Fortified Region, and the 1st Mechanized Corps' 1st Tank Division, which Popov had temporarily assigned to him. In addition, Frolov controlled the Northern Fleet, five border-guards detachments (the 35th, 100th, 82d, 72d, and 101st), the 104th RGK (High Command Reserve) Gun Artillery Regiment, and, for air support, the 1st Mixed Aviation Division.[26]

To the south, the 7th Army, commanded by Lieutenant General F. D. Gorelenko, constituted Covering Region No. 2, which was responsible for defending the sector from north of Lake Onega to Lake Ladoga with the 54th, 71st, 168th, and 237th Rifle Divisions and the 26th (Sortavalo) Fortified Region. Four border guards detachments (the 1st, 73d, 80th, and 3d), the 55th Mixed Aviation Division, and a variety of supporting subunits were subordinate to Gorelenko's army.[27] Gorelenko's force was to defend the state border north of Lake Onega and between Lakes Onega and Ladoga, with priority to the approaches axes toward Sortavalo, Ukhta, Rebol'sk, and Petrozavodsk and the vital Kirov rail line, which connected Leningrad with Murmansk.

The most powerful of Popov's forces was Covering Region No. 3, manned by Lieutenant-General P. S. Pshennikov's 23d Army. Pshennikov's army defended the main threat axis across the Karelian Isthmus from Vyborg to Leningrad's northern approaches. His forces included the 19th Rifle Corps' 115th and 142d Rifle Divisions, the 50th Rifle Corps' 43d and 123d Rifle Divisions, and the 27th (Keksholm) and 28th (Vyborg) Fortified Regions. The 10th Mechanized Corps, which consisted of the 21st and 24th Tank and 198th Motorized Divisions, provided Pshennikov with a mobile armored capability. Three border-guards detachments (the 102d, 5th, and 33d), the 101st, 108th, and 519th RGK Howitzer Artillery Regiments, the 573d RGK Gun Artillery Regiment, the 5th Mixed Aviation Division, and other supporting subunits were also subordinate to the Covering Region No. 3. By 22 June, Popov had reinforced this region with the 70th Rifle Division.

Southwest of Leningrad, the 65th Rifle Corps, commanded by Major General K. V. Komissarov, manned Covering Region No. 4, which was responsible for defending the coast of the Baltic Sea east and west of the Estonian SSR's capital at Tallin. Komissarov had at his disposal the 11th and 16th (Lithuanian) Rifle Divisions and a modest number of supporting units and subunits, including elements of the 4th Mixed Aviation Division to provide necessary air support. By 22 June the General Staff had transferred the 65th Rifle Corps' headquarters to Baltic Special Military District control and its rifle divisions to the latter's 11th and 27th Armies. Finally, the 8th Separate Rifle Brigade defended Covering Region No. 5 on the Hango Peninsula with only limited artillery, air, and naval support.

In accordance with his original defense plan, Popov retained the 70th, 177th, and 191st Rifle Divisions and the 1st Mechanized Corps' 3d Tank and 163d Motorized Divisions as his reserve directly subordinate to the military district's headquarters. In addition, his military district controlled the 21st and 22d (Karelian), 25th (Pskov), and 29th Fortified Regions and the 4th Mixed, 39th Fighter, and 3d and 54th PVO Fighter Aviation Divisions. The PVO divisions were responsible for defending the skies over Leningrad proper.

On the eve of war, the NKO and General Staff were relying on the Baltic Special Military District, which was designated to become the Northwestern Front in wartime, to defend the approaches toward Leningrad from East Prussia through the Baltic republics. Thus, the Leningrad Military District was only responsible for defending the Leningrad region against any Finnish advance through the Karelian Peninsula and enemy attack from the air. Sadly for Popov and his forces, the NKO's and General Staff's assumption that the Northwestern Front could contain any enemy advance at the state border or, at least, along the line of the Western Dvina River line well short of Leningrad, proved grossly incorrect.

Because of these false assumptions and the accepted wisdom that the primary threat to Leningrad emanated from the north, Popov and his military district staff paid scant attention to the necessity of preparing ground defenses along the southern approaches to the city. Only on the morning of 23 June, 24 hours after the German invasion began, did Popov begin displaying any concern about a possible enemy thrust against Leningrad from the south. That day, he dispatched his deputy, Lieutenant General K. P. Piadyshev, to inspect the southern approaches to the city and recommend sites where new, precautionary defense lines could be erected. Even though Piadyshev subsequently recommended the Kingisepp-Luga-Lake Il'men' line as the logical location of the new defense line, severe shortages of manpower and material rendered the issue moot until the worsening combat situation impelled Popov to action.

MILITARY FORCES

Although, as required by Soviet war plans, Leningrad Military District's forces were clearly adequate to defend the Leningrad region against any Finnish attack, Popov's forces were not prepared to deal with aggression by the *Wehrmacht,* which in 1941 was the most formidable and accomplished military force in Europe. Like the Red Army as a whole, district forces were in serious disarray in June 1941, conceptually, organizationally, and with regard to the competence of its leaders and the effectiveness of its command and control organs. Conceptually, the Red Army's overall military strategy as expressed in Defense Plan 1941 was clearly defensive in nature. As such, it was wholly incompatible with the offensive tactical and operational concepts of deep battle and deep operation, which the Red Army had developed in the 1930s and which still dominated Soviet military thought on the eve of war.

In addition, in the wake of its abysmally poor performance in the Finnish War, the Red Army was simultaneously reforming, expanding, reorganizing, and reequipping its forces, but doing so poorly in all respects. Worse still, the military purges, which had begun in 1937 and were still ongoing, produced a severe shortage of trained and experienced commanders and staff officers capable of implementing any concepts, either offensive or defensive. In contrast to the German belief in subordinate initiative, the purges and other Soviet ideological and systemic constraints convinced Red Army officers that any show of independent judgment was hazardous to their personal health.[28]

Because political considerations required that it defend every inch of Soviet territory, by June 1941 the Red Army had largely abandoned and cannibalized its pre-1939 defenses along the former Soviet frontier and were erecting new "fortified regions" in the western portions of the territories they occupied in 1939 and 1940. Despite prodigious efforts, the new defenses were far from complete when the Germans and Finns attacked. Nor were Red Army forces permitted to do anything that would provoke their potential enemies. To ensure that no provocations occurred, the Red Army manned the Soviet Union's frontier defenses primarily with NKVD (People's Commissariat of Internal Affairs) border guards troops and token rifle forces, while the bulk of its main forces were garrisoned far to the rear.

Organizationally, the Red Army's force structure was severely flawed. Its largest armored formations, the mechanized corps, were structured rigidly and contrasted unfavorably with the more flexible German motorized corps. Hastily formed in late 1940 and still forming when war began, each massive mechanized corps consisted of two tank divisions and one motorized division. Since the tank divisions, which had a strength of 10,940 men and 375 tanks, were tank-heavy and lacked sufficient support, the NKO added a motorized division and various supporting units to each mechanized corps. At least on paper, each of the unwieldy mechanized corps totaled 36,080 men and 1,031 tanks.[29] Not only that, most of the mechanized corps in the border military districts were mal-deployed, with their divisions stationed far apart from one another. The Leningrad Military District's two mechanized corps suffered from the same problem. Worse still, the military district's cadre of armored and mechanized force officers had not learned the lessons of the Winter War: that large mechanized forces could not operate effectively in the heavily woody and often swampy terrain of northern Russia.[30]

Soviet rifle forces were also in disarray. The principal building blocks of the Red Army were its rifle divisions. On the eve of war, these were organized into three rifle regiments of three battalions each plus two artillery regiments, a light tank battalion, and supporting services, for a strength on paper of 14,483 men and 16 light tanks. In reality, however, rifle divisions were 8,000–10,000 men strong, and they had no tanks, inadequate supporting artillery, and only rudimentary logistical support at best.[31] Both the Red Army rifle corps, which was supposed to contain two or three rifle divisions, and the field army, which was supposed to consist of three rifle corps, one mechanized corps, several artillery regiments, and an antitank brigade, were also understrength and lacked much of their heavy equipment.[32]

In late May 1941, the Soviet government attempted to remedy this problem by calling up 800,000 additional reservists and accelerating the graduation of various military schools. However, these additional personnel were just joining their units when the German attack materialized. In practice, when war began, the LMD's armies could muster only four to five divisions each and had woefully inadequate artillery, armor, engineer, logistical, and maintenance support.

The Red Army Air Force (*Voenno-vozdushnye sily*—VVS), in general, and the Leningrad Military District's Air Force, in particular, suffered from many of the same problems as the ground forces. Overall, the VVS (and VMF) fielded 24,488 aircraft (18,759 of which were combat aircraft) on 22 June 1941, 21,030 (16,052 combat) of which were operable. Of this number, 10,743 aircraft (10,266 combat) were assigned to operating forces in the Western Theater of Military Operations (*Teatr voennykh deistvii*—TVD). The Western TVD included forces in the Leningrad, Baltic Special, Western Special, Southwestern Special, and Arkhangel'sk Military Districts, the Odessa Military District's 9th Army, and the Northern, Baltic, and Black Sea Fleets. Of this number, 9,099 (8,696 combat) aircraft were operable. The Leningrad Military District's share of aircraft was 1,342 (1,336 combat) planes, 1,222 (1,216 combat) of which were operable.[33] Worse still, many of these aircraft were obsolete and suffering from prolonged use.

The Great Purge had also affected aircraft manufacturers and designers as well as military commanders, ending the previous Soviet lead in aeronautics.[34] Newer types of aircraft, such as the swift MiG-3 fighter and the excellent Il-2 *Shturmovik* ground attack airplane, which were, in some ways, superior to their German counterparts, were just entering service in spring 1941, leaving the Air Force with a mixture of old and new equipment. Transition training to qualify pilots to fly these new aircraft lagged since Air Force commanders feared that any training accidents would lead to their arrest for "sabotage."[35] When Barbarossa began, many Soviet fighter pilots in the forward area had as few as four hours' experience in their aircraft. The changeover to new equipment was so confused that numerous Soviet pilots had not become familiar with the appearance of new Soviet bombers and erroneously fired on their own aircraft on 22 June.

Other factors reduced the combat effectiveness of the Red Army Air Force. The Soviet occupation of eastern Poland in 1939 and Soviet successes in air combat against the Japanese and Finns in 1939 and 1940 generated a false sense of superiority among many senior aviation officers. Widespread Soviet acceptance of doctrinal concepts for the massed employment of air power as expressed by A. N. Lapchinsky, the "Russian Douhet," in the 1930s only compounded the ill effects of this feeling of overconfidence. In the event of war, Soviet military leaders expected to launch a massive air offensive against any enemy from their newly acquired territories. However, when war began, relatively few airfields were operational in the forward area, many others were being torn up for expansion in the spring of 1941, and the few that existed lacked revetments and antiaircraft defenses necessary to protect the crowded parking aprons.

The VVS was also plagued by disunity of command and severe command turbulence. Some air divisions supported specific ground armies or *fronts,* others were directly subordinate to the General Staff, and still others were dedicated to the regional air defense of the Soviet Homeland. Within the context of the chaotic initial campaign, when tenuous communications and chains of command evaporated, such divisions made it difficult to bring coordinated air power to bear at key points. Nor did most Soviet aircraft have radios in 1941. Worse still, the military purges had liquidated three successive Air Force commanders and many other senior officers, and the rippling effect of promotions left inexperienced officers in command at all levels. Few of these officers were capable of correcting the VVS's overly rigid and essentially outdated tactics.[36]

Thus, as was the case with the Red Army as a whole, on the eve of war, the Leningrad Military District, the Baltic Fleet, and other organizations tasked with the defense of Leningrad were only marginally capable of performing their assigned missions. However, what neither they nor Stalin and central Soviet defense organs understood was the speed and destructiveness of the *Wehrmacht*'s advance once Operation Barbarossa began. Within days, the deteriorating situation converted their mild concern into near panic.

CHAPTER 2

Target Leningrad

German Operation Barbarossa and the *Wehrmacht*'s Advance
through the Baltic Region, 22 June–7 August 1941

PLAN BARBAROSSA

Hitler embarked on Operation Barbarossa as a virtual crusade against Russian Bolshevism, which he perceived as a threat to Germany and all of Western civilization. Emboldened by the success of his diplomacy and the *Wehrmacht*'s numerous victories in Central and Western Europe during the late 1930s, he also set out to achieve the ambitious aims he had enunciated years before in his personal testament, *Mein Kampf*. In this memoir of his personal struggle, he had argued that the German people were historically entitled to the acquisition of "living space," most of which, he perceived, existed in the vast Soviet Union. While conquest of the Soviet Union would provide that essential living space, it would also rid the world of the scourge of Bolshevism.

Militarily, however, the ground invasion and conquest of the Soviet Union was a formidable task. The German Armed Forces had achieved their previous military victories in Western Europe, a theater of operations that was well developed and distinctly limited in terms of size. They had done so by employing minimal forces against poorly prepared armies that were utterly unsuited to counter or endure blitzkrieg and whose parent nations often lacked the will to fight and prevail. The conquest of the Soviet Union was an entirely different matter. Plan Barbarossa required that the German Armed Forces vanquish the largest military force in the world and ultimately advance to a depth of 1,750 kilometers (1,087 miles) along a front of over 1,800 kilometers (1,119 miles) in an underdeveloped theater of military operations whose size approximated all of Western Europe. Hitler and his military planners assumed that blitzkrieg would produce a quick victory and planned accordingly.

To achieve this victory, the Germans planned to annihilate the bulk of the Soviet Union's peacetime Red Army before it could mobilize its reserves by conducting a series of dramatic encirclements near the Soviet Union's new western frontier. Although German military planners began contingency planning for an invasion of the Soviet Union in the summer of 1940, Hitler did not issue his Directive No. 21 for Operation Barbarossa until 18 December 1940 (see Appendixes). When he finally did so, his clear intention was to destroy the Red Army rather than achieve any specific terrain or political objectives:

The mass of the [Red] army stationed in Western Russia is to be destroyed in bold operations involving deep and rapid penetrations by panzer spearheads, and the withdrawal of combat-capable elements into the vast Russian interior is to be prevented. By means of rapid pursuit, a line is to be reached from beyond which the Russian air force will no longer be capable of attacking the territories of the German Reich.[1]

In one of his many planning conferences for Barbarossa, Hitler had noted that, in comparison with the goal of destroying the Soviet Armed Forces, "Moscow [is] of no great importance."[2] Together with his military advisers, Hitler believed that, if his forces did destroy the Red Army, Stalin's Bolshevik regime would collapse, replicating the chaos that engulfed Russia in 1918. This assumption, however, woefully underestimated the Soviet dictator's control over the population and the Red Army's capacity for mobilizing strategic reserves with which to replace the forces that the German Army destroyed in its anticipated initial encirclements. Only later, after the Red Army and Soviet government displayed disturbing resilience in the face of unmitigated military disasters, did the Germans begin believing that the captures of Leningrad and Moscow were the key to achieving a quick victory.

To destroy the Red Army, Hitler massed 151 German divisions (including 19 panzer and 15 motorized infantry divisions) in the East, equipped with an estimated 3,350 tanks, 7,200 artillery pieces, and 2,770 aircraft.[3] The Finns supported Barbarossa with 14 divisions, and the Rumanians contributed 4 divisions and 6 brigades to the effort, backed up by another 9 divisions and 2 brigades.[4] The German Army High Command (*Oberkommando des Heeres*—OKH) controlled all Axis forces in the Eastern Theater. The OKH, in turn, subdivided these forces into an Army of Norway operating in the far north and Army Groups North, Center, and South, with four panzer groups, deployed from the Baltic Sea southward to the Black Sea. A German air fleet supported each of these four major commands.

German military planners sought to exploit Russia's lack of decent roads and railroads laterally across the front and into the depths to prevent the mass of Soviet forces from regrouping from one sector to another or from withdrawing eastward before they were surrounded. However, German intelligence overestimated the degree of Red Army forward concentration and was totally unaware of the groups of reserve armies, which the Soviets were already deploying east of the Dnepr River. Once the battle of the frontier had ended, Plan Barbarossa required the three German army groups to advance along diverging axes: Army Group North toward Leningrad, Army Group Center toward Moscow, and Army Group South toward Kiev. Thus, from its inception, Plan Barbarossa anticipated dangerously dissipating the *Wehrmacht*'s military strength in an attempt to seize all of Hitler's objectives simultaneously.

Plan Barbarossa, which incorporated the recommendations of the Armed Forces High Command (*Oberkommando der Wehrmacht*—OKW), required the three *Wehrmacht* army groups to attack the Soviet Union simultaneously. Army Groups North and Center were to deliver the main attack along the Leningrad and Moscow axes north of the Pripiat' Marshes, and Army Group South was to attack along the Kiev axis south of the marshes. The army groups were to envelop, trap, and annihilate the bulk of the Red Army close to the frontier and prevent combat-capable enemy forces from withdrawing into "the vast Russian interior." Once Army Group Center had destroyed enemy forces in Belorussia, it was to assist Army Group North in the capture of Leningrad and Kronshtadt. "Only after accomplishing this priority mission," read the directive, "should we initiate operations to seize Moscow."[5]

The directive's final objective was "the establishment of a defensive barrier against Asiatic Russia along the general line of the Volga and Arkhangel'sk." Based upon its previous military performance and the presumed dilapidated state of the opposing Red Army, German military planners assumed the *Wehrmacht* could accomplish this task within a period of from 8 to 10 weeks. So confident was Hitler of victory that, on 11 June 1941, he issued yet another Fuehrer directive (no. 32), which ordered 60 divisions be left on security duty in occupied Russia so that the bulk of the *Wehrmacht* could be deployed elsewhere.[6]

THE OPPOSING FORCES

German Army Group North, commanded by Field Marshal Ritter von Leeb, was to conduct the *Wehrmacht*'s advance along the Leningrad axis with the mission of destroying Red Army forces in the Baltic region and capturing Leningrad. Leeb's powerful army group consisted of the Eighteenth and Sixteenth Armies and the Fourth Panzer Group with a total of six army and two motorized corps, backed up by three security divisions and an army corps in reserve. So configured, his army group fielded 21 infantry, 3 panzer, and 3 motorized divisions, and 3 security divisions with another 2 infantry divisions in OKH reserve.[7] Colonel General Erich Hoepner's Fourth Panzer Group, which formed Army Group North's armored spearhead, was to advance rapidly northwestward along the Tilsit-Daugavpils axis. Hoepner's panzer group consisted of Colonel General Hans Reinhardt's XXXXI Motorized Corps, which consisted of the 1st and 6th Panzer and 36th Motorized Divisions, and Colonel General Erich von Manstein's LVI Motorized Corps, which included the 8th Panzer and 3d Motorized Divisions. Colonel General Georg von Kuechler's Eighteenth Army, with the XXVI, XXXVIII, and I Army Corps, and Colonel General Ernst Busch's Sixteenth Army, with the

X, XXVIII, and II Army Corps, were to advance along the flanks and in the wake of Hoepner's advancing panzers. Leeb retained the XXIII Army Corps in army group reserve and could, if need be, call on the L Army Corps, which was deployed in his sector as the OKH reserve.[8] This cast of players would initiate the Battle for Leningrad.

Even though the German Army seemed at the height of its power in June 1941 by virtue of its stunning victories in 1939 and 1940, it was by no means invincible. The German officer corps had traditionally prided itself on its doctrine, a unity of training and thought that allowed junior officers to exercise initiative because they understood their commander's intentions and knew how their peers in adjacent units would react to the same situation. Although disagreements about the correct employment of armor had disrupted doctrinal unity in the mid-1930s, subsequent victories vindicated the minority of younger German theorists' faith in mechanized warfare. The *Wehrmacht*'s panzer forces clearly demonstrated that massed mobile, offensive power could penetrate enemy's defenses in narrow front sectors, exploit to the rear, disrupt enemy logistics and command and control, and encircle large enemy forces. While follow-on infantry destroyed the encircled enemy forces, the panzers could then continue to exploit success deep into the enemy rear area.

In practice, however, earlier campaigns had also demonstrated that the enemy could often escape from these encirclements if the infantry failed to advance quickly enough to seal the encirclement. This had occurred because Germany never had enough motor vehicles to equip more than a small portion of its infantry troops. The vast majority of the German Army throughout the Second World War consisted of foot-mobile infantry and horse-drawn artillery and supplies, sometimes forcing the mechanized and motorized spearheads to pause while their supporting units caught up by forced marches.

Since panzer forces were vitally important to the implementation of German offensive doctrine, Hitler created more of them prior to Barbarossa by reducing the number of tanks in existing and new panzer divisions. The 1941 German panzer divisions consisted of two or three tank battalions each with an authorized strength of from 150 to 202 tanks per division (in practice, an average of 125 operational tanks). In addition, the panzer division included five infantry battalions, four truck-mounted and one on motorcycles. Few of these motorized infantry units were equipped with armored personnel carriers; hence the infantry suffered higher casualties. The panzer division, which also included armored reconnaissance and engineer battalions and three artillery battalions equipped with guns towed behind trucks or tractors, and communications, antitank, and antiaircraft units, totaled roughly 17,000 men.

The slightly smaller German motorized infantry divisions consisted of one tank battalion, seven motorized infantry battalions, and three or four artillery battalions.[9] The organization of the first four *Waffen* (combat) SS divisions was identical to that of regular army motorized infantry divisions, although they later evolved into lavishly equipped panzer divisions. The 1941 German motorized (panzer) corps consisted of two panzer and one motorized infantry division, and two to four of these motorized corps formed a panzer group. During Barbarossa, several of the panzer groups, which were augmented by the addition of army (infantry) corps, were renamed panzer armies.

Since German operations in 1939 and 1940 were predominantly offensive in nature, German defensive doctrine remained largely based on techniques employed during the later stages of the First World War. Defending infantry relied on deep and elaborate prepared defenses, kept the bulk of forces in reserve, and relied on elastic defense and rapid counterattacks to defeat the attacker. Defensive doctrine rested on three assumptions, all of which proved invalid in Russia. The assumptions were that sufficient infantry would exist to establish defenses in depth, the enemy would make his main attack with dismounted infantry, and German commanders would be allowed to choose where to defend and be permitted to defend flexibly as the situation required.

The typical German infantry division in 1941 consisted of three regiments of three infantry battalions each, plus four horse-drawn artillery regiments, for an overall strength of 15,000 men. Since the division's principal infantry antitank weapon, the 37mm antitank gun, had already proved inadequate against French and British heavy armor, infantry divisions had to employ their 100mm or 105mm medium artillery battalion and the famous 88mm antiaircraft guns against enemy tanks.[10]

The German *Luftwaffe* (Air Force) shared in the German Army's lofty reputation. The 2,770 *Luftwaffe* aircraft deployed to support Barbarossa represented 65 percent of Germany's first-line strength.[11] Although the Messerschmidt Bf-109f fighter was a superb aircraft, other German models were rapidly approaching obsolescence. The famous Ju-87 *Stuka* dive bomber could survive only when the enemy air force was helpless, and the Dornier-17 and Ju-88, Germany's primary bombers, and the versatile Ju-52 transport, were inadequate both in range and load (bomb) capacity. Since German industry had not made up for losses during the Battle of Britain, in 1941 Germany actually had 200 fewer bombers than it had possessed the previous spring.[12] Given these shortages and the requirement to operate from improvised forward airfields, it was exceedingly difficult for German pilots to provide effective air superiority or offensive air strikes over the vast expanse of European Russia. In short, the *Luftwaffe* was primarily a tactical air force, capable of supporting short-term ground offensive operations but not a deep and effective air campaign.

Germany's greatest weaknesses lay in the logistical realm. Only 40,000 miles of hard-surfaced, all-weather roads and 51,000 miles of railroads spanned the vast Soviet Union, and the railroads were of a wider gauge than those in Germany. Even though they frantically converted captured rail lines to Western gauge as they advanced, German logistical organs had to transfer most of their supplies forward by employing whatever Soviet-gauge rolling stock they could capture. Nor did the panzer and motorized forces possess adequate maintenance capacity for a long campaign. The mechanical complexity of the tanks and armored personnel carriers, coupled with numerous models with mutually incompatible parts, confounded the German supply and maintenance system. Worse still, earlier campaigns had depleted stocks of repair parts, and trained maintenance personnel were also in short supply. Therefore, it was no wonder that German blitzkrieg had lost much of its sharp armored tip by late 1941.

Perhaps Germany's most fundamental logistical vulnerability was the fact that it had not mobilized its economy for war. Severe shortages of petroleum and other raw materials limited German production and transportation throughout the war. The German industrial economy was already dependent on 3 million foreign workers by June 1941, and the labor shortage became more acute with each new draft of conscripts for the army. As in his previous campaigns, Hitler was banking on achieving a quick victory rather than preparing for a prolonged struggle. In fact, he was already looking beyond the 1941 campaign, planning to create new mechanized and air formations for follow-on operations in North Africa and Asia Minor. Hitler dedicated virtually all of German new weapons production to such future plans, leaving the forces in the east chronically short of matériel. The *Wehrmacht* had to win a quick victory or none at all.[13]

Leeb's strong and experienced force faced Colonel General F. I. Kuznetsov's Baltic Special Military District, which was to become the Northwestern Front at the outbreak of war. When war broke out, Kuznetsov's forces were responsible for defending the northwestern strategic axis through the Baltic region and the approaches to Leningrad. Kuznetsov's *front,* which was the weakest of the three deployed along the Soviet Union's western frontier, consisted of three armies and two mechanized corps. The 8th Army, commanded by Lieutenant General P. P. Sobennikov, and the 11th Army, commanded by Lieutenant General V. I. Morozov, supported, respectively, by Major General A. V. Kurkin's 3d and Lieutenant General N. M. Shestapolov's 12th Mechanized Corps, formed Kuznetsov's first echelon. Major General M. E. Berzarin's 27th Army constituted Kuznetsov's second echelon.

On the eve of war, Kuznetsov's military district fielded 369,702 men (including 44,143 in schools and training institutions), 7,019 guns and mortars, 1,549 tanks (of which 1,274 were operational), and 1,344 combat aircraft (of which 1,150 were operational).[14] These forces faced all of German Army Group North and Army Group Center's Third Panzer Group, which fielded a total of 655,000 men, 7,673 guns and mortars, 1,389 tanks, and 1,070 combat aircraft.[15]

Although the strength of Kuznetsov's *front* looked powerful on paper, his forces suffered from the same debilitating deficiencies that plagued the entire Red Army on the eve of war. In the midst of Timoshenko's reforms, which were scheduled to be completed by mid-1942, his forces were only partially reorganized, trained, and reequipped. Worse still, since Stalin's direct orders prevented him from taking prudent defensive precautions and ensured that his forces were not deployed for combat, Soviet mobilization and defense plans utterly failed. Given the circumstances, the results were utterly and painfully predictable. The German force that Hitler designated to capture Leningrad quickly and efficiently crushed and eliminated the Soviet forces responsible for defending the northwestern axes and, within weeks, turned the approaches to Leningrad into a virtual war zone in its own right.

THE BORDER BATTLES, 22 JUNE–9 JULY

The massed panzers and infantry of Leeb's army group advanced across the Neiman River into Lithuania early on 22 June, catching Soviet border guards and Red Army troops manning the fortified regions and forward rifle division positions along the border totally by surprise. The advancing German forces ripped apart the only partially manned Soviet defenses and plunged deep into Soviet territory, preempting Soviet defense plans and producing total chaos and disorder among the defending Red Army forces. Although his forces were incapable of effective organized resistance, Kuznetsov tried to implement his defense plan, but given the precipitous and violent German assault, did so in wooden and haphazard fashion. The forward rifle divisions of Sobennikov's 8th and Morozov's 11th Armies manned the border defenses with only a regiment each, with the division's remaining regiments situated in peacetime garrisons to the rear. German forces first overwhelmed these forward regiments and the troops of the border guards detachments and fortified regions, and then defeated the division's remaining regiments as they frantically tried to deploy forward.

In utter disregard for the actual situation, on the evening of 22 June, the NKO dispatched to Kuznetsov the now famous Directive No. 3, which ordered his forces, "While firmly holding on to the coast of the Baltic Sea, deliver a powerful blow from the Kaunas region into the flank and rear of the enemy Suvalki grouping [Hoepner's Fourth Panzer Group], destroy it in cooperation with the Western Front, and capture the Suvalki region by day's end on 24 June."[16]

Even before receiving the directive, at 1000 hours on 23 June, Kuznetsov ordered his two mechanized corps into action in a futile attempt to implement his defensive plan, but without knowing where the advancing German forces were actually located or headed. Over the next two days, the 23d and 28th Tank Divisions of Shestapolov's 11th Mechanized Corps struck southward piecemeal without infantry support and with insufficient ammunition or fuel against a phantom enemy. In three days of heavy but confused fighting, the two divisions were decimated by antitank fire from the I Army Corps' 11th and 21st Infantry Divisions, losing 704 of the 749 tanks the divisions had fielded on 22 June.[17] Utterly overwhelmed, the decimated armored force withdrew northward in disorder toward Siauliai. On the 11th Mechanized Corps' left flank, Major General P. V. Bogdanov's 48th Rifle Division, in the army's second echelon, hastily deployed forward from reserve positions, only to be crushed and dismembered by the XXXXI Motorized Corps' 1st and 6th Panzer Divisions. After losing 70 percent of its men and all of its equipment, this division also joined the massive flow of disorganized Red Army soldiers retreating northeastward toward Raseinai and Siauliai.

To the south, Kurkin's 3d Mechanized Corps attempted to "march to the sounds of the guns," but in two separate directions. The corps' 5th Tank and 84th Motorized Divisions moved to bolster the 11th Army's forward defenses, which had already been shattered by the Third Panzer Group's ferocious assault out of East Prussia. At the same time, Major General E. N. Soliankin's 2d Tank Division, by itself, marched blindly northward into the teeth of the XXXXI Motorized Corps' advancing panzers. Late on 24 June, the tank division's forward elements reached the Dubysa River, 9.7 kilometers (6 miles) east of Raseinai, where it encountered the 6th Panzer Division's reconnaissance battalion, which was occupying a small bridgehead on the river's eastern bank. The fighting that ensued threw a fright into the defending Germans but also served as a microcosm of Red Army experiences elsewhere across the front during the harrowing first week of war.

Soliankin's tank division, which was equipped with approximately 300 tanks, including several battalions with about 50 of the new KV-1 heavy models, reached the German bridgehead late in the afternoon of 24 June and immediately attacked. In 20 minutes of fierce fighting, the more than 100 Soviet tanks overwhelmed the bridgehead's defenders and rolled across the river literally crushing the defenders:

> The battalion might have held out longer, had it not been for the monster tanks, whose 27.3-inch tracks literally ground into the dirt everything in their path—guns, motorcycles, and men. There was not a weapon in

the bridgehead that could stop them. After the massacre, the tanks waded through the Dubysa, crawling up the 45 degree banks with ease.

When the Soviet tanks lurched over the lip of the west bank of the Dubysa, they were met by fires from the entire 6th Panzer Division artillery and enfilade fire from every antitank gun the division could bring to bear. Enveloped by a tornado of fire and smoke, the mass tank attack rolled on. With growing apprehension, then in instances of near panic, the grenadiers began to realize that their weapons were useless against the big tanks. Soon some Soviet tanks split off from the main assault force and took on the antitank guns on the flanks of the armored column, rolling over the dug-in guns. The main force meanwhile drove straight toward Raseinai and broke into the artillery positions on the heights just east of the village.[18]

The 6th Panzer Division's harrowing experience continued for three more days. On 25 June the division engaged the Russian force with more than 100 tanks, one third of them Mark IV's from its 11th Panzer Regiment, in an attempt to halt the Russians' iron monsters, but their shells bounced harmlessly off the Russian tanks. The *Luftwaffe* could not help since the struggling tanks were hopelessly intermingled. New Soviet assaults pushed the defenders back to the eastern outskirts of Raseinai, where German forces finally halted the attack by using direct fire of 88mm antiaircraft guns to destroy a few of the Russian tanks. There the Soviet force halted and, to the Germans' surprise, remained in place.

The XXXXI Motorized Corps finally parried the Soviet assault by enveloping Soliankin's force with the 1st Panzer and 36th Motorized Divisions and neighboring infantry divisions, while the Soviet tank force obligingly remained immobile on the outskirts of Raseinai, where, it turned out, they had run out of fuel and ammunition. During the ensuing two days of fighting, Soliankin's tank division was completely encircled in a large pocket east of Raseinai and Soliankin perished along with many of his troops. German sappers then destroyed the monster tanks one by one with explosive charges. After the fighting was over, the Germans reported destroying or capturing more than 200 tanks, including 29 KVs, 150 guns, and hundreds of trucks and vehicles. Soviet reports indicated that 400 men and 1 BT-7 tank escaped destruction at Raseinai.[19] The Germans later determined that many of the KV tanks had not fired their guns not only because they had run out of fuel and ammunition but because they were not bore-sighted. Instead, the tanks' commanders had received orders to defeat the German forces by ramming their tanks and crushing the accompanying infantry under their treads.

By late on 25 June, Kuznetsov's counterattacks had failed, and his surviving forces were in full retreat toward Siaulai, Riga, and S'ventsiany, leaving the Daugavpils region with its important crossing sites along the Western Dvina River completely unprotected. By this time, led by its 8th Panzer Division, Manstein's LVI Motorized Corps had captured Kedainiai and Ukmerge and was approaching the Western Dvina River deep in the Soviet rear. Manstein's deep thrust cut off the withdrawal routes of Morozov's 11th Army, forcing it to withdraw in disorder to the east, and separated it from Sobennikov's 8th Army to the west.

In haste, on 25 June the newly formed Soviet *Stavka* sought to establish new defensive positions to the rear of Kuznetsov's smashed *front* by ordering him to organize a "stubborn defense" along the Western Dvina River from Riga to Vitebsk. He was to do so with the 27th Army from his reserve, the already shattered 8th and 11th Armies, and the 22d Army, the former reinforced by Major General D. D. Leliushenko's fresh 21st Mechanized Corps. However, Berzarin's 27th Army failed to occupy its defenses in time. Advancing abreast, the 8th Panzer and 3d Motorized Divisions reached the Western Dvina River on the morning of 26 June and by nightfall had seized a sizable bridgehead across the river. By doing so, they threatened the viability of the Northwestern Front's entire strategic defense. Heavy fighting raged in the Daugavpils region from 26 through 30 June as Sobennikov's infantry and Leliushenko's armor tried repeatedly to eliminate Manstein's bridgehead. Leliushenko's mechanized corps lost 79 of his 107 tanks in the heavy fighting but failed to dislodge Manstein's forces.[20]

Deprived of his last major defensive barrier protecting the northwestern axis, Kuznetsov had no choice but to withdraw his 8th Army northward toward Estonia and the 11th and 27th Armies eastward to Opochka on 27 and 28 June, leaving the Pskov and Ostrov axis on the direct approach to Leningrad virtually unprotected. Hitler ordered Hoepner's Fourth Panzer Group to advance on Ostrov, but instead Leeb ordered a 12-hour delay to permit the Sixteenth Army to catch up with his advancing panzers. Faced with the imminent loss of the Western Dvina River line, on 29 June the *Stavka* ordered the Northwestern Front to organize new defenses along the Velikaia River near Ostrov (the former Stalin Line), anchored on the Pskov and Ostrov Fortified Regions. It then reinforced these defenses with Major General I. S. Kosobutsky's 41st Rifle Corps from its reserve, Major General M. L. Cherniavsky's 1st Mechanized Corps from Popov's Northern Front (the former Leningrad Military District), and the 234th Rifle Division.

However, once again Kuznetsov's forces failed to occupy their new defenses in time to block the German advance. Reinhardt's XXXXI Panzer Corps seized crossings over the Western Dvina at Jacobpils and Livany from the 8th Army on 30 June, while Manstein's LVI Panzer Corps expanded its bridgehead at Daugavpils and repelled futile counterattacks by Leliushenko's now decimated 21st Mechanized Corps. By this time, the armored strength of

Kuznetsov's *front* had fallen to 150 tanks, and only 154 aircraft remained to provide his forces with air support.[21]

In an attempt to stem Northwestern Front's apparent collapse, at month's end the *Stavka* shuffled the *front*'s senior command cadre by replacing Kuznetsov with Sobennikov, the former 8th Army commander, and by appointing Lieutenant General F. S. Ivanov in Sobennikov's stead. At the same time, it sent Lieutenant General N. F. Vatutin, the deputy chief of the General Staff, who had played a vital role in preparing prewar Soviet defense plans, to serve as Sobennikov's chief of staff. Vatutin's instructions were to restore order to the *front* and actively resist the German advance "at all cost."[22]

Meanwhile, on 2 July the OKH ordered Leeb's army group to erect blocking positions north and south of Lake Chud (Peipus) and advance with his main force through Pskov to Leningrad and the southeastern shore of Lake Ladoga to invest Soviet forces defending Leningrad. Hoepner's Fourth Panzer Group was to spearhead the advance northward and northeastward from Pskov while Kuechler's and Busch's infantry cleared Soviet forces from Estonia and Soviet bases on the Baltic coast and protected its right flank against attack from Nevel'. Hours later, the OKH also ordered Hoepner's panzer group to seize the area between Velikie Luki and Lake Il'men' while it extended its lines to Pskov, but not to advance farther without special authorization so as not to become isolated and destroyed before the follow-on infantry arrived.

Hoepner's panzer group advanced from its bridgeheads on the Western Dvina River on 2 July in a driving rainstorm. The weather improved after two days of slow movement, and the 1st Panzer Division of Reinhardt's XXXXI Panzer Corps captured Ostrov on 4 July, piercing Soviet defenses along the former Stalin Line and approaching the southern limits of Leningrad region. At the same time, the corps' 6th Panzer Division crushed Soviet defenses along the Velikaia River south of Pskov. To the south, the 8th Panzer Division of Manstein's LVI Panzer Corps captured Rezekne on 3 July after heavy fighting but then bogged down for two days while trying to traverse the swampy terrain along both banks of the Velikaia River. This delay prompted Hoepner to order Manstein's 3d Motorized Division to regroup northward and join Reinhardt's corps, which was advancing along the Ostrov axis.

Concluding that he had no choice but to do so, Manstein ordered his 8th Panzer Division and the SS "Totenkopf" Motorized Division to continue to fight their way through the swamps toward Opochka despite Hoepner's increasingly shrill entreaties that Manstein join Reinhardt's advance at Ostrov. While Manstein and Hoepner argued over future strategy and Manstein's forces struggled to overcome the Velikaia River swamps, Reinhardt's XXXXI Motorized Corps fended off heavy Soviet counterattacks at Ostrov on 6 and 7 July. Successfully expanding their bridgehead, his forces captured Pskov on 8 July, penetrating into the southern portion of Leningrad region. Despite the daunting terrain problems and increasingly desperate Soviet resistance, by 9 July Hoepner's panzer group had successfully slashed its way through the entire depth of the vaunted Stalin Line.

Subsequently, a portion of Kuechler's Eighteenth Army spread into Latvia against diminishing resistance from the severely weakened 8th Army, while the remainder of his infantry hastened after the advancing panzer corps. To the south, Busch's Sixteenth Army supported Manstein's armor between Opochka and Sebezh and protected the army group's right flank.

By 7 July the border battles were at an end. Leeb's army group and Hoepner's panzers had preempted *Stavka* mobilization and defense plans, utterly defeated Kuznetsov's Northwestern Front, and advanced northeastward through the Stalin Line. The first three weeks of dramatic combat along the northwestern strategic axis proved costly to Kuznetsov's *front*. Leeb's army group had advanced 450 kilometers (279.6 miles) and captured much of the Soviet Union's Baltic region. During this period, Kuznetsov's *front* lost 90,000 soldiers, more than 1,000 tanks, 4,000 guns and mortars, and more than 1,000 combat aircraft.[23] Worse still, his forces had not been able to establish credible defenses anywhere, and Leeb's forces now posed a deadly threat to Popov's Northern Front.

Popov was acutely aware of the new threat and realized that Leningrad would now have to fight for its very survival. He was so concerned that on 23 June, the day before the *Stavka* transformed his military district into the Northern Front, he dispatched his deputy, Lieutenant General K. P. Piadyshev, southwestward to determine if, where, and how the *front* could erect defenses to protect the southern approaches to the city. Piadyshev recommended the Kingisepp-Luga-Lake Il'men' line as the most suitable location for the defenses, but neither he nor his commander knew where forces to defend the line would come from.[24] However, the gravity of the threat had become so great by 25 June that Popov and the rest of his *front*'s Military Council accepted Piadyshev's proposals and appointed him to command the as yet phantom defense. The council did, however, promise a large force of laborers to construct the new Luga Line. Piadyshev, who was described as "a brilliant, rather sardonic man of great military experience and few illusions," needed all the help he could get.[25]

To make matters worse for Popov, he was distracted by enemy operations in other sectors of his *front*'s theater of operations. In mid-July, his forces operating along the Murmansk, Ukhtinsk, and Kandalaska axes halted an advance by the German Army of Norway and the Finnish III Army Corps, which penetrated 25–30 kilometers (15.5–18.6 miles) deep into the Soviet defenses. However, he was certain that enemy action in these sectors, as well as along the vital approaches to Leningrad on the Karelian Isthmus, would soon resume. In addition, the fighting in the Baltic region had forced the Baltic Fleet to transfer its ships from the ports of Liepaia and Ventspils to Tallin in Estonia.

THE DISTANT APPROACHES TO LENINGRAD AND
THE SOVIET COUNTERSTROKE AT SOL'TSY,
10 JULY–7 AUGUST

Leeb's army group resumed its rapid advance from the Pskov and Ostrov regions toward Leningrad early on 9 July with its Eighteenth Army, Fourth Panzer Group, and a portion of the Sixteenth Army. Having advanced roughly 450 kilometers (279.6 miles) during the first two weeks of Operation Barbarossa, he fully expected to cover the remaining 250 kilometers (155.3 miles) just as rapidly. His army group's mission was to advance toward Leningrad, destroy the Northwestern and Northern Fronts, sever Leningrad's communications from the east and southeast, and capture the city.[26]

Forming the cornerstone of the army group's advance, Hoepner's Fourth Panzer Group was to advance northeast toward Lake Il'men' with Reinhardt's XXXXI Motorized Corps attacking from Pskov toward Luga and Manstein's LVI Motorized Corps advancing toward Lake Il'men'. Busch's Sixteenth Army was to protect the army group's right flank against any Soviet attack from the Staraia Russa and Velikie Luki regions, and Kuechler's Eighteenth Army was to clear Soviet forces from Courland, Latvia, and Estonia. Neither Hitler nor General Franz Halder, the chief of staff of the OKH, believed that any further concentration of forces was necessary since, in their view, the Red Army was already defeated. Consequently, OKH ordered the Third Panzer Group to remain with Army Group Center and did not release the panzer group's XXXIX Panzer Corps to Army Group North until 12 August (Map 3). To the north, the Finnish Army was to assault along the northwestern approaches to Leningrad between Lakes Onega and Ladoga to assist Army Group North in the capture of Leningrad.

Soviet defenses along the northwestern axis were indeed shaky in early July. The Northwestern Front's 8th Army defended southern Estonia from Parnu on the Gulf of Riga to Tartu on Lake Chud, and the 11th and 27th Armies held what remained of the Stalin Defense Line east of the Velikaia River from Pskov to Opochka. The *front*'s mission was to protect the approaches to Leningrad and Tallin with armies that had already suffered serious defeat, many of whose divisions numbered fewer than 2,000 men.[27]

To shore up the Northwestern Front's defenses, on 4 July, Zhukov, who was still the Red Army's chief of staff, ordered Popov's Northern Front to "immediately occupy a defense line along the Narva-Luga-Staraia Russa-

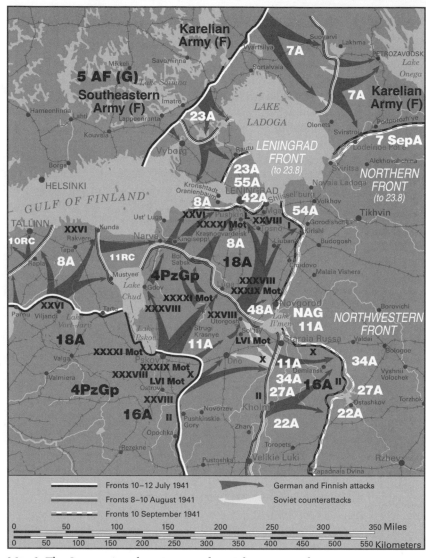

Map 3. The German Assault on Leningrad, 10 July–10 September 1941

Borovichi front."[28] The heart of the new Luga Defense Line was supposed to be a defense 10–15 kilometers (6.2–9.3 miles) deep of barriers, minefields, and antitank guns behind the Luga River 100 kilometers (62.1 miles) south of Leningrad. All the while, Popov had to defend the city's northern approaches along the Karelian Isthmus with his 23d Army and the approaches into central Karelia and Murmansk in the far north with his 7th and 14th Armies. Popov also had at his disposal the Baltic Fleet, assigned to his control on 28 June, and the 8th Army, transferred to his *front* on 14 July.[29]

Popov officially formed the Luga Operational Group (LOG) on 6 July with the experienced Piadyshev as its commander. The group—which initially consisted of the 70th, 171st, 177th, and 191st Rifle Divisions; the 1st, 2d, and 3d People's Militia Divisions (*diviziia narodnogo opolcheniia*—DNO); the 1st Separate Mountain Rifle Brigade; and supporting artillery—occupied its defense positions between 6 and 9 July.[30] By 14 July the LOG consisted of the 177th and 191st Rifle Divisions; the 90th, 111th, 118th, and 235th Rifle Divisions of Major General I. S. Kosobutsky's 41st Rifle Corps; the 1st Mountain Rifle Brigade; the 1st, 2d, and 4th DNOs; and the Leningrad "S. M. Kirov" Infantry and Rifle–Machine Gun School. Popov also placed the 10th Mechanized Corps' 21st and 24th Tank Divisions in *front* reserve with orders to provide the LOG with critical armor support.

Construction work on the Luga Line had begun after 29 June, when the Northern Front's Military Council formed the Rear Line Construction Directorate (USTOR), which was headed by Major General P. A. Zaitsev, Popov's Deputy Commander for Fortified Regions. After halting all ongoing construction in Leningrad, Zaitsev mobilized all construction forces and 30,000 civilians to work around the clock on the new defenses.[31] The Luga Line itself, which was never fully completed, extended from the Gulf of Narva to Lake Il'men' with a gap left between Luga and Krasnogvardeisk through which the Northwestern Front's forces could withdraw. Behind the first line was a second "outer circle," which extended from Petergof on the Gulf of Finland through Krasnogvardeisk to Kolpino and was anchored on the Krasnogvardeisk Fortified Region. A third line, which formed the city's inner defense, ran along the rail line from Avtovo to Rybatskoe on the Neva River.

When the first of the defending divisions, Colonel A. F. Mashoshin's 177th Rifle, arrived south of Luga on 4 July, the line was so incomplete that an additional 25,000 laborers had to be mobilized to accelerate its construction. Thereafter, additional forces occupied the defenses while the combat front inched perilously northward toward it. Colonel D. A. Luk'ianov's 191st Rifle Division occupied the Kingisepp sector and Colonel I. M. Ivanov's 111th Rifle Division, which had already been shattered in heavy fighting east of Pskov, withdrew to back up the 177th south of Luga. Piadyshev's remaining forces filtered into position from 10 to 14 July.

North of Leningrad, the Northern Front's 7th Army defended the border north of Lake Ladoga with three rifle divisions. To the south, the 23d Army, consisting of the 19th and 50th Rifle Corps with four rifle divisions, and the 198th Motorized Division, defended from the Gulf of Finland to west of Lake Ladoga. To generate additional forces for the defense, on 29 June the *Stavka* approved Popov's request for permission to form DNOs.[32] The next day his *front* formed the Leningrad National Militia Army, a provisional organization complete with a military council and staff, tasked with recruiting and training militia forces. Within days, however, the deteriorating situation prompted the militia army to defer the orderly creation of 15 DNOs and instead raise three divisions for employment on the Luga Line by 7 July. Formed on a voluntary basis from students, workers, professionals, and anyone else who wished to join, the divisions' regiments took the names of the districts or factories in which they were formed. Although the DNOs had a small nucleus of trained regulars and high morale, they lacked training, experience, and any heavy weapons. The fate of the Leningrad DNO and those formed elsewhere across the Soviet Union symbolized the price the populace would have to pay for Soviet lack of preparedness for war. They also vividly demonstrated the Soviet population's capacity for suffering and sacrifice, as John Erickson describes in *The Road to Stalingrad:* "The dispatch to inevitable destruction of men scarcely trained, committed against and butchered by crack, battle-tested German divisions, blotted out by tank and dive-bomber attacks and shredded by artillery, shaped gruesomely into enormous tragedy. Four divisions were ultimately wiped out."[33]

All of the frenzied activity to shore up Leningrad's defenses reflected and, in turn, were affected by Stalin's determined efforts to rationalize Red Army command and control from Moscow. On 30 June he established the State Defense Committee (*Gosudarstvennyi komitet oborony*—GKO), a virtual war cabinet, to control the state's management of the war more effectively. The same day, he appointed Vatutin as the new Northwestern Front chief of staff effective 4 July, with orders to restore order in the badly shaken *front,* and replaced Kuznetsov with Sobennikov as Northwestern Front commander. Less than a week later, on 10 July, Stalin reorganized the *Stavka* of the Main Command (SGK), which had been organized on 24 June to centralize control of military operations, into the *Stavka* of the High Command (SVK) with himself as its chairman.[34] Also on 10 July, Stalin ordered the People's Commissariat of Defense to organize the Main Command of the Northwestern Direction to coordinate the Northern and Northwestern Fronts' and the Northern and Baltic Fleets' operations. Stalin appointed Marshal of the Soviet Union K. E. Voroshilov as the Main Command's commander; A. A. Zhdanov, secretary of the Communist Party's Central Committee and Leningrad Party chief, as its member of the Military Council (commissar); and Major General M. V. Zakharov as its chief of staff.[35]

Literally simultaneously, Popov's Northern Front was beset by enemy assaults from north and south as Army Group North resumed its advance along the Luga, Novgorod, and Staraia Russa axes and into Estonia, and Finnish forces began an offensive toward Petrozavodsk and Olonets north of Lake Ladoga. Faced with the new German onslaught, with *Stavka* approval, on 13 July Voroshilov's Northwestern Direction High Command reorganized the command and control of its forces operating southwest of Leningrad.

First, Voroshilov ordered the 8th Army and the 41st Rifle Corps of Morozov's 11th Army transferred from Northwestern to Northern Front control to help block the German advance on Leningrad. Ivanov's 8th Army was to defend Estonia and the coast of the Gulf of Finland, while Kosobutsky's 41st Rifle Corps was to reinforce Piadyshev's Luga Operational Group. Deployed along the 300-kilometer (186.4-mile) front from Narva to Shimsk on Lake Il'men', Piadyshev's group was to defend the southwestern approaches to Leningrad, and Sobennikov's Northwestern Front was to halt any German advance on Novgorod, Staraia Russa, and Velikie Luki.[36] To the south, Morozov's 11th Army and the newly formed 34th Army, commanded by Brigade Commander N. I. Pronin, were to defend along the Novgorod and Staraia Russa axes, and Berzarin's 27th Army was to defend along the Velikie Luki axis. Voroshilov's headquarters then acted to stiffen the defense by issuing Order No. 3, dated 14 July, which demanded that all Red Army formations and units hold Leningrad "at all cost."[37]

On 10 July Hoepner's Fourth Panzer Group resumed its advance from its bridgehead east of the Velikaia River at Pskov and Ostrov. The summer heat, which often exceeded 90°F, and the rugged terrain acted as an effective brake on the accustomed fast pace of Blitzkrieg:

> Though slower than earlier phases, progress was still measured in about twenty miles a day. The roads were abominable, leading through sand, bog, swamp, forest, and dense undergrowth, favoring at every turn the defender. . . .
>
> Leaving the road to Porkhov meant leaving the Twentieth Century for the Middle Ages. The tracks the Germans had to use had never seen a motor vehicle before. The German maps (on a scale of 1:300,000) were hopelessly out of date and completely wrong. . . .
>
> The weather was oppressively hot. The days in these northern regions were interminably long, and even the brief hours of semi-darkness brought little relief from the sweltering heat. The area was sparsely populated. Drinking water became a problem at the incredibly primitive settlements, but dug wells of up to one hundred feet provided excellent drinking water. To their surprise, the troops still found there was ice at the bottom.[38]

Reinhardt's XXXXI Motorized Corps advanced toward Kingisepp with the XXXVIII Army Corps' infantry of Kuechler's Eighteenth Army in its wake. The motorized corps' 1st and 6th Panzer Divisions advanced rapidly through Liady toward Luga against light resistance from the LOG's western group and on 13 July a combat group of the 6th Panzer Division captured a small bridgehead across the Luga River. After securing additional bridgeheads across the river at Porech'e, Ivanovskoe, and Sabsk southeast of Kingisepp, only 110 kilometers (68.6 miles) from Leningrad, Reinhardt's advance stalled for six days in the face of fanatical Soviet resistance, resistance he could not overcome without assistance from Manstein's LVI Motorized Corps. Faced with the surprise German advance toward Kingisepp, Popov had tried to block it with the only forces at his disposal, the 2d DNO and two companies of the Leningrad Red Banner Infantry School.[39]

Unfortunately for Reinhardt, Manstein was unable to help because he too had encountered stiffer than anticipated Soviet resistance. While Reinhardt's panzer corps sped forward toward the Luga River, Manstein's LVI Motorized Corps, supported by infantry from the Eighteenth Army's I Army Corps, advanced along the Luga axis through Sol'tsy toward Novgorod, Chudovo, and Staraia Russa. The motorized corps' vanguard, the 8th Panzer Division, penetrated 30–40 kilometers (18.6–24.8 miles) along the Shimsk road and reached the town of Sol'tsy late on 13 July. Here, the panzer division's advance ground to a halt in the face of spirited resistance by Mashoshin's 177th Rifle Division and Major General I. G. Lazarev's 10th Mechanized Corps of the LOG, which skillfully exploited the difficult terrain. By nightfall, the 8th Panzer Division found itself isolated from the 3d Motorized Division to its left and the SS "Totenkopf" Division, which was still lagging well to its rear.

Ever alert for an opportunity to strike back at the Germans, by this time, the *Stavka* had already ordered Voroshilov's Northwestern Direction High Command to launch a counterstroke against the overexposed German force. In a scathing critique of the Northwestern Command's previous conduct of its defense, on behalf of the *Stavka*, on 10 July Zhukov ordered Voroshilov and Vatutin, the Northwestern Front's new chief of staff, to attack the exposed German panzer force:

> The *Stavka* of the High Command and the State Defense Committee are completely dissatisfied with the work of the Northwestern Front's command and headquarters.
>
> First, up to this time, commanders who have not fulfilled our orders and, like criminals, have abandoned their positions and withdrawn from their defensive lines without orders have not been punished. You cannot defend with such a liberal attitude toward cowardice.

To date, your destroyer detachments have not performed well, and the fruits of their labors are not apparent. The Northwestern Front's units are constantly rolling to the rear because of the division, corps, army commanders, and *front* commanders' inactivity. It is time for this shameful matter to cease. Immediately commence active operations, in the first place, night destroyer operations with small detachments.

The commander and the member of the Military Council, the [military] prosecutor, and the chief of the 3d Directorate will immediately go to the forward units to deal with cowards and criminals on the spot. Organize active operations on the spot to destroy the Germans and to attack and destroy them at night.

For the time being, one tank division is being sent forward to Porkhov. Two rifle divisions will be sent forward to the Porkhov region only when you have restored the situation in the Pskov region. It will not be possible to take two divisions from the Luga region until the penetration has been liquidated. Attach the tank units to your rifle divisions to add greater durability and activity to your rifle corps. Beginning this morning you must burn the enemy's motor-mechanized units, artillery, and rear services with air strikes.

[signed] Army General Zhukov, Chief of the General Staff[40]

The *Stavka*'s stinging rebuke spurred Voroshilov to action and precipitated the ensuing action around Sol'tsy. On 13 July he and his chief of staff, Vatutin, ordered Morozov's 11th Army to counterattack along the Sol'tsy-Dno axis with two shock groups. The northern group, which consisted of the 10th Mechanized Corps' 21st Tank Division and the 16th Rifle Corps' 70th and 237th Rifle Divisions, were to attack the 8th Panzer Division's exposed positions around Sol'tsy from the north.[41] Other LOG forces to the west and the 1st DNO and 1st Mountain Rifle Brigade, which were operating along the Novgorod axis, were to support and reinforce the northern group's assault.

The southern group, which consisted of the 180th, 182d, and 183d Rifle Divisions of Major General A. S. Ksenofontov's 22d Rifle Corps, was to attack the 8th Panzer Division's defenses from the east. Colonel S. I. Karapetian's 183d Rifle Division was to strike directly westward toward Sol'tsy, and Colonels I. I. Missan's and I. I. Kuryshev's 180th and 182d Rifle Divisions were to attack toward the 8th Panzer Division's lines of communications to the southwest. Farther to the south, the divisions of Berzarin's 27th Army were to support Morozov's assault by attacking the German Sixteenth Army's forces west of Kholm.

The Soviet assault, launched in oppressive 90°F (32°C) summer heat and massive clouds of dust, caught the 8th Panzer Division and its neighbor to the left, the 3d Motorized Division, totally by surprise. The violent assault isolated the two German divisions from one another and forced the 8th Panzer to fight a costly battle in encirclement for four days. It also disrupted the Germans' offensive plans by forcing Hoepner's Fourth Panzer Group to divert the SS "Totenkopf" Motorized Division from the Kingisepp and Luga axes to rescue the beleaguered 8th Panzer at Sol'tsy. Manstein, the LVI Panzer Corps commander, later recalled the perilous situation:

> 8 Panzer Division was to drive through Zoltsy to seize the vital crossing point where the Mshaga River ran into Lake Ilmen. In a series of battles, most of them fierce ones, the advance was kept going for the next few days . . . the enemy had so far not made his presence felt on our open flank in the south. That same day, at my insistence, 8 Panzer Division, which had taken Zoltsy after a battle against an enemy well equipped with artillery and armour, pushed on to the Mshaga sector. It found the bridge already blown. . . .
>
> Early on 15th July we received a number of most unpleasant reports at the corps command post on the Shelon, west of Zoltsy. The enemy had launched a powerful attack from the north into the flank of 8 Panzer Division, now strung out to the Mshaga, and simultaneously driven up from the south over the Shelon. This meant that the bulk of 8 Panzer Division's fighting troops, who were located between Zoltsy and the Mshaga, were cut off from the division's rear echelons, in whose area corps H.Q. was located. But that was not all. The enemy had closed the trap behind ourselves, too, by pushing strong forces from the south to straddle our supply route. . . .
>
> Our corps' position at that moment was hardly an enviable one, and we could not help wondering whether we had taken rather too great a risk this time. . . . As matters stood, the only course open to us was to pull 8 Panzer Division back through Zoltsy to escape the encirclement that now threatened. . . . The next days proved critical, with the enemy straining every nerve to keep up his encirclement and throwing in, besides his rifle divisions, two armoured divisions enjoying strong artillery and air support. 8 Panzer Division nevertheless managed to break through Zoltsy to the west and re-group, despite having to be temporarily supplied from the air.
>
> By 18th July the crisis was as good as over, the corps being by then firmly established around Dno on a front facing roughly east by northeast.[42]

Another observer echoed the seriousness of the situation:

> Both of Manstein's divisions were cut off. Only now did Hoepner return the SS division to him. It took several days of fierce fighting—in a single day the 3d Panzer Grenadier [Motorized] Division turned back seven-

teen attacks—before the divisions could disengage and fight their way out of encirclement. It was a clear case of isolated armor having surged ahead without regard for either flank protection or the gap between the mobile forces and the slower, marching infantry.[43]

The Northwestern Front's Sol'tsy counterstroke, which cost the 8th Panzer Division 70 of its 150 tanks destroyed or damaged, represented the first, albeit temporary, success achieved by Soviet forces on the path to Leningrad. It also cost the German command a precious week lost to regroup and resume its advance. Although Soviet losses are not known, they must have been high given the intensity of the fighting. For example, after being either wounded or relieved of their commands, in the midst of the fighting on 17 July, Fediunin of the 70th Rifle Division was replaced by a major and Kuryshev of the 182d Rifle Division was also replaced. Two days later, Popov of the 237th Rifle Division also relinquished his command.

While the 8th Panzer, 3d Motorized, and SS "Totenkopf" Motorized Divisions were repelling the heavy Soviet assaults, Soviet forces to the south were experiencing a major setback. In the region west of Kholm, the XXVIII Army Corps of Busch's Sixteenth Army succeeded in defeating, encircling, and destroying a large portion of Berzarin's 27th Army west of Kholm.[44]

Once the crisis at Sol'tsy had ended, the Eighteenth Army's I Army Corps continued its advance along the Novgorod axis against the Luga Operational Group's 1st DNO and the 1st Separate Mountain Rifle Brigade, capturing Shimsk and reaching the southwestern shore of Lake Il'men' on 30 July. The corps' determined advance also forced the 22d Rifle Corps of Morozov's 11th Army and the remnants of Berzarin's 27th Army to break off contact and withdraw precipitously to the Staraia Russa–Kholm line. The II and X Army Corps of Busch's Sixteenth Army pursued, occupying Kholm on 2 August and Staraia Russa on 6 August. By this time, Busch's Sixteenth Army had managed to exploit the 27th and 11th Armies' defeat and established a continuous German front from Lake Il'men' to Velikie Luki.

Vatutin's counterstroke at Sol'tsy forced Leeb to halt his army group's advance for about three weeks along the Narva, Luga, and Mshaga River lines, while he and his subordinate commanders argued over the army group's future course of action. After advancing 450 kilometers (279.6 miles) in two weeks, Leeb's forces had spent almost an entire month covering 120 kilometers (74.6 miles) and were still over 100 kilometers (62.1 miles) from Leningrad. While the *Stavka* was pleased that Vatutin's Sol'tsy-Dno counterstroke had had an adverse impact on the Germans' offensive timetable, Soviet critiques of the operation lamented that only appallingly poor command, control, and coordination by the attacking forces had prevented the operation from accomplishing far more.

While the bulk of Leeb's army group was advancing along the main attack axis toward Leningrad, lesser groups of forces were clearing Soviet forces from the army group's left flank in Estonia and along the coast of the Baltic Sea. The Germans conducted these seemingly peripheral operations to secure the army group's left flank and deprive the Soviets of naval and air facilities in the Baltic region.[45] Between 11 July and 28 August, the Eighteenth Army's XXVI and XXXXII Army Corps, each consisting of two infantry divisions, defeated the 8th Army's 10th Rifle Corps in Estonia and occupied Tartu, Parnu, and Tallin.[46] The *Stavka* finally ordered its forces to evacuate Tallin on 26 August. At a cost of heavy losses, including roughly 20,000 prisoners taken by the Germans, the Soviet defense of Estonia tied down four German divisions but only marginally weakened the German Luga and Novgorod groupings. Thereafter, in September and October, German forces seized the Moon Islands off the Estonian coast, while Finnish forces eliminated the Soviet naval base at Hango.[47]

After failing to inflict a major defeat of German forces with its counterstroke toward Sol'tsy, the *Stavka* demanded the Northwestern Direction High Command strengthen its Luga Line defenses along the immediate approaches to Leningrad. In response, Voroshilov assembled a new reserve consisting of the 272d, 265th, 268th, and 281st Rifle Divisions and the 1st Tank Division, which had been sent southward from northern Karelia. He concentrated this force at Batetskii Station, 20 kilometers (12.4 miles) east of Luga, and ordered it to help repel any German advance along the Novgorod and Luga-Leningrad axes.[48] However, the Finnish Army's advance in Karelia and German Eighteenth Army's drive into Estonia forced the Northwestern Command to commit the four rifle divisions elsewhere.[49] Reluctantly, Voroshilov transferred the 272d Rifle Division to reinforce the 7th Army at Petrozavodsk, the 265th Rifle Division to the 23d Army on the Karelian Isthmus, the 268th Rifle Division to the 8th Army in Estonia, and the 281st Rifle Division to the Kingisepp defensive sector. He then positioned Major General V. I. Baranov's 1st Tank Division south of Krasnogvardeisk (Gatchina) as his only reserve.

At the same time, the *Stavka* began simplifying its military command structure in an attempt to improve command and control throughout all of its operating forces. In its Directive Letter No. 1 dated 15 July, it informed Voroshilov:

War experience indicates that the presence of such large and cumbersome armies with a great number of divisions and with intermediate corps headquarters severely hinders the organization of combat and command and control of forces in combat, particularly considering the youth and inexperience of our staffs and command cadre. The *Stavka* believes that, gradually and without any prejudice to current operations, we ought to make the transition to a system of smaller armies of five or a maximum of six divisions without the corps headquarters and with the divisions directly subordinate to the army commanders.

The *Stavka* obliges the *front* commanders to consider these conclusions from the first three weeks of war with German fascism and implement them under the leadership of the High Commands.[50]

Following the *Stavka*'s advice, Popov relieved and arrested General Piadyshev on 23 July, ostensibly for dereliction of duty, and split his Luga Operation Group into three separate and semi-independent sector commands. The Kingisepp Sector, commanded by Major General V. V. Semashko, was responsible for defending the Kingisepp axis along the Luga River southwest of Leningrad. It consisted of the Baltic Fleet's coastal units, the 90th and 191st Rifle Divisions, the 2d DNO and 4th Light DNO, the Leningrad Infantry School, the 14th Antitank Brigade, Armored Train No. 60, and the 519th RVK (*Stavka* reserve) Howitzer Artillery Regiment. The Luga Sector, commanded by Major General A. N. Astinin, had the mission of protecting the Luga highway axis south of the city. Astinin's force consisted of the 111th, 177th, and 235th Rifle Divisions, the 2d Tank Division, the 3d DNO's 1st Rifle Regiment, the 260th and 262d Machine Gun Artillery Battalions, and the Leningrad Artillery School's Rifle–Machine Gun School and associated battalion. Finally, the Eastern Sector, consisting of the 1st DNO, the 1st Separate Mountain Rifle Brigade, and the 261st and 263d Machine Gun Artillery Battalions under Major General F. N. Starikov's command, was to protect the Novgorod axis and Leningrad's southeastern approaches.[51]

Simultaneously, a team from the Northwestern Direction High Command inspected the Luga Defense Line and determined that it was wholly inadequate for an effective defense. Therefore, on 29 July the Northwestern Command ordered its two *fronts* to strengthen the Krasnogvardeisk Fortified Region and subdivide the fortified region into three distinct sectors, which it named the Krasnoe Selo, Central, and Slutsk-Kolpino defensive sectors. It tasked General Zaitsev, the chief of the Northern Front's Engineers, with constructing the fortified region and created a new military-civilian Special Defense Works Commission, headed by A. A. Kuznetsov, the Leningrad Party chief, with overall responsibility for building all defensive works around Leningrad.[52] However, even the new construction effort was inadequate, primarily because Voroshilov objected to building defenses so close to the city and instead insisted that defensive work be concentrated on the Luga Line. Dissatisfied with the defensive effort, on 30 July Stalin summoned Voroshilov and Zhdanov to Moscow, where he sharply criticized them for their "lack of toughness" in conducting operations in the Northwestern Theater.

Meanwhile, the *Stavka* and General Staff acted vigorously to strengthen the defenses south of Leningrad. By early August the *Stavka* had already dispatched nine rifle and two cavalry divisions to the Northwestern Front, and on 6 August it assigned it Pronin's 34th Army with five rifle and two cavalry divisions, four artillery regiments, and two armored trains.[53] The accompanying instructions required both Voroshilov and Popov to employ the new army as a single entity rather than frittering it away piecemeal on peripheral operations. The next day, the General Staff formed the 48th Army, commanded by Lieutenant General S. D. Akimov, which consisted of the 1st DNO, the 70th, 128th and 237th Rifle Divisions, the 1st Separate Mountain Rifle Brigade, and the 21st Tank Division, and assigned it as well to the Northwestern Front. Akimov's new army was responsible for protecting the Northern Front's left flank north of Lake Il'men'. To protect the lake itself, the Northwestern Front formed the Il'men' Detachment of Ships subordinate to the 48th Army.[54] In addition, Voroshilov still retained the 1st Tank Division at Krasnogvardeisk, even though it had already been weakened in previous heavy fighting at Kandalaska north of Lake Onega.

The Red Army's defense of the Soviet Union's state borders was an unmitigated disaster. In only six weeks, the *Wehrmacht* utterly shattered the Red Army's border defenses and the bulk of the Northwestern Front's forces that manned these defenses. Although Kuznetsov attempted to implement his defense plan, his clumsy counterstrokes gave the lie to both the requirements of the NKO's ambitious defense plans and the Red Army's capabilities for successfully implementing them. At first glance, the 2d Tank Division's brave but futile counterstroke at Raseinai was indicative of what might have occurred in more favorable circumstances. In reality, however, the dramatic tank battle symbolized the overall dismal performance of Soviet forces along the northwestern axis, the utter futility of its resistance, and the frustration the *Stavka* would experience throughout the entire initial period of the war here and elsewhere across the front. Within a brief period of only six weeks, the Germans largely demolished Kuznetsov's *front,* forcing its shaken remnants to defend and withdraw as best they could.

The Northwestern Front's precipitous collapse created an immense gap in Soviet strategic defenses. The *Stavka* tried but failed to plug the gap by deploying forward a confusing array of partially mobilized and poorly controlled reserve forces. Despite its strenuous efforts in late July, the *Stavka* and Northwestern Direction High Command succeeded only in slowing the German advance, however, at immense cost in terms of lost men and material. By that time the *Wehrmacht* had cleared virtually the entire Baltic region of Red Army forces and reached to within 100 kilometers (62.1 miles) of Leningrad's southern outskirts.

The only bright spot for the *Stavka* in the midst of this most depressing period was the limited success the Northwestern Front achieved in its counterstroke at Sol'tsy, where, for the first time in the war, an attacking Red Army force managed to encircle and severely damage a sizable German panzer force. At the same time the counterstroke seriously disrupted the Germans' ambitious but vitally important offensive timetable. Although the Soviet success at Sol'tsy was fleeting, the violent counterstroke inflicted such damage on the 8th Panzer Division that it would be hors de combat for several weeks and not available to participate fully in the decisive operations that would occur south of Leningrad in August and early September. On the other hand, the ultimate failure of the Sol'tsy counterstroke encouraged the *Stavka* to order its forces to conduct numerous subsequent offensive operations along the same axis, most of which achieved the same mixed results.

Worse still for the Red Army, by early August the forces of Popov's Northern Front were in direct contact with the advancing Germans, finding themselves fighting unexpectedly and ill prepared on the front lines in the Battle for Leningrad. A situation that neither Popov nor the *Stavka* had anticipated and that both dreaded had suddenly materialized. The victorious *Wehrmacht* forced Popov to make the best of a bad situation and attempt to defend Leningrad from his shaky, fragile, and incomplete defense line along the Luga River.

CHAPTER 3

The Defense of Leningrad

8 August–10 September 1941

GERMAN OFFENSIVE PLANNING

Hitler and his senior commanders formulated their plans for the final assault on Leningrad during the second half of July. During this period, Hitler issued three directives that collectively refined his concept for future *Wehrmacht* military operations. In his Fuehrer Directive No. 33, dated 19 July, Hitler provided general and specific guidance as to how the offensive was to develop:

1. The second offensive to the east has been completed by the penetration of the "Stalin Line" along the entire front and by a further deep advance by the panzer groups to the east. Army Group Center requires considerable time to liquidate the strong enemy groups, which continue to remain between our mobile formations.

The Kiev fortifications and the operations by the Soviet 5th Army's forces in our rear have inhibited active operations and free maneuver on Army Group South's northern flank.

2. The objective of further operations should be to prevent the escape of large enemy forces into the depth of the Russian territory and to annihilate them. To do so, prepare [as follows] along the following axes. . . .

    c. *The Northern sector of the Eastern Front.* Resume the advance toward Leningrad only after the Eighteenth Army has restored contact with the Fourth Panzer Group and the Sixteenth Army's forces are protecting its eastern flank. When that is accomplished, Army Group North must strive to prevent Soviet forces, which are continuing to operate in Estonia, from withdrawing to Leningrad. It is desirable to capture as rapidly as possible the islands in the Baltic Sea, which can be Soviet fleet strong points.[1]

In a supplement to the directive issued on 23 July, Hitler reiterated his intention to capture Leningrad before marching on Moscow and assigned the Third Panzer Group to Army Group North for the duration of the operation against Leningrad:

After the report of the OKW on 22 July 1941, I order [the following] as an addition to and broadening of Directive No. 33. . . .

3. *The Northern sector of the Eastern Front.* Having received control of the Third Panzer Group, Army Group North will be capable of allocating large infantry forces for the advance on Leningrad and thus avoid expending mobile formations on frontal attacks in difficult terrain.

Enemy forces still operating in Estonia must be destroyed. While doing so, it is necessary to prevent their transport by ship and penetration through Narva toward Leningrad.

Upon fulfilling its mission, the Third Panzer Group must be once again transferred to Army Group Center's control.

4. Subsequently, but as soon as conditions permit, the OKW will fix its attention on withdrawing part of Army Group North's forces, including the Fourth Panzer Group, and also part of Army Group South' s infantry force to the Homeland.[2]

Finally, Hitler provided even more detailed instructions on how Army Group North was to capture Leningrad in yet another Fuehrer directive, No. 34, which he issued on 30 July:

The course of events in recent days, the appearance of large enemy forces before the front, the supply situation, and the necessity of giving the Second and Third Panzer Groups 10 days to restore and refill their formations has forced a temporary postponement of the fulfillment of aims and missions set forth in Directive Nr. 33 of 19 July and the addendum to it of 23 July.

Accordingly, I order:

I. Army Forces:

In the northern sector of the Eastern Front, continue the offensive toward Leningrad by making the main attack between Lake Il'men' and Narva to encircle Leningrad and establish contact with the Finnish Army.

North of Lake Il'men', this offensive must be limited by the Volkhov sector and, south of this lake, continue as deeply to the east as required to protect the right flank of forces attacking to the north of Lake Il'men'. In advance, restore the situation in the Velikie Luki region. All forces that are not being employed for the offensive south of Lake Il'men' must be transferred to the forces advancing on the northern flank.

Do not begin the anticipated offensive by the Third Panzer Group to the Valdai Hills until its combat readiness and the operational readiness of its panzer formations have been fully restored. Instead, the forces on Army Group Center's left flank must advance northeastward to such a depth as will be sufficient to protect Army Group North's right flank.

The priority missions of all of the Eighteenth Army's forces are the clearing of all enemy forces from Estonia. After this, its divisions can begin to advance toward Leningrad.[3]

A still optimistic OKW issued a special communiqué on 6 August that summed up the *Wehrmacht*'s achievements and lauded its performance during the first six weeks of war. The communiqué noted that Army Group North had almost cleared Red Army forces from the entire region of the Baltic states, broken through the Stalin line, and occupied jumping-off positions along the Lake Il'men'–Narva line for the offensive on Leningrad. It also claimed that, during this period, Army Group North had killed or captured 35,000 Soviet soldiers, 355 tanks, 655 guns, and 771 aircraft.[4]

Given the favorable prospects for seizing the city, on 8 August Hitler reinforced Army Group North with large armored forces and with the VIII Air Corps from Army Group Center and ordered Leeb to initiate the offensive on Leningrad, encircle the city, and link up with the Finnish Army. Leeb was to conduct his main attack between the Narva River and Lake Il'men' with three shock groups formed from Hoepner's panzer group and Kuechler's Eighteenth Army and a secondary attack south of Lake Il'men' with Busch's Sixteenth Army. Reinhardt's XXXXI and Manstein's LVI Motorized Corps of Hoepner's Fourth Panzer Group, supported by the Eighteenth Army's XXXVIII Army Corps, were to attack between the Narva River and Lake Il'men' on 9 August. The Sixteenth Army's I and XXVIII Army Corps and other Eighteenth Army forces were to join the advance as soon as they became available after completing operations toward Tallin. Leeb organized his forces into three separate but mutually supporting groups to conduct the final offensive on Lenin's city.[5]

The Northern Group, consisting of Reinhardt's XXXXI Motorized and XXXVIII Army Corps, later reinforced by the 8th Panzer Division, was to attack from the Porech'e and Sabsk bridgeheads across the Luga River through Kingisepp toward Leningrad, supported on the left flank by the 58th Infantry Division. The Luga Group, which consisted of three divisions of Manstein's LVI Motorized Corps, with the 8th Panzer Division in reserve, was to attack Leningrad from the south via the Luga axis. Finally, the Southern Group, with the Sixteenth Army's I and XXVIII Army Corps, was to attack along the Shimsk-Novgorod-Chudovo axis against the Soviet 48th Army to envelop Leningrad from the east and sever its communications with Moscow.

On the offensive's left flank, five infantry divisions of the Eighteenth Army were to attack toward Narva, and the army's XXXXII Army Corps was to complete clearing Soviet forces from the Estonian coast and Tallin. The Sixteenth Army's X, II, L, and XXIII Army Corps, deployed on a broad front south of Lake Il'men', were to attack eastward on the army group's right flank. Their mission was to drive the Soviet 11th, 34th, 27th, and 22d Armies from their defenses at Staraia Russa and Velikie Luki and penetrate through the Valdai Hills to sever the vital Moscow-Leningrad rail line. Leeb and his subordinate armies retained only three security divisions in reserve.[6]

THE SOVIET STARAIA RUSSA COUNTERSTROKE, 8–23 AUGUST

The *Stavka* and Northwestern Direction High Command prepared vigorously for the Germans to resume their offensive, which they knew they would. Therefore, on 9 and 10 August, the *Stavka* ordered Voroshilov and Sobennikov, the Northwestern Front commander, to employ the reinforcement provided to them in late July and early August to orchestrate yet another counterstroke aimed at destroying German forces in the Sol'tsy, Staraia Russa, and Dno regions. Vatutin responded characteristically, recommending a massive offensive south of Leningrad involving forces from both the Northern and Northwestern Fronts. However, the *Stavka* quickly intervened, ordering him to curb his ambition and adopt a more modest plan, which it dictated to him at 2030 hours on 9 August:

> 1. The operational plan presented by the Northwestern Front commander is unrealistic at this time. It is necessary to take into account those forces that you have at your disposal, and, therefore, you must assign the [more] limited mission of attacking enemy forces grouped in the Sol'tsy, Staraia Russa, and Dno regions, capturing Staraia Russa and Dno station, and consolidating along the latter line.
> 2. Employ the 34th, 48th, and 11th Armies to conduct this operation.
> 3. The 34th Army will occupy jumping-off positions in the Kulakovo and Kolomna sector along the eastern bank of the Lovat' River by the evening of 11 August. Have only forward units and reconnaissance detachments along the Porus'ia River west of the Lovat' River.
> 4. Conduct your main attack with the 34th Army and a simultaneous attack by the 11th Army's left flank in the direction of Vzgliady and the 48th Army along the Utorgosh and Peski axis. The 34th Army will deploy one rifle division behind its right flank to protect the junction between the 11th and 34th Armies and the 181st Rifle Division behind the junction of the 34th and 27th Armies.
> The offensive by all armies will begin on the morning of 12 August.
> 5. Your notion of an operational tempo of 15 kilometers [9.3 miles] per day is clearly beyond your capability to fulfill. Experience indicates that, during our offensive, the enemy will deliberately withdraw in front of our shock group. Then, while creating the appearance of a rapid and easy

offensive, he will simultaneously regroup his forces to the flanks of our shock group with the mission of subsequently encircling it and cutting it off from the main front lines. Therefore, I *order* you not to go too far forward during the offensive—the daily movement tempo should be 4–5 kilometers [2.5–3.1 miles] per day. Pay attention to reconnaissance and protect our flanks and rear, and consolidate the territory you seize.

Dig in firmly along the Nikolaevo, Dno, and Lake Polisto front.

6. Simultaneously with the 34th Army's assault from the Lovat' River line, dispatch the 25th Cavalry Division along the Dedovichi and Dno axis to operate in separate squadrons against the enemy rear area.

7. The 27th Army, reinforced by the 256th Rifle Division and the 54th Cavalry Division, will capture the Kholm region and dig in along the Lake Polisto and Podberezy line.

8. At the present time, it is not possible to fulfill the Northwestern Front's request for three to four divisions and additional aviation. It is necessary to rely on your existing forces.

9. Prepare the operation with the utmost secrecy, abstain from telephone conversations and superfluous correspondence so that the enemy, as so often happens, does not discover our plan and the beginning of the operation and does not disrupt our offensive.

Confirm receipt.

[signed] High Commander, I. Stalin
[signed] Chief of the General Staff, B. Shaposhnikov[7]

As Vatutin ultimately planned it, the Staraia Russa–Dno offensive was still clearly overly ambitious. It required the *front*'s 48th, 34th, 11th, and 27th Armies to launch concentric attacks on 12 August against the Sixteenth Army's X Army Corps, which was defending the town of Staraia Russa. Akimov's 48th Army was to attack southward toward Shimsk and Utorgosh from positions north of Lake Il'men', while Morozov's 11th Army, the 34th Army, now commanded by Major General V. M. Kachanov, and Berzarin's 27th Army were to attack westward south of the lake.[8] The twin pincers were to cut off and destroy the German X Corps and capture Sol'tsy, Dno, and Kholm, thereby disrupting the German advance on Leningrad.

Despite careful preparations, Vatutin's offensive achieved only fleeting success, largely because the Sixteenth Army and X Army Corps attacked toward Novgorod and eastward from Staraia Russa on 10 August, preempting and disrupting the 48th and 11th Armies' attacks and tying down the forces on the 11th Army's right flank. Despite the unanticipated difficulties, Kachanov's 34th Army, the remainder of Morozov's 11th Army, and Berzarin's 27th Army attacked early on 12 August. The results were indeed mixed. In the south, the 12th, 32d, and 123d Infantry Divisions of the Six-

teenth Army's II Army Corps occupied all-round defenses at Kholm that sty-
mied the 27th Army's advance. To the north, Kachanov's army, spearheaded
by the 202d and 163d Motorized and 25th Cavalry Divisions, lunged 40 kilometers (24.8 miles) westward through the German defensive cordon, reaching the Dno–Staraia Russa rail line early on 14 August. The determined assault
enveloped the X Army Corps in Staraia Russa, separated it from the II Army
Corps on its right flank, and threatened the rear of the German main panzer
force advancing on Novgorod.[9]

Manstein later recorded the harrowing circumstances of the operation:

> The picture we were given on our arrival at H.Q. Sixteenth Army was the
> following: 10 Corps, fighting on the right wing of the army south of Lake
> Ilmen, had been attacked and pushed back by far superior enemy forces
> (Thirty-Eighth [in reality, the 34th] Soviet Army, comprising eight divi-
> sions and cavalry formations). It was now fighting a difficult defensive
> battle south of Lake Ilmen on a front facing west. 56 Panzer Corps was to
> provide urgently needed relief.
>
> What our corps had to do—if possible without attracting the attention
> of the enemy—was to introduce its two mechanized divisions into his
> western flank east of Dno in order to roll up the front while he was busy
> attacking our own 10 Corps in the north. The task confronting us was a
> pretty one, and it was gratifying to see how pleased the SS were to come
> back under our command. It was only a pity that we could not get 8 Panzer
> Division released for such a worth-while operation.
>
> By 18th August the carefully concealed move of the two divisions into
> camouflaged assembly areas in the enemy's western flank had been suc-
> cessfully completed, and when the corps unleashed its attack early the
> next day the enemy was obviously taken by surprise. Our plan to roll up
> the enemy front from the flank proved entirely successful, and in the
> engagements that followed we and 10 Corps, which had now returned to
> the attack, jointly succeeded in roundly defeating Thirty-Eighth [34th]
> Soviet Army. By 22d August we had reached the Lovat south-east of
> Staraya Russa, despite the fact that in that sandy terrain, with its almost
> complete absence of roads, the infantry of the two motorized divisions
> had had to advance most of the way on foot. During those few days
> 56 Panzer Corps alone captured 12,000 prisoners, 141 tanks, 246 guns
> and several hundred automatic weapons and motor vehicles.[10]

Despite its auspicious beginning, the Soviet counterstroke soon floundered
due to the roadless and difficult terrain and the almost total loss of command
and control by all of the army commands participating in the counterstroke.
While the 11th Army's offensive against the X Corps' defenses around Staraia

Russa was faltering, on 14 August Leeb diverted the SS "Totenkopf" Motorized Division from the Novgorod axis to Dno to block the Soviet advance. The following day he transferred the LVI Motorized Corps headquarters and the 3d Motorized Division from the Luga sector, along with the VIII Air Corps, with orders to counterattack against the 34th Army's penetrating forces late the next day. The counterattack against the disorganized Soviet force was immediately successful and by 25 August had driven the 34th and 11th Armies' forces back to the Lovat' River line. In the process, the Germans reported capturing 18,000 Red Army soldiers and either capturing or destroying 200 tanks, 300 guns and mortars, 36 antiaircraft guns, 700 vehicles, and the first *Katiusha* multiple rocket launchers to fall intact into German hands.[11]

Vatutin's counterstroke was indeed a costly venture. The 11th, 27th, and 34th Armies lost 30 percent of their personnel and over 80 percent of their weapons between 10 August and 1 September, although these figures also include the 27th Army's losses in the subsequent German advance into the Valdai Hills (see Table 1). During its battle around Staraia Russa, the 34th Army lost 60 percent of its men and an equally immense amount of equipment (see Table 2). However, Vatutin's counterstroke delayed Army Group North's drive on Leningrad for another 10 days.

Despite this limited success, the operation fell well short of achieving its objectives, largely due to poor command and control of the attacking forces. Writing for the *Stavka*, Shaposhnikov noted as much in a message he sent to Voroshilov on 15 August:

> As experience demonstrates, you have organized command and control of forces poorly. During the course of two days, your headquarters has not been able to provide the actual situation of the *front's* forces. Troop control has been lost by the destruction of wire communications, and, apparently, you are not employing radio communications. The forces have remained uncontrolled for a prolonged period.

Table 1. Soviet Strengths and Losses in the Staraia Russa and Valdai Operation, 10 August–1 September 1941: 11th, 27th, and 34th Armies

	Strength on 10 Aug.	Strength on 1 Sep.	Losses (%)
Personnel	327,099	198,549	128,550 (30.3)
Tanks	541	60	481 (88.9)
Machine guns	1,667	250	1,417 (85)
Rifle weaponry	385,441	52,420	333,021 (86.4)

Source: A. A. Volkov, *Kriticheskii prolog: Nezavershennye frontovye nastupatel'nye operatsii pervykh kampanii Velikoi Otechestvennoi voiny* [Critical prologue: Incomplete *front* offensive operations in the first campaigns of the Great Patriotic War] (Moscow: Aviar, 1992), 69.

Table 2. The 34th Army's Losses in the Staraia Russa Offensive Operation,
10–28 August 1941

	Strength on 10 Aug.	Strength on 26 Aug.	Losses (%)
Personnel	54,912	22,043	16,551 (60)
Tanks	83	9	74 (89)
Guns and mortars	748	120	628 (84)
Machine guns	1,601	148	1,453 (91)
Rifles	43,220	11,875	31,345 (73)
Vehicles	1,300	630	670 (58)
Horses	16,933	2,021	14,912 (88)

Source: A. A. Volkov, Kriticheskii prolog: Nezavershennye frontovye nastupatel'nye operatsii pervykh kampanii Velikoi Otechestvennoi voiny [Critical prologue: Incomplete front offensive operations in the first campaigns of the Great Patriotic War] (Moscow: Aviar, 1992), 69.

I demand continuous command and control from the army commanders and from *your* staff, by using all communications means, and that you bring order to your forces, especially, your headquarters.

Employ decisive measures for the receipt of timely and accurate reports.

Report the measures *you* have undertaken.[12]

Vatutin's offensive failed because of the difficult terrain, poor command and control of forces at all levels, lack of adequate antiaircraft support, and the quick reaction of Army Group North. It did, however, have an adverse effect on the subsequent German advance on Leningrad. First, the crisis produced by the violent counterstroke forced the OKH to shift additional forces quickly from Army Group Center to Army Group North and also to accelerate the transfer of the XXXIX Motorized Corps northward from Smolensk to reinforce the drive on Leningrad. In addition, the diversion of the LVI Motorized Corps to Staraia Russa seriously weakened and delayed the German advance on Leningrad while the fighting itself exacted a significant toll on German strength. By this time, Army Group North's losses had reached 80,000 men.[13]

In a larger sense, Vatutin's failed Soviet Staraia Russa counterstroke also diverted forces from both Army Group North and Center away from the vital Leningrad axis, as the OKH sought to eliminate the threat south of Lake Il'men'. On 24 August the OKH ordered Army Group North's LVI Motorized, II, and X Army Corps and Army Group Center's LVII Motorized Corps to advance through Demiansk and Velikie Luki toward the Valdai Hills and Toropets against the Soviet 11th, 34th, 27th, and 22d Armies. Ostensibly, this offensive was designed both to support Army Group North's offensive toward Novgorod and to straighten the lines of Army Group Center, then fighting east of Smolensk, by eliminating the 22d Army, whose forces hung threateningly over Army Group Center's left flank. The operations in the region between Staraia Russa, Velikie Luki, and Toropets proved daunting since the few available roads were in terrible condition and were surrounded by dense forests and impenetrable swamps. So difficult were the conditions that the regrouping German forces had to employ roads far to the rear.

THE GERMAN PENETRATION OF THE LUGA DEFENSE LINE, 22–25 AUGUST

After several days of delay caused by heavy rains, on 22 August, the 19th and 20th Panzer Divisions of General of Panzer Troops Adolf Kuntzen's LVII Motorized Corps of Army Group Center's Third Panzer Group struck northward southeast of Velikie Luki. Supported by the XXXX Army Corps and screened by the 251st and 253d Infantry Divisions of Army Group North's II Army Corps west of Velikie Luki, the two panzer divisions captured Velikie Luki, encircled most of the Soviet 22d Army, and wheeled eastward toward Toropets. By 1 September, the attacking force had captured Toropets and plugged the gap between the Sixteenth Army's left flank at Kholm and the Ninth Army's and Third Panzer Group's left flank north of Smolensk.

Meanwhile, by 30 August, Kuntzen's LVII Motorized Corps had regrouped its 19th Panzer Division northwestward to Kholm, where on 31 August it struck northward toward Demiansk with three infantry divisions of the Sixteenth Army's II Army Corps. Soon after, Manstein's LVI Motorized Corps and the Sixteenth Army's X Army Corps struck eastward from Staraia Russa. Within a week, the 19th Panzer Division captured the vital and heavily defended town of Demiansk on the road eastward to Ostashkov and the important land bridge across Lake Seliger, the 105-kilometer (65-mile) barrier to any subsequent German advance to the east. The LVII Motorized Corps' 20th Panzer Division then also struck from the south, linked up with the X Army Corps divisions advancing from the west, and encircled the bulk of Berzarin's 27th Army and a portion of the 11th and 34th Armies in the Molvotitsy region south of Demiansk. Within days, the combined force reached the headwaters of the Volga River, captured Ostashkov, and slammed shut the gap between Army Groups North and Center.

As a result of this operation, the OKW claimed it had destroyed the bulk of the 11th, 34th, and 27th Armies (18 divisions) and captured or destroyed 53,000 men, 320 tanks, and 659 guns in a month. It recorded another 35,000 men, 117 tanks, and 334 guns captured or destroyed during the operations into the Valdai Hills.[14] Once the operation ended, the OKH ordered the LVI and LVII Motorized Corps to join Army Group Center's advance on Moscow. By this time, General Schaal had replaced Manstein as commander of the LVI Motorized Corps.

While the Velikie Luki and Valdai diversions were absorbing the attention of the better part of two German motorized corps, Army Group North resumed its advance on Leningrad, achieving immediate and spectacular success despite its setback at Staraia Russa. Reinhardt's XXXXI Motorized Corps, supported by the XXXVIII Army Corps, began the assault along the Kingisepp-Krasnogvardeisk axis on 8 August in a driving rain. His objective was the open country south of the Narva-Leningrad railroad from which his shock group, reinforced by the reserve 8th Panzer and 3d Motorized Divisions, could wheel eastward toward Leningrad. Two days later, elements of Manstein's LVI Motorized Corps, supported by the I and XXVIII Army Corps, advanced along the Luga and Novgorod axes toward the southern and southeastern approaches to the city.[15]

On 11 August, Reinhardt's XXXXI Motorized and XXXVIII Army Corps' 1st and 6th Panzer, 36th Motorized, and 1st Infantry Divisions quickly penetrated the 2d DNO and 90th Rifle Divisions' defenses along the Luga River at Kingisepp, Ivanovskoe, and Bol'shoi Sabsk. However, the three days of heavy fighting against well-dug-in Soviet troops cost the attackers 1,600 casualties.[16] The Germans then committed the 8th Panzer Division (detached from Manstein's Corps), which lunged forward and severed the Kingisepp-Krasnogvardeisk rail line the next day. Reinhardt's motorized corps then wheeled his main force eastward toward Krasnogvardeisk, while the accompanying infantry launched a supporting attack westward toward Kingisepp.

At his Northwestern Direction Command's headquarters, Voroshilov responded by reinforcing the Kingisepp sector with Baranov's 1st Tank Division and Colonel I. M. Frolov's 1st Guards DNO on 9 August and with Colonel I. V. Burbo's 281st Rifle Division on 13 August. At the same time, the Northern Front occupied the Krasnogvardeisk Fortified Region with Lieutenant General F. S. Ivanov's 2d and Colonel V. P. Kotel'nikov's 3d Guards DNOs on 17 August. The next day, he reinforced the fortified region with Colonel N. A. Trushkin's 291st Rifle Division and formed a Separate Aviation Group to provide air support under Northern Front control.[17] Soviet forces launched repeated counterattacks along the Kingisepp axis from 13 to 15 August, but all of the attacks failed.

Beginning on 16 August, the 6th, 1st, and 8th Panzer Divisions of Reinhardt's XXXXI Panzer Corps repeatedly and violently assaulted the approaches to the Krasnogvardeisk Fortified Region for six days, but failed to crack the Soviet defenses. To the west, German infantry forces occupied Kingisepp on 16 August, forcing the 8th Army to withdraw its five rifle divisions defending the Kingisepp axis from the Narva region to the western bank of the Luga River on 21 August. The 8th Army reported losing all of its regimental and battalion commanders and their staffs in the vicious fighting around Kingisepp.[18]

The Germans' inability to destroy Soviet forces at Narva and Kingisepp left a worn-down yet still sizable Red Army force threatening the left flank of the XXXXI Motorized Corps' forces attacking Krasnogvardeisk. This force included the remnants of the 8th Army's 48th, 125th, 191st, 268th, 11th, and 118th Rifle Divisions and the 1st Naval Infantry Brigade and the Kingisepp Defensive Sector's 2d DNO, 1st Guards DNO, and the 1st Tank and 281st Rifle Divisions.[19] Consequently, Army Group North ordered the attacks on Krasnogvardeisk temporarily postponed while the Eighteenth Army's infantry forces eliminated the threat and, at the same time, threatened Kronshtadt and Leningrad from the sea.

The Eighteenth Army's XXVI and XXVIII Army Corps attacked northward toward the Gulf of Finland between 22 and 25 August. By 1 September the assaulting infantry had forced the 8th Army's forces to withdraw to new defenses forming a tight bridgehead south of Oranienbaum, a bridgehead that Soviet forces would retain until 1944. During the period from 21 August to 9 September, the Eighteenth Army reported capturing 9,774 prisoners and destroying or capturing 60 tanks and 77 guns.[20] The vigorous assault left Ivanov's 8th Army in a shambles. For example, the intense fighting reduced Colonel A. I. Safronov's 118th Rifle Division to a strength of only 3,025 men, 14 76mm field guns, 3 152mm howitzers, and 7 heavy and 47 light machine guns. Ivanov reported to Popov on 25 August, "The main danger now in the command and control of units is the absence of almost 100 percent of our regimental commanders and their chiefs of staff and battalion commanders."[21]

While the forces on Leeb's left flank were smashing the Northern Front's defenses at Kingisepp and assaulting Krasnogvardeisk, Manstein's truncated LVI Motorized Corps (with only the 3d Motorized Division) and the L Army Corps' 269th and SS Police Divisions began their attack along the Luga axis on 10 August. To the east, the XXVIII and I Army Corps advanced the same day along the Novgorod axis on Manstein's right flank. The three German corps tore into and through the partially prepared defenses of the Luga Operational Group and 48th Army forward of Luga and Novgorod. After the 3d Motorized Division was diverted to deal with the crisis at Staraia Russa, the L Army Corps' 269th Infantry Division, reinforced by the 8th Panzer Division, broke through the Luga defense line and outflanked and captured Luga on 24 August, after two weeks of heavy fighting. The German command reported that the toll of captured Soviet soldiers and equipment reached 16,000 men, 51 tanks, 171 guns, and 1,000 vehicles.[22]

While Manstein's forces were savaging Voroshilov's defenses around Luga, the XXVIII and I Army Corps penetrated the 48th Army's defenses along the

Mshaga River on 10 August and captured Shimsk late on 12 August. After repelling repeated futile counterattacks by Akimov's 48th Army against their left flank from 13 through 15 August, the XXVIII Army Corps swung to the northeast, outflanking the hapless Soviet defenders of Luga from the east. The I Army Corps captured Novgorod on 16 August and raced northward to capture Chudovo on 20 August, severing the Moscow-Leningrad rail line and communications between the 48th Army and the remainder of the Northwestern Front, whose offensive at Staraia Russa was already faltering. In two weeks of fighting, the XXVIII and I Army Corps took 16,000 prisoners and destroyed or captured 74 tanks and 300 guns and reached the desolate terrain along the Volkhov River.[23] In particular, Akimov's 48th Army was a wreck, with only 6,235 men, 5,043 rifles, and 31 artillery pieces remaining with which to defend the southeastern approaches to Leningrad.[24]

Faced with looming disaster, Voroshilov subordinated Akimov's 48th Army to the Northern Front on 23 August so that it could coordinate its actions with those of the other forces defending Leningrad proper.[25] He then ordered Akimov's withered army to defend the Gruzino-Liuban' sector to protect the main axis into Leningrad from the southeast. The same day the *Stavka* once again attempted to improve command and control, this time by subdividing the Northern Front into the Leningrad Front under General Popov's command and the Karelian Front under the command of Lieutenant General V. A. Frolov.[26] The new Leningrad Front assumed control over the 8th, 23d, and 48th Armies; the Kopor, Southern, and Slutsk-Kolpino Operational Groups; the Baltic Fleet; and *front* air forces. The Karelian Front, which was responsible for operations north of Lake Ladoga, controlled the 7th and 14th Armies and the Northern Fleet.

The Northwestern Direction High Command also tightened up its organization for the defense of Leningrad, although not in the manner Voroshilov had envisioned. Voroshilov first acted alone and on 24 August set up a special military council to deal with the existing crisis.[27] However, at Stalin's insistence, he was soon forced to create a formal Military Council for the Defense of Leningrad, whose mission was to mobilize all forces necessary for the city's defenses and whose members, by implication, would be responsible for failing to do so. Council members included the Northwestern Command commander, Voroshilov, its commissar, Zhdanov, Admiral N. G. Kuznetsov, the naval commissar, and others.

Within days, however, Stalin once again preempted Voroshilov's attempt to retain control of his own fate. To bring all matters of defense under stricter *Stavka* control, on 27 August the GKO abolished Voroshilov's Northwestern Direction High Command and merged its remnants into the Leningrad Front, which was still under Popov's command.[28] By doing so, the GKO assumed direct control over the Karelian, Leningrad, and Northwestern Fronts' operations. This directive, which was unique in Soviet wartime command and control, effectively ended Voroshilov's and Zhdanov's satrapy over military affairs at Leningrad. Voroshilov, who had displayed his military incompetence on numerous occasions prior to and during the war, would not feel the directive's full effects until almost two weeks later.

THE GERMAN ADVANCE TO LAKE LADOGA, 25 AUGUST–8 SEPTEMBER

By late August, German forces were pounding on Soviet defenses at Krasnogvardeisk, only 40 kilometers (24.9 miles) south of Leningrad, and had reached Chudovo, on the main Leningrad-Moscow rail line, 100 kilometers (62.1 miles) southeast of the city. Worse still for the Red Army, it seemed likely to the *Stavka* that the German forces exploiting east of Leningrad might link up with Finnish forces and encircle the city. To protect against that eventuality, on 27 August the *Stavka* began deploying fresh forces along and east of the Volkhov River east and southeast of Leningrad. These included the newly formed 54th and 52d Armies, which were commanded by Marshal of the Soviet Union G. I. Kulik and Lieutenant General N. K. Klykov, and, later, the 4th Army, commanded by Lieutenant General V. F. Iakovlev. These three new armies were responsible for protecting the Volkhov axis and preventing German forces from advancing to Tikhvin and the Svir River and linking up with Finnish forces, which were advancing eastward through the Karelian Isthmus.[29] Finally, ostensibly in the interests of unity of command, on 5 September the GKO appointed Voroshilov to command the Leningrad Front, with Popov as his chief of staff.

While the *Stavka* was desperately attempting to shore up its defenses at Leningrad, Army Group North prepared to resume its offensive. Leeb had intended to do so once the crisis at Staraia Russa had passed and after General Rudolf Schmidt's XXXIX Motorized Corps (the 12th Panzer and 18th and 20th Motorized Divisions) had completed its transfer from Army Group Center. In the meantime, the Sixteenth Army's I and XXVIII Army Corps and Schmidt's motorized corps, supported by the First Air Fleet and VIII Air Corps, concentrated in the Chudovo and Novgorod region from 24 through 26 August with orders to penetrate into Leningrad from the southeast along the Leningrad-Moscow road. Schmidt's corps was to encircle Leningrad from the southeast, Hoepner's Fourth Panzer Group was to attack Leningrad from the south, and Kuechler's Eighteenth Army was to attack Leningrad from the west. The remainder of Busch's Sixteenth Army was to defend the army group's right flank in the Valdai Hills and along the Volkhov River.[30]

Opposite the assembled German force, the Leningrad Front's defenses were a shambles. Ivanov's 8th Army clung precariously to its defenses west of Leningrad, and the remnants of the Luga Operational Group attempted to man the Krasnogvardeisk Fortified Region. Meanwhile, most of the 41st Rifle Corps, now commanded by Major General V. K. Urbanovich, was half encircled between Luga and Krasnogvardeisk to the south. Akimov's pathetically weakened 48th Army defended the 40 kilometer (24.9 miles) sector from Gruzino-Liuban' north of Chudovo, and the Northwestern Front's hastily assembled Novgorod Army Group (NAG), screened along the Volkhov River north of Novgorod.[31]

Schmidt's XXXIX Motorized Corps, with the XXVIII Army Corps' 121st, 122d, and 96th Infantry Divisions on its left flank, broke through the 48th Army's defenses and captured Liuban' on 25 August. Having uncovered the southeastern approaches to Leningrad, Schmidt's corps fanned out in three directions: the 18th Motorized Division northeastward toward Kirishi, the 12th Panzer Division westward toward Kolpino, and the 20th Motorized Division northwestward toward Volkhov. The next day the *Stavka* allocated the Leningrad Front four days' worth of Leningrad's tank production, four aviation regiments, and ten march battalions with which to reinforce the defense.[32] Popov himself attempted to plug the yawning gap southeast of Leningrad by reinforcing his Slutsk-Kolpino Group with Colonel A. L. Bondarev's 168th Rifle Division transferred from north of Lake Ladoga and Colonel V. A. Lansky's 4th DNO transferred from Krasnogvardeisk. He ordered the reinforced group and the 48th Army "to organize a reliable system of rifle, machine gun, and artillery fire, employ engineer obstacles, especially mines, extensively, and skillfully conduct counterattacks."[33]

Despite Popov's precautions, Schmidt's 12th Panzer and 20th Motorized Divisions, followed by the 121st, 96th and 122d Infantry Divisions, raced forward toward Tosno, and the 20th and 18th Motorized Divisions toward Mga Station and Kirishi. The 20th Motorized Division captured Tosno and reached the eastern bank of the Neva River on 29 August, threatening to sever the last Leningrad rail line running east from Leningrad and splitting apart Soviet forces defending southeast of Leningrad.

With his left flank torn apart, Popov's staff inspected the Krasnogvardeisk Fortified Region and on 31 August requested and received *Stavka* permission to split the fortified region into two armies. The 55th Army, commanded by Major General I. G. Lazarev and consisting of the 168th, 70th, 90th, and 237th Rifle Divisions, the 4th DNO, and the Slutsk-Kolpino Fortified Region, was to defend the western portion of the sector. The 42d Army, under Lieutenant General F. S. Ivanov, was to defend the eastern sector and Krasnogvardeisk proper with the 2d and 3d DNOs, the 291st Rifle Division, and the Krasnogvardeisk Fortified Region.[34] The reorganization simplified command and control of forces defending south of Leningrad and in doing so significantly influenced the course and outcome of the Battle for Leningrad.

East of Leningrad, after piercing the 48th Army's defenses, the attacks by Schmidt's XXXIX Motorized Corps and the XXVIII Army Corps' infantry developed along two distinct axes: the latter toward Leningrad proper and the former northeastward toward Mga south of Lake Ladoga and Kirishi along the Volkhov River. The XXVIII Corps' three infantry divisions, supported by the 12th Panzer Division's tanks, repeatedly attacked the 55th Army's defenses west of Tosno and southeast of Krasnogvardeisk and the Neva River between 30 August and 8 September and succeeded in pushing the defenders slowly back to the Izhora River. However, the 55th Army's resistance stiffened and finally contained the German assaults at the river line on 9 September after fierce fighting raged for several days at Iam-Izhora on the Tosno-Leningrad road.

Further east, after seizing Chudovo and Liuban' on 25 August, the 20th and 18th Motorized Divisions of Schmidt's XXXIX Motorized Corps advanced simultaneously toward Mga, Volkhov, and Kirishi against Akimov's weakened 48th Army in an attempt to sever the rail line east of Leningrad and link up with Finnish forces. The fierce German attacks forced the 48th Army to withdraw and abandon Mga, but only temporarily. An irate Voroshilov reacted to the loss of the key railroad station by ordering Akimov to recapture the town by 6 September at all costs. Akimov was to attack and recapture the town with his hastily refitted 311th and 128th Rifle Divisions and 1st Separate Mountain Rifle Brigade, reinforced by an NKVD Rifle Division made up of former Karelian border guards, which Voroshilov had just assigned to him. On 30 August Akimov's forces drove German forces from Mga, while other elements of the fresh NKVD Rifle Division engaged and repelled the 122d Infantry Division's assaults around Ivanovskoe and the mouth of the Mga River.

The seesaw fighting continued on 31 August, when the 20th Motorized Division recaptured Mga Station from the 1st Separate Mountain Rifle Brigade and began a slow, grinding advance northward through the dried-up swamps, thickets, and scrub grass that dominated the flat landscape south of Lake Ladoga. During the ensuing week, the NKVD Rifle Division and 1st Separate Mountain Rifle Brigade fought stubbornly to block the 20th Motorized Division's northward advance and hold on to the critical Neva River defenses. However, on 7 September Schmidt reinforced the 20th Motorized Division with a portion of the12th Panzer Division, and the combined force overwhelmed the border guards, forcing them to withdraw westward to the Neva River. Too weak to halt or even slow the German offensive avalanche, the worn-out 1st Separate Mountain Rifle Brigade withdrew eastward to

Siniavino. The 20th Motorized Division quickly exploited the breach, captured Siniavino after heavy fighting on 7 September, and on 8 September occupied Shlissel'burg, the fortress on the south shore of Lake Ladoga.[35] The OKW announced triumphantly in a communiqué, "The iron ring around Leningrad has been closed," signaling the fact that the blockade of Leningrad had begun.[36]

A Leningrad diarist recorded his impressions on that fateful day:

> *Monday, 8 September.* The Hitlerite forces have captured Shlissel'burg. Leningrad is under blockade. On this day, 2,544,000 inhabitants are located in the city.
>
> And yet another calamity—at 1855 hours, for the first time, enemy aviation managed to subject the city to a massive air raid. In the Moscow District alone, 5,000 incendiary bombs fell. 178 fires broke out. One of these, the largest, enveloped the wooden sheds of the Badaev Warehouses. The fire there blazed for five hours; 3,000 tons of grain and 2,500 tons of sugar burned up.
>
> The raid was repeated at 2235 hours. Incendiary bombs destroyed 12 houses. The city's main water supply station was threatened. Two reservoirs of fresh water and several water supply lines were destroyed. On this night the Vodokanal Service's emergency reconstruction battalion endured its first combat education with honor. Within a short period, it eliminated the very serious damage.
>
> Many in the city were wounded or burned. Twenty-four persons perished.
>
> The consequences of the raid would have been far more serious if our pilots had not delivered a strike beforehand on the Lisino airfield, where squadron commander Senior Lieutenant Osipov discovered up to 50 enemy aircraft earlier in the morning. By subjecting the enemy airfield to bombing and strafing, our aviators destroyed and burned 25 Fascist aircraft. In addition, one Junkers and one Messerschmitt were shot down over the airfield.
>
> On 8 September, an English radio station sent out the message: "Listen Leningrad! London is speaking! . . . London is with you. Every one of your shots echoes in London. London salutes Leningrad's heroism. . . . All hail to Leningrad!"
>
> The Londoners hardly knew then how difficult this day has been in Leningrad.[37]

The loss of Shlissel'burg was a disaster for both Voroshilov and Leningrad's now besieged population and placed Leningrad's defenders in a precarious situation indeed. The presence of German forces at Shlissel'burg, Siniavino, and along the Volkhov River cut off all of Leningrad's land communications with Moscow and the rest of the country, or what Russians termed the Great Land *(bol'shaia zemlia)*. Henceforth, resupply of the city's population and its Red Army defenders was possible only by water routes across Lake Ladoga or by air. Worse still, German forces were poised to attack and possibly capture the towns of Volkhov and Staraia Ladoga, thereby taking control of the railroad terminus on Lake Ladoga's eastern shore. If they could do so, they would sever all of Leningrad's communications, and if direct assault failed to capture the city, they could easily, quickly, and inevitably starve it into submission. Voroshilov, however, took some consolation in the fact that the timely arrival of Major General V. F. Kon'kov's 115th Rifle Division west of Shlissel'burg permitted the Neva Operational Group to hold firmly to its defenses along the Neva River. Farther east, Kulik's 54th Army, just deployed forward by the *Stavka* to fill the gap between the Leningrad and Northwestern Fronts, halted the German drive east of Mga and Siniavino and held firmly to the town of Volkhov.

Due south of Leningrad, however, an even greater disaster loomed. There, the German advance to Krasnogvardeisk and the 48th Army's loss of Chudovo and Tosno had severed the communications and lines of withdrawal of Piadyshev's Luga Operational Group (the 41st Rifle Corps) to Leningrad. Subsequently, the group abandoned Luga on 20 August, was encircled, and had to cut its way out to the north and east in small parties. The encircled forces included the 41st Rifle Corps' 111th, 177th, and 235th Rifle Divisions; the 90th, 70th, and 235th Rifle Divisions; the 1st and 3d DNO; and the 24th Tank Division.[38] During the group's attempted escape, the 8th Panzer and SS Police, 269th, and 96th Infantry Divisions hounded the encircled forces unmercifully by conducting constant converging attacks on the group from all sides. The Germans estimated Red Army losses in the bloody encirclement battle at 30,000 men, 120 tanks, and 400 guns.[39]

The loss of Shlissel'burg on 8 September and, with it, all ground communications between Leningrad and the rest of the country convinced the *Stavka* and the Leningrad Front that the fight for Leningrad was fast approaching its climax. However, most in the German camp believed that the climax had already passed and that Leningrad was German for the taking. On 5 September Halder wrote in his diary, "Leningrad: Our objective has been achieved. Will now become a subsidiary theater of operations."[40] Given these strategic realities, two days before German forces captured Shlissel'burg, Hitler had already decided to avoid unnecessary casualties by assaulting a city that was already doomed. Enticed by new opportunities in Army Group Center's sector, he ordered Leeb to encircle Leningrad and starve it into submission rather than seizing it by costly frontal assaults. Accordingly, on 6 September he issued Fuehrer Directive No. 35, which ordered Army Group Center to embark on its Moscow adventure, Operation Typhoon:

The initial successes in the operations against enemy forces located between the adjoining flanks of Army Groups South and Center, combined with further successes in the encirclement of enemy forces in the Leningrad region, have created prerequisites for the conduct of a decisive operation against Army Group Timoshenko, which is unsuccessfully conducting offensive operations in front of Army Group Center. It must be destroyed decisively before the onset of winter within the limited time indicated in existing orders.[41]

Hitler's directive then assigned Leeb Army's Group North its missions in subsequent operations:

Encircle enemy forces operating in the Leningrad region (and capture Shlissel'burg) in cooperation with Finnish forces attacking on the Karelian Isthmus so that a considerable number of the mobile formations and the First Air Fleet's formations, particularly the VIII Air Corps, can be transferred to Army Group Center no later than 15 September. First and foremost, however, it is necessary to strive to encircle Leningrad completely, at least from the east, and, if weather conditions permit, conduct a large-scale air offensive against Leningrad. It is especially important to destroy the water supply stations.

As soon as possible, Army Group North's forces must begin an offensive northward in the Neva River sector to help the Finns overcome the fortifications along the old Soviet-Finnish border, and also to shorten the front lines and deprive the enemy of the ability to use his air bases. In cooperation with the Finns, prevent enemy naval forces from exiting Kronshtadt into the Baltic Sea (Hango and the Moonzund Islands) by using mine obstacles and artillery fire.

Also isolate the region of combat operations at Leningrad from the sector along the lower reaches of the Volkhov [River] as soon as forces necessary to perform this mission become available. Link up with the Karelian Army on the Svir River only after the enemy forces have been destroyed in the Leningrad region.[42]

Anticipating Hitler's directive, on 4 September German forces began shelling Leningrad daily with 240mm guns from the region north of Tosno, and four days later German aircraft began pounding the city with daylight air raids. In response, the *Stavka* ordered the Leningrad Front to form the Ladoga PVO Brigade Region.

Finnish Army operations in Karelia complicated the defense of Leningrad. Although the Finns were supposed to help capture Leningrad, from 22 June through 10 July, they conducted only limited-objective operations. Then, beginning on 10 July, they began more extensive operations against Gorelenko's 7th Army defending the sector between and forward of Lakes Onega and Ladoga. Beginning on 31 July, Finnish forces attacked Pshennikov's 23d Army defending the Karelian Isthmus, forcing his army to withdraw to new defensive positions astride the isthmus only 30 kilometers (18.6 miles) from Leningrad's northern defenses.[43] Although the Finns advanced no farther, the mere threat of a Finnish attack adversely affected the Leningrad Front's defense in other sectors. For example, at a time when Popov most needed reserves, Finnish operations forced him to transfer the 265th Rifle Division, the 48th Army's reserve, and the 291st Rifle Division from the Krasnogvardeisk Fortified Region to bolster the 23d Army's defense against the Finns.

At the end of the first week of September, the *Wehrmacht* began operations to isolate and destroy Leningrad and its defenders. As anticlimactic as it seemed to the German, no Russian doubted that the battle was nearing its climax.

THE DEFENSE OF LENINGRAD, 8–30 SEPTEMBER

Both the Soviet defense of Leningrad proper and the German blockade formally began on 8 September, when German forces captured Shlissel'burg and reached the southern shore of Lake Ladoga. Hitler's directive and several critical *Stavka* decisions set the stage for the climactic battle that would follow.

Pursuant to Hitler's orders, Leeb formulated a plan to encircle Leningrad by conducting offensive operations designed to seize the entire southern and eastern shores of Lake Ladoga. By doing so, his forces would deprive the Soviets of the vital railheads on the lake's eastern shore, transshipment points that were necessary for the Soviet government to supply its troops and the city's population. Originally, Leeb planned to encircle Leningrad by sealing off its access routes from the east and west. Hoepner's panzer group was to establish a tight inner encirclement line around the city with the 1st, 6th, and 8th Panzer and the 36th Motorized Divisions of Reinhardt's XXXXI Motorized Corps and the 12th Panzer and the 18th and 20th Motorized Divisions of Schmidt's XXXIX Motorized Corps. Simultaneously, the XXVI, XXXVIII, L, and XXVIII Army Corps of Kuechler's Eighteenth Army were to establish a broader encirclement line extending from the Koporskii Gulf (adjacent to the Gulf of Finland) to Lake Ladoga east of Leningrad.

However, Hitler's 6 September directive complicated Leeb's task by requiring him to transfer the Fourth Panzer Group's XXXXI, LVI, and LVII Motorized Corps and Richtofen's VIII Air Corps to Army Group Center, effective on 15 September. That meant Leeb would retain only the XXXIX

Motorized Corps and, as a later concession, the 8th Panzer Division. The Eighteenth Army would then take over the Fourth Panzer Group's sector south and west of Leningrad. Soon to be deprived of most of his armor, Leeb decided to envelop the city from the east immediately with Schmidt's XXXIX Motorized Corps and attack with the Eighteenth Army south and west of Leningrad. Reinhardt's XXXXI Motorized Corps would spearhead the advance on Leningrad from the southwest before its departure to Army Group Center.[44]

On 29 August Leeb ordered his forces to encircle Leningrad by capturing bridgeheads over the Neva River and the towns of Uritsk, Pulkovo, Pushkin (Detskoe Selo), Kolpino, and Izhora and to establish a tight ring around the city itself before the bulk of Hoepner's Fourth Panzer Group departed for Army Group Center. To do so, he organized his attacking forces into two shock groups, the Krasnogvardeisk and the Slutsk-Kolpino Groups. The Krasnogvardeisk group consisted of the Eighteenth Army's XXXVIII and L Army Corps and the Fourth Panzer Group's XXXXI Motorized Corps. The group formed with the motorized corps' 1st and 6th Panzer and 36th Motorized Divisions in the center; the XXXVIII Army Corps' 1st, 58th, 291st, and, later, 254th Infantry Divisions on its left flank; and the L Army Corps' SS Police and 269th Infantry Divisions on its right. The 8th Panzer Division, which was refitting after its heavy losses the previous month, was in reserve. The group's mission was to capture Krasnogvardeisk, advance northward along the Krasnoe Selo axis against Ivanov's 42d Army, and reach the Gulf of Finland, thereby isolating Soviet forces west of Leningrad from the city.

The Slutsk-Kolpino group, under Hoepner's command, consisted of the XXVIII Army Corps' 121st, 96th, and 122d Infantry Divisions, supported by elements of the 12th Panzer Division. Deployed in the Iam-Izhora sector, the group was to penetrate the defenses of Lazarov's 55th Army along the Izhora River, advance along the Moscow-Leningrad Highway toward the Neva River, and capture Slutsk and Kolpino. Further east, the 20th Motorized Division and the bulk of the 12th Panzer Division of Schmidt's XXXIX Motorized Corps were to widen the corridor to Shlissel'burg and Lake Ladoga, screen the Neva River front, and drive Soviet forces eastward from the Mga and Siniavino regions.

Voroshilov defended the southern approaches to Leningrad and the Krasnogvardeisk and Slutsk-Kolpino Fortified Regions with his 42d and 55th Armies, flanked to the west by the 8th Army.[45] The 8th Army, now commanded by Major General V. I. Shcherbakov, defended the coastal bridgehead in the northern portion of the Koporskii plateau with his 191st, 118th, 11th, and 281st Rifle Divisions, all of which were seriously weakened from previous combat. Shcherbakov's forces faced the XXXVIII Army Corps, which

Kuechler ordered to deliver his main attack. Lieutenant General F. S. Ivanov's 42d Army, supported by the Baltic Fleet, defended the Krasnogvardeisk Fortified Region from the Gulf of Finland to Pustoshka. The 2d Guards DNO, now commanded by Colonel V. A. Trubachev, and Kotel'nikov's 3d Guards DNO were situated opposite the German main attack axis.

Finally, Major General of Tank Forces I. G. Lazarov's 55th Army defended the Slutsk-Kolpino Fortified Region from Pustoshka to the Neva River, with the 90th, 70th, and 168th Rifle Divisions and the 4th DNO deployed along the intended German main attack axis. Completing Leningrad's immediate defensive perimeter, the 155th Rifle and 1st NKVD Rifle Divisions defended the Neva River front east of the city from the southern shore of Lake Ladoga to the westward bend in the Neva southeast of the city.

Voroshilov's small reserve consisted of the 10th and 16th Rifle Divisions, the 5th DNO, the 8th Rifle and 1st Naval Infantry Brigades, the 48th Separate Tank Battalion, and the 500th Separate Rifle Regiment. As of 11 September, the Leningrad Front's strength was 452,000 men, about two thirds of which were deployed south of Leningrad facing an equal number of German troops. East of the Shlissel'burg corridor, Kulik's 85,000-man 54th Army was still assembling at and around Volkhov in the rear of the decimated 48th Army, which was now commanded by Major General M. A. Antoniuk.[46]

Reinhardt's XXXXI Motorized and the XXXVIII Army Corps began their assault along the Krasnogvardeisk–Krasnoe Selo axis toward the Baltic coast on 9 September. An entry in the Leningrad diary captured the intensity of the attack and the desperation of the defense (see Map 4):

Tuesday, 9 September. Today, the danger hanging over our city grew still larger. Having regrouped his forces, the enemy has launched a decisive offensive. He is making his main attack from the region west of Gatchina [Krasnogvardeisk] in the direction of Krasnoe Selo. Having repelled the initial attacks, our units were not fully able to repel the subsequent attacks. Exploiting his numerical superiority, particularly in tanks, the enemy is penetrating directly forward. The artillery of the 3d Guards DNO destroyed and burned 27 fascist tanks, but, nevertheless, the Hitlerites succeeded in wedging into the People's Militia's defenses. . . .

Battle is also raging south of Kolpino and along the Oranienbaum axis. Enemy forces enveloping Leningrad from the east are attempting to force the Neva River. That operation has far-reaching aims—to link up with Finnish forces operating on the Karelian Isthmus. But the Hitlerites' idea has been disrupted. They underestimated the assistance that the ships of the Red Banner Baltic Fleet are providing to our ground forces standing along the Neva.[47]

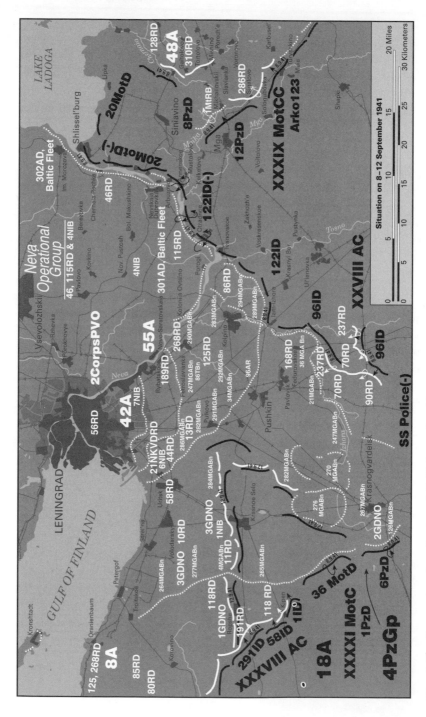

Map 4. The German Assault on Leningrad, 8–12 September 1941

The 36th Motorized Division, in the vanguard of Reinhardt's XXXXI Motorized Corps, struck and penetrated the 3d DNO's defenses at Bol'shie Skvoritsy and advanced 10 kilometers (6.2 miles) before being halted by heavy artillery fire late in the day. At the same time, in accordance with Hitler's orders, the *Luftwaffe* began three days of heavy aerial bombardment of the city (8–11 September) to supplement the heavy artillery shelling that had begun on 1 September. The effectiveness of the shelling, however, was limited by the fact that it could not range the heart of the city. During the ensuing three days, the *Luftwaffe* rained 8,000 incendiary bombs on the city, causing heavy damage and many fires. The air strikes destroyed the Badaev Warehouses, where most of Leningrad's foodstuffs were stored.[48]

In response, Voroshilov ordered Ivanov's 42d Army to fire a strong artillery counterpreparation on 10 September and counterattack vigorously with Kotel'nikov's 3d DNO. Reinhardt committed the XXXXI Motorized Corps' 1st Panzer Division into the action late on 10 September, and the panzers managed to reach the Krasnogvardeisk–Krasnoe Selo road, forcing Kotel'nikov's militia to withdraw northward. However, the intensifying Soviet resistance made it readily apparent to Reinhardt that reinforcements were essential if his forces were to overcome the 42d Army's prepared defenses. However, since his most logical reinforcing force, the 6th Panzer Division, was still engaged in heavy fighting for Krasnoe Selo, Leeb reinforced the 1st Panzer Division with the only forces he had at hand, a single tank battalion from the 8th Panzer Division, instead of the fresh panzer division that Reinhardt so desperately needed and desired.[49]

As the battle reached a crescendo, Voroshilov poured his last available reserves into the battle in an increasingly desperate attempt to cling to his sagging defenses. He reinforced Ivanov's 42d Army with the 500th Rifle Regiment on 10 September, the 1st Naval Infantry Brigade on 12 September, and the newly formed 5th DNO on the same day.[50] Nevertheless, the 1st Panzer Division captured Dudergof from the 2d DNO and 500th Rifle Regiment on 11 September and Krasnoe Selo from the 3d DNO and 1st Naval Infantry Brigade on 12 September, but was then halted by the 5th DNO at Pulkovo in Leningrad's southwestern suburbs. By this time, the 1st Panzer and 36th Motorized Divisions had outflanked the defenses of the 42d Army's 2d Guards DNO at Krasnogvardeisk and were threatening the rear of the 55th Army's forces defending the Slutsk-Kolpino Fortified Region. The way was now open for Reinhardt's XXXXI Motorized and the L Army Corps to seize Krasnogvardeisk, exploit toward Slutsk and Pushkin, and link up with the XXVIII Army Corps, which was attacking Pushkin from the east, now under Hoepner's control. However, he had to have reinforcements to do so.

Once again, however, the reinforcements were not available since, at this critical moment, the 8th Panzer Division was still reorganizing and was unable to exploit the motorized corps' success.[51] Worse still for Leeb, on 12 September the 55th Army's 168th Rifle Division halted the XXVIII Army Corps' advance toward Slutsk at Fedorovskoe after it had registered only minimal gains. Voroshilov then transferred the Krasnogvardeisk sector, together with the 2d DNO and all other forces defending it, to the 55th Army's control and, the next day, ordered Lazarov's army to defend Pushkin, Krasnogvardeisk, and Kolpino at all cost. As one critic noted, Leeb faced a serious command and control problem:

> [Leeb's] organization for the attack was flawed, since Hoepner could not control Kuechler's corps on the left, nor Schmidt's group (which came under increasing pressure from Forty-eighth Army outside of the Leningrad perimeter, and from Fifty-fifth Army from inside) on the right, nor, as it turned out, his only reserve, the 8th Panzer Division. The attack was not synchronized because L Corps, still struggling north of Luga, was not ready in time. Finally, the 254th Infantry Division, which should have reinforced Reinhardt's panzer corps, instead was shifted by the Army Group to Kuechler. Such disarray was serious and could have jeopardized the operation if the Russians themselves had not also reached the end of their tether.[52]

The only saving grace for Leeb was the fact that Voroshilov was in a similarly weak position.

To make matters worse for Leeb, the OKH's 10 September order requiring he transfer Reinhardt's XXXXI Motorized Corps to Army Group Center "in good condition" finally arrived, and Schmidt reported that the Russian 54th Army and a cavalry division were threatening Leeb's right flank.[53] Thus, with Halder's approval, Leeb adjusted his defenses by dispatching the 8th Panzer Division to assist Schmidt's motorized corps. However, when the panzer division arrived three days later, it was no longer needed. Leeb also deployed his fresh 254th Infantry Division to the Eighteenth Army to fill the gap once Reinhardt's corps departed to Army Group Center.

Despite these vexing problems, Leeb persisted in pushing his attack forward by ordering the XXVIII Army Corps to advance westward toward Pushkin, Slutsk, and Mar'ino and the 6th Panzer Division to attack Pushkin from the west. After a day of regrouping, the rest of Reinhardt's XXXXI Motorized Corps was to remain in place south of the Pushkin-Petergof road until the neighboring XXXVIII Army Corps on the left and the L Army Corps on the right had caught up with his panzer spearheads. The combined force would then launch one final attempt to breech Leningrad's southern defenses south of the Pushkin-Petergof road.

With the German noose tightened around Leningrad, on 9 September an angry Stalin made wholesale changes to the Leningrad Front's command structure. Although he issued the official directive two days later, that day he appointed Army General G. K. Zhukov to command the Leningrad Front in place of the hapless Voroshilov, whose incompetence was becoming more evident each day.[54] Stalin was particularly angered over Voroshilov's failure to inform him about the fall of Shlissel'burg, a fact which Stalin first read about in a German communiqué. Stalin also learned of the Leningrad Military Council's decision to demolish Leningrad's military installations in anticipation of the city's fall to the Germans. While meeting with Admiral Kuznetsov, whom he had summoned to Moscow to prepare preliminary instructions for scuttling the Baltic Fleet, Stalin admitted, "It is possible that it [Leningrad] may have to be abandoned." Before Zhukov's departure to Leningrad, Stalin informed him, "It is an almost hopeless situation. By taking Leningrad and joining up with the Finns the Germans can strike Moscow from the northeast and then the situation will become even more critical." Handing Zhukov a slip of paper, Stalin said, "Give this to Voroshilov." The paper read, "To Voroshilov. The GKO is appointing Army General Zhukov command of the Leningrad Front. Turn over command of the *front* to Zhukov and fly back to Moscow immediately."[55]

Indicative of his dark mood, Stalin had sent a letter to Churchill on 3 September describing the deteriorating situation in the Ukraine and at Leningrad, lamenting the absence of a second front and large-scale material aid, and describing the likely effects on Britain of a Soviet defeat. In the letter, Stalin suggested that Churchill send 25–30 divisions to Arkhangel'sk or via Iran to help the Red Army. Churchill noted the letter's "utter unreality" in a remark of 15 September.[56]

At the same time, the *Stavka* also disbanded the Leningrad Front's 48th Army, which had already been demolished by the advancing Germans and, on 12 September, assigned its forces to Kulik's new 54th Army, which was still assembling at Volkhov. Stalin ordered Kulik to restore the broken front south of Lake Ladoga and Iakovlev's 4th and Klykov's 52d Armies to defend the Volkhov River line north of Lake Il'men'.

Zhukov arrived at Leningrad late on 9 September, accompanied by his trusted lieutenants from his Khalkhin-Gol days, Major Generals I. I. Fediuninsky and M. S. Khozin, and took command of the Leningrad Front.[57] Upon his arrival, he appointed Khozin as his chief of staff and established his new headquarters in the famed Smol'ny Institute. Zhukov then suspended Voroshilov's plans to demolish Leningrad, even though the *Stavka* reiterated the instructions several days later. On 17 September Zhukov enlarged the Leningrad Military Council by adding to it Admiral I. S. Isakov, chief of the Main Naval Staff and *Stavka* representative, and ordered his forces, "Not a step back! Do not give up a single verst of land on the immediate approaches to Leningrad!" under penalty of being shot.[58]

By the time Zhukov reached Leningrad, the situation his *front* faced was indeed grave. In the vicinity of Leningrad proper, German forces had captured Krasnoe Selo, broken into the western portion of Krasnogvardeisk Fortified Region, and advanced to Uritsk, only 10 kilometers (6.2 miles) from Petergof and Strel'na on the coast of the Gulf of Finland. They had also reached the outskirts of Pulkovo, 12 kilometers (7.5 miles) due south of the city, and Pushkin, 18 kilometers (11.2 miles) southeast of the city. Farther east, German forces had captured Shlissel'burg and Siniavino and were threatening to capture Volkhov and link up with the Finns. Once in command, Zhukov assessed that the Uritsk and Pulkovo sectors posed the greatest threat, reinforced these sectors, and ordered relentless counterattacks to blunt the 1st Panzer and 36th Motorized Divisions' advance.

The Germans resumed their advance along the Krasnogvardeisk–Krasnoe Selo axis early on 13 September, almost four days after Zhukov arrived in Leningrad. The 1st and 58th Infantry, 1st Panzer, and 36th Motorized Divisions of Reinhardt's XXXXI Motorized and XXXVIII Army Corps attacked toward Uritsk and penetrated the 3d Guards DNO's and 1st Naval Infantry Brigade's defenses just north of Krasnoe Selo (Map 5). They then captured Konstantinovka, Sosnovka, and Finskoe Koirovo, producing a genuine crisis in Ivanov's 42d Army. The next day Zhukov reinforced the 42d Army with the 10th Rifle Division from his reserve, and Ivanov's army recaptured Sosnovka and Finskoe Koirovo in a series of desperate counterattacks.[59] Although Ivanov's actions temporarily halted the German drive, his army was perilously close to collapsing, a fact Zhukov seemed to sense.

In an attempt to regain the initiative or at least stave off disaster, on 15 September Zhukov ordered Lazarov's 55th Army to defend Pushkin, Krasnogvardeisk, and Kolpino stubbornly and established new priority missions for his entire *front:*

1. Smother the enemy with artillery and mortar fire and air attacks, permitting no penetration of the defenses.

2. Form five rifle brigades and two rifle divisions by 18 September and concentrate them in four defense lines for the immediate defense of Leningrad.

3. Strike the enemy in the flank and rear with the 8th Army.

4. Coordinate the 8th Army's operation with the 54th Army, whose objective is to liberate the Mga and Shlissel'burg regions.[60]

The same day, however, the 58th and 1st Infantry, 1st Panzer, and 36th Motorized Divisions resumed their assault, penetrated the defenses of the 42d Army's 10th and 11th Rifle Divisions, and reached the outskirts of Volodarskii and Uritsk. With the Germans only 4 kilometers (2.5 miles) from

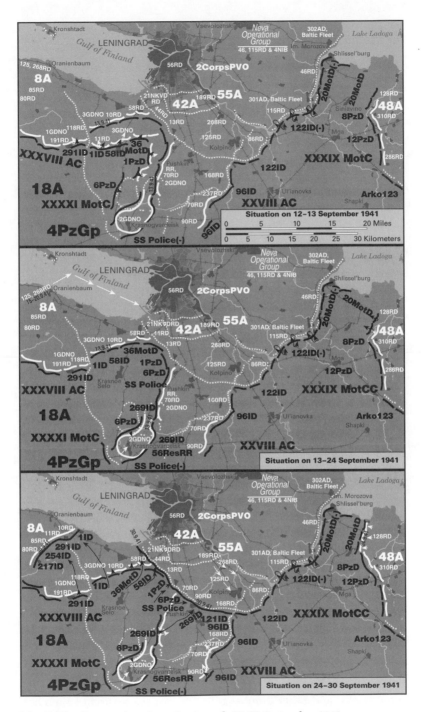

Map 5. The German Assault on Leningrad, 13–30 September 1941

the Baltic coast, Zhukov immediately reinforced Ivanov's army with the newly formed 21st NKVD Rifle Division, the 6th DNO, two naval rifle brigades, and ad hoc formations of PVO troops. On 16 September this hastily assembled force occupied second-echelon positions behind the 42d Army's defenses from the Gulf of Finland through Ligovo, the Meat Factory, and Rybatskoe to the Neva River. Zhukov categorically forbade his commanders from removing any of their forces from this line without his express permission, and Stalin reinforced Zhukov's prohibition by issuing a draconian order of his own dealing mercilessly with "saboteurs" and "German sympathizers" who withdrew from combat without authorization.[61]

Soon after, Zhukov sent his deputy Fediuninsky to investigate the situation in the 42d Army, but when Fediuninsky arrived at the army's headquarters, he found General Ivanov sitting with his head in his hands, unable to report where his troops were located. Major General Larionov, Ivanov's chief of staff, reported that the 42d Army was holding, "literally by a miracle."[62] Ivanov requested permission to move his headquarters to the rear, but Fediuninsky categorically refused. Fediuninsky reported to Zhukov that the 42d Army's morale, as well as the morale in the 8th and 55th Armies, was cracking. Learning that Ivanov had relocated his headquarters to a safer location farther behind the lines in the basement of the Kirov factory, Zhukov ordered Fediuninsky, "Take over the 42d Army—and quickly."[63]

Zhukov's 14 September decision to attack was based on his perception that the Germans' precipitous advance to Uritsk had exposed the left flank of the German force pounding the 42d Army and left it vulnerable to a flank attack. Therefore, he intended to catch the attacking German shock group between the 8th Army's "hammer" and the 42d Army's "anvil." Shcherbakov's 8th Army was to attack toward Krasnoe Selo against the German shock group's left flank with his 191st and 281st Rifle Divisions, reinforced by the 10th and 11th Rifle Divisions and the remnants of the 42d Army's 3d DNO. While doing so, he was supposed to protect his extended right flank by withdrawing the 5th Naval Infantry Brigade to new defenses along the Kovashi River and retain the 125th and 286th Rifle Divisions in reserve. However, when Shcherbakov demurred, claiming that his force was too weak to launch the counterattack, Zhukov relieved him on the spot, together with his commissar, I. F. Chukhnov, and appointed Lieutenant General T. I. Shevaldin to command the army.[64]

However, the Germans foiled Zhukov's plan by preempting the 8th Army's counterattack. On 16 September the Germans resumed their attacks against the 42d Army and the 8th Army's left flank before Shevaldin's army had completed its regrouping preparations for the counterattack on Krasnoe Selo. The German attack encountered strong and continuous Soviet resistance and counterattacks, and fierce combat raged on for possession of Volodarskii, Uritsk, and Pulkovo Heights until late September. By 30 September, however, Fediuninsky's 42d Army had managed to solidify its defenses along the Ligovo, Nizhnoe Koirovo, and Pulkovo line.

To the west, however, the 58th Infantry and 1st Panzer Divisions of Reinhardt's XXXXI Motorized and the XXXVIII Motorized Corps, reinforced by the 254th Infantry Division, attacked and defeated the 8th Army's 10th Rifle Division and, on 16 September, forced it to abandon Volodarskii and withdraw toward Strel'na. The three attacking German divisions reached the Gulf of Finland and captured Petergof, Strel'na, and Uritsk that very day, completing the isolation of the 8th Army in the so-called Oranienbaum pocket, cut off from Leningrad proper. The Leningrad diary laconically recorded the day's grim events:

> *Tuesday, 16 September. Leningrad Pravda* appeared today with head-lines which spoke about the threat hanging over the city—"The Enemy Is at the Gates." The headline is also emblazoned on leaflets. They are being pasted up around the city and at the front.
>
> The enemy is really at the very gates of the city. Uritsk has fallen. How-ever well our forces resisted, they did not succeed in holding on to it. And only the day before, one was able to travel from Uritsk to Leningrad by tram. . . .
>
> Worst of all, the Hitlerite forces have penetrated to the coast of the Gulf of Finland between Uritsk and Strel'na. The 8th Army, which is operating around Oranienbaum, has been cut off from the *front's* main forces.
>
> Workers' formations have occupied positions in the Kirov and Moscow districts. Urgent resettlement of the populations of these districts has begun.
>
> Fierce fighting is under way in the Kolpino region. Three times the Izhorsk militia went over to the attack, fighting hand to hand. It required great efforts to clear the enemy from the houses that they had occupied yesterday on the outskirts of Kolpino Colony No. 3.
>
> On this day, the men of Kolpino are missing many of their comrades. It was especially difficult when they suffered the death of a sixteen-year-old girl, Zhenia Stasiuk. She not only dressed the wounded. When the platoon commander was killed, and machine-gun fire pinned the soldiers to the ground, the young girl threw herself forward and led them in the attack. A woman died in that battle. An enemy bullet pierced her breast. . . .
>
> The formation of the 6th People's Militia Division has been completed in timely fashion. It occupied defenses in the sector from the Meat Fac-tory to the village of Rybatskoe. On this day, around 5,000 Baltic Fleet troops arrived at the ground front. The 6th Naval Infantry Brigade, formed by the fleet command, entered combat literally from the march.

The Workers' Detachment from the Kirov Factory is ready for combat. At the same time, the men of the Kirov factory are providing the front with tanks. And they have transformed their factory into a fortress. They have constructed 1,053 meters of barricades, 18 artillery pillboxes, 27 blindages, and 13 mortar nests on factory grounds. In the factory's wall, the workers have punched through embrasures and set up 47 machine guns.

The factory does not differ much from the front lines. On 16 September 34 enemy shells exploded on its grounds.[65]

Undeterred by the setback and whipped on by an insistent Zhukov, Shevaldin completed regrouping the forces on his 8th Army's left flank on 18 September and, the next day, attacked toward Krasnoe Selo with four rifle divisions. However, yet another German assault struck Shevaldin's army on 20 September, halted its attack, and sent its forces reeling back to the Novyi Petergof, Tomuzi, Petrovskaia line, where the front stabilized once and for all.

While heavy fighting raged along the Uritsk axis, Leeb began a two-pronged assault on the vital Soviet strong point at Pushkin. His intent was to destroy the main force of Lazarov's 55th Army in the Slutsk, Pushkin, and Krasnogvardeisk regions by concentric attacks from east and west, and then strike the left flank of Fediuninsky's 42d Army and smash open the door to Leningrad. On 12 September the XXXXI Motorized Corps' 6th Panzer Division and the L Army Corps' SS Police and 169th Infantry Divisions attacked eastward toward Krasnogvardeisk and Pushkin. Simultaneously, the XXVIII Army Corps' 96th and 121st Infantry Divisions attacked westward from the Izhora River toward Slutsk and Pushkin. Soviet accounts claim that the Leningrad Front and its army commands were forewarned of the attack by intelligence and hence were able to deal with it.[66]

Whether or not the Soviet claim was true, after capturing Krasnogvardeisk on 13 September, the two attacking German forces fought for possession of the Slutsk-Kolpino Fortified Region for three days without achieving any measurable success. During the fighting, on 14 September soldiers of the SS Police Division reported finding the dead bodies of General Ivanov, the former 42d Army commander, and his commissar in a bunker. However, the reports were mistaken. In reality, Ivanov survived the fighting and, after Zhukov relieved him from command, on 21 September he became the chief of the Leningrad garrison and commander of Leningrad's Internal Defense Forces. Ever vengeful, the Leningrad Military Council stripped Ivanov of his command on 15 December 1941, and on 22 February 1942, arrested, tried, and convicted him of dereliction of duty.[67]

German forces resumed their assaults against Lazarov's defensive positions at Slutsk and Pushkin on 17 September. After tremendous exertions, the 1st Panzer and SS Police Divisions finally managed to capture Pushkin

late in the day, and the XXVIII Army Corps captured Slutsk the next morn-
ing, forcing the 55th Army to withdraw to new defenses at Pulkovo, Bol'shoe
Kuz'mino, Novaia, and Putrolovo. A final desperate assault by the 1st Panzer
Division captured Pulkovo and Aleksandrovka, the terminus of the Leningrad
southwest tram line, only 12 kilometers (7.5 miles) from the city's center.
However, there, on the southern slopes of Pulkovo Heights, the 1st Panzer
Division's assault faltered when it encountered Soviet tanks that had just rolled
off the Kolpino Tank Factory's assembly line:[68]

> *Thursday, 8 September.* Pressing our forces back, the enemy occupied
> Pushkin at 0200 hours. Continuing their fierce attacks, the Hitlerites tried
> to envelop Pulkovo Heights from the left and Kolpino from the right. But
> in spite of their numerical superiority, they did not succeed in penetrat-
> ing into Leningrad. The 42d Army's forces stopped the enemy and dug
> in on the northeastern outskirts of Uritsk and Staro-Panova.[69]

At least in part, the German attack faltered because on 17 September
Zhukov issued yet another draconian order to steel the backbones of Leningrad's
defenders. His Combat Order No. 0064 succinctly captured both Zhukov's will
and his command style:

> 1. Considering the particularly great importance of Ligovo, Kiskino,
> Verkh. Koirovo, Pulkovo Heights, and the Moskovskaia Slavianka, Shushary,
> and Kolpino regions' line to the defense of Leningrad's southern sector,
> the Leningrad Front's Military Council announces to all commanders and
> political and line cadres defending the designated line that all command-
> ers, political workers *[politruk],* and soldiers who abandon the indicated
> line without a written order from the *front* or army military council will
> be shot immediately.
> 2. Announce this order to command and political cadres upon receipt.
> Disseminate [it] widely among the rank and file.
> 3. Report fulfillment of the order by 1200 hours 18 September by cipher.
> [signed] Zhukov, Zhdanov, Kuznetsov, and Khozin[70]

Three days later, Stalin himself chimed in, directing Zhukov and his other
council members to rid Leningrad ruthlessly of disloyal elements:

> To Zhukov, Zhdanov, Kuznetsov, and Merkulov:
> It is said that, while advancing to Leningrad, the German scoundrels
> have sent forward among our forces individuals [delegates]—old men, old
> women, wives, and children—from the regions they have occupied with
> requests to the Bolsheviks to give up Leningrad and restore peace.

It is said that people can be found among Leningrad's Bolsheviks who do not consider it possible to use weapons and such against these individuals. I believe that, if we have such people among the Bolsheviks, we must destroy them, in the first place, because they are afraid of the German fascists.

My answer is, do not be sentimental, but instead smash the enemy and his accomplices, the sick or the healthy, in the teeth. The war is inexorable, and it will lead to the defeat, in the first instance, of those who demonstrate weakness and permit wavering. If anyone in our ranks permits wavering, he will be the main culprit in the fall of Leningrad.

Beat the Germans and their creatures, whoever they are, in every way and abuse the enemy; it makes no difference whether they are willing or unwilling enemies. [Show] no mercy either to the German scoundrels or their accomplices, whomever they are.

Request you inform commanders and division and regimental commissars and also the military council of the Baltic Fleet and the commanders and commissars of ships.

[signed] I. Stalin[71]

As severe as they were, orders like this one achieved their desired effect.

As the German assaults expired in utter exhaustion, a resigned Halder noted the setback in his diary:

The ring around Leningrad has not yet been drawn as tightly as might be desired, and further progress after departure of the 1st Armored Division and 36th Motorized Division from that front is doubtful. Considering the drain on our forces before Leningrad, where the enemy is concentrating large forces and great quantities of material, the situation will remain tight until such time when hunger takes effect as our ally.[72]

He then added, "I remind him [General Brennecke, chief of staff, Army Group North] of the necessity to turn over the armored divisions to AGp. Center on schedule."[73]

Although fighting lasted until 30 September, the tenacious Soviet defense at Pulkovo Heights by the 5th DNO and 500th Rifle Regiment convinced Leeb to halt his attacks, although, as Halder indicated, the scheduled departure of Reinhardt's XXXXI Motorized Corps, which he had dreaded so much, was also an important factor. Even though the ground action waned, as Hitler had mandated, the German *Luftwaffe* began a massive air offensive against the Baltic Fleet and Kronshtadt from 21 through 23 September.

By 30 September Zhukov's forces were indeed hemmed into Leningrad, but not as tightly as Hitler, the OKH, and Leeb wished. German forces had dented but not penetrated Zhukov's defenses in the city's southern suburbs, the Leningrad Front's Neva River defenses remained intact, and the Finns had yet to attack. Zhukov's iron will had produced a "Miracle on the Neva," and Leeb clearly understood that he had lost his best opportunity to seize Leningrad. Worse still, from Leeb's perspective, rather than resting on his defensive laurels, Zhukov set about exacting an even greater toll on Leningrad's tormentors by attacking once again. On Zhukov's recommendations, the *Stavka* ordered Kulik's 54th Army, still operating under its direct control, and Zhukov's Neva Operational Group to launch converging attacks toward Siniavino and Mga to raise the Leningrad blockade.[74]

The Leningrad Front had formed the Neva Operational Group on 2 September from the 46th and 115th Rifle Divisions and the 4th Armored Car Regiment and deployed it facing east along the western bank of the Neva River. On the same day, the *Stavka* had created the 54th Army under Kulik's command. Initially, Kulik's army consisted of the 285th, 286th, 310th, and 314th Rifle Divisions (from the 52d Army), the 27th Cavalry Division, the 122d Tank Brigade and 119th Separate Tank Battalion, the 881st and 882d Corps Artillery Regiments, the 150th Pontoon-Bridge Battalion, and four motorized engineer battalions. By the end of September, the *Stavka* had reinforced Kulik's army with the 3d and 4th Guards Rifle Divisions, the 21st Tank Division, and the 16th Tank Brigade.[75]

After repeated delays, Kulik's 54th Army began its attack on 10 September but advanced only 6–10 kilometers (3.7–6.2 miles) toward Siniavino in 16 days of off-and-on heavy fighting, while Zhukov and the *Stavka* castigated him repeatedly for his army's dismal performance. Ultimately, Schmidt's XXXIX Motorized Corps forced Kulik's forces to withdraw from the Mga-Kirishi rail line to new defensive positions along the Nasiia River. Angrily, Zhukov insisted Stalin replace Kulik with his protégé, Khozin.[76] Although court-martialed for his failure and reduced to the rank of major general, later the politically loyal general would return to army command with predictably poor results. Meanwhile, the Neva Operational Group's 115th Rifle Division and 4th Naval Infantry Brigade crossed the Neva River on 20 September and seized a small bridgehead in the Moskovskaia Dubrovka region on the river's left bank, but accomplished little more.

Although Zhukov's so-called First Siniavino Offensive indeed failed, it did offer some positive gains from the Soviet perspective. First, it prompted the Germans to transfer to the Siniavino region from Western Europe two parachute regiments of the 7th Parachute Division from Germany, one infantry regiment from Army Group Center, the Spanish 250th "Blue" Division, and the 72d Infantry Division from Western Europe. In addition, it delayed somewhat the transfer of Reinhardt's XXXXI Motorized Corps southward to reinforce Army Group Center, and it forced Leeb to transfer the 8th Panzer

Division and part of the 96th Infantry Division from south of Leningrad to the Siniavino sector.

After fighting in the Leningrad region died out in late September, the front south of Leningrad stabilized temporarily. Both sides licked their wounds, counted their casualties, and prepared for future operations, which the situation around Leningrad dictated must continue. Despite the spectacular gains it had recorded since crossing the Western Dvina River in early July, Army Group North had suffered heavy losses. Although Soviet sources claim that the army group lost between 40 and 50 percent of its forces dead or wounded in the battles for the coastal bridgehead and the Krasnogvardeisk and Slutsk-Kolpino Fortified Regions, the army group reported 60,000 men lost.[77]

However, Leningrad's poorly organized, badly trained, and ill-equipped defenders lost far more. The Northern Front reported suffering 55,535 casualties between 10 July and 23 August out of 153,000 men engaged. The Leningrad Front lost 116,316 soldiers from 23 August to 30 September out of 300,000 engaged. Finally, the Northwestern Front's casualty toll from 10 July through 30 September added another 144,788 men out of 272,000 engaged to the gruesome toll.[78] By any count, the opposing forces were exhausted. Nevertheless, as both sides ministered to their troops and counted their casualties, they prepared to resume operations, knowing full well that, since Army Group North had failed to achieve its Barbarossa objectives, the struggle would inevitably continue.

Unfortunately for Leeb, the resources available for him to do so also dwindled. On 15 September Hoepner's Fourth Panzer Group began departing for Army Group Center. Reinhardt's XXXXI Motorized Corps, with the 1st, 6th, and 8th Panzer and 36th Motorized Divisions, the LVI and LVII Motorized Corps, and Richtofen's VIII Air Corps, departed for Army Group Center on 15 September to take part in Operation Typhoon. The 6th Panzer Division deployed southward late on 15 September, and the 1st Panzer Division on 19 September. A day later, the 36th Motorized Division and the corps headquarters joined the southward march. By this time, only Schmidt's XXXIX Motorized Corps, with the 12th Panzer and 18th and 20th Motorized Divisions and, as a later concession, the 8th Panzer Division, remained to provide Leeb with armor support. On 24 September he reported candidly to OKH that the situation had "worsened considerably," he could no longer continue offensive operations toward Leningrad, and his forces had no other choice but to go on the defensive, a declaration that Hitler would not accept.[79]

The Red Army's painful defense along the Leningrad axis lasted from 10 July to 30 September, a period that seemed an eternity to Stalin, the *Stavka,* and the Northwestern, Northern, and Leningrad Fronts' beleaguered commanders and forces. After 30 September the front north and south of Leningrad stabilized and remained stable until January 1943. During the 50 days of often desperate and usually costly defense that characterized the summer operations, Red Army forces disrupted Hitler's plan to seize Leningrad from the march by delivering concentric blows from the south and north.

Combat steadily intensified during this period as the Red Army increased its resistance and began conducting counterstrokes of its own. As a result, the tempo of the German advance decreased from a daily rate of advance of 5 kilometers (3.1 miles) in July, to 2.2 kilometers (1.37 miles) in August, and 1.4 kilometers (.87 miles) in September. The Red Army improved its defensive forces and techniques throughout this period by adopting extraordinary and sometimes draconian mobilization measures and by committing virtually all of its available manpower to combat. During July and August, it raised and fielded four DNOs, three guards DNOs, and an NKVD Rifle Division and was reinforced by four weak rifle divisions dispatched by the *Stavka*.

The strength and complexity of German offensive operations increased as the offensive developed. In July Army Group North and its Finnish allies attacked simultaneously along the Petrozavodsk, Olonets, and Leningrad axes. In mid-August the Germans penetrated Soviet defenses along the Novgorod axis, cut off and isolated much of the 8th Army in Estonia, and attacked simultaneously along the Krasnogvardeisk and Karelian Isthmus axes. In late August and early September, German forces attacked simultaneously along the Mga, Krasnogvardeisk, and Karelian axes. The Red Army tried but failed to mount effective large-scale counterstrokes at Sol'tsy, Staraia Russa, Krasnoe Selo, and Siniavino, but achieved little more than delaying the German advance. Even after the Red Army halted the German juggernaut on Leningrad's doorstep and frustrated their attempts to capture the city by direct attack, there was no doubt in either camp that the city remained in mortal danger of being encircled and destroyed.

There was also little doubt concerning German intentions regarding the city. Directive No. 1a 1601/41, "Concerning the Future Existence of the City of Leningrad," issued by a higher German headquarters on 22 September, starkly announced those intentions:

1. The Fuehrer has decided to erase the city of Petersburg from the face of the earth. I have no interest in the further existence of this large population point after the defeat of Soviet Russia. Finland has also said the same about its disinterest in the further existence of this city located directly on its new border.

2. The previous demands by the fleet concerning the maintenance of dockyards, harbors, and similar important naval facilities are well known

to the OKW; however, the satisfaction of these does not seem possible in view of the general line of conduct with regard to Petersburg.

3. We propose to closely blockade the city and erase it from the earth by means of artillery fire of all caliber and continuous bombardment from the air.[80]

Nor did the German air and artillery campaign that began in late August lessen in intensity in September or thereafter. Driven by ambition, frustration, and sheer hatred, Hitler would force Leeb's army group to make one last exertion to encircle the city before the onset of winter.

Adolf Hitler

I. V. Stalin

Colonel General Erich Hoepner,
Commander, Fourth Panzer Group

Colonel General Franz Halder, Chief,
German Army General Staff

Field Marshal Ritter von Leeb,
Commander, Army Group North

Colonel General Erich von Manstein,
Commander, LVI Motorized Corps

Army General G. K. Zhukov, Commander,
Leningrad Front

Lieutenant General A. M. Vasilevsky,
Deputy Chief, General Staff Operational
Directorate, Deputy Chief, General
Staff, and *Stavka* representative

Marshal of the Soviet Union
B. M. Shaposhnikov, Chief,
Red Army General Staff

Lieutenant General N. F. Vatutin,
Deputy Chief, General Staff, and
Chief of Staff, Northwestern Front

Marshal of the Soviet Union K. E. Voroshilov, Commander, Northwestern Direction High Command, and Commander, Leningrad Front

Colonel General F. I. Kuznetsov, Commander, Baltic Special Military District, and Commander, Northwestern Front

Lieutenant General P. P. Sobennikov, Commander, 8th Army, and Commander, Northwestern Front

Lieutenant General V. I. Morozov,
Commander, 11th Army

Major General M. E. Berzarin,
Commander, 27th Army, and
Commander, 34th Army

Lieutenant General M. M. Popov,
Commander, Leningrad Military
District; Commander, Northern Front;
and Commander, Leningrad Front

A. A. Zhdanov, Communist Party chief in Leningrad

Red Army T-26 light tank

Red Army T-28 medium tank

Red Army T-35 heavy tank

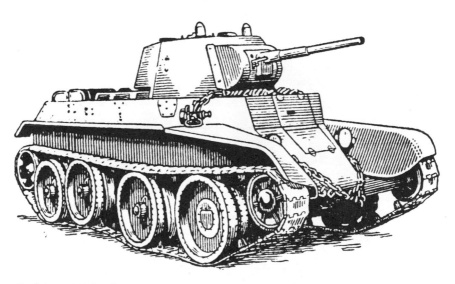

Red Army BT-7 tank

Red Army T-34 medium tank

Red Army KV-1 heavy tank

Red Army soldiers on parade (1939)

Soviet propaganda poster, "The beginning . . ." Hitler's sword is labeled "Plan Barbarossa."

German infantry advancing during the border battles

Advancing German artillery

Red Army infantry deploying to the front (June 1941). The sign reads, "Our cause is just. The enemy will be defeated. The victory will be ours."

Red Army poster (1941), "Under the banner of Lenin—Onward to victory!"

Red Army poster (1941), "The Motherland calls!"

Dead Red Army soldiers, July–August 1941

Red Army troops deploying past the Kirov factory to defend Leningrad

The Encirclement Struggle

The Miracle at Tikhvin, 30 September–30 December 1941

THE SITUATION ON 1 OCTOBER

As summer heat began to give way to the chill of fall in northern Russia, for the first time in the war, German forces in the Leningrad region found themselves playing second fiddle to more momentous developments elsewhere in the Eastern Front. With the *Wehrmacht*'s drive on Leningrad at a standstill and the operation to encircle Soviet forces at Kiev about to begin, on 6 September, Hitler had issued Directive No. 35 announcing his intention to seize Moscow and much of the Ukraine before the onset of winter. The directive provided necessary context for what Hitler expected Army Group North to accomplish during the early fall:

> 1. *On the southern wing of the Eastern Front.* Destroy the enemy located in the Kremenchug, Kiev, and Konotop triangle with the forces of Army Group South, which have crossed the Dnepr to the north, in cooperation with the attacking forces of Army Group Center's southern flank. As soon as the situation permits, freed-up formations of Second and Sixth Armies and also the Second Panzer Group should be regrouped to carry out new operations.
>
> No later than 10 September, mobile formations on Army Group South's front, reinforced with infantry and supported along the main axes by the Fourth Air Fleet, are to begin a surprise offensive northwestward through Lubna from the bridgehead created by the Seventeenth Army. At the same time, the Seventeenth Army will advance along the Poltava and Khar'kov axis.
>
> Continue the offensive along the lower course of the Dnepr toward the Crimea supported by the Fourth Air Fleet. . . .
>
> 2. *In Army Group Center's sector.* Prepare an operation against Army Group Timoshenko as quickly as possible so that we can launch an offensive in the general direction of Viaz'ma and destroy the enemy located in the region east of Smolensk with a double envelopment by powerful panzer forces against his flanks.
>
> To that end, form two shock groups:

The first on the southern flank, presumably in the region southeast of Roslavl', with an attack axis to the northeast. The composition of the group [will include] forces subordinate to Army Group Center and the 5th and 2d Panzer Divisions, which will be freed up to fulfill that mission.

The second in the Ninth Army's sector with its attack axis presumably through Belyi. Insofar as possible, this group will consist of large Army Group Center formations.

After destroying the main mass of Timoshenko's group of forces in this decisive encirclement and destruction operation, Army Group Center is to begin pursuing enemy forces along the Moscow axis while protecting its right flank on the Oka River and its left on the upper reaches of the Volga River. The Second Air Fleet, reinforced in timely fashion by transferred formations, particularly from the northern sector of the front, will provide air support for the offensive. While doing so, it will concentrate its main forces on the flanks while employing the principal bomber formations (Eighth Air Corps) for support of the mobile formations in both attacking flank groupings.

3. *In the northern sector of the Eastern Front.* Encircle enemy forces operating in the Leningrad region (and capture Shlissel'burg) in cooperation with an offensive by Finnish forces on the Karelian Isthmus so that a considerable portion of the mobile and First Air Fleet formations, particularly, the VIII Air Corps, can be transferred to Army Group Center no later than 15 September. First and foremost, however, it is necessary to strive to encircle Leningrad completely, at least from the east, and, if weather conditions permit, conduct a large-scale air offensive on Leningrad. It is especially important to destroy the water supply stations.

As soon as possible, Army Group North's forces must begin an offensive northward in the Neva River sector to help the Finns overcome the fortifications along the old Soviet-Finnish border, and also to shorten the front lines and deprive the enemy of the ability to use his air bases. In cooperation with the Finns, prevent enemy naval forces from exiting Kronshtadt into the Baltic Sea (Hango and the Moonzund Islands) by using mine obstacles and artillery fire.

Also isolate the region of combat operations at Leningrad from the sector along the lower course of the Volkhov as soon as forces necessary to perform this mission become available. Link up with the Karelian Army on the Svir River only after enemy forces in the Leningrad region have been destroyed.

4. During the further conduct of operations, ensure that the southern flank of Army Group Center's offensive along the Moscow axis is protected by an advance to the northeast by a flank protection grouping in Army Group South's sector created from available mobile formations. [Also

ensure] that Army Group North's forces are directed to protect Army Group Center's northern flank and also the advance along both sides of Lake Il'men' to link up with the Karelian Army.

5. Any curtailment of the period for preparing and accelerating the operation's commencement will accompany the preparation and conduct of the entire operation.

[signed] Hitler[1]

Despite these instructions, Hitler had not abandoned Leningrad as a target of his wrath. Instead, grudgingly admitting that the conquest of Leningrad would be far more difficult than originally thought, he turned to the seizure of Kiev and Moscow as far more lucrative and achievable goals, leaving the bewildered Leeb the mission of encircling Leningrad. Leeb had to do so in deteriorating weather and without the Fourth Panzer Group, on which he was accustomed to rely.

By early October Leeb's army group fielded 53 divisions (including 2 panzer and 2 motorized divisions) and 7 brigades along the northwestern strategic axis, half of which were deployed in the Leningrad region. Having already informed Hitler that his forces were in no state to conduct major offensive operations, Leeb then debated the issue of what sort of limited offensive Army Group North could conduct before deteriorating weather conditions required him to consolidate his positions for the winter.

Ultimately, Leeb suggested two offensive options. His forces could either eliminate the Soviet 8th Army's bridgehead at Oranienbaum, or they could advance eastward and northeastward from Chudovo and Kirishi to Tikhvin and Volkhov to block the last remaining Soviet access route to Leningrad and, perhaps, link up with the Finns. Leeb chose a lesser variant of the latter, specifically, a limited attack with Schmidt's XXXIX Motorized Corps, reinforced by infantry, northward from Kirishi to Volkhov to dislodge and perhaps to destroy the Soviet 54th Army. He proposed that the attack begin on 6 October.[2]

Hitler, however, rejected Leeb's proposal on the grounds that such an attack would traverse poor terrain unsuited for armored operations. Instead, he ordered Leeb to advance northeastward from Chudovo to Tikhvin and then northwestward along the road and railroad to Volkhov to encircle the Soviet 54th Army. This offensive option projected German forces twice as far forward as the one proposed by Leeb and required greater forces than Leeb actually possessed. Nevertheless, Leeb reluctantly acceded to Hitler's desires and ordered Schmidt's XXXIX Motorized Corps, with the 12th and 8th Panzer and the 20th and 18th Motorized Divisions, to conduct the army group's main attack from Chudovo to Tikhvin on 16 October. At the same time, the I Army Corps' 11th, 21st, 254th, and 126th Infantry Divisions would either support Schmidt's motorized corps or conduct a secondary attack northward from Kirishi toward Volkhov. Ultimately, the two forces were to capture Tikhvin and Volkhov and the southeastern shore of Lake Ladoga to cut the Soviet's remaining rail line to Lake Ladoga and Leningrad. The operation was also designed to assist Army Group Center, whose Operation Typhoon toward Moscow was not developing as rapidly as the OKH had anticipated.

Not everyone in the OKH was enthusiastic about Leeb's planned offensive. For example, on 2 October, Halder noted that the Fuehrer "makes proposal to rectify the situation on the Ladoga front by an armored thrust on Tikhvin, which subsequently would swing around across the Volkhov River, into the enemy's rear. (Fantasy!)"[3] Halder continued to track the debate between Hitler and Leeb on 5 October: "In AGp. North the attack against the Ladoga front planned for 6 October has been called off by OKH, and an order has been issued to take the armored divisions, which would needlessly burn themselves out in that terrain. The attack will be launched with infantry as soon as sufficient strength has been built up with the newly arrived divisions. Meanwhile the armored divisions will rest and refit."[4] Unfortunately, a gap in Halder's diary between 9 October and 3 November deprives us of his perspective on the wisdom of Hitler's final decision to launch the Tikhvin venture despite the obvious hazards.

Stalin, too, was concerned about the situation on the Soviet Union's northern flank, particularly as it related to the *Wehrmacht*'s thrust toward Moscow that began in early October. His clear intent was to defend Leningrad, conduct an offensive to raise the blockade of the city, prevent the Germans from transferring forces from Leningrad to the Moscow axis, and block any German attempt to link up with the Finns and completely encircle Leningrad. Days after the Germans began their advance on Moscow, on 5 October, Stalin recalled Zhukov to Moscow to take command of the crumbling Western and Reserve Fronts. Zhukov turned temporary command of the Leningrad Front over to his favorite, Fediuninsky, and flew to Moscow the following day.[5] Several days later, Stalin dispatched Colonel General N. N. Voronov, a deputy people's commissar of defense and chief of Red Army Air Defense (PVO), to the city as his representative, with orders to prepare an operation to raise the blockade of the city.[6] The most important question confronting Stalin, Voronov, and Fediuninsky, however, was whether the Leningrad Front, which had just endured a costly defense, had sufficient strength to mount a successful offensive.

On 1 October the Leningrad Front's forces were indeed stretched thin. The 23d Army, now commanded by Lieutenant General A. I. Cherepanov, defended Leningrad's northern and western periphery, only 30 kilometers (18.6 miles) from the city's northern outskirts.[7] By this time, Cherepanov's army fielded six rifle divisions, an NKVD brigade, a fortified region, and two separate tank battalions.[8] The 8th Army, still under Shevaldin's command, was isolated in the coastal bridgehead at Oranienbaum. It consisted of a rifle corps with three rifle divisions, four additional rifle divisions, a naval infantry brigade, rifle and tank regiments, and an armored car battalion.[9]

The battle-weary 42d and 55th Armies and the Neva Operational Group defended Leningrad itself. South of the city, Fediuninsky's 42d Army defended the 17-kilometer (10.6-mile) sector from Ligovo to Pulkovo with two rifle divisions in first echelon and three rifle divisions and one naval infantry and one rifle brigade in second echelon, supported by the Baltic Fleet.[10] Lazarov's 55th Army defended the 30-kilometer (18.6-mile) sector from east of Pulkovo to the Neva River at Putrolovo with five rifle divisions in first echelon and one in second echelon, with a fortified region (seven separate artillery–machine gun battalions) occupying cut-off positions to the rear.[11] Finally, the Neva Operational Group, which consisted of one rifle and one NKVD rifle division, one naval infantry brigade, three destroyer battalions, and a s eparate tank battalion, defended northward along the Neva River to Lake Ladoga.[12]

East of the German corridor, which extended from Shlissel'burg along the southern shore of Lake Ladoga, Khozin's 54th Army, now under Leningrad Front control, was still conducting desultory attacks toward Siniavino. Khozin's army, which manned the 35-kilometer (21.8-mile) sector from Lipka to Maluksinskii Swamp, consisted of six rifle divisions (two of which were guards), a mountain rifle brigade, one tank division, and two tank brigades, all woefully understrength after weeks of heavy fighting.[13] Iakovlev's 4th and Klykov's 52d Armies, still under *Stavka* control, and the Northwestern Front's Novgorod Army Group defended eastward from Maluksinskii Swamp to the Volkhov River at Kirishi and southward along the river's eastern bank to Lake Il'men'. Iakovlev's force, which occupied a 50-kilometer (31-mile) sector from Maluksinskii Swamp through Kirishi and southward along the Volkhov River to the mouth of the Pchevzha River, consisted of four rifle divisions, one cavalry division, one tank brigade, one tank battalion, and supporting artillery and engineers. His forces were in the same understrength state as Khozin's.

Klykov's army, which manned an 80-kilometer (49.8-mile) sector from the mouth of the Pchevzha River to Dubrovka, included four rifle divisions and artillery and engineers but no armor.[14] His forces were between 65 and 70 percent strength. Neither the 4th nor the 52d Armies had significant reserves. The small Novgorod Army Group (NAG), which was still operating under the Northwestern Front's control, fielded three rifle divisions, a separate rifle regiment, and a tank division (without tanks) in the relatively narrow sector from Dubrovka to the northern shore of Lake Il'men'.[15]

THE RED ARMY'S FIRST SINIAVINO OFFENSIVE, OCTOBER

On 12 and again on 14 October, the *Stavka* ordered the Leningrad Front to prepare and conduct a two-pronged offensive operation beginning on 20 October to crush German forces in the Shlissel'burg corridor, capture Siniavino, and restore land communications between Leningrad and the Soviet rear.[16] Lazarov's 55th Army, organized into the so-called Eastern Sector Operational Group (ESOG), was to conduct the western prong of the attack by assaulting across the Neva River, advance toward Siniavino, and link up with the 54th Army advancing from the east. The Neva Operational Group was to conduct a supporting attack on the 55th Army's left flank. Khozin's 54th Army was to attack westward from the Naziia River, capture Siniavino, and link up with the 55th Army's operational group and the Neva Operational Group. Once they had effected link-up, the three forces were to destroy German forces in the Shlissel'burg corridor. In reality, since the new effort at Siniavino was but a continuation of the September action, Soviet military historians have lumped together the twin operations under the rubric of the First Battle of Siniavino.

The ESOG, which Fediuninsky had formed from the 55th Army and *front* reserves, consisted of the 265th, 86th, 20th, 191st, and 177th Rifle Divisions, the 123d and 124th Tank Brigades, the 107th Separate Tank Battalion, and supporting artillery. The group's mission was to assault across the Neva River in the 5-kilometer (3.1-mile) sector between Peski and Nevskaia Dubrovka on the army's right flank, advance toward Siniavino, and help encircle and destroy the German force by the end of the second day of the operation. The Neva Operational Group was to defend the northern sector of its Neva River defenses with its 1st Rifle Division and 11th Rifle Brigade. Meanwhile its shock group, consisting of the 115th Rifle Division and 4th Naval Infantry Brigade, was to attack eastward through Gorodok No. 1 toward Siniavino from its bridgehead on the eastern bank of the Neva near Moskovskaia Dubrovka to support the ESOG and help destroy German forces in the corridor.[17]

To the east, Khozin's 54th Army was to penetrate German defenses between Workers Settlement No. 8 and Tortolovo on the Volkhov-Leningrad rail line with his army's shock group, capture Siniavino, link up with the ESOG and NOG, and destroy German forces in the corridor.[18] Khozin's shock group consisted of the 3d and 4th Guards and 310th Rifle Divisions, the 16th and 122d Tank Brigades, and two artillery regiments. The 286th and 294th Rifle Divisions provided support by attacking on the shock group's flanks, and the 128th Rifle Division, 1st Mountain Rifle Brigade, and 21st Tank Division either conducted local attacks or defended the remainder of the army's sector.[19]

Fediuninsky's attacking force totaled nine rifle divisions, one rifle brigade, four tank brigades, and one separate tank battalion with 71,270 men, 97 tanks (including 59 heavy KV tanks), 475 guns, including all available heavy artillery and *Katiusha* multiple rocket launchers, and aircraft and artillery from the Baltic Fleet. The assaulting force faced 54,000 German soldiers occupying fortified positions in depth flanked by swampy terrain, supported by 450 guns, but no tanks.[20]

Despite Fediuninsky's careful attack preparations, the Germans preempted his offensive by beginning their thrust toward Tikhvin on 16 October. Nevertheless, the *Stavka* insisted the Leningrad Front's shock groups begin their assaults on 20 October as planned. A Leningrad diarist laconically kept track of the offensive's meager progress:

> *Sunday, 19 October.* The 115th Rifle Division and 4th Naval Infantry Brigade have been fighting in the Neva "pocket" for a month already. One can say it has been a month of severe and inhuman education. Today at 2010 hours, two regiments of the 86th Rifle Division and the 169th and 330th Rifle Divisions began crossing from the Nevskaia Dubrovka side into the bridgehead. The 86th Rifle Division is the former 4th People's Militia Division, which formed in Leningrad's Dzerzhinsky District. Until now the division held defenses in the Ust' Tosno–Pokrovskoe sector. Now, having routinely replaced exhausted units, it will defend a bridgehead, which will play a significant role in penetrating the blockade.
>
> *Monday, 20 October.* According to a plan approved by the *Stavka* VGK [Supreme High Command], the *front's* forces began an offensive along the Siniavino axis to raise the blockade.
>
> The Neva Operational Group and the 55th Army are conducting the offensive from Leningrad. The 54th Army is meeting them from the external side of the blockade ring. . . .
>
> The crossing by the 86th Rifle Division into the Neva "pocket," which began yesterday evening, was successful. The losses were minimal—several wounded and dead. The regiments attacked at 1000 hours. Although the Hitlerites opened furious fire, our forces wedged into the enemy's foxholes and began throwing hand grenades. Hand-to-hand fighting then began. By the end of the day, we managed to push the Germans back a bit and expanded the bridgehead somewhat.
>
> *Thursday, 23 October.* Having begun the battle to penetrate the blockade three days ago, the forces of the Leningrad Front's 54th Army pressed the enemy back in places. But the enemy succeeded in overcoming the resistance of the 4th Army and captured Budogosh'. Tikhvin is now directly threatened.[21]

Although his attacking forces achieved only meager gains in three days of heavy but futile fighting, Stalin repeatedly ordered Fediuninsky to complete his operation successfully, regardless of the deteriorating situation along the Volkhov River.[22] The only redeeming feature of the failed offensive was that it tied down five German infantry divisions in the Siniavino salient.

On 23 October, the *Stavka*'s nerves finally cracked, and it ordered Khozin to dispatch two rifle divisions to assist other Soviet forces beleaguered at Tikhvin.[23] Three days later, it assigned Fediuninsky to command the 54th Army and appointed Khozin as Leningrad Front commander.[24] Ostensibly Stalin made this decision because the latter outranked the former, but it is more likely that he did so because Fediuninsky had developed a well-deserved reputation as a fighter—and a fighter was what was needed most along the Tikhvin axis. On 28 October the *Stavka* finally ordered Fediuninsky's 54th Army to cease its offensive at Siniavino and, instead, diverted its forces to defend Volkhov.[25] By then, the *Stavka*'s optimism over prospects for raising the blockade of Leningrad had faded, replaced by a deep foreboding over the prospects of the city's total isolation. It seemed as if the Germans might actually reach Tikhvin and Volkhov and perhaps even link up with the Finns.

THE GERMAN ADVANCE TO TIKHVIN,
OCTOBER–NOVEMBER

The *Stavka*'s concerns were very real indeed. Leeb's mission was to exploit apparent Soviet weakness along the Volkhov River and Tikhvin axis and complete operations around Leningrad as quickly as possible in order to free up forces to reinforce the ongoing offensive against Moscow. The OKH ordered him to regroup his forces, attack through Tikhvin to Lake Ladoga to sever Leningrad's last rail links to Moscow, and completely encircle Leningrad. If successful, it was remotely possible that the German force could link up with the elusive Finns on the Svir River. In either case, both Hitler and Leeb reasoned that Leningrad's fate would then be sealed.

To conduct the offensive, Leeb concentrated Schmidt's XXXIX Motorized Corps and most of the I Army Corps' infantry at Kirishi, Liuban', and southward along the Volkhov River. Schmidt's motorized corps was to conduct the main attack from Chudovo through Gruzino, Budogosh', and Tikhvin to Lodeinoe Pol'e on the Svir River with its 12th Panzer and 20th Motorized Divisions and the I Army Corps' 21st and 126th Infantry Divisions. On Schmidt's left flank, the 11th Infantry Division was to advance from Kirishi northward toward Volkhov. To the south, the motorized corps' 8th Panzer and 18th Motorized Divisions were to attack toward Malaia Vishera and Bologoe to link up with forces operating on Army Group Center's left flank, which were to attack northwestward along the Moscow-Leningrad railroad from Kalinin through Vyshnii Volochek to Bologoe. Even if Schmidt's forces failed to reach the Svir River, they would threaten the Karelian Front's communications east of Lake Ladoga and would likely encircle and destroy the 54th Army, which was operating west of the Volkhov River.[26]

In mid-October the Leningrad Front's 54th Army, the 4th and 52d Armies under *Stavka* control, and the Northwestern Front's Novgorod Army Group defended a 200-kilometer (124.2-mile) front from Lipka on Lake Ladoga to Kirishi and southward along the eastern bank of the Volkhov River to Lake Il'men'. Khozin's 54th Army defended the 35-kilometer (21.7-mile) sector from Lipka halfway to Kirishi and, once again, was preparing to attack toward Siniavino. Iakovlev's 4th Army occupied shallower defenses and was conducting local operations along the 50-kilometer (31-mile) front west of Kirishi and southward along the Volkhov River to the mouth of the Pchevzha River. His army consisted of the 285th, 311th, and 292d Rifle Divisions, the 27th Cavalry Division, the 119th Separate Tank Battalion, one corps artillery regiment, and one pontoon bridge battalion, all of which were understrength, and he had only a single rifle regiment in reserve. Klykov's 52d Army defended the 80-kilometer (49.7-mile) sector along the Volkhov River from the Pchevzha River to Dubrovka, 25 kilometers (15.5 miles) north of Novgorod. He deployed the understrength 288th and 267th Rifle Divisions in defensive sectors 46 and 34 kilometers (28.9 and 21.1 miles) wide and supported them with four corps artillery regiments and one antitank artillery regiment. Klykov's army had no reserve. Finally, the Novgorod Army Group defended the 30-kilometer (18.6-mile) sector along the Volkhov from Dubrovka to Lake Il'men' with the 305th and 180th Rifle Divisions and the 43d Tank Division, which had no tanks.

The bulk of Khozin's 54th Army, specifically, six rifle divisions, one tank division, one mountain rifle and two tank brigades, and two artillery regiments, fully 70 percent of all Soviet forces deployed between the southern shore of Lake Ladoga and Lake Il'men', were concentrated for employment in the Siniavino offensive. This left only five rifle divisions, one cavalry division, one tank battalion, five artillery regiments, and one antitank regiment in the 130-kilometer (80.8-mile) sector opposite the impending German main attack.[27] As subsequent operations soon indicated, this force was wholly inadequate to deal with Leeb's impending offensive.

However, the harsh terrain in the Tikhvin region mitigated against the *Stavka*'s deployment mistakes and would have a significant impact on the forthcoming operations. In fact, Hitler's perception of the difficulties German forces were likely to experience when operating in the Tikhvin region was right on the mark. The Tikhvin region, which encompassed the northeastern part of Leningrad region, was a vast forested and swampy territory dotted with many lakes and swamps and crisscrossed by numerous rivers and streams. Forests, swamps, and lakes covered approximately 60 percent of the region. The region's main communications arteries were the Tikhvin-Volkhov-Luga, Rybinsk-Khvoinaia-Budogosh', Tikhvin-Budogosh', and Oktiabr'skaia rail lines, which were the only decent routes permitting movement throughout the region. During the fall the few dirt roads that existed in the region quickly became sodden because of the abundant rains and unsuited for movement by vehicular transport. This could only be remedied by the construction of corduroy (wooden) roads.

Most towns, villages, and hamlets in the region were located in dry places, on hills and ridges, which were quite low and rolling, and along the roads. Since these populated points dominated all movement routes, they became key terrain and thus objectives for any attacking force.

The entire region abounded with rivers and streams, which varied in size and significance. Because of its width and depth, the Volkhov River, which ran from Lake Il'men' northward past Kirishi and Volkhov to Lake Ladoga, was a serious obstacle and, as the Germans later appreciated, could serve as the base for an imposing defense line. On the other hand, the Bol'shaia and Malaia Vishera rivers, which ran parallel to and roughly 16–24 kilometers (9.9–15 miles) east of the Volkhov River, were not serious obstacles and could be forded at numerous points. Although smaller, other rivers, including the Tigoda, Pchevzha, Sias', Tikhvinka, and Oskuia, had steep banks and adjacent swamps, which could be exploited in defensive operations. Taken together, the region's many rivers, streams, and impenetrable swamps hindered maneuver by attacking forces but assisted forces on the defense. Adding to the inherent terrain problems, once they occupied the region, German forces systematically destroyed all towns, villages, bridges, and other installations, severely hindering Red Army operations.

Nor did the climate facilitate military operations. In addition to the chowdered roads caused by the October rains, in November bitter cold weather arrived, leaving an average snow cover of 50 centimeters (19.7 inches) on the ground by mid-December. With careful preparation, the snow cover improved road mobility, but frequent snowstorms often disrupted road movement. Once the countryside and swamps froze solid, forces could and did construct corduroy roads and tracks across open terrain and swamp alike. However, the plentiful forests and occasional thaws still hindered military operations.[28]

Despite Hitler's reservations, early on 16 October, German infantry of the 21st and 126th Infantry Divisions stormed across the Volkhov River, followed later in the day by the XXXIX Motorized Corps' 12th Panzer and 20th Motorized Divisions. The assaulting forces penetrated the 4th Army's fragile defenses in four days of heavy fighting in roadless terrain covered by 9–10 centimeters (3–4 inches) of snow. The assault forced the 4th Army's 288th and 267th Rifle Divisions to withdraw eastward and northeastward and turned the left flank of the 292d Rifle Division defending to the north, ultimately shattering this division. The German assault created an immense gap between the 4th and 52d Armies that, given the lack of reserves, the defenders were unable to close. Nevertheless, that was what the *Stavka* ordered the two armies to do in a directive it sent to Iakovlev and Klykov on 20 October (Map 6).[29]

In spite of the *Stavka*'s unrealistic directive, from 21 through 23 October, the attacking force fanned out: the 12th Panzer and 20th Motorized Divisions advancing toward Budogosh' and Tikhvin, the 21st Infantry Division toward Kirishi, and the 126th Infantry Division toward Bol'shaia and Malaia Vishera. The advance, however, was tediously slow because the few roads were often impassable, and periodic thaws turned the adjacent terrain into a thick, gluey mass that severely inhibited movement and resupply of the advancing force.[30]

Despite these problems, on 23 October the 12th Panzer and 20th Motorized Divisions captured Budogosh' on the 4th Army's left flank, but the 285th and 311th Rifle Divisions on the 4th Army's right flank halted the 11th Infantry Division's attacks north of Kirishi the following day. To the south, 18th Motorized and 126th Infantry Divisions forced the 52d Army to abandon Bol'shaia Vishera and withdraw to the southeast.

Given the obvious and increasing threat to Tikhvin, the *Stavka* reinforced the 4th and 52d Armies and ordered them to halt the German advance, counterattack, and restore the Volkhov River defenses. In accordance with the *Stavka*'s instructions, Khozin's 54th Army transferred its 310th and 4th Guards Rifle Divisions to the 4th Army on 23 October. At the same time, the *Stavka* quickly moved to back up the crumbling 4th Army. It moved the Leningrad Front's 191st Rifle Division to Sitomlia, 40 kilometers (24.9 miles) southwest of Tikhvin and the 44th Rifle Division to Tikhvin by air to occupy defenses along the Sias' River, 20 kilometers (12.4 miles) to the rear of the 191st Rifle Division's hastily erected defenses. In addition, the *Stavka* sent the 92d Rifle and 60th Tank Divisions to the Tikhvin region from its reserves on 30 October. Meanwhile, on 20 October the Northwestern Front reinforced the 52d Army with its 259th Rifle Division and a battalion of *Katiusha* multiple rocket launchers. Despite the parlous state of the 4th Army's defenses, the *Stavka* ordered the 54th Army to continue its attacks at Siniavino to tie down German forces.[31]

Once reinforced, Iakovlev's 4th and Klykov's 52d Armies should have been capable of driving German forces back to the Volkhov River. Convinced that this was the case, at 1345 hours on 26 October, the *Stavka* sent Klykov a blistering directive criticizing his army's performance and demanding it stiffen its defenses:

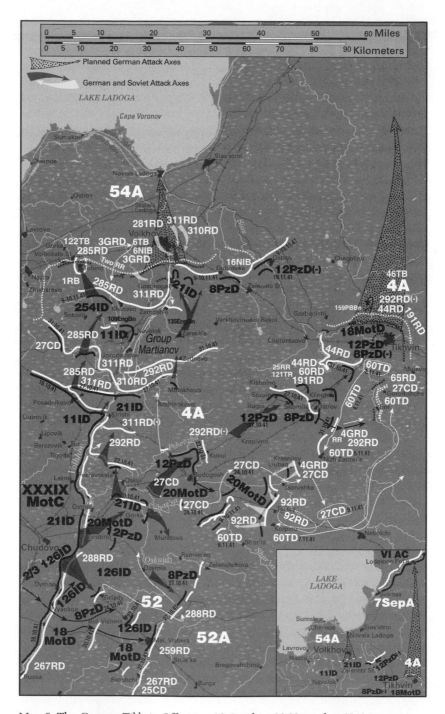

Map 6. The German Tikhvin Offensive, 16 October–10 November 1941

98

The *Stavka* of the Supreme High Command considers [that]:

1. The withdrawal of the 52d Army beyond the Msta and Mda rivers is untimely.

2. The decision to withdraw to the Zelenshchina, Okzovo, Kuz'minka, and Zador'e line is incorrect since it is based on unverified aviation reconnaissance data.

By 27 October you must present an explanation of the reasons for the unprovoked circumstances of the army's withdrawal to the Zelenshchina, Okzovo, Kuz'minka, and Zador'e line.

3. The army's forces will firmly defend their occupied positions.

[signed] Vasilevsky[32]

However, the two armies' defenses continued to collapse because they committed their reserves into combat in piecemeal fashion and without adequate preparation or effective command and control. For example, on 27 October, Colonel D. A. Luk'ianov's 191st Rifle Division and elements of Major General A. I. Andreev's 4th Guards Rifle and Major General A. F. Popov's 60th Tank Division attacked the 12th Panzer Division's vanguard near Sitomlia on the road to Tikhvin. The counterattack failed because it was poorly coordinated, although it did force the 12th Panzer to halt its advance and regroup. By this time, Schmidt's motorized corps reported capturing 12,500 prisoners and seizing or destroying 66 Russian guns.[33]

Farther south, the 52d Army's 288th and 267th Rifle Divisions, by now reinforced by the 259th Rifle Division, delayed the 8th Panzer and 18th Motorized Divisions' advance long enough to occupy new defenses along the Malaia Vishera River north and south of Malaia Vishera. So strenuous was their defense that, by 27 October, the German advance in this sector ground to a halt. At this juncture, increasing Soviet resistance west of Tikhvin forced Schmidt to regroup his 8th Panzer and 18th Motorized Divisions from Malaia Vishera to Sitomlia to reinforce his main attack. The following day he reinforced the 11th Infantry Division, whose attack north of Kirishi had bogged down with part of the 21st Infantry Division, and renamed the force Group von Boeckmann. He then ordered Boeckmann's new group to attack northward toward Volkhov from the sector between Maluksinskii Swamp and Kirishi and make its main attack along the Volkhov River to protect the left flank of Schmidt's main force operating along the Tikhvin axis.

With the pace of his offensive slowing, on 26 October Leeb visited with Hitler and the OKH staff at Hitler's headquarters in the Wolf's Lair *(Wolfsschance)*. He requested that Army Group Center support his offensive by attacking from Kalinin through Vyshnii Volochek to Bologoe with its Third Panzer Group and the northern wing of its Ninth Army. While Leeb's request seemed reasonable at the time, violent Soviet counterattacks at Kalinin soon made such support impossible.[34] In any case, Hitler, whose attention was riveted on Moscow, categorically refused Leeb's request. However, he did agree to cancel plans for an attack to eliminate the Oranienbaum bridgehead, in so doing saving three of Leeb's divisions. Before leaving Hitler's headquarters, Leeb expressed doubts to Hitler that his forces could take Tikhvin. Hitler, however, insisted that the advance continue.[35]

In late October the *Stavka* began planning and orchestrating a series of counterstrokes it hoped would culminate in the defeat of German forces operating along the Tikhvin axes. After two days of exchanging often acrimonious messages, on 29 October, the *Stavka* ordered Iakovlev's 4th Army to concentrate two shock groups, each of roughly two divisions, southwest of Tikhvin, with which to conduct a major counterstroke. Once formed, the first shock group consisted of Luk'ianov's 191st Rifle Division and one regiment each from the 44th Rifle and 60th Tank Divisions deployed in the vicinity of Sitomlia.[36] The second shock group, made up of Andreev's 4th Guards Rifle Division and the remaining two regiments of Popov's 60th Tank Division, assembled 25 kilometers (15.5 miles) to the south. The two shock groups were to attack toward Budogosh' and Gruzino on 1 November together with the 92d Rifle Division already operating to the south, destroy the German forces advancing on Tikhvin, and restore Soviet positions along the Volkhov River. The northern shock group began its attack on 2 November, and the southern joined the action on 4 and 6 November. However, both attacks failed in the face of massive German air and artillery strikes and heavy counterattacks.[37]

Undeterred by the fresh Russian counterattacks and taking advantage of a vicious blast of cold weather on 6 November that began freezing rivers and streams in the region, Schmidt's motorized corps resumed its advance toward Tikhvin on 5 November. Now reinforced by the 8th Panzer and 18th Motorized Divisions, the 12th Panzer Division brushed aside the 191st Rifle Division on 6 November and captured Tikhvin during a snowstorm on 8 November, severing the last rail line from Moscow to Lake Ladoga. In the process, the corps reported capturing, since the beginning of the operation, 20,000 Russian prisoners and seizing or destroying 96 tanks, 179 guns, and an armored train. In addition, the Germans claimed the 4th Army headquarters had abandoned its records and all of its vehicles in its haste to escape Tikhvin.[38]

Despite Schmidt's success, it was also increasingly clear that his forces had already "shot their bolt." The prolonged advance had seriously weakened his mobile divisions, the ravages of winter weather and the terrible terrain conditions were taking their toll on soldiers and armored vehicles alike, and Soviet resistance was perceptively stiffening both north of Tikhvin and at Malaia Vishera. Even before the Germans captured Tikhvin, the temperature had fallen to as low as 40° below zero (Centigrade and Fahrenheit), and many soldiers were frostbitten or simply froze to death.

Compounding Leeb's and Shmidt's discomfiture, the Finns failed to resume offensive operations after reaching the northern outskirts of Leningrad
and the Svir River line north of Lake Ladoga in early October. Without Finnish
assistance, it was sheer folly for Schmidt to continue his drive toward the lake's
eastern shore and the Svir in such appalling weather conditions.

By 8 November menacing Russian troop concentrations hemmed the 12th
Panzer and 18th Motorized Divisions into Tikhvin from three sides and the
German force was unable to muster the strength or will necessary to continue the attack northward. To the southwest, the 8th Panzer, 20th Motorized, and 126th Infantry Divisions manned strong-point defenses scattered
throughout the 100-kilometer (62.1-mile) snow-covered gap between Tikhvin
and Malaia Vishera, and Soviet forces were intensifying their counterattacks
against the 126th Infantry Division, dug in at Malaia Vishera. To the west,
Group von Boeckmann continued to advance along the Volkhov axis, but at
a snail's pace, reaching within 14 kilometers (8.7 miles) of Volkhov before its
attack totally bogged down.

Leeb's entire offensive ground to a halt on 8 November literally locked
in the embrace of the bitter cold weather. His forces had neither eliminated
the Soviet 54th Army nor reached the Finns, and although they had captured
Tikhvin and cut the Moscow-Ladoga rail line, his entire force was now overextended and threatened from every direction. With the temperature falling
to –20°F (–29°C) and the terrain deep in snow, the frost produced more
casualties than Russian bullets.

Hitler, however, permitted Leeb no respite. Goaded on by Hitler, Leeb
stoically reinforced Group von Boeckmann south of Volkhov with the 254th
Infantry Division and dispatched the 61st Infantry Division to Tikhvin to
reinforce Schmidt's exhausted motorized corps.[39] He then altered his offensive plan by shifting the focal point of his offensive away from Tikhvin. His
revised plan called for Group von Boeckmann to capture Volkhov with its
vital aluminum plant and power station and then Novaia Ladoga on the southern shore of Lake Ladoga to cut off the transport of supplies to Leningrad
via Lake Ladoga and encircle and destroy the Russian 54th Army.

Boeckmann's group, reinforced by the 254th Infantry Division, had been
attacking along the Kirishi-Volkhov axis since 28 October, slowly driving the
4th Army's 285th, 311th, and 310th Rifle Divisions and part of the 292d Rifle
Division northward toward Volkhov. On 8 November Boeckmann's group
approached the southern outskirts of Volkhov, driving a deep wedge between
the 54th Army, which was now commanded by Fediuninsky, and Iakovlev's
4th Army. At this point, Leeb dispatched a task force from the 8th Panzer
Division to support Boeckmann's advance. However, a desperate counterattack by the 310th Rifle Division at Zelenets Station thwarted the 8th Panzer
Division's attempt to outflank Soviet defenses east of the town.[40]

The appearance of 8th Panzer Division units near Volkhov, which threatened both Volkhov and the 54th Army's rear, once again forced the *Stavka* to act. On 9 November it appointed Army General K. A. Meretskov, just released from NKVD captivity on groundless charges of treason, to replace Iakovlev as the commander of the 4th Army.[41] At the same time, the *Stavka* ordered the Leningrad Front to halt the 54th Army's offensive at Siniavino and employ the bulk of Fediuninsky's army to destroy German forces in the Volkhov region. Fediuninsky, in turn, requested that the *Stavka* assign to him the 4th Army's Volkhov Operational Group, which consisted of the 285th, 310th, 311th, and 292d Rifle Divisions, the 6th Naval Infantry Brigade, and the 3d Guards Rifle Division, which were operating on the 4th Army's right flank. The *Stavka* approved Fediuninsky's request on 12 November and ordered him to form a new shock group to defeat Group von Boeckmann's advance toward Volkhov.[42] However, Fediuninsky's task became more challenging when, on 18 November, Leeb reinforced Boeckmann's force with yet another combat group, this time from the 12th Panzer Division.[43]

Shortly after receiving his new attack orders, Fediuninsky moved his auxiliary army command post nearer to Volkhov, began assembling a shock group on the western bank of the Volkhov River southwest of the town, and ordered the group to attack Boeckmann's forces no later than 25 November. However, while Fediuninsky was regrouping his forces to deliver the counterstroke, Boeckmann ordered his 254th Infantry Division to attack northwestward toward Voibokalo Station in the 54th Army's rear along the shortest route to Lake Ladoga. Reacting quickly, Fediuninsky countered by dispatching Colonel T. A. Sviklin's 285th Rifle Division and Lieutenant Colonel M. I. Rudoi's 122d Tank Brigade to block Boeckmann's thrust. The combined force managed to do so, but only barely, in late November just south of Voibokalo Station. This local success set the stage for Fediuninsky's army to participate in the general Soviet Tikhvin counteroffensive, which was already beginning to ripple across the entire front in the Volkhov and Tikhvin regions.

Leeb's offensive along the Tikhvin and Volkhov axes had bogged down by mid-November in the face of intensified Soviet resistance, debilitating weather, and his forces' heavy losses. Over the course of 30 days, his front east of the Volkhov River had expanded from 70 to 350 kilometers (43.4 to 223.6 miles), his forces were exhausted, woefully overextended, and at the end of their logistical tether, and Schmidt's main shock group was half encircled in Tikhvin. Leeb's only consolation—the fact that his forces held the Moscow-Ladoga and Tikhvin-Volkhov rail lines in a stranglehold and, by doing so, posed a mortal threat to Leningrad—however, was illusory. His reckless advance deep into the Soviet rear area in the dead of winter created favorable conditions for a concerted Soviet counteroffensive, a circumstance that the watchful *Stavka* decided to exploit to full advantage.

Halder expressed his growing appreciation of Leeb's precarious position in his diary on 16 November:

> Field Marshal von Leeb (AGp. North) on the phone: The situation between Lake Ilman and Lake Ladoga has taken a bad turn. Very heavy pressure on Malaya Vishera and Vishera. No threat to Tikhvin last night. Today very large movements from the east again. Pressure from the south, from Kostruna Plesso. Situation at Tikhvin not very acute, but may become so within the next few days. Enemy also coming from the north. Twenty-first Division thinks it can get as far as Volkhovstroi, but will not be able to advance further unless it receives reinforcements.
>
> The attack by 254th and 223d divisions [of Group Boeckmann] has miscarried. The divisions had to return to their lines of departure; 223d is not yet equal to such a task; it was caught on its northern flank, and then also the 254th Division had to fall back. The Volkhov front needs reinforcements. The only thing available is one-third of 61st Division, but it too will take a long time to move into line (initial elements day after tomorrow). Commander of army group wants to await today's developments. He is considering abandoning Tikhvin in favor of strengthening the "Volkhov front." I emphasized OKH's interest in holding Tikhvin at all costs. Two medium artillery battalions have been withdrawn from the Kronstadt front. Infantry line very thin. Enemy has three to four divisions and some MG [machine gun] battalions opposite Hangoe.[44]

Despite the heavy fighting under way along the Moscow axis, the correlation of forces east of Leningrad was indeed shifting significantly in the Red Army's favor. Furthermore, Army Group Center's 15 November assault on Moscow made it essential that the Red Army go on the offensive in the Leningrad region, if for no other reason than to tie down German forces. It did so after mid-November by unleashing a series of counterattacks and counterstrokes that inevitably grew into a full-fledged counteroffensive.

THE SOVIET TIKHVIN COUNTERSTROKE, NOVEMBER–DECEMBER

When it began orchestrating its counterattacks and counterstrokes northeast of Leningrad, the *Stavka* focused intently on achieving two priority aims. First and foremost, it sought to save Leningrad by destroying the German forces at Tikhvin and Volkhov and restoring communications between Leningrad and Moscow via the Tikhvin-Volkhov railroad. Second, it tried to tie down as many German forces as possible along the northwestern axis in the interest of the Moscow defense (Map 7).

In late November the Leningrad Front's 54th Army and the 4th and 52d Armies, which were still operating under *Stavka* control, faced a German force of 10 infantry, 2 motorized, and 2 panzer divisions deployed between Lakes Ladoga and Il'men'. The German force, whose divisions were at about 60 percent strength, numbered roughly 120,000 men, 100 tanks and assault guns, and 1,000 artillery pieces. The *Stavka* was able to concentrate 17 rifle and 2 tank divisions, 1 cavalry division, 3 rifle and 2 tank brigades, and 3 tank and 2 ski battalions, organized into 3 armies and fielding 192,950 men, against this German force.[45] While the Soviets enjoyed a considerable superiority in manpower and guns, they were slightly inferior in armor.

The *Stavka* ordered the 54th, 4th, and 52d Armies to destroy the opposing German forces, drive them back to the Volkhov River, and establish bridgeheads on the river's western bank by conducting concentric attacks toward Kirishi and Gruzino.[46] Conducting the main attack, Meretskov's 4th Army was to encircle the XXXIX Motorized Corps at Tikhvin, exploit through Budogosh' to the Volkhov River, link up with the 54th Army at Kirishi and the 52d Army at Gruzino, and capture bridgeheads over the river. His army faced the 12th Panzer, 18th and 20th Motorized, and 61st Infantry Divisions, and one third of the 8th Panzer Division.

Meretskov divided his army, which consisted of five rifle, one tank, and one cavalry division, one rifle and one tank brigade, and three separate tank battalions, into Northern, Southern, and Eastern Shock Groups, and assigned each a specific mission.[47] The Northern Group, consisting of two regiments of Colonel P. A. Artiushenko's 44th Rifle Division, the 1067th Rifle Regiment, Major General V. A. Koptsov's 46th Tank Brigade, and the 159th Pontoon-bridge Battalion, was to attack German forces at Tikhvin from the north. The Eastern Group, with one regiment of the 44th Rifle Division, the 191st Rifle Division, now commanded by Colonel P. S. Vinogradov, Major General G. T. Timofeev's 27th Cavalry Divisions, the 60th Tank Division's 120th Regiment, and the 128th Separate Tank Battalion, was to attack Tikhvin from the east. Finally, the Southern Group, with Colonel A. N. Larychev's 92d Rifle and Andreev's 4th Guards Rifle Divisions and one regiment of the 292d Rifle Division, was to assault the Germans' communications routes southwest of Tikhvin. Once it captured Tikhvin, the Northern Group was to advance northwestward to assist the 54th Army attack on Boeckmann's forces south of Volkhov, while Meretskov's main force advanced toward Gruzino to link up with the 54th Army's main force and envelop Boeckmann's forces from the south.[48]

By this time, Fediuninsky's 54th Army consisted of eight rifle divisions, one tank division without tanks, two rifle and two tank brigades, and two ski battalions, the bulk of which were to conduct the army's main attacks west of

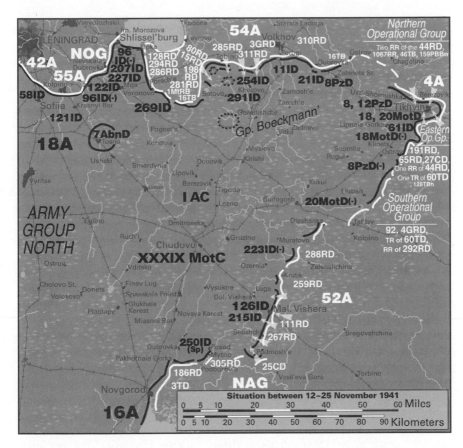

Map 7. The Soviet Tikhvin Counterstroke: The Situation on 12 November 1941

Volkhov and at Voibokalo Station against Boeckmann's left flank and center. After smashing Boeckmann's defenses, Fediuninsky's forces were to link up with the 4th Army's forces near Kirishi, and encircle and destroy Group Boeckmann.[49] His remaining forces were to defend the army's extended right flank toward Siniavino and Lake Ladoga. If successful, the 54th and 4th Armies' converging attacks would also sever the German XXXIX Motorized Corps' withdrawal lines westward from Tikhvin and destroy the already weakened motorized corps.

To the south, the four divisions of Klykov's 52d Army and the two divisions of the Northwestern Front's Novgorod Army Group were to destroy German forces in the Malaia Vishera region, advance to the Volkhov River, capture bridgeheads over the river, and help cut German withdrawal routes from Tikhvin.[50] The Novgorod Army Group was to defend its southern sector with its tankless 3d Tank Division and support the 52d Army's assault by attacking in its northern sector with its 180th and 305th Rifle Divisions.[51]

Since the chaotic operational situation and the shortage of forces prevented the *Stavka* from initiating the offensive operation simultaneously in every sector, it began the attacks in piecemeal fashion, building it into a crescendo of a full counteroffensive as the month progressed. The 52d Army initiated the process on 12 November by attacking along the Malaia Vishera axis, the 4th Army unleashed its attacks around Tikhvin on 19 November, and the 54th Army attacked west of Volkhov on 3 December.

As the Soviet attacks rippled across the front, Schmidt's motorized corps was too weak and deployed in too dispersed a fashion to deal effectively with the expanding torrent of attacks. While his 12th Panzer and 18th Motorized Divisions were bottled up in Tikhvin proper, his 8th Panzer, 20th Motorized, and the newly arrived Spanish 250th "Blue" Infantry Division clung precariously to a string of strong points scattered along the corps' long right flank from Tikhvin southwest to Malaia Vishera. Throughout this entire period the unrelenting Soviet pressure forced Leeb to withdraw portions of his armor from Tikhvin, reinforce Group Boeckmann south of Volkhov with parts of the 8th Panzer Division, and shore up the vulnerable defenses on his right flank. When these measures proved inadequate to stem the Soviet tide, on 3 December Leeb subordinated Boeckmann's three divisions to the I Army Corps headquarters, recently transferred from Leningrad, and reinforced the army corps with additional 8th Panzer Division forces.

The situation was no better on the flanks of Army Group North's Tikhvin penetration. To the west, south of Leningrad proper, the infantry forces of Kuechler's Eighteenth Army manned an extended front from the Gulf of Finland to Shlissel'burg on Lake Ladoga and eastward to the Volkhov-Tikhvin railroad. To the south, Busch's Sixteenth Army, also vastly overextended, defended the long front from Lake Il'men' southward to the Valdai Hills. Nor did the weather cooperate with Leeb's defense. As the temperature dropped another 10 degrees, his men were soon fighting in desperation as machine guns and artillery jammed and horses collapsed, freezing solid in a matter of minutes.

The *Stavka* began its series of incessant attacks early on 12 November in the sector of Klykov's 52d Army, while Meretskov's forces were still struggling to contain German forces in Tikhvin. Klykov's four rifle divisions repeatedly assaulted the German 126th Infantry Division's defense on a broad front north and south of Malaia Vishera for four days, but made no appreciable progress. Failing to concentrate his forces properly, instead Klykov employed fruitless frontal attacks with inadequate artillery support against poorly reconnoitered German strong points. For example, Klykov attacked with four divisions deployed across the 48-kilometer (29.9-mile) front, while only two regiments of Colonel A. V. Lapshov's 259th Rifle Division assaulted the key German strong point at Malaia Vishera.[52] The OKH responded to these attacks by transferring a regiment of the 61st Infantry Division from Army Group Center's reserve and the 223d Infantry Division from France to reinforce its defenses at Malaia Vishera and protect the right flank of its forces struggling at Tikhvin.[53] The Novgorod Army Group's initial assault on 12 November also failed for many of the same reasons.

Urged on by the *Stavka,* Klykov regrouped his forces on 16 and 17 November and resumed his attack overnight on 17–18 November. This time he infiltrated two detachments formed from Lapshov's 259th and Colonel S. V. Roginsky's 111th Rifle Divisions into the German rear area west of Malaia Vishera, and the two divisions successfully stormed and captured the village the next morning. The assault unhinged the 126th Infantry Division's defenses and forced it to withdraw westward. Although Klykov's forces pursued the retreating Germans toward Bol'shaia Vishera, Gruzino, and Selishchenskii Poselok on the Volkhov River, the pursuit was too slow to prevent Leeb from reinforcing his forces at Tikhvin, then under assault by 4th Army forces, with the 61st Infantry Division. Within days, Leeb also reinforced the 126th Infantry Division with the 215th Infantry Division transferred from France.

While Klykov's 52d Army was occupying Schmidt's attentions with its assaults at Malaia Vishera, the three shock groups of Meretskov's 4th Army attacked German forces defending Tikhvin on 19 November. Advancing through deep snow at an agonizingly slow pace against determined German resistance, Meretskov's northern shock group finally fought its way to the outskirts of Tikhvin on 7 December. By this time the attack by his eastern shock group had stalled, locked in heavy combat west of the Tikhvinka River and to the south along the Tikhvin-Tal'tsy road with the 20th Motorized and 61st Infantry Divisions, the latter having just arrived from Malaia Vishera. Schmidt's 12th Panzer and 18th Motorized Divisions in Tikhvin were now enveloped from three sides and were suffering heavy losses fighting in the deep snow and bitter cold. The 18th Motorized Division alone had lost 5,000 men in the fierce fighting, leaving it with a combat strength of fewer than 1,000 men. The 30th Panzer Grenadier Regiment's 3d Battalion had already lost 250 men, most of whom froze to death during the advance from Chudovo to Tikhvin.[54]

Halder recorded the deteriorating situation on 6 December, noting, "Enemy before Tikhvin has been reinforced. Very severe cold (38 degrees below freezing); numerous cases of death from cold."[55] The next day, he added, "Very tight situation at Tikhvin. Army group thinks it cannot hold the town and is preparing to take back its defense positions to the baseline of the salient."[56] Worse still, Meretskov's southern group had penetrated the 18th Motorized Division's defenses along the rail line to the south on 7 December and was approaching Sitomlia, threatening the Tikhvin group's communications with the rear.

After withdrawing additional troops from Schmidt's beleaguered forces at Tikhvin to defend their vital communications lines to the rear, Leeb requested permission from the OKH to withdraw Schmidt's forces back to the Volkhov River. Shortly after midnight on 7 December, Halder informed Leeb that Hitler still insisted the original plan be fulfilled: "[You] must not withdraw farther than artillery range from Tikhvin."[57] At 1000 hours the next morning, Leeb repeated his request, informing Hitler his forces at Tikhvin were outnumbered by more than two to one, and adding that, if he did not agree to a withdrawal, they might be destroyed. By this time, the Red Army had already begun its massive counteroffensive at Moscow, rendering Hitler's order for Leeb to continue his offensive utterly futile. Bowing to the inevitable, at 0200 hours on 8 December, exactly one month after the 12th Panzer Division captured Tikhvin, Hitler consented to Leeb's request. Hours before, a distraught Leeb had already issued the evacuation order. That night Halder cryptically wrote in his diary, "Evacuation of Tikhvin in progress," without further comment or elaboration.[58]

The 12th Panzer and 18th Motorized Divisions began their painful withdrawal westward from Tikhvin toward the Volkhov River on 9 December, along roads clogged with deep snow. Leeb raced reinforcements to Sitomlia, Gruzino, and Volkhov to support the withdrawal, which Schmidt was supposed to complete by 22 December. By this time Schmidt's 8th and 12th Panzer Divisions had dwindled to regimental strength, with 30 tanks apiece.[59] As they withdrew, Meretskov's northern and eastern groups assaulted German rear guards and captured Tikhvin late in the day. While Schmidt's three mobile divisions withdrew in orderly fashion, the 61st Infantry Division's 151st Infantry Regiment, supported by the 11th and 12th Companies of the 18th Motorized Division's 51st Panzer Regiment, attempted to block the pursuing Russians. During the heavy fighting, the regiment suffered heavy losses, and the two panzer grenadier companies were wiped out to the last man.[60]

After capturing Tikhvin, on 10 December, Meretskov's 4th Army began pursuing German forces westward and southwestward, but its forces, too, were severely hindered by the deep snow. To the south, Klykov's 52d Army attacked westward, captured Bol'shaia Vishera on 16 December, and pushed the two defending German divisions westward toward new defenses, which the army group was erecting along the Volkhov River. The pursuit was not an easy one since the withdrawing Germans halted their pursuers at an intermediate "swamp" position in mid-December (Map 8). Ultimately, however, the Germans had no choice but to withdraw since fresh and even more dangerous Soviet attacks were materializing to the north against their exposed left flank.

While one act of the *Stavka's* multi-act drama was playing out around Tikhvin, another was developing in the Volkhov sector to the west. By 25 November Fediuninsky's 54th Army had halted the German I Army Corps' advance 6 kilometers (3.7 miles) south of Volkhov and farther to the west at Voibokalo Station. The next day Fediuninsky's main shock group, which consisted of the 3d Guards, 310th, and 311th Rifle Divisions and the 6th Naval Infantry Brigade, attacked the I Army Corps' 21st Infantry Division south of Volkhov. The assault drove the 21st Infantry Division back several kilometers south of the town by 29 November. Halder noted the failure in his diary, "In AGp. North it is becoming increasingly obvious that the attack on Shum [location unknown but presumably between Volkhov and the Svir River] has miscarried. The main effort by von Boeckmann's group must be shifted against Volkhovstroi [near Voibokalo Station]. An order to this effect is issued."[61]

Several days later, Khozin, the Leningrad Front commander, reinforced Fediuninsky's forces with the 80th Rifle Division from Leningrad and ordered him to form yet another shock group at Voibokalo Station by 1 December and strike the I Army Corps' left flank. The new shock group, which consisted of the 80th, 311th, and 285th Rifle Divisions, the 6th Naval Infantry Brigade, and the 122d Tank Brigade, attacked on 3 December and drove the German I Army Corps's left flank southward, successively encircling and destroying several companies of the 254th Infantry Division. The 115th and 198th Rifle Divisions, transferred from Leningrad, joined the army's assault on 15 December and drove the Germans back to Olomny by 17 December, enveloping the I Army Corps' left flank on the western bank of the Volkhov River.[62]

At the same time, the northern group of Meretskov's 4th Army penetrated German defenses along the Tikhvin-Volkhov railroad and reached the Lynka River southeast of Volkhov, enveloping the I Army Corps' right flank and forcing the beleaguered German corps to withdraw southward toward Kirishi.

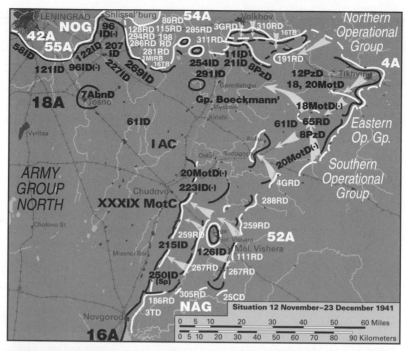

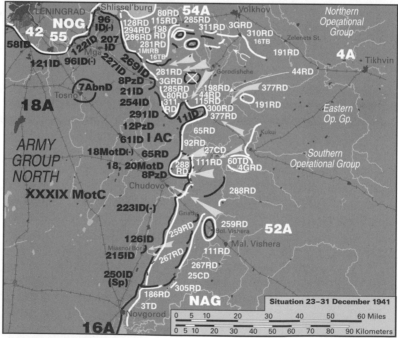

Map 8. The Soviet Tikhvin Counterstroke, 12 November–31 December 1941

During its withdrawal, the 54th Army's 1st and 2d Ski Battalions constantly harassed the Germans' flanks and rear. Although the I Army Corps attempted to hold on to the critical Mga-Kirishi rail line, the 54th Army's 311th, 80th, and 285th Rifle Divisions penetrated across the railroad, forming a shallow salient in the German defenses west of Kirishi. The remainder of the 54th Army struggled to expel German forces from Kirishi and surrounding villages until 28 December but, despite suffering heavy casualties, failed to dislodge the defenders. During this fighting, Leeb reinforced his strong point at Kirishi with the 291st and 269th Infantry Divisions transferred from Leningrad, transforming it into the vital apex of German defenses along the Volkhov River.

While the Soviet's Tikhvin counteroffensive was reaching its climax, the *Stavka* reorganized its forces in the Volkhov region to facilitate future operations. Two days after Tikhvin fell, Stalin summoned Meretskov, his chief of staff Major General G. D. Stelmakh, Khozin, and Zhdanov to Moscow to discuss how the offensive could best be expanded.[63] The first order of business was to reorganize Red Army forces in the region into a proper *front* structure capable of controlling multiple armies in a major new offensive push. When the conference ended on 11 December, the *Stavka* formed the new Volkhov Front, effective 17 December, with Meretskov as its commander and Stelmakh as its chief of staff.[64] In addition to Meretskov's 4th and Klykov's 52d Armies, the *Stavka* assigned the new *front* Lieutenant General G. G. Sokolov's 26th Army (which was redesignated the 2d Shock Army in late December) and Major General I. V. Galanin's 59th Armies, both of which had just been formed in the *Stavka* Reserve.

The Moscow meeting produced ambitious new plans for an expanded offensive to accomplish nothing less than the complete lifting of the Leningrad blockade. The *Stavka* issued a formal directive to that effect at 2000 hours on 17 December:

> The Volkhov Front, consisting of the 4th, 59th, 2d Shock, and 52d Armies, will launch a general offensive to smash the enemy defending along the western bank of the Volkhov River and reach the Liuban' and Cholovo Station front with your armies' main forces by the end of [left blank]. The armies' main forces will reach the Liuban'-Cholovo station line.
>
> Subsequently, attacking to the northwest, encircle the enemy defending around Leningrad, destroy and capture him in cooperation with the Leningrad Front, and, if the enemy resists, capture or destroy him. . . .
> [signed] I. Stalin, B. Shaposhnikov[65]

A companion directive dispatched to Khozin the same day ordered his Leningrad Front "to help the Volkhov Front in the destruction of the enemy defending around Leningrad and raise the Leningrad blockade by active operations with the 42d, 55th, 8th, and 54th Armies and the Coastal Operational Group."[66] In addition, the *Stavka* ordered the Northwestern Front to conduct a major offensive to capture Demiansk, Novgorod, and Dno.[67] The twin offensives were to begin shortly after Meretskov's forces reached the Volkhov River and seized bridgeheads on its western bank. The perilous situation at Leningrad, which was being subjected to near-constant German artillery fire and air bombardment and whose population was facing famine, and his desire to maintain the initiative prompted Stalin to demand that Meretskov begin his offensive with the forces he had at hand.

However, the seamless expansion of the Tikhvin counteroffensive into the vastly larger and far more ambitious Volkhov-Leningrad offensive depended entirely on Meretskov's armies reaching and establishing adequate bridgeheads across the Volkhov River. To Stalin's obvious disgust, Meretskov's armies, in particular, Fediuninsky's 54th Army, did so too slowly. After Stalin sent them numerous, increasingly caustic messages ordering them to accelerate their advance, the 4th and 52d Armies finally reached the river near Kirishi, Gruzino, and north of Novgorod on 27 December, seized bridgeheads, and began expanding the bridgeheads against determined German resistance.[68] However, despite Stalin's exhortations, Fediuninsky's 54th Army failed to capture Kirishi, and the 4th Army, now under the command of Major General P. A. Ivanov, was not able to capture Tigoda Station. By 30 December Meretskov's three armies had driven the two German corps back to positions from which they had begun their Tikhvin offensive on 16 October. Utterly exhausted and at the end of their logistical umbilicals, Meretskov's forces had no choice but to dig in, fortify their positions, and go over to the defense. The grand new offensive would have to await the New Year.

While the fateful struggle was unfolding at Tikhvin and along and east of the Volkhov River, Red Army forces in the Leningrad region conducted military operations in support of their comrades' far more dramatic actions to the east. Although relegated to the status of mere footnotes to the Tikhvin operations and seldom mentioned in past Soviet accounts of the Battle for Leningrad, these battles too contributed to the Red Army's November and December victories.

In response to *Stavka* demands that Soviet forces in Leningrad support operations east of the Volkhov River more vigorously, on 31 October Khozin proposed a two-stage operation to capture Siniavino, Mga, and Tosno and regain control of the Shlissel'burg corridor.[69] During the operation's first stage, five rifle divisions from the Neva Operational Group were to play the most important role in Khozin's offensive by widening the bridgehead at Moskovskaia Dubrovka. After being reinforced by four rifle divisions and a tank brigade, the force was to attack eastward, capture Workers Settlement No. 6 and Siniavino, and by 4 or 5 November link up with the 8th and 54th Armies' forces advancing from the east. While this operation was taking place, Lazarov's 55th Army was to attack on 2 November with a shock group of seven rifle divisions and one tank brigade, whose four first-echelon divisions were to capture Ust'-Tosno, Ivanovskoe, and Pokrovskoe and seize bridgeheads across the Tosno River. Subsequently, by 6 November the three second-echelon divisions were to exploit and capture Mga Station in support of the 54th Army. Once the operation had succeeded, the 55th, 8th, and 54th Armies were to capture Tosno, thereby raising the Leningrad blockade. The *Stavka* approved Khozin's plan on 1 November.[70]

Khozin's forces went into action on 2 November, launching heavy assaults from the bridgehead at Moskovskaia Dubrovka against the defenses of the German 96th Infantry Division. However, the five divisions failed to dent the German defenses around the bridgehead at a cost of extremely heavy casualties. For example, Major General A. L. Bondarev's 168th Rifle Division, which entered the bridgehead on 5 November, had fallen in strength to 200 men by 7 November. During the same period, the 20th NKVD Rifle Division lost all but 300 of its men.[71] Despite the heavy losses, the offensive faltered, prompting Stalin to contact Khozin's commissar Zhdanov by telephone on 8 November and caustically criticize both him and Khozin for their forces' dismal performance:

> We are very dissatisfied with your slowness in conducting the operation. You were given a period of several days. If you do not force your way to the east in several days, you will ruin the Leningrad Front and the population of Leningrad. They inform us that, after the artillery preparation, the infantry decided not to advance forward. But you should realize that the infantry will not advance without tanks. After the artillery preparation, you must commit the tanks, and only after the tanks can the infantry go into action. The artillery must smash the enemy 3–4 kilometers east of the front lines in advance of our tanks. . . . Without such an organized offensive you will go nowhere.[72]

Zhdanov responded that his advancing infantry had struck "rather well-prepared enemy defenses." Each time the artillery preparation was sufficient, but the infantry attacks stalled, and the seven tanks that made it into the bridgehead were quickly destroyed. Nor had any of the KV tanks, upon which they were relying for success, made it across the river because of heavy losses in bridging equipment. Worse still, since the artillery could not cross the river, either, it could not range deeply enough into the German defenses to support any breakout from the bridgehead. After relating his casualties, Zhdanov emphasized, "no one has yet deserted, and no one declined to enter the battle."[73]

In a telephone conversation the next day, Khozin and Zhdanov presented the *Stavka* with yet another attack plan, this time promising to commit 40

medium and heavy tanks into the bridgehead overnight on 9–10 November.
The tanks were to support an assault by "three newly formed volunteer regiments of crack troops." Khozin then outlined his plan:

> The offensive will be ready to begin on 10–11 November. We will also create shock volunteer regiments along the axis of the 55th Army's secondary attack. The army's assigned immediate mission is to clear the enemy from the western bank of the Tosno River and, subsequently, capture crossings over the Tosno River, attack toward Mga, and link up with the 8th and 54th Armies' formations.[74]

A key element in the new offensive plan was the role played by Shevaldin's 8th Army, whose headquarters had just been transferred from the Oranienbaum bridgehead to take control of forces operating east of the Shlissel'burg corridor on the 54th Army's right flank.[75] Shevaldin's army was to assault toward Siniavino along with a shock group from the 54th Army to link up with the Neva Operational Group attacking from the west.

Khozin's forces began their assault on 9 November against the 96th and 227th Infantry Divisions defending the western and eastern faces of the Shlissel'burg corridor. The first of the NOG's volunteer shock groups went into action in the Moskovskaia Dubrovka bridgehead, supported by the 86th and 168th Rifle Divisions and the 8th Rifle Brigade attacking in the NOG's first echelon. The second shock group, which was supported by the second-echelon 177th Rifle Division, went into action on 11 November along an altered attack axis toward Gorodok No. 1. This attack also faltered after the assaulting forces gained a small foothold on the western outskirts of the strong point. The third shock group went into action on 13 November, supported by the 10th, 80th, and 281st Rifle Divisions. Once again, only 11 of the planned 50 tanks made it into the bridgehead to support the attack, and the German defenders had destroyed over half of these by 12 November. Despite suffering heavy casualties, the gains were meager, and the NOG's forces were unable even to dent the German defenses.[76]

To the east, five rifle divisions of Shevaldin's 8th Army attacked toward Siniavino on 11 November against the 227th Infantry Division. Once again the attack failed, according to Khozin, because the Germans committed the 223d Rifle Division newly arrived from France (as well as a rumored parachute division) to block the advance and because of poor command and control by the army commander. In the sector of Lazarov's 55th Army, the shock groups formed from the 43d and 85th Rifle Divisions managed to gain a foothold over the Tosno River but were unable to expel the German 122d Infantry Division's forces from the stone houses in Ust'-Tosno. Nor were they able to seize bridgeheads over the Tosno River. Eventually, the 55th Army also committed the 70th, 90th, 125th, and 286th Rifle Divisions and the 84th and 86th Tank Battalions into the fighting, but to no avail. Ultimately, the German assault toward Tikhvin prevented Fediuninsky's army from joining the effort to capture Siniavino and Mga, and the entire venture collapsed in bloody failure.

In his diary, Halder underscored the futility of Khozin's assaults by simply ignoring mention of them throughout early November and, finally, by stating in his 19 November entry, "On the Leningrad front, the usual attack was repelled."[77] After these futile operations, the *Stavka* replaced Shevaldin as 8th Army commander with Bondarev, the former commander of the 168th Rifle Division, and Lazarov at 55th Army with Lieutenant General V. P. Sviridov. However, these command changes made little difference to the fate of Khozin's offensive efforts. The 55th Army's forces assaulted German defenses at Putrolovo and Iam-Izhora on 2 and 7 December in yet another attempt to capture Tosno and threaten the rear of the German Mga grouping. Halder noted the operations, stating in the first instance, "Violent enemy attacks across the Neva, which we were able to repel. Enemy concentration in the Ladoga sector for an attack toward the Neva River," and, in the second instance, "Violent attacks at Leningrad."[78] Although this operation too failed, both the November and December offensives tied down German forces in the Leningrad region and denied vital reinforcements required by Schmidt's XXXIX Motorized Corps struggling at Tikhvin and Volkhov.

The Soviet Tikhvin defense and counteroffensive were component parts of a far greater strategic duel, which was taking place along the entire expanse of the Soviet-German front, but particularly along the Moscow axis. Army Group North's bold but risky lunge toward Tikhvin symbolized the fatal optimism that gripped Hitler and the OKH when they launched Operation Typhoon in October 1941. The ensuing *Wehrmacht* defeats at Tikhvin and Moscow were sober reminders that this optimism was misplaced. In reality, the Red Army's victory at Tikhvin represented the culmination of a process begun at Sol'tsy in July and continued at Staraia Russa and Luga in August and at Leningrad in September. Although costly in terms of lives, the *Stavka's* insistence on an active defense and merciless counterattacks and counterstrokes finally caught up with an exhausted *Wehrmacht* in November and December. At the same time, the *Wehrmacht* learned, to its everlasting consternation, that warfare in Russia was far from the sport it had been in the West.

The Tikhvin counteroffensive was the Red Army's first large-scale military success in the Great Patriotic War. In addition to ending Hitler's dream of encircling Leningrad in 1941, the counteroffensive assisted in the defeat of German forces at Moscow and drove home to German leaders, political and military alike, the realization that this war would not be easily won. The victory had been difficult to achieve and very costly to those forces that participated in its achievement. According to official tallies, the 54th, 4th, and 52d Armies suffered 40,589 casualties, including 22,743 killed, captured, or missing in their Tikhvin defense, out of 135,700 men initially engaged. The Tikhvin counteroffensive cost the Red Army another 48,901 casualties, including 17,924 killed, captured, or missing, out of 192,950 men engaged. In addition, the 54th Army and Neva Operational Group lost 54,979 men, including 22,111 killed, captured, or missing, out of 71,270 men involved in the October sideshow at Siniavino. However, Soviet sources have provided no tally of the 55th and 8th Armies' and NOG's losses in the November and December fighting along and east of the Neva River, which must have totaled at least 50,000 men.[79]

Thus, the Red Army employed roughly 300,000 troops in the Tikhvin defense, the Tikhvin counteroffensive, and the associated offensives around Leningrad. When the fighting ended, it had suffered roughly 190,000 casualties, including about 80,000 dead, captured, or missing. The Germans also suffered heavy losses in the Tikhvin venture. Leeb committed over 100,000 troops in the advance to Tikhvin and Volkhov and another 80,000 in the defense of Siniavino and Mga and suffered roughly 45,000 casualties.

Despite his defeat, Leeb issued a proclamation to his forces on Christmas Day proclaiming his army group's victories:

> In the battles on and to the east of the Volkhov—as well as in the withdrawal of the front into a secure winter position behind the Volkhov—you have again met the highest requirements of defensive power and of physical resiliency in fulfilling the mission. The enemy arrives at the Volkhov empty-handed.
>
> Since 22 June and up to 20 December, Army Group North has taken 438,950 prisoners and captured or destroyed 3,847 tanks and 4,590 guns.
>
> We reverently bow our heads to those who have given their lives. The Homeland thanks us for having protected it and counts on us in the future.
>
> We shall justify this trust. The New Year will find us ready to repel all enemy breakthrough efforts until the Fuehrer calls on us again to resume the attack.[80]

Leeb's inspirational message belied the grim reality that German forces had failed to achieve the missions that Hitler had assigned to them. Less than two weeks later, Leeb's tired forces would have to respond to their commander's bold summons when, on 7 January, the Red Army assaulted their defenses along the Volkhov River with renewed determination. Leeb's Christmas message was also his swan song. As the new Soviet offensive began, he submitted his resignation to Hitler. After five days of indecision, on 18 January 1942, Hitler replaced Leeb with Kuechler.

PART II
BLOCKADE

CHAPTER 5

Winter under Siege

1941–1942

DEFENSE

In the Soviet Union as a whole, the German invasion struck like a thunderbolt, catching government and population alike by surprise. Worse still, the speed and devastating effects of the *Wehrmacht*'s initial advance disrupted defense and mobilization plans and quickly transformed cities like Leningrad, presumed to be relatively safe rear areas, into active war zones. As the front collapsed, the first order of business was defense and mobilization. At 0500 hours on 22 June, Major General D. N. Nikishev, the Leningrad Military District's chief of staff, summoned his army commanders and authorized implementation of the mobilization plans, which when opened seemed utterly irrelevant to the situation at hand.[1] From this point forth, the mobilization and preparation of the city's defenses was largely an ad hoc and increasingly frantic business.[2]

The Leningrad Party organization, under Party chief A. A. Zhdanov, began the mobilization process in accordance with 29 June directives of the USSR's Council of People's Commissars and the Communist Party.[3] These directives required the Party to supervise preparation of the city's defenses, mobilize industry, raise people's militia forces, and form and field partisan forces in close cooperation with the military councils of appropriate military commands, Leningrad's Communist Party Committee, and the leadership of the city's Workers' Council. Militarily, this meant the Northern Front's Military Council, the Leningrad Party Committee, and the city's Workers' Council initially, and, later, the Northwestern Direction High Command's and Leningrad Front's Military Councils.

The most urgent task, which became particularly critical after German forces pierced the Stalin Line in early July, was to organize Leningrad's military defenses. In late June and July, this involved primarily organizing defenses, first, along the Luga Line, during which all construction within Leningrad halted, and then around and within the city itself. To do so, the authorities mobilized most of the city's population. On 27 June 1941, the Leningrad City Council's Executive Committee *(ispolkom)* issued an order specifying the work responsibilities of the city's inhabitants:

In accordance with the 22 June 1941 order of the Presidium of the USSR's Supreme Soviet, "Concerning the Military Situation," and on the basis of the orders of the military authorities, the Executive Committee of the Leningrad City Council of Workers' Deputies has decided:

1. To enlist the services of able civilians of both sexes between the ages of 16 and 50 for men and between the ages of 16 and 45 for women, excluding workers working in defense industries, in [defensive] work. . . .

5. To establish the following work routine for the fulfillment of work obligations:

    a. Nonworking able-bodied civilians of both sexes—eight hours per day.

    b. Office workers, other workers, and laborers—three hours per day after work.

    c. Students of functioning educational institutions—three hours per day after class.[4]

Work details began constructing defenses on Leningrad's southern outskirts and within the city itself in late July. Ultimately, the population helped to build the Pskov and Ostrov Fortified Regions, the Luga Defense Line and associated cut-off positions at Kingisepp, Luga, Batetskii, Chudovo, and Kirishi, and defensive regions and lines closer to Leningrad. These included extensive fortifications and defensive positions at Krasnogvardeisk, Uritsk, Pulkovo, Kolpino, and along the right (western and southern) bank of the Neva River.[5] An average of 125,000 Leningraders per day expended a total of 8,757,600 man-days working on defensive belts and fortified regions on the approaches to the city in July, August, and the first 10 days of September (Map 9).[6]

Even though military authorities organized and supervised the massive construction effort, the population, organized into teams formed from workers in Leningrad's factories, performed the actual labor. These teams built a staggering quantity of defensive works ranging in scale from simple slit trenches to two-ton reinforced concrete artillery firing positions, half-ton to three-ton machine-gun firing points, armored artillery and machine-gun pillboxes, and reinforced concrete pyramid antitank obstacles weighing up to two tons each.

During the first six months of war, civilian labor and military forces together prepared an immense number of defensive works. For example, from 22 June through 13 September, Trusts Nos. 16, 53, and 55, Factory No. 5, and the Barrikady, Kirov, Ordzhonikidze, and Izhorsk factories constructed 378 armored and reinforced concrete gun firing points, and 678 machine-gun firing points in and around Leningrad. In addition, these same organizations built 24,046 reinforced concrete antitank pyramids, primarily in the Luga, Kingisepp, Krasnogvardeisk, and Slutsk-Kolpino Fortified Regions. By official count, Leningrad's population built 592 kilometers of open antitank

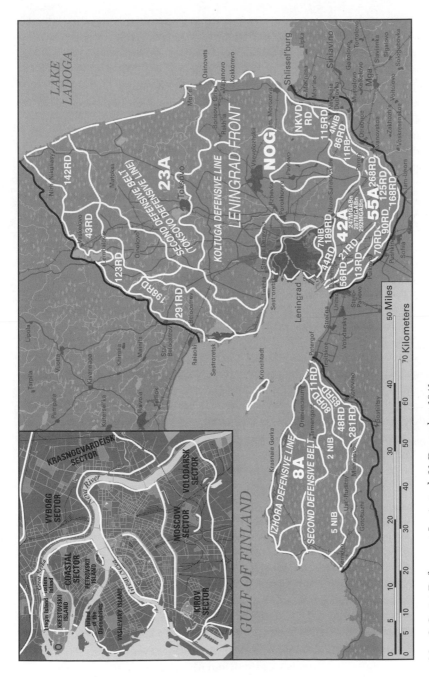

Map 9. Soviet Defenses at Leningrad, 31 December 1941

ditches, 459 kilometers of escarpments and counter-escarpments, 48 kilometers of antitank obstacles, 134 kilometers of blockades, 24 kilometers of barricades, 667 antitank hedgehogs and chevaux-de-frise, 329 kilometers of barbed wire entanglements, 11,500 squad foxholes, 772 kilometers of communications trenches, 1,527 shelters, 2,072 command, observation, and medical points, and about 4,500 pillboxes and small and large bunkers.[7]

Despite accomplishing a prodigious amount of work, the construction effort was fraught with numerous problems and even danger, particularly during July and August, when the rapidly changing military situation prevented sound planning and preempted much of the work done. Worse still, the work was often poorly organized, and there was a chronic shortage of qualified supervisors and labor to accomplish the work.[8] Since most weaponry and explosives were required at the front, the new defenses were deficient in antitank and antipersonnel mines and other explosive obstacles. The defensive construction effort went on long after the front reached Leningrad, with an average of 45,000 people per day expending a total of 6,596,000 mandays preparing the defenses between 1 August and 31 December.[9]

The Communist Party's city and regional committees, together with supporting factories, began defensive work within the city's boundaries in late July and early August 1941. The Leningrad Front's Military Council accelerated the work on 3 September, when German forces reached the city's outskirts, by ordering the creation of an elaborate "sector defense."[10] Once work began, the forward edge of the city's defenses ran along the rail line that ringed the city. Within the railroad ring, the defense was divided into six sectors, each corresponding to one of the city's six districts (raion). These included the Kirov, Moscow, and Volodarsk sectors in the south and the Primorskii, Vyborg, and Krasnogvardeisk sectors in the north. Each sector consisted of several defensive positions 1.2–2 kilometers (0.3–1.24 miles) apart, and each defensive position consisted of separate but mutually supporting battalion defensive regions. In total, the six sectors encompassed 99 distinct battalion regions.

A defense staff made up of the secretary of the district Party organization, the chairman of the district executive committee, and local NKVD and workers organizations commanded each defensive sector.[11] Local NKVD forces, Leningrad Fire Security forces, city militia personnel, and workers formations manned the sector's defensive regions, but only as the combat situation dictated. An elaborate system of barricades and antitank defenses formed the backbone of each sector's defense. The defenders erected barricades up to 2.5 meters high and 3.5 meters deep between blocks of houses and individual buildings within each sector. For example, the Kirov sector built 17.2 kilometers (10.7 miles) of barricades protected by antitank ditches around its circumference.[12]

Since antitank defenses were particularly vital given the Germans' reliance on armor, construction forces attempted to erect continuous antitank defenses echeloned in depth along all dangerous tank approaches. For example, by 1 November 1941, the 42d Army, whose sector included the most dangerous tank axis, built 41 mutually supporting antitank regions in addition to those antitank regions already created on the edge of the city. These regions fielded 342 antitank guns, for an average density of 17 guns per kilometer of front. The 42d Army deployed 50 percent of its antitank guns in its main defensive belt, 20 percent in its second belt, and 30 percent on the city's outskirts.[13] The antitank defense also included an extensive network of antitank obstacles and barriers that exploited unique terrain features such as rivers, ravines, streams, and forested regions for antitank defense, and covered them with over-watching fires. Where no such natural obstacles existed, engineers filled in the gaps in the defense with obstacles such as dragon's teeth, escarpments, and antitank ditches.

Leningrad's defenders also had to counter the *Luftwaffe*'s potentially devastating capability for pounding the city into submission with air attacks. Although quite weak in the summer of 1941, Leningrad's air defense (PVO) capabilities improved markedly in the fall. Initially, four organizations were responsible for air defense in the Leningrad region. The 2d PVO Corps and 7th Fighter Aviation Corps defended Leningrad proper, the Ladoga Brigade PVO Region defended water routes across Lake Ladoga, and the Svir Brigade PVO Region defended the rail line from the depths of the country to Lake Ladoga.[14]

In an effort to improve Leningrad's air defense by centralizing control over it, in November 1941 the State Defense Committee reorganized the Soviet Union's National Air Defense (PVO *Strany*), converting the 2d PVO Corps into the Leningrad Corps PVO Region. While the reorganization left the Svir and Ladoga Brigade PVO Regions in their former configuration, it subordinated the three regions to the Leningrad Front rather than to the commander of PVO *Strany*.[15] This facilitated concentration of air defense resources and fostered better fire coordination between PVO and air force defense, which was especially critical for a successful city defense. Subsequently, air defense forces operated independently only when protecting specific objectives within their own zones of fire.

PVO fighter aviation concentrated on repelling German air attacks on the city as far forward as possible, and the associated searchlight batteries supported the aircraft at night. Antiaircraft artillery regiments subordinate to the Leningrad Front's armies established antiaircraft artillery fire zones on the city's outskirts and within the city itself, which were concentrated primarily along the western and southwestern approaches to the city. PVO also mounted antiaircraft batteries on ships in the Gulf of Finland to strengthen and add depth to the western defense sector and protected the approaches to the city and the city itself with aerostatic (barrage) balloons.

The city's military defenders also had to counter the threat of German artillery fire once German forces advanced to within artillery range of the city. At that point, an extensive counter-battery program was necessary to halt or impede the destructive fire the Germans delivered against the city's population, factories, and buildings. The Leningrad Front responded in late September by developing a single unified artillery and air fire plan to deal with this threat. The plan allocated specific targets to artillery and aircraft, the most distant obviously to aircraft. In October, the *front* also formed counter-battery artillery groups, each consisting of two to three antiaircraft artillery battalions. These groups, which included all of the 42d and 55th Armies' antiaircraft artillery and all coastal and naval guns, were directly subordinate to the *front's* chief of artillery. When the threat became especially critical in the fall, the *Stavka* sent Colonel General of Artillery N. N. Voronov to Leningrad to advise on the counter-battery struggle.

During the winter, when the surface of the Gulf of Finland and the lakes and rivers in and around Leningrad froze, permitting German and Finnish forces to traverse their surfaces, coastal defense became a major concern. The Leningrad Front countered this threat by forming the Internal Defense of the City (*Vnutrenniaia oborona goroda*—VOG), which consisted initially of a rifle brigade, a ski detachment, two machine-gun companies, 8 45mm gun batteries, 18 sail (ice) boats, and 4 reserve companies.[16] Commanded by Major General S. P. Ivanov, the former commander of the 42d Army whom Zhukov had relieved of army command in September, the VOG's mission was to organize continuous defenses in Leningrad's western sector, prevent the enemy from reaching the city from the Finnish Gulf, and ensure normal communications between Leningrad and the forces isolated in the Oranienbaum bridgehead.

During the same period, the *Stavka* ordered the Leningrad Front to move the bulk of the Baltic Fleet's ships from Kronshtadt to Leningrad. While this decision strengthened Leningrad's defenses, it also necessitated the reinforcement of Kronshtadt's ground defenses with army troops. The task of countering possible German air assaults against the city fell to ground commanders of all defensive sectors and special anti-*desant* (air assault) detachments. Headed by a special troika formed from representatives from militia, fire, and Komsomol elements, these detachments included forces from each type force.

Leningrad was in the greatest danger in September, when German forces approached the city's suburbs and after Zhukov had assumed command of the Leningrad Front. During this period, the *Stavka* directed Khozin, Zhukov's chief of staff, to prepare the city's bridge and factories for destruction and the city's defenses for final German assault by 17 September. On 13 September Stalin issued instructions, "Plan of Measures in the Event of the Forced

Withdrawal from Leningrad on Ships and Boats," which ordered deliberate destruction of all installations of value to the Germans:

1. In the event of a forced withdrawal from Leningrad, all ships of the naval fleet, commercial, industrial, and technical vessels will be subject to destruction.
2. Carry out the destruction in order to:
   a. Deny their use by the enemy.
   b. Exclude the possibility of the enemy sailing to the Kronshtadt and Leningrad regions and the use to them of channels, road-steads, harbors, and canals.
3. Carry out the destruction with maximum damage for the longest period possible, that is, blow up and sink the objectives and ships.
4. Execute the destruction according to a strict sequential plan at the moment the High Command gives the signal. . . .

[signed] I. Stalin
Approved 13 September 1941[17]

However, the failure of the final German assault and Hitler's decision to encircle the city ended the immediate crisis and prevented the destruction of the city.

MOBILIZATION

In response to GKO instructions to exploit the city's "local resources for its defense," from July through September, military and Party officials instituted an ambitious and extensive mobilization program to generate military manpower necessary for the city's defense. The centerpiece of this program was the formation of people's militia (*narodnoe opolchenie*) forces, primarily in divisional configuration, and armed workers detachments. Regional Communist Party committees and district military commissariats issued individual and collective appeals to form a people's militia immediately after war began. Days later, on 30 June the Leningrad Communist Party began forming the Leningrad People's Militia Army (*Leningradskaia armiia narodnogo opolcheniia*—LANO), and the Leningrad Front appointed Major General A. I. Subbotin as its commander and Colonel M. N. Nikitin as its chief of staff. Originally, Subbotin's army was to be made of 15 divisions, each consisting of 12,000–13,000 men drawn from the "best workers, students, and teachers" in Leningrad between the ages of 18 and 50 years.[18]

The collapse of the Northwestern Front's defenses in early July, however, forced the Party to accelerate the formation process, and LANO dispatched the first three militia divisions southward to man the Luga Defense Line by 7 July. A total of 45,183 men had voluntarily joined militia formations by 2 July. During the seven days from 30 June through 6 July, a total of 96,776 Leningraders joined the People's Militia Army, including 20,647 Communist Party and 13,457 Komsomol members, and 32,000 women for auxiliary services.[19] By 8 July this figure had risen to 101,037 men and women.[20]

LANO fielded its subordinate forces in three distinct stages. During the first stage, from 4 through 18 July, the army formed three people's militia divisions (DNOs), designated as the 1st, 2d, and 3d DNOs, with strengths of 12,102, 8,721, and 10,094, respectively, for a total of 30,917 men. However, this number fell 2,000–3,000 men short of the stated requirements.[21] During the same period, it formed 16 machine gun–artillery battalions and 6 destroyer regiments with a total of 16,800 men and 5,000 men, respectively. Since the first levy was clearly inadequate, on 16 July the Northwestern Direction High Command issued a new directive ordering the formation of five new divisions over the three-week period from 18 July through 20 August. The 4th DNO was a light division formed from three destroyer regiments, and the 1st, 2d, 3d, and 4th Guards DNOs (GDNOs) were made up of men from former workers' volunteer detachments. The four GDNOs numbered 10,538, 11,489, 10,334, and 8,924 men, respectively, with the 2d GDNO actually 653 men above its required strength.[22] The 4th Guards DNO was renamed the 5th DNO on 11 September.

The third and final stage of militia formation began when the Northwestern Direction High Command ordered the 6th and 7th DNOs be formed between 1 and 15 September, also on the basis of existing workers' battalions. Since the two divisions numbered 8,189 and 8,454 men, respectively, both were roughly 2,500 men short of their authorized strength. Thus, by 15 September the Northwestern Direction High Command had organized and fielded 10 DNO divisions and 16 separate machine gun–artillery battalions manned by a total of 135,400 men.[23]

Each DNO resembled a normal rifle division and was manned primarily by reservists and volunteers, most of whom had received some prior military training while serving in the reserve. Each DNO consisted of three rifle regiments, one artillery regiment, a reconnaissance detachment, a communications company, a sapper battalion or company, a medical battalion, and an auto transport company. The divisions' senior command cadre, roughly 20 officers per division, was generally inexperienced, poorly trained, and unfamiliar with the employment of modern military equipment. The divisions' mid- and low-level cadre was former Red Army sergeants or enlisted men from the ranks. The DNOs were woefully short of machine guns and antitank and antiaircraft artillery. To compensate for these shortages, the divisions formed antitank destroyer groups of men armed with antitank grenades or antitank mines.

The Northwestern Direction High Command sent the DNOs to the Luga front from 10 through 20 July, immediately after their formation and without providing the officers or soldiers with any combat refresher training. The results were predictable. Despite the enthusiasm and ardor of their officers and soldiers, the divisions had no staying power, and their soldiers died like flies. Since all of its divisions had been assigned to the front, the Direction High Command disbanded the militia army at the end of September. Ultimately, those DNOs which survived the heavy fighting south of Leningrad in late August and early September provided the nuclei for the 42d and 55th Armies and the Neva Operational Group. In late September the General Staff renumbered the seven surviving DNOs as regular Red Army rifle divisions and formally disbanded the 1st DNO and the 2d and 4th GDNOs, which had already been annihilated in combat.[24]

While the people's militia was forming, the Party and industrial enterprises created armed workers' detachments and instituted routine military training for all workers. Large factories like the Kirov and Lenin factories formed workers' detachments headed by troikas, consisting of the factory director, the local Party secretary, and the trade union chairman. About 107,000 workers received military training during July and August while on the job in Leningrad's factories and then formed armed detachments on the basis of one company raised per factory shop or section. In this fashion the Party organized 123 workers' detachments totaling 15,460 worker-soldiers by 1 November.[25] Since most of these detachments proved to be combat ineffective, on 9 October the authorities reorganized some of these detachments into rifle battalions, companies, and platoons and, later, into five workers' brigades, and assigned the brigades responsibility for the city's internal defense. These workers' battalions also served as manpower reservoirs from which the DNOs and later the Leningrad Front's line formations and units were replenished.

When the Germans intensified their air offensive against the city in early 1942 and manpower shortages became acute, Party and military authorities began employing women, particularly Komsomol members, in combat assignments in addition to performing in their more traditional noncombat roles. Based on GKO instructions issued on 23 March and 13 April 1942, the Leningrad Front's Military Council initially accepted 1,000 women into the PVO.[26] The Leningrad Komsomol regional committee raised the female volunteers through special committees established in each district and also accepted volunteers from among the nonunion youth. The PVO commands assigned the women primarily to PVO antiaircraft artillery batteries, projector (searchlight) stations, balloon-obstacle subunits, telephone and radio stations, and aerial reconnaissance and radio location points and installations. An additional 1,000 women had joined the ranks of the Leningrad PVO by May 1942.

In addition to mobilizing militia, workers' detachments, and women, Party, military, and Komsomol organs provided the population as a whole with minimal military training to increase the combat readiness of workers' formations. On 3 March 1942, the City Party Bureau ordered factory directors and Party secretaries to help regional military commissariats improve universal military training and strengthen Leningrad's defenses. While Party organizations were responsible for meeting the minimal needs of the DNOs and the workers' and destruction detachments, factories provided weapons, equipment, uniforms, and supplies to mobilizing units from their own internal resources above and beyond the requirements of normal production plans.[27]

One of the most ubiquitous tasks performed by large segments of Leningrad's population was local air defense (MPVO) supervised by local authorities. Soon after war began, the Party assigned the Leningrad's Council of Workers' Deputies responsibility for organizing MPVO. In turn, on 27 June the Council's Executive Committee ordered workers in all factories, installations, schools and universities, social organizations, and housing authorities to organize around-the-clock MPVO sentry duty. On-duty sentries were to issue air raid warnings to the population, organize fire fighting, and enforce blackouts (light discipline) to protect against enemy air attack. All lights were prohibited on the city's streets and in buildings, and protective covers masked necessary road and rail signals. MPVO personnel also prepared specially equipped collective air-raid shelters and field air-raid shelters throughout the city manned by a permanent cadre charged with maintaining them and controlling their use. For example, the population of Oktiabr'skii District dug more than 4,000 linear meters of slit trenches, prepared 214 basement bomb shelters, painted around 1 million square attic covers with superphosphates, and performed hundreds of other tasks during the first 45 days of war.[28]

Later, the MPVO formed brigades to fight fires in factories and other installations and self-defense groups and fire teams to perform the same functions in homes and apartment blocks. More than 3,500 of these groups were operating by early September, manned by 270,000 men and women, and 16,000 women were serving in this capacity in the Frunze District alone.[29] Finally, on 27 July, the Leningrad City Council's Executive Committee expanded the MPVO effort by ordering the entire able-bodied population of Leningrad to receive MPVO training.

All of these measures paid off, particularly when the *Luftwaffe* began its intense bombing campaign on the night of 6 September and continued the intense bombing through 27 September. Early during this period, Richtofen's VIII Air Corps, which was scheduled for transfer to Army Group Center in mid-October, also attacked the Baltic Fleet, damaging the battleships *Marat* and *Oktiabr'skaia Revoliutsiia* and the cruisers *Kirov* and *Maksim Gor'kii*.

However, these attacks too failed to achieve their goal of destroying Leningrad's floating batteries before Richtofen's departure.[30]

Thereafter, the *Luftwaffe* concentrated its efforts on the city itself. For example, on 19 September alone, 280 German aircraft dropped 528 explosive and 135 incendiary bombs during 6 separate air raids on the city and more than 200 explosive bombs in 3 separate raids on 27 September. During this period, the *Luftwaffe* conducted 11 day and 12 night air raids, and 480 of the total 2,712 attacking German aircraft successfully penetrated the city's air defenses.[31] However, Soviet aircraft and antiaircraft artillery claimed to have shot down 272 of the penetrating aircraft, forcing the *Luftwaffe* to bomb from ever-increasing heights and increasingly at night to cut down on aircraft losses. The *Luftwaffe* conducted 108 air raids during the rest of the year, and 1,499 aircraft (79 percent) managed to penetrate the city's defenses. The 3,295 explosive and 67,078 incendiary bombs these aircraft dropped caused 88 percent of the casualties Leningrad's population suffered from air attack throughout the entire war.[32]

The German air bombardment decreased sharply from January through March 1942, when the attacks dwindled to individual sorties by single aircraft. For example, 572 aircraft attacked the city in April, and only 95 made it through the city's antiaircraft defenses. The Germans ceased their air attacks entirely in May and did not resume them until October. Thereafter, German air activity was light through the end of the year. The marked decrease in German air activity, the German air blockade's collapse, and associated decreases in civilian losses due to air attack largely resulted from the growing strength and resilience of Leningrad's PVO and the efforts of the MPVO.

DEFENSE PRODUCTION AND EVACUATION

Before war began, Leningrad was one of the most important centers for weapons production in the Soviet Union, and it remained so after the war began, as State and Party officials tasked the city's factories with supplying the Red Army with weapons, ammunition, and other supplies and equipment, under the slogan "Everything for the front." Immediately after war began, the government ordered the city's industries to shift to production of military products only, a process that took two to three months to complete. Factories such as the Kirov, Frunze, and Bol'shevik accelerated their production after 22 June, enlisting large numbers of women into their workforces.

While the factories' workload increased, the working conditions deteriorated sharply as the front neared the city. German artillery pounded Leningrad and its factories 272 times from 4 September to 31 December, firing more than 13,000 shells into the city, exacerbating the devastation produced by the more than 70,000 aerial bombs dropped on the city.[33] The shelling sometimes endured for more than 18 hours in a single day, reaching a crescendo on 15 September, when it lasted 18 hours and 32 minutes and on 17 September when it endured 1 minute more. Another 21,000 artillery shells and more than 950 bombs struck the city in 1942. This prolonged enemy bombardment killed 5,723 civilians and wounded 20,507 from September 1941 through the end of 1943.[34]

Soviet heavy industry was the primary target for German artillery and aerial bombardment. Artillery fire struck the Elektrosila Factory, which was located along the southern ring railroad, 9 times from September through November 1941, and 73 of the 333 shells fired struck the factory's buildings. Artillery struck the Kronshtadt Factory 114 times from 22 September 1941 through 25 January 1942, and the 1,420 incoming shells killed 26 persons and wounded 58. The artillery raids finally tapered off after July 1942 as a consequence of successful Red Army ground operations. Thereafter, a total of 15,462 artillery shells hit the city during the first half of 1943 and 5,535 during the last six months of the year.[35]

Despite the appallingly dangerous working conditions, factory production remained substantial through 31 December 1941 and included 491 tanks (from the Kirov Factory), many of which rolled off the assembly line and drove directly into the front lines. Weapons production from 22 June to 31 December 1941 included thousands of mortars and submachine guns, 3 million shells and mines, 40,000 multiple rocket launcher rounds, more than 42,000 aerial bombs, great quantities of rifle ammunition, 491 tanks, and 317 artillery pieces.[36] In addition to supplying the Northern and Leningrad Fronts' needs, the factories produced a thousand guns and mortars and millions of shells needed in the defense of Moscow.

After the Germans captured Shlissel'burg in early September and began their land blockade of the city, on 4 October the GKO ordered Zhdanov and Kuznetsov to begin evacuating as many as possible of the city's key industries and technical personnel from Leningrad to the Volga and Ural regions.[37] The evacuation of heavy tank and armored vehicle factories and many other plants with their qualified workers, which had begun in August, accelerated in October when German forces began operations to cut off the remaining communications routes east of the city and began bombarding these routes. The evacuation routes extended by rail to Lake Ladoga, by barge across the lake, and by rail through Volkhov and Tikhvin to Vologda and the depths of the country. By 31 August 282 trains had departed Leningrad, but the German capture of Mga complicated movement plans, forcing Lieutenant General of Technical Services V. A. Golovko, who was in charge of the evacuation effort, to rely more heavily on barges to ferry the equipment across Lake Ladoga from Shlissel'burg. The subsequent German capture of Shlissel'burg closed these evacuation routes, leaving tons of industrial equipment strewn along rail sidings and roads leading from Leningrad to the lake. Ultimately the Kirov and Izhora tank factories relocated to Cheliabinsk and Sverdlovsk in the Urals region. At the same time, aircraft evacuated 10,500 of the most qualified workers and technical personnel.[38] These factories and technicians soon resumed production in their new locales.

Despite severe personnel shortages and constant enemy aerial and artillery bombardment, the factories continued producing during the evacuation by using locally procured resources. Beside the Germans' intense bombardment in September, the most trying period for the factories was from November 1941 through early 1942, when fuel and electricity shortages and personnel losses due to famine forced many of them to cease producing entirely. At the height of the famine, 50–60 percent of the workers were absent from work at any given time. This had a devastating impact on the availability of ammunition at the front. Even during this period, however, Leningrad's factories continued supplying Red Army forces in other critical regions, particularly the Moscow sector. On GKO instructions, in October and November, Leningrad transported vital weapons and ammunition to Moscow via Lake Ladoga and by air. The Special Northern Aviation Group, which flew key Kirov and Izhora factory technicians to the Urals, participated in the airlift of critical supplies to Moscow.[39]

Factory production improved significantly in spring 1942, when supplies transported across Lake Ladoga on the ice road permitted some factory production and city transport to resume. However, since the shortage of trained managers and workers still limited full production, the Party and city government established technical schools and new worker training programs. Understandably, the authorities focused on restoring weapons and munitions production, and the number of functioning weapons factories rose from 50 in April to 57 in May and 75 in June, although most remained quite small.[40] Arms production rose modestly from 1 January through 30 September 1942, although it primarily involved only light weaponry and munitions. Production during the first nine months of 1942 totaled 1,935 mortars, 1,975 heavy machine guns, 22,000 submachine guns, 187 tanks (repaired), and 360 guns (repaired). For the entire year, ammunition production totaled 1,700,000 shells and mines, 22,000 bombs, and 1,260,000 hand grenades.[41]

Thus, although arms production decreased drastically during the first 18 months of war, Leningrad's factories were able to satisfy the city's basic defensive needs despite experiencing the harshest rigors of war, blockade, and famine.

THE POPULATION UNDER SIEGE

The German blockade of Leningrad trapped over 3 million souls in the city. With winter approaching, food and fuel supplies cut off, and their inadequate reserves of foodstuffs dwindling, the city's inhabitants faced a frozen hell of starvation and disease while they struggled to survive under intense enemy fire. It was indeed fortunate that the Germans failed to draw the noose tight around Leningrad by severing all of the city's communications lines east of Lake Ladoga. This failure came back to haunt the Germans and, in the end, saved the city and its population from utter starvation and destruction. Nor did the Germans reach close enough to the city to destroy it by artillery fire.

With the bulk of Leningrad's male population at or on the way to the front, the first crisis faced by the Leningrad Defense Council was to care for the soldiers' families. To do so, the council established special departments in regional, city, and district executive councils, which were responsible for the support and welfare of the soldiers' families. These departments distributed benefits and pensions and determined and attempted to satisfy the families' legal benefits and material and social needs, a process that became quite difficult during the winter famine. During the first winter, these special departments supplied 17,000 soldiers' families with fuel, more than 9,000 families with daily monetary payments, more than 20,000 persons with shoes and clothing, and more than 10,000 families with living quarters.[42] In addition, Komsomol "social" brigades and the Red Cross provided medical and food assistance to many families. Despite this special assistance, the soldiers' families shared many the blockade's rigors and hardships with the population at large.

Leningrad's population suffered immensely during the German blockade, particularly during the first winter, when shortages, famine, and disease ravaged the city. The blockade's most immediate impact was to reduce drastically the supply of food, ammunition, fuel, fat, and other materials necessary to sustain human life. Even though the GKO, the Party, and the city government were preoccupied with the desperate situation at the front, they attempted to mobilize all of the city's resources to save it and its population.

When the Germans first disrupted Leningrad's supply lines in early September, the city's reserves were insufficient to meet the population's needs. Since bread and flour reserves totaled 35,000 tons on 26 September, and daily requirements were at least 1,101 tons of flour, the city had just over one month's supply of this staple remaining.[43] Reserves of other foodstuffs were just as low. Thus, the authorities' first priority was to ensure that some essential supplies reach the city.

The only routes by which supplies could reach the city were by water across Lake Ladoga and by air. The Lake Ladoga route relied on flimsy and slow barges and cutters to cross the lake around the clock, in stormy weather, and under constant German air attack. From 1 October through 30 November, these fragile ships transported 45,000 tons of food, 6,208 tons of ammunition, 6,638 tons of fuel and lubricants, and 2,363 tons of other cargo across the lake. This totaled 60,000 tons of supplies or 1,791 wagonloads, at a rate of 30 wagons per day. Aerial resupply by 30–50 aircraft per day during the period 14–28 November managed to transport 1,200 tons of high-calorie foods to the city.[44] However, these deliveries fell far short of meeting the city's requirements.

The establishment of the blockade on 8 September and the destruction of the city's Badaev Warehouses by German bombardment on 12 September created a food supply crisis in the city. Consequently, Stalin sent D. V. Pavlov, a member of A. A. Mikoian's Food Commissariat, to Leningrad with orders to institute food rationing and conservation systems.[45] Pavlov remained in the city and established and managed the city's food and fuel rationing system for two years in close cooperation with the city's administration and Party.

Pavlov's rationing system established strict norms for all supplies based on the military function or work status of each soldier or inhabitant in the city. The following table shows the norms in grams (ounces) for each category of recipient for specific types of foodstuffs as decreed on 10 September 1941.[46]

	Ration Period	Workers	Employees	Dependents	Children up to 12 Years
Baked bread	Per day	500 (17.6)	300 (10.6)	250 (8.8)	300 (10.6)
Groats and macaroni	Per month	1,500 (52.9)	1,000 (35.3)	800 (28.2)	1,200 (42.3)
Meat and meat products	Per month	1,500 (52.9)	800 (28.2)	400 (14.1)	600 (21.2)
Fish and fish products	Per month	800 (28.2)	600 (21.2)	400 (14.1)	500 (17.6)
Fat	Per month	950 (33.5)	500 (17.6)	300 (10.6)	500 (17.6)
Sugar and preserves	Per month	1,500 (52.9)	1,200 (42.3)	1,000 (35.3)	1,500 (52.9)

However, these norms proved illusory, and they had to be steadily decreased to match the dwindling food supplies. For example, bread norms that had been established even before his arrival were reduced five times between 2 September and 20 November, specifically, on 2 and 7 September, 1 October, and 13 and 20 November. In decreasing order in terms of the amount of bread provided, the norms applied to five categories of people, including frontline soldiers, rear-area troops, priority workers, engineers and technical personnel, and employees, dependents, and children.[47]

The 20 November daily bread ration amounted to a bare minimum of 375 grams (13.2 ounces) for workers in priority shops, 250 grams (8.8 ounces) for engineers and technical workers, and 125 grams (4.4 ounces) for employees, dependents, and children.[48] Compared with bread supplies available on 22 June 1941, this represented a 60 percent decrease in the workers' bread ration norm and an over 80 percent decrease in the employees' norm. The 20 November norm endured until 25 December. During the same period, the bread norm for soldiers was reduced three times, on 2 October, and 7 and 20 November. This represented a decrease of 44.5 percent for line soldiers, who received 500 grams (17.6 ounces) each after 20 November, and 62.5 percent for troops in rear service units and installations. On 20 November, the city required 510 tons of bread per day to support its population of 2.5 million souls.[49] On 25 December Pavlov adjusted the bread ration once more, this time reducing the ration for workers and engineer-technical personnel to 350 grams (12.2 ounces) and establishing a norm of 200 grams (7 ounces) for employees, dependents, and children.[50]

The city's bakeries used their imagination to compensate for the bread shortage. First, they increased the bread's baked weight compared with the amount of flour used by shifting from hearth baking to form baking, a measure that increased the bread's baked weight by 68 percent. Then, on 23 September the Leningrad Front ceased beer production and ordered all malt, barley, soybeans, and bran reserves sent to the bread factories to economize on the use of flour.[51] However, these measures only eased rather than solved the shortages. Therefore, on 24 September the *front* ordered the bakeries to adulterate the bread further (40 percent of the bread already consisted of such additives as malt, oatmeal, and husks). Finally, in late November the bakeries began adding edible cellulose to the bread, which, depending on the day, constituted 20–50 percent of the bread's volume. The use of additives and decreasing norms extended the bread supply more than one and a half months.[52]

The early onset of an abnormally severe winter sharply curtailed navigation on Lake Ladoga in late November and significantly worsened the supply situation in the city and at the front. More than 1,000 tons of daily cargo was required just to sustain the city's population, and the ice road, which was just beginning to operate in mid-January, could not satisfy these supply requirements. In addition, forage was also in short supply, and this shortage exhausted the horses, reduced their capability for work, and finally led to cattle plague.

This forced the city's authorities to search for new ways to increase the volume of cargo transported across Lake Ladoga and further mobilize Leningrad's internal resources. First, in late December the *front* released to the population 300 tons of food reserves stored at Kronshtadt and other forts and islands. At the same time, soldiers assigned to the fleet, forts, and the

54th Army reduced their rations voluntarily for the sake of the population.[53] All the while, search parties scoured all buildings formerly used for food and bread storage for food remnants.

As supplies dwindled and the Germans intensified their bombardment of Soviet supply depots and the ice road, the city's population began suffering from hunger and famine, casualties rose, and a normal work became difficult and then impossible. As hunger spread, fuel supplies also ran out in January 1942, electricity became unavailable, the city's trams ceased operating, water supply was interrupted, ferry and boat transport ended, and all business activity ceased. Thereafter, the city's inhabitants had to obtain their water from the icy Neva River, walk to work from one end of the city to the other or live in the factories, and operate machine tools by hand or by generator. Since the population had no choice but to use wood stoves to cook their food and heat their lodgings, numerous fires broke out, which were no less dangerous than the German bombardment and were difficult to fight because of the lack of water. The government reacted by establishing numerous fire commands tasked with advising the population on the fire danger and fighting fires.

Spreading disease was a natural outgrowth of the famine. The percentage of the population ill with scurvy and malnutrition (dystrophia) increased dramatically, and the death toll rose inexorably and catastrophically.[54] The same number of people perished in December 1941 that had died in all of 1940, and in January 1942, 3,500–4,000 persons succumbed to disease and famine daily.[55] After the famine began in November, the monthly death toll rose from 10,000 in November to more than 50,000 in December and to more than 120,000 in January. During the winter of 1941–1942, the worst period of the siege, when scurvy was rampant, the authorities decided to produce vitamin C from pine needles and produced 738,500 liters of pine extract in the first half of 1942.[56]

To help alleviate the population's plight, the population of Leningrad region provided food to the Leningraders through the porous blockade. For example, the inhabitants of the region's southeastern district smuggled 300 tons of foodstuffs into the city from 28 to 30 January, and Leningraders received more than 500 tons of bread, meat, and other products from occupied regions in May 1942.[57] This was possible because rivers, lakes, and swamps, which were impenetrable most of the year, froze and could be traversed during much of the winter. The city's fuel supplies also remained critically short, largely due to the *front*'s and fleet's requirements. Despite strict rationing and conservation, all fuel supplies were exhausted by 1 January 1942. The authorities then launched a major effort to collect firewood and peat from all neighboring districts, in particular from the city's suburbs and the northeast, where they gathered more than 3.5 million cubic meters of firewood in 1942.[58]

The experiences of a single Leningrader, Valentina Fedorovna Kozlova, typify the hardships the city's population had to endure during the terrible famine and blockade. Born in 1923, Valentina Fedorovna was 18 years old when the blockade began.[59] She describes her recollections of the rigors of those dark days:

First and foremost, the blockade meant hunger. I suffered from a state of extreme malnutrition. My prewar weight of 60 kilograms [132 pounds] fell to 39 kilograms [86 pounds] by July 1942. There was no running water or sewer system. Hunger dominated, and the winter of 1941–1942 was intensely cold. German bombers raided frequently. Buildings burned and collapsed, and people perished. There was no city transport. The first trams began operating in spring 1942.

I have many memories of the blockade. I have forgotten some things, but one can never forget the overall picture of that terrible time, and no words can adequately convey the true nature of those things we had to live through. First there was the famine. One constantly wanted to eat. I dreamed (on the way to work on foot) of suddenly finding a box of fat or an entire horse lying around. Mama helped our family somehow survive, except for Papa, who died on 30 March 1942 at the age of 62. Her wisdom and diligence arranged three square meals a day, even if it was hot water with some grain and cabbage and bits of bread (625 grams— 22 ounces) for the four of us (Mama, Papa, my sister Nina, and me). As soon as they announced that the war had begun, my parents bought some products: 5 kilograms [11 pounds] of sugar and several kilograms of groats. In the fall they fermented between 30–40 kilograms [66–88 pounds] of cabbage, that is, green leaves and cabbage stalks. This also helped us endure our strict nourishment regime. Those who, having received a bread ration of 125 grams [4.4 ounces], ate it all, and then, when there was nothing left, died. The authorities parceled the foodstuffs out according to the ration card—lentils, flour, some sort of fat, even if just a little.

When Lake Ladoga froze, the "Road of Life" opened. Trucks brought supplies along it from the "Great Land," meaning the territory unoccupied by the Germans. The Germans bombed the "Road of Life" unmercifully, and many vehicles sunk under the ice, not reaching Leningrad. But we began to receive chocolate, powdered eggs, tinned goods, and other foodstuffs. The partisans drove sledges with provisions across the ice. We always appreciated the entire country's concern for us—the "blockaded." However, this was inadequate for normal nourishment, the famine continued, and by May 1942 I was very weak. I could not climb the steps of the tram and lay down often. I was filled with foreboding thoughts.

In the winter of 1941–1942 there was little water, and our room was cold and almost dark. The lamp burned as long as there was kerosene, and then a homemade wick sunk in some sort of fat—an oil lamp of sorts and a torch. It was difficult to obtain water. We melted snow to bathe. I went to the street fountains behind several blocks of buildings for water. There were two water pails on the sled. Often I fetched only water from the ground. Along the road the water spilled from the snowdrifts and iced over the narrow tracks, which became ever smaller. In the morning we washed only our faces and hands. We did not wash our hair and bodies for several months. The public baths opened in spring 1942. Men, women, and children washed in one room. They were skeletons covered with skin—what a shame it was.

The greatest invention of all was the "small stove" [burzhuika]. It consisted of a 15-liter zinc tank, several bricks as a base, a carved-out the door for small pieces of firewood, a small opening on the top for cooking, and

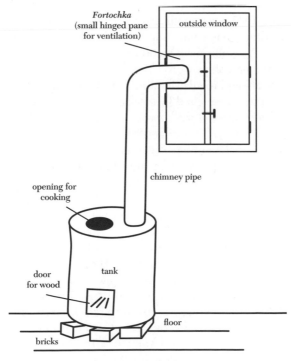

Burzhuika (small stove)

Diagram of a *burzhuika* (small stove)

a pipe to serve as a chimney. Papa did all of this. We prepared our food on the stove, it warmed the room, and the bread dried on the flue.

We went outdoors through the front doors into the snowdrifts. In the spring of 1942, the city was cleared of vermin and bodies by the efforts of the weak population. This was done to eliminate the possibility of the outbreak of epidemics.

Despite the immense human suffering, being a young and small part of the people as a whole, I believed in victory and gave no thought whatsoever to the surrender of Leningrad. All those who surrounded me at home, at work, and in military service maintained a high moral spirit.[60]

Valentina Fedorovna was called up by the Leningrad Military Commissariat on 1 July 1942, despite her obvious malnutrition, was trained in a school for young Red Army women, and was assigned to a PVO balloon obstacle detachment, where she served until 14 August 1945. She describes the circumstances of her military service and her attitude toward Stalin, the war, and the German invaders:

Then in June 1942 a summons arrived from the Military Commissariat. Mama and sister accompanied me. They took us gaunt, weak, and young slips of girls to Vsevolozhnaia Station for two weeks to restore our health.

Many of the hardships were alleviated during my service in the Red Army. Adequate and regular feeding cured my malnutrition, and within a year I once again weighed 60 kilograms. The water supply began to work. Only the constant artillery fire and bombing still threatened our lives. . . .

My aerostatic balloon regiment was located in Leningrad itself or in the city's suburbs, depending on the situation. The greatest danger we faced during our service was perishing from either the artillery or aerial bombardments. Our associated antiaircraft guns shot down some German aircraft, but perhaps not many. Today it is hard to recall exactly how many, but we did shoot down some. Our obstacle balloons, which were launched into the air during favorable weather, frightened off German pilots and, by doing so, protected the city. There were Heroes of the Soviet Union among the PVO aviation corps pilots, and that meant that they contributed to the achievement of victory. As I recall, we suffered few personnel losses, but perhaps there were minor losses of equipment.

The only news I received about the situation at Leningrad came from the newspapers and the radio. I knew that the German plan to take the city by starving it into submission did not succeed even though they were preparing for a celebration parade in our city's squares, and they even printed invitation tickets to celebratory assemblies. However, the selfless steadfastness of our soldiers and officers turned out to be stronger than the Germans' will to conquer. In spite of very heavy losses, first the blockade of the city, our beloved city, was penetrated (in January 1943) and later decisively raised (January 1944).

All of our exertions and thoughts during the war years were only of victory. We believed in Stalin and our military leaders and also in the motto, "Our cause is just, victory will be ours."

After many years there is talk that we should have surrendered Leningrad in order to avoid such loss of human life. But if you ask me about this, I will answer, "No!" It was better to die than to live "under the Germans." We heard much about the death camps and gas chambers. The Germans were a brutal enemy for us all and for me as well. I simply hated the Germans for a very long time. Now, at the age of 77 years, the emotion has become blunted, and, yes, Germany has become quite different—repentant for what occurred. But God forbid such a war ever again occur.[61]

Like the 2.5 million Leningraders around her, Valentina Fedorovna was caught up in the vortex of a dramatic struggle and devoted her energies to what emerged as the indelible and unforgettable spirit of the city's population. Unlike hundreds of thousands of her compatriots, she did so and survived.

SUPPLY, TRANSPORT, AND THE "ROAD OF LIFE"

Leningrad's sole ground supply route during the first harsh winter was the "Ladoga ice road" (*Ladozhskaia ledovaia trassa*), which crossed the surface of Lake Ladoga. This legendary road, which began operating during the most difficult period of the winter, earned the well-deserved sobriquet "The Road of Life" (*Doroga zhizni*), because it was vital to Leningrad's survival. The *Stavka* ordered work to begin on the construction of a supply route across the lake in early November, even before the lake froze, after it became apparent that the Leningrad Front's initial attempts to raise the blockade had failed. On 19 November the Leningrad Front ordered a military-vehicular road [*voenno-avtomobil'naia doroga*—VAD], designated the 101st VAD, be built from Kobona on the eastern shore of Lake Ladoga across the ice of Shlissel'burg Bay to Vaganovo on the lake's western shore. It appointed Engineer 1st Rank V. G. Monakhov, the deputy chief of the *front*'s Automobile Road Department, as the 101st VAD's commander.[62]

At the time the situation was extremely precarious because the railroad connecting Kobona with Vologda and the Soviet interior was the last available rail route to the rear, and it ran through Volkhov, then threatened by

German forces, and Tikhvin, which German forces had already captured. This forced the Leningrad Front to build the much longer 102d VAD, which bypassed Tikhvin to the north, and rely on it until Soviet forces could recapture the town. The 102d VAD, which was commanded by Major General of the Quartermaster Service A. M. Shilov, absorbed the 101st VAD on 7 December, after the Red Army recaptured Tikhvin.[63]

The ice road itself followed the shortest possible route (28–32 kilometers, or 17.4–19.9 miles) across the lake and was constructed in extremely difficult conditions. Units constructing the road had to contend with nearly constant German artillery fire and air bombardment, which required extensive use of camouflage and reliable antiaircraft defense. The constructors also had to contend with ever-changing ice conditions on the lake, frequent and numerous cracks and fissures in the ice, periodic thaws that affected the ice's thickness, and recurring storms (Map 10).

Major A. S. Mozhaev's road exploitation regiment began reconnoitering and marking primary and alternative routes across the ice once Shlissel'burg Bay began freezing over in mid-November. The first reconnaissance group, consisting of the 88th Separate Bridge Construction Battalion under Military-Technician 1st Rank V. Sokolov marked the first route on 17 and 18 November, and the second group under Major Mozhaev himself reached Kobona the same day.[64] However, the groups determined that the 100mm (3.9 inches) of ice was not sufficiently thick to support heavy transport, which required a minimum of 200mm (7.8 inches); therefore, most of the supply transports had to wait for the ice to thicken. During the delay, light carts transported the first cargoes of flour across the lake from Kobona on 19 November, with each cart carrying a modest load of two to four sacks of flour. The next day, Major General of the Quartermaster Service F. N. Lagunov, the chief of the Leningrad Front's rear services, twice traveled across the lake's ice from Kokkorevo to Kobona by light vehicle to test the ice's load-carrying capacity. The first substantial vehicular column (60 cargo trucks with 33 metric tons of flour) crossed the lake on 22 November despite a heavy snowstorm. Traveling in column formation along tracks prepared by horse transport, the trucks reached Leningrad on 23 November. A second column carrying 19 tons reached Leningrad the next day.[65]

Subsequently, harsh and ever-changing weather conditions continually battered the routes and limited their carrying capacity, requiring *front* engineers to work constantly to repair, improve, and expand them. Between 18 and 28 November, the engineers managed to build a second route extending 27 kilometers (16.8 miles) across the lake from Kokkorevo via Kloch'ia Island to Kobona. As the ice thickened, the engineers also created multiple new routes to the north. By the end of December, the ice had thickened to 1 meter (39.4 inches) and was covered by 30 centimeters (11.8 inches) of snow cover,

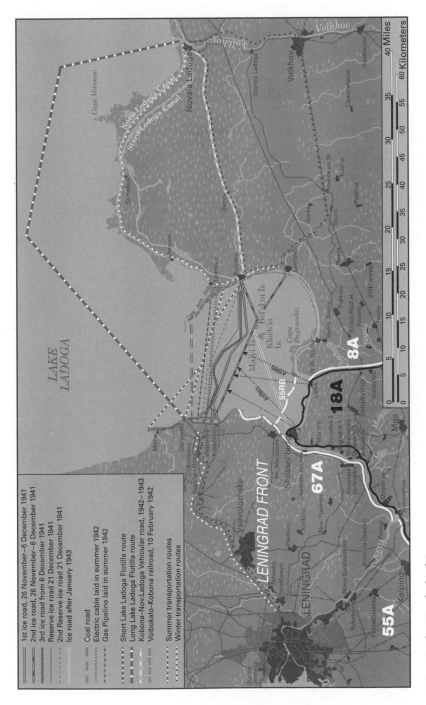

Map 10. The "Road of Life"

permitting almost unlimited use. Thereafter, the routes were able to sustain the weight of almost any type of military vehicle up to and including heavy KV tanks.

The engineers configured the ice roads to accommodate around-the-clock, two-way traffic in any weather. When construction was complete, the roads extended a total of 1,770 kilometers (1,099.8 miles), 1,650 (1,025.3 miles) of which had to be repeatedly cleared of snow. This required clearing and reclearing ice hummocks and snowdrifts from more than 33,000 square meters of roadway. During this process, the *front*'s road service leveled 824 kilometers (176.5 miles) of ice and snow walls, cleared snow from 2,200 kilometers (1,367 miles) of road surface, and built 260 kilometers (161.6 miles) of detours around intersections and dangerous sectors. The *front* also had to create and deploy an elaborate network of road guides, communications points, road service commandant posts, medical and rescue service points, feeding points, and combat security posts along the routes to ensure the routes functioned reliably. The communications network alone extended 168 kilometers (104.4 miles).[66]

At least initially, however, the new ice road fell far short of satisfying Leningrad's needs and the Leningrad Front's plan for supplying 2,000 tons of supplies to the city per day. For example, the road supplied 70 tons on 25 November, 154 on the 26th, 126 on the 27th, 196 on the 28th, and 128 on the 29th, an insignificant amount compared with the requirements.[67] Worse still, a thaw that began on 30 November limited vehicular movement and reduced the shipment that day to only 62 tons. Even after the ice thickened, the supply effort was plagued by congenitally poor and ineffective organization, which reduced food, ammunition, and fuel reserves to catastrophically low levels and threatened the survival of soldier and civilian alike in the city.

Therefore, Party leaders Zhdanov and Kuznetsov took personal charge of the supply effort, after which the situation slowly improved. Daily supply shipments rose to 700 tons on 22 December and 800 tons on the 23d, for the first time exceeding Leningrad's daily consumption rate. Since Leningrad and its defending *front* and the fleet were being fed "on wheels," the effort could not diminish, since even the slightest disruption in the flow of supplies had immediate adverse consequences for the population and the troops.

On 25 December the flow of supplies had improved enough for the *front*'s Military Council to increase the bread ration by 100 grams (3.5 ounces) for workers and engineer and technical personnel and 75 grams (1.8 ounces) for employees, dependents, and children.[68] However, the increased bread ration alone did not satisfy the exhausted population's food needs, and they continued to endure incredible deprivation well into January 1942. In early January Leningrad's food reserves shrank to two days' supply: 980 tons of flour, 2.9 tons of barley, 815 tons of soybeans, 11 tons of malt, 427.7 tons of slab fat, and 1.1 tons of bran. At the same point, fuel supplies amounted to only 217,000 tons, well short of the required 1,700 wagonloads per day, which was equivalent to 36 trainloads of fuel or 120 trainloads of wood.[69]

Given these catastrophic shortages, the *front* accelerated work on the ice road, expanding its capacity and usage to two or three convoys per day along multiple routes and increasing the speed of convoy movement. As a result, deliveries doubled, and by 18 January road traffic finally fulfilled the *front*'s mandated norms, permitting it to increase daily rations and begin to build up its reserves. By 20 January the Leningrad Front had amassed 10–11 days' worth of flour, 5 days of grain, 9–10 days of butter, 4 days of fat, and 8 days of sugar in city warehouses, at Ladoga Station on the lake's western shore, and cn route across the ice. A like quantity was stored on the lake's eastern shore and at Voibokalo and Zhikharevo on the rail line to Volkhov.[70]

The improved supply transport prompted the *front* to double the population's and soldiers' daily bread rations on 24 January. By this time, workers were receiving 400 grams (14 ounces) per day, employees 300 grams (10.5 ounces), dependents and children 250 grams (8.8 ounces), and workers in priority shops 575 grams (20.3 ounces) (up from 500 grams, or 17.5 ounces) per day. At the same time, the daily rations of front-line forces increased to 600 grams (21.1 ounces) (up from 500 grams, or 17.5 ounces), and rear service troops to 400 grams (14.1 ounces) (up from 300 grams, or 10.5 ounces). All categories of rations increased once again on 10 February. By this time, front-line soldiers were receiving 800 grams of bread daily, and rear service troops 600 grams.[71]

The effort to increase the number of ice routes and their carrying capacity continued unabated until the road was no longer needed. This required tremendous exertion. "Two convoys per driver per day" became a slogan that 261 drivers achieved in January and another 627 in March. During March, 355 drivers completed three trips per day, and 100 completed five.[72] The supply flow across the lake increased further in the second half of January 1942, with foodstuffs making up 75 percent of the cargo. At the same time, convoys began evacuating women, children, sick, wounded, and other valuable cargoes from the city.

However, the ice road's usefulness began decreasing rapidly after the spring thaw set in. On 25 March the ice's thickness began eroding, pools of water and numerous cracks began appearing on and in the ice, and transport had to be curtailed. Buses could not use the road after 15 April, and tanker trucks after the 19th. The *front* ordered all movement across the ice halted, effective 1200 hours on 21 April.[73] Despite the order, a 64-ton shipment of spring onions made it to Leningrad on 23–24 April.[74] That, however, was the end, and all vehicular traffic finally halted the next day.

The ice road contributed enormously to the city's defense and its population's survival before the spring thaw ended its usefulness. By February Leningrad's civilians were receiving daily food rations comparable to those received by workers elsewhere in the country, and bread adulteration fell to 1.7 percent of each loaf during the first quarter of 1942.[75] During the final three weeks the road was functioning, it transported four and a half times as many supplies as it had in November and December 1941. The road carried 361,109 tons of cargo during the winter, including 262,419 tons of food, 8,357 tons of forage, 31,910 tons of ammunition and explosives, 34,717 tons of fuel and lubricants, 22,818 tons of coal, and 888 tons of other cargo. In addition, 2,000 tons of anti-scurvy and other health-enhancing, high-calorie products such as chocolate and eggs made it into Leningrad across the ice road.[76] Furthermore, the reserves amassed during its operations were sufficient to feed the population from the time the ice road melted until water transport across the lake resumed.

Beside vital ammunition, food, and fuel supplies, the ice road also served as a means for evacuating civilians, key personnel, and factories.[77] As soon as the ice road opened, the Leningrad Front began a massive evacuation of those who were not capable of working, in particular, women, children, and the disabled. The number evacuated rose from 11,296 persons in January to 117,434 in February, 221,947 in March, and 163,392 in April. By April the total number of evacuees reached 514,069, an average rate of 5,000–6,000 persons per day.[78] Industrial evacuation also began in December. From December 1941 through April 1942, the Leningrad Front sent 3,677 railroad cars loaded with dismantled factory machine equipment, valuable cultural items, and cargo destined for the "mainland" from Leningrad to Lake Ladoga's eastern shore. About 20 percent of these transfers occurred along the ice road.[79]

Since the ice road operated under almost constant German air attack, road security and defense were immensely important. The Leningrad Front deployed rifle units and naval infantry brigades along the lake's shores to defend against German or Finnish diversionary attacks and aircraft and antiaircraft units to defend against air attacks. These forces defended the road's many routes, roads and railroads adjacent to the lake, and bases and warehouses on the lake proper or on its approaches. PVO fielded 200 mid-caliber antiaircraft guns, 50 small caliber guns, 100 antiaircraft machine guns, and 100 searchlights to defend against enemy aircraft.[80]

Forces from the 54th Army defended the lake's southern shore, and the 10th Rifle Division, 4th Naval Infantry Brigade, and 23d Army units, reinforced by armored cutters and coastal artillery of the Baltic Fleet, defended the western shore. These forces organized observation points, patrols, outposts, and local security along the ice road and also organized ski patrols and mined all approaches to the lake and ice road. German air attacks on the road and its associated installations intensified through March 1942, and on some days German aircraft attacked the road repeatedly, around the clock. The Leningrad Front PVO countered with all means at its disposal, including the entire 13th Fighter Aviation Regiment.

The Leningrad Front's Road Commandant Service maintained and regulated traffic along the ice road. Initially, it established 20 traffic control posts 300–400 meters (984–1,312 feet) apart to control traffic but increased their number to 45 within days and to 75 by 1 January. By the beginning of the new year, the service had deployed 350 regulators to control vehicle intervals, movement, and dispersion and to verify the thickness and condition of the ice. The regulators also placed between 150 and 200 blackout lanterns along the routes to light the way. Later, when the weather became more settled and high snow walls flanked the roads, traffic control became easier, the number of regulators decreased, and posts were deployed 1–2 kilometers (0.6–1.24 miles) apart.[81] The regulators contributed significantly to the ice road's success, doing so while stoically enduring the extreme cold and German air strikes.

THE PARTISAN MOVEMENT

Hand in hand with the military defense of the city itself, the Party and military leadership worked to establish a partisan movement in the German rear area, which it hoped could disrupt German operations and logistics and gather intelligence on enemy troop movements and intentions. Initially, the suddenness of the German offensive and Army Group North's rapid advance toward the city paralyzed the Soviet authorities, leaving them little time to consider partisan operations. However, the Germans' subsequent harsh treatment of the population and the large number of Soviet soldiers bypassed in the German rear created partisan forces spontaneously. In time, the *Stavka* and *front* came to appreciate the potential value of partisans and moved decisively to create and expand a partisan movement. They did so first by exploiting underground party organizations left in the German rear area and, later, by sending specially trained teams and detachments into the German rear to organize partisan formations.

Initially, from late June through mid-July, the Northwestern Direction High Command and Leningrad Communist Party Committee met with provisional partisan command and political cadre, formed initial partisan detachments, and assigned missions to partisan forces through the Northern and Northwestern Fronts' headquarters. Among the first partisan forces formed were 13 partisan detachments made up of students and faculty of Leningrad's Lesgaft Institute of Physical Culture, which were formed from 24 to 28 June.[82] By September 1941 Party and Komsomol regional and district committees formed, deployed, and directed the operations of 227 partisan detachments and smaller diversionary groups composed of carefully selected volunteers totaling about 9,000 men. During August and September, the two *fronts* inserted 67 of these detachments totaling 2,886 men into the German rear area and disbanded the remaining detachments, using their personnel to man newly formed destroyer detachments and GDNO divisions.[83]

The Leningrad Party Regional Committee established a troika headed by G. Kh. Bumagin, the regional secretary, to direct partisan operations, and on 2 August the Leningrad Front appointed Lieutenant Colonel E. N. Artoshchenko to head an Operational Group to direct the *front*'s partisan detachments. Later, on 27 September, the Leningrad Front and the Party issued a joint directive establishing a partisan headquarters headed by M. N. Nikitin, the secretary of the Regional Party Committee, to control partisan actions and coordinate them with *front* operations.[84]

Initially, Party members formed the nucleus of these partisan detachments and diversionary groups, and Party secretaries at each level directed both the partisan units and Party underground groups operating in territories under their jurisdiction. For example, the Glovsk District fielded 3 partisan detachments, 6 diversionary groups, and several underground Party groups and the Luga District, a total of 17 partisan detachments and diversionary groups. By the end of 1941, 88 regional and district secretaries, 29 chiefs of district and city committees, and hundreds of other local officials were directing the underground effort.[85] By 22 October 1941, this increasingly elaborate partisan effort encompassed 38 district Party and 38 district Komsomol organs composed of 125 Party and 100 Komsomol groups and 84 partisan detachments numbering 3,164 men operating in the region west and southwest of Leningrad.[86]

Although scarcely operational and lacking even rudimentary command and control, these early partisan detachments initiated a series of low-level sabotage and diversionary actions in June and July. For example, the Lesgaft Institute student partisan detachment blew up the railroad bed on the Luga-Siverskii railroad in July. In late July and August, the 5th Leningrad Partisan Regiment destroyed 40 trucks and light vehicles on the Pskov-Luga road, blew up the Pskov-Porkhov rail line, damaged Lokot' Station, and conducted numerous small ambushes. Also in July the Leningrad University and Art Institute Student Detachment destroyed the railroad bridge across the Igol'nyi River on the Shapki-Tosno road and damaged several trains. To the south, six detachments in Luga District destroyed several German tanks and aircraft, 24 ammunition trucks, 4 motorcycles, 36 bicycles, and 7 bridges and destroyed the German garrison at Voloshovo.[87]

The most significant partisan action during this period took place in the southern reaches of Leningrad region. There the 2d Partisan Brigade, commanded by N. G. Vasil'ev, seized and held most of the Belebelka, Ashevsk, and Dedovichi regions, which became one of the first "Partisan *krai*," a *krai* beng an administrative subdivision under district control.[88] The area under the 2d Brigade's control extended 120 kilometers (74.6 miles) from north to south and 90 kilometers (55.9 miles) from east to west, encompassing the area bounded by the towns of Dno, Staraia Russa, Bezhanits, and Kholm. Throughout July and August, the partisans successfully parried German attempts to penetrate and occupy this region, and during October and November the Party reestablished village councils, many collective farms, 53 schools, and many medical points within the region.

Although Army Group North organized several punitive expeditions against the Partisan *krai* in August and September, its use of SS units only inflamed partisan activity, and German forces were unable to reestablish control over the region. In the final analysis, however, at best, partisan activities during the first few months of the war were crude, poorly organized, sporadic, and, hence, only marginally effective. Nevertheless, their limited actions and the Germans' often arrogant and brutal response toward the inhabitants paved the way for the emergence of an even more effective partisan movement in the future.

Soviet sources claim that, during this period, the partisans killed 11,493 German soldiers and officers, captured 5 guns, 30 machine guns, 98 tanks and armored cars, 1,632 vehicles, 316 motorcycles, 71 aircraft, 66 locomotives, 807 wagons, platforms, and railroad cars, 8 warehouses, 320 bridges, and 8 garrisons and headquarters and captured many prisoners.[89] These figures, however, are probably apocryphal.

THE HUMAN TOLL

While fierce debates still rage over the numbers of civilians who perished from famine or enemy fire during the first year of the Battle for Leningrad, no one can question the horror of the first terrible winter under blockade. The gruesome toll rose from at least 10,000 dead in November, to 50,000 in December, to in excess of 120,000 in January. Dmitriy Pavlov, who fed the Leningraders during the blockade, states that 199,187 people were officially reported to have perished during the winter. Although the Funeral Trust, which was responsible for individual and mass burials, maintained no records for January and February, it recorded 89,968 bodies buried in March 1942, 102,497 in April, and 53,562 in May. The average of 4,000–5,000 bodies per month buried through autumn 1942 brought the count of total dead from February 1941 through February 1942 to 460,000 persons. In addition, individual work teams of civilians and soldiers estimated that they transported an additional 228,263 bodies from morgues to cemeteries from December 1941 through December 1942.[90]

When the winter evacuations via the Ladoga ice road ended in April 1942, Leningrad's population had fallen from about 2,280,000 persons in December 1941 to an estimated 1,100,000 souls, a decline of 1,180,000. Subtracting the 440,000 who were evacuated during the winter and the 120,000 sent to the front or evacuated in May and June, the city's civilian population suffered at least 620,000 deaths by 1 July 1942, not counting the many who perished in the city's suburbs.

As far as military casualties were concerned, official figures indicate that the Red Army and Baltic Fleet lost 344,926 personnel during the Leningrad strategic defensive operation from 10 July through 30 September 1941.[91] This included 214,078 dead and 130,848 wounded or sick. The 54th Separate Army lost 54,979, including 22,211 dead and 32,768 wounded or sick in the Siniavino offensive (10 September–28 October).[92] Total losses during the Tikhvin defense and offensive (16 October–30 December) were 89,490, including 40,667 dead and 48,823 wounded or sick.[93] The Liuban' offensive and subsequent encirclement (7 January–10 July 1942) cost the Red Army 403,118 more casualties, including 149,838 dead, and 253,280 wounded and sick.[94] This grim toll in major operations amounted to 825,513 casualties, including 426,794 dead and 465,719 wounded and sick. Losses during other periods were likely to have raised the military death toll during the first year of the Battle for Leningrad to in excess of 500,000 and the total military and civilian death toll to in excess of 1.1 million.

Regardless of the actual death toll, these figures accord the Battle for Leningrad and its associated winter blockade the dubious distinction of being the most terrible and costly siege in recorded history.

Red Army antiaircraft positions along the Neva River

Workers from the Kirov factory erect a barricade, September 1941

A Leningrad workers battalion heads for the front, October 1941

Leningrad's first civilian victims of German artillery fire, September 1941

Red Army infantry marching along the Neva River, fall 1941

Trucks on the "Road of Life" across Lake Ladoga, winter 1941–1942

German artillery shells exploding in Leningrad's streets, fall 1941

The evacuation of Soviet industry to the east, August 1941

Women working in a Soviet arms factory, 1941

CHAPTER 6

False Dawn

The Red Army's Winter Offensive,
January–April 1942

THE SITUATION ON 1 JANUARY

The Red Army's victories at Moscow, Rostov, and Tikhvin in December 1941 made it possible for the *Stavka* to expand its ongoing offensive operations in these regions into a general winter offensive encompassing virtually the entire Soviet-German front. Along the northwestern axis, Khozin's Leningrad Front and Tributs's Baltic Fleet had formed a dense and continuous front protecting the southern approaches to Leningrad and the Neva River line just east of the city and were conducting organized counter-battery fire against German artillery bombarding the city. Having defeated the German Tikhvin Volkhov grouping in December, the Leningrad Front's 54th Army and the 4th, 59th, and 52d Armies of Meretskov's new Volkhov Front manned continuous defenses from the southern shores of Lake Ladoga to Kirishi and southward along the Volkhov River to Lake Il'men'. Meretskov's forces tried repeatedly to expand their bridgeheads west of the Volkhov River throughout December but gave up the effort on 3 January because of the determined German resistance.

To the south, Lieutenant General P. A. Kurochkin's Northwestern Front defended the sector between Lakes Il'men' and Selizharevo with its 11th, 34th, and 27th Armies and was preparing to attack westward along the Staraia Russa and Velikie Luki axes. Along the vital western axis, the Kalinin and Western Fronts were pressing German Army Group Center westward from Moscow, threatening to envelop the army group's flanks. In southern Russia, the bulk of the Briansk, Southwestern, Southern, and Caucasus Fronts were on the defensive, tying down German forces and defending Sevastopol' and the Kerch peninsula.

The *Stavka* began planning for a full-fledged winter campaign in mid-December 1941 during the midst of its Tikhvin, Moscow, and Rostov counteroffensives. On 10 January 1942, it ordered the Red Army to commence a general offensive to exploit its December successes. The *Stavka*'s directive sketched out the situation and established a series of new offensive aims:

> After the Red Army has succeeded in sufficiently exhausting the German-Fascist forces, it will make the transition to a counteroffensive and begin to drive the German invaders to the west.

In order to stop our advance, the Germans are going over to the defense and have begun to construct defensive lines with foxholes, obstacles, and fortifications. In this manner, the Germans count on holding back our offensive until the spring, so that, having assembled his forces, in the spring they can once again launch an offensive against the Red Army. Consequently, the Germans want to win time and get a breathing spell.

Our mission is to deny the Germans that breathing spell, drive them to the west without a halt, and force them to expend their reserves before spring, when we will have large fresh reserves and the Germans will not have greater reserves. In this manner we will assure the complete destruction of Hitlerite forces in 1942.[1]

The *Stavka*'s primary objective during its winter campaign was to capture Smolensk and destroy German Army Group Center. Simultaneously, however, it also hoped to liberate the Donbas region of the Ukraine, recapture the Crimean Peninsula, rescue its forces encircled in the city of Sevastopol' in the south, and defeat German Army Group North and raise the Leningrad blockade in the north. While reflecting Stalin's ambitious political aims, these objectives in no way accorded with the Red Army's real military capabilities. Worse still, as Stalin, the *Stavka,* and the Red Army's *front* commanders prepared their offensives, rather than concentrating their forces decisively along the most critical operational axes, they dispersed their forces and attacked along every conceivable axis.

On 17 December the *Stavka* ordered Khozin's Leningrad Front, Meretskov's Volkhov Front, and the right wing of Kurochkin's Northwestern Front to prepare to conduct the "Leningrad-Novgorod offensive" by launching three concentric attacks against Army Group North to defeat the army group and raise the Leningrad blockade. Within the context of the larger offensive, the Leningrad and Volkhov Fronts were to conduct the Leningrad-Volkhov offensive to cut off and destroy German forces in the Mga, Tosno, and Liuban' regions and, by extension, in the Shlissel'burg corridor, by attacking southeastward from Leningrad and northwestward from the Volkhov River.[2] To the south, the Northwestern Front was to attack westward to capture Demiansk and Staraia Russa, exploit toward Sol'tsy and Dno, and cut off German withdrawal routes from Novgorod and Luga in cooperation with the Volkhov Front.[3] Since Meretskov's Volkhov Front was to play the lead role in raising the Leningrad blockade, the *Stavka* provided it with significant reinforcements.

Meretskov recalled the scope of the ambitious operation in his memoirs:

We received the *Stavka*'s operational directive late in the evening of 17 December, according to which the *front* was to deliver its main attack in the center, along the Gruzino, Siverskii, and Volosovo axis, completing a deep envelopment of Leningrad from the south. The 59th and 2d Shock Armies were designated to fulfill this mission. The 4th Army on the right flank was supposed to attack in the general direction of Kirishi and Tosno to encircle and destroy the enemy that had advanced north of Mga to Lake Ladoga in cooperation with the Leningrad Front's 54th Army. The 52d Army on the left flank received the mission of capturing Novgorod and then advancing in the direction of Sol'tsy to protect the advance of the Volkhov Front to the northwest.[4]

What Meretskov failed to mention was that the timing and objectives of his *front*'s assault were congruent with those of the Northwestern Front, a fact hitherto generally concealed in most Soviet histories. In fact, the twin offensive operations reflected the *Stavka*'s intent to crush German Army Group North's Eighteenth and Sixteenth Armies and propel Soviet forces westward in unison to the Leningrad (Volosovo)-Luga-Sol'tsy-Dno line by the end of January 1942.

In early January, the *Wehrmacht* was already facing increasingly powerful and violent Red Army assaults across the breadth of its Eastern Front, some of which jeopardized large groups of its forces. Therefore, Hitler and the OKH ordered the *Wehrmacht* to hold on to its positions, rest and replenish its forces, form new strategic and operational reserves, and be prepared to resume decisive offensive operations in the spring and summer of 1942. Hitler had already ordered his commanders to implement such a strategy in his Directive No. 39, which he issued on 8 December 1941, only days after the Red Army began its counteroffensive at Moscow:

> The early arrival of cold winter on the Eastern Front and resupply difficulties associated with it are forcing us to halt immediately all offensive operations and go on the defense. The manner of this defense's conduct depends on the aims that it pursues, namely:
> a. Hold on to those regions that have important operational and military-economic importance for the enemy.
> b. Rest and replenish the forces.
> c. By doing so, create conditions necessary to resume large-scale offensive operations in 1942.

Accordingly I order: . . . Army Group North will shorten the front of its eastern and southeastern defense line north of Lake Il'men'. However, it is to do so while denying the enemy the road and railroad from Tikhvin to Volkhovstoi and Kolchanovo that support restoring, reinforcing, and improving his positions in the region south of Lake Ladoga. Only by doing

so can we finally complete encircling Leningrad and establishing communications with the Finnish Karelian Army.

    d. If we determine that the enemy has withdrawn his main forces
       from the coastal belt on the southern coast of the Gulf of Fin-
       land and does not intend to offer serious resistance there, we
       should occupy that sector of the coast to economize forces.[5]

Along the northwestern axis, Hitler ordered Leeb's Army Group North
and the Finnish Southeastern Army to blockade Leningrad and hold firmly
to the Volkhov River line. While weathering the onslaught of winter, Army
Group North was to rest and refit its forces and prepare for an offensive to
capture Leningrad in the summer. Hitler issued specific missions to Leeb's
army group on 16 December 1941, even before the Tikhvin operation had
ended:

Army Group North is permitted to withdraw the Sixteenth and Eighteenth
Armies' internal flanks to the Volkhov River line and the rail line running
northwest from Volkhov Station. Establish continuous communications
with the XXVIII Army Corps' right flank along that rail line.

    The army group's mission is to defend that line to the last soldier, do
not withdraw a single step, and, at the same time, continue to blockade
Leningrad.

    I especially call your attention to reinforcing air defenses south and
southeast of Leningrad.[6]

German forces operating along the northwestern axis in early January 1942
numbered 26 infantry, 2 panzer, 2 motorized, and 3 security divisions, and
2 brigades concentrated primarily south and east of Leningrad, in the Kirishi
strong point, and along the Demiansk and Staraia Russa axis.[7] Kuechler's Eighteenth Army with 17 divisions, including the 8th and 12th Panzer and 20th
Motorized Divisions, was deployed along the front extending from south of the
Oranienbaum bridgehead and Leningrad proper to the Shlissel'burg corridor
south of Lake Ladoga and southeastward to the Volkhov River at Kirishi. The
army's XXVI and L Army Corps contained the Soviets' Oranienbaum bridgehead and occupied defenses south of Leningrad. The XXVIII Army Corps
occupied the vital Shlissel'burg-Mga-Siniavino corridor and the sector to the
southeast, and the I Army and XXXIX Motorized Corps defended the Kirishi
region.

    Busch's Sixteenth Army with 11 divisions, including the 18th Motorized,
protected a 350-kilometer (217.5-mile) front along the Volkhov River from
the Kirishi region to Lake Il'men' and eastward through the Valdai Hills to

Ostashkov on Lake Seliger. The army's XXXVIII Army Corps defended the Volkhov River line; the X Army Corps, backed up by the 18th Motorized Division, defended the Staraia Russa sector; and the army's II Army Corps defended the region from east of Demiansk to Ostashkov.

The two German armies occupied strong and deep defenses organized around numerous strong points along the front and in the depths. The most formidable strong points were located at Ropsha, Krasnoe Selo, Iam-Izhora, Mga, Siniavino, Liuban', Spasskaia Polist', Staraia Russa, Demiansk, and Vatolino. The German defenses skillfully integrated the many terrain obstacles in the region, in particular, the numerous rivers, lakes, and swamps, into their defenses. While the hard freeze of winter reduced the obstacle value of many of these terrain features, it also created terrible conditions for both sides.

PLANNING THE LENINGRAD-VOLKHOV OFFENSIVE

The Leningrad and Volkhov Fronts' Leningrad-Volkhov offensive was the centerpiece of the *Stavka*'s winter campaign along the northwestern axis. But, at the same time, it was only part of a larger effort to liberate the entire region from Leningrad southward to Staraia Russa, an effort that involved the Northwestern Front as well. As originally conceived in December, the operation was aimed primarily at raising the Leningrad blockade and clearing German forces from virtually all of Leningrad region and Demiansk, Staraia Russa, and Dno in the south. The missions the *Stavka* assigned to its operating *fronts* were ambitious and, given the Red Army's real capabilities, unattainable.

The *Stavka* assigned the leading role in the forthcoming offensive to Meretskov's Volkhov Front. Lieutenant General G. G. Sokolov's newly formed and fresh 2d Shock Army was to conduct Meretskov's main attack westward from the Volkhov River in the Spasskaia Polist' sector, supported by Major General I. I. Galanin's 59th Army, which was also newly formed. Galanin's army was supposed to begin the assault and penetrate German forward defenses, after which Sokolov's 2d Shock Army was to exploit Galanin's success. Thereafter, the two armies were to advance on the towns of Liuban', Dubovik, and Cholovo, sever the Leningrad-Dno and Leningrad-Novgorod railroads, and destroy German forces in the Liuban' and Chudovo regions in cooperation with the Leningrad Front's 54th Army attacking from the north. Subsequently, the three armies were to advance northwestward to raise the Leningrad blockade in cooperation with the Leningrad Front's other armies.[8]

Klykov's 52d Army, on Meretskov's left flank, was to attack across the Volkhov River north of Novgorod and assist the Northwestern Front's 11th Army in the destruction of the German Sixteenth Army's forces in the Novgorod, Sol'tsy, and Dno regions. Major General P. A. Ivanov's 4th Army, which was deployed along the Volkhov River east of Kirishi, was to support the main and secondary attacks and protect the Volkhov Front's left flank. Frontal aviation was to support the offensive with 52 aircraft, most of which were in disrepair. The aircraft were under army control since the *front*'s air staff, which had been created in December 1941, lacked means to control the aircraft.

Meretskov, the Volkhov Front commander, was a "survivor" of Lavrenti Beriia's NKVD and the purges the NKVD orchestrated in the early days of the war. Known to be an impulsive and caustic officer who was often short-tempered with his subordinates, Meretskov was arrested by Beriia's NKVD shortly after war began on trumped-up charges of treasonous activity. After severe physical and certainly mental mistreatment, he was released in September 1941 on Stalin's personal orders. No doubt this experience significantly influenced the former chief of the Red Army General Staff. At the least, it prompted him to obey Stalin's every command. Accordingly, a combination of fear and desire impelled Meretskov to fulfill every instruction from Moscow, however unrealistic it was. Meretskov "even showed excessive zeal, urging the *Stavka* to speed up the implementation of Stalin's ideas. If their realization met with difficulties, Meretskov would use Front Military Council statements as a cover instead of adopting bold personal decisions."[9]

As for Sokolov's new 2d Shock Army, it had begun its formation in late October 1941 in the Volga Military District. Most of its personnel came from the southern and steppe regions of Russia, and its personnel saw forests and marshes for the first time when they were assigned to the Volkhov Front. "Afraid of the forest thickets, the army's soldiers preferred to concentrate in clearings, where they were excellent targets for the enemy. Many of the army's soldiers lacked even elementary military training and were poorly trained to operate on skis. Some of them, for example, preferred to traverse areas covered by deep snow on foot, carrying their skis as an unnecessary load on their shoulders. Much had to be done to turn these rookies into skilled soldiers."[10] The 2d Shock Army's commander, Sokolov, was a former NKVD officer who had served in various capacities in the NKVD since 1920, finally becoming Beriia's deputy. His only military service occurred in October 1941, when he had served for 10 days as the 26th Army's chief of staff. Hence he was woefully unfit to either plan, coordinate, or conduct such a complex operation. Characteristically, when informed by his chief of staff that his army was experiencing deployment and supply problems when moving its forces forward into their jumping-off positions for the attack, Sokolov shrugged, pointed to the ceiling, and responded, "This is Stalin's order, we should fulfill it."[11]

Galanin's new 59th Army was somewhat better suited to operate in the forested swamps west of the Volkhov River. It had begun forming in early November 1941 in Vologda in the Arkhangel'sk Military District and was made up of soldiers raised in the Ural and Siberian Military Districts and in the Far East. Many of its officers and senior enlisted men had served in combat during the summer of 1939 against Japanese forces at Khalkhin Gol. After its formation, it underwent extensive training in the forests of northern Russia, although most of the training was of a defensive nature. It began deploying by rail to the Volkhov region on 17 December.[12] Its commander, Galanin, had served in the Red Army since 1919 and had attended the Vystrel tactical school in 1931 and the Frunze Academy in 1936. He began the war as a corps commander and in August 1941 was assigned to command the Southern Front's 12th Army after German forces destroyed the original 12th Army in the Uman' pocket in late July and early August 1941. Galanin had been in army command for three months when he took command of the 59th Army in November.[13]

The *Stavka* ordered Khozin's Leningrad Front to conduct one major attack east of the Shlissel'burg corridor in support of Meretskov's offensive and secondary assaults in the Leningrad region. Fediuninsky's 54th Army was to penetrate German defenses east of Kirishi and advance southward and southwestward in tandem with the 4th Army to assist Meretskov's force in encircling German forces in the Liuban' region. At the same time, Fediuninsky's forces were to link up with the 55th Army's forces attacking southeastward from Leningrad, capture Tosno, encircle and destroy German forces in the Shlissel'burg corridor, and raise the Leningrad blockade. The 8th Army, now commanded by Major General A. V. Sukhomlin, which was situated along the Neva River east of Leningrad, was to attack eastward against German forces in the Shlissel'burg corridor. At the same time, Lieutenant General I. F. Nikolaev's 42d Army and Lieutenant General V. P. Sviridov's 55th Army, which were defending south of Leningrad, were to attack southeastward toward Tosno once Meretskov's 54th, 2d Shock, and 59th Armies reached the Leningrad-Dno railroad near Chashcha Station. The 345 aircraft assigned to the Leningrad Front, the Baltic Fleet, and PVO were to protect Leningrad, Kronshtadt, the Tikhvin-Leningrad sector, and the ice road from the air and support the attacking ground forces. The force numbered 82 bombers, half of which were older models, 5 assault, and 258 fighter aircraft. The Leningrad Front allocated 67 fighters to protected its communications and 25 to cover Leningrad proper. The remaining 166 fighters, half of which were in disrepair, were to support the ground forces.[14] When the operation began, Khozin's and Meretskov's *fronts* committed 325,700 troops to combat and reinforced them with upward of 100,000 more during the offensive.[15]

Kurochkin's Northwestern Front was to attack German forces at Staraia Russa, Demiansk, and Toropets, simultaneously, with two shock groupings. The first shock group, Morozov's 11th Army deployed on the *front*'s right wing, was to advance through Staraia Russa to Dno, link up with the Volkhov

Front's 52d Army, and destroy German forces in the Novgorod region. The second shock group, Lieutenant General M. A. Purkaev's 3d and Colonel General A. I. Eremenko's 4th Shock Armies (formerly the 60th and 27th Armies) on the *front*'s left wing, was to advance through Toropets to Rudnia and destroy German forces in the Rzhev and Viaz'ma regions in cooperation with the Kalinin and Western Fronts. The 34th Army, deployed in the *front*'s central sector and now commanded by Berzarin, was to encircle and destroy German forces in Demiansk. A total of 89 aircraft, many in disrepair, were to provide the *front* with air support. Initially, Kurochkin committed 105,700 men to the offensive but reinforced the operations with another 200,000 men during its course.[16]

According to Soviet planning documents, on the eve of the offensive, Red Army forces outnumbered opposing German forces in the entire offensive sector by factors of 1.5 in personnel, 1.6 in guns and mortars, and 1.3 in aircraft. In the 2d Shock Army's penetration sector, the respective ratios of Soviet numerical superiority were 5:1 in infantry, 3:1 in tanks, 3:1 in heavy machine guns, 4:1 in light machine guns, and 6:1 in automatic weapons.[17] Despite their clear numerical superiority, however, none of the attacking *fronts* was prepared for the attack, as became abundantly evident when the assaults finally began.

THE JANUARY OFFENSIVE

The *Stavka* ordered the forces participating in the offensive to seize jumping-off positions and complete concentrating their forces by 26 December. However, neither the Germans nor the weather cooperated, forcing the *Stavka* to delay the main operation until 6 January. Meanwhile, Fediuninsky's 54th Army was to begin its assault west of Kirishi. Because of the innumerable delays, the *Stavka* decided to launch its main offensive in staggered sequence, with the 59th, 4th, and 52d Armies attacking on 6 January and the 2d Shock Army joining the effort on 7 January. Even so, the attacking forces completed few of their offensive preparations on time. Meretskov did not complete concentrating his infantry and armor until 7 and 8 January, his artillery until 10 through 12 January, and his rear services until well after the operation began. Despite the delays and the incomplete attack preparations, Stalin insisted Meretskov begin his assault on 6 January as planned, before his forces were fully concentrated and without necessary artillery and logistical support. The results were predictable (Map 11).

From the very beginning, the overly ambitious offensive encountered recurring and insurmountable difficulties, the most serious of which was Stalin's unwavering insistence that it begin on time. Inevitably, from the very

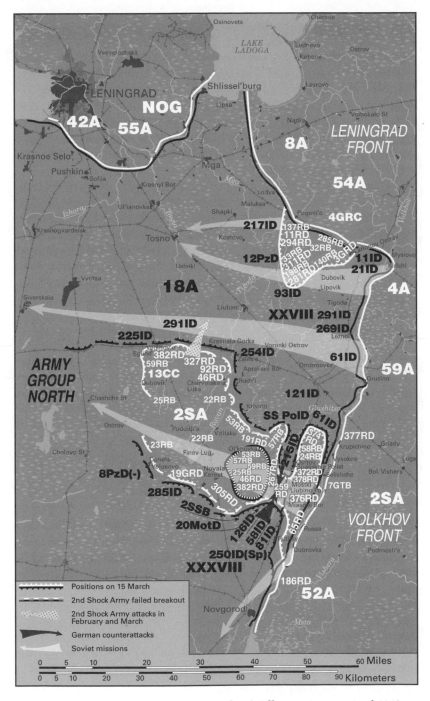

Map 11. The Soviet Leningrad-Volkhov (Liuban') Offensive, January–April 1942

start, the attacking forces suffered from acute and persistent ammunition and fuel shortages, the unavailability of reserves necessary to exploit success, and congenitally poor command and control and coordination of forces. Worse still, as the offensive developed, the three *fronts'* axes of advance diverged sharply in three separate directions, and combat developed in three sectors separated by both space and time. The Volkhov Front's 2d Shock and 59th Armies advanced into the frozen swampy wastelands south of Liuban', where they fought in relative isolation from January through June. During the same period, the Northwestern Front's armies bypassed and encircled German forces in Demiansk and reached the eastern outskirts of Staraia Russa before becoming engaged in prolonged and fruitless operations in both regions. The Leningrad Front's 54th Army became locked in a fruitless struggle west of Kirishi, and the *front's* armies south and southwest of Leningrad made no progress whatsoever, in part because conditions within Leningrad made them too weak to do so.

Fediuninsky's 54th Army initiated the offensive on 4 January by attacking the defenses of the German I Army Corps' 269th and 11th Infantry Divisions near Pogost'e, west of Kirishi. After the attacking forces advanced only 4–5 kilometers (2.5–3.1 miles) in 48 hours of heavy fighting, German infantry and elements of the reinforcing 12th Panzer Division counterattacked and drove Fediuninsky's troops back to their jumping-off positions. The attack seemed so insignificant that neither the German nor the Soviet chronicler paid much attention to it. Halder noted in his diary, "North. Continued enemy attacks, but nothing on a major scale."[18] The Leningrad war diary recorded: "In spite of the difficult conditions, the Leningrad Front's forces are continuing offensive operations. The scale of the battle was not so great that the Informburo [Information Bureau] reported on it, but it went on. On 7 January it [combat] was particularly fierce in the region of Zharok Station on the Mga-Kirishi rail line."[19]

Although the 54th Army's failure seemed insignificant, it set the pattern for what was to come and, worse still, prevented Fediuninsky's army from supporting the Volkhov Front's main attack once it began.

Meretskov's and Khozin's forces attacked on 6 and 7 January as Stalin demanded, but their initial assaults aborted almost immediately after achieving only meager gains. Galanin's 59th Army began Meretskov's main attack early on 6 January, when its lead divisions attempted to seize and expand the *front's* bridgeheads west of the Volkhov River so that Sokolov's 2d Shock Army could exploit westward the next day. While a portion of Galanin's forces struggled west of the river, Meretskov completed concentrating the remainder of the 59th and 2d Shock Armies on the river's eastern bank. By day's end Galanin's initial assault had expired midst the heavy German resistance. The 59th Army history described the first day's action:

The regiments of the army's first-echelon divisions rose up to attack in the morning after short artillery barrages. Deep snow hindered the advance, and the subunits managed to cross the Volkhov River, whose width reached up to 400 meters, on the ice, and were immediately exposed to enemy flanking fire.

The enemy met the attackers with intense fire from large-caliber machine guns from pillboxes located along the forward edge and from all of types of rifle weapons. Artillery and mortars fired from the depths. Wounded and dead began appearing in the combat ranks. However, despite the enemy's strong resistance, separate subunits managed to overcome the river and dig in on the Volkhov River's western bank.

The battle lasted many hours. The soldiers rose up to attack time and time again but, after encountering destructive fires, were forced back. At nightfall, in many sectors the attacking units withdrew to their jumping-off positions.[20]

Meretskov provided his own description of the futile initial attacks in a report he sent to the *Stavka* at 0700 hours on 7 January:

The 59th Army's offensive is developing slowly, and units are encountering strong enemy resistance.

Today the enemy twice launched division-scale counterattacks from the Tushin Island, Chudovo station, and Chudovo region. All enemy attacks along the 59th Army's front were beaten back, the enemy's 8th Motorized Regiment was destroyed, and other counterattacking regiments suffered heavy losses.

The divisions of the 59th Army's main force occupied the following positions by day's end on 6 January:

The 8th Rifle Division—the Vodos'ia region on the left bank of the Volkhov;

After repelling repeated enemy attacks, the 376th and 288th Rifle Divisions are along the Meneksha River line;

The 111th Rifle Division is continuing to liquidate enemy strong points at the mouth of the Liubun'ka River; and

Two regiments of the 372d Rifle Division are along the western bank of the Volkhov River four kilometers south of Krasnofarforny.

All divisions are prepared to conduct night operations.

The 2d Shock Army occupied its jumping-off positions along the eastern bank of the Volkhov River in readiness to begin its offensive on the morning of 7 January with five brigades and the 259th Rifle Division.

In spite of the fact that the concentration is not complete, the 2d Shock Army will attack on 7 January.

The principal difficulties are: the 2d Shock Army's army artillery has not arrived, its guards divisions have not arrived, aviation is not concentrated, auto-transport has not arrived, ammunition reserves have not been stockpiled, and the serious situation regarding foodstuffs and fuel has not yet been corrected.

At the same time he has counterattacked against the 59th Army's front, the enemy has also counterattacked against the 4th Army's left flank. Although the counterattacks there were repelled, and the enemy suffered heavy losses, the 65th and 4th Rifle Divisions were driven back 2–3 kilometers.

[signed] K. Meretskov, G. Stel'makh[21]

Undeterred, Meretskov committed the remainder of the 59th Army and Sokolov's 2d Shock Army to combat on 7 January, however, in piecemeal and uncoordinated fashion. Reinforcing failure, the two armies attempted to penetrate German defenses along the Volkhov River and at Posadnikov Ostrov, but the hapless attacking forces immediately bogged down with heavy losses, and both armies had to retreat to their original positions. So heavy was the fighting that the 2d Shock Army alone lost more than 3,000 men in the first 30 minutes of its ill-fated assault.[22] Driven on by Stalin's incessant orders, exhortations, and threats, the two armies struggled for two days more before the attacks collapsed in utter exhaustion and confusion.

Consequently, at Meretskov's request, on 10 January the *Stavka* called a three-day halt in the attacks.[23] Soviet after-action critiques dryly noted that the attacks failed because of the fierce German resistance and the *front*'s congenital penchant for dissipating its strength in fruitless and repetitive assaults on German strong points. Halder confirmed this judgment in his diary: "The attack against the Volkhov front was repulsed. It seems that both here and on the Ladoga front, the main attack is yet to come."[24] The Leningrad war diary accurately noted on 10 January, "The hope that the Volkhov Front's 7 January offensive would complete the penetration of the Leningrad blockade has not been realized. Unfavorable circumstances forced the command to cease the offensive on 10 January. Supposedly, it will resume in several days."[25]

Nonplused by the failures, Stalin ordered Meretskov to regroup his forces and conduct a fresh assault in more coordinated fashion on 13 January, this time leading the assault with the full 2d Shock Army. To ensure his orders were carried out to the letter, Stalin dispatched L. Z. Mekhlis, the chief of the Red Army's Main Political Directorate and his special emissary and personal hatchet man, to supervise Meretskov's attack preparations. Once there, "The 'guest' began to go deeply into all matters, even trifles, continuously urging on the *front* commander, as assiduous enough as he already was."[26]

As evil and universally feared and loathed as he was, Mekhlis played a role in preparing the operation that was not altogether negative. "For example, when he learned that the attacking armies were without artillery and that the available guns lacked vital parts, including optical instruments and communications equipment, Mekhlis informed Stalin. Soon, General N. Voronov, the chief of the Red Army's Artillery, was sent to Malaia Vishera with several railway cars containing the missing equipment."[27] Mekhlis, who had almost immediately recognized the incompetence of Sokolov, the 2d Shock Army commander, was also instrumental in his removal and replacement by the more experienced Major General N. K. Klykov, the former 52d Army commander. Unfortunately, Sokolov left his command on 10 January, three days after the offensive had begun.

However, the arrival of Mekhlis did not bode well for the operation's success. His legendary vile temperament and military incompetence were only exceeded by his ruthless treatment of commanders and soldiers alike. Here, along the Volkhov, the dreaded Mekhlis would begin earning his well-deserved reputation as a harbinger of military disaster.

After regrouping his forces and forming new shock groups, Meretskov's 2d Shock and 59th, 4th, and 52d Armies and the Leningrad Front's 54th Army resumed the offensive early on 13 January, this time almost simultaneously with and preceded by proper artillery preparations. Even so, ammunition was still woefully inadequate to sustain the new attack. Attacking across swampy, roadless, and snow-covered terrain in bad weather, none of the attacking forces was able to maneuver freely or to be resupplied with essential fuel, ammunition, or food. Newly released Volkhov Front combat reports vividly capture the frustrating nature of the offensive.[28] During this period Meretskov repeatedly asked for and received *Stavka* assistance to facilitate his advance. For example, on 19 January the *Stavka* sent him 3,000 PPSh submachine guns and 300 antitank rifles and released 9 ski battalions and an aerosleigh transport battalion to his control.[29]

Halder did note the increased Soviet activity on 13 January and immediately recognized its gravity: "The southern wing of AGp. North came under heavy pressure today as the result of an attack against 123d Division by elements of four divisions across the frozen lakes. Von Leeb is at once thinking of withdrawing. Fuehrer disapproves."[30]

The Leningrad diary simply noted the action without enthusiasm: "The Volkhov Front's forces resumed offensive operations interrupted on 10 January. Simultaneously, the Leningrad Front's 54th Army once again went over to the attack. The recent attempt to penetrate the blockade turned out unsuccessful. How will conditions be now? On the first day of the offensive there was little of comfort. The enemy is resisting stubbornly."[31]

In the 2d Shock Army's sector, the artillery preparation and subsequent ground assault shattered German defenses at the junction of the XXXVIII Army Corps' 126th and 215th Infantry Divisions, producing panic in the former, which had only recently arrived from the West. In heavy fighting from 13 through 16 January, the 2d Shock Army's forces managed to carve small wedges in the Germans' defenses west of the Volkhov and Tigoda rivers. They were not able, however, to capture key German strong points on the rivers' western banks and penetrate the Germans' defenses. Once again, Meretskov and his army commanders had failed to concentrate their attacking forces, and the *front*'s forces continued to experience debilitating shortages of ammunition. On the 2d Shock Army's flanks, the 4th and 52d Armies also failed to record any progress and went over to the defense on 14 and 15 January.

After completing its regrouping, Fediuninsky's 54th Army also attacked early on 13 January with full kit but immediately encountered determined resistance by XXVIII Army Corps' 269th Infantry Division, which was reinforced by elements of the 223d and 291st Infantry and 12th Panzer Divisions. Although Fediuninsky's forces captured Pogost'e on 17 January, they failed to penetrate the German defenses, reportedly because, despite repeated *Stavka* instructions to do so, Fediuninsky also failed to concentrate his forces and, instead, attacked in dispersed fashion across a 30-kilometer (18.6-mile) front.[32] The failure, which the General Staff also attributed to poor command and control, prompted Stalin to subdivide Fediuninsky's army into the 54th and 8th Armies in late January to tighten command and control.

The new 8th Army, now commanded by Major General A. V. Sukhomlin, manned what formerly had been the 54th Army's right flank south of Lake Ladoga. Sukhomlin's army, together with the 54th Army on its left flank, was to smash German defenses in the Lodva area east of Siniavino and advance westward to Tosno, where it was to link up with the 55th Army, whose forces were attacking Tosno from the northwest. The *Stavka* left Fediuninsky's mission unchanged. His 54th Army was to advance southwestward from Pogost'e, link up with the 2d Shock Army at Liuban', and destroy German forces at Liuban', Chudovo, and Kirishi. However, the 54th Army's attack developed too slowly, while the 8th Army's attack faltered entirely.

On 17 January, the same day Fediuninsky's forces captured Pogost'e, Klykov's 2d Shock Army resumed its attack. Supported by more than 1,500 aircraft sorties, the army finally penetrated the Germans' first defensive position on the left bank of the Volkhov River, advanced 5–10 kilometers (3.1–6.2 miles), and created conditions Meretskov deemed favorable for developing success. However, once again the attacking forces failed to capture key German strong points because of poor command, control, and coordination, the dispersed nature of the assaults, and deteriorating weather conditions, and the offensive faltered with heavy losses. The only consolation for Meretskov was the fact that, although they aborted from the very start, the assaults by the Leningrad Front's 8th and 55th Armies tied down German forces operating south of Leningrad.

At this stage of the operation, the Germans too began to experience command turbulence prompted by the unexpected Soviet assault. With his *front* under assault from the Volkhov line in the north and south of Lake Il'men', "Leeb asked either that he be relieved or that he be allowed to order the retreat [south of Lake Il'men'] while he still had some room for maneuver."[33] Through Halder, Hitler responded, "Put all of the powers of the General Staff in motion . . . and extirpate this mania for operation. The army group has a clear mission to hold, and the highest command will assume all the risk."[34] The die was cast for Leeb. Hitler relieved him on 17 January "for reasons of health" and appointed Kuechler to command Army Group North.

On 21 January, after a four-day halt to regroup its forces and integrate reinforcements, Klykov's 2d Shock Army resumed its struggle, this time focusing on capturing the German strong points at Spasskaia Polist', Mostki, Zemtitsy, and Miasnoi Bor at the base of the shallow penetration. While Klykov's forces were pounding the German strong points, early on 22 January, Meretskov reported his *front*'s progress to the *Stavka,* requesting permission to regroup his forces so that they could begin to exploit westward:

> The penetration is developing successfully, albeit slowly, along the 2d Shock and 52d Armies' front. The penetration has developed along a 12-kilometer (7.5-mile) front from Selishchenskoe village to Krasnyi Udarnik State Farm, which is encircled. The forces have advanced to a depth of 10 kilometers (6.2 miles) and are approaching the Leningrad road.
>
> The operations along the 4th and 59th Armies' axes have become more prolonged. Despite the fact that we concentrated 12 divisions and more than 400 guns in the 12-kilometer (7.5-mile) sector on the main attack axis on 21 January 1942, we have not succeeded in penetrating the enemy defense. The enemy has prepared strong defenses along this axis and has concentrated up to four infantry divisions (the 291st, 81st, 61st, and 215th) and four regiments from other divisions (the 139th Jager, 9th SS Infantry, and the 322d and 311th Infantry) in them. If the repetitive attacks along the 4th and 59th Armies' fronts do not achieve success on 22 January 1942, we consider it essential to exploit the 2d Shock and 52d Armies' success in order to develop further the Volkhov Front's offensive. It is necessary to regroup the 59th Army, reinforced by three divisions from the 4th Army, to the right flank of the 2d Shock Army as quickly as possible to develop the offensive on Tosno in the rear of the enemy Mga grouping.

We propose that you approve the following plan for regrouping the *front*'s forces and weaponry:

1. Leave the 4th Army with the 44th, 310th, and 190th Rifle Divisions and the 80th Cavalry Division along the Kirishi and Gruzino front and add to it the 59th Army's 288th and 376th Rifle Divisions, which are operating along the western bank of the Volkhov River north of Gruzino. The 4th Army will temporarily conduct local operations to tie down enemy forces.

To the extent that the offensive by the *front*'s shock group south of Oktiabr'skoe develops successfully, the 4th Army can also join in the general offensive.

2. Regroup the 59th Army with the 372d and 378th Rifle Divisions to the Dubtsy Station and Selishchenskoe village sector and add to it the 327th Rifle division, operating west of Selishchenskoe, and the 65th, 92d, and 4th Guards [Rifle] Divisions from the 4th Army.

The 59th Army will deploy its main forces on the western bank of the Volkhov River for an attack from behind the 2d Shock Army's right flank.

The 59th Army's offensive sector is [delineated] on the right by the Pshenichishche (on the Volkhov River), Tushin Ostrov (inclusive), and Bol'shaia Kunest' line and on the left by the Arefino (on the Volkhov River) (inclusive), Priiutino, Sennaia Kerest', and Apraksin Bor line.

Reinforce the 59th Army with the 881st Corps Artillery Regiment and the 827th and 367th RGK Artillery Regiments and bring up the 37th and 430th High-powered Artillery Regiments after the passage of the rifle divisions. The army will then have 100 guns of 76 caliber or greater.

The *front* reserve will consist of the 46th Tank Brigade and the 377th Rifle Division in the Glady region and the 87th Cavalry Division in the Bol'shaia Vishera region.

When this proposal is approved, we can begin relieving units on the night of 22–23 January and begin the regrouping on 23 January. If so, the 59th Army will be ready to launch its attack on 27 January with the 327th, 372d, 65th, and 4th Guards [Rifle] Divisions. The 378th and 92d [Rifle] Divisions will be committed to combat two days later. Furthermore, as the divisions arrive in their designated regions, they will be introduced quickly into the penetration, not expecting the approach of others.

[signed] Meretskov, Zaporozhets, Stel'makh[35]

Later that day, the *Stavka* approved Meretskov's request:

The *Stavka* of the Supreme High Command approves your proposal to develop the 2d Shock Army's success by regrouping the 4th and 59th Armies and, while doing so, *demands:*

1. Conduct the planned regrouping secretly from the enemy.

2. In no way cease the 2d [Shock] and 52d Army offensive operations during the regrouping, but, on the contrary, develop the operations.

[signed] I. Stalin, A. Vasilevsky[36]

On the night of 23–24 January, Meretskov finally convinced himself that Klykov's forces had blasted enough of a hole through German defenses to commit his exploitation force. The next morning Major General N. I. Gusev's 13th Cavalry Corps, consisting of the 25th and 87th Cavalry Divisions and an attached rifle division from the 59th Army, lunged through the narrow gap into the German rear area. However, once Gusev's cavalry and Klykov's infantry made it through the gap, the XXXIX Motorized and XXXVIII Army Corps hurriedly assembled forces to hold the flanks of the penetration and contain the exploiting 2d Shock Army and accompanying cavalry in the forested swamps south of Liuban'. The 59th and 52d Armies struggled to widen the narrow gap at the base of the 2d Shock Army's penetration but were unable to capture the German strong points along the flanks of the gap.

Even though Gusev's 13th Cavalry Corps made it into the Germans' rear area, Meretskov's offensive once again stalled after several days of heavy fighting, this time with about 30,000 Soviet troops lodged precariously in the German rear area. From Meretskov's perspective, this force was in an ideal position to perform its vital mission if he could reinforce it and secure its supply lines. From the Germans' perspective, although the large Soviet force threatened the viability of the entire German defense south of Leningrad, it also represented an enticing target for destruction if they could contain it and sever its tenuous logistical umbilical.

Early on 27 January, Meretskov acted to end the stalemate, issuing orders he hoped would settle the issue once and for all:

In connection with the successful arrival of the 13th Cavalry Corps in the enemy's rear west of the Kerest' River line and the further development of the 2d Shock Army's penetration, I *order:*

1. The 59th Army to attack on 28 January 1942 from the Dymenka River line in the direction of Selishchenskii village, Tregubovo, Piatnitsa, and Aleksandrovka to envelop the enemy Chudovo grouping from the west.

To develop the attack more rapidly, move the 92d Rifle Division through the *front*'s penetration in the 2d Shock Army sector in the direction of Lesopunkt, height marker 38.9, and Priiutino by 28 January 1942. Simultaneously, complete clearing the enemy from the western bank of the Volkhov River to the Polist' River line with the 53d Rifle Brigade and the 374th Rifle Division's 374th Rifle Regiment. The main forces should reach the Korlovo, Piatnitsa, and Sennaia Kerest' region by day's end on 30 January 1942, with one rifle division echeloned from behind in the Bol'shoe Opochivalovo region.

Withdraw the 53d Rifle Division to the Vysokoe region for replenishment when it reaches the Polist' River line. The boundary to the left is unchanged. The 2d Shock Army will form the following operational groups to improve command and control:

    a. Operational Group Korovnikov will consist of the 327th, 374th, and 111th Rifle Divisions and the 22d [Tank] Brigade. The group's mission is to complete liquidating the enemy strong points in the Spasskaia Polist' and Liubino Pole sector along the Leningrad road, after which it will be possible to move the main forces to the Novaia Derevnia, Vditsko, and Finev Lug regions.

    b. Operational Group Privalov will consist of the 191st and 382d Rifle Divisions and the 57th Brigade (Ski). The group's mission is to move the 191st Rifle Division and the 57th Brigade through the penetration in the Lesopunkt region on the night of 27 January 1942, and advance through Ol'khovka and Krivino to the Malaia Brontitsa, Chervino, and Ruch'i regions as rapidly as possible.

After leaving one rifle regiment subordinate to Comrade Korovnikov, on the night of 27 January 1942, the 382d Rifle Division will advance from its occupied region through Priiutino and Sennaia Kerest' to the Podsoson'e and Krapivino region. The operational group's main forces will reach the Kerest' River line by day's end on 28 January 1942.

    c. Comrade Zhil'tsov's Operational Group will consist of the: 23d, 24th, and 58th Brigades. Its mission is to liquidate the enemy in the Zemtitsy and Liubtsy region and, later, sever the Leningrad-Novgorod rail line not later than day's end on 29 January 1942, by developing the attack in the direction of Maloe Zamosh'e and Selo Gora. After capturing the Piatilipy region and Gorenka platform, reliably protect the 2d Shock Army's left flank against attack from the upper reaches of the Luga River.

The 13th Cavalry Corps will continue to perform its existing mission to reach and capture the Liuban' region. Transfer the 53d Rifle Brigade to the 59th Army commander at 0800 hours on 27 January 1942.

The left boundary is Russa, Liubtsy, Maloe Zamosh'e, and Gorenka platform.

3. The 52d Army will capture the Bol'shoe Zamosh'e, Veshki, and Koptsy region no later than day's end on 29 January 1942. Subsequently, it will reach the Tatino Station, Bol'shevodskoe, and Kotovitsy front to protect the *front's* shock group [against attack] from the Novgorod axis.

4. The *front* air force commander will direct the main efforts of aviation to assist the 59th and 2d Shock Armies' offensive and to protect the 13th Cavalry Corps and the 2d Shock and 59th Armies' main forces.

Prevent the approach of enemy reserves from Liuban' and Chudovo and continue to destroy centers of resistance in the Leningrad road sector.

[signed] Meretskov, Zaporozhets, Stel'makh[37]

Meretskov's hope was that, after regrouping, his forces would be able to capture the German strong points, widen the neck of the penetration, and seize Liuban'. Most important, Korovnikov's and Zhil'tsov's operational groups were to seize the German strong points at Spasskaia Polist' and Zemtitsy and then fan out with the third group deep into the German rear area. Simultaneously, Gusev's 13th Cavalry Corps was to advance directly on Liuban', while Meretskov's other armies attacked to distract German attention from his plan's central objective.

However, once again, the 2d Shock Army's assaults on Spasskaia Polist' and Zemtitsy failed, due to what the General Staff described as weak cooperation, ineffective employment of tanks and artillery, and undue reliance on costly frontal attacks. Nevertheless, the remainder of Klykov's force penetrated between the two strong points, advanced 75 kilometers (46.6 miles), and joined Gusev's cavalry. Now over 100,000 Red Army troops were in the German rear area, poised to advance on Liuban' and threatening the very survival of German forces in the Liuban', Chudovo, and Kirishi regions. However, the army's failure to seize Spasskaia Polist' and the difficulties it encountered in moving through terrain covered with frozen swamps and peat bogs seriously hindered the Soviet advance and permitted German forces to contain the thrust.

Kuechler did so effectively on 22 January by assigning Busch's Sixteenth Army responsibility for defending the southern flank of the penetration and Lindemann's Eighteenth Army the northern flank. Busch's XXXVIII Army Corps erected strong defenses south of Miasnoi Bor and at Zamosh'e, and Lindemann's I Army Corps did the same at Spasskaia Polist', Miasnoi Bor, and south of Liuban'. In early February the I Army Corps cordoned off the salient's northern face with its 225th, 212th, 254th, 61st, and 215th Infantry and SS Police Divisions, and the XXXVIII Army Corps the southern face with the 285th and 126th Infantry and 20th Motorized Divisions.[38]

EXPANDING THE OFFENSIVE, FEBRUARY–MARCH

In early February, the *Stavka* dispatched A. V. Krulev, Deputy People's Commissar of Defense for Logistics, to the Volkhov Front to help Meretskov solve his persistent logistical problems. Meretskov then prepared a special assault group under the command of Colonel S. V. Roginsky, which consisted of the 11th Rifle Division and 22d Tank Brigade, and ordered the group to attack the German strong points at Liubino Pole and Mostki, south of Spasskaia Polist'.[39] Roginsky's assault group captured the two strong points on 12 February, thereby widening the mouth of the army's penetration to 14 kilometers (8.7 miles), and Meretskov immediately threw fresh forces into the penetration with orders to advance on Liuban'.[40] On 19 February the 2d Shock Army's 327th, 46th Rifle, and 80th Cavalry Divisions and the 39th and 42d Ski Battalions attacked northward toward Liuban', managing to envelop and capture Krasnaia Gorka at the junction of the German 291st and 254th Infantry Divisions' defenses. Klykov then ordered the two rifle divisions to capture Liuban', which was only 10 kilometers (6.2 miles) distant, and his cavalry and ski forces to cut the Leningrad-Liuban' railroad at Riabovo, 10 kilometers (6.2 miles) northwest of Liuban'.[41]

The 2d Shock Army's advance toward Liuban' and the northwest posed a serious danger to German defenses by threatening to separate the I Army Corps from the rest of Eighteenth Army, destroy it, and open the road to Leningrad. However, the I Army Corps' 291st Infantry Division and Group Haenicke (the 215th and 61st Infantry Divisions) attacked the flanks of the small penetration, recaptured Krasnaia Gorka on 27 February, and encircled the Soviet 327th Rifle and 80th Cavalry Divisions in Riabovo. Although most of the encircled Soviet forces escaped, the Germans claimed bagging 6,000 Russian prisoners by 15 March.[42]

During the weeks of fighting during February, Klykov's forces were able to expand the 2d Shock Army's "pocket" west of the Volkhov River but were unable to break out decisively toward Leningrad. Consequently, an increasingly frustrated Stalin weighed in with a series of new directives exhorting the Volkhov Front to complete their encirclement of German forces in the Liuban' and Chudovo regions and move westward to capture Tosno and raise the Leningrad blockade. He sent Meretskov the first of these directives at 0230 hours on 26 February:

> The *Stavka* of the Supreme High Command does not object to your proposed strengthening of the 2d Shock and 59th Armies' Liuban' and Chudovo groupings.
>
> At the same time, the *Stavka* categorically demands that, under no circumstances are you to cease the 2d Shock and 59th Armies' offensive operations along the Liuban' and Chudovo axes in the expectation of reinforcements. On the contrary, it demands that, after receiving reinforcements, you reach the Liuban'-Chudovo railroad by 1 March in

order to liquidate the enemy Liuban' and Chudovo groupings completely
by no later than 5 March.

[signed] I. Stalin, B. Shaposhnikov[43]

Less than an hour later, Stalin ordered Zhozin's Leningrad Front to accelerate its offensive in support of the Volkhov Front:

The Volkhov Front's forces have begun an operation to destroy the enemy Liuban'-Chudovo grouping.
The *Stavka* of the Supreme High Command *orders:* after the 54th Army's
shock group has been reinforced on 26–27 February, the 54th Army will
launch a decisive offensive in the general direction of Liuban' no later than
1 March. By combining the 54th Army's attack with an attack by the Volkhov
Front's forces, the *fronts'* united forces will completely liquidate the enemy's
Liuban'-Chudovo grouping and capture the Liuban'-Chudovo rail line.
Report the receipt of this order.

[signed] I. Stalin, B. Shaposhnikov[44]

Despite these orders, by late February Meretskov's forces had utterly
failed in their multiple attempts to destroy German forces in the Kirishi,
Liuban', and Chudovo region and raise the blockade of Leningrad. They failed
because they attacked the complex network of German points frontally and
in dispersed and uncoordinated fashion without adequate fire or logistical
support. Because of the *front*'s repeated failures, Stalin dispatched his crony,
Marshal Voroshilov, and GKO member G. Malenkov to Meretskov's headquarters in mid-February to oversee planning for a renewed offensive. With
them was Lieutenant General A. A. Vlasov, who had recently distinguished
himself as commander of the 20th Army in the fighting west of Moscow, who
was to become Meretskov's deputy.[45] One of Malenkov's first acts was to
remove many of the 2d Shock Army's command personnel, including the army
chief of staff and some of his associates.[46] Clearly, Malenkov's mission was to
find scapegoats for past and future failures.

At 0200 hours on 28 February, the *Stavka* once again ordered Voroshilov,
Meretskov, and Khozin to prepare a new plan to accelerate their liquidation
of German forces in the Liuban' and Chudovo region and provided detailed
guidance on how they were to conduct the offensive:

To capture or destroy the enemy's Liuban'-Chudovo grouping and to liberate the Leningrad railroad to Liuban' more rapidly, the *Stavka orders:*
1. Reinforce the 2d Shock Army with no fewer than two rifle divisions
from the 59th Army.

2. Create a single shock group consisting of no fewer than five rifle divisions, four rifle brigades, and one cavalry division reinforced with tanks, artillery, and aviation to deliver a decisive attack in the direction of Liuban' and to the north.

3. The 59th Army will attack with a shock group of no fewer than three rifle divisions in the direction of Torfianoe Station to the west of the Leningrad road to sever the Leningrad road and railroad in the Torfianoe Station region and to capture or destroy the enemy's Chudovo grouping.

4. Create a shock group of no fewer than two rifle divisions on the 4th Army's right flank to attack in the general direction of Larionov and beyond to Smerdynia to link up with the 2d Shock Army's Liuban' group.

5. During the operation, under no circumstance permit the dissipation of the shock groups' forces to protect flanks and rear. Instead, employ units that are not included in the shock groups to that end.

6. Capture and firmly consolidate defenses at Liuban' Station and Liuban' without fail no later than 4–5 March.

7. Report all orders you issue.

[signed] I. Stalin, B. Shaposhnikov[47]

Stalin then reinforced Fediuninsky's 54th Army with Major General N. F. Gagen's newly formed 4th Guards Rifle Corps, which consisted of the 3d Guards Rifle Division and 32d and 33d Rifle Brigades, so that he could accomplish his mission.

Once formulated, Voroshilov's plan required the 2d Shock Army to attack northwest toward Liuban' with a shock group of five rifle divisions, one cavalry division, and four rifle brigades, reinforced with tanks and artillery. The shock group was to cut the Leningrad-Liuban' rail line, link up with the Leningrad Front's 54th Army, and encircle and destroy German forces in the Liuban' and Chudovo regions. Fediuninsky's 54th Army, reinforced by Gagen's 4th Guards Rifle Corps, and Sukhomlin's 8th Army were to attack Liuban' from the north and west. At the same time, the 59th Army, now commanded by Major General I. T. Korovnikov, was to attack and destroy the German force defending Chudovo. The bulk of the Leningrad Front's aircraft were to strike German defenses and rear area installations prior to the attack, which was to commence simultaneously in all sectors on 4 March.

Despite the growing intrigue at Meretskov's headquarters and the *Stavka*'s constant entreaties, the combined force struck as ordered early on 4 March, but once again achieved only limited gains against strong German resistance. During the 54th Army's assault, on 8 March the *Stavka* tried to assist the advance by ordering an intense air bombardment in support of Fediuninsky's army:

The *Stavka* of the Supreme High Command *orders:*

During the period from 10 through 20 March, organize massive air strikes against the enemy's combat formation and defenses in the forward area and in the depth of the offensive sectors of the Volkhov Front's 4th, 59th, and 2d Shock Armies and the Leningrad Front's 54th Army and also against the enemy's main road arteries. To do so:

1. Lieutenant General Novikov, deputy commander of the Red Army Air Forces, is responsible for organizing the air strikes, and Major General of Aviation Comrade Golovanov, the commander of the *Stavka's* Long-range Aviation, is subordinate to him.

2. Insofar as possible, employ eight High Command reserve aviation regiments, Long-range Aviation, and aviation of the participating *fronts* and armies to conduct the strikes, all under the supervision of Deputy Air Force Commander Novikov.

3. Closely coordinate the massive air strikes with ground force operations, conducting them in the following sequence: first, against combat formations and defensive works in front of the 59th Army's shock group along the Chudovo axis; second, in front of the 4th Army's shock group in the Kirishi and Larionov Ostrov region; and third, in front of the 2d Shock and 54th Armies' shock groups in the Krasnaia Gorka region and south of Pogost'.

Simultaneously with these strikes, a portion of the aviation will systematically bomb the Leningrad road and railroad and all associated bridges in the Liuban' and Chudovo region and also indicated cities and towns to end any sort of enemy transport along these roads.

[signed] I. Stalin, B. Shaposhnikov[48]

While these air strikes were being conducted, the heavy ground fighting continued with only meager gains. On 14 March Khozin described his intentions to the *Stavka* and detailed some of the difficulties he was experiencing:

In fulfillment of the *Stavka's* directive to encircle and destroy the enemy Liuban'-Chudovo grouping, we plan to:

1. Withdraw no fewer than four rifle divisions from the Liuban', Chudskoi Bor, and Cheremnaia Gora regions to fulfill the mission of encircling and destroying the enemy's Liuban'-Chudovo grouping in cooperation with the Volkhov Front.

2. At the same time, form a shock group of three to four rifle divisions, one guards rifle division, and three tank brigades from the 54th Army, which is currently operating along the Chudovo axis, by withdrawing forces into second echelon in the Smerdynia, Vas'kiny Nivy, and Ramtsy regions during the battle. [This shock group] will attack along the Tosno axis

between the Makar'evskoe and Pel'gorskoe swamps, while the 8th Army's left flank will simultaneously attack toward Erzunovo and Tosno.

When implemented, these measures will seek to liquidate the Leningrad blockade immediately before the spring thaw begins.

3. An offensive along the Tosno axis only with the forces mentioned above will clearly be inadequate. Strong second echelons will be necessary to strengthen the combat formations from the depths. For this purpose we need a *front* reserve consisting of one to three rifle divisions, three to four rifle brigades, and one tank brigade that can constitute the shock group's second echelon while the operation is developing along the Tosno axis.

While raising this question, we request that you approve the proposed measures and place two to three rifle divisions, three to four rifle brigades, and one tank brigade at our disposal in Volkhov. At the same time, we request that you undertake timely measures to replenish the 54th and 8th Armies' forces with personnel, tanks, and also motors and reserve parts for KV and T-34s in accordance with our two telegrams of 13 March.

[signed] Khozin, Zhdanov[49]

The *Stavka* responded at 0200 hours on 15 March, approving most of Khozin's request but denying him his requested reinforcements:

The main mission of the *front's* 54th Army remains the same. Seize Liuban' and destroy the enemy Liuban' grouping in cooperation with the Volkhov Front's forces. The army's main forces must be committed there.

Before the seizure of Liuban', the *Stavka* of the Supreme High Command considers it expedient to allocate one to two rifle divisions and one tank brigade for operations along the Tosno axis to cover and tie down enemy forces.

When Liuban' is seized, depending on the situation, the main forces of the 54th Army's main grouping can be turned toward Tosno.

At this moment the *Stavka* cannot allocate the additional forces you requested for the 54th Army.

[signed] I. Stalin, B. Shaposhnikov[50]

After several days of intense fighting, Fediuninsky's 54th Army finally managed to penetrate the German 269th Infantry Division's defenses near Pogost'e on 15 March and advanced 22 kilometers (13.7 miles) southward, reaching positions only 10 kilometers (6.2 miles) north of Liuban'. The Leningrad war diary mentioned Fediuninsky's initial success on 13 March, 15 March, and 21 March, devoting more space than usual to his army's feats:

Friday, 13 March. General I. I. Fediuninsky's 54th Army has not ceased its attempts to penetrate to Leningrad from the external side of the encirclement ring. Heavy combat is raging. 39 enemy blindages and bunkers, 8 tanks, and 10 guns were destroyed in this sector in the course of only a single day. Our artillery fire neutralized 5 artillery and 6 mortar batteries. The enemy left more than 500 bodies, 3 guns, 38 machine guns, 360 ammunition boxes, and 2,000 mines on the field of battle. Our forces took prisoners.

Sunday, 15 March. The Volkhov Front's 2d Shock Army and the Leningrad Front's 54th Army are conducting offensive combat with the aim of encircling the enemy Liuban' grouping, which can considerably ease the blockade of Leningrad.

Saturday, 21 March. Attacking in the direction of Liuban', the 32d Rifle Brigade [of the 4th Guards Rifle Corps] encountered swamps that it could not overcome in the winter. With an impenetrable marsh in their front, the enemy was not worried. However, Sergei Polikarpovich Ketiladze, the brigade commander, outwitted the Hitlerites. He led the soldiers in an envelopment and the brigade struck the enemy by surprise at first light on 21 March. The Fascists were forced back, not even managing to withdraw their warehouses from Milaevka and Didvina.

It was only 11 kilometers straight from Didvina to Liuban'. During the next three hours, the 32d Brigade captured yet another village, Kordynei. This considerably eased the situation in the neighboring division, and it occupied the villages of Zenino and Dobroe.[51]

Halder also mentioned the Russian attack in his diary on 18 March but dismissed the action as inconsequential: "In the Volkhov bulge, the enemy attacking power seems to be gradually weakening, but at Pogostye his continual small local gains are not adapted to alter our view of the seriousness of the situation."[52] Less than a week later, on 25 March, Halder took greater note of Fediuninsky's gains but was still not overly alarmed: "Enemy attack at Pogostye resulted in fairly deep penetration, which seems to have been temporarily checked. Mountain infantry is moving up the counterattack."[53]

However, once again heavy German resistance thwarted further Soviet success. Because other Soviet forces in the region, particularly the 4th Army, remained inactive, the Germans were able to shift forces quickly to the threatened sector from Leningrad proper, from the Sixteenth Army, and from the West. These forces, which included the 5th, 93d, 217th, and 21st Infantry Divisions, successfully contained Fediuninsky's advance by 31 March. The other Soviet assaults utterly failed. As described by a Soviet participant in the operation:

The offensive by the Volkhov Front and the Leningrad Front's 54th Army in March and April did not produce optimal results. It once again developed slowly, often halting due to the absence of reserves and material and equipment resources (tanks, ammunition, self-propelled artillery, etc.). These halts and pauses were rather considerable, and they occurred unequally for both *fronts*. For example, having expended its reserves, the Leningrad Front ceased its attacks, and, conversely, having replenished and refitted [its units] with men and equipment, the Volkhov Front continued the attack after the pause. But when the Leningrad Front's 54th Army began its attack, the Volkhov Front's forces had already halted theirs. Thus, the lack of coordination between the *fronts'* operations played into the hands of the enemy. Possessing required auto transport and exploiting the good road network, he could maneuver his reserves, concentrate his forces on our attack axes, and easily parry them.[54]

THE GERMANS' MARCH COUNTERSTROKE

While Meretskov and Voroshilov were orchestrating their March offensive, Kuechler's Army Group North was preparing a counterstroke of its own. During a meeting with his army group commander on 2 March, Hitler ordered Kuechler to mount an operation between 7 and 12 March to close the penetration gap and encircle the Soviet's Liuban' force in conjunction with a counterstroke to relieve German forces encircled at Demiansk.[55] By this time, Kurochkin's Northwestern Front had reached the outskirts of Staraia Russa and had encircled the German Sixteenth Army's II Army Corps in the Demiansk region. In addition, on 23 February Kuechler had assigned the entire defensive sector north and south of the Soviet penetration at Miasnoi Bor to the Eighteenth Army. The new boundary between the Eighteenth and Sixteenth Armies extended due west from Lake Il'men'.[56]

The objectives of Kuechler's attack were two narrow snow-packed Soviet supply lines, which the Germans nicknamed Erika and Dora, that ran through the 10-kilometer- (6.2-mile-) wide corridor between the 2d Shock Army and the Soviet front lines along the Volkhov River. Hitler gave Kuechler 5–10 days to plan the counterstroke, which the OKH code-named Operation Beast of Prey (*Raubtier*).[57] Halder, the chief of OKH, recorded German intent in mounting Operation Raubtier in a diary entry on 2 March: "Start of operations on the Volkhov front: 7 March to last until 12 March. Concentration of air force in that sector is requested for period 7–14 March. Fuehrer specifies air preparation beginning several days before opening of offensive (heaviest bombs against camps in forest). After elimination of the Volkhov salient, no blood is to be wasted on reducing the enemy in the marshes; he can be left to starve to death."[58]

If successful, the German counterstroke against the neck of the Volkhov Front's penetration would thwart the 2d Shock Army's attack on Liuban' and totally encircle Klykov's isolated army. Although Army Group North was ready to begin the operation on 9 March, Kuechler had to delay the operation for one day since the *Luftwaffe* was tied down in dealing with Soviet attacks on Kholm to the south.[59]

Understanding the implications of a successful German counterattack, the *Stavka* ordered vigorous action to counter the German efforts. At 2000 hours on 17 March, while the 54th Army's assault was still under way, it issued new instructions to Meretskov:

> The enemy is attempting to cut off the 2d Shock Army from its commu-
> nications by counterattacks from Spasskaia Polist' toward Miasnoi Bor.
> The *Stavka* of the Supreme High Command *orders:*
>
> 1. While employing all means possible to support the 59th Army's op-
> eration to seize Chudovo and destroy the enemy's Chudovo grouping, at
> the same time, prevent the enemy from severing the 2d Shock Army's
> communications and also completely defeat and destroy the enemy's coun-
> terattacking forces with the 59th Army's left flank and the 52d Army.
>
> 2. The *Stavka* of the Supreme High Command has decided to trans-
> fer the 4th Army's 376th Rifle Division to the Miasnoi Bor region to ful-
> fill this mission.
>
> 3. Comrade Meretskov will be personally responsible for directing the
> operations for the liquidation of the enemy counterattacks from Spasskaia
> Polist', Liubtsy, and Zemtitsy.
>
> 4. To liquidate the enemy counteroffensive rapidly, we envision an op-
> eration by the 52d Army's forces to capture Novgorod before the onset
> of the spring thaw. Submit your views concerning this operation to the
> *Stavka* no later than 20 March.
>
> [signed] I. Stalin, B. Shaposhnikov[60]

However, the warning came too late for Meretskov to do anything about the German counterstroke except what Fediuninsky's army was already doing.

The Eighteenth Army began its counterstroke at 0730 hours on 15 March, when two shock groups totaling five divisions with strong air support attacked from Spasskaia Polist' and Zemtitsy, at the base of the 2d Shock Army's pene-tration, toward Liubino Pole. The northern shock group, with the I Army Corps' SS Police, 61st, and 121st Infantry Divisions, advanced 3 kilometers (1.8 miles) on the first day of its attack, and the southern shock group, made up of the XXXVIII Army Corps' 58th and 126th Infantry Divisions, advanced

1 kilometer (0.6 miles).[61] After two days of agonizingly slow movement through boggy terrain against heavy resistance, the northern shock group severed route Erika on 18 March, and the southern shock group Dora the following day. The two groups linked up on 20 March, trapping the 2d Shock Army in the half-frozen wasteland south of Liuban'. Curiously, the Leningrad chronicles lapse into silence about the German's success, utterly neglecting mention of the 2d Shock Army's predicament.

Even though it successfully slammed shut the door on the 2d Shock Army, the success was tenuous at best. For example, on 23 March, just after the thaw began in the region, the Eighteenth Army's chief of staff reported to the OKH, "It was gradually becoming impossible for the army to keep the Russians from taking Lyuban because it did not have enough men to do so."[62] Worse still for the Eighteenth Army, the Soviets positioned their tanks so that they could rake route Erika with constant fire, preventing the Germans from actually capturing it and turning it into a bloody no-man's-land.

While the German counterstroke was under way, Meretskov frantically formulated plans to thwart the threat and submitted a new proposal to the *Stavka* at 0821 hours on 21 March:

> To complete the destruction of the enemy who are conducting the counter-offensive, the 52d Army can begin the Novgorod operation with the 366th, 305th, 376th, and 65th Rifle Divisions, supported by five RGK artillery regiments, three guards-mortar regiments, and one tank battalion.
>
> Before the operation begins, it will be necessary to replenish all of these divisions, since today they are extremely understrength (together with rear services they have only 5,000 men each). Each division requires 2,500–3,000 replacements.
>
> In favorable conditions, and if the movement of trains with replacements is accelerated, the 52d Army can receive and integrate them by 27–28 March 1942. Simultaneously, during this period we will conduct regrouping, road building, and replenishment of supplies. We propose the offensive commence on 29 March.
>
> The offensive with the 366th, 305th, and 376th Rifle Divisions and a portion of the 65th Rifle Division will begin from the Piatilipy and Bol'shoe Zamosh'e line and develop along the Bolotnaia Platform and Novgorod axis. The overall depth of the offensive along this axis to the northwestern approaches to Novgorod will amount to 34 kilometers (21.1 miles). It will require eight to nine days to traverse this distance. During the final stage of the offensive, the immediate attack on Novgorod will begin on 6–7 April.
>
> When the *front's* main forces reach the Bolotnaia Platform and Nekokhovo front, it will be necessary to conduct an air assault operation with

one airborne brigade to cut approach routes into Novgorod from Bashkovo and Borka. Simultaneously, the 225th Rifle Division will allocate one reinforced regiment and conduct an attack from Slutka to the Volkhov River's western bank to sever the Leningrad highway.

As the operation develops, the 366th Rifle Division will protect it from the west, and the 225th Rifle Division will do so from the east and the north. One regiment of the 372d or 378th Rifle Division will remain in reserve north of Liubtsy. Inasmuch as the 52d Army lacks any sort of second echelon, it is necessary to envision the provision of replacements during the operation so that we do not exhaust the attacking divisions and so that they will be fully combat capable when they approach Novgorod.

I request:

1. Approve the plan for the conduct of the Novgorod operation.

2. Move 12,000 replacements from those already en route to Malaia Vishera Station by 23 March.

3. Provide 10,000 replacements during the period from 28 March through 3 April 1942, to cover losses incurred during the operation.

4. Provide transport aviation for the conduct of the air assault operation and approve the allocation of an airborne brigade for the assault.

In the event you approve our proposals, we will submit a detailed operational plan.

[signed] Meretskov, Zaporozhets, Stel'makh[63]

Within hours the *Stavka* approved his plan:

The *Stavka* of the Supreme High Command basically agrees with your proposals for the conduct of the Novgorod operation. Submit a detailed operational plan by 22 March.

On our orders, the Arkhangel'sk Military District is dispatching one rifle division and the Moscow Military District two rifle brigades as a second echelon for the development of your offensive. These units will begin moving immediately. Familiarize Marshal Comrade Timoshenko with this directive.

[signed] I. Stalin, B. Shaposhnikov[64]

Despite Meretskov's exertions, by 26 March German forces had formed outer and inner encirclement lines along the Glushitsa and Polist' rivers, respectively, around the hapless 2d Shock Army. A Soviet critique held Meretskov directly responsible for the failure:

Thus, the communications of the 2d Shock Army and several 59th Army formations were cut. The tragedy for our forces, which were now practically encircled, began from that moment. This could have been avoided had our command paid more attention to protecting the flanks of the attacking shock group. The persistent enemy counterattacks that began as early as February, as well as the transfer of reserves to the Spasskaia Polist' and Liubtsy region, provided an opportunity to determine the enemy's intent, the more so as our forces' development of the penetration into the depths became prolonged.[65]

THE ENCIRCLEMENT BATTLE, APRIL

Faced with this catastrophic situation, while still planning his Novgorod operation by Iakovlev's 52d Army, Meretskov ordered the partially encircled 2d Shock Army to form a special operational group to spearhead a breakout against the German forces that had cut the 2d Shock Army's communications. The operational group, which was commanded by Major General Korovnikov, consisted of the 372d Rifle and 4th and 24th Guards Rifle Divisions, the 24th and 58th Separate Rifle Brigades, and the 7th Tank Brigade, all from the 59th Army. The group was to attack and link up with the 52d Army's forces and then clear all German forces from the Miasnoi Bor–Novaia Kerest' road at the base of the salient.

Meretskov's new assault with the 2d Shock and 52d Armies, which employed all of his reserves, began early on 27 March. By day's end the desperate and costly assaults drove through the gap, managing to carve a narrow but tenuous gap 3–5 kilometers (1.9–2.5 miles) wide through the German cordon near the village of Miasnoi Bor. At 0815 hours on 30 March, Meretskov dispatched a situation report to the *Stavka*, which detailed the 2d Shock Army's successful reopening of its supply routes and presented recommendations for future operations:

1. The liquidation of the enemy penetrating at the junction of the 52d and 59th Armies is developing successfully. The 2d Shock Army's communications routes have been cleared of the enemy, and in the future we can expect to complete the destruction of his grouping defending southwest of Spasskaia Polist' and restore the situation in the Zemtitsy region in the 52d Army's sector. All of this will permit us to develop the *front's* main operation.

2. The 2d Shock Army's offensive along the Krasnaia Gorka axis toward Liuban' has not developed. The many days of offensive combat in extraordinarily difficult conditions of no roads and forested terrain have yielded no results. The enemy along that axis has succeeded in creating a strong system of strong points in the forests, and further attempts to penetrate the enemy's defenses will lead to still greater exhaustion of our forces.

Therefore, within the shortest possible period, it is necessary for the 2d Shock Army along the Liuban' axis to regroup its forces to its right flank in the Malaia Bronitsa, Dubovoe, and Korovii Ruchei sector. We will concentrate 4 rifle divisions, 2 rifle brigades, and 1 tank brigade and 200 guns, 250 mortars, and 2 heavy guards-mortar regiments in this sector, strike the enemy with massed mortar-artillery fire and air strikes, penetrate the front, and approach Liuban' from the south by attacking to the northeast. Simultaneously, we will cut the highway and rail line between Babino Station and Liuban' to sever the withdrawal routes of the enemy Chudovo grouping. After capturing Liuban' in cooperation with the Leningrad Front's forces, a portion of the 2d Shock Army will attack along the highway to Chudovo and assist the 59th Army in completing the destruction of the enemy's Chudovo grouping.

The 2d Shock Army, organized in its new grouping, will be ready to begin the offensive on Liuban' on the morning of 2 April. This period is necessary for the transport of ammunition, the bringing forward of replacements by auto-transport, and the organization for combat in the new sector.

3. On the 59th Army's front, we will continue operations to destroy the enemy in the Tregubovo, Priiutino, and Spasskaia Polist' regions as the initial stage of the attack on Chudovo. After liquidating the enemy, the 59th Army will conduct an attack toward Turfianovo and cut off Chudovo from the north. Simultaneously, we will conduct local operations to seize the railroad bridge over the Volkhov River.

We will reorganize command and control within the 59th Army on 1 April. We will employ the operational group's headquarters to form the 6th Guards Rifle Corps headquarters, and, at that time, the 4th Guards Rifle Division will be withdrawn into reserve in the Selishchenskii village region for replenishment and refitting. The 377th, 374th, 378th, 267th, 24th Guards, and 372d Rifle Divisions will remain in the 59th Army. The 52d Army can no longer conduct an attack toward Novgorod.

4. Therefore, I intend to conduct the Novgorod operation on the following basis. Before the 2d and 170th Rifle Divisions have arrived, the 52d Army's available forces will conduct local operations to liquidate the bulges in the enemy's positions in the Tiutitsy, Liubtsy, Zemtitsy, and Veshki region with the 376th, 65th, and elements of the 305th and 225th Rifle Divisions. We will attack from the east in order to press the enemy into the swamps and destroy him. Simultaneously, the 366th Rifle Division (the 19th Guards) will liquidate the enemy strong points in the Piatilitsy and Grzi regions. The local operations can begin on 2 April. We will begin the general offensive against Novgorod only after the 2d and 170th Rifle Divisions have arrived.

5. The 4th Army, consisting of four rifle divisions, will continue to defend along a broad front and conduct active reconnaissance. In the event the enemy withdraws, it will prepare detachments for pursuit.

6. The 24th and 58th Rifle Brigades are being withdrawn to the Liubino Pol'e and Miasnoi Bor region for replenishment and, after replenishment, will be dispatched to the 2d Shock Army.

7. Request you approve the ideas stated above on the further conduct of the *front* operation.

[signed] Meretskov, Zaporozhets, Stel'makh[66]

The following day, the *Stavka* once again approved Meretskov's plans.[67] However, as Khozin later noted, Meretskov's report to the *Stavka* was less than completely candid:

On 30 March the Volkhov Front commander reported to the *Stavka* that the liquidation of the enemy who had penetrated at the junction of the 52d and 59th Armies was developing successfully and that communications with the 2d Shock Army had already been opened. [He also reported] that the *front* command intended to complete the destruction of the enemy grouping in the next few days. However, in no way did this report exactly reflect the actual situation. The penetration had been made, but its width did not exceed 1.5–2 kilometers (.4–1.2 miles). Small groups of soldiers, equipment, and supplies could move along such a narrow corridor only at night by using column routes employing wooden planks in the swampy places. In January, at a time when the width of the penetration reached 8–10 kilometers (5–6.2 miles), narrow-gauge was used to supply the 2d Shock Army with all necessities and to withdraw the sick and wounded, and also to evacuate unserviceable equipment. They did not manage to complete this [task], and, later, all that was accomplished was destroyed in the ensuing heavy combat.[68]

Meanwhile, Kuechler relieved his XXXVIII Army Corps commander for failing to seize route Erika, and, over Kuechler's strenuous objections, Hitler demanded that the 58th Infantry Division commander also be relieved.[69] While Kuechler protested, Meretskov struck once again, this time also recapturing route Dora. Losing no time, at 1835 hours on 8 April, Meretskov submitted yet another report to the *Stavka,* once again including proposals for renewing the overall offensive:

The situation along the front on 8 April is characterized as follows:
    a. The communications of the 2d Shock Army have been freed of enemy, and a gap 6 kilometers (3.7 miles) wide has been created in the enemy's defenses at the junction of the 59th and

52d Army, which is clearly not adequate for reliable protection of communications.

b. The 59th Army is attacking in the region southwest of Spasskaia Polist', and a portion of the 52d Army in the region west of Teremets-Kurliandskii in order to widen the penetration further. The 59th Army's attack is developing unsatisfactorily, and, in spite of heavy losses, the enemy is continuing to resist steadfastly in the forests.

c. Along the Liuban' axis, the 2d Shock Army has been unsuccessful after encountering an organized enemy defense on the Tigoda River line. The main reason is the poor organization for combat, the fatigue of the forces following the constant prolonged battle, and the 2d Shock Army commander's fear for his communications.

In accordance with the situation, I propose the following operational plan in the near term:

In the first place, widen the penetration along the Chudovo axis. Subsequently, develop the attack along that axis to reach the Chudovo-Liuban' railroad and capture Chudovo.

The 52d Army will reliably protect the 2d Shock Army's communications from the south and, to do so, dig in along existing positions and form reserves. Part of the force will clear the enemy from the forests south of the line from Height Markers 43.1 to 40.2.

The 2d Shock Army will temporarily cease its attack along the Tigoda River, rest and refit its forces, conduct reconnaissance of enemy forces, and prepare to resume the offensive. During this period conduct local operations to capture the Ruch'i strong point.

Conduct the following measures to strengthen the 59th Army: transfer the 58th Rifle Brigade from the 52d Army to the 59th Army and replenish the brigade with 3,000 men; withdraw the 7th Tank Brigade from combat for two days for reorganization, rest, and replenishment, and then transfer it to the 59th Army; refit the 24th Rifle Brigade; and withdraw the 376th Rifle Division into *front* reserve for replenishment, temporarily deploying it in the Miasnoi Bor region.

Four days are required to conduct the organizational measures to strengthen the 59th Army and to prepare it for an offensive. The general offensive will begin on 12 April. The main attack will be from the west from the region of Height Markers 38.9, 37.8, and 18.4 (see the attached 50,000 scale map) toward Spasskaia Polist' and, simultaneously, from the east from Lesopunkt to height marker 37.8. Concentrate 250 guns, 200 mortars (82 mm or greater), and 3 guards-mortar regiments to support and protect the attack. *Front* aviation will be employed day and night to assist the 59th Army. At the same time, prepare local operations to secure the railroad bridge on the Volkhov River in the Sosninskaia Pristen' region. Before launching the general offensive, conduct local operations from the west to clear the enemy from the column route of the 378th Rifle Division, which is operating southwest of Maloe Opochivalovo, and to strengthen and widen the sector captured in the Mikhalevo and Tregubovo region to halt all movement along the highway and dirt road in those regions.

I request you approve the proposed *front* operational plan.

[signed] Meretskov, Zaporozhets, Stel'makh[70]

At 1500 hours on 9 April, the *Stavka* approved Meretskov's plans for future operations. However, in early April the spring rainy period set in, the roads became impassable for all but foot traffic, and German fire paralyzed virtually all Soviet movement along a corridor 3–4 kilometers (1.9–2.5 miles) wide. Within days, routes Erika and Dora were both underwater; the 2d Shock Army was running short of ammunition, fuel, and food supplies; and command, control, and communications within the 2d Shock Army had become impossible. These appalling conditions left the Leningrad and Volkhov Fronts no choice but to halt their offensive in late April, dig in, and await more favorable conditions to resume the offensive and rescue the 2d Shock Army. As one observer described the situation:

The benefit the Russians gained from retaking the two lanes, however, did not quite equal the pain the loss occasioned for the Germans. The XXXVIII Corps and I Corps held the corridor to a width of less than two miles, and by mid-April, the thaw and constant air and artillery bombardment had turned the lanes into cratered ribbons of mud. Second Shock Army was not strangled but it was choking. Eighteenth Army, for its part, reported that continuing hold on Lyuban owed entirely to "luck and unfounded optimism" both of which could be dispersed at any time by Soviet infantry "and a few tanks."[71]

Given the emerging stalemate, Khozin then asked Stalin to centralize control over all forces operating in the region under his Leningrad Front. Stalin agreed over Shaposhnikov's objections, and on 21 April the *Stavka* ordered the Leningrad and Volkhov Fronts be combined into a larger Leningrad Front consisting of a Leningrad Group of Forces and a Volkhov Group of Forces, effective 23 April:

The *Stavka* of the Supreme High Command *orders:*
1. At 2400 hours on 23 April 1942, combine the Leningrad and Volkhov Fronts into a single Leningrad Front consisting of two groups:

   a. A Group of Forces on the Leningrad Axis (the 23d, 42d, and 55th Armies and the Coastal and Neva Groups of Forces).

   b. A Group of Forces on the Volkhov Axis (the 8th, 54th, 4th, 2d Shock, 59th, and 52d Armies, the 4th and 6th Guards Corps, and the 13th Cavalry Corps).

The Baltic Red Banner Fleet is subordinate to the Leningrad Front commander through the commander of the Group of Forces on the Leningrad Axis.

2. Lieutenant General Khozin is appointed as the commander of the Leningrad Front, and he and his command group are [also] responsible for the Group of Forces on the Volkhov Axis.

3. Lieutenant General Govorov, the [former] 5th Army commander, is appointed commander of the Group of Forces on the Leningrad Axis.

4. Army General Meretskov is relieved from command of the Volkhov Front and appointed deputy high commander of the Western Direction.

[signed] I. Stalin, B. Shaposhnikov[72]

Within days, Meretskov departed his command to become deputy commander of Zhukov's Western Direction High Command.

Although designed to streamline command and control of forces in the Leningrad and Liuban' regions, the new force configuration only served to confuse matters further. Only days before, on 20 April, with Stalin's permission, Meretskov dispatched General Vlasov, his deputy, into the pocket to assume command of the 2d Shock Army from the ailing General Klykov.[73] Vlasov's mission was to reinvigorate the 2d Shock Army's offensive or, failing that, to extricate the beleaguered army from its perilous position.

In four months of intense fighting in terrible terrain and weather conditions, Meretskov's Volkhov Front managed to penetrate German defenses along the Volkhov River, insert a full army into the German rear area, and threaten the German I Army Corps with encirclement. However, skillful and resolute German resistance and numerous severe problems with command and control, fire support, and logistics prevented Soviet forces from exploiting the opportunity and jeopardized over 100,000 troops of the 2d Shock Army in the swamps west of Miasnoi Bor.

THE DEMIANSK DIMENSION

Although the Leningrad-Volkhov offensive failed to meet *Stavka* expectations, the Northwestern Front accomplished considerably more in its portion of the Leningrad-Novgorod offensive. Even so, Kurochkin's *front* fell far short of achieving the ambitious mission the *Stavka* had assigned to it. Morozov's 11th Army began its advance along the Staraia Russa axis on the *front*'s right flank on 7 January.[74] The army penetrated German defenses and advanced 6–7 kilometers (3.7–4.3 miles) on the first day of the operation and almost 50 kilometers (31 miles) in two days of heavy fighting, reaching the eastern outskirts of Staraia Russa. Army ski battalions bypassed German strong points, crossed frozen Lake Il'men' north of the city, and cut the road leading from Staraia Russa to Shimsk, while other army forces dug in along the Lovat' River to the south. Thereafter, however, the army's attack faltered against heavy German resistance.

Berzarin's 34th Army attacked along the Demiansk axis on 7 January, penetrated German defenses, and advanced very slowly through heavy snow in tandem with the Kalinin Front's 3d Shock Army on his left flank. The 34th and 3d Shock Armies reached the Vatolino and Molvotitsy region south of Demiansk, enveloping the German II Army Corps in the town from the south. Halted by heavy German resistance south of Demiansk, Kurochkin ordered his forces to bypass German strong points and, instead, sever German communications. By late January Kurochkin's armies had almost completely encircled the II Army Corps in Demiansk, leaving only the narrow Ramushevo corridor connecting the beleaguered corps with Sixteenth Army's main force at Staraia Russa.

By this time, Red Army forces had utterly demolished the Sixteenth Army's front from Staraia Russa to Ostashkov, and all that stood between the Red Army and Smolensk was a series of unconnected strong points northwest of the city. Kurochkin's forces threatened Demiansk and Staraia Russa, and the Kalinin Front's 3d Shock Army encircled German forces in Kholm.

However, the *Stavka* realized that the fate of its Leningrad-Novgorod offensive depended on its ability to capture Demiansk and Staraia Russa. Accordingly, on 26 January it reinforced the Northwestern Front with the 1st Shock Army and the 1st and 2d Guards Rifle Corps and ordered Kurochkin to seize both towns. His 34th Army and the two reinforcing Guards Rifle Corps were to complete encircling German forces in Demiansk, and the 1st Shock and 11th Armies were to advance toward Sol'tsy and Shimsk to cut the communications line of German forces defending Novgorod and Staraia Russa.

On 29 January the 1st and 2d Guards Rifle Corps attacked the Ramushevo corridor from the north, and the 34th and 3d Shock Armies from the south. After almost a month of complex and bloody fighting, the two forces linked up near Zaluch'e on 26 February, encircling 70,000 Germans in the Demiansk pocket. Soviet sources claim that the Germans lost 3 divisions, 12,000 dead, 185 guns, 135 mortars, 29 tanks, 340 machine guns, 4,150 submachine guns and rifles, 320 motorcycles, 560 bicycles, and 125 supply wagons during the encirclement battle.[75]

With Demiansk encircled, the *Stavka* ordered Kurochkin to reduce the encircled German forces as quickly as possible and advance northwest to help the Leningrad and Volkhov Fronts to raise the Leningrad blockade. This meant that Kurochkin's forces had to destroy the II Army Corps before it fortified its defenses around Demiansk and before the spring thaw set in. To assist Kurochkin, the *Stavka* combined all forces taking part in the reduction of Demiansk, including the Kalinin Front's 3d Shock Army, the 34th Army, and the 1st Guards Rifle Corps, under his control. It also reinforced his forces with five artillery and three mortar regiments in early March and an aviation shock group in mid-March.

Kurochkin's new offensive, during which he employed elite airborne forces in a joint air-ground role, lasted from 6 March until 9 April and ended in failure.[76] The Germans resisted skillfully and resupplied their encircled forces by air. Nor did Kurochkin's forces escape the problems that plagued their neighbors to the north. Soviet critiques credited the failure to weak air and artillery support and poor command, control, and communications. Kurochkin prepared the offensive too quickly, in part because his intelligence reported that the Germans were about to mount an effort to relieve their Demiansk garrison.

Worse still for Kurochkin, true to the intelligence assessment, on 16 March Army Group North assembled a force of five divisions under Group Seydlitz with orders to advance east from Staraia Russa and relieve the encircled II Army Corps. Group Seydlitz attacked on 20 March, linked up with their Demiansk force on 21 April after weeks of prolonged fighting in quagmire conditions, and established a 4-kilometer (2.5-mile) corridor through Ramushevo linking the II Army Corps with the Sixteenth Army's main forces. Urged on by the *Stavka,* Kurochkin's forces attacked incessantly from 3 through 20 May attempting to close the corridor, but all of the attacks failed with heavy losses.[77]

The front in the Northwestern Front's sector finally stabilized along the Lovat' River at the end of May. Soviet after-action critiques blamed the Demiansk failure on inexperience in the reduction of large encircled forces, poor command, control, and coordination, congenital underestimation of German capabilities and intentions, and a failure to fortify the junctions between cooperating forces.[78]

While this immense mosaic of operations was playing out along and west of the Volkhov River and at Staraia Russa and Demiansk, the German Eighteenth Army added insult to Soviet injury by capturing the Leningrad Front's small bridgehead across the Neva River at Nevskaia Dubrovka on 29 April.[79] Meanwhile, the Baltic Fleet conducted operations to shore up Leningrad's defense from the sea, which seemed vulnerable to German attack at the beginning of 1942. The Leningrad Front had lost many of the islands in the Gulf of Finland, the Kronshtadt fortress was isolated, the Germans had mined the seas, and the early frost, which froze the gulf's surface, raised the specter of a German assault on Leningrad across the gulf's frozen surface.

The Leningrad Front and Baltic Fleet responded by organizing all-round defenses of Kotlin Island and Kronshtadt and conducting counter-battery fire against German artillery bombarding Leningrad, Kronshtadt, and the fleet's ships and installations. The fleet also provided artillery and air support for Soviet forces conducting ground operations around Leningrad and protected the ice road. In late December 1941 and early January 1942, fleet naval infantry forces captured several islands in the gulf and defended them against German counterattacks. However, German forces mounted new assaults and recaptured the islands in March, successfully defending them against Soviet counterattacks in April. German aircraft subjected the Baltic Fleet and Kronshtadt to heavy aerial bombardments on 4–5, 24, 25, and 27 April, and struck ships at the mouth of the Neva River with heavy artillery fire, but failed to inflict heavy damage.[80]

When all was said and done, although the Leningrad-Novgorod offensive failed spectacularly, it provided a virtual model for future *Stavka* offensives in the region, in particular, Zhukov's Operation Polar Star the following winter.

As had been the case in the summer and fall of 1941, Red Army military operations along the northwestern axes were closely related to those along other more critical axes. In fact, the Leningrad-Novgorod offensive was but one segment of a far grander *Stavka* scheme designed to defeat three German army groups, raise the blockade of Leningrad, and recapture many lost cities, including Smolensk, Briansk, Orel, Kursk, Khar'kov, and Dnepropetrovsk. Ultimately, the *Stavka*'s aim was to drive German forces back to the Narva, Pskov, Vitebsk, and Gomel' line and southward along the Dnepr River to the Black Sea. However, as the course of events indicated, this aim clearly exceeded the Red Army's capabilities.

During the winter campaign, Stalin and the *Stavka* colleagues displayed congenital over-optimism that would continue to characterize their strategic planning well into the future. Unwarranted rashness, unrealistic objectives, and frustration from not being able to achieve them combined to generate much of the ensuing carnage and damaged the Soviet war effort by squandering precious human and material resources, such as the 2d Shock Army, that more patient leaders could have put to better use.

The Volkhov and Leningrad Fronts lost 308,367 casualties during the ill-fated operation, including 95,064 killed, captured, or missing. The Northwestern Front lost 245,511 more casualties, including 88,908 killed, captured, or missing. In the end neither the Volkhov nor the Leningrad Fronts fulfilled its mission, and the Leningrad-Novgorod operation faltered in the frozen swamps southeast of Leningrad, failing to match the major accomplishment achieved by their neighboring *fronts* to the south. The only saving graces were that the offensive inflicted modest damage on German Army Group North and forced the OKH to reinforce the Leningrad and Demiansk regions at the expense of other more important sectors. While materially assisting the Kalinin and Western Fronts west of Moscow, the offensives denied Army Group North the opportunity to complete its blockade of Leningrad. Finally, contrary to one school of thought, the scope, intensity, duration, and cost of these operations clearly indicated that Stalin wished to raise the Leningrad blockade and made every attempt to do so.

As even Soviet open-source studies indicate, in addition to underscoring Stalin's and the *Stavka*'s blindness, the course and outcome of the offensive revealed gross errors Meretskov, Khozin, and their subordinate commanders made when planning and conducting the offensive. First and foremost, lacking experience in conducting major offensive operations, they neglected to exploit their numerical superiority by concentrating their forces at decisive points, although the orders they received somewhat mitigated their guilt. In this regard, Stalin ordered them to do on a smaller scale precisely what he was doing on a larger scale. As a result, the *fronts* did not coordinate their offensives among themselves, and the armies frequently attacked one after the other in separate sectors where previous attacks had already failed. Throughout the offensive, command, control, and communications often collapsed, and the attacking forces had wholly inadequate fire and logistical support.

All in all, it was a depressing beginning to the new year, and it bode ill for Red Army performance in the coming summer months. Most tragically of all, the offensive's failure condemned Leningrad's civilian and military defenders alike to the specter of unrequited famine, misery, and death during the winter and spring to follow.

CHAPTER 7

Frustrated Hopes

May–October 1942

THE SITUATION ON 1 MAY

In late April the Red Army's winter offensive collapsed in utter exhaustion before fulfilling the ambitious objectives assigned to it by the *Stavka*. Nevertheless, the massive offensive had saved Moscow, denied Hitler his Barbarossa objectives, and inflicted an unprecedented defeat on the *Wehrmacht*.

The Red Army's multiple offensives left the Soviet-German front a crazy quilt of interlocking and often overlapping forces arrayed from the Leningrad region to the Black Sea. Along the northwestern axis, the Leningrad Front's 2d Shock and 54th Armies were deep in the Eighteenth Army's rear but were themselves enveloped from three sides by German forces, and Northwestern Front's forces threatened the flanks and rear of the Sixteenth Army's forces occupying the Demiansk salient and Ramushevo corridor. Along the western (Moscow) axis, Soviet forces, which occupied a deep salient jutting westward from Ostashkov toward Velikie Luki, threatened Army Group Center's forces with encirclement but were themselves threatened with encirclement. In the south, the Southwestern and Southern Fronts' forces in the Barvenkovo salient south of Khar'kov threatened Army Group South's defenses at Khar'kov and in the Donbas, and on the Crimean Peninsula, the North Caucasus Front threatened to relieve Sevastopol' from its forces' bridgehead on the Kerch Peninsula.

The configuration of the front itself, disfigured by numerous salients and large Soviet forces lodged deep in the Germans' rear area, illustrated the unfinished nature of the first six months of wartime operations. Understandably, neither Hitler nor Stalin could accept the winter decision as final, instead viewing it as an aberration that could be corrected in the summer. In short, both sides planned to seize the strategic initiative and complete the missions left unfilled during the first six months of the war.

After considerable deliberation, in spring 1942 the *Stavka* decided to conduct a strategic defense along the vital western axis in the summer against an anticipated new German offensive toward Moscow, while conducting spoiling offensives of their own in southern Russia during the spring. At the same time, Hitler ordered the *Wehrmacht* to conduct Operation *Blau* [Blue], a major offensive by Army Group South to conquer the Stalingrad and oil-rich Caucasus regions. Fuehrer Directive No. 41, issued on 5 April 1942, set the parameters of the offensive, which was to begin in late June:

> The winter battles in Russia have come to an end. Thanks to their distinguished bravery and selfless actions, the soldiers on the Eastern Front have managed to achieve a great success of German arms in the defense.
>
> The enemy has suffered huge losses in personnel and weaponry. This winter he has squandered the majority of those reserves, which were earmarked to conduct subsequent operations, trying to develop imaginary successes.
>
> As soon as the weather and terrain conditions become favorable, the German command and its forces must exploit their superiority once again, seize the initiative, and impose our will on the enemy.
>
> The aim is to destroy conclusively the remaining forces under Soviet control and deprive the Russians of as great a number of important military-economic centers as possible.
>
> All of the German Armed Forces' forces and those of her allies are to be employed to this end. While doing so, everything is to be done in all circumstances to ensure the security and defense of our occupied territory in Western and Central Europe, and especially the sea coast. . . .
>
> While Army Group Center conducts holding operations, capture Leningrad and link up with the Finns in the north and, on the southern flank, penetrate into the Caucasus region, adhering to the original main aim in the march to the east.
>
> Rather than achieving these missions simultaneously along the entire front, instead we will achieve them in separate sectors depending on the situation that resulted from the consequences of the winter battles and also in accord with existing forces and weaponry and transport capabilities.
>
> Initially, it is necessary to concentrate all existing forces for the conduct of a main operation in the southern sector of the front to destroy enemy forces west of the Don River and, subsequently, capture the Caucasus oil regions and the passes across the Caucasus Mountains.[1]

While establishing Stalingrad and the Caucasus region as the *Wehrmacht*'s priority targets in summer 1942, Directive No. 41 also provided context and rationale for Army Group North's summer operations: "We will refrain from the final encirclement of Leningrad and the capture of Ingermannland [Oranienbaum] until such time as the situation in the enveloped areas or the availability of otherwise sufficient forces permits."[2]

Accordingly, Army Group North's initial mission was to improve the Eighteenth Army's operational situation by liquidating the Red Army's bridgeheads on the western bank of the Volkhov River. Subsequently, after the *Wehr-macht*'s offensive in southern Russia began successfully, the OKH planned to reinforce Army Group North so that it could launch its summer offensive. Kuechler's army group was to capture Leningrad, establish contact with the Finnish Army on the Karelian Isthmus, and seize Ingermannland in accordance with Plan *Nordlicht* (Northern Lights), which Army Group North had already prepared early in the previous winter. After seizing Leningrad and establishing contact with the Finns, Army Group North's Eighteenth Army was to sever Soviet rail communications between Moscow and Murmansk. Simultaneously, the army group's Sixteenth Army was to attack southeastward from the Demiansk region in tandem with an attack by Army Group Center's Ninth Army northward from Rzhev. The twin assaults were to encircle and destroy Soviet forces occupying the large salient in the Ostashkov, Kholm, and Toropets regions, which threatened Smolensk and Army Group Center's rear area.

In accordance with Stalin's strategy, the *Stavka* conducted its Khar'kov and Crimean offensive operations in May. However, both operations ended catastrophically with the complete defeat and destruction of both attacking forces. German forces then captured Sevastopol' and the Kerch Peninsula in the Crimea, advanced eastward across the Northern Donets River, and initiated Operation *Blau* on 28 June, totally collapsing Red Army defenses in southern Russia. The German victories at Khar'kov, in the Crimea, and across southern Russia between May and July enabled the OKH to dispatch substantial reserves to the Leningrad region with which to mount Operation *Nordlicht*. However, at the same time, Soviet operations around Leningrad and Demiansk between January and May ended any German hopes of enveloping Leningrad by an advance northeastward from Demiansk. Conversely, the failure of the Soviet Leningrad-Novgorod offensive and the successful German relief of Demiansk worsened the Soviet situation along the northwestern axis and encouraged Army Group North to mount serious new operations in the region.

INITIAL SOVIET ATTEMPTS TO RESCUE THE 2D SHOCK ARMY

In May, with combat raging in southern Russia, the *Stavka* ordered the Leningrad Front to strengthen Leningrad's defenses, conduct local operations to weaken German forces besieging the city, and liberate the 2d Shock Army from the German trap south of Liuban'. Since both the *Stavka* and Khozin well understood how weak the 2d Shock Army actually was, on 30 April Khozin ordered Vlasov's encircled force to occupy an all-round defense, with Gusev's 13th Cavalry Corps in reserve.[3] In the meantime, Khozin, now in command of all Soviet forces east and west of the 2d Shock Army's Liuban' pocket, developed a fresh plan of action to rescue the encircled forces and to hold on to the narrow gap between Spasskaia Polist' and Miasnoi Bor (Map 12). At 0240 hours on 2 May, Khozin submitted his report and proposals for doing so to the *Stavka:*

> I am reporting my views on the conduct of operations by the Leningrad Front along the Volkhov axis.
>
> 1. The *front's* principal mission—to raise the Leningrad blockade—will be carried out by conducting a series of successive *front* operations. In the first place, the operation along the Volkhov axis to complete the destruction of the enemy Chudovo-Liuban' grouping with the 54th, 4th, 59th, and 2d Shock Armies and reach the Maluksa Station, Liuban', Krasnaia Gorka, and Eglino Platform front must be brought to an end. We can conduct this operation by subjecting the enemy to piecemeal destruction by attacking with superior forces in decisive *front* sectors. At present the decisive *front* sectors are:
>
> > a. The Kirishi, Lipovik, and Tigoda Station sector. Liquidation of the enemy in this sector will make it possible to regroup the 4th Army's forces to the western bank of the Volkhov River for subsequent attacks on Chudovo from the north and to regroup the 54th Army's forces to the right flank for an attack on Liuban'.
> >
> > b. The Maloe Opochivalovo, Spasskaia Polist', and Priiutino sector. While the enemy controls the Spasskaia Polist' region, we will not be able to remove the threat to the 2d Shock Army's communications, and any advance by the 2d Shock Army on Liuban' will be constrained by focusing too much on the narrow gate between Spasskaia Polist' and Miasnoi Bor.
>
> In accordance with the operational situation along the Volkhov axis, I request you approve the following plan for immediate operations:
>
> > a. Having completed liquidating the enemy in the forests southwest of Spasskaia Polist', the 59th Army will quickly conduct an operation to liquidate the enemy in the Tregubovo, Spasskaia Polist', and Priiutino regions. The 2d and 377th Rifle Divisions and the 29th Tank Brigade will attack from the east, and the 191st, 259th, 267th, and 24th Guards Rifle Divisions [will attack] from the west. This operation will tentatively begin on 6 May.
> >
> > b. The 54th Army will continue to develop its attack on Lipovik and beyond to Kholmogor State Farm to liquidate the enemy operating in the Kirishi, Posadnikov Ostrov, Lipovik, and mouth of the Tigoda River regions jointly with the 4th Army. At the same

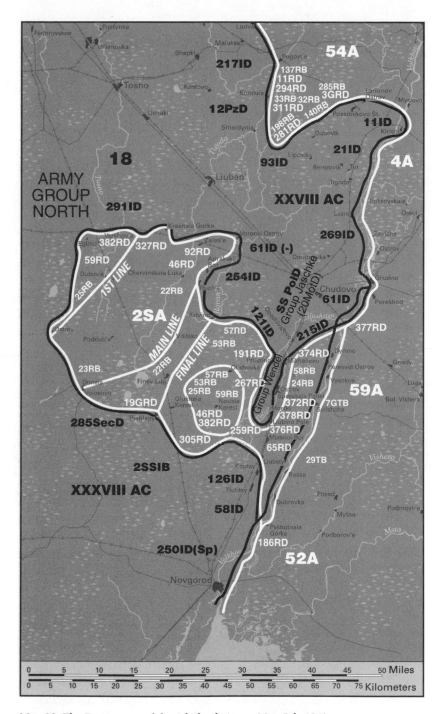

Map 12. The Destruction of the 2d Shock Army, May–July 1942

time, the 54th Army will begin to prepare a subsequent operation along the Smerdynia and Liuban' axis. The 54th Army is rehabilitating the 198th and 311th Rifle Divisions for this operation. Tentatively, the 54th Army can begin the Liuban' operation during the second half of May.

c.   The 4th Army must complete local operations to liquidate the enemy in the Kirishi and Gruzinskii Park regions on the eastern bank of the Volkhov River, after which it will move the 311th Rifle Division to the western bank of the Volkhov River. Subsequently, I intend to assign the 115th and 285th Rifle Divisions to the 4th Army so that it can conduct an offensive toward Chudovo with the 44th, 310th, 115th, and 285th Rifle Divisions.

d.   The 2d Shock Army will temporarily defend its present front. I am detaching the 191st and 259th Rifle Divisions from that army and subordinating them to the 59th Army to form a shock group during the period when the operation to liquidate the enemy in the Tregubovo and Spasskaia Polist' region is being conducted. Simultaneously, the 2d [Shock] Army will prepare to conduct the Liuban' operation. To do so, the army will include, when it is available, the 6th Guards [Rifle] Corps, consisting of the 4th and 24th Guards and 165th Rifle Division and the 24th and 58th Rifle Brigades, which must be refitted by mid-May (besides the 165th Rifle Division). Depending on the 6th Guards Rifle Corps' readiness, tentatively the 2d Shock Army can launch its offensive in the final 10 days of May, that is, at the same time as the 54th Army. The 2d Shock Army's main attack axis will be from the Krivino and Ruch'i regions toward Babino Station so as to cut off and liquidate the enemy Chudovo grouping in cooperation with the 59th Army.

I also intend to employ the 13th Cavalry Corps, which will be concentrated in the Poddub'e, Finev Lug, Vditsko, and Nanezhno regions in reserve by 4 June, to exploit success on the 2d Shock Army's front. The 13th Cavalry Corps will be replenished in that region and tentatively will be ready to participate in the operation by 15 May.

2. The 372d Rifle Division, which, when rehabilitated, can be employed to reinforce the 2d Shock Army, and the 378th Rifle Division, which requires replacements, will be in *front* reserve. The 378th Rifle Division will be deployed in the Liubino Pole region (behind the 52d Army's front) in the event the enemy attacks from the south along the Novgorod-Chudovo railroad.

While presenting these views for approval, I request [that you]:

a.   Confirm the inclusion of the 4th and 24th Guards and 165th Rifle

Divisions and the 24th and 58th Rifle Brigades in the 6th Guards Rifle Corps.

b. Rehabilitate the 24th Guards and 378th Rifle Divisions, the 24th and 58th Rifle Brigades, and also the 7th, 122d, 124th, and 16th Tank Brigades.

c. In view of the rifle forces' extreme weakness, assign 50,000 personnel and 5,000 junior commanders to the *front* reserve during the operation as replacements for 10 divisions.

d. Assign one combat load of ammunition above the established norm during the month of May.

e. Reinforce the Air Force on the Volkhov axis with three fighter aviation regiments and two assault and bomber aviation regiments (a total of 100 aircraft).

f. Strengthen force and fixed air defenses (PVO) by attaching 3 anti-aircraft artillery divisions and 20 batteries of MZA [antiaircraft artillery guns] to fill out rifle division MZA batteries to establishment requirements.

[signed] Khozin, Zaporozhets, Tiurkin, and Stel'makh[4]

Shortly before receiving Khozin's report, at 0040 hours on 3 May, the *Stavka* completed its final command and control arrangements in the Leningrad and Volkhov regions:

As an addendum to *Stavka* Directive No. 170301, dated 21 April 1942, the *Stavka* of the Supreme High Command *orders:*

1. Henceforth, the Group of Forces on the Volkhov Axis, consisting of the 8th, 54th, 4th, 59th, and 2d Shock Armies, is named the Leningrad Front's Volkhov Group of Forces. The Group of Forces on the Leningrad Axis, which consists of the 23d, 42d, and 55th Armies and the Neva and Coastal Operational Groups, is named the Leningrad Front's Leningrad Group of Forces.

2. The Leningrad Front's headquarters and staff, stationed in Malaia Vishera, is the control headquarters for the Volkhov Front. The Leningrad Front Military Council will nominate candidates for the positions of chief of staff, chief of the political directorate, chief of artillery, chief of auto-armored forces, chief of rear, chief of communications, and commander of the Leningrad Front Air Force, and submit the list of candidates to the *Stavka* for approval by 5 May.

3. The Leningrad Group of Forces' headquarters and staff will be in keeping with *front* headquarters and staff establishment No. 02/215 without changes in personnel pay.

[signed] B. Shaposhnikov[5]

Later on the same day, Stalin and Shaposhnikov also approved Khozin's proposals for conducting operations during May, even though they refused to comment on his request for reinforcements.[6] Thus, even before the operation to rescue the 2d Shock Army began, Khozin envisioned withdrawing the 13th Cavalry Corps, four rifle divisions and the 7th Tank Brigade, all of the wounded and sick, and also as much of the army's rear installations as possible through the narrow gap to safety. Ultimately, he was able to do so.

At midday on 12 May, Khozin once again notified the *Stavka* that the Germans were reinforcing their positions at Spasskaia Polist' and north of Liubtsy by deploying the 121st and 61st Infantry Divisions to those regions. To Khozin this was incontrovertible evidence that the Germans were once again about to attack to sever the 2d Shock Army's communications routes through the Miasnoi Bor corridor. Energized by this intelligence, at 2050 hours on 12 May, Khozin ordered the 2d Shock Army to begin planning its breakout:

> For the purpose of allocating additional forces from the 2d Shock Army to destroy the enemy threatening the 2d Shock Army's communications from the north and, subsequently, developing success along the Spasskaia Polist' and Chudovo axis together with the 59th Army, I *order:*
>
> 1. The 2d Shock Army to withdraw its forces successively to the Ol'khovskie, Rogavka, and Lake Tigoda line and occupy that line with two divisions for a strong defense. Pay special attention to the Ol'khovskie axis. Immediately make engineer preparations of that line.
>
> The army's remaining forces, consisting of two rifle divisions and four brigades with two regiments of RGK artillery, will concentrate in the Krechno, Marker 43.7, and Marker 39.8 regions to attack successively from the [Marker] 39.8 and 40.3 line toward Lesopunkt.
>
> 2. Begin withdrawing the army's forces to the new line upon receipt of the order "forward" and conduct it while observing the following requirements:
>
>> a. Covering detachments must occupy the main defense line ahead of time.
>>
>> b. First, withdraw forces from the Chervinskaia Luka, Korovii Ruch'ei, Krasnaia Gorka, Verkhov'e, Konechki, and Veret'e sector to the Chervinskaia Luka, Radofinnikovo Station, Polosatyi Swamp intermediate line. Subsequently, plan on withdrawing all of the army's forces to the intermediate line from Krivino through Nanezhno to Iazvonka. When they arrive at that intermediate line, two rifle divisions and two brigades must be assigned to occupy a main defense line.

    c. Withdraw the forces from their currently occupied positions se-
cretly by leaving covering detachments, reinforced automatic
weapons, and antitank weapons in the positions.

    d. As the forces withdraw, create antipersonnel and antitank ob-
stacles on all march routes and existing and newly constructed
roads and bridges and put brushwood roads out of commission.

3. Upon receipt of this [directive], begin withdrawing the army's
rear service units and installations and also excess troop transport in the
Aleksandrovskaia Colony No. 1, Gorelovo, Ottenskii, and Aleksandrovskoe regions without waiting for orders concerning the withdrawal of
forces to the new line. Leave with those forces only that which is strictly
necessary to sustain the strength of troop formations. Immediately transfer two sapper battalions to the *front's* chief of rear services to support
the passage of the rear services along the Novaia Kerest'–Miasnoi Bor
march-route.

4. Bear in mind that, when it reaches the new defense line, the 2d Shock
Army will include all of the 59th Army's forces that are operating along
the Glushitsa River line and the 52d Army's 19th Guards Rifle Division.

5. Confirm receipt and propose a plan of action promptly by 2400 hours
14 May 1942.

[signed] Khozin, Tiurkin, Stel'makh[7]

On the same day, Khozin summoned the 2d Shock Army's chief of staff
and commissar to his headquarters to coordinate future operations. Together,
they studied the proposed withdrawal plan and agreed on the respective lines
and objectives. Thirty-six hours later, at 0250 hours on 14 May, the *Stavka*
responded to Khozin's proposal and the 2d Shock Army's plan by issuing its
own directive that authorized 2d Shock Army to break out but recommended
some major alterations to Khozin's proposed breakout plan:

The 2d Shock Army's withdrawal to the Ol'khovskie and Lake Tigoda line
will not benefit us greatly since it will require no fewer than four rifle divisions to hold on to that line. Besides, the withdrawal of the army to the
Ol'khovskie and Lake Tigoda line will not eliminate the threat to army
communications in the Miasnoi Bor region.

Therefore, the *Stavka* of the Supreme High Command *orders:*

1. Withdraw the 2d Shock Army from the region it occupies and destroy enemy forces in the Priiutino and Spasskaia Polist' bulge by simultaneous attacks by the 2d Shock Army from west to east and by the 59th
Army from east to west.

2. Upon completion of this operation, the 2d Shock Army will concentrate in the Spasskaia Polist' and Miasnoi Bor region (inclusive) and, together with the 59th and 52d Armies, firmly consolidate its position along the Leningrad railroad and highway on the western bank of the Volkhov River.

3. Confirm receipt.

[signed] I. Stalin, A. Vasilevsky[8]

By authorizing this breakout attempt, the *Stavka* tacitly admitted the error it had made on 21 April when it had united the two *fronts* under a single command and also acknowledged the terrible consequences of that error. This recognition, however, did little to alleviate the 2d Shock Army's current dilemma.

Having received the fresh *Stavka* guidance, at 1901 hours on 15 May, Khozin sent yet another plan to the *Stavka* for its approval:

The operation for the withdrawal of the 2d Shock Army will consist of several phases. The operation's first phase is set forth in Appendix No. 24 [to our 12 May directive]. The main mission of this phase is to disengage forces for an attack by the 2d Shock Army from west to east against the bulge south of Spasskaia Polist' by successive withdrawals from the lines. The Ol'khovskie and Lake Tigoda line has been selected as most favorable for that purpose. Only by securing that line can the 2d Shock Army deliver an attack to the east.

The 2d Shock Army must hold on to that specific line because it covers the sole road (Ol'khovka–Novaia Kerest') necessary for the deployment of the 2d Shock Army's shock group during its operations to the east.

The operation's second phase will fulfill the operation's final aim—the subsequent withdrawal of the 2d Shock Army and also part of the 59th and 52d Armies to positions that protect the Leningrad railroad, highway, and bridgehead on the western bank of the Volkhov immediately to their rear. I will present a specific operational plan for that phase as the situation becomes clearer as a result of the operation's first phase.

I request that you approve [Appendix] No. 24 as the first phase of the *front's* operation as fully responding to the contents of your first Directive No. 170379 of 14 May 1942.

[signed] Khozin, Zaporozhets, Stel'makh[9]

The *Stavka* approved Khozin's revised plan at 1430 hours on 16 May, and Khozin then authorized Vlasov's 2d Shock Army to begin its breakout in concert with the 59th Army's attacks from the east.[10] Heavy, chaotic, but mostly futile combat raged for several days as the ragged remnants of Vlasov's once proud 2d Shock Army, in large and small groups, tried desperately to reach the Volkhov Front's lines. However, Korovnikov's 59th Army could not fulfill its mission, primarily because its formations were woefully under strength and lacked both tanks and reserves. Worse still, the narrow corridor was at the junction of the 59th and 52d Armies, and it was virtually impossible to coordinate their operations with those of the 2d Shock Army.

In the midst of the 2d Shock Army' death throes, at 1720 hours on 21 May, the *Stavka* sent its last directive to Khozin demanding that the 2d Shock Army break out once and for all:

The *Stavka* of the Supreme High Command *orders:*

1. The immediate missions of the Leningrad Front's Volkhov Group are to:

    a. Firmly defend the 8th and 54th Armies' fronts to prevent an enemy penetration from Mga Station to Volkhov.

    b. Clear the enemy from the eastern bank of the Volkhov River in the Kirishi and Gruzino regions no later than 1 June 1942. Personally prepare and provide fire support for these operations. Destroy the railroad bridges over the Volkhov River at Kirishi and Volkhovo Station and 6 kilometers (3.7 miles) southeast of Chudovo during the next four to five days with the help of specially assigned long-range aviation.

    c. Withdraw the 2d Shock Army's forces, while reliably protecting them against attacks from the west along the Ol'khovskie and Lake Tigoda line, and destroy the enemy in the Priiutino and Spasskaia Polist' bulge with simultaneous attacks by the 2d Shock Army from the west and the 59th Army from the east.

    d. Prevent the enemy from penetrating along the Leningrad highway from Novgorod to Kerest' by a reinforced defense, in particular, antitank, on the 52d Army's left flank.

2. When the enemy in the Kirishi and Gruzino regions and in the Priiutino and Spasskaia Polist' salient have been destroyed, the Volkhov Front's principal missions are to:

    a. Reliably protect the Mga and Liuban' axes with the 54th and 8th Armies to prevent the enemy from attacking Volkhov and, subsequently, Lodeinoe Pole and, at the same time, reliably protect Leningrad's communications. To that end, you may reinforce that front sector with one or two rifle divisions from the 59th and 2d Shock Armies. Form a rear defensive line along the eastern bank of the Volkhov River.

    b. Reliably defend the eastern bank of the Volkhov River in the Kirishi and Gruzino sectors with the 4th Army to prevent any enemy attempt to force the Volkhov River and attack in the direction of Budogosh' and Tikhvin.

c. Reliably protect the bridgehead on the western bank of the Volkhov River in the Spasskaia Polist', Miasnoi Bor, and Zemtitsy regions and the Leningrad railroad and road with the 59th and 2d Shock Armies and the 52d Army's right flank to prevent the enemy's Novgorod and Chudovo groups from linking up along that road and restoring the Novgorod-Leningrad railroad.

d. Reliably protect the Novgorod and Krestitsy axis with 52d Army's center and left wing.

The *Stavka* of the Supreme High Command requires that the Leningrad Front Military Council's pay special attention to strengthening the 54th, 8th, and 52d Armies' engineer defenses as quickly as possible.

While doing so, pay attention to the construction of observation and command posts, pillboxes, and reserve firing positions for machine guns, mortars, antitank weapons, antitank rifles, and artillery batteries. The system of blocking fires in front of the forward edge and in the depth of the defense must guarantee cooperation between the firing points and protect the guns of the antitank defense.

Pay special attention to the reliable fortification of population points, defiles, and intersections and road junctions. Dig ditches in all roads and, along the forward edge, mine them so that they can be cleared in any sector, and open passages for our forces in case we conduct offensive operations. Note down precisely on 100,000 or 50,000 maps all work associated with the employment of explosives and mining, the latter in the headquarters of divisions and armies. Construct the defenses of populated points on the basis of a system of intersecting and flanking fire by machine guns and antitank rifles with extensive employment of mine obstacles, fougasse, and MZP [*malozametnye prepiatsviia*—hidden obstacles].

While doing so, rear service units and installations will prepare populated points in the depth of the defense up to the rear defensive belt.

Require that the troops and all chiefs carefully camouflage weapons and command posts and observe camouflage discipline in all defensive belts.

4. For the sake of command and control, after liquidating the enemy in the Spasskaia Polist' region, reorganize the Volkhov Group of Forces into two groups. The Ladoga Group, consisting of the 54th and 8th Armies, will deploy along the front from Lake Ladoga to the Volkhov River at Kirishi. The Volkhov Group, consisting of the 4th, 59th, 2d Shock, and 52d Armies, will deploy along the Kirishi, Gruzino, Spasskaia Polist', and

Zemtitsy front and, farther, along the Volkhov River to Lake Il'men'. Appoint commanders and staffs for these groups. The Leningrad Front's Military Council and headquarters are freed from command of Volkhov Group's forces. Present your views on this reorganization and the personnel appointments to the *front* military council to the *Stavka* for approval by 1 June 1942.

5. Assign the following to the Leningrad Front to strengthen the Volkhov Group:

    a. The chief of the General Staff and the chief of the Main Directorate for Manning [will assign] 25 battalions of equal size, including 6 by 30 May and the remaining 19 in June, to reinforce the 54th, 8th, 4th, and 52d Armies.

    b. The chief of the Main Artillery Directorate [will assign] 6 antitank regiments from the USV by 5–10 June, 500 heavy machine guns during June, 1,000 submachine guns in June, and 5,000 PPSh by 1 June.

    c. The chief of the Auto-Armored Directorate will replenish the 7th Guards and 29th Tank Brigades by 26 May by sending them the missing quantity of tanks and send two tank brigades (without motorized rifle battalions) consisting of 50 tanks each to the 4th Army by 27 May. During June replenish the group's remaining four tank brigades, two of them by 10 June.

[signed] I. Stalin, A. Vasilevsky[11]

THE RED ARMY'S TRAGEDY AT MIASNOI BOR

In accordance with the *Stavka*'s directive, the entire Leningrad Front and the Leningrad and Volkhov Groups of Forces went over to the defense. While doing so, Khozin also agreed with a *Stavka* request to dispatch the fresh 6th Guards Rifle Corps, which Meretskov had intended to employ in the relief of 2d Shock Army, to reinforce the Northwestern Front's operations at Demiansk.[12] By this time, Vlasov's beleaguered army had decreased in strength by 60–70 percent and lacked tanks, artillery, ammunition, and food supplies. Because of the lack of requisite manpower and weaponry, the Leningrad Front also ceased active operations to raise the Leningrad blockade. The *Stavka* also finally realized that the earlier unification of the Leningrad and Volkhov Fronts had been a mistake that had only complicated command and control of forces in the region. The directive's provision to divide the Volkhov Front into two parts was a belated attempt to remedy this problem.

Despite its obvious weakness, Vlasov's army repeatedly attempted to resume its offensive over the next few days in accordance with the *Stavka's* and *front's* instructions. Throughout this heavy fighting, once the roads and columns routes had dried out a bit, some of the encircled forces made their way out of the pocket to safety. For example, on 16 May, Gusev's 13th Cavalry Corps, the 24th and 58th Guards Rifle Brigades, the 4th and 24th Guards Rifle Divisions, the 378th Rifle Division, and the 7th Guards and 29th Tank Brigades managed to make their way eastward out of the Liuban' pocket through the treacherous corridor.[13]

On 24 May Vlasov's army began to withdraw to its first designated position from the middle course of the Tigoda River through Ravan' to Vditsko. The 92d and 327th Rifle Divisions and the 22d and 23d Rifle Brigades reached and occupied the main defense line from Ruch'i along the Ravan' River to Vditsko, Rogavka Station, to Lake Tigoda on 28 May. The 2d Shock Army's remaining forces continued to withdraw to jumping-off positions north of Novaia Kerest' to launch an attack to link up with the 59th Army, which was set to begin on 5 June.[14] In the meantime, the 181st and 328th Rifle Divisions and an army artillery regiment accompanied by many sick and wounded and some heavier equipment managed to escape from the pocket by 1 June.[15]

However, at this critical juncture, the Germans detected the Soviet movement and quickly organized attacks with strong air support along the Novgorod-Chudovo railroad from the north and south that slowly squeezed the narrow passage at the junction of the 59th and 52d Armies. According to a German account:

> In mid-May, the number of deserters increased, which could have been taken as a sign of disintegration. Some of them said that *Second Shock Army* was being evacuated, but probing attacks met sharp resistance all around the perimeter. The first outward movement, of about a thousand men, was seen on the 21st.
>
> Another thousand went out on the 22d, and General Vlasov's radio closed down, a sign that he was shifting his *Twentieth Army* [should read: *Second Shock Army*] command post.[16]

Consequently, on 24 May, Kuechler called Lindemann, informed him that it would be "awfully bad" to let the Russians escape and ordered him to launch an attack to trap the remainder of Vlasov's army.[17] The next day Lindemann assigned this task to his XXXVIII and I Army Corps. The I Army Corps' 254th, 61st, 121st, and SS Police Divisions and the XXXVIII Army Corps' 58th Infantry Division, 2d SS Infantry Brigade, and 20th Motorized Division were to participate in the offensive.[18] After a rain delay, the two corps began their joint attack against the base of the 2d Shock Army's pocket on 30 May. Despite suffering 30 percent casualties, the XXXVIII Army Corps continued its assault into the night, linking up with the I Army Corps' forces at 0130 hours on 30 May, severing vital route Erika. The two corps established a continuous front facing east at 1200 hours on 31 May and a front facing west later in the day.[19]

Finding themselves now totally trapped, the remnants of Vlasov's once proud army desperately made one final lunge eastward toward safety. The 2d Shock and 59th Armies' shock groups, which, according to German reports, consisted of troops who were all "drunk," struck German defenses east and west of the Polist' River at 0200 hours on 5 June. Although most of the 59th Army's shock group managed to reach the Polist' River's eastern bank, the 2d Shock Army's poorly organized attack faltered and then failed in the face of well-organized German resistance and counterattacks. In fact, the German counterattacks actually penetrated the 2d Shock Army's positions and captured Ruch'i, Vditsko, and Rogavka Station, while other advancing German forces captured Finev Lug and threatened the shock group's rear area north of Novaia Kerest'.[20]

An enraged Khozin demanded in vain that Vlasov's army repel the attacks and restore their defenses by day's end on 6 June.[21] Instead, the Germans resumed their attacks on the morning of 6 June and totally severed the corridor between the trapped Soviet forces and freedom. The trap contained seven rifle divisions and six rifle brigades, totaling up to 20,000 men.[22]

When Khozin reported the sad news to the *Stavka*, Stalin simply admitted failure by issuing yet another directive at 0300 on 8 June, which abolished the obviously ineffective existing command and control arrangements and censored key command figures involved in the disaster:

The *Stavka* of the Supreme High Command *orders:*
  1. Divide the Leningrad Front into two independent *fronts:* the Leningrad Front will consist of the Leningrad Group of Forces' present forces, and the Volkhov Front will consist of the Volkhov Front's present forces.
  2. Abolish the Leningrad and Volkhov Groups of Forces.
  3. Establish the existing line between the Leningrad and Volkhov Groups of Forces as the boundary line between the Leningrad and Volkhov Fronts.
  4. Relieve Lieutenant General Khozin of his command of the Leningrad Front for his failure to fulfill the *Stavka's* order regarding the timely and rapid withdrawal of the 2d Shock Army, for his bureaucratic control methods, and for isolating himself from his forces. As a result, the enemy cut off the 2d Shock Army's communications and placed the latter in an exceptionally grave situation. Appoint [Khozin] to command the Western Front's 33d Army.

5. Dismiss Comrade Tiurkin from his position as member of the Leningrad Front's Military Council for his inability to cope with his duties and place him at the disposal of the Leningrad Front Military Council.

6. After releasing him from command of the 33d Army, appoint Army General Comrade Meretskov to command the Volkhov Front.

7. Appoint Lieutenant General Comrade Govorov, the commander of the Leningrad Group, to command the newly formed Leningrad Front.
[signed] I. Stalin, A. Vasilevsky[23]

Immediately after restoring Meretskov to Volkhov Front command and appointing Govorov to Leningrad Front command, Stalin dispatched Vasilevsky as *Stavka* representative to redeem what he could of the parlous situation. That was not very much since it was simply too late to correct the situation. By this time, Vlasov's encircled army was threatened as much by starvation as by German forces. For example, on 19 June, Division Commissar I. Zuev, a member of the 2d Shock Army's Military Council (commissar), reported to Meretskov, "Aviation failed to deliver foodstuffs today. As of 19 June 1942, there is not a single gram of food left. Many are disabled by emaciation. In spite of this, the people's mood is sound. The units are fighting very heroically."[24] Two days later, Zuev reported, "For three weeks now, the army's forces have received 50 grams (1.6 ounces) of dried bread per day. During the past three days we have had no food at all. . . . The personnel are famished to excess. . . . There is no ammunition."[25] A letter from a soldier named A. Baziuk underscored the seriousness of Zuev's distressing reports: "We ate everything that could be eaten . . . [including] tree leaves and fir cones. We boiled old horse bones and gnawed on them. I say nothing about the bark—all the trees around us were stripped. Any insects, worms, and frogs were used as food. Birch sap was of great help, but, in the middle of May, it disappeared, and we suffered distressingly until the end of June."[26]

Despite the deprivations it suffered, the 2d Shock Army continued its desperate fight to escape destruction. For example, the army's 46th Rifle Division and 25th and 57th Rifle Brigades made brief contact with the 59th Army's 25th Cavalry Division during an attack on 19 June, thereby briefly establishing a corridor 300 meters wide through which some of the soldiers escaped. Once again Red Army soldier Baziuk described the scene: "No imagination can recreate what was happening in the Valley of Death. A continuous wall of fire, unceasing howling and roaring, a stupefying stench of burnt human flesh . . . and thousands of people rushing into this fiery corridor. We all thought that it would be better to die in fire than be captured by the Germans. But only those who could move tried to escape. Many collapsed from famine or could not move because of wounds, and all of them still lie there."[27]

Yet another joint attack by the 59th and 2d Shock Armies on 21 June resulted in 6,000 more troops escaping from the trap by overnight on 21–22 June.[28] However, that night Vlasov's encircled army lost communications with the Volkhov Front's headquarters, and German forces once again penetrated the encirclement ring and advanced toward Novaia Kerest'. All escape attempts had ceased by 0935 hours on 25 June, and Vlasov's forces were never again able to restore communications. Soon after, Vlasov himself fell into German hands and with him thousands of his exhausted soldiers. Soviet sources claim that another 9,322 soldiers escaped to Soviet lines singly and in small groups while the 2d Shock Army was in its death agony.[29]

Although the *Stavka* was unaware of Vlasov's fate, it did everything in its power to determine the army's fate and ensure its continued resistance if its collapse continued and retrieve the general and his staff in obvious fear that they would fall into German hands. For example, on 24 June the General Staff notified the Volkhov Front:

> It is known from the Volkhov Front's reports that healthy soldiers from the 2d Shock Army's units are exiting through the penetration and are being placed in reserve behind the 59th Army's front lines.
>
> The General Staff considers that such a practice of withdrawing the 2d Shock Army can lead to healthy people withdrawing from the encirclement, while abandoning their weapons to the enemy. It recommends you not weaken the 2d Shock Army by prematurely withdrawing healthy soldiers with weapons from it but instead accelerate their provision with necessary amounts of reinforcements, ammunition, and foodstuffs.
>
> [signed] Bodin, Bokov[30]

On 13 July the General Staff sent a message to the Volkhov Front's chief of staff ordering him to accelerate the rescue of the 2d Shock Army's command cadre and staff:

> The withdrawal of groups and individuals from the 2d Shock Army's units is continuing. Among those withdrawing are persons from mid- and senior-level command cadre, who undoubtedly possess information, which when carefully analyzed and compared, can reveal the state of the 2d Shock Army.
>
> Despite this fact, the Volkhov Front does not have this information and has reported nothing concerning the situation of the 2d Shock Army's units, which remain in encirclement.

Undertake immediate measures to gather this data from those who have escaped from encirclement and also personally interrogate the withdrawing command cadre and present their views on this matter by 20 July 1942.

[signed] Tikhomirov, Ryzhkov[31]

As late as 17 July, Stalin ordered Meretskov to do all in his power to save the army commander:

According to your reports, Vlasov, his chief of staff, and his chief of communications are located with Comrade Sazanov's partisan detachment.

The *Stavka* of the Supreme High Command *orders:*

You are personally responsible for undertaking all possible measures to see to it that Vlasov and his people are delivered to the *front's* territory [rear] no later than 19 July.

The *Stavka* considers it a matter of honor for you to fulfill this mission.

The *Stavka* orders you to employ all of the *front's* aviation in the fulfillment of this mission.

Report fulfillment.

[signed] I. Stalin, A. Vasilevsky[32]

In their memoirs both Vasilevsky and Meretskov blamed Vlasov for much of the 2d Shock Army's tragedy, and virtually all Soviet sources have since echoed their condemnation. In addition to accusing Vlasov of treason during the operation, they also condemned him for being unable to unite his men and hold the corridor open. However, they were incorrect on both counts. For example, Meretskov admitted that his own attempts to "form detachments from retreating units and use them to protect the corridor also proved futile."[33] Yet some 2d Shock Army units did fight their way out of encirclement, including the 92d Rifle Division, which brought 83 utterly exhausted men out of the trap.[34]

Nor did Vlasov commit treason in June 1942. For example, as late as 21 June, the army newspaper *Otvaga* (Courage) published army orders that awarded 31 of the 2d Shock army's soldiers with the medals "For Valor" and "For Combat Merit." Vlasov himself, along with Military Council Members Zuev and N. Lebedev and army chief of staff Colonel P. Vinogradov, signed the orders, hardly an act of traitors. Reports also make it clear that Vlasov was still in command on 25 June, the day that the Germans finally closed the corridor forever. As for the fate of the surrounded troops, all information indicates they suffered with courage and selflessness. Accordingly: "Surrounded by the Nazis, Division Commissar I. Zuev shot himself, Divi-

sion Commissars S. Bulanov and F. Chornyi were killed when leading their men in attacks. Unwilling to expose his friends to additional risk, badly wounded A. Shashkov, chief of the 2d Shock Army's Special Department [Counterintelligence], committed suicide. Many other heroes preferred death in a mortal clash with the enemy to shameful captivity."[35]

As for Vlasov, recent accounts describe his fate:

But what had really become of Vlasov? Soviet scouts and partisans were looking for him to help him cross the front line, but he disappeared. One can get the impression that the army commander finally lost his head and was in no hurry to return. Why?

An answer to this question can be found in the reminiscences of T. Tokarev, [Vlasov's] "official biographer." Scolding Vlasov, this journalist mentions one interesting detail. It turned out that after the Germans finally closed the gap on 25 June, Meretskov sent a coded order to arrest Vlasov, evidently intending to use him as a scapegoat to bear the blame for the defeats of army troops.

A reasonable question arises: Could Meretskov have given such an order? Let us reason out the situation he was in. Only six months had elapsed since Stalin had mercifully released Meretskov from the NKVD's prison cellars. His command over *front* forces was far from ideal. He remembered well the dismal end of the Western Front commander [Pavlov] shot by Stalin's order at the beginning of the Great Patriotic War. And it was Meretskov himself who recommended the appointment of Vlasov as the commander of the 2d Shock Army. In those troubled times, when, by a single order, Stalin could declare hundreds of thousands of his soldiers to be traitors, Meretskov *could* issue the order to arrest Vlasov to save his own reputation.

If Vlasov knew about Meretskov's order, he naturally understood that his career and life itself were at stake. He got cold feet and for a long time hesitated to show up. According to the testimonies presented at the court-martial trying his case, only on 11 July, i.e., after more than two weeks wandering in the forests, did he surrender to the enemy and embark on the path of treachery. By that time, part of the 2d Shock Army would have forced its way to its own troops, and the bulk would have perished. Vlasov's betrayal would have played no part in its fate.[36]

German forces reported capturing 15,000 Red Army troops at the Miasnoi Bor corridor's eastern end in mid-June and another 33,000 by 28 June. Official Russian sources indicate that the Red Army lost 308,367 men during the Liuban' operation from 7 January through 30 April 1942, and another 94,367 men during the May and June relief operations (see Table 3). Of this figure,

Table 3. Soviet Losses on the Volkhov Front in the Liuban' Operation, 1942

	7 Jan.–30 Apr.	13 May–10 July[*]
Soviet forces committed to combat	325,700	231,906
Irrevocable losses	95,064	54,774
Medical losses	213,303	39,977
Total losses	308,367	94,751

[*]Operation to free encircled 2d Shock Army.

Source: G. F. Krivosheev, ed., *Grif sekretnosti sniat: Poteri vooruzhennykh sil SSSR v voinakh, boevykh deistviiakh, ivoennykh konfliktakh* [The classification secret is removed: Losses of the USSR armed forces in wars, combat operations, and military conflicts] (Moscow: Voenizdat, 1993), 224–225.

the total casualty count in Vlasov's 2d Shock Army was more than 66,000 men killed, missing, or captured.

Once Soviet and Russian analysts and historians officially recognized the existence of the Liuban' disaster, they agonized over who should take the blame. Initial assessments made during the Khrushchev period assigned blame evenly to the *Stavka* and Soviet force commanders. Writing after the war, Khozin offered criticisms that were equally applicable to virtually all Red Army operations during the winter campaign:

> Speaking of the causes of the unsuccessful winter offensive by the Leningrad and Volkhov Fronts, it would not be entirely correct to refer only to the *Stavka.* To a great degree these failures depended on the *front,* army, and formation commanders and on the training of the staffs and the troops. The organization and command and control of combat operations by army and division headquarters were not sufficiently high.
>
> One of the main [reasons for the failure] was the overall serious situation faced by our country and armed forces as a result of the defeats we suffered during the summer-fall campaign. The enemy approached Moscow, occupied the Ukraine, Crimea, and the Donbas, and captured many regions of economic and strategic importance to our country. Military production sharply decreased, and there were very few tanks and aircraft and insufficient ammunition, fuel, and even rifle weaponry. These severe conditions forced the commitment into combat of reserve formations and units lacking adequate training and cohesion. . . .
>
> Objectively discussing the activities of the Supreme High Command during the winter campaign of 1941–1942, one must say that it was in a very difficult situation: it needed to throw the enemy back from Moscow, raise the Leningrad blockade, and prevent the Hitlerites from penetrating into the Caucasus. Gathering up reserves, the Supreme High Command struck the German-Fascist forces along the decisive axis during the Battle for

Moscow. In difficult conditions it launched counteroffensives at Tikhvin and Volkhov that completed the defeat of German forces and prevented them from reaching the Svir River and linking up with the Finnish Army. But despite these rather large-scale successes, it was not possible to penetrate the Leningrad blockade without the use of considerable forces from other *fronts* and the *Stavka* reserve. At that time the enemy was at the zenith of his power.[37]

According to Khozin, a host of structural problems compounded these grim strategic realities:

Great deficiencies existed in force organization and in the operational and tactical training of command cadre, staffs, and forces. The heavy losses that we suffered in the initial months of the war and the reduction in military production associated with the evacuation of industry from the western and southern regions to the east led to the creation of new formations that lacked required quantities of artillery, mortars, tanks, and other equipment. This prevented the Supreme High Command from forming rifle, motorized, and tank divisions. Instead, they formed separate rifle and tank brigades and two-company tank battalions (20 tanks). The absence of self-propelled artillery was a great minus. The abolition of the corps level complicated troop command and control by army commanders. Armies operating along main attack axes consisted of 10–15 varieties of formations. In these conditions with so many subordinate formations, it was a complex task and practically impossible for army commanders and their staffs to look after and organize command and control in all of their divisions and brigades.[38]

Nor was the situation any better operationally:

There were also blunders in the operational direction of forces. In an operation as serious as the raising of the Leningrad blockade . . . the Volkhov Front's forces performing the main mission in that operation had a single echelon operational formation without strong *front* reserves. There were no groups at all in the *front's* operational formation to exploit the penetration. General N. I. Gusev's 13th Cavalry Corps was subordinate to the 2d Shock Army and employed like a rifle formation. With such an operational formation, the *front* could neither strengthen the attack nor parry counterattacks. The low densities of tanks in the units' and formations' combat formations (three to four tanks per kilometer of front) and insufficient densities of artillery fire had an [adverse] impact on offensive tempo. . . . A great deficiency in the organization and conduct of the Volkhov Front's offensive operation was the weak flank protection for the 2d Shock Army's shock grouping, which ultimately led to catastrophe and the failure of the entire offensive operation.[39]

Khozin also criticized Red Army tactics:

Shortcomings also existed in the tactical training of the troops and their command cadre. These were a direct result of the heavy losses our cadre forces suffered earlier in the war. Hastily created rifle units and formations suffered heavy losses in combat, and, if they achieved success, the cost was high. The forces conducted offensive battle unskillfully. Often the attacks ended with the capture of the first trenches since the soldiers did not know how to fight close combat in the trenches and communications trenches. The artillery offensive had not yet been mastered, and cooperation had not been arranged between infantry, artillery, and tanks within subunits, units, and formations. All of this affected the results of combat and, consequently, entire operations. Only after our forces and commanders had acquired the necessary habits for conducting war in the course of the war did they learn how to conquer.[40]

This remarkably candid critique of the Leningrad-Novgorod operation, which was published in 1966, remained the only serious commentary on the operation until the late 1980s.

Reflecting the new candor of the Gorbachev period, in 1989 a short article on the operation began the painful process of rediscovery and reassessment. Its opening passages expressed a mixture of frustration and anger, shared collectively by the Russian people over the obscurity of their own history and suffering:

The exploratory expedition of Komsomol members and youth, which has now been working for several years at the locations where the 2d Shock Army fought, is called "Dolina" [Valley]. Terse, but not quite clear. The valley of what? Perhaps, the "Valley of Death," as Soviet soldiers who had managed to break out of that killing ground and impassable swamps dubbed those places? Or maybe the "Valley of Oblivion," as this dreary place can rightly be called, because many glorious defenders of the homeland who perished there half a century ago still remain unburied, thus placing a heavy moral burden on all of us? Or maybe the name "Valley of Courage" better suits this region through which Soviet soldiers forced their way to Leningrad.[41]

More to the point:

The prolonged hushing up of our military failures in the Great Patriotic War and attempts to screen our bitterness and sorrow at not always justifiable losses are incongruous and abusive for our people and its armed forces. This silence was used as a cover for grievous mistakes in troop control, Stalin's stubbornness and incompetence, and disorganized logistics. At the same time, it unjustifiably belittled the great exploits performed by thousands of soldiers, officers, and generals, as, for example, those of the 2d Shock Army, who saved Leningrad in the winter of 1942, displaying such courage as would do credit to any army in the world. But especially lamentable and blasphemous is that, for many years, the 2d Shock Army's veterans have been bearing the stigma of betrayal for Army commander General Vlasov's going over to the enemy.[42]

Regarding blame for the operation itself, the author's comments summed up contemporary judgments about the operation:

The facts and eyewitnesses clearly indicate that the greater part of the blame for the tragedy of the 2d Shock Army should be laid on the *Stavka* headed by Stalin and his closest associates. They are to blame for the incorrect assessment of the military-strategic situation at the end of 1941 and for assigning the *fronts* unrealistic missions. They are to blame for the poor organization of the offensive and unsatisfactory supply of troops, first and foremost the Volkhov Front troops. They are to blame for curbing the will of commanders and the frequent reshuffling of cadre (in the period from January to June alone, the 2d Shock Army was led successively by three commanders, three members of the Military Council, and four chiefs of staff). It was due to their stubbornness that the 2d Shock Army was not withdrawn in due time from the killing ground, which resulted in unjustifiable death and capture of tens of thousands of our people.

Through Stalin's military incompetence and miscalculations, in 1942 our country would lose, besides the destruction of the 2d Shock Army, the Crimea. . . . The enemy would reach the Volga and Caucasus. However, on 28 July 1942, Stalin would sign his notorious Order No. 227, which laid blame for the defeats on panic-mongers and cowards and which contained the following ominous instructions: "The commanders of companies, regiments, divisions and corresponding commissars and political workers abandoning combat positions without a senior commander's order are traitors of the Homeland, and therefore such commanders and political workers should be treated as traitors of the Homeland." Although the order was supposedly aimed at restoring the lost staunchness of the army, it is easy to imagine how it curbed the initiative of the command and political staff, how many battles were to be fought in unfavorable situations, and how many thousands of needless victims it cost the Homeland.

Clearly, part of the blame for 2d Shock Army's tragedy should be assigned to K. Meretskov, the commander of the Volkhov Front, for his lack of courage and firmness in defending the interests of his subordinate troops, for his hasty commencement of the unprepared offensive, and for his inadequate control of his subordinate forces.

Are some of the soldiers, officers, and generals of the 2d Shock Army to blame for this tragedy? I am sure they are not. If some of them wavered in a difficult moment, they redeemed themselves in the fires of the Volkhov battles. . . . There are tragic pages in the chronicles of the Great Patriotic War, but the terrible ordeals that fell to the lot of the 2d Shock Army are difficult to compare with anything. Nevertheless, the servicemen of this army fulfilled their duty to the end. Honor and glory to them. May their memory live on forever.[43]

Little more need be said about this tragic, forgotten operation.

GERMAN PLANNING FOR OPERATION *NORDLICHT*

With Operation *Blau* well under way in southern Russia and apparently successful, the Germans began planning for new offensive operations in the Leningrad region. On 30 June, Kuechler briefed Hitler at his headquarters, the *Wolfsschanze* (Wolf's Lair), detailing offensive options other than *Nordlicht* that his army group was capable of undertaking. These operations included two in the Leningrad region and two additional operations to the south. In the Leningrad region, the first operation, code-named Operation *Moorbrand* (Moor Fire), involved either capturing the Pogost'e salient west of Kirishi, which was still defended by the 54th Army, or totally destroying the entire Soviet force west of the Volkhov River. The second operation, code-named Operation *Bettelstab* (Beggar's Staff), called for eliminating the Soviet bridgehead south of Oranienbaum.[44]

At the same time, Kuechler assigned the code names *Brueckenschlag* (Bridge Blow) and *Schlingpflanze* (Vine) to the two operations he proposed to conduct to the south. The former involved a joint attack with Army Group Center against the Soviet salient in the German rear southwest of Ostashkov, and the latter an assault to widen the northern flank of the Ramushevo corridor to Demiansk. Kuechler added more details to these proposed operations when he returned to his headquarters on 1 July and ordered his staff to begin work first on *Moorbrand* and *Schlingpflanze* and, later, *Bettelstab*. In the meantime, the OKH ordered its siege artillery batteries, named Dora, Gamma, and Karl, regrouped from Sevastopol' to Leningrad between 2 and 23 July so that they could assist in the reduction of Kronshtadt fortress.[45]

On 23 July, Hitler issued revised guidance for *Wehrmacht* offensive operations in late summer in his Fuehrer Directive No. 45.[46] The directive ordered Army Group South, now split into Army Groups A and B, to conduct Operation *Braunschweig* to liquidate Red Army forces in the great bend of the Don River. In addition, it included yet another offensive option for Army Group North, Operation *Feuerzauber* (Fire Magic), which required the army group to capture Leningrad by early September. To do so, Hitler ordered Manstein's Eleventh Army headquarters with five infantry divisions transferred northward from Sevastopol' to reinforce the Eighteenth Army and the heavy artillery already dispatched to the region. One week later, the OKH renamed Operation *Feuerzauber* Operation *Nordlicht,* which was code-named *Georg* (George) within the Eighteenth Army.[47] Hitler then ordered Kuechler to conduct operations *Schlingpflanze, Moorbrand,* and *Bettelstab* in "short order" before embarking on *Nordlicht* and to complete them all by early September.

Since conducting all of these operations was beyond the army group's capability, Kuechler convinced Hitler and the OKH to delay Operation *Bettelstab* until after the successful completion of Operation *Nordlicht.* Ultimately, the OKH canceled Operation *Moorbrand* later in the summer because by then the situation had changed substantially and also postponed Operation *Schlingpflanze* on 4 August because of poor weather conditions in the Demiansk region. Hitler, however, insisted that *Nordlicht* go ahead as scheduled. On 23 August he assigned Manstein responsibility for conducting *Nordlicht* and ordered him to execute it in any way feasible with his fresh Eleventh Army as long as he linked up with the Finns and "leveled Leningrad to the ground."[48] To ensure that his orders were carried out, Hitler subordinated Manstein's forces directly to the OKH rather than Army Group North. The Finnish Army on the Karelian Isthmus was to assist the operation with artillery support and by conducting a feint north of Leningrad.

Once formulated, the plan for Operation *Nordlicht* required three army corps to penetrate Soviet defenses south of Leningrad after a powerful artillery and air preparation and advance to the city's southern outskirts. Once through the Soviet defenses, while one corps cordoned off Leningrad from the south, the other two corps were to wheel eastward, cross the Neva River, and destroy Soviet forces between the river and Lake Ladoga. Thereafter, the two corps were to envelop Leningrad from the east to capture the city without having to engage in costly street fighting.[49]

THE RED ARMY'S SECOND SINIAVINO OFFENSIVE, AUGUST

After the Germans destroyed the 2d Shock Army in late June, the *Stavka* and Leningrad Front anticipated renewed German offensive operations in the Leningrad region sometime during mid-summer. The new Leningrad

Front commander, Lieutenant General of Artillery L. A. Govorov, was well equipped to deal with the crisis in the wake of the Liuban' defeat. An experienced artilleryman, Govorov was a graduate of the Higher Academy Course (1930), the Frunze Academy (1933), and the General Staff Academy (1938) and, despite a brush with the NKVD during the purges, survived to rise to senior command during the war. After war began, he commanded the Western Direction (July 1941) and Western Front's artillery (August–October 1941), and then the 5th Army with distinction during the Battle for Moscow, during which his army captured Mozhaisk for his *front* commander Zhukov. He rose to command the Leningrad Front after a short stint as commander of the Leningrad Group of Forces, in part based on the judgment that his artillery experiences would benefit the Red Army in a theater where armor was of limited utility.

With the *Stavka*'s approval, Govorov's first action was to reconstitute the 2d Shock Army, which he did on 14 July around the nucleus of the 13th Cavalry Corps and its 25th, 80th, and 87th Cavalry Divisions, and assign Klykov to command the resurrected force.[50] In early July, Soviet intelligence reported a buildup of German forces in the Siniavino and Chudovo regions, possibly in preparation for a major advance on Volkhov. To forestall the German offensive and pave the way for a larger offensive of its own, the Leningrad Front mounted several "local" offensives of its own in late July and early August against German forces south of Leningrad.

In the first of these attacks, the 109th and 85th Rifle Divisions of Nikolaev's 42d Army attacked in the Staro-Panovo sector of 20 July, precipitating several days of heavy combat but producing little in the way of results.[51] The Leningrad war diary captured the essence of the action:

> *Monday, 20 July.* The 42d Army's forces began an attack against the strongest enemy strong point in the Staro-Panovo region, less than 10 kilometers (6.2 miles) from the outskirts of Leningrad. The operation's primary aim, as with others conducted in the summer of 1942, was to attract part of the enemy forces concentrated in the Mga and Tosno regions for an assault on Leningrad, deliver an answering blow against them, and, at the same time, prepare conditions to penetrate the blockade.
>
> The regiments that received the immediate mission of capturing Staro-Panovo occupied their jumping-off positions at night. Once the artillery preparation ended in the morning, they advanced forward, supported by artillery, tanks, and aircraft. Thanks to this, they were soon able to capture Staro-Panovo.
>
> By evening separate groups of our forces reached Uritsk. However, the danger of a flank counterattack forced the groups to withdraw so that enemy forces would not be able to cut them off.

The enemy counterattacked fiercely. In addition, as a countermeasure the enemy bombarded Leningrad with artillery three times. They also tried to deliver air strikes, but to no avail.

Tuesday, 21 July. The enemy once again conducted repeated counterattacks against our forces that have captured Staro-Panovo. The Fascists clung to every patch of ground. . . .

Thursday, 23 July. Having occupied Staro-Panovo, the 42d Army tried to advance further. They managed to gain a foothold in the southeastern section of Uritsk. Street fighting is under way.[52]

In the wake of Nikolaev's assault, the 268th Rifle Division and 220th Tank Brigade of Sviridov's 55th Army attacked in the Putrolovo and Iam-Izhora sectors on 23 July. The Leningrad war diary also recorded the fate of Sviridov's assault.

Thursday, 23 July. The 55th Army began the Putrolovo operation south of Kolpino. Like that at Staro-Panovo, it has only local significance but is designed to attract enemy reserves designated to conduct the assault on Leningrad.

Colonel S. I. Donskov's 268th Rifle Division, which is well known to Leningraders, is conducting the battle for Putrolovo. . . . After four hours of combat, the 268th Rifle Division supported by the 220th Tank Brigade captured the enemy's Putrolovo fortified center. . . .

The enemy did not resign himself to the fall of Putrolovo. Counterattacking, he concentrated his blow against the road junction in the center of the village. . . . The enemy was driven back.

Saturday, 25 July. The Hitlerites are in no way resigned to the loss of the Putrolovo fortified center. At first light today, they launched a strong counterattack. Our infantry repulsed the attack with the help of artillery and tanks. However, the danger of the enemy forcing the Izhora has not lessened. Seizure of the bridge will give the enemy the opportunity to cross from the right bank of the river to the left—into Putrolovo. [Sappers had to blow up the bridge.]

Sunday, 26 July. Once again, the enemy attempted to force the Izhora and take back Putrolovo. The attacks were repelled.

Tuesday, 28 July. The Hitlerites are still not resigned to the loss of Putrolovo. Today they decided to subject our forces, which have dug into new positions, to air attacks.[53]

The fighting south of Leningrad was serious enough for Halder to note in his diary on 23 July, "Local attacks by enemy debouching from western part of Leningrad against Jaeckeln's group and Kolpino. Also thrusts against 58th Division on the Ingermann [Oranienbaum] front."[54]

Although the fighting south of Leningrad proved costly and inconclusive, Govorov did not halt the 55th Army's operation until 4 August and the 42d Army's until 26 August. Although the twin offensives achieved very little more than capturing the German strong points at Putrolovo and Iam Izhora, they did force German Eighteenth Army to shift its 121st and 61st Infantry, 5th Mountain Division, and part of the 12th Panzer Division to the threatened regions. During the same period, the Northwestern Front conducted near-constant offensive operations against German forces at Demiansk and Staraia Russa, both to eliminate the German salient and to decrease the likelihood of a German offensive at Leningrad. These operations, which took place from 3 to 20 May, 17 to 24 July, 10 to 21 August, and 15 to 16 September, failed to make any progress, but they did tie down the Sixteenth Army and prevented it from taking any action to support the Eighteenth Army at Leningrad.[55]

The growing fear of impending German offensive operations against Leningrad prompted the *Stavka* to demand that Govorov's and Meretskov's *fronts* conduct a larger-scale offensive to preempt a possible German offensive and, if possible, raise the German blockade of the city.[56] The *Stavka* and the two *fronts* chose the Germans' Shlissel'burg, Siniavino, and Mga salient south of Lake Ladoga as its target. The offensive plan required the Leningrad and Volkhov Fronts, supported by the Baltic Fleet and Ladoga Flotilla, to conduct concentric attacks to defeat and destroy German forces in the salient and restore ground communications with Leningrad. By doing so successfully, the *Stavka* hoped it could forestall any German offensive farther east and draw German reserves away from the Stalingrad region.

The task Govorov and Meretskov faced was not an easy one, since Lindemann's Eighteenth Army had erected strong and deep defenses in and around its Siniavino "bottleneck." The bulk of Lindemann's army, which consisted of 21 infantry divisions, 1 panzer division (the 12th Panzer), and 1 infantry brigade, was concentrated south of Leningrad and in the Mga-Siniavino salient. The XXVI Army Corps' 227th and 223d Infantry Divisions defended the sector from Lodva to Lipka on the salient's eastern flank opposite the Volkhov Front's 8th Army. It was flanked on the left by the L Army Corps' SS Police Division, which defended along the Neva River opposite the Neva Operational Group, and on the right by the I Army Corps' 96th Infantry Division. A second German defense line was anchored on the Siniavino strong point, and a third line was located forward of the Mga River, which had elements of the 12th Panzer and 5th Mountain Divisions situated nearby.[57]

The German defense consisted of a dense network of strong points and centers of resistance protected by extensive obstacles, interconnected by trenches, and protected by interlocking artillery and mortar fire. The most important German strong points were at Workers Settlements Nos. 7, 8, and 4 and the villages of Tortolovo and Porech'e. The most powerful German defense line extended from Workers Settlements Nos. 4 and 8 through Kruglaia Woods, Tortolovo, and Porech'e to Voronovo. The Siniavino Heights, which rose 150 meters above the surrounding flat terrain, dominated the entire area. A large mossy swamp protected the southeastern approaches to Siniavino, making a tank assault along that approach impossible.

Worse still for the Soviets, on the eve of their offensive, the OKH alerted Kuechler to intensified Soviet preparations for an attack and ordered him to move the 170th Infantry Division, one of the Eleventh Army's divisions preparing for Operation *Nordlicht,* northward from Mga into the bottleneck. It also assigned Kuechler control of several new Tiger tanks that were en route by rail from Pskov.[58] Despite these precautionary measures, however, a complacent Halder noted in his diary on 6 August, "For the time being there are no signs of another major Russian attack [in the region]."[59] Nor did he note any extraordinary Soviet preparations for an attack in the region prior to 19 August, when he noted only "local attacks as usual."[60]

Although at first sight the Soviet offensive plan seemed simple and direct, Govorov and Meretskov tried to eliminate the glaring deficiencies so evident in their previous offensives. In the Leningrad Front's sector, Sviridov's 55th Army and the Neva Operational Group were to attack toward Tosno and Siniavino to link up with the Volkhov Front's forces and destroy German forces in the salient. Initially, naval infantry and boats from the Baltic Fleet were to cross the Neva River and secure bridges and crossing sites for the Leningrad Front's main shock groups. While the main attack was under way toward the east, Nikolaev's 42d and other elements of the 55th Army were to attack toward Uritsk and Staro-Panovo to tie down German forces.[61]

East of the Shlissel'burg corridor, the Volkhov Front's 8th Army, now commanded by Major General F. N. Starikov, was to penetrate German defenses west of Gaitolovo at the base of the salient. Its shock group, consisting of Major General S. T. Biiakov's 6th Guards Rifle Corps with the 3d, 19th, and 24th Guards Rifle Divisions and the 265th Rifle Division, was to destroy German forces at Siniavino, exploit the attack toward Mga, and link up with the Leningrad Front's 55th Army. Gagen's 4th Guards Rifle Corps, which was in second echelon behind Starikov's 8th Army, was to strengthen the 8th Army's assault, help capture the German strong point at Siniavino, and begin the subsequent exploitation. Klykov's 2d Shock Army, just reestablished after its predecessor's destruction at Liuban', was in third echelon with the mission of destroying German forces at Mga, linking up with the Leningrad Front's forces near Krasnyi Bor, and exploiting the offensive southward toward Tosno.

In addition to this triple-echelon assault force, Meretskov established a strong reserve of five rifle divisions and one rifle brigade and positioned it in

the Volkhov region in Starikov's deep rear. The Volkhov Front's deeply echeloned formation was designed both to overcome the heavy German defenses
quickly and to sustain the attack into the depths. Meretskov's forces were to
begin their attack on 28 August. However, Govorov's forces were to attack to
seize bridgeheads over the Neva River on 19 August and conduct their main
attack on the 28th.

Unlike the case in previous offensives, Meretskov provided Starikov's
8th Army with significant armor and artillery support so that, at least in
theory, it could penetrate the entire depth of the German defense and capture Siniavino. This support included 2 tank brigades, 5 separate tank battalions, 12 artillery and 9 mortar regiments, 4 separate mortar battalions, 3 M-13
Katiusha regiments, and 7 M-30 *Katiusha* battalions.[62] Meretskov's third
echelon, Klykov's 2d Shock Army, was to complete the destruction of German forces at Mga, link up with Leningrad Front forces along the Moskovskaia
Dubrovka–Krasnyi Bor front, and, subsequently, develop the offensive southward toward Tosno.

During its assault, the 8th Army was to deploy strong screening forces to
protect the shock group's left and right flanks as it advanced. Starikov assigned
that task to the 128th Rifle Division, which was to screen from Workers Settlement No. 7 to Moskovskaia Dubrovka on the right and the 11th and 286th
Rifle Divisions, which were to do the same from Turyshkino to Krasnyi Bor
on the left. Meretskov's remaining armies, deployed southward through
Kirishi to Lake Il'men', were to conduct diversionary attacks to tie down
German forces.

Although Govorov and Meretskov spent roughly 30 days regrouping and
preparing their forces for the offensive, five rifle divisions, four tank brigades,
and many specialized forces failed to complete their movement into assembly
areas by the appointed time. The regrouping effort involved the movement
of 479 trains and 233 supply convoys from 7 August through 17 September.[63] The delays occurred due to the limited carrying capacity of the rail lines
into concentration areas, poor command and control, and the slow regrouping itself, when units had to be moved to the rear to refill and then back to
the front. Since only two rifle divisions and one rifle brigade designated for
Meretskov's reserve had reached Volkhov by the time the offensive began,
both his first and second echelons had to defend their own flanks as they
conducted the breakthrough and exploitation.

Nevertheless, when the offensive preparations were complete, the Soviet
forces outnumbered the opposing Germans by a factor of better than four to
one in the 8th Army's 15-kilometer (9.3-mile) penetration sector. By then the
tactical density in the penetration sector was up to 5 rifle battalions, more than
100 guns and mortars, and 9 tanks per kilometer (.62 miles) of front, which
accorded the attacking forces significant superiority over the defending Ger-

man forces.[64] However, to succeed the offensive had to develop quickly, since the Germans had six to seven divisions in operational reserve, including those assigned to the Eleventh Army, with which they could reinforce the threatened sector by the eighth or ninth day of the operation.

Sviridov's 55th Army began its offensive early on 19 August, when Major General S. I. Donskov's experienced 268th Rifle Division attacked across the Neva River and seized small bridgeheads at Ivanovskoe and Ust'-Tosno.[65] However, Donskov's division was unable to develop the offensive due to poor command and control, inadequate artillery and engineer support, and the German SS Police Division's stout resistance. Although elements of the 43d, 70th, and 136th Rifle Divisions ultimately reinforced the attack, the 55th Army was not able to expand the bridgehead. Lindemann reinforced the SS Police Division with the 61st Infantry Division's 151st Infantry Regiment on 19 August and the 12th Panzer Division's 25th Panzer Grenadier Regiment on 23 August. The skillful commitment of these reinforcements utterly frustrated Sviridov's efforts to break out to the east from the Neva bridgehead. With his preliminary operations to cross the Neva unsuccessful, Govorov postponed further operations until Meretskov's forces penetrated German defenses east of Siniavino (Map 13).

To the east in the Volkhov Front's sector, Starikov's 8th Army attacked at 0210 hours on 27 August, striking at the junction of the German 227th and 223d Infantry Divisions. The army's main shock group, consisting of the four rifle divisions of Biiakov's 6th Guards Rifle Corps, conducted the *front*'s main attack, supported by one division on its right flank and two on its left. On the first day of the assault, Colonel P. K. Koshevoi's 24th Guards Rifle Division and Colonel B. N. Ushinsky's 265th Rifle Division of Biiakov's shock group penetrated between the German 227th and 223d Infantry Divisions and forced their way across the Chernaia River. By day's end Biiakov's force had captured Tortolovo and enveloped the German strong point at Porech'e from the south, driving a 3-kilometer (5.6-mile) wedge into the German defenses.[66] Early the next day, Colonel D. M. Barinov's 19th Guards Rifle Division exploited the neighboring divisions' success and advanced 5–6 kilometers (3.1–3.7 miles), reaching the southeastern approaches to Siniavino by nightfall.

The attack caught the Germans by surprise, since the 55th Army's violent assaults at Ust'-Tosno had just failed.[67] Shortly before 1200 hours, Lindemann reported to Kuechler that attacks were under way along the entire front north of the railroad, 20 enemy tanks had achieved a small penetration, but no discernible enemy main attack was as yet apparent.[68] Kuechler's main concern at this point was over the fate of Operation *Nordlicht,* which a prolonged Soviet offensive might disrupt. Therefore, he began pushing all of his available reserves forward into the threatened sector.

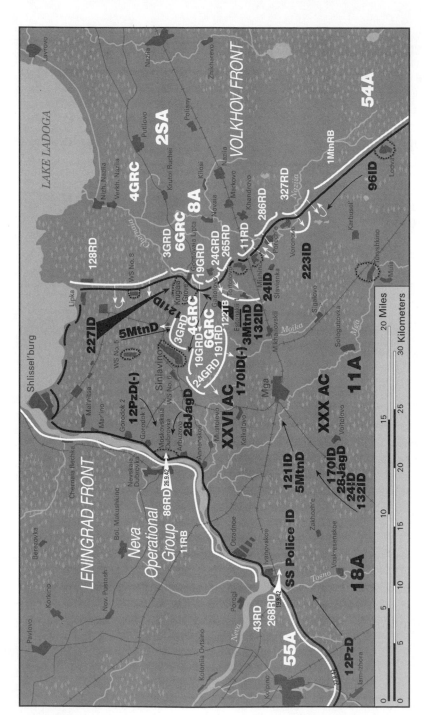

Map 13. The Soviet Second Siniavino Offensive, 19 August–15 October 1942

Starikov's shock group advanced slowly and painfully toward Siniavino from 28 to 30 August in the face of heavy German counterattacks, finally reaching the southern approaches to Siniavino in the center of his attack sector on 31 August. At this point the banks of the Neva River were only 7 kilometers (4.3 miles) to his front. While the shock group gnawed its way forward through the German defenses, Colonel L. G. Sergeev's 128th Rifle Division, on the shock group's right flank, and Colonel I. V. Gribov's 11th and Colonel D. L. Abakumov's 286th Rifle Divisions on its left tried in vain to expand the penetration.[69] The strong German defense, which was anchored on a series of strong points on both of the shock group's flanks, tied down Soviet forces and weakened the strength of the main effort toward Siniavino and Mga. Despite the modest progress Starikov's forces recorded, the intense fighting produced heavy casualties and severe attrition. Reinforcements were clearly essential if the offensive was to continue successfully.

Fearing that the attacking Soviets were heading for the Neva River by way of Siniavino, on 28 August Kuechler ordered his 5th Mountain and 28th Jager Divisions to move forward to Mga from their staging areas for Operation *Nordlicht*. Later in the day, Hitler diverted the 3d Mountain Division, which was en route by sea from Norway to Finland, to Reval, Estonia, and Kuechler brought up the 12th Panzer Division to protect the Neva River front and accelerated the 170th Infantry Division's movement to Siniavino.[70] These forces and part of the 96th Infantry Division assembled at Siniavino between 27 and 30 August. Finally, Kuechler committed his four Tiger tanks to combat south of Siniavino Heights on 29 August, although two of the new tanks broke down almost immediately.[71] The redeployment and commitment of these forces succeeded in slowing the Volkhov Front's offensive, prompting Lindemann to report that the crisis had passed and the penetration had been contained.

By that time, Meretskov had already begun frittering away his second echelon and reserve forces to sustain the 8th Army's advance. He began committing portions of his second-echelon 4th Guards Rifle Corps in support of Biiakov's 6th Guards Rifle Corps prior to 30 August, long before it was called for by his original plan. At the time, Gagen's 4th Guards Rifle Corps consisted of the 259th Rifle Division, the 22d, 23d, 32d, 33d, 53d, 137th, and 140th Rifle Brigades, and the 98th and 122d Tank Brigades.[72] Major General M. F. Gavrilov's 259th Rifle Division and a tank brigade went into action on 29 August, and the additional rifle brigades joined battle in piecemeal fashion beginning on 30 August, although too late to affect the penetration since Starikov's initial shock group had already been severely weakened. By late on 31 August, the shock group was assaulting several strong points on the southern approaches to Siniavino but simply lacked the strength to overcome the fierce and skillful German resistance.

Although reinforced, Starikov's main attack finally faltered south of Sinia-vino on 1 and 2 September in the face of heavy and constant counterattacks by the 28th Jager Division and elements of the 170th Infantry Division.[73] On its right flank, Sergeev's 128th Rifle Division managed to surround and then capture Workers Settlement No. 8 in brutal hand-to-hand combat but was halted on 3 September after advancing only 2–3 kilometers (1.2–1.9 miles). On its left, Gribov's 11th Rifle Division captured the German strong point at Mishino, but Abakumov's 286th Rifle Division failed to seize Voronovo, which was defended by the 223d Infantry Division and a task force from the 12th Panzer Division.

Thus, despite three days of heavy fighting against strong German resistance, on 3 September the Volkhov Front's secondary attacks faltered with heavy losses only 2–3 kilometers (1.2–1.9 miles) deep into the German defense. By this time Starikov's shock group, now reinforced by Gagen's entire 4th Guards Rifle Corps, was lodged in the woods southwest of Siniavino Heights almost 10 kilometers (6.2 miles) deep into the German defenses and only 5 kilometers (3.1 miles) from the Neva River.

An increasingly frustrated Meretskov then took measures to restore some momentum to his offensive. First, on 5 and 6 September, he regrouped his shock forces. He withdrew Starikov's worn-out 19th and 24th Guards Rifle Divisions from the 6th Guards Rifle Corps and replaced them with Lieutenant Colonel N. I. Artemenko's fresh 191st Rifle Division and Lieutenant Colonel A. V. Zazimko's 122d Tank Brigade from the *front*'s reserve. However, these fresh forces were severely damaged by intense German air strikes even before they entered combat as they deployed forward through a gauntlet of German fire. Although these forces managed to reach the swamps southeast of Siniavino on 7 September, their ordeal deprived them of the strength necessary to mount a credible assault on the German strong point.

While Starikov's shock group was waging its brutal but futile struggle to capture Siniavino and its adjacent heights, the forces on his left flank did achieve some modest success. There, Colonel N. A. Poliakov's 327th Rifle Division enveloped German forces defending the strong point at Voronovo and, together with Abakumov's 286th Rifle Division, was able to capture the strong point and dig in late on 7 September.[74]

With Meretskov's assault faltering, Govorov's 55th Army and Neva Operational Group once again joined the assault on 3 September, attacking across the Neva River and assaulting from the bridgeheads on its eastern banks.[75] Sviridov's 55th Army attacked in the Iam-Izhora sector with two rifle divisions but failed to penetrate the German defenses, largely due to poorly organized command and control and weak combat support. At the same time, other elements of Sviridov's army and the Neva Operational Group attacked north and south of Moskovskaia Dubrovka in an attempt to capture Mustolovo, advance to Siniavino from the west, and link up with Meretskov's shock group. Two rifle divisions managed to force their way across the Neva River in the sector from Annenskoe to Gorodok No. 1, where they wedged into the German SS Police Division's defense. Once again, however, poor command and control and weak fire support caused the attack to bog down and finally expire. Admitting failure, the *Stavka* authorized these forces to withdraw to their jumping-off positions on 12 September.

Hitler was "exasperated" by the fact that the Soviet assault had tied up in the Mga-Siniavino bottleneck four of the divisions earmarked to conduct Operation *Nordlicht* but without achieving any appreciable effect on the Soviet offensive. Noting these "atrocious developments," he ordered Manstein and his Eleventh Army to take command in the bottleneck and "restore the situation offensively."[76] Hitler also ordered the OKH to take direct control over Manstein's Eleventh Army headquarters and required Manstein to "report immediately failures on the part of any commanders."[77]

Meanwhile, berated unmercifully by a dissatisfied *Stavka*, an increasingly desperate Meretskov proceeded to commit the remainder of Klykov's 2d Shock Army into combat on 5 September. However, neither Starikov's nor Klykov's armies was able to report any further progress. Worse still, the combined forces of the German XXVI Army Corps' 121st Infantry, 5th Mountain, 28th Jager, and 223d Infantry Divisions contained the Soviet attacks in heavy fighting from 6 through 9 September and began launching counterattacks of their own to regain lost territory.

The initial German counterattacks struck the right flank of Starikov's struggling shock group on 6 September. Lacking sufficient flank defenses, the Germans were able to capture Kruglaia Grove, a feat that prompted Meretskov to subordinate the 4th and 6th Guards Rifle Corps to Klykov and his 2d Shock Army. However, this attempt to replace one army command with another proved unsuccessful and failed to improve the situation.

Having halted the Soviet advance on Siniavino, Manstein concentrated his 24th and 170th Infantry and 12th Panzer Divisions and ordered them to attack the Soviet penetration from the southeast on 10 September. However, this counterattack collapsed almost immediately when the advancing infantry encountered heavy artillery and mortar fire and his tanks stumbled into extensive Soviet minefields and suffered heavy losses. Consequently, Manstein canceled the attacks planned for the following day and, instead, ordered his army to neutralize the Soviet artillery and prepare another attack from both north and south.[78] Meanwhile, from 4 through 20 September, counterattacks by the 121st Infantry and 5th Mountain Divisions from the north, the 28th Jager Division from the west, and the 170th Infantry Division from the south compressed the attacking Soviet forces back into a tight salient extending from southeast of Siniavino to Gaitolovo.

THE GERMANS' SINIAVINO COUNTERSTROKE, SEPTEMBER

After heavy rains forced a three-day delay, on 21 September Manstein began a more carefully planned counterstroke involving pincer attacks from both north and south toward Gaitolovo at the base of the Soviet's penetration. The XXVI Army Corps' 121st Infantry Division formed the northern prong of the pincer, and the XXX Army Corps 24th, 132d, and 170th Infantry Divisions formed the southern prong, while the 3d Mountain and 28th Jager Divisions contained Soviet forces in the penetration. Overcoming desperate Soviet resistance, the counterattacking German forces linked up near Gaitolovo on 25 September, encircling the bulk of Meretskov's 8th and 2d Shock Armies. However, before Manstein could begin mopping-up operations west of Gaitolovo, Govorov's forces attacked once again eastward across the Neva River.

When Manstein launched his counterstroke, imperiling Meretskov's shock group east of Gaitolovo, the *Stavka* had immediately ordered both Meretskov and Govorov to mount fresh operations to thwart Manstein's effort. Meretskov's revised plan of action, which he submitted to the *Stavka* on 21 September, scarcely altered his original objectives:

> Considering the correlation of forces and the existing groupings of enemy forces on the flanks of the penetration sector, I recommend the following plan for the further conduct of operations:
>
> 1. The immediate mission—to destroy the enemy Siniavino grouping, to capture Kruglaia Grove and the Siniavino fortified center in succession, which will widen the penetration front, and to create more favorable conditions for a subsequent offensive to the west or northwest up to the Neva. During the period the Siniavino operation is being conducted, firmly defend with the 8th Army to prevent an enemy penetration into the shock group's rear. I consider it possible to conduct the Siniavino operation with the *front's* existing forces. To that end, while digging in on its left flank northwest of Lake Siniavino, the 2d Shock Army will regroup to reinforce its grouping in the Kruglaia Grove region. In addition, the 2d Shock Army will be given the 376th Rifle Division from the *front* reserve for the capture of Kruglaia Grove. The 2d Shock Army will be reinforced with the 372d Rifle Division from *front* reserve to capture the Siniavino region.
>
> 2. The subsequent stage of the operation will seek to penetrate the front toward Moskovskaia Dubrovka, reach the eastern bank of the Neva River, and clear the enemy from the region along the southern shore of Lake Ladoga.

To conduct this operation, I request you:
  a. Transfer the 314th and 256th Rifle Divisions and the 73d Bri-
     gade to the front for employment in the operation after the cap-
     ture of Siniavino.
  b. Reinforce frontal aviation with three fighter regiments.
  c. Provide 100 heavy and medium tanks.
  d. Issue an additional one combat load of ammunition. The request
     will be presented to the chief of the General Staff tonight.
          [signed] Meretskov, Kochetkov, Stel'makh[79]

The *Stavka* approved Meretskov's plan at 0110 hours on 24 September
and authorized him to employ the 314th and 256th Rifle Divisions and 73d
Rifle Brigade in the advance from Siniavino to the Neva River but postponed any decision on additional air support for the operation.[80] Later in
the day, Govorov notified the *Stavka* that his forces were prepared to force
the Neva River whenever it gave the order, and at midnight Vasilevsky re-
layed Stalin's permission for Govorov to begin his assault at dawn on 25 September.[81] For inexplicable reasons, however, Govorov delayed the assault
for another 24 hours. By the time it did begin, Manstein's counterattacks
east of Siniavino prevented Meretskov's forces from attacking since they
had their hands full coping with the German assault. Govorov's forces, therefore, had no choice but to go it alone.

At 0300 hours on 26 September, the 55th Army's and the Neva Operational Group's shock groups assaulted across the Neva River against the
12th Panzer Division's defenses at Annenskoe and Gorodok No. 1. Colonel A. A. Krasnov's 70th and Colonel P. S. Fedorov's 86th Rifle Divisions and the 11th Separate Rifle Brigade of the Neva Group managed
to capture small bridgeheads at Arbuzovo, Annenskoe, and Moskovskaia
Dubrovka, into which they brought 28 guns, 281 mortars, and 12 tanks.[82]
These forces continued assaulting German defenses through the end of
September but failed to expand the bridgehead despite suffering heavy
losses.

Adding insult to injury, the 12th Panzer Division launched a counterattack against the bridgehead on 29 September and recaptured both Arbuzovo
and Annenskoe. After a week more of futile fighting, on 7 October, Govorov
ordered the 55th Army to abandon its bridgehead and withdraw back across
the Neva. Although the 28th Jager Division recaptured most of the Neva
Operational Group's bridgehead at Moskovskaia Dubrovka, a single company
of the group's 70th Rifle Division, later reinforced by Major General E. V.
Kozik's 46th Rifle Division, retained a small foothold over the Neva, which
Soviet forces retained until January 1943.[83]

Govorov's assault across the Neva River delayed the German destruction of Meretskov's shock group in the Gaitolovo pocket by forcing Manstein to move the 28th Jager Division from Siniavino to the Neva front, but accomplished little more. In heavy fighting from 30 September through 15 October, Manstein's forces systematically reduced the encirclement, recaptured all previously lost strong points, and restored the original front. The German success was costly, however, since German forces suffered 26,000 casualties in the fighting.[84] Although far fewer than Soviet estimates that the Germans lost 60,000 men, 200 tanks, 200 guns, 400 mortars, 730 machine guns, and 260 aircraft, the losses were unprecedented.[85] Worse still, the counterstroke totally "burned out" several divisions earmarked for participation in Operation *Nordlicht,* and as a result, Hitler would never issue an order to initiate the operation.[86]

Belatedly, on 29 September, the *Stavka* sent Meretskov a directive ordering him to withdraw his forces from the Siniavino-Gaitolovo pocket, a directive that underscored the confusion prevailing in both headquarters:

> For several days, the Volkhov Front and 2d Shock Army commands have not been able to provide a precise and clear answer concerning the situation with the passages south of the Gaitolovo-Kelkolovo road.
>
> As a result of such criminal carelessness and false complacent information regarding the situation, an impression has been created that nothing special has occurred and the forces can withdraw along the passage south of the Gaitolovo-Kelkolovo road. Indeed, the forces in that passage have become engaged in combat with some sort of unknown "small groups" of enemy. Moreover, given the completely fresh reinforcing 314th Rifle Division and 73d Rifle Brigade and the five divisions which have withdrawn from the west, these groups have not been destroyed but instead are continuing to stop up the passage and are not permitting the 2d Shock Army to withdraw.
>
> Such a situation can exist only as a result of the absence of command and control of forces. As is evident, the *front* and 2d Shock Army commands do not wish to acknowledge the situation that exists west of the Chernaia River and in the passage southwest of Gaitolovo with any seriousness. They are getting away with issuing orders regarding the supposedly possible withdrawal of the 2d Shock Army to the region east of Gaitolovo that are out of touch with the actual situation.
>
> The *Stavka* of the Supreme High Command *orders:*
>
> 1. Report in all honesty about the true situation of the units west of the Chernaia River and about the passages in the bottleneck southwest of Gaitolovo by 1000 hours 29 September 1942.

2. You and your staff will immediately take over direction of the with-drawal of the 2d Shock Army into the region east of Gaitolovo.

Present such a withdrawal plan by 1800 hours 29 September 1942.

[signed] Vasilevsky[87]

Within days after the remnants of his two armies escaped encirclement, on 1 October, an undaunted Meretskov noted the continued German threat to Leningrad, recounted the serious damage his forces had inflicted on the Germans, and requested permission to mount new "local" operations to re-duce that threat:[88]

1. At present . . . the enemy is preparing to continue his operations against Leningrad, and the Volkhov Front's offensive has forced him to turn his forces to the Mga axis. Bloody and fierce combat has been raging along the Mga axis for more than a month. Along with defensive operations, the enemy has undertaken local counterattacks and has launched a general counter-offensive. Our forces have displayed stubbornness in combat. The enemy has suffered heavy losses from all types of fire and, in particular, from mas-sive artillery and guards-mortar [Katiusha] fire. Prisoner-of-war reports in-dicate that the 24th, 170th, 28th, and 132d Infantry Divisions, which were superbly refitted after the Crimean operations, have been so exhausted in these battles that only 18–20 men remain in the companies of the 24th, 170th, and 5th Infantry Divisions and 50–70 men in the companies of the 132d Infantry Division. The 223d and 227th Infantry Divisions were smashed in our forces' initial attacks.

The total enemy losses for the entire operation amount to 51,700 men killed and wounded and 260 aircraft, 144 guns, 300 mortars, 400 machine guns, and 197 tanks destroyed. In addition, our forces captured 72 guns of all caliber, 105 mortars, 330 machine guns, 7 tanks, 2 aircraft, and half a million bullets. It is clear from these losses that the enemy grouping that was preparing to storm Leningrad has been seriously weakened in com-bat with the Volkhov Front and at present is not capable of conducting such a large-scale operation without reinforcements. However, this group-ing has sufficient strength for a defense along the Mga axis. Therefore, I consider that, in the near future, the enemy along the Mga axis will limit himself to local operations and attempt to withdraw a large portion of his forces from combat for rest and replenishment and subsequent employ-ment for the struggle for Leningrad.

2. After withdrawing part of our forces to the eastern bank of the Chernaia River, our forces will hold on to the Voronovo and Workers Settlement No. 8 centers of resistance, which we captured from the

enemy. After more than 30 days of battle, our divisions are exhausted. In addition to personnel losses, our forces have suffered considerable losses in equipment, from enemy artillery and heavy mortar fire, and especially massive bombing raids.

3. Considering the situation existing at Leningrad and along the Mga axis, I believe that the Volkhov Front's forces must remain active along the Mga axis. Therefore, while the forces are resting and refitting, we must conduct local operations to tie down enemy forces along the Mga axis and prevent them from transferring forces against Leningrad. In addition, the seizure of individual enemy centers of resistance will create more favorable jumping-off positions for a transition to a general offensive.

4. I intend to conduct local operations to seize the "Lipka" center of resistance, the Kruglaia Grove center of resistance, and the "Mishino" and "Porech'e" centers of resistance. The forces designated to conduct these local operations will be replenished first and will conduct special training in the storming of centers of resistance.

5. Request you approve these proposals. I will present plans for the conduct of these local operations.

[signed] Meretskov, Zaporozhets, Kochetkov, Stel'makh[89]

The *Stavka* categorically refused Meretskov's request on 3 October: "The *Stavka* of the Supreme High Command *orders* that you conduct no local operations whatsoever without the express permission of the *Stavka*."[90] Instead, it ordered him to reestablish new defenses along the Chernaia River and forbade him from undertaking any new operations until he gave his forces the rest they clearly required.

Although the Siniavino offensive utterly destroyed any German hopes of conducting Operation *Nordlicht* and capturing Leningrad, the operation exacted a heavy toll on Red Army forces. In addition to losing the 2d Shock Army for a second time in less than single year, the two *fronts* lost 113,674 men, including 40,085 dead, captured, and missing, out of a total force of 190,000 committed to combat.[91] Combined with the almost 400,000 casualties the two *fronts* had suffered earlier in the year, both urgently required a respite.

Candid Soviet after-action critiques attributed the failure in its second Siniavino offensive to a variety of causes. The General Staff formally critiqued Meretskov's conduct of the operation in a message it sent to him on 15 September:

The Red Army General Staff has received information about the facts, which, to a considerable degree, affected the success of individual units' and formations' combat operations in the operation that your *front* conducted.

The principal [judgments] are:

1. Inadequate ammunition support. Thus, when it was committed into combat, the 191st Rifle Division had .02–.03 combat loads of mines and 45mm shells and units of the 259th Rifle Division entered battle with no hand grenades.

2. An absence of the required organization of cooperation and command and control in combat. The 259th Rifle Division's commander lost control over his regiments and provided false information about the situation of the division's units. From 2 through 9 September, the commander of the 944th Rifle Regiment of the same division did not have communications with his battalions and for three days was unable to locate his regiment's mortar company. The 70th Army Artillery Regiment and 117th Mortar Regiment, which should have supported the 131st and 140th Rifle Brigades, did not establish communications with the brigades and did not support the brigades with their fires.

3. The tank brigades and battalions operated in small groups across a broad front and, as a result, lost 105 tanks.

4. The piecemeal and tardy commitment of the second echelons and the 2d Shock Army into combat held back the operation's development and accorded the enemy the opportunity to reinforce his forces along the Siniavino axis and launch counterattacks. As a result, the 19th Guards Rifle Division and 4th Guards Rifle Corps' units withdrew 2–3 kilometers (1.2–1.9 miles) from Siniavino and the railroad. The *front's* headquarters did not inform the General Staff about the withdrawal of these units.

We request that you report to the General Staff on the essence of these matters and about the measures that the Military Council takes toward the specific culprits of the aforementioned deficiencies.

[signed] Ivanov, Ryzhkov[92]

On 6 October the General Staff issued yet another critique, which underscored serious deficiencies in the employment of tank forces in the operation:

The Red Army General Staff has received information regarding fundamental deficiencies in the employment of tank units in the offensive and the heavy tank losses in combat.

During the initial days of the Siniavino operation, tank units which were operating as a part of the 8th Army suffered 29 tanks burned, 15 blown up, 11 stuck in the mud, and 4 missing, for a total of 59 tanks.

The 124th Tank Brigade, which was operating with the 80th Rifle Division (of the 54th Army), lost 24 of its 27 tanks taking part in the fighting in the course of a single day.

In the 286th Rifle Division's sector (8th Army), 6 tanks were blown up in our own minefields.

The main reasons for such excessive tank losses are:

1. The dispersal of the tanks across a broad front and the absence of echeloning in the tank units' combat formations, which permits the enemy's antitank guns to cope rather easily with a quantity of tanks attacking across the front. This circumstance hampers the concentrated accompaniment of the tank attack with all sorts of fires, aviation, and sappers.

2. The employment of tanks on terrain unsuited for tank operations (the majority of tanks in the 124th Tank Brigade became stuck in the swamps and were shot up by the enemy).

3. The loss of contact between the tanks and the infantry (in the 286th Rifle Division, the infantry lagged 500 meters behind the tanks), which permitted the enemy to cut off the infantry from the tanks.

Take immediate measures to prevent the aforementioned deficiencies in the employment of tanks.

[signed] Ivanov, Ryzhkov[93]

Despite Meretskov's careful preparations, command and control, reconnaissance, concentration, and cooperation among attacking forces continued to be poor. Meretskov and his subordinate army commanders committed their second echelons and reserves to combat in piecemeal fashion and often too late to make a difference. The critiques credited these failures to inexperienced command cadre and staffs, particularly at the platoon and company level, and poor staff procedures. On the other hand, the critiques noted the offensive's positive effect of forcing the Germans to cancel their planned offensive to capture the city and divert forces from the south. The offensive also seriously eroded German strength, weakened their defenses, and paved the way for a more successful offensive in the future by imparting necessary experience to the Soviet command cadres and staffs.[94]

On 14 October the OKH issued its Operations Order No. 1, which ordered Army Group North over to the defense during the upcoming winter, but left Operation *Nordlicht* as a future option.[95] Given the state of Manstein's Eleventh Army, however, soon after, Hitler had no choice but to postpone the operation and, instead, order Manstein to smash the Soviet defenses at Leningrad by concentrated artillery fire. Manstein remained the custodian of a dormant front until 20 November, when he was summoned south to deal with the growing crisis in the Stalingrad region. The front in the Leningrad region stabilized after 15 October and remained stable until the end of the year.

As during previous periods, the Red Army's operations around Leningrad in the summer of 1942 had significant consequences for German operations elsewhere along the front. The most important consequence was Hitler's decision to transfer the Eleventh Army to the Leningrad region, which he deemed essential if Army Group North was to have any chance to fulfill his aim of seizing the city in 1942. However, this decision had the distinctly negative impact of depriving the *Wehrmacht* of critically important reserves in southern Russia at a time when it most needed them. After the Eleventh Army failed to capture Leningrad, the OKH transferred its divisions to the south, but they arrived too late to help prevent the disasters that befell German forces in that region in the fall of 1942.

Although most Soviet accounts ignore the 1942 Siniavino offensive or mention it only in passing, the operation had far greater significance than simply imparting valuable military experience to the commanders and staffs who conducted the offensive operations. More importantly, the operation underscored Stalin's preoccupation with the offense, even at a time when the Red Army faced a major crisis in southern Russia. It also vividly illustrated Stalin's continued determination to raise the Leningrad blockade, regardless of cost.

Finally, operations in the summer and fall of 1942 brutally revealed how much more the Red Army's command cadre, staffs, and forces would have to learn if they ever hoped to defeat German forces and raise the Leningrad blockade. In the summer and fall of 1942, the two *fronts* repeated many of the mistakes they had made in previous operations, with the same adverse effects. The catalogue of command errors, staff mistakes, and force deficiencies was long, disturbing, and all too familiar.

First and foremost, Govorov and Meretskov failed to synchronize their offensives, allowing the Germans to shift forces between threatened sectors and defeat each attack in detail. Ineffective preliminary reconnaissance failed to "reveal" the true nature of German defenses and largely negated the effectiveness of carefully planned and more massive artillery and air preparations. During the offensive, the two *fronts* employed artillery in too decentralized a fashion to provide effective, concentrated, and flexible artillery support. Commanders failed to concentrate their forces properly before the offensive, to control and coordinate infantry, tank, and artillery forces effectively before and during the offensive, and to maneuver their forces properly during the operations. Often, they committed their forces to battle piecemeal and without adequate flank protection, they failed to anticipate German counterattacks, and they belatedly shifted forces from secondary to main attack sectors. Poor logistical support throughout the offensive made it difficult if not impossible to sustain the operations, and equally inadequate movement planning and engineer support led to excessive losses of tanks to enemy mines. Finally, the difficult terrain conditions and the virtual absence of anything resembling suitable roads required far more painstaking engineer planning and support throughout the offensive.

The two *fronts* would have to address and solve these and other glaring problems before they could achieve any success in future operations. They did not have long to do so, for in October 1942, Stalin was already planning for even larger-scale offensives in the Leningrad region.

Army General K. A. Meretskov,
Commander, 7th Separate and 4th
Armies, and Commander, Volkhov Front

Army General L. A. Govorov, Commander, Leningrad Front *(left)*, and his commissar,
A. A. Zhdanov *(right)*

Red Army snipers on the Leningrad Front, 1942

Red Army wounded receiving assistance

Tanks repaired at the Kirov factory head to the front

German prisoners march down Nevsky Prospect, 1942

German "Bertha" siege gun

A Russian "highway"

A building in Leningrad damaged by German artillery

A women's volunteer unit marching through Leningrad

A Soviet propaganda poster (1942), "Fight to the death!"

A Soviet propaganda poster (1942), "Soldiers of the Red Army, save us!"

A Red Army antiaircraft gun firing on German aircraft

KV heavy tanks being built at Leningrad's Kirov factory, 1942

A Soviet poster on a destroyed building, "Death to the child killers!"

Civilians evacuating Leningrad by way of Lake Ladoga, summer 1942

CHAPTER 8

The Continuing Siege
1942–1943

REFINING LENINGRAD'S DEFENSES

While the Red Army struggled to raise the blockade of Leningrad in 1942 and 1943, the *Stavka* exploited its experiences in other sectors of the front to progressively strengthen and deepen the city's defenses. All the while, the General Staff collected and analyzed techniques employed in the defense of Odessa, Sevastopol', and Stalingrad and provided these vital data to the Leningrad Front.

Ultimately, Leningrad's defenses consisted of several distinct defensive belts, echeloned in depth and equipped with numerous antitank obstacles, integrated firing artillery positions, and a mature system of interlocking antiaircraft positions and fires. The backbone of the defense during the first half of 1942 was a continuous trench system that connected separate battalion defensive regions and fortified strong points and other lesser defensive lines into a single mutually supporting defense network. Collectively, the battalion defensive regions, each of which consisted of a rifle battalion, supporting weapons, and a well-developed system of combat and communications trenches, formed the tactical foundation of each separate defensive belt.

Throughout the remainder of 1942 and into 1943, the Leningrad Front improved the strength and resiliency of its defenses, largely because it organized the defensive work more effectively. Under its supervision, the city's civilian population constructed additional defensive works along the city's southern, southeastern, and northern approaches, which formed both main and second defensive belts, and a series of cut-off positions and fortified regions in the 23d, 42d, and 55th Armies' and the Neva Operational Group's defensive sectors.[1]

By the end of 1942, these defenses included 150 kilometers (93.2 miles) of antitank ditches, escarpments and counter-escarpments, 202 kilometers (125.5 miles) of barbed wire entanglements, 7,178 rifle squad trenches, and 627 kilometers (389.6 miles) of communications trenches. Interspersed throughout this system were 140 prefabricated iron and reinforced concrete works, 487 armored firing points, 176 encasements for tanks and tank turrets, 1,500 antitank obstacles (pyramids), 1,395 earth and timber bunkers, 809 firing points in buildings, and 1,089 command and observation posts or blindages.[2]

The Leningrad Front finally completed its entire system of continuous defensive belts around the city during the second half of 1942. The heart of the system was three defensive belts around the city proper and a series of intermediate lines and cut-off positions linking the three belts, which were themselves equipped with extensive engineering works and fortifications. By this time, the *front*'s forces were able to occupy all three belts in depth. For example, the 42d and 55th Armies' defensive sectors south of Leningrad encompassed 350 kilometers (217.5 miles) of communications trenches by October 1942. In addition, the two armies' defenses incorporated 656 artillery and 2,094 machine gun bunkers, 536 mortar firing positions, 800 antitank rifle firing positions, 2,000 blindages and bunkers, 600 kilometers of antitank and anti-infantry obstacles, and 350 kilometers of communications trenches.[3]

Forces from the defending armies' first and second echelons and fortified regions occupied the first and second defensive belts, *front* and army reserves occupied the third defensive belt and the intermediate and cut-off positions, and NKVD forces manned positions within the city itself. This complete defense system permitted the armies to maneuver their forces and weaponry laterally and in the depths, improved ammunition resupply, and provided better protection against German artillery and air attack. By the end of the year, the *front* had sufficient resources to organize the entire defense on the basis of field fortified regions (FFRs), whose attached transport made them more mobile than the earlier wartime fortified regions.

The Leningrad Front's, Baltic Fleet's, and Ladoga Flotilla's artillery materially assisted in the city's defense by conducting better-organized counterbattery fires against German artillery. This fire forced the Germans to move their artillery 10–15 kilometers (6.2–9.3 miles) from the front lines and curtailed the frequent fire raids on the city. The Baltic Fleet and Ladoga Flotilla, which were operationally subordinate to the Leningrad Front, concentrated their fires against German forces, communications, and supply routes, and the fleet had seized complete superiority in the Gulf of Finland by the end of 1942. The Ladoga Flotilla protected the supply routes across the lake to facilitate the buildup of supplies necessary for the city's survival during the winter.

Throughout the year, the Leningrad Front's Military Council issued a series of orders that converted Leningrad into a virtual "military city." An order issued on 5 July 1942 defined what that term meant:

> The Leningrad Front's Military Council considers the completion of all measures necessary for the transformation of Leningrad into a military city within the shortest possible time to be the most important and urgent mission of the *front*'s Military Council, the city's Party Committee, and

Leningrad City Council of Workers' Deputies' Executive Committee. The fulfillment of this mission requires that only the essential minimum self-employed population remain in Leningrad [necessary to]:

   a. Service industries producing ammunition, weaponry, communications equipment, and supplies for the Leningrad Front's and Baltic Fleet's needs.
   b. Man Leningrad's fuel and energy industry and transport.
   c. Ensure the production of products satisfying the basic needs of the city's remaining population.
   d. Continue uninterrupted work by the most important branches of the city's economy and council, administrative, economic, and cultural-educational institutions.
   e. Satisfy the needs of local PVO and the city's antifire security.
   f. Conduct necessary defensive work in and around Leningrad.[4]

This order required the authorities to evacuate 300,000 of the city's inhabitants after 5 July, and it established fixed limits on the number of those who remained to perform each essential function. A subsequent letter issued by Zhdanov on 6 July established 800,000 persons as the amount of manpower necessary to perform these essential duties and sketched out the production parameters.[5]

During 1941 the military commands and city administration had formed a considerable number of armed workers' detachments to provide for the city's internal defense. However, by early 1942 the Leningrad Front had incorporated most of the members of these detachments into the Red Army as combat replacements. A major effort was therefore required to replace them with new formations. The Party addressed this need in a report it issued on 7 July 1942:

Armed workers' detachments were formed in July and August 1941, which numbered 102,000 men. By virtue of a *front* Military Council decision in the fall of that year, the workers' detachments were disbanded, and five separate workers' brigades and one *Vseobuch* [reserve training] brigade were formed from them. . . .

However, the workers' brigades ceased to exist in the spring of 1942. One brigade was completely mobilized into the Red Army, and the Kirov and Moscow Detachments (which totaled around 1,000 men) were entirely transferred with their weapons [into the Red Army]. Several units of people were taken from the reserves and mobilized on a general basis. The main reason for ending the detachments' existence was the massive evacuation of workers with their industries and the consequences of the blockade of the city during the winter. . . .

At present, with regard to the improved situation in Leningrad (in the first place, regarding food, water, and other products), work has begun anew on forming workers' detachments.

At the present time, there are 77 detachments numbering 8,482 men. Some of these are already conducting military training. The best of these are located in the Kirov region, where there are 5 detachments numbering 1,968 men; in the Krasnogvardeisk region, with 15 detachments and 1,184 men; in the Moscow region, with 12 detachments and 1,200 men; in the Smolensk region, with 9 detachments and 847 men; and in Volodarsk region, with 12 detachments and 850 men. We have not yet begun work in the Vasileostrovi, Vyborg, Oktiabr', Petrograd, and Primorskii regions. However, workers' detachments in these regions can be formed from reserves of people in the city's remaining factories, those under age for service in the Red Army, and some number of women.

These detachments can be armed with weapons and ammunition existing in the city and those that are produced above the plan by Saturday workers [subbotniki]. Detachments in several regions already possess powerful weaponry. For example, the detachments in the Kirov region have 1,100 rifles, 1 Maxim machine gun, 71 submachine guns, 51 automatic weapons, 5,000 grenades, 10,000 bottles with flammable liquid, 552 hunting rifles, and 183 light caliber rifles.

Overall in the city, the workers' detachments have 1,953 combat training rifles of various types, 6 combat training Maxim machine guns, 8 DT [Degtarev machine guns], 85 combat training submachine guns, 57 automatic weapons, 33,800 grenades (various types), 119,000 bottles with flammable liquid, 9,325 hunting rifles, and 8,000 small caliber rifles. . . .

All work in forming and equipping workers' detachments and, in particular, their military training will now be on a larger scale, given the special decision of the bureau of the Leningrad Party City Committee.

[signed] Pavlov[6]

Leningrad's armed workers' forces indeed increased in strength during 1942, as the number of workers battalions rose to 52 by year's end, which were manned by 26,897 personnel, including more than 10,000 women.[7] In early 1943 the commander of the Internal Defense of the City (VOG) recommended that the Leningrad Front improve the city's defense by forming 12 workers' battalions modeled on the existing machine gun–artillery battalions and another 40, which resembled the Red Army's automatic weapons battalions. Govorov approved and implemented this proposal on 18 April.[8]

After the Red Army cracked the German blockade in January 1943 and established a narrow land corridor connecting Leningrad with the country as a whole, on 2 April the Stavka ordered the Leningrad and Volkhov Fronts to dig in and defend the corridor and strengthen the city's defenses.[9] The Leningrad Front responded by constructing ever deeper and better-organized defenses and converting the 42d Army's final defense line into a reinforced concrete defensive belt, which was manned by VOG forces. This measure converted the defense line, which had previously consisted of antitank obstacles and armored and wooden fortifications, into a series of permanent fortified regions. Govorov also erected new fortifications and cut-off positions along the eastern (left) bank of the Neva River north of the villages of Gorodok No. 1 and Gorodok No. 2. To the east, Meretskov's Volkhov Front established continuous and deeply echeloned defenses anchored on numerous strong points and obstacles, which extended to a depth of 80 kilometers (49.7 miles) on its right wing and 35–50 kilometers (21.7–31.1 miles) on its left wing.[10] This eliminated any possibility of German forces threatening either the corridor north of Siniavino or the city of Volkhov.

THE ORDEAL CONTINUES

After enduring the terrible famine of winter 1941–1942, the city's civilian and military leadership worked frantically to eliminate the famine's effects and restore as much normalcy as a city under siege could expect. At the same time, however, they had to prepare to defend the city against an expected German summer assault. This meant they had to balance carefully the city's defensive requirements, particularly the soldiers' needs, against the needs of the city's shrunken, surviving population.

The most serious problem facing Leningrad other than its food supply dilemma was the specter of epidemic produced by the city's appalling living conditions and the spring thaw. Already during the winter, on 11 February 1942, the city's Party Committee formed an extraordinary commission under the direction of P. S. Popkov to study methods for either preventing or coping with epidemics.[11] On 31 March Popkov's commission issued a report detailing the main reasons for deaths among the city's population. The report identified malnutrition [emaciation] and what he called "elementary dystrophy" as the cause of about 70 percent of the deaths in the city. A gruesome chart summarized his findings and discounted the impact of infectious diseases on the beleaguered population (Table 4).[12]

On 2 April the NKVD issued a summary report of deaths in the city during the first quarter of 1942, broken down by date and the age distribution of those who perished (Table 5).[13]

The spring thaw, which released a veritable flood of bodies, garbage, and debris from the grip of the winter's ice, produced immense numbers of rodents and other vermin. It also prompted Popkov's organization to under-

Table 4. Deaths from Infectious Diseases in Leningrad, January–March 1942

	January		February		March	
	1941	1942	1941	1942	1941	1942
Spotted typhus	99	24	34	31	61	269
Typhoid fever	137	30	74	77	101	131
Dysentery	2,225	1,982	2,202	3,688	1,489	4,270
Measles	5,527	451	3,789	149	1,831	90
Scarlet fever	1,245	32	1,198	25	700	34
Diphtheria	695	100	734	134	450	105
Whooping cough	1,662	207	1,400	83	784	48
Total	11,640	2,826	9,431	4,187	5,416	4,917

Source: A. P. Dzeniskevich, ed., *Lenigrad v osade: Sbornik dokumertov o geroicheskoi oborone Leningrada v gody Velikoi Otechestvennoi voiny 1941–1944* [Leningrad under siege: Collection of documents about the heroic defense of Leningrad in the Great Patriotic War 1941–1944] (St. Petersburg: Liki Rossii, 1995), 297–298.

take immediate measures to reduce the likelihood of disease decimating what was left of Leningrad's population. Due to his efforts and those of the government and Party, the city managed to avoid major outbreaks of disease throughout 1942 because the authorities implemented a series of stringent hygienic measures to prevent it. Between 27 March and 15 April 1942, the city government and Party and factory organizations organized an extensive public effort to remove all vermin and garbage from the city's streets, basements, homes, buildings, and waterways. During the massive cleanup operation, more than 300,000 people cleaned 16,000 buildings and 3 million square meters of streets, squares, and alleys and removed about 1 million tons of refuse and garbage.[14]

Despite this massive cleanup effort, on 11 May 1942, Zhdanov received a letter from Lieutenant General Kabanov, the commander of Leningrad's garrison, indicating that the cleanup effort had failed and underscoring the seriousness of the problem:

The exceptionally grave health-epidemic state of Leningrad demands extraordinary measures to cease the further growth of infectious disease among the city's population.

In comparison with the previous year, the number of various diseases has risen sharply in April. Based on a calculation of 1,000 inhabitants, in April of this year, the quantity of those sick with dysentery and typhoid fever has increased 5- to 6-fold and spotted typhus 25-fold against April of last year. . . . Because of the poor organization of help to the sick in apartments and the inadequate clinic help, the focal points of spotted typhus have been identified too late, thus hindering the struggle to eliminate it.

Table 5. Civilian Deaths in Leningrad, January–March 1942

	January (%)	February (%)	March (%)
Period			
1st five days	11,217	17,610	14,530
2d five days	16,860	19,686	12,751
3d five days	15,073	17,660	12,984
4th five days	16,963	17,192	15,275
5th five days	17,172	14,556	12,253
6th five days	19,466	9,311	13,714
Total	96,751	96,015	81,507
Men	70,853 (73.2)	57,990 (60.4)	38,664 (47.4)
Women	25,898 (26.8)	38,025 (39.6)	42,843 (52.6)
Total	96,751 (100)	96,015 (100)	81,507 (100)
Age (years)			
Under 1	7,267 (7.5)	5,949 (6.2)	3,696 (4.5)
1–4	2,953 (3.0)	5,022 (5.3)	4,840 (5.9)
5–9	1,833 (2.0)	2,955 (3.1)	3,132 (4.0)
10–14	2,487 (2.5)	3,977 (4.0)	4,477 (5.5)
15–19	5,146 (5.4)	6,699 (7.0)	5,359 (6.6)
20–29	5,506 (5.7)	5,967 (6.2)	5,572 (6.8)
30–39	12,642 (13.1)	12,302 (13.0)	10,150 (12.4)
40–49	16,683 (17.3)	14,513 (15.1)	11,725 (14.4)
50–59	18,853 (19.4)	14,693 (15.3)	11,815 (14.4)
60 and older	20,362 (21.0)	17,590 (19.0)	15,924 (19.5)
Unknown	3,019 (3.1)	6,348 (5.7)	4,817 (6.0)
Total	96,751 (100)	96,015 (100)	81,507 (100)

Source: A. P. Dzeniskevich, ed., *Lenigrad v osade. Sbornik dokumertov o geroicheskoi oborone Leningrada v Velikoi Otechestvennoi voine 1941–1944* [Leningrad under siege: Collection of documents about the heroic defense of Leningrad in the Great Patriotic War 1941–1944] (St. Petersburg: Liki Rossii, 1995), 298.

An apartment-by-apartment search of many tens of thousands of citizens has determined that a considerable segment of the population is lice-ridden, reaching in some regions to 30 percent. At present many living spaces also remain unclean. Only 6–7 percent of the apartments have running water. The sewers operate in only 9 percent of the apartments. Because of the inoperable healthy sewer system, a considerable part of the population throw their garbage in waste collection pits.

The absence of an operable water supply and sewers in the homes hinders the regular cleaning of apartments and fosters the further pollution of living spaces. The washing of clothes in laundries is seldom done because of the absence of water and the disrepair of the sewers in the laundries. Of the city's 65 baths that are operating, about one half do so with great interruptions. Of the 14 first aid points, only 6 are operating but with interruptions.

Preventative health measures and the medical work being conducted by the city health department is far from sufficient for achieving a turn-around in the health-epidemic state of the city and eliminating outbreaks of contagious diseases among the population.

At the present time, separate instances of sickness with spotted typhus are appearing in the garrison's units, whose source is the close contact between the soldiers and the city's population. The outbreaks of the sickness of spotted typhus among the civilian population at Shushmary Station and the village of Rybatskii in the immediate vicinity of Leningrad will also cause the appearance of the illness in the forces quartered in these population points. In these conditions, there is a real threat that infectious diseases will penetrate and massively spread throughout the garrison's forces.[15]

[signed] Lieutenant General Kabanov
Chief of the Leningrad Garrison

Clearly, the measures undertaken in March and April had not been adequate to eliminate the threat of spreading epidemics. Several documents underscore the depressing consequences of the ensuing epidemic as it swept across Leningrad in summer 1942. For example, Brick Works No. 1 reported on 9 December 1942 that its furnaces had cremated 117,300 bodies from 7 March through 1 December.[16] Even more damning, a detailed report, which the city's Statistical Directorate issued in February 1943, summarized in tabular form by month the number of infectious illnesses recorded in all of Leningrad's 15 districts throughout 1942:[17]

Typhoid fever	1,939	Cerebral meningitis	160
Paratyphoid	211	Epidemic encephalitis	5
Dysentery	31,648	Poliomyelitis	2
Spotted typhus	3,516	Infectious jaundice	498
Measles	1,401	Scurvy	814
Scarlet fever	621	Malaria	113
Diphtheria	2,380	Influenza [grippe]	64,233
Whooping cough	5.201		

The only ameliorating circumstance associated with these grim statistics was the fact that the death toll from malnutrition dwarfed the number of deaths from disease.

Another natural but tragic by-product of the immense death toll was a burgeoning number of homeless and neglected children. A report prepared by the city's Executive Committee and sent to A. I. Kosygin, deputy chairman of the Council of People's Commissars, in Moscow on 28 July 1943 summarized the problem:

The conditions of the Leningrad blockade have caused considerable growth in the quantity of children who have lost their parents or who have temporarily been deprived of parental supervision. . . .

In December 1941 the Executive Committee of the Leningrad City Council made a decision concerning the expansion of the contingent [capacity] in children's homes and the opening of two new children's homes. In January 1942 we increased the enrollment in children's homes by 2,725 children and opened 23 new children's homes with an overall capacity of 5,550 children. By March 1942 the actual number of children in children's homes reached 14,300 persons. . . .

The NKVD's Children's Receiver-Distributors *[Detskie priemniki-raspredeliteli]*, which were organized in February 1942 in every city district, have accomplished great work on the organization of children left without parents. Since the Children's Receiver-Distributors began work and up to the end of 1942, 26,250 children have passed through them. The Children's Receiver-Distributors were also completely staffed and equipped with teachers, medical and technical workers, and equipped with necessary stock and kitchen utensils.

The quantity of children in children's homes grew so much during the second half of March 1942 that it became necessary to unload them both because it was impossible to create appropriate living conditions for the children and to save the children's lives. The evacuation of the children's foundling hospitals was begun im March 1942. In all, 38,080 children located in children's homes were taken from Leningrad in the spring and summer.[18]

The net effect of famine, epidemic, and German artillery fire and air strikes was a sudden and inexorable rise in the death rate and a corresponding abrupt and staggering decrease in the city's population. A report by the city's Bureau of Ration Cards dated 13 October 1943 placed Leningrad's population at 621,000 persons, including 575,400 with ration cards, 16,000 in hospitals, and 30,600 without cards.[19] Numerous reports prepared in 1943 and 1944 documented the human suffering the population endured.

Despite the winter's hardships, some life returned to the city after winter's end. During spring 1942, the city's transport system once again began to operate, its population returned to work, and the authorities and the public at large worked frantically to improve the city's still scarce food supplies. The trams, water supply, canals, and many factories began working on 15 April, and the city government ordered the population to plant gardens on every possible patch of open land. It exploited every park and vacant area in the city to assign plots of land to the population on which to grow vegetables. Ultimately, more than 200,000 Leningraders planted 2,000 hectares (4,942 acres).[20]

Factories too began production, albeit slowly, particularly those producing weaponry, to which the government assigned priority in the allocation of critical resources. Weapons factories increased their production from 5 machine guns, 649 submachine guns, and 67,900 shells and mines in April to 150 machine guns, 2,875 submachine guns, and 150,700 shells and mines in May.[21] As indicated by a report submitted by the defense industry on military production throughout 1942, this also included heavy weaponry, in particular tanks:[22]

KV-1 tanks	46	Pillboxes	1,439
T-26 and SU-26 tanks	14	Rocket launchers	386
Repaired KV-1 tanks	108	Mine detectors	4,708
Repaired tanks of various types	262	Firing and bombing sights	1,483
Armored trains and armored		Trench periscopes	10,200
platforms	3	Helmets	1,704
Repaired armored trains and		50mm, 82mm, 120mm	
armored platforms	4	mortar shells	861,300
Naval artillery systems	9	M-28, M-30, M-32 rocket	
Repaired naval artillery systems	74	shells	5,765
76mm guns, 1927 model	692	Antitank and antipersonnel	
Repaired ground artillery systems	285	mines	955,700
Repaired railroad batteries	23	Imitation mines	4,500
Platforms for naval systems	65	Shells, 45mm to 406mm	827,155
MTV gun chassis	310	20- to 100-kilogram	
160mm mortars	3	aviation bombs	22,230
50mm and 82mm mortars	1,555	Explosives of various types	3,235,660
Repaired 50mm, 82mm, 107mm,		Hand grenades	1,260,820
and 120mm mortars	555	Fuses for various systems	5,630,000
Maxim machine guns	2,692	Percussion caps	115,102,300
DP submachine guns	139	Detonator caps	3,554,000
PPD automatic rifles	34,936	TB-2 tank destroyer	
PPS automatic rifles	620	mechanisms	36,000
Nagan revolvers	70	KV-4 tank bushings	980,000
Rifle bayonets	21,699	Specialized bullets	831,000
Machine gun cartridge belts	9,164		

Since coal and other fuels were still in short supply, factories and other enterprises used only wood and peat as fuel. Once again, the authorities mobilized the entire population in the effort, and they gathered 1 million cubic meters of fuel during the summer. Since this amount was still insufficient, the authorities ordered all buildings not suited for occupancy to be torn down for use as fuel.

In the fall of 1942, as the second winter under siege approached, the city's entire population, together with soldiers and sailors, helped the city prepare. Every able-bodied man and woman repaired buildings and gathered foodstuffs, including 76,000 tons of vegetables, which considerably lightened the transport requirements across Lake Ladoga in the summer and early fall. Labor detachments repaired 81,531 square meters of roofs and 48,000 furnaces, cleaned out 220,000 chimneys, and glazed over and sealed 550,000 square meters of flues, walls, and windows. The same workforce repaired 50,000 water hydrants and repaired 489,688 meters of water pipes and other conduits. By winter, theses groups also restored 6,131 building to a habitable state.[23]

To help solve the fuel shortage, on 25 April 1942, the GKO ordered Red Army's engineers to lay a welded fuel pipeline across the floor of Lake Ladoga. When it went into operation on 18 June, the pipeline, 35 kilometers (21.7 miles) long and 12 meters (39.4 feet) deep, carried 300 tons of fuel per day to Leningrad. Finally, in September the power station at Volkhov began sending the city electrical power, which was transmitted across the lake by underwater cable.[24]

RESUPPLY IN SUMMER 1942

While the population and military struggled to make Leningrad as safe and self-sufficient as possible, the Leningrad Front and Ladoga Flotilla worked with equal determination during the summer to expand transport capacity into the city. On 9 April 1942, the GKO approved a new transport plan that established daily targets for shipment of food, ammunition, military equipment, and fuel and lubricants into the city and evacuees and some cargoes out of the city. These targets involved the transfer of 2,500 tons of food, 300 tons of ammunition, 100 tons of military equipment, 100 tons of coal and fuel oil, and 300 tons of lubricants to the city and the shipment of 1,000 tons of cargo and 3,000 people daily from the city to the Soviet rear.[25]

The Ladoga Military Flotilla was responsible for organizing and managing this transport effort. The flotilla and the Baltic Fleet personnel repaired ships during the winter; Leningrad's shipbuilders constructed 14 metal barges, 31 towed wooden boats, and 118 small-capacity self-propelled boats for use on the lake; and fishermen provided 17 self-propelled boats and 4 towed boats. Similar work went on at docking facilities, which were greatly expanded.[26]

Navigation across the lake began on 22 May 1942, when the steamer *Gidrotekhnik* towed a string of barges from Kobona on the lake's eastern shore to Osinovets on its western shore. Soon other ships began traveling the 150 kilometers (93.2 miles) from Gostinopol' through Novaia Ladoga to Osinovets and the 29 kilometers (18 miles) from Kobona to Osinovets. The first full convoy left Novaia Ladoga on 28 May. From May through 31 December 1942, more than 200 ships with a total carrying capacity of 32,000 tons made uninterrupted trips across the lake carrying a total of 779,586 tons of cargo. Of this cargo, 50 percent was foodstuffs, 15.4 percent coal, 16.7 percent lubricants, and 17.9 percent weaponry and other military cargoes. The foodstuffs primarily consisted of flour, grain, macaroni, butter, fat, meat, sugar, preserves, and chocolate. In addition, the city received 4,186 sheep and goats, 7,723 small cattle, 4,388 horses, 41,638 cubic meters of wood, 5,967 tons of various goods, and 1,300 tons of medical supplies.[27]

Once the Ladoga routes became operational, the evacuation of factory equipment and critical technical personnel increased dramatically. During the summer the flotilla and associated lake transport evacuated 539,597 persons and 292,900 tons of factory equipment across the lake. On its return trips, it transported 310,000 combat replacements for the Leningrad Front, turning the city into an immense military encampment.[28] These shipments materially improved the city's food supply, avoided new famine in the winter of 1942–1943, and permitted industry to resume operations.

Since Leningrad remained in the grips of a tight siege throughout 1942, defense of the supply lines remained a critical requirement, particularly against air attack. During the summer, in conjunction with their anticipated Operation *Nordlicht* against the city, the Germans tried to interdict the flow of supplies into the city, primarily by bombing its port facilities and vital supply umbilicals across Lake Ladoga and the Gulf of Finland between Leningrad and Oranienbaum. The Germans began their air campaign on 4 April, when they conducted heavy attacks on the ships of the Baltic Fleet and Ladoga Flotilla. They repeated the attacks on 24, 25, and 27 April in conjunction with a heavy artillery bombardment of the city's port facilities. For example, about 100 German aircraft struck the port of Kobona on 28 May, but antiaircraft gunners shot down an estimated 19 German aircraft.[29]

The heaviest German air attacks, however, occurred in early fall 1942, when Hitler ordered Manstein to pound the city into submission. In September alone, German aircraft dropped 120 bombs in several raids on the Kobona region and neighboring port and transshipment facilities. Throughout the fall, the Germans conducted a total of 122 daylight and 15 night raids involving 80–130 aircraft each and dropped a total of 6,400 bombs on the city.[30] However, PVO antiaircraft gunners and Red Army aircraft inflicted increasingly heavy aircraft losses on the *Luftwaffe,* forcing it to reduce sharply the size and number of its raids. In the end, these raids had only a negligible effect on transport and resupply, reducing cargo shipments by only .4 percent, at a cost of an estimated 160 aircraft lost by the Germans.[31]

The ground defenses of Lake Ladoga's southern shore and the approaches to the shores east and west of the lake remained vital to the defense of the water routes through mid-January 1943, since the Germans' front lines still clung to the lake's southern shores, perilously close to the city. Throughout 1942 the Ladoga Flotilla manned the Oreshek Fortress opposite Shlissel'burg to defend the southwestern shore of the lake and maintained a naval garrison on Sukho Island to protect the lake's southeast shore. The Leningrad and Volkhov Fronts protected the ground approaches to these routes, in particular, the critical road and railroad between Novaia Ladoga and Volkhov. The 55th Rifle Brigade and 16th Fortified Region of the Leningrad Front's Neva Operational Group (later the 67th Army) provided security forces for the water route and ground approaches and the ice road itself once the lake froze. Largely due to the effective defense, the Ladoga water routes managed to function normally throughout 1942 despite constant navigation difficulties caused by storms, rough water, and German air and artillery action.

Frustrated by their inability to halt or even slow the flow of vital supplies across the lake, on several occasions the Germans attempted direct action to close the lake routes. For example, in April and May 1942, they convinced the Finns to deploy a small naval and amphibious force on the lake. This force consisted of 4 Italian torpedo boats, 4 German cutters, 7 self-propelled amphibious assault boats, 12 self-propelled landing barges, and 1 headquarters, 1 medical, and 4 transport ships.[32] Soviet intelligence detected the presence of these ships and a landing force of 3,000 men at the ports of Sortavala, Lakhdenpokh'ia, and Impilakhti the following month.

In addition, the Germans deployed a detachment of landing barges to Keksholm in August and began conducting reconnaissance and diversionary actions on the lake in late September. They laid magnetic mines on the sea routes on 27 September and also attempted to cut communications west of Sukho Island in September and October by landing a small force on the island. Govorov responded by beefing up Soviet defenses on the lake and islands between May and September and by deploying a naval detachment of 100 men and three 100mm guns into defensive positions on Sukho Island.

Soon after, in early October, the Finns formed an amphibious force of 23 boats and 7 cutters armed with 88 37mm guns and 22mm automatic guns and prepared to land the force on the island, supposedly on 13 October. However, Soviet aircraft discovered and heavily damaged the flotilla on 9 October and forced postponement of the operation. The Leningrad war diary described the action:

> *Friday, 9 October.* On Ladoga the enemy is clearly attempting to carry out an amphibious operation. Seventeen of his landing boats were discovered on the banks of the Severnaia Goloveshka [River] on the night of 1 October. Our ships drove them back. Another 16 enemy barges and 7 cutters appeared once again east of Konivets Island on the night of 9 October. The crews of two "sea hunters" discovered this flotilla. In spite of the enemy's superiority, they took them under fire. . . .
>
> Two of our cutters began unequal battle with the enemy flotilla. Soon cutter MO-175, commanded by Lieutenant V. Iu. Pustynnikov, was destroyed. Cutter MO-214 was encircled. Its crew continued firing until its ammunition ran out . . . [and soon our aircraft appeared and engaged the enemy].
>
> The enemy quickly retreated. He lost an amphibious barge, and many of his boats were damaged.[33]

The Finns began a new landing attempt from Sortavala on 22 October, concealed by a storm on the lake. Once again, two Soviet patrol cutters discovered the force in time, and the Soviet garrison repelled the attack, sinking 17 Finnish boats, shooting down 14 enemy aircraft, and capturing 61 prisoners. This small victory ended all enemy attempts to operate on the lake.[34]

RESUPPLY IN WINTER 1942–1943 AND SUMMER 1943

When winter began in late 1942, German forces defending the Mga-Siniavino salient east of the city still had all land routes into the city in a stranglehold. Once again, it seemed as if Leningraders would have to rely on the ice road as their lifeline during the coming winter. Since few Leningraders had forgotten the horrors of the previous winter's famine, they and the city's authorities redoubled their efforts to avoid repeating the catastrophe that had befallen them the previous year.

However, four, and ultimately five, factors combined to alleviate the situation. First, and tragically, because of the previous year's death toll and the summer evacuations, the size of Leningrad's population was far smaller in November 1942 than it had been in November 1941. Leningrad now had only 700,000 civilians and about 420,000 soldiers' mouths to feed. Second, the Leningraders were able to amass far greater reserves in 1942 than had existed in 1941. Third, the winter of 1942–1943 was far less severe than the winter of 1941–1942. The freeze arrived later in 1942, and, as a result, navigation and transport on the lake continued until 27 November 1942, and, in some instances, until 7 January 1943 farther north on the lake, where the ice formed later. Fourth, despite the late freeze, the authorities were far more experienced with the exploitation of the ice road. Fifth, the Red Army finally cracked the blockade in mid-January 1943.

When the lake finally did freeze, the Leningrad Front and Ladoga Flotilla exploited their experiences of the previous winter to improve the road and also began constructing rail lines to supplement the existing road routes. The increased reliance on rail precluded the painstaking and time-consuming transfer of cargoes from railroad cars to ships and boats. Red Army engineers began building the rail line simultaneously from east and west and by mid-January had laid 15 kilometers (9.3 miles) of operational track across the western extremity of the lake. However, after Red Army forces reopened the land corridor to Leningrad in January 1943, the engineers halted construction of the lake route and instead moved the railroad to a land route through the corridor, even though the land corridor remained quite narrow and was subject to constant German artillery fire. All construction on the ice railroad halted on 19 January, although work on the lake's ice roads continued, as did vehicular traffic across the lake.

Despite the late freeze and frequent thaws, which complicated construction on the ice road, it finally opened for traffic on 19 December. The first convoy passed over it on 20 December, but the 160 transports carried only 300 kilograms (660 pounds) of cargo each. Subsequently, larger columns of 300 GAZ-AA trucks, each carrying 1,000 kilograms of cargo, and 143 ZIS-5s trucks traveled the route on 27 December and 8 January.[35] After 8 January the convoys ended due to weak ice. Ice road traffic resumed on 12 January but again ended on 30 March, when the Leningrad Front was forced to close the road because of yet another thaw. Over the course of the winter, the ice road was serviceable for only 101 days between 20 December and 30 March and suitable for massive movements on only 97 days.

During this period, trucks transported 214,539 tons of cargo, predominantly food and ammunition, and over 200,000 personnel and evacuees.[36] The total tonnage reaching Leningrad by way of the ice road during the winter of 1942–1943 included 111,813 tons of food, 54,355 tons of ammunition, and 18,603 tons of coal. In addition, 12,368 horses, 1,431 vehicles, and 133,144 personnel reinforcements entered the city via the road, and the road carried 10,126 tons of cargo and 88,932 evacuees from the city.[37] Even after the rail line through the Shlissel'burg corridor became operational, the ice road still functioned as a reliable communications route for the Leningrad Front. The Germans continued their air attacks on the ice road throughout the winter, even after the Red Army recaptured the narrow land link into the city. Despite mounting 140 air raids and dropping more than 280 bombs, they failed to hinder movement over the ice road. To the relief of the road's defenders, German artillery fire ended after the Red Army seized a land corridor to the city in January.

After completing Operation Spark in January, the Leningrad Front worked feverishly to restore reliable ground communications between Leningrad and the Soviet rear area. In accordance with a GKO directive of 18 January, the very next day the Leningrad Front's Military Council began planning to construct a rail line along the southern shore of Lake Ladoga from Shlissel'burg to Poliana.[38] Railroad forces and specialized construction formations began work on the rail line on 21 January. The railroad bed, which ran through rough terrain only 6–8 kilometers (3.7–5 miles) from the front lines at Siniavino, was constructed under constant artillery fire and air attack in severe winter conditions. Despite the difficulties, military construction troops managed to build a 33-kilometer (20.5-mile) line from Volkhovstroi on the Volkhov River through Poliana to Shlissel'burg that opened on 6 February.[39] Thereafter, the rail line and lake water routes supplied Leningrad's military and civilian needs.

In terms of its capacity, the rail line was far more important than the water routes across Lake Ladoga.

Construction forces continued to improve rail passage as spring approached, building a new railroad bridge across the Neva River in the dead of winter. When it opened on 18 March, the bridge permitted through traffic along the entire rail line. However, incessant German artillery fire inflicted heavy casualties and constantly forced the constructors to repair and restore the lines. The Ladoga water routes took over the transport task while the railroad was being repaired. Construction troops built a second rail line parallel to the first in May 1943. This 18-kilometer (11.2-mile) rail line, which was closer to the lake, improved the efficiency, capacity, and safety of rail transport through the Shlissel'burg corridor.[40] At first, all rail transport along the two railroads took place at night on the basis of special schedules for one-way and two-way movement. By the end of June, however, all rail traffic was running two ways almost constantly.

The Germans did everything in their power to disrupt or halt rail movement by conducting artillery fire and air strikes on the roadway, bridges, and other rail installations. Since the Germans believed that they could cut off supplies both to Leningrad and the Volkhov Front by destroying the bridges across the Volkhov River, in May and June they mounted heavy air raids against these bridges by as many as 100 bombers and 40 fighters at a single time. Although they succeeded in destroying one bridge on 1 June, construction troops and engineers had replaced the destroyed bridge with a wooden bridge within five days and a metal bridge by 19 June. German aircraft destroyed the wooden bridge again on 19 June and the metal bridge on 21 June. However, these bridges were again restored on 23 June and 2 July, respectively.[41] Subsequently, the Shlissel'burg-Volkhovstroi railroad played an immense role in supplying Leningrad's population and defenders. During the period between its opening in February 1943 through 6 March 1944, 5,334 cargo trains with 225,859 railroad cars filled with various cargoes traversed the land route to Leningrad.[42]

With the new land route into Leningrad functioning effectively, resupply of the city and defense of the supply lines became a far easier process during the spring and summer of 1943. In addition, the nature of transported cargo also changed considerably as the Leningrad Front used the lake routes to transport primarily wood and wood products. The total volume of supplies amounted to 515,500 tons, over half of which was wood. Shipments during spring and summer included 78,109 tons of wood, 52,886 tons of food, 4,436 tons of fuel, and 12,532 tons of coal sent into Leningrad and 41,300 tons of cargo shipped out of Leningrad.[43]

The supply routes across Lake Ladoga gradually lost their military importance after September 1943, when the Leningrad Front transferred all berths, ports, and cargo means on the lake's eastern and western shores to the control of the civilian Northwestern River Ferry Service. Throughout the entire Leningrad blockade, the water routes across Lake Ladoga transported 2,275,000 tons of cargo, including 1,870,000 tons of cargo sent to the city.[44]

THE PARTISAN MOVEMENT IN 1942

Although the partisan movement in Leningrad region grew significantly in 1942 and 1943, its military importance remained relatively limited. On 1 January 1942, an estimated 1,994 partisans, men and women, were operating, primarily in the northwestern, western, and southern parts of the region. The most extensive and successful partisan activities took place in the Partisan *krai* far south of the city. These forces were loosely organized into the Leningrad, Valdai, and Volkhov Operational Groups, each of which consisted of separate detachments. The Leningrad Operational Group, which consisted of partisan detachments operating in the Tosno and Liuban' regions, was organized into two battalions commanded by E. F. Tuvalovich and K. I. Volovich. The Valdai Operational Group consisted of partisan detachments in the Staraia Russa, Polovsk, Zaluch'e, and Molvotitsy regions in the southwestern and southern reaches of Leningrad region, and the third operational group operated in the Volkhov Front's sector.[45]

Despite the growing array of partisan detachments, the detachments were weak and poorly organized, and the heavy snow and extreme cold severely hindered their operations. Therefore, the Leningrad partisan headquarters spent the winter attempting to improve their organization, command and control, and firepower. In March, for example, it combined the Leningrad and Volkhov Operational Groups under A. A. Guzeev's command to improve command and control. The following month it reorganized the Valdai Operational Group's detachments into the 3d Partisan Brigade, commanded by A. V. German, and the 4th Partisan Brigade, commanded by A. P. Luchin.[46]

During winter 1941–1942, partisan operations were weak and episodic and only loosely coordinated with *front* operations. For example, the Tosno and Liuban' detachments operated against German communications lines, but with only limited effectiveness, during the Volkhov Front's Liuban' offensive. Farther south, in January and February, partisans in the Gdov region supported the Northwestern Front's Demiansk offensive by disrupting German communications between Pskov and Gdov and Gdov and Kingisepp. In addition, partisans operating near Ostrov, Dno, Porkhov, Soshikhin, and Belebelka supported the Northwestern Front operations around Demiansk and Kholm. These partisans achieved signal success when they assisted Red Army forces in the seizure of Kholm on 18 January, Iasski on 5 February, and Dedovichi on 22 February. However, in each case, German relief attacks ultimately forced the partisans and Red Army forces to abandon the towns.[47]

At the same time, however, partisans operating in and around the Partisan *krai* gathered and sent foodstuffs to Leningrad, the first delivery of which reached the city by a circuitous route on 25 February.[48] Partisan detachments also sent representatives and delegations to and from the city to receive instructions and coordinate their actions with the Leningrad Front.

Despite its relative inactivity, the partisan movement and the closely associated Party underground structure grew throughout the winter. By April 1942, 50 new partisan detachments had formed and begun operating in the Leningrad region, and the Party formed and fielded 25 special partisan groups of seven to nine men each in Gdov, Pskov, Luga, Oredezh, Pliussa, Strugo-krasnensk, Kingisepp, and other regions to establish underground communications, liaison, and infrastructure with partisan detachments.[49] During this period, Soviet records indicate that partisan actions inflicted 15,000 losses on German troops and destroyed 114 rail and road bridges, 26 warehouses, 69 tanks, 500 vehicles, and 13 aircraft.[50]

Partisan organization and operational effectiveness improved during the summer and fall of 1942, primarily because the Party, GKO, and Red Army exercised more effective centralized control over partisan organizations and operations. On 30 May 1942, the Communist Party and GKO formed the Central Headquarters of the Partisan Movement to centralize state control over all partisan organizations and detachments:[51]

> 1. The Central Headquarters of the Partisan Movement is created under the *Stavka* of the Supreme High Command for the purpose of unifying the direction of the partisan movement in the enemy rear and for the further development of this movement.
>
> 2. The following headquarters of the partisan movement are created in the *fronts'* Military Councils for direct control over partisan detachments:
>> a. The Ukrainian Headquarters of the Partisan Movement
>> b. The Briansk Headquarters of the Partisan Movement
>> c. The Western Headquarters of the Partisan Movement
>> d. The Kalinin Headquarters of the Partisan Movement
>> e. The Leningrad Headquarters of the Partisan Movement
>> f. The Karelo-Finnish Headquarters of the Partisan Movement
>
> The headquarters indicated above are subordinate to the Central Headquarters of the Partisan Movement.
>
> 3. In their practical activities in the control of the partisan movement, the Central Headquarters of the Partisan Movement must proceed from

the premise that the main mission of the partisan movement is the disorganization of the enemy's rear area [by]:

a. Destroying enemy lines of communications (blowing up bridges, damaging rail lines, wrecking trains, and attacking enemy automobile and truck transport).
b. Destroying communications lines (telephone, telegraph, and radio stations).
c. Destroying warehouses—ammunition, supplies, fuel, and foodstuffs.
d. Attacking headquarters and other troop installations in the enemy's rear.
e. Destroying equipment at enemy airfields.
f. Notifying Red Army units about the dispositions, strength, and movements of enemy forces.

4. Include P. K. Ponomarenko (a member of the Party Central Committee), V. T. Sergienko (NKVD) as chief of staff, and T. F. Korneev (NKO Intelligence Directorate) in the Central Headquarters of the Partisan Movement.

5. Include the following comrades in the headquarters of the partisan movement in the *fronts:*

a. Ukrainian Headquarters—head, Strokach (NKVD); chief of staff, Spivak (Central Committee, Ukrainian Communist Party); and Vinogradov (chief of the Southwestern Front's Intelligence Department).
b. Briansk Headquarters—head, Matveev (secretary of the Orel Party Executive Committee); chief of staff, Gorshkov (NKVD); and Chermazov (chief of the Briansk Front's Intelligence Department).
c. Western Headquarters—head, Bel'chenko (NKVD); chief of staff, Kalinin (Central Committee, Communist Party); and Il'nitsky (chief of the Western Front's Intelligence Department).
d. Kalinin Headquarters—head, Ratsenko (NKVD), chief of staff, Ryzhikov (Central Committee, Communist Party); and Aleshin (chief of the Kalinin Front's Intelligence Department).
e. Leningrad Headquarters—head, Nikitin (Leningrad Communist Party Executive Committee); chief of staff, Evstigneev (chief of the Leningrad Front's Intelligence Department).
f. Karelo-Finnish Headquarters—head, Vershinin (NKVD), chief of staff, Khoroshaev (Central Committee, Karelo-Finnish SSR); Almazov (NKVD); and Povetkin (chief of the Karelian Front's Intelligence Department).

[signed] I. Stalin[52]

The new headquarters established an elaborate hierarchy of command and control organs, which extended from Moscow through operating *fronts* to individual partisan headquarters in the German rear, and dispatched Red Army and NKVD officers to create new partisan forces and control all partisan operations. The new structure increased the effectiveness of partisan warfare, brought partisan actions under more effective centralized control, and permitted better coordination between partisan activities and Red Army operations.

At Leningrad, Govorov established the Leningrad Headquarters of the Partisan Movement in July 1942, in accordance with a Central Headquarters order dated 2 July, which mandated the formation of specific operational group headquarters within major subordinate headquarters:

> In accordance with NKO Order No. 00125 of 16 June 1942 I *order:*
>
> The Leningrad Headquarters of the Partisan Movement will create operational groups in the Military Councils of the 23d, 54th, 59th, 4th, 52d, 11th, 53d, 1st Shock and 7th Separate Armies and also in the Leningrad Front's Primorskii Group of Forces.
>
> I am establishing operational groups of the headquarters of the partisan movement, consisting of a chief of the operational group, an operational representative, and a chauffeur, in the indicated army military councils.
>
> [signed] Ponomarenko, Timoshenko[53]

As of 3 July 1942, the Leningrad Headquarters of the Partisan movement had fielded 58 detachments totaling 5,024 partisan fighters.[54]

The Leningrad Headquarters of the Partisan Movement exercised command and control over all partisan forces operating in the Leningrad region and the headquarters was tasked with centralizing all planning for and control over partisan warfare in the region. A new unified partisan operational plan created new partisan detachments and diversionary groups, ordered these forces to sabotage and destroy German garrisons, installations, and communications and attack German headquarters, supply depots, airfields, and communications centers, and established priority intelligence collection requirements in support of *front*-controlled ground combat operations.[55]

The strength of partisan forces and the scope of their activities in the Leningrad region increased sharply in the summer of 1942. Throughout the year, the number of partisan brigades and the strength of partisan forces operating in the German rear area grew from 2 partisan brigades and 30 weak detachments with 2,000 fighters to 4 brigades and numerous separate detachments with 3,000 personnel.[56] The 2d Partisan Brigade operated southeast of Dno, and the 3d Partisan Brigade operated south of Opochka Station. Detachments commanded by A. I. Iakumov, M. I. Shchurov, L. P. Durygin, D. A. Shakhrinsky, and F. S. Makarov and tens of diversionary groups operated in the forests east of Pskov. Detachments led by B. M. Prokhorov, T. Ia. Pechatnikov, S. A. Sergeev, G. F. Bol'shov, A. A. Zabelina, G. I. Bogdanov, the 1st Partisan Brigade, and tens of other detachments operated northeast of Gdov. Finally, the 4th Partisan Brigade operated in the southern part of the region.[57]

Although these forces engaged primarily in low-intensity sabotage and diversionary operations, their actions were bothersome enough to provoke an organized German response in the form of formal antipartisan operations. In Fuehrer Directive No. 46 issued on 18 August 1942, Hitler declared, "The bandit monstrosity in the East has assumed a no longer tolerable scope and threatens to become a serious danger to front supply and exploitation of the land."[58] Hitler assigned Heinrich Himmler responsibility for rooting out partisan activity, charged the OKH chief of staff with conducting antipartisan warfare, and ordered the Replacement Army be employed as antipartisan forces as they completed their training.

Subsequently, the Germans mounted numerous operations against partisans, but particularly against the Partisan *krai*. A German punitive expedition consisting of the 218th Infantry Division, the 4th Blocking Regiment, security units, and punitive detachments, with a total strength of 6,000 men, began a major operation to pacify the Partisan *krai*. In combat that lasted until 10 September, German forces captured villages in the Belebelka, Dedovichi, and Poddorsk regions; destroyed villages, farms, and buildings; and persecuted local inhabitants, turning the Partisan *krai* into "a desert."[59]

The German punitive operation inflicted significant casualties on the partisans and forced the partisan movement to move its forces to safer locales out of harm's way. Subsequently, the 2d and 3d Partisan Brigades moved to the Ostrov, Slavkovichi, and Novorzhensk regions; the 1st and 4th Brigades relocated to Gdov and Slantsy; and the remaining detachments moved to the Novgorod, Sol'tsy, Utorgosh', and Luga regions for their own protection.[60] However, the fury of the German operation generated a backlash by prompting virtually all of the region's inhabitants to join the partisan movement. Before its destruction, the Partisan *krai* had existed unmolested for about one year, during which Soviet records claim the partisans killed an estimated 9,000 German troops and destroyed 130 vehicles, 18 depots, and 37 railroad trains.[61]

A 31 October report prepared by the Central Headquarters of the Partisan Movement summarized the strength and activities of partisan forces in Leningrad region in 1942:

There are 73 partisan detachments and 133 diversionary groups with a total of 5,129 partisans. The partisans are operating in difficult conditions in the enemy's immediate rear.

They practiced procuring ammunition and clothing in the winter of 1941–1942. The partisans obtained foodstuffs and even organized the supply of Leningrad. They practiced the withdrawal of detachments for short rests in the Soviet rear area and sent them back into the enemy rear area for combat operations.

During this year the food resources of the population have been significantly exhausted by German confiscation everywhere in these regions. Huge segments of the population itself have been evacuated or destroyed and are already experiencing food shortages. Therefore, the partisan detachments have not been able to exist on the basis of local resources during the winter. In addition to foodstuffs seized by the partisans from smashed and derailed trains, the Leningrad, Volkhov, and Northwestern Fronts must provide assistance to the partisan detachments operating in the enemy rear. The resupply can be carried out [by land] from the Northwestern and Kalinin Fronts in the Kholm region and also by aircraft.

It is necessary to disperse the large brigades of Vasil'ev and Orlov and others by detachments during the winter.[62]

Despite destroying the Partisan *krai,* German losses to partisan actions continued to mount in a vicious circle that ignited revolt throughout the entire German rear area. Worse still for the Germans, the near-constant heavy fighting in and around Leningrad and to the south around Demiansk forced Army Group North to reduce the size and number of its own rear-area security installations, while significantly improving partisan morale.

THE PARTISAN MOVEMENT IN 1943

The partisan movement in the Leningrad region strengthened significantly throughout 1943 and became far better organized than had previously been the case. The strength of the partisan movement in the Leningrad region increased from 2,993 enrolled fighters on 1 January 1943 to 4,203 on 1 August and 14,358 on 1 November.[63] So also did the scope of diversionary, reconnaissance, and underground activities. By 1 January 1943, the Leningrad Party Regional Committee had established 11 interregional underground Party centers at Ostrov, Pskov, Dno, Strugkrasnensk, Dedovichi, Gdov, Kingisepp, Luga, Oredezh, Novgorod, and Porkhov.[64] Headed by a first secretary and equipped with a full staff, each center was responsible for coordinating the activities of all partisan groups, detachments, and underground organizations operating in each region and consolidating these forces into larger and more effective formations. Partisan formations on 1 May 1943 included five partisan brigades, a separate partisan regiment, and tens of detachments and groups.

The 5th Partisan Brigade, commanded by K. D. Karitsky, had formed in the Slavkovichi region in the winter of 1942–1943 from the Staraia Russa and Dedovichi detachments. A. D. Kondrat'ev's 4th Partisan Brigade formed from the 5th Brigade in mid-1943 to conduct operations in the southern part of Leningrad region. The 11th Partisan Brigade, first commanded by A. P. Luchin and, later, by N. A. Brednikov, combined the Oredezh, Novgorod, Bataisk, and other detachments operating at the junction of the Leningrad and Volkhov Fronts. The 3d "A. V. German" Partisan Brigade continued to operate in the Ostrov and Soshikhin regions, and the 2d "N. G. Vasil'ev" Partisan Brigade, commanded successively by M. I. Timokhin, A. N. Rachkov, and N. I. Sinel'nikov, redeployed from the Novgorod to the Pskov region in summer 1943. In addition, several separate partisan regiments and detachments operated throughout the region. By 1 August five partisan brigades, a separate partisan regiment, and tens of detachments totaling 4,203 partisan fighters were operating throughout the Leningrad region.[65]

Additional partisan formations formed after 1 August 1943. The 6th Partisan Brigade, under V. P. Ob'edkov, formed in September from the 2d Brigade and the 7th and 8th Partisan Brigades under A. V. Alekseev and L. B. Tsinchenko in the regions administered by the Pskov, Ostrov, and Porkhov Party District Committees. The 9th Partisan Brigade, commanded by N. G. Svetlov, formed during the fall in the Gdov, Slantsy, Liady, Os'mino, and Luga regions. T. A. Novikov's 10th Partisan Brigade formed in the Dno and Struga regions, and A. A. Inginen's 12th Partisan Brigade formed from detachments in the Kingisepp region also in late fall. Finally, the 13th Partisan Brigade, under A. V. Iurtsev, which was the last to form, organized on 11 January 1944 in the southern portion of Dedovichi region. On 1 December these forces totaled 35,000 active fighters and thousands of auxiliaries.[66]

The new brigades combined partisan detachments, Party underground cells, Komsomol, and other antifascist groups into an elaborate structure subordinate to central Party district and interdistrict organizations. This expanded partisan and underground structure organized local governmental organs and conducted a propaganda war by publishing underground newspapers and pamphlets. All the while, it intensified its reconnaissance and diversionary operations in support of Red Army operations.

In addition to frequent low-level diversionary and sabotage activities, in mid-1943 partisan brigades and detachments began conducting coordinated larger-scale raids and attacks on German lines of communications and military installations. For example, on 1 August 1943, partisan forces began Operation Railroad War, which involved concerted attacks on German rail communications across the entire Soviet-German front controlled by the Central Staff of the Partisan Movement in Moscow and the *Stavka*.[67] For example, as a part of the general partisan offensive, in the Leningrad region, the 3d Partisan Brigade conducted multiple attacks against the Pskov-Porkhov rail line on 21 August that put the rail line out of commission for eight days. In September several partisan brigades conducted Operation Large Concert against the Luga-Pskov rail line. Soviet sources claim that the partisans killed an estimated 17,000 German troops from 1 January through 1 September 1943 and destroyed or damaged a considerable amount of German equipment.[68]

So successful were these partisan operations and so confident were the Leningrad partisans of imminent victory that in September the partisan movement began speaking openly about the Red Army's forthcoming liberation of the region and accelerated its activities against German rear-area installations. For example, the 2d Partisan Brigade raided Pliussa Station on the Leningrad-Pskov rail line, blowing up a bridge, destroying a train, freeing Soviet prisoners of war, and killing a reported 136 Germans. Also in September, 775 partisan fighters of the 5th Partisan Brigade fomented popular uprisings in many villages in its area of operations, and partisan activities then intensified in other regions, igniting a full-scale popular uprising in the entire Leningrad region by October. Meanwhile, the 5th Partisan Brigade captured the town of Pliussa and the southern portion of Luga and Bataisk regions, preventing German occupying authorities from either gathering the harvest or removing much of the population to forced labor camps in Germany or German-occupied territory.[69]

The 9th Partisan Brigade produced similar havoc in the Gdov, Slantsy, Liady, Os'mino, and Kingisepp regions in early October by organizing uprisings in Utorgosh, Pliussa, Luga, Gdov, Slantsev, Os'min, Liady, Volosovo, and elsewhere in cooperation with the 12th Brigade. Soon the uprising spread to the Pekovets region, where the 2d and 3d Partisan Brigades were operating. The ferocity and scope of this partisan revolt had a singularly adverse effect on German control of the region and hastened Hitler's decision to permit Army Group North first to construct and then to withdraw to the Panther Line.[70]

Although the Germans at first treated the partisans' actions with contempt, comparing their impact to the mere discomfort produced by "red lice under the German's hide," ultimately, partisan warfare had a seriously adverse impact on their military operations. While the Germans could and did dismiss the hundreds of pinprick partisan attacks as inconsequential, the cumulative effect was debilitating. At the least, they tied down an ever-increasing number of German security troops at a time when manpower was becoming critically necessary at the front. They also gave the lie to the Germans' stated intent regarding the future political, economic, and social organization of captured territories and rendered German propaganda utterly ineffective.

However, a less tangible aspect of partisan warfare had a more telling effect on the Germans. As partisan operations expanded in scope from mere harassment to concerted attacks that produced real pain, they tended to undermine the Germans' will for victory. By early 1944, as the Red Army mounted its major assaults that liberated Leningrad region, the partisan movement assumed proportions that accurately reflected the immense suffering of their countrymen confined for three years in the prison that was Leningrad.

CHAPTER 9

Breaking the Blockade

January–April 1943

THE SITUATION IN JANUARY 1943

The most important region on the Soviet-German front at the end of 1942 was southern Russia, where fighting whose outcome would have a fundamental impact on the subsequent course and outcome of the entire war, raged. The massive *Wehrmacht* legions Hitler had dispatched across southern Russia to seize the Soviet Union's most vital economic regions had suffered unprecedented defeat at the hands of a revived and reinforced Red Army. After marching triumphantly eastward in late June, two German army groups and four satellite armies defeated the Red Army, crossed the Don River, captured most of Stalin's namesake city on the Volga, and, simultaneously, lunged southward, reaching the high peaks of the Caucasus Mountains. Then, in November, the Red Army struck back at its tormentors by conducting massive counteroffensives code-named Uranus and Mars in the Stalingrad region and at Rzhev, west of Moscow.[1]

Although the Soviets' Mars counteroffensive against German forces in the Rzhev salient west of Moscow failed, Operation Uranus succeeded, encircling and destroying three Axis armies and leaving Hitler and the *Wehrmacht* stunned in utter disbelief. Heavy combat raged for months in the Don and Donbas regions as the *Stavka* exploited its Stalingrad victory and the Germans strained to avoid collapse and contain the Red Army torrent. Quite naturally, the momentous strategic operations occurring in central and southern Russia eclipsed operations elsewhere along the German Eastern Front.

By January 1943 Stalin and the *Stavka* believed that an opportunity was at hand to exploit the Axis defeats by expanding its offensive operations to encompass virtually the entire German Eastern Front. Understandably, the *Stavka* included the Leningrad region in its offensive plans since the city's defenders faced a second harsh winter in blockade and a continued, if reduced, threat of German attack. Therefore, the *Stavka* decided to conduct a major offensive in the Leningrad region timed to coincide with the expanded Red Army offensive in southern Russia. Although its initial aim was to raise the Leningrad blockade, by February 1943, the *Stavka* hoped to defeat Army Group North decisively and drive its forces from the entire Leningrad region. By this time, the Leningrad offensive was part of a grander scheme aimed at defeating all three German army groups in the East and driving them back to the Narva, Vitebsk, Kiev, and Dnepr River line, the same objectives the Red Army had failed to achieve in the winter of 1941–1942.

On 1 January 1943, the Red Army's strategic situation in the Leningrad region was serious but no longer grave. Throughout the previous year, the *Stavka* had twice launched major offensives to raise the Leningrad blockade, only to fail miserably on both occasions. In the process, its 2d Shock Army twice suffered the indignity of being encircled and destroyed, and tens of thousands of Red Army soldiers had either perished or marched off into German captivity. Although the threat of a major German offensive against the city had lessened, German forces still encircled the city from three sides, and Finnish forces threatened it from the north. The front lines stood a mere 4 kilometers (2.5 miles) south of the city and only 30 kilometers (18.6 miles) to the northwest and southeast.

Govorov's Leningrad Front defended the isolated Oranienbaum bridge-head west of the city and the city's southern, southeastern, and eastern approaches. The city was still cut off from the country as a whole, the Baltic Fleet was bottled up in the eastern Gulf of Finland, and German artillery continued to pound Leningrad's dwindling population. To the east, Meretskov's Volkhov Front defended vital communications lines extending to the eastern shore of Lake Ladoga and the broad sector between Lakes Ladoga and Il'men'.

Major General A. I. Cherepanov's 23d Army defended the northwestern approaches to the city along the Karelian Isthmus against possible Finnish attack, and the Coastal Operational Group (COG, formerly the 8th Army) defended the isolated Oranienbaum bridgehead west of the city. Cherepanov's army consisted of five rifle divisions, one rifle brigade, two fortified regions, and one tank brigade, and COG fielded two rifle divisions, two rifle and two naval infantry brigades, two separate machine gun–artillery battalions, and one separate tank battalion.[2] COG's bridgehead protected the approaches to Kronshtadt with long-range artillery and threatened the left flank of German forces south of Leningrad. The Internal Defense of the City and the Baltic Fleet's Kronshtadt Naval Defensive Region protected the sea approaches to Leningrad, in conjunction with the 23d Army and COG. The Kronshtadt Naval Defensive Region defended the forts and islands in the Gulf of Finland and maintained communications between these islands by aircraft and aerosleigh.

Colonel General I. I. Maslennikov's 42d and Lieutenant General V. P. Sviridov's 55th Armies defended the southern and southeastern approaches to the city along a front extending from Uritsk on the Gulf of Finland through Pushkin and Kolpino to the Neva River. The 42d Army fielded five rifle divisions, one fortified region, one tank brigade, and one separate tank regiment, and the 55th Army consisted of four rifle divisions, one fortified region, and one tank brigade. Major General M. P. Dukhanov's 67th Army, which had been formed in October 1942 from the Neva Operational Group, occupied a

55-kilometer (34.2-mile) sector northward along the Neva River to Shlissel'burg on the *front*'s left flank. It also defended Lake Ladoga's western shore north of the Neva River's mouth.

The 67th Army consisted of three rifle divisions, two rifle brigades, one ski brigade, one fortified region, two separate tank battalions, and supporting artillery. The army's 46th Rifle Division defended the Porogi–Vyborgskaia Dubrovka sector and a small bridgehead across the Neva River near Moskovskaia Dubrovka, and the 11th Rifle Brigade was deployed from Vyborgskaia Dubrovka to the Gannibalovka River, 4 kilometers (2.5 miles) south of Shlissel'burg. The army's 16th Fortified Region defended the western shores of Lake Ladoga, the 55th Rifle Brigade defended the ice road across Lake Ladoga along with the Ladoga Flotilla, and a small garrison manned Oreshek Fortress at the mouth of the Neva opposite Shlissel'burg. Dukhanov retained the 45th Guards and 86th Rifle Divisions and the 35th Ski Brigade in army reserve. The 67th Army's divisions varied in strength from 7,000 to 10,000 men each and the brigades from 3,000 to 5,800 men each, and the army as a whole fielded 850 guns and mortars, 400 M-30 multiple rocket launchers, and slightly more than 50 tanks. The army's operational density was 12 kilometers (7.5 miles) per defending division.[3]

Govorov retained two rifle divisions (the 136th and 268th), two rifle brigades (the 162d and 250th), a ski brigade (the 34th), one fortified region (the 13th) and two tank brigades (the 61st and 122d) in the *front*'s reserve in the Leningrad region for employment on the Karelian Isthmus.

The Leningrad Front's air forces consisted of the 13th Air Army and Baltic Fleet's aviation, which protected the Leningrad Front and naval base. The 13th Air Army, which had been formed in November 1942, consisted of three aviation divisions (the 275th Fighter, 276th Bomber, and 277th Assault), five separate aviation regiments (the 196th and 286th Fighter, 23d Guards and 897th Bomber, and 13th Reconnaissance), and the 12th Mixed Aviation Regiment, which was still forming. It had 150 combat aircraft at its disposal, augmented by the 235 aircraft from the Baltic Fleet's three aviation brigades.[4]

The Leningrad PVO Army and the Ladoga Division PVO Region defended Leningrad and its environs against air attack. The Leningrad PVO Army's 7th Fighter Aviation Corps and antiaircraft artillery and machine gun regiments fielded 550 antiaircraft guns and 150 heavy antiaircraft machine guns, supplemented by 180 antiaircraft guns and 60 heavy antiaircraft machine guns assigned to the Ladoga Division PVO Region. The Leningrad PVO Army included the 7th Fighter Aviation Corps, with its 80 aircraft operationally subordinate to the 13th Air Army, 6 medium- and 1 small-caliber antiaircraft artillery regiments, and 1 heavy machine gun artillery regiment.[5]

The Baltic Fleet, still subordinate to the Leningrad Front, consisted of the Kronshtadt Naval Base and adjacent forts; the Izhorsk and Ostrov Fortified Sectors; the Leningrad Naval Base, which repaired fleet ships, squadron ships, and submarines based at Kronshtadt and Leningrad; and the Ladoga Military Flotilla, coastal defenses, and aviation units. The Baltic Fleet performed multiple missions designed to protect the sea approaches to Leningrad and the vital Lake Ladoga supply route. First, it prevented German forces from seizing Kotlin Island and other islands in the Gulf of Finland by an attack across the ice and protected the sea approaches to Leningrad in cooperation with the 23d Army, the Coastal Operational Group, and the Internal Defense of the City. In addition, it protected the ice roads across the Gulf of Finland, helped defend Lake Ladoga's western shore and the ice roads across the lake with coastal artillery and the Ladoga Military Flotilla's ships, and defended Novaia Ladoga on the lake's eastern shore.[6]

Meretskov's Volkhov Front defended the 300-kilometer (186.4-mile) sector from Lake Ladoga to Lake Il'men' with six armies. Starikov's 8th Army defended the 50-kilometer (31.1-mile) sector on the *front*'s right flank from the Novo Ladoga Canal to the Kirov railroad and was backed up by Lieutenant General V. Z. Romanovsky's 2d Shock Army, which was in second echelon preparing for new offensive operations. The 8th Army consisted of eight rifle divisions, one rifle brigade, one tank regiment, and two separate tank battalions, and the 2d Shock Army fielded two rifle divisions, two rifle infantries, one naval infantry, two tank brigades, four separate tank battalions, and supporting artillery. The 54th, 4th, 59th, and 52d Armies, commanded, respectively, by Lieutenant General A. V. Sukhomlin, Major General N. I. Gusev, Lieutenant General I. T. Korovnikov, and Lieutenant General V. F. Iakovlev, were deployed from the Kirov railroad southward to Lake Il'men'.

The operational density in the Volkhov Front's 8th and 2d Shock Armies' sectors was one division per 4 kilometers (2.5 miles) of front. The 8th Army's divisions numbered from 3,800 to 9,500 men (5,400 on average), and the 2d Shock Army from 6,500 to 7,000 men. The two armies fielded 1,700 guns and mortars, approximately 130 *Katiushas,* and more than 100 tanks.[7] Meretskov retained the 71st Rifle Division and the 37th and 39th Ski Brigades in his *front* reserve. The 14th Air Army, which had formed in July 1942, provided air support to the Volkhov Front, with a total of over 200 aircraft organized into three aviation divisions and seven separate aviation regiments.

After the *Wehrmacht*'s defeats in southern Russia, the OKH deferred further action in the Leningrad region until the situation stabilized in the south. In the meantime, the OKH ordered Kuechler's Army Group North to go on the defense and weakened it considerably by transferring the Eleventh Army to Army Group Center in October. In addition, it transferred nine divisions from the Eighteenth Army to other front sectors during October and November 1942.[8]

On 1 January 1943, Lindemann's Eighteenth Army consisted of 26 divisions deployed on a 450-kilometer (279.6-mile) front from the Baltic Sea to

Lake Il'men' opposite the Red Army's Leningrad and Volkhov Fronts. Severe force shortages required that Lindemann deploy virtually all of his divisions in a single line, with each division defending roughly a 17-kilometer (10.6-mile) front. Each defending division maintained its own tactical reserve of one or two battalions, and Lindemann retained portions of two divisions (the 96th Infantry and 5th Mountain) in reserve at Mga and west of Krasnoe Selo. The OKH tried to compensate for the shortage in manpower by sending Lindemann the 10th *Luftwaffe* Field Division, which, on 1 December, was en route from Kingisepp to Krasnogvardeisk. In addition, five Finnish Army divisions threatened the 23d Army's defenses north of Leningrad. The *Luftwaffe*'s First Air Fleet provided Lindemann's army with air support by conducting a limited number of reconnaissance and bombing sorties against Leningrad. The air fleet conducted 4,700 bombing sorties against Leningrad with flights of three to six aircraft each from 1 October through 31 December.[9]

The Eighteenth Army's L Army Corps defended the sector south of Leningrad from the western edge of the Oranienbaum bridgehead to Pushkin with its 225th and 215th Infantry, 9th *Luftwaffe* Field, and 2d SS Divisions. Farther east the LIV Army Corps defended the sector from Pushkin to Annenskoe on the Neva River with the 250th Spanish "Blue," SS Police, and 5th Mountain Divisions. The XXVI Army Corps manned fortifications from Annenskoe to south of Voronovo in the Mga-Siniavino salient south of Shlissel'burg. The corps' 170th Infantry Division and one regiment of the 227th Infantry Division defended along the Neva River facing west, and the remainder of the 227th and the 1st and 223d Infantry Divisions were deployed from Shlissel'burg past Voronovo facing north and east. The I Army Corps' 69th, 132d, 61st, 11th, 217th, and 21st Infantry Divisions defended from south of Voronovo to the Volkhov River south of Kirishi. Finally, the XXVIII Army Corps' 24th and 121st Infantry and 28th Jager Divisions and the XXXVIII Army Corps' 254th and 212th Infantry Divisions and 1st *Luftwaffe* Field Division defended the front southward along the Volkhov River to Lake Il'men'. The 285th Security Division protected the army group's rear area as a whole.

The German defenses were strongest in the Shlissel'burg-Siniavino bottleneck, which was defended by the XXVI Army Corps' 1st, 227th, and 170th Infantry Divisions, the LIV Army Corps' SS Police Division, part of the 5th Mountain Division, and the Eighteenth Army's reserve 96th Infantry Division. Here, five experienced German divisions with from 10,000 to 12,000 men each manned strongly fortified defenses in the region's forested and swampy terrain. The depth and width of the Neva River, which was partially frozen during the winter, and the nearly impassable forested and swampy terrain in the Mga-Siniavino salient, which was laced with many fortified stone villages, facilitated German defense and the maintenance of the blockade as a whole. Even in early 1943, Hitler considered the salient an important launching pad for future attacks against the ice road and Leningrad from the east and a vital link in the blockade, since it blocked communications between the Leningrad and Volkhov Fronts.[10]

Therefore, the Germans established three strong defense lines within the salient, each consisting of three trench lines, and formed defensive regions and large centers of resistance anchored on numerous fortified villages. The Germans constructed defensive regions at Workers Settlements Nos. 1 and 2, Shlissel'burg, and Siniavino. The five centers of resistance at Shlissel'burg, Gorodok No. 1, Gorodok No. 2, Arbuzovo, and Annenskoe faced the 67th Army, and another at Lobanovo protected the rail line to Mga Station. In addition, the six centers of resistance at Lipka, Workers Settlement No. 8, Gontovaia Lipka, Tortolovo, Mishino, and Porech'e faced the 8th Army. Finally, the Germans formed deep defensive positions anchored on Workers Settlements Nos. 1 and 5 and Siniavino in the depths and numerous additional rear defense lines.[11] These strong defenses in the salient represented the "nut" Soviet forces had to crack if they were to raise the blockade of Leningrad.

PLANNING OPERATION SPARK

Govorov and Meretskov began planning their offensive to raise the Leningrad blockade in late November and early December 1942 under the watchful eye of *Stavka* representative Voroshilov, just as the Red Army was beginning to exploit its Stalingrad victory by conducting a major winter offensive in southern Russia. Originally, on 18 November, Govorov proposed conducting two separate offensives.[12] The first, the Shlissel'burg operation, was designed to penetrate the blockade and restore rail communications south of Lake Ladoga, and the second, the Uritsk operation, sought to reestablish communications between the Coastal Operational Group and the 42d Army by liquidating the gap between the two forces. In the Shlissel'burg offensive, the Leningrad Front's 67th Army was to penetrate the Germans' defenses between Gorodok No. 2 and Shlissel'burg and along the shores of Lake Ladoga; simultaneously, the Volkhov Front's 2d Shock and 8th Armies were to penetrate German defenses between Lake Ladoga and Mishino. The two *fronts'* shock groups were to link up near Siniavino to raise the Leningrad blockade and then protect the reconstruction of the rail line along the Ladoga Canal. By doing so, they would restore normal ground communications between Leningrad and the country as a whole and provide freedom of maneuver to both *fronts'* forces.

In the Uritsk offensive, the Leningrad Front's 42d Army was to penetrate German defenses in the Uritsk and Pushkin sector and link up with the Coastal Operational Group to reestablish communications between the Oranienbaum bridgehead and Leningrad. If successful, the offensives would halt the German artillery bombardment of Leningrad, provide the Baltic Fleet's ships freedom of maneuver between Leningrad and Kronshtadt, restore a continuous front west of the city, and significantly widen the southern sector of Leningrad's defenses. As originally planned, the operations were to be conducted successively, the Shlissel'burg operation in the second half of December and the Uritsk operation in mid-February 1943. Although the two *fronts'* staffs planned both operations in detail, the ultimate attack dates depended on ice conditions on the Neva River and Lake Ladoga.

On 18 November Govorov requested the *Stavka* approve his plans, and four days later he submitted concrete recommendations concerning its conduct.[13] Since a strong ice cover was required to move infantry, artillery, and heavy tanks across the Neva River (river-crossing equipment was in short supply), Govorov recommended that the operations begin in mid-January. Further, he stated his forces should penetrate German defenses in the 10-kilometer (6.2-mile) sector from Gorodok No. 1 to Shlissel'burg, while the Volkhov Front's forces should do so in the Lipka-Mishino sector between the Mga rail line and Lake Ladoga. Both forces should then advance to Siniavino to prevent a German flank attack from Lake Ladoga.

Govorov urged that both *fronts* attack simultaneously with powerful shock groups to avoid repeating the problems his forces had experienced in August 1942. He recommended each shock group consist of seven to eight rifle divisions, with four divisions in first echelon, three in second echelon, and one in reserve, and be supported by substantial tank, artillery, and engineer forces.[14] Govorov intended to employ more than 700 guns and mortars in the operation to generate an artillery density of 70 guns and mortars per kilometer of front. Finally, Govorov requested the *Stavka* reinforce his *front* with three to four rifle divisions and bring the 13th Air Army to full strength.

The *Stavka* approved Govorov's plan on 2 December with only minor amendments.[15] Specifically, it ordered Govorov and Meretskov to complete their planning by 1 December and assigned the code name "Spark" *(Iskra)* to the offensive. It designated Romanovsky's 2d Shock Army as the Volkhov Front's shock group and Dukhanov's 67th Army as the Leningrad Front's shock group and ordered Fediuninsky, now the deputy *front* commander, to supervise Romanovsky's operation and Govorov himself to direct Dukhanov's operation. Finally, the *Stavka* sent Marshal Voroshilov from Moscow to act as its representative and coordinate the offensive as a whole.

The *Stavka* assigning specific missions to each *front* on 8 December.[16] Initially, the *fronts'* two shock groups were to destroy German forces defending the Shlissel'burg-Siniavino bottleneck (the Lipka, Gaitolovo, Moskovskaia Dubrovka, and Shlissel'burg regions), penetrate the Leningrad blockade, and reach the Moika River, Mikhailovskii, and Tortolovo line by the end of January, where they were to dig in. After successfully completing the Shlissel'burg operation, during the first half of February, the two *fronts* were to conduct a new operation to destroy German forces in the Mga region, clear the Kirov railroad, and reach the Voronovo, Voskresenskoe, Sigalovo, and Voitolovo line by month's end. By doing so, the two *fronts* would establish a land corridor to Leningrad and, hence, more reliable communications with the city.

Responding to Govorov's earlier request, the *Stavka* provided Govorov and Meretskov with significant reinforcements during December. Govorov's *front* received the 224th Rifle Division, the 102d, 123d, 138th, 250th, and 142d Rifle Brigades, the 7th Antiaircraft Artillery Division, and three aerosleigh battalions. Meretskov's *front* was assigned the 18th, 147th, 239th, 364th, and 379th Rifle Divisions and the 53d Engineer-Sapper Brigade from Moscow, the 11th, 12th, and 13th Ski Brigades from Arkhangel'sk, and four aerosleigh battalions.

The NKO also provided the two *fronts* with the equipment necessary to form sizable new artillery and armored forces. These included 4 artillery divisions, 10 mortar regiments, 2 antiaircraft artillery regiments, and 1 tank regiment in the Volkhov Front and 1 artillery division, 1 artillery brigade, 3 artillery regiments, 5 guards-mortar battalions, 3 mortar regiments, 1 tank regiment, and 4 separate tank battalions in the Leningrad Front. These reinforcements increased the Volkhov Front's personnel strength by 22 percent, its guns by 20 percent, and its mortars by 30 percent and the Leningrad Front's personnel strength by 10 percent.[17]

Although the two *fronts* managed to complete their offensive preparations by 1 January, on 27 December poor ice conditions on the Neva forced Govorov to request the offensive be delayed. The *Stavka* approved Govorov's request and postponed the offensive until 10–12 January. According to the final offensive plan, the two shock groups were to destroy German forces defending the Shlissel'burg-Siniavino salient and raise the Leningrad blockade. Thereafter, in early February they were to attack southward, destroy German forces in the Mga region, and establish a broad land corridor to Leningrad through which to restore reliable ground communications with the city. The precise second-stage mission was to clear German forces from the Kirov rail line and reach the Voronovo, Voskresenskoe, Sigalovo, and Voitolovo line by month's end.

Govorov's shock group, Dukhanov's 67th Army, was to penetrate German defenses in the 13-kilometer (8.1-mile) sector between Moskovskaia Dubrovka and Shlissel'burg, defeat German forces in the western portion of the salient, and link up with the Volkhov Front's shock group to restore ground communications with Leningrad. Dukhanov's shock group was to attack along the Mar'ino-Siniavino axis to destroy German strong points on the left bank of the Neva River and capture Arbuzovo, Workers Settlement No. 2, and Shlissel'burg. Thereafter, Dukhanov was to commit his second-echelon forces and overcome the German centers of resistance at Annenskoe, Mustolovo,

Workers Settlement No. 6, Siniavino, and Workers Settlements Nos. 5 and 1. Subsequently, his forces were to wheel southward and occupy new defenses along the Moika River from its mouth at the Neva River to Kelkolovo. Dukhanov's army consisted of 8 rifle divisions, 5 rifle, 2 ski, and 3 tank brigades, 1 fortified region, 22 artillery and mortar regiments, 15 engineer-sapper and pontoon battalions, and other specialized units deployed in two echelons to strengthen the force of its attack. His shock group was to attack early on 10 January and operate around the clock so as to penetrate the blockade in three to four days' time.[18]

Meretskov's shock group, Romanovsky's 2d Shock Army, was to smash German defenses in the 12-kilometer (7.5-mile) sector from Lipka to Gaitolovo, destroy German forces in the eastern part of the salient, and link up with the Leningrad Front, while defending firmly across the remainder of its front. Romanovsky's immediate mission was to destroy German forces in the Lipka, Kruglaia Grove, and Gaitolovo regions with his strong left flank and capture the German strong points at Workers Settlements Nos. 1 and 5 and the center of resistance at Siniavino to disorganize the entire German defense. Subsequently, its forces were to dig in, protect the Shlissel'burg axis and its left flank, and link up with the Leningrad Front's 67th Army. Romanovsky's army consisted of 11 rifle divisions, 1 rifle, 2 ski, 4 tank, and 2 engineer-sapper brigades, 37 artillery and mortar regiments, and other specialized units deployed in two echelons with specific forces assigned to capture specific objectives.[19]

Starikov's 8th Army, deployed on Romanovsky's left flank, was to penetrate German defenses in the Gaitolovo and Mishino sectors, advance westward and southwestward to the Kelkolovo, Mikhailovskii, and Mishino line, protect the 2d Shock Army's left flank, and establish new defenses in tandem with the 67th Army northwest of Mga. Although Meretskov originally planned to begin his attack on 7 January, the *Stavka* also postponed his attack to 12 January.

On 27 December Voroshilov approved Govorov's and Meretskov's plan for coordinating their assaults, which required the *fronts'* two shock groups to link up along a line passing through Workers Settlements Nos. 2 and 6. The completed plan of cooperation, which was far more detailed than previous cooperation plans, instructed the two shock groups on every aspect of the operation and established detailed guidelines for every aspect of staff planning.[20]

Dukhanov and Romanovsky did most of their planning on the basis of the two *fronts'* warning orders, even before they received the formal *front* directives, and submitted their own plans to Govorov and Meretskov by 1 January. Dukhanov's plan required his army's shock group to cross the Neva River's ice and penetrate German defenses between Moskovskaia Dubrovka and Shlissel'burg. His shock group would then attack toward Siniavino, destroy German forces in Shlissel'burg and Siniavino, and capture the strong points at Arbuzovo, Marker 22.4, Workers Settlement No. 6, Siniavino,

Workers Settlement No. 1, and Shlissel'burg. Subsequently, his shock group was to link up with the Volkhov Front's shock group, restore a continuous front south of Lake Ladoga, and attack southeastward to capture the Moika River line. While doing so, his 46th Rifle Division, 55th Rifle and 35th Ski Brigades, and 16th Fortified Region were to defend the western bank of the Neva River and the ice road across Lake Ladoga. The Baltic Fleet reinforced the 67th Army with 23 batteries of fixed and railroad artillery. These included 88 long-range 130mm–356mm guns from the fleet training grounds and 4 minesweeper squadrons and 3 cannon ships positioned on the Neva River.[21]

Romanovsky's plan required his shock group to penetrate German defenses between Lipka and Gaitolovo, destroy German forces in the Lipka, Workers Settlement No. 8, Kruglaia Grove, and Gaitolovo regions, and capture Workers Settlements Nos. 1 and 5 and Siniavino. Subsequently, while protecting its right flank against German attacks from Shlissel'burg and its left flank against attacks from Kelkolovo, the shock group was to reach the Neva River and link up with the Leningrad Front's shock group. During the offensive, the army's 22d Rifle Brigade was to protect the southern shore of Lake Ladoga east of Lipka. On Romanovsky's left flank, Starikov's 8th Army planned to penetrate German defenses in the Gaitolovo and Mishino sector with two rifle divisions and one rifle brigade, advance toward Mga to protect the 2d Shock Army's left flank, and defend elsewhere in its sector.[22]

To conduct so complex an offensive against enemy forces occupying strong defenses in very difficult terrain and weather conditions necessitated careful and effective command and control and massive but thoroughly integrated and coordinated artillery, air, armor, engineer, and logistical support. The fact that the two shock groups were attacking toward one another against objectives that were only 13–15 kilometers (8.1–9.9 miles) apart made coordination both essential and difficult. This was particularly true since previous offensives had often illustrated what not to do in similar circumstances. Consequently, *front* and army staffs paid special attention to organizing and coordinating combat and combat service support.

At this stage of the war, effective artillery fire (and aviation) was the key to softening up a well-prepared defense before and during the attack and was vital to a successful exploitation and consolidation at final objectives. The absence of accurate targeting and effective fire was a prime reason why earlier Soviet offensives had failed. Therefore, both Govorov and Meretskov planned to provide massive artillery support to their shock groups before and during the offensive. Govorov regrouped his artillery extensively prior to the attack, ultimately concentrating 1,873 guns and mortars (76mm or above) in the 67th Army's sector. This produced a density of 144 guns and mortars per kilometer of front. He reinforced this fire with 3 guards-mortar regiments and 12 battalions in the penetration sector to increase the preparation's effectiveness. In addition, he formed long-range action and special designation artillery groups, which were to destroy enemy artillery and engage important targets in the depth, and a guards-mortar group, which was to support the second echelon during their commitment into the penetration. Finally, to improve infantry support, Govorov formed counter-mortar groups in each attacking division to supplement the fires of usual infantry support groups.[23]

Govorov planned to conduct artillery preparation for 140 minutes prior to the assault. Initially, this involved firing simultaneous barrages to a depth of 1 kilometer (.6 miles). After the barrages ended, artillery was to fire successive fire concentrations and lay down a dense zone of final protective fire 200–250 meters from the Neva River's bank to protect the advancing infantry. Before and during the infantry assault, 22 guns per kilometer of front were to fire massed direct fires over open sites to prevent the Germans from destroying the ice cover over the Neva River. The *front* allocated 3 full combat loads of artillery to the 67th Army and retained 1.5–5.0 loads at *front* and army depots and planned to employ 3.3–5.0 combat loads during the penetration to a depth of 5 kilometers (3.1 miles).[24] This far exceeded the quantities of ammunition allocated for previous offensives.

Meretskov concentrated 2,885 guns and mortars in his offensive sector, providing for a density of 180 guns and mortars per kilometer of front, not including the two heavy brigades and four guards-mortar brigades, and allocated 2,206 guns and mortars to support the 2d Shock Army. He employed the same types of artillery groups as Govorov and planned to conduct a 140-minute preparation in the 2d Shock Army's sector and a 160-minute preparation in the 8th Army's sector organized in the same fashion as in the Leningrad Front. His artillery preparation also relied on intense direct fire along the forward edge by 18 guns deployed per single kilometer of front. The *front* supplied the 2d Shock Army with from 2–2.5 to 5.0 combat loads of ammunition and ordered all regimental and divisional artillery to be mounted on skis or sleighs and heavy machine guns on skis or snow carts to improve their mobility.[25]

The aircraft assigned to both *fronts* concentrated on supporting the ground offensive and bombing key targets in the German rear area. Major General S. D. Rybal'chenko's 13th Air Army—which was reinforced by Baltic Fleet aircraft, the Leningrad PVO Army's 7th Fighter Aviation Corps, and the four mixed aviation divisions assigned to the armies—supported Govorov's offensive with 414 planes, predominantly fighter aircraft.[26] Given the relatively small proportion of bombers and assault aircraft, Rybal'chenko concentrated his air sorties during the preparation against targets in the forward edge and, later, against enemy reserves and artillery positions during the assault. Thereafter, aircraft was to support the advancing troops in small groups and on an on-call basis when absolutely needed. The fighters concentrated on attaining air superiority and providing air cover for the troops.

Major General I. P. Zhuravlev's 14th Air Army—which was reinforced by the 2d Fighter Aviation Corps, the 232d Assault Aviation Division, and three mixed aviation regiments assigned to the subordinate armies—supported Meretskov's offensive with 395 aircraft, most of which were assault planes and fighters.[27] The greater proportion of assault aircraft permitted Zhuravlev's air army to provide more effective ground support while striking German strong points.

As was the case in earlier offensives, large tank forces could not operate in the broken, forested, and swampy terrain around Leningrad, and the short distances to the shock group's objectives denied tank forces adequate room to maneuver. Therefore, both *fronts* assigned tank brigades, regiments, and separate battalions to their shock groups simply to support the infantry advance. Initially, Govorov assigned the 152d, 220th, and 61st Light Tank Brigades and the 189th and 119th Separate Tank Battalions, with a total of 222 tanks and 37 armored cars, to support the 67th Army.[28] He distributed these tank forces and their accompanying sapper (combat engineer) groups equally between the first- and second-echelon rifle forces, with the predominance of light tanks forward to negotiate the Neva River's icy surface.

Meretskov attached the 16th, 98th, 122d, and 185th Tank Brigades, the 32d Guards Tank Penetration Regiment, and the 500th, 501st, 503d, and 507th Separate Tank Battalions, with a total of 217 tanks, to the 2d Shock Army. In addition, the 92 tanks assigned to the 25th Separate Tank Regiment and the 107th and 502d Separate Tank Battalions supported the 8th Army's secondary attack. The 32d and 44th Aerosleigh Battalions, which were equipped with lightly armored machine-gun aerosleighs, were to conduct reconnaissance and raids in the German rear. Romanovsky deployed the bulk of his tank brigades and battalions on his shock group's left flank to ensure swift capture of the vital German Siniavino center of resistance. Therefore, the 372d, 256th, and 191st Rifle Divisions, which were attacking in his center, lacked any armor support.[29]

Given the strong German defenses, the absence of roads, and the difficult off-road terrain, extensive engineer support, which had been largely ineffective in previous operations, was vital for the offensive's success. The Leningrad Front's engineers had to assist in the crossing of the Neva River, prepare movement routes through the roadless terrain, and organize jumping-off and assault positions. Govorov supported the 67th Army with 15 engineer-sapper, pontoon, and other battalions, 7 river-crossing parks, and camouflage and hydro-technical companies. Prior to the offensive, the engineers and sappers widened and deepened existing trenches and constructed an elaborate system of ditches 400–600 meters from the river to protect the movement of troops from the railroad to the jumping-off positions along the river.[30] They also built an extensive system of command and observation points, numerous covered gun firing positions, particularly for direct fire over the river, and heating and rest bunkers and cabins covered with waterproof canvas for entire infantry platoons.

While the army regrouped for the attack, the engineers constructed up to 50 kilometers (31.1 miles) of winter roads so that each division would have two routes to its jumping-off positions and cut paths through the minefields using specially prepared overhead explosives. During the attack, usually under enemy fire, they built wooden crossings over the Neva with a capacity of up to 60 tons so that medium and heavy tanks could cross the river. Their most important combat contribution, however, was the employment of assault and destruction groups specially tailored to destroy specific German strong points and engineer obstacle battalions and miner battalions to fortify occupied lines and protect the flanks.

Meretskov allocated two complete engineer-sapper brigades, one separate mine-sapper battalion, and one motorized engineer battalion to the 2d Shock Army and an engineer-miner brigade and a separate RGK motorized engineer battalion to support Starikov's 8th Army. These engineers performed the same basic functions as their counterparts in the Leningrad Front except for the provision of river-crossing support. During the preparatory period, the Volkhov Front's engineers constructed 20 kilometers (12.4 miles) of approach roads and many crossings and bridges across frozen rivers and streams and removed mines and cut lanes through minefields at the rate of one per attacking company.[31]

Since reconnaissance had been a serious weakness in previous operations, both *fronts* conducted extensive observation, raids, "snatches" (to capture prisoners), daily inspections of the Neva ice, and aerial photography of enemy positions prior to the offensive. By the time of the attack, the Leningrad Front's Intelligence Department had formed a reliable picture of enemy defenses, except artillery firing positions on the flanks.

In comparison with previous operations, the task of antiaircraft defense was considerably easier because, with several exceptions, the 13th and 14th Air Armies were able to maintain air superiority over the relatively restricted battlefield. The Leningrad Front allocated 400 fighters to provide its shock groups with air cover. In addition, it allocated one full antiaircraft artillery division, one PVO artillery regiment, six separate antiaircraft artillery battalions, and two railroad batteries to provide antiaircraft gun support. The 67th Army formed all of these guns into a single antiaircraft artillery group, which organized three layers of antiaircraft fire over the heads of the attacking forces. The Volkhov Front supported its shock group with two PVO antiaircraft artillery divisions, two antiaircraft artillery battalions, and one battery organized in two equal antiaircraft artillery groups deployed one behind the other, which provided multilayered antiaircraft fire.[32]

Another capability absent in many earlier operations was effective anti-tank defense during the course of the attack and exploitation, particularly against enemy counterattacks. While both *fronts* employed antitank guns as they had the year before, this time they reinforced their antitank defense by employing artillery in a direct fire role and by increasing the number of direct fire weapons by assigning extra antitank regiments to their shock groups.

Matériel and technical support remained a severe problem, particularly for the Leningrad Front, which was still feeling the adverse effects of the blockade and was hindered by the difficult terrain and weather conditions. Specifically, the Leningrad Front lacked an adequate depot system and was short of vehicular transport, fuel, and medical supplies. The Volkhov Front was also experiencing supply and transport difficulties because of the great distance to its bases and the main supply sources in the depth of the country.

Despite these challenges and with considerable effort, both *fronts* managed to amass required reserves. When the offensive began, the Leningrad Front's 67th Army had 22 days' supply of food and forage and three refills of fuel. Vehicles assigned to individual formations and to army transport units conducted resupply and evacuation along a single road allocated to each first-echelon division. In addition to its own hospitals and beds, the *front* had a hospital base consisting of seven hospitals with 8,000 beds. The Volkhov Front's 2d Shock Army had a 20-day supply of food, a 58-day supply of forage, and 2–3 refills of fuel per fighting vehicle. It had at its disposal four dirt roads, supplemented by one winter road constructed for each first echelon rifle division. The *front*'s vehicular park had 260 operational trucks, and its road transport units had 20–85 percent of their authorized trucks. The *front*'s hospital base consisted of 12,000 beds, which was considered adequate for this scale of operation.[33]

Operational security prior to the offensive was extremely tight in both *fronts*. Only a limited number of senior officers were involved in planning the operations, written documents were kept to a minimum, and all movement associated with force regrouping took place at night or in bad weather under a strict regime of light discipline. Between 16 December 1942 and 11 January 1943, the front-line forces employed direct fire artillery to eliminate obstacles the Germans had placed along the Neva and did so on a broad front so as to conceal the intended attack sectors. In addition, the Volkhov Front commander simulated attack preparations 30–35 kilometers (18.6–21.7 miles) southeast of Mga in an attempt to confuse the Germans as to the offensive's real objective. Although the Germans were certainly aware of the attack preparations, these and other measures prevented the Germans from determining the precise date of the assault.

To improve secrecy, as well as command and control, which had been major problems in past operations, both *fronts* strictly centralized all command and control of forces under the *front* commanders through the army and division commanders to lower-level units. Both *fronts* relied on advanced oral warning orders and personal meetings between respective commanders and followed up these meetings by issuing more detailed written orders. The principal operational documents at army level were combat orders and graphic combat planning tables.

During the preparatory period for the offensive, both *fronts* conducted specialized training in combat techniques unique to the operation, such as the assault across the Neva River's ice and assaults on specific strong-point objectives. They also conducted practice attacks against specific objectives, which involved numerous rehearsals and combat exercises in the rear area, which were conducted against detailed mock-ups of each attack target.

On the eve of the offensive, the *fronts'* shock groups regrouped and concentrated gradually to help conceal the exact location and timing of the offensive. Artillery occupied forward firing positions by 5 January, rifle divisions moved into their jumping-off positions by 11 January, and first-echelon tanks moved into their advanced positions on 12 January.

ZHUKOV'S OPERATION SPARK: THE THIRD SINIAVINO OFFENSIVE, JANUARY

The Leningrad and Volkhov Fronts' third Siniavino offensive took place within the context of the Red Army's expanding winter campaign in southern Russia. Because of his previous experience in the region, shortly before the offensive began, on 10 January, the *Stavka* sent Zhukov to Leningrad as its representative to coordinate the operation. Less than a month before Zhukov had coordinated Operation Mars, the Western and Kalinin Fronts' unsuccessful attempt to smash Army Group Center's defenses in the Rzhev salient.[34] Zhukov supervised the last-minute preparations for Operation Spark and its conduct from 12 through 24 January. After Spark ended, in February, Zhukov developed plans for the even more ambitious Operation Polar Star.[35]

While Operation Spark was under way, the Red Army was either conducting or preparing to conduct major offensive operations along the entire Soviet-German front. Along the southern axis, the Don Front was destroying German Sixth Army encircled at Stalingrad, the Voronezh and Southwestern Fronts were driving German forces westward from the Don River, and the Southern Front was advancing on Rostov. Along the southwestern axis, the Briansk Front was preparing to strike German Second Army at Voronezh, and along the western axis the Kalinin Front was battling with German forces near Velikie Luki. All of these operations were occurring simultaneously and were part of an overall *Stavka* plan to collapse German defenses in the East and reach the Dnepr River line by summer 1943.

The forces of the Leningrad and Volkhov Fronts attacked simultaneously early on 12 January. The night before, Soviet night bombers pounded German forces, artillery positions, headquarters, airfields, and communications centers (Map 14). Govorov's almost 2,000 artillery pieces and *Katiushas* began firing their preparation at 0930 hours on 12 January. Artillery conducting indirect fire blasted German positions 200 meters or more from the rivers so as to avoid damaging the ice on the Neva River, while direct fire artillery engaged German targets on the river's far bank. At 1150 hours, five minutes before the artillery preparation ended with an earsplitting *Katiusha* barrage, massed Soviet infantry from four 67th Army rifle divisions with armor support advanced to exploit the destructive fires and crossed the Neva. The day was clear and the temperature at dawn was –23°C (–9°F). A German account described the awesome scene:

> Between Shlusselburg, Lipka, and Sinyavino there was only smoke and fire. The swamps and the thick forest on the Neva and on the Volkhov Front were once again plowed up. From 4,500 barrels the Russians unleashed a hurricane of fire over the German positions, a bombardment of an intensity hitherto not experienced at this northern end of the eastern front. . . .
> A total of 4500 barrels! From Leningrad and from the Volkhov Front they were firing at the two German sectors of only nine miles each. That meant one gun for every twenty feet. For two hours and twenty minutes the hurricane of steel howled, flashed, and crashed down on the Neva Front, and for an hour and forty-five minutes it swept the eastern side of the bottleneck.
> "They aren't joking this time," the men said in their dugouts, their strong points, their foxholes, and their trenches. . . . And then they attacked. Immediately behind the slowly lifting artillery barrage, the Soviets charged the German lines. With them came ground-support aircraft.[36]

Led by special assault groups and exploiting the hurricane of artillery and machine-gun fire laid down by the troops of the 16th Fortified Region, Colonel V. A. Trubachev's 86th Rifle Division assaulted across the Neva River south of Shlissel'burg. To the south, Major General N. P. Simoniak's 136th and Colonel S. N. Borshchev's 268th Rifle Divisions, supported by accompanying tanks and artillery, captured the German defensive positions on the Neva River's far bank between Mar'ino and Gorodok No. 1, as the protective artillery fire slowly shifted into the depths. Despite the dense clouds and falling snow that arrived at midday, assault aircraft flew more than 100 sorties in support of the advancing infantry on the first day of the attack.

Simoniak's and Borshchev's troops captured the Germans' first defensive position on the first day, seizing a bridgehead 5 kilometers (3.1 miles) wide and 3 kilometers (1.9 miles) deep across the river between Shlissel'burg and

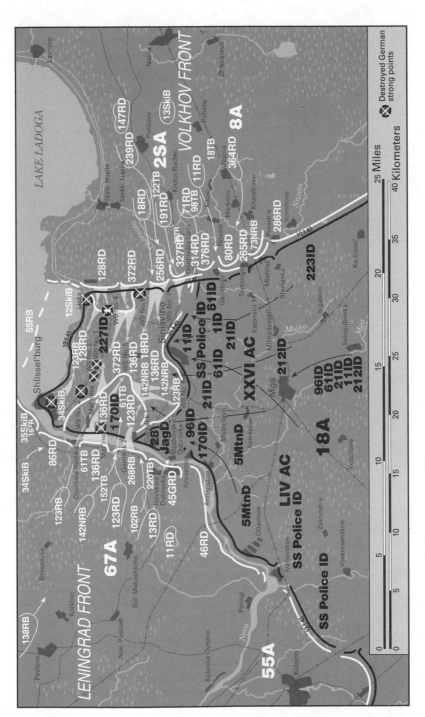

Map 14. Soviet Operation Spark, 12–24 January 1943

Gorodok No. 2. The successful assault split the Germans' defenses at the junction of the 170th and 227th Infantry Divisions and seriously damaged the regiment on the 170th Division's right flank. Simoniak's riflemen rushed forward, captured Pyl'naia Mel'nitsa and Mar'ino from the German 170th Infantry Division and by day's end was fighting in the woods north of the Beliavskoe Swamp. At 1800 hours sappers erected bridges over the Neva River north and south of Mar'ino for the passage of the heavy tanks in Simoniak's second echelon. Borshchev's riflemen also assaulted across the river successfully, penetrated the 170th Infantry Division's defenses to a depth of 1.5–2 kilometers (.9–1.2 miles), and began to envelop German defenses at Gorodok No. 1 and Gorodok No. 2 from the northeast.[37]

However, Dukhanov's shock group achieved considerably less success on its flanks. On the right flank, Major General A. A. Krasnov's 45th Guards Rifle Division, which was attacking through the 46th Rifle Division's forces already in the Moskovskaia Dubrovka bridgehead, captured the first German trench line but was halted shortly thereafter by fierce German counterattacks. This clearly indicated that the Germans had expected the attack. On the left flank, Trubachev's 86th Rifle Division encountered heavy fire and was able to insert only two of its battalions across the river. Later in the day, his division regrouped, crossed the river to the south, in the 136th Rifle Division's sector, and began a slow advance on Shlissel'burg. The battle subsided when the early winter night set in, only to be resumed the next day with increased ferocity after both sides had regrouped and reinforced their forces. A German account poignantly described the dramatic Red Army assault:

> How did things go at Gorodok, that key point of the German defenses on the Neva? Corporal Luhrsen survived the artillery barrage unscathed in his narrow trench. As the creeping barrage moved on towards the hinterland he rose and shook off the dirt and snow which had half buried him. Then he scrambled out of the trenches.
>
> And then he saw them coming—the regiments of the Soviet 13th [136th] and 268th Rifle Division. In close line abreast they were charging across the perfectly flat snow-covered ice of the Neva. There was less than a yard between each man and his neighbor. Veritable giants in front— sailors of the Red Banner Baltic Fleet. They were employed particularly at Gorodok and Maryino. With them came mine-clearing parties with their detectors, working their way forward in leaps and bounds. . . .
>
> General Krasnov's three guards regiments [the 45th Guards Rifle Division] reached the first shattered German trenches. But that was as far as they got. In the deep and cunningly planned trenches of the main defense zone the Russians were thrown back in hand-to-hand fighting with grenades, trenching tools, and submachine guns. . . .

At Maryino, however, at the junction between Captain Irle's Reconnaissance Battalion 240 and the 2d Battalion, 401st Grenadier Regiment, the Russians succeeded with their fifth wave and at the enormous cost of 3,000 dead and wounded, in breaking into the German positions and in gaining a foothold near the *dacha* north of Gorodok. . . .

Major-General Dukhanov, the C-in-C of the Soviet 67th Army, perceived his opportunity and instantly threw everything he had into the penetration area. He withdrew the remnants of 86th Rifle Division from Shlusselburg and employed them at Maryino. There he concentrated the bulk of three divisions, and with hurriedly brought-up tank battalions he fanned out to the north, south, and east.[38]

General Karl Hilpert, the commander of the German XXVI Army Corps, whose forces defended the Shlissel'burg salient, reacted quickly to the Soviet assault despite his lack of significant reserves. With Lindemann's approval, he moved five battalions of his 96th Infantry Division from Mga to Gorodok No. 2 and the forest east of Gorodok. Supported by a battery of 88mm guns from the 36th Flak Regiment, a battery of 150mm howitzers, and a company of Tiger tanks (four tanks) from the 502d Panzer Battalion, the composite force reinforced the sagging defenses on the 170th Infantry Division's beleaguered right flank.[39] At the same time, a combat group from the neighboring 5th Mountain Infantry Division reinforced the defenses south of Moskovskaia Dubrovka. The partially shattered 170th Infantry Division consolidated its forces along a line running west of Gorodok No. 1, and the shaken 227th Division withdrew its shattered left flank to new defenses facing south at Workers Settlements Nos. 2 and 3. Another combat group from the 96th Infantry Division attempted to plug the gaps on the 227th Division's left flank and rear by occupying defenses near Workers Settlement No. 1.

After regrouping and replenishing his forces overnight, Dukhanov's troops resumed their offensive along the entire front on 13 January after another short artillery preparation. Simoniak's 136th Rifle Division, supported by tanks from Lieutenant Colonel V. V. Khrustitsky's 61st Light Tank Brigade, enveloped the 96th Infantry Division's right flank in Beliavskoe Swamp from the north and slowly advanced 4 kilometers (2.5 miles) eastward. After heavy fighting with the 96th Infantry Division, its forward battalions reached the region 1.5 kilometers (.9 miles) west of Workers Settlement No. 5, forming a deep salient only 4–5 kilometers (2.5–3.1 miles) west of the advancing 2d Shock Army. Simultaneously, Trubachev's 86th Rifle Division, now following Simoniak's 136th, advanced 1–1.5 kilometers (.6–1 mile) and approached Workers Settlement No. 3 and Preobrazhenskoe Hill, the main German strong point protecting the southern approaches to Shlissel'burg, before being halted by heavy resistance from the 227th Infantry Division.

As had been the case the previous day, the attack on the 67th Army's right flank once again faltered. Borshchev's 268th Rifle Division, attacking on Simoniak's right flank, failed to dislodge the German 170th Infantry Division's troops defending Gorodok No. 1 and Gorodok No. 2, suffering heavy losses in the process. Worse still, at 1615 hours, the 96th Infantry Division, supported by 15 tanks, launched a surprise counterattack, forcing Borshchev's division to withdraw 2 kilometers (1.2 miles) in near panic.[40] On Borshchev's right flank near Moskovskaia Dubrovka, Krasnov's 45th Guards Rifle Division once again made no progress in the Moskovskaia Dubrovka region and, in fact, lost ground to counterattacks by the German 5th Mountain Division. At nightfall, Dukhanov ordered his attacking divisions to repel the German counterattacks and prepared to commit his army's second echelon the next morning.

To the east, Meretskov began his artillery preparation at 0930 hours on 12 January with more than 2,000 artillery pieces, 300 of which conducted direct fire against German defensive positions on the forward edge. While the artillery preparation was wreaking havoc on German defenses, special groups of snipers picked off German officers and soldiers. Forty minutes before the end of the artillery preparation, bombers and assault aircraft from the 14th Air Army struck German strong points at and around Workers Settlements Nos. 4, 5, and 7 and Siniavino. Simultaneously, sappers cut lanes through the German minefields. The ground and aerial bombardment disorganized the German defenses. A captured sergeant from the 227th Infantry Division's 366th Infantry Regiment captured the scene:

> It was a nightmare. In the morning, the Russians opened fire from guns of all caliber. The shells impacted precisely where the bunkers were located. Even before the Russians attacked, many were killed and wounded in the 10th Company. Lieutenant Dehl, the company commander, and his senior sergeant and sergeant were killed. The soldiers were overcome by panic. The Russians had hardly approached when those located in the trenches greeted them with raised hands.[41]

Romanovsky's five first-echelon rifle divisions assaulted at 1115 hours across the entire sector from Lipka to Gaitolovo under the cover of a final artillery barrage and air strikes. The assault groups from two divisions on the right flank of Starikov's 8th Army joined the attack at 1135 hours. Against heavy resistance, the assaulting infantry and infantry support tanks penetrated the forward edge of the 227th Infantry Division's defenses and attacked the German strong points at Lipka, Workers Settlement No. 8, and Kruglaia Grove. On the right flank, Major General F. M. Parkhomenko's 128th Rifle Division penetrated the first German trench line but was halted south of Lipka by heavy fire from the 96th Infantry Division's 2d Battalion, 287th Infantry

Regiment. This battalion, which had only recently reinforced the 227th Infantry Division, manned snow-covered bunkers in a cemetery on a hill adjacent to the 128th Rifle Division's right flank, and the snow prevented the attacking troops from detecting the bunkers. Soviet critiques later noted that the 128th Rifle Division's attacking battalions failed to maneuver properly, exploit their heavy weaponry, concentrate their direct fires, or cooperate properly with their supporting tanks.[42]

In Romanovsky's center, Colonel P. I. Radygin's 372d and Colonel A. P. Baraboshkin's 256th Rifle Divisions penetrated the 227th Infantry Division's forward defenses and advanced 2 kilometers (1.2 miles) north and south of Workers Settlement No. 8. In the process, Radygin's division overran the 1st Battalion, 374th Infantry Regiment, which had been attached to the 227th Infantry Division, but then encountered heavy fire from Workers Settlement No. 8. The 372d Rifle Division repeatedly assaulted the settlement, which was defended by the 374th Regiment's 2d Battalion, but failed to crack the strong point and suffered heavy losses. To the south, despite the heavy flanking fire from Workers Settlement No. 8 and Kruglaia Grove, Baraboshkin's right flank regiment managed to wedge between the two strong points but could advance no farther through the murderous fire.[43]

With the attack in his center faltering, Romanovsky asked for and obtained Meretskov's permission to commit Major General M. N. Ovchinnikov's 18th Rifle Division, supported by the 98th Tank Brigade, into combat from the second echelon early on 13 January. The fresh forces were to bypass Workers Settlement No. 8 from the south, attack toward Workers Settlement No. 5, and link up there with the 67th Army's advancing forces. Although committed in timely fashion, these reinforcements were clearly inadequate to outflank Workers Settlement No. 8 from the north and south. Making matters worse, heavy snow and strong winds disrupted the supporting artillery fire and tank attack and caused Romanovsky's fresh assault to fail.

Meanwhile, to the south, Colonel N. A. Poliakov's 327th Rifle Division, supported by the 32d Heavy Tank Regiment and the 507th Tank Battalion, assaulted Kruglaia Grove at daybreak on 12 January and captured it by day's end after heavy and often fierce hand-to-hand fighting. However, the 227th Infantry Division's 366th Infantry Regiment clung desperately to its defensive works at Workers Settlement No. 7 on the left flank of the Soviet penetration and was reinforced by the 28th Jager Division's 83d Jager Regiment. The combined force successfully defended the settlement for days, effectively blocking the Soviet advance toward Siniavino.[44] On the 2d Shock Army's extreme left flank, Major General N. E. Argunov's 376th Rifle Division and the 80th and 265th Rifle Divisions and 73d Naval Rifle Brigade of Starikov's 8th Army penetrated the forward edge of the German defense but were halted by heavy fire from the 1st Infantry Division. Repeated attempts to resume the offensive in this sector utterly failed in the face of repeated German counterattacks.[45]

Overnight on 12 January and on the morning of the 13th, Hilpert assembled a combat group from the 1st Infantry Division and employed it in counterattacks to recapture Kruglaia Grove and the strong points covering the Siniavino road. Meretskov countered by reinforcing the 376th Rifle Division's thrust toward Siniavino with Major General N. M. Zamirovsky's 71st Rifle Division. As the battle raged on, deteriorating weather conditions and the dense forests hindered the delivery of coordinated and accurate artillery fires. Having flown 550 air sorties on 12 January, the 14th Air Army was prevented by bad weather from flying any sorties the next day.

By day's end on 13 January, Romanovsky's 2d Shock Army had penetrated German defenses in two sectors along the 10-kilometer (6.2-mile) front between Lipka and Gaitolovo. Two of his divisions had driven a wedge 3 kilometers (1.9 miles) deep into the 227th Infantry Division's defenses southeast of Workers Settlement No. 5, and two other divisions carved a smaller penetration south of Lipka. The attackers had almost encircled Lipka and Workers Settlement No. 8, captured most of Kruglaia Grove, and had almost reached Workers Settlements Nos. 4 and 5, where the 227th and 1st Infantry Divisions struggled to avoid encirclement.

Faced with this determined and clearly better organized Soviet offensive, Kuechler desperately sought to defend the Shlissel'burg bottleneck at all costs and prevent the two attacking *fronts* from linking up. To that end, he ordered the 61st Infantry Division at Kirishi to reinforce German defenses at Workers Settlement No. 6 and Gorodok No. 1 and Gorodok No. 2 and elements of the 5th Mountain Division and SS Police Divisions to reinforce his defenses at Siniavino. Meretskov, too, threw fresh forces into combat from his second echelon.

Early on 14 January, Govorov ordered Dukhanov to commit his 67th Army's second echelon to combat, strengthen his first echelon, attack to link up with the Volkhov Front's forces, and capture Gorodok No. 1 and Gorodok No. 2. At dawn, Colonel A. P. Ivanov's 123d Rifle Division, Colonel P. I. Pinchuk's 152d Tank Brigade, and Lieutenant Colonel F. F. Shishov's 123d Rifle Brigade advanced into combat on the left and right flanks of Simoniak's 136th Rifle Division. To the south, first, a regiment of Colonel V. P. Iakutovich's 13th Rifle Division and Lieutenant Colonel A. V. Batluk's complete 102d Rifle Brigade and, later, the remainder of Iakutovich's division and Lieutenant Colonel Koshchienko's 142d Naval Rifle Brigade reinforced Borshchev's 268th Rifle Division. Govorov ordered the entire force to crush German resistance at Gorodok No. 1 and Gorodok No. 2 once and for all.

In addition, Govorov ordered Lieutenant Colonel Ia. F. Potekhin's 34th Ski Brigade to support the assault of Trubachev's 86th Rifle Division on

Shlissel'burg. However, the piecemeal commitment of his second echelon across so broad a front to reinforce already exhausted forces was a mistake that actually slowed the 67th Army's forward progress. Once again, the two *front* commanders were ignoring past experience.[46]

Subsequently, beginning on 14 January, Dukhanov's forces gnawed their way through the German defenses, suffering heavy losses as they did so. In four days of bitter fighting, the infantry and tanks of Simoniak's 136th Rifle Division and Khrustitsky's 61st Tank Brigade advanced up to 2.5 kilometers (1.6 miles), reaching the western outskirts of Workers Settlement No. 5 late on 17 January. To the south, Shishov's 123d Rifle Brigade approached Workers Settlements Nos. 1, 2, and 3, capturing No. 3 on 17 January, but faltering on the outskirts of the two other settlements. The 13th Air Army flew 919 air sorties on 14 and 15 January as the weather improved markedly.

Despite the improved air support, German reserves prevented Borshchev's 268th Rifle Division from capturing Gorodok No. 1 and Gorodok No. 2, even after his division had been reinforced. After four days of combat, Ivanov's 123d Rifle Division and Batluk's 102d Rifle Brigade captured the woods east of Gorodok No. 2 but could accomplish nothing more. On Dukhanov's left flank, Trubachev's 86th Rifle Division finally stormed Preobrazhenskoe Hill at 1500 hours on 15 January and in heavy fighting fought its way into the southern portion of Shlissel'burg proper at 1200 hours the next day. For the next two days, Trubachev's riflemen fought intense street battles with the rear guard forces of the 227th Infantry Division, which had just received orders to withdraw.[47]

Meanwhile, to the east, Romanovsky's forces advanced at a snail's pace in intense fighting, largely because both he and Meretskov had repeated Govorov's mistake of dissipating their forces over a broad front and committing their second echelon and reserve forces in piecemeal fashion. On Meretskov's orders, Romanovsky committed Ovchinnikov's 18th and Colonel V. N. Fedorov's 71st Rifle Divisions, supported by Lieutenant Colonel Z. G. Papkin's 98th Tank Brigade, into combat on 13 January. Then Colonel P. A. Popapov's 191st Rifle Division went into combat against German defenses north of Kruglaia Grove on 14 January. Finally, Major General P. N. Chernyshev's 239th and Colonel I. V. Gribov's 11th Rifle Divisions, the 12th and 13th Ski Brigades, and Colonel Ia. A. Davydov's 122d Tank Brigade went into action over the next three days.[48]

Despite the piecemeal commitments, Baraboshkin's 256th Rifle Division captured Podgornyi Station on 14 January and, wheeling its front to the southwest, attacked German positions on the approaches to Siniavino. After regrouping overnight, the next morning Radygin's 372d Rifle Division captured Workers Settlement No. 8, and the remnants of the German garrison fought their way out to the west with heavy casualties. Radygin's forces pursued, reaching Workers Settlement No. 1 late on 17 January. Simultaneously, Ovchinnikov's 18th

Rifle Division fought its way to the outskirts of Workers Settlement No. 5. By this time, the Germans' defensive front was split asunder and Govorov's and Meretskov's forces were only 1.5–2 kilometers (.9–1.2 miles) apart, threatening to encircle German forces in the Shlissel'burg salient.

Both Kuechler at Army Group North and Lindemann at Eighteenth Army understood the perilous situation they faced late on 17 January. Clearly, one more determined Soviet thrust would cut off and destroy German forces in the Shlissel'burg region. By this time, Group Huhner, under Lieutenant General Huhner, the commander of the 61st Infantry Division who had two regimental groups under his command, had forced its way northward from Siniavino and Workers Settlement No. 5 in an attempt to link up with the encircled 227th and 96th Infantry and 5th Mountain Divisions. Once in the pocket, however, Group Huhner was too weak to hold open the corridor, while defending what was left of the Shlissel'burg pocket. Therefore, with Kuechler's approval, Lindemann ordered Group Huhner to hold on to Workers Settlement No. 5 and then break out southward through the narrow forested corridor north of Siniavino in conjunction with an attack by the SS Police Division against the 67th Army's right flank near Workers Settlement No. 5.[49]

The breakout had to be accomplished quickly if it was to succeed because Soviet forces were also about to sever Group Huhner's withdrawal routes to the south. In fact, at 0930 hours on 18 January, the lead elements of Ivanov's 123d Rifle Division from the 67th Army and Radygin's 372d Rifle Division from the 2d Shock Army linked up just east of Workers Settlement No. 1. Less than an hour later, after repelling a strong German counterattack, Simoniak's 136th Rifle Division captured Workers Settlement No. 5. To the north, the division's 269th Rifle Regiment made contact with the 424th Rifle Regiment of the 2d Shock Army's 18th Rifle Division at 1145 hours and at noon south of the village.[50] A Soviet account captured the ferocity of the fighting at Workers Settlement No. 5:

> The units of the 136th Rifle Division twice broke through into Settlement No. 5 but were unable to gain a foothold. Three times during the night of 16 January, the regiments of the 2d Shock Army's 18th Rifle Division assaulted the settlement from the east but had no success. A few of the division's subunits [battalions] got within 15 or 20 meters of the fortified position but had to fall back time and again. The Germans were fighting with the courage of desperation, but their position became more and more hopeless. By the evening of the following day, the division's regiments, supported by the 61st Tank Brigade, reached the eastern edge of the settlement and began to fight for each single house. On the morning of 18 January, the fighting flared up again with renewed violence around Workers Settlements Nos. 1 and 5. The Soviet units continued to attack

the village from the east and west. The Eighteenth Army commander hurriedly transferred separate battalions and units from other sectors of the front and threw them into battle from the march trying in every way possible to halt a further Soviet advance. . . .

Since they were still not completely cut off, the northern units of the enemy's Shlissel'burg-Siniavino grouping emerged from the forests and swamps along the coast of Lake Ladoga and tried several times to penetrate the narrow corridor in the vicinity of the settlements. Early in the morning, when a narrow corridor remained, they once again attempted to drive through it to the south to the main force of their Eighteenth Army. But it was already too late. Soviet forces had cut the corridor. Having repelled the last desperate enemy counterattack, on 18 January, the units of the Leningrad Front's 136th Rifle Division and 61st Tank Brigade burst into Workers Settlement No. 5 on the heels of the crushed enemy, where at midday they linked up with units of the Volkhov Front's 18th Rifle Division.[51]

The struggle now reached a crescendo as Soviet forces sought to destroy German forces desperately trying to escape from the pocket around Shlissel'burg and Lipka. Trubachev's 86th Rifle Division of Dukhanov's army captured Shlissel'burg at 1400 hours on 18 January after intense street fighting and then set about liquidating German forces scattered through the forests south of Lake Ladoga. At the same time, Major General F. N. Parkhomenko's 128th and Radygin's 372d Rifle Divisions of Romanovsky's army captured Lipka and cleared German forces from the forests northeast of Workers Settlement No. 1. Trapped between the 67th and 2d Shock Armies' vanguards, Group Huhner ran the gauntlet of fire southward past Workers Settlement No. 5 and Podgornyi Station and finally reached the relative safety of Siniavino on 19 and 20 January. The breakout was costly for both sides:

> At daybreak General Huhner finally ordered his combat group at P. 5 [Workers Settlement No. 5] to disengage. The heavy losses which the Soviets had suffered during the night in the continuous hand-to-hand fighting reduced his risk. The withdrawal was less dangerous than the general had feared. The German flank cover held out. Even the Russian tanks only followed up hesitantly. . . . On 20 January Huhner's men reeled into the intercepting line. The companies of the 151st and 162d Regiments now numbered thirty to forty men each. The 1st Company, 162d Grenadier Regiment, which had gone into battle with one hundred and twenty-eight men on 15th January, was by now reduced to a mere forty-four.[52]

After linking up, Dukhanov and Romanovsky wheeled their armies' main forces southward and ordered them to capture Siniavino, Gorodok No. 1, and

Gorodok No. 2. In turn, Lindemann reinforced his defenses at Siniavino with the SS Police and 21st Infantry Divisions and, soon after, with the 11th Infantry Division and, simultaneously, ordered the 28th Jager Division to reinforce the Gorodok sector.

Spurred on by an impatient Zhukov, beginning on 20 January, the 67th and 2d Shock Armies delivered attack after attack on German defenses across a broad front from Gorodok No. 1 and Gorodok No. 2 through Siniavino to Gontovaia Lipka. The fighting increased day by day in both intensity and cost. Govorov ordered Dukhanov's 67th Army to dig in along its existing lines and, at the same time, widen the penetration front southward toward Siniavino. He then deployed his 16th Fortified Region from Gorodok No. 2 to Workers Settlement No. 5, where it quickly constructed battalion defensive regions necessary to hold the newly won corridor to Leningrad.

Dukhanov's army attacked southward east of Gorodok No. 1 and Gorodok No. 2 on 20 January in an attempt to capture Mustolovo, cut the road and railroad from Siniavino to Mga, and outflank Siniavino from the west. At the same time, the army's 142d Naval Infantry and 123d Rifle Brigades attacked toward Siniavino, while the 102d Rifle and 220th Tank Brigades and 123d Rifle Division struck violently at German defenses at Gorodok No. 1. Although the advance on Mustolovo failed after heavy fighting, the force attacking Siniavino managed to advance southward 2 kilometers (2.1 miles) against heavy resistance, severing the rail line southeast from Gorodok No. 1 and capturing Workers Settlement No. 6 just west of Siniavino. However, try as they did, Dukhanov's forces were not able to overcome German defenses at Siniavino proper.

Nor was Romanovsky successful in developing his attack further. At the cost of immense losses in men and material, his forces managed to drive a wedge into German defenses south of Workers Settlement No. 7 but were not able to achieve a clean breakthrough. With exhaustion gripping both of their forces, Govorov's and Meretskov's attacks collapsed on 31 January.[53] The front then stabilized along a line running north and east of Gorodok No. 1 and Gorodok No. 2, south of Workers Settlement No. 6 and Podgornyi to Gontovaia Lipka.

Operation Spark was a clear and signal Red Army victory. As far as military accomplishments were concerned, during the operation Soviet forces penetrated German defenses to a depth of 15 kilometers (9.3 miles) during a period of seven days and captured Shlissel'burg, Mar'ino, Lipka, Workers Settlements Nos. 1, 2, 3, 4, 5, 6, 7, and 8, and Podgornyi Station. Although they failed to capture Siniavino, they succeeded in pushing German forces away from the southern shore of Lake Ladoga and tore open a corridor 8–10 kilometers (5–6.2 miles) wide between Leningrad and the rest of the country. The successful offensive also vastly improved the Soviets' strategic situation along the northwestern strategic axis by eliminating the possibility of German-Finnish linkup and improving cooperation between the Leningrad and Volkhov Fronts. Most important to Leningraders themselves, the victory opened supply links between Russia, the city, and the city's defenders. For their contributions to the victory, the GKO awarded the designations of 63d and 64th Guards to Simoniak's 136th and Poliakov's 327th Rifle Divisions and 30th Guards to Khrustitsky's 61st Tank Brigade and promoted Khrustitsky to the rank of colonel.[54] However, to Zhukov's consternation, the elusive target of Siniavino and the adjacent Siniavino Heights remained in German hands.

If the third Siniavino offensive was a victory, it was a costly one for both sides. The attacking Soviet forces suffered 115,082 casualties, including 33,940 killed, captured, or missing, and 81,142 wounded, out of 302,800 troops engaged.[55] Several senior Soviet officers were among the casualties, including Meretskov's deputy, Fediuninsky, who was seriously wounded by mortar fire on 20 January, and Major General of Tank Forces N. A. Bolotnikov, Meretskov's Chief of Armored and Mechanized Forces, who was killed by a German air strike on 26 January.[56] The Germans, too, suffered greatly, admitting to 12,000 dead and many more wounded, losses the Eighteenth Army could ill afford.[57]

General Zhukov, whom Stalin promoted to Marshal of the Soviet Union on 18 January, the same day that Govorov's forces captured Shlissel'burg, conducted the operation in characteristically brutal fashion and suffered characteristically heavy losses. An undocumented exchange between Zhukov and Simoniak, the commander of the 67th Army's 136th Rifle Division, vividly describes Zhukov's command style:

> Rows broke out among the Soviet generals. Marshal of the Soviet Union Georgi Zhukov, hero of the Battle of Moscow, hero of Stalingrad, had been sent in to "coordinate" between the Volkhov front and Moscow. He got on the VC high security line to General Simoniak of the 136th Division. Why didn't Simoniak attack the Sinyavino Heights? The Nazi positions there were holding up the Second Shock Army.
>
> "For the same reason the Second Army doesn't attack them," Simoniak replied. "The approach is through a marsh. The losses would be great and the results small."
>
> "Trotskyite! Passive resister!" shouted Zhukov. "Who are those cowards of yours? Who doesn't want to fight? Who needs to be ousted?"
>
> Simoniak angrily replied that there were no cowards in the Sixty-seventh Army.

"Wise guy," snapped Zhukov. "I order you to take the heights."

"Comrade Marshal," Simoniak rejoined. "My army is under the command of the Leningrad front commander, General Govorov. I take orders from him."

Zhukov hung up. Simoniak got no orders to attack the Siniavino Heights.[58]

Despite the high cost of victory, the offensive did crack the Leningrad blockade, but only barely. The Soviets were able to restore ground communications with the city, but those communications lines remained tenuous at best and subject to German artillery interdiction. During the ensuing days, the Soviets constructed a rail line through the corridor from Shlissel'burg to Poliany and on 6 February opened regular rail communications between Leningrad and the rest of the Soviet Union. Despite the construction of the new rail line, the corridor was only 8–10 kilometers (5–6.2 miles) wide, it was subject to constant German artillery fire, and the German interdiction meant that its carrying capacity remained low. Mga Station, the most important point on the old main rail line from Leningrad to Volkhov, was still in German hands, and heavy German troop concentrations still posed a threat to the tenuous corridor.

Although the third Siniavino offensive was a relatively small-scale component of the much vaster Soviet winter campaign, the operation had more than symbolic significance. For example, it marked the first time in the modern era when large-scale offensives from within and without raised the siege of a large city and port. What made this feat more impressive was the fact that the attacking forces had to assault well-prepared enemy defenses on the far bank of an ice-covered river that was 500–600 meters wide.

Red Army infantry played the most important role in the offensive, since terrain and weather precluded the large-scale employment of tanks and other heavy weaponry. Artillery also played a vital role by creating the requisite conditions for the infantry to penetrate the strong defense. The 2d Shock Army's artillery alone fired 630,000 artillery and mortar shells from 12 to 18 January, and the Baltic Fleet engaged and damaged 14 enemy strong points, 43 firing points, and 8 artillery batteries.[59] Although relatively weak in comparison with operations in other front sectors, individual tank brigades and regiments as well as separate tank battalions did provide critical support to the infantry despite the difficult terrain and weather conditions. For example, Khrustitsky's 61st Tank Brigade distinguished itself while supporting the 136th Rifle Division and Davydov's 122d Tank Brigade did likewise for the 2d Shock Army. More often than not, however, poor integration of tanks and infantry led to inordinate tank losses.

Combat engineers and sappers also played a vital part in the operations, particularly by supporting the assault across the Neva River, removing mines, penetrating prepared defenses, and reducing German strong points. Poor weather hampered the employment of aviation throughout the operation. Nevertheless, the 13th Air Army conducted 910 sorties and dropped around 13,700 bombs and rockets on the Germans between 12 and 18 January.[60]

ZHUKOV'S OPERATION POLAR STAR, FEBRUARY

The third Siniavino offensive served only as prelude for an even more ambitious Red Army offensive in the Leningrad region. By early February 1943, the Red Army had smashed German Army Groups "B" and Don west and south of the Don River, and German Army Group "A" was in full retreat from the Caucasus region. The *Stavka* was already planning to expand its winter offensive to encompass the region from Rzhev in the north to Khar'kov in the south during February and March 1943 and soon would plan an advance to the Vitebsk region and the Dnepr River from Gomel' to the Black Sea. It was only reasonable that the *Stavka* would include the Leningrad region in its offensive plans.

At Leningrad, the third Siniavino offensive had created conditions the *Stavka* considered conducive to the conduct of an even larger offensive. The fighting around Siniavino had forced the Eighteenth Army to concentrate its forces in that region and weaken its forces elsewhere. For example, on 31 January 1943, only two regiments of the Spanish 250th "Blue" Infantry Division defended the sector from Pushkin to Ivanovskoe south of Leningrad opposite the Leningrad Front's 55th Army. At the same time, only the 69th, 132d, and 81st Infantry Divisions defended the sector 100 kilometers (62 miles) wide opposite the Volkhov Front's 54th Army. Worse still, the Eighteenth Army was overextended, it had only two security divisions in reserve, and since its strongest forces faced the 67th and 2d Shock Armies, the flanks of the German Siniavino-Mga salient appeared vulnerable.

After its victory in Operation Spark, the *Stavka* carefully assessed the strengths and vulnerabilities of German forces in the Leningrad region. Both Govorov and Meretskov had already proposed defeating Army Group North by employing their forces to cut off, encircle, and destroy the entire German Mga-Siniavino grouping by delivering concentric attacks against the weak flanks of the German salient from the region south of Mga. However, the *Stavka* well understood the difficulties entailed in mounting an offensive solely in the immediate vicinity of Leningrad. The experiences of previous offensives vividly underscored how difficult it would be to overcome strong German defenses in such difficult terrain.

Marshal of the Soviet Union S. K. Timoshenko, who had replaced Kurochkin as commander of the Northwestern Front, unwittingly provided a solution to the dilemma when on 14 January he proposed a new general offensive by his *front* to destroy German forces in the Demiansk and Staraia Russa regions.[61] Zhukov immediately perceived an opportunity to defeat Army Group North as a whole and raise the Leningrad blockade by conducting a broad envelopment of Army Group North with offensives from both the Demiansk and Staraia Russa regions and Leningrad proper.

Therefore, on Zhukov's recommendation, the *Stavka* decided to broaden the scope of the offensive to completely destroy Army Group North and liberate the entire Leningrad region. Under Zhukov's direction and close supervision, by early February the *Stavka* had developed plans for Operation Polar Star, a multi-*front* offensive whose objective was nothing short of the complete destruction of Army Group North. The *Stavka* timed the operation to coincide with a major offensive by the Red Army's Kalinin, Western, Briansk, and Central Fronts toward Briansk and Smolensk and by the Voronezh, Southwestern, and Southern Fronts to the Dnepr River line. Operation Polar Star required the Northwestern Front to attack from the Demiansk region through Dno and Luga to Pskov and Narva on the Gulf of Finland. Simultaneously, the Leningrad and Volkhov Fronts were to attack the Eighteenth Army around Leningrad and, ultimately, link up with Northwestern Front's forces to encircle almost all of Army Group North south of Leningrad (Map 15).

The official Soviet history of the war accurately describes the nature and intent of Operation Polar Star:

> Along the northwestern axis, the *Stavka* intended to employ the Leningrad, Volkhov, and Northwestern Fronts to destroy Army Group North. According to the plan for Operation Polar Star, the Northwestern Front's left wing would deliver the main attack in the general direction of Pskov and Narva. Initially, the intention was to sever the so-called Ramushevo corridor by concentric attacks from the north and south and destroy the enemy Demiansk grouping. At the same time, the forces of the Leningrad and Volkhov Fronts were to liquidate the Mga salient. General M. S. Khozin's Special Group, which consisted of the 1st Tank and 68th Armies and also a number of other formations and units, was entrusted with a very crucial mission. It was to be committed into the penetration in the 1st Shock Army's sector with the mission of advancing rapidly to the northwest, severing the enemy Leningrad-Volkhov grouping's communications by reaching the Luga, Strugi Krasnye, Porkhov, and Dno regions and preventing the approach of enemy units to assist the enemy's Demiansk and Leningrad-Volkhov groupings. Subsequently, reinforced by the Northwestern Front's formations, this group was to exploit success to Kingisepp and Narva with part of its forces, while the main force encircled and destroyed the enemy Volkhov and Leningrad grouping in cooperation with

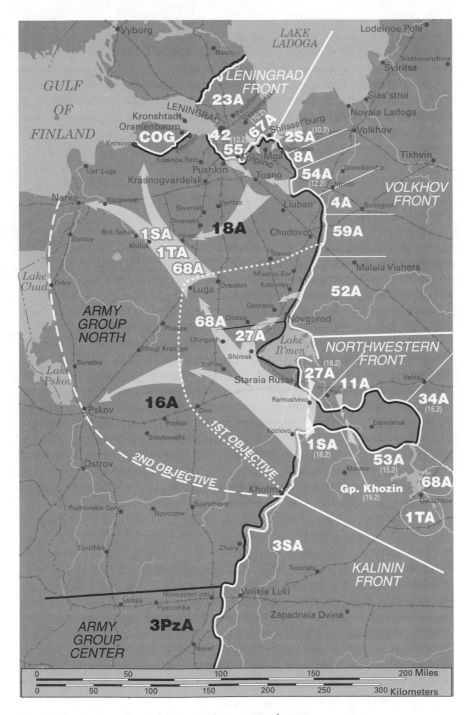

Map 15. Soviet Operation Polar Star, February–March 1943

the Volkhov and Leningrad Fronts. Marshal of the Soviet Union G. K. Zhukov was entrusted with coordinating the operations of the *fronts* operating along the northwestern axis.[62]

However, Zhukov is singularly silent about the operation in his memoirs, devoting just two paragraphs to his role in the operation, and saying nothing about either Operation Polar Star or the operation's grand intent:

A representative of the *Stavka* at that time, I was on the North-Western Front, which was under the command of Marshal Timoshenko. Having reached the Lovat River, our forces were preparing to cross.

Stalin rang the command post of the North-Western Front on either the 13th or 14th of March.

I described to the Supreme High Commander the situation on the River Lovat and told him that the river had become impassable owing to the early thaw and that the troops of the North-Western Front would evidently have to cease their offensive operations for a while.[63]

In reality, Zhukov spent all of February and half of March actively involved in planning and supervising the Northwestern Front's offensive operations. According to Zhukov's plan, Govorov's and Meretskov's *fronts* were to begin Operation Polar Star in early February to distract German attention northward to Leningrad and away from the Demiansk region. Then, in mid-February, Timoshenko's *front* was to commence its assault to cut the Ramushevo corridor, and, shortly thereafter, Group Khozin would exploit toward Pskov and Narva. The combined forces of the three *fronts* would then destroy German Army Group North and raise the Leningrad blockade.

Timoshenko's Northwestern Front was to play the major role in Polar Star by destroying the German II Army Corps lodged in the Demiansk salient and advancing through Staraia Russa and Dno to Pskov and Narva. The *Stavka* issued its final order for the offensive to Timoshenko at 0140 hours on 6 February:

To destroy the enemy Demiansk grouping, the *Stavka* of the Supreme High Command *orders:*

1. The 1st Shock Army, consisting of eight rifle divisions, one tank brigade, four tank regiments, one artillery division, seven RGK artillery regiments, five mortar regiments, and the 1st Guards-Mortar Division, will penetrate the enemy defense in the Shotovo and Ovchinnikovo sector on 19 February 1943. [It] will reach the Onufrievo and Sokolovo region by attacking to the north and northeast.

2. The 27th Army, consisting of seven rifle divisions, five rifle brigades, four tank regiments, three ski brigades, two tank brigades, one artillery division, two RGK artillery regiments, two mortar regiments, and one guards-mortar brigade, will penetrate the enemy defense in the Penno and Borisovo sector on 19 February 1943. [It] will reach the Onufrievo and Sokolovo region by attacking to the south and southeast, where it will close the encirclement ring around the enemy's Demiansk grouping.

3. After closing the encirclement ring, the 1st Shock Army will attack to the east with two rifle divisions from the 27th Army subordinate to it with the mission of destroying the enemy deployed in the Ramushevo corridor.

4. After penetrating the enemy defense and while attacking with part of its force to the south and southeast, the 27th Army's main forces will turn to the west to envelop Staraia Russa with the mission of encircling and destroying the enemy Staraia Russa grouping. After destroying the enemy in the Staraia Russa region, the 27th Army will become subordinate to Colonel General Khozin, the commander of the Special Group of Forces.

5. After destroying the enemy in the Ramushevo corridor and having quickly regrouped the *front's* forces and weapons, the *front* commander will destroy the encircled Demiansk grouping.

6. After the 1st Shock Army has penetrated the enemy defense, it will support the passage of Group Khozin to Dno Station.

7. The Northwestern Front is entrusted with the material support of Khozin's group of forces.

8. Confirm receipt and report your decision on 10 February 1943.

[signed] I. Stalin, G. Zhukov[64]

The Northwestern Front's left wing, consisting of the 27th, 11th, 34th, 1st Shock, and 53d Armies, was to make Timoshenko's main attack through Staraia Russa toward Luga and Dno. During the first stage of the operation, these armies were to sever the Ramushevo corridor, which connected German II Army Corps with its parent Sixteenth Army, and destroy German forces at Demiansk. Subsequently, a Special Operational Group made up of one tank and one combined arms army under Colonel General M. S. Khozin's command was to advance northwest, capture Pskov and Narva, and cut off and destroy the German Eighteenth Army in cooperation with the Leningrad and Volkhov Fronts:

The *Stavka* of the Supreme High Command *orders:*

1. Complete concentrating your group of forces, consisting of the 1st Tank and 68th Armies and the reserve group, in the Marevo, Usad'ba,

and Slautino region by day's end on 16 February 1943. Deploy the group for commitment into the penetration in the Ryto, Nikulino 2, Kursko, and Bol'shoi Ostrov region by day's end on 18 February 1943. Be fully prepared to commit the group into the penetration in the Khodyki and Sluchino sector on the morning of 19 February 1943.

2. The group's main mission is to cut the enemy Leningrad-Volkhov grouping's communications by reaching the Luga, Strugi Krasnye, Porkhov, and Dno regions and to prevent enemy units from approaching to assist his Demiansk and Leningrad-Volkhov groupings.

Seize and hold the city of Pskov with a group of forces consisting of two rifle divisions, two ski brigades, two tank regiments, two RGK artillery regiments, and one engineer brigade.

3. After destroying the enemy in the Staraia Russa region, the 27th Army will become subordinate to the commander of the Special Group of Forces for an attack on Luga together with the 68th Army. However, in addition, part of the 27th Army's forces will be employed to seize Novgorod in cooperation with the Volkhov Front's 52d Army.

4. After seizing the Luga and Strugi Krasnye line, seize the Kingisepp and Narva line with part of the group's forces, thus cutting off the enemy's withdrawal routes into Estonia.

Encircle and destroy the enemy Volkhov and Leningrad groupings with the main forces in cooperation with the Volkhov and Leningrad Fronts.

5. Confirm receipt and report fulfillment by 16 February 1943.

[signed] I. Stalin, G. Zhukov[65]

Special Group Khozin, whose forces and commanders were handpicked by the *Stavka,* consisted of Lieutenant General M. E. Katukov's newly formed 1st Tank Army and Lieutenant General F. I. Tolbukhin's fresh 68th Army. The Northwestern Front was to begin its offensive on 15 February. The fact that the *Stavka* assigned Zhukov, Timoshenko, Katukov, and Tolbukhin to plan or participate in Operation Polar Star was indicative of the importance the *Stavka* attached to the offensive.

The *Stavka* issued the Leningrad and Volkhov Fronts their attack orders at 2355 hours on 1 February:

In view of the fact that, up to this time, the frontal attacks in the Siniavino region have not produced the proper results, it is necessary to organize additional attacks by the Volkhov and Leningrad Fronts' forces from the flanks.

The *Stavka* of the Supreme High Command *orders:*

1. The Volkhov Front will penetrate the enemy's defenses in the Makar'evskaia Pustyn', Smerdynia, and Korodynia region on 8 February

1943 with a force of six rifle divisions with *front* reinforcements and will attack in the direction of Vas'kiny Nivy and Shapki to reach the rear of the enemy Siniavino grouping.

Cut the highway and railroad in the Liuban' region with part of your forces.

2. The Leningrad Front will attack from the Ivanovskoe and Rozhdestveno region toward Mga Station on 8 February with a force of five to six rifle divisions with *front* reinforcements to reach the rear of the enemy Mga-Mstolovsk grouping.

3. Without waiting for these flank attacks, the Volkhov and Leningrad Fronts will continue to destroy the enemy and seize the Siniavino and Gorodok No. 1 and Gorodok No. 2 regions by means of an envelopment of Siniavino Heights and the Gorodok No. 1 and Gorodok No. 2 regions.

4. Upon the fulfillment of these missions, destroy the enemy Mga-Siniavino-Shapki grouping in cooperation with the flank attacks and reach the Ul'ianovka, Tosno, and Liuban' line.

5. The boundary lines are as before. Confirm receipt. Report on the beginning of the operation.

[signed] I. Stalin, G. Zhukov[66]

In the Leningrad Front's sector, Sviridov's 55th Army was to attack southeastward along the Oktiabr' rail line from the Kolpino region through Krasnyi Bor to Tosno, wheel its forces east across the Tosno River, and link up with the Volkhov Front's 54th Army. Simultaneously, Sukhomlin's 54th Army was to attack westward from the Smerdynia region through Shapki and subsequently advance toward Tosno to link up with Sviridov's army. The twin pincers were to encircle all German forces in the Mga-Siniavino region, widen the narrow land corridor to Leningrad, and, subsequently, serve as a hammer to smash the bulk of Army Group North against an anvil formed by the Northwestern Front advancing in the south. In addition, part of the 54th Army was to attack Liuban' both to distract the Eighteenth Army and to tie down its forces.

While the 55th and 54th Armies were conducting their pincer maneuver toward Tosno, the Leningrad Front's 67th and the Volkhov Front's 2d Shock Armies were to attack Gorodok No. 1, Gorodok No. 2,, and Siniavino and capture Mga and the Leningrad-Volkhov railroad. Before the operation began, the *Stavka* transferred the 2d Shock Army and its sector north of Siniavino to the Volkhov Front to provide for more unified command and control.[67] The Leningrad and Volkhov Fronts were to begin their offensive on 8 February, one week before the Northwestern Front, to draw Army Group North's reserves northward to Leningrad and away from the Northwestern Front's main attack sector.

Sviridov's 55th Army, which formed the Leningrad Front's arms of the pincer, consisted of eight rifle divisions, two rifle and two ski brigades, and one separate tank regiment.[68] Sviridov planned to lead the assault with his 45th and 63d Guards and 43d Rifle Divisions and 34th Ski Brigade in first echelon, supported by the 31st Tank Regiment, a force numbering roughly 33,000 men and 30 tanks. Once his first-echelon forces had smashed German defenses at Krasnyi Bor, a mobile group consisting of the 35th Ski and 122d Tank Brigades under the command of Major General I. M. Liubovtsev was to advance along the Oktiabr' railroad, capture Ul'ianovka Station, and lead the advance on Tosno. Sviridov's forces faced the L Army Corps' 250th Spanish "Blue" Infantry Division and the 4th SS Police Division deployed in the sector 32 kilometers (19.9 miles) wide from Krasnyi Bor to the Neva River east of Kolpino. General Esteban-Infantes's Spanish division had a reinforced regiment and three infantry battalions totaling 4,500 men with no tanks facing the 55th Army's main attack.[69]

The Volkhov Front's arm of the pincer, Sukhomlin's 54th Army, consisted of 10 rifle divisions, 3 rifle brigades, and 2 tank brigades, with a strength of over 70,000 men and 60 tanks.[70] Sukhomlin's forces were to assault a sector defended by the XXVIII Army Corps' 96th Infantry Division flanked on the left by the 69th Infantry Division and on the right by the 132d Infantry Division. General Noeldechen's 96th Infantry had been assigned this "quiet" sector after being decimated in the previous fighting at Siniavino Heights.

Although imposing on paper, the Leningrad Front's 67th and 2d Shock Armies, which were designated to attack at Gorodok No. 1, Gorodok No. 2, and Siniavino, were still woefully under strength after the January fighting. Nevertheless, they were to join the offensive, based on the assumption that the fighting in the 55th and 54th Armies' sectors would draw German reserves away from the Siniavino region. Romanovsky's 2d Shock Army consisted of 12 understrength rifle divisions, 1 rifle, 1 ski, and 2 tank brigades, 1 tank regiment, and 4 separate tank battalions for a total of roughly 60,000 men and 50 tanks. Dukhanov's 67th Army consisted of 6 rifle divisions, 8 rifle, 2 ski, and 4 tank brigades, 2 tank regiments, 2 separate tank battalions, and 1 fortified region, about 40,000 men and 30 tanks strong.[71] The German XXVI Army Corps (Group Hilpert) defended the salient around Gorodok No. 1 and Gorodok No. 2 with its 28th Jager and 21st Infantry Divisions and the Siniavino region with the 11th and 61st Infantry Divisions, with a combined strength of roughly 35,000 men.

Sviridov's 55th Army attacked early on 10 February along the Kolpino, Krasnyi Bor, Tosno axis after a two-hour artillery preparation by about 1,000 guns and mortars. Catching the Germans by surprise, Simoniak's 63d Guards Rifle Division captured Krasnyi Bor at 1200 hours, and Major General A. A. Krasnov's 45th Guards Rifle Division captured Mishkino later in the day.

By day's end, but against fierce Spanish resistance, Sviridov's first-echelon forces had advanced 4–5 kilometers (2.5–3.1 miles) and captured Krasnyi Bor, Mishkino, Staraia Myza, Chernyshevo, Stepanovka, and Popovka Station. The Leningrad war diary described the action:

> *Wednesday, 10 February.* In the morning the enemy, who were occupying positions in the vicinity of Krasnyi Bor, were stunned by a squall of explosions. Two hours after the beginning of the artillery preparation, the forces of the Leningrad Front's 55th Army began an offensive from the Kolpino region. By midday our forces had captured the village of Krasnyi Bor. Advancing several kilometers forward, during the day they captured the villages of Staraia Myza, Chernyshevo, Popovka Station, and the outskirts of Stepanovka.[72]

Satisfied by the progress, Sviridov then committed his mobile group into action late on 10 February to exploit the 45th Guards Rifle Division's success. However, heavy German resistance and an unexpected thaw, which prevented the ski brigades from operating off the road, halted the mobile group attack short of its objective. Sviridov's tanks and infantry bogged down in hand-to-hand fighting with Spanish forces defending along the Izhora River and the narrow roads south of Krasnyi Bor. During the later stages of the operation, the Germans reinforced the Spaniards' defenses with regimental combat groups from the 212th and 215th Infantry Divisions transferred from Chudovo and Uritsk.

The forces on Sviridov's left flank fared little better. Colonel Ia. P. Sinkevich's 43d Rifle Division and the 34th Ski Brigade advanced 3–4 kilometers in two days of heavy fighting, driving the SS Police Division's forces back toward the Tosno River. Once again, however, the Germans reinforced their defenses with the 24th Infantry Division, portions of the 2d SS Motorized Infantry Brigade, the Flanders Legion, and remnants of the 11th, 21st, and 227th Divisions that had been badly damaged in the earlier fighting at Siniavino. The reinforcements stopped the Soviet advance far short of its objectives. Sviridov's forces had advanced 4–5 kilometers (2.5–3.1 miles) on a front of 14 kilometers (8.7 miles) by 13 February but could advance no more, having lost an estimated 10,000 casualties and most of their tanks in the heavy fighting. The Spanish 250th Infantry Division's gallant defenses cost it 3,200 casualties, and its Fusilier Battalion lost almost 90 percent of its initial strength.[73]

While Sviridov's forces were conducting their futile attacks at Krasnyi Bor, Sukhomlin's 54th Army went into action early on 10 February in the sector north of Smerdynia and the Tigoda River, aiming its thrust at the rail line south of Tosno. Sukhomlin ultimately attacked the 96th Infantry Division's defenses with the 166th, 198th, 311th, and 378th Rifle Divisions, the 14th and 140th Rifle Brigades, the 6th Naval Rifle Brigade, and the 124th Tank Brigade. Despite employing overwhelming force, Sukhomlin's shock group penetrated only 3–4 kilometers (1.9–2.5 miles) into the German defense along a 5-kilometer (3.1-mile) front in three days of heavy fighting. The Germans halted the assault by reinforcing the 96th Infantry Division with regimental combat groups from the 61st Infantry Division at Siniavino, from the 121st Infantry and 217th Infantry Divisions, transferred from the Volkhov River front, and from the adjacent 132d Infantry Division.

The 67th and 2d Shock Armies joined the assault early on 12 February, capitalizing on the fact that the Eighteenth Army had transferred forces from the Siniavino region to reinforce the defensive sectors, which were already under assault. Dukhanov's shock group struck the German 28th Jager and 21st Infantry Divisions' forces dug in around Gorodok No. 1 and Gorodok No. 2 at the same time that Romanovsky's shock group struck German defenses east and west of Siniavino proper. The Leningrad war diary recorded the ferocious and bloody nature of the fighting:

> *Saturday, 13 February.* Once again fighting along the Siniavino axis. Even after the penetration of the blockade, Siniavino, for which so much blood had flowed, remained in enemy hands. And somewhat to the west, where the enemy had managed to halt the 67th Army's right flank, a salient had been formed that projected into our dispositions. Units of the Volkhov Front's 2d Shock Army and the Leningrad Front's 67th Army began an attack—from the Siniavino swamps to the west toward the Neva and from the Neva (from Moskovskaia Dubrovka) to the east toward the Siniavino swamp, trying to cut off that salient.[74]

After six days of heavy fighting, Dukhanov's forces finally succeeded in capturing the smashed ruins of Gorodok No. 1 and Gorodok No. 2 and advanced several kilometers southward to the outskirts of Arbuzovo:

> *Sunday, 14 February.* Along the Siniavino axis around Leningrad, battle is raging for the little known village of Arbuzovo and the even lesser known Gorodok No. 1 and Gorodok No. 2. However, the fighting is heavy. Here the enemy has sunk his teeth so far into the ground that he has to be pried out of every fortification. The Hitlerites exploit every opportunity to deliver an answering blow. Today the counterattacks were especially fierce. . . .
> *Wednesday, 17 February.* The formations on the 67th Army's right flank have completed the destruction of the enemy in Gorodok No. 1, Gorodok No. 2, and the region around Hydroelectric Station No. 8. This has been facilitated by the 55th Army's offensive in the Krasnyi Bor region, to which the enemy has transferred considerable forces. Exploiting

this fact, the 67th Army's 102d, 138th, and 142d Rifle Brigades successfully stormed the so-called Gorodok center of resistance.

Saturday, 20 February. As a result of the battles that began a week ago, we have succeeded in cutting off the bulge in our defenses west of Siniavino. Having dug in on the northern outskirts of Arbuzovo, in truth, where there once was a village, our units have straightened out the front. Conditions have been created for a further offensive to the south. However, the hopes that we could widen the corridor, which had been formed during the penetration of the blockade, were not realized.[75]

Although they had finally pinched off the small German salient on the eastern bank of the Neva River that pointed menacingly toward Shlissel'burg, Dukhanov's forces were too exhausted to accomplish anything more. To the east, however, the assault by Romanovsky's forces on Siniavino and the adjacent Siniavino Heights faltered immediately with heavy losses. The Soviet fourth Siniavino offensive ended with the Siniavino strong point still firmly in German hands.

The Leningrad and Volkhov Fronts' Tosno and Siniavino offensives failed for a variety of familiar reasons. Soviet critiques credited the defeat to the strongly fortified enemy defenses, faulty reconnaissance, poor command and control at all levels of command, clumsy employment of tanks (which invariably became separated from the infantry), and ineffective artillery support. In a directive it issued on 27 February, the *Stavka* noted, "The basic shortcoming was the fact that the 67th and 2d Shock Armies operated separately. . . . They dispersed their forces . . . and suffered unjustifiable casualties."[76] In reality, Govorov's and Meretskov's forces were so exhausted by previous fighting that they lacked the strength and endurance necessary to fulfill the *Stavka*'s overly ambitious objectives.

Despite the obvious failure of the secondary attacks to the north, Zhukov decided to capitalize on their diversionary effect and unleash the Northwestern Front's main attack. However, while Timoshenko's armies were completing their final preparation for the offensive between 11 and 14 February, deteriorating weather prevented the 1st Shock and 53d Armies and Group Khozin from concentrating on time, leaving Zhukov no choice but to delay the operation. No sooner had he authorized the delay than Soviet intelligence detected German preparations to withdraw from the Demiansk salient. Therefore, Zhukov ordered Timoshenko to begin his offensive prematurely with the forces he had at hand. Thereafter, the offensive developed in piecemeal fashion with predictable results.

The 11th and 53d Armies, now commanded by Kurochkin and Major General E. P. Zhuralev, began their assaults against the flanks of the Ramushevo corridor on 15 February, while Lieutenant General A. I. Lopatin's 34th Army began harassing attacks on German positions northeast of Demiansk. After the initial assaults failed, with the *Stavka*'s approval, Zhukov threw Lieutenant General S. G. Trofimenko's 27th and Lieutenant General G. P. Korotkov's 1st Shock Armies into combat on 23 February, the former just south of Staraia Russa and the latter at the base of the corridor. However, both armies' attacks faltered against the strong defenses German forces had erected to protect their withdrawal from the Demiansk salient.

In fact, the Germans had already begun Operation Tsitin, the planned withdrawal of their forces from the Demiansk salient on 19 February, and by 23 February the operation was almost complete, in the process, totally disrupting Zhukov's Operation Polar Star.[77] Urged on by Zhukov, the 27th and 1st Shock Armies tried to resume their offensives on 27 February, but once again failed with heavy losses. Upset by the heavy casualties and only limited gains, Stalin halted the offensive on 27 February and ordered Zhukov to orchestrate a new offensive in March. The defeat cost Zhukov and Timoshenko's forces 33,663 casualties, including 10,016 dead, captured, or missing, out of a committed force of 327,600 troops.[78]

IN THE WAKE OF OPERATION POLAR STAR, MARCH–APRIL

Neither Zhukov nor the *Stavka* was prepared to abandon the offensive as long as Red Army forces in central and southern Russia were still advancing successfully. Therefore, on Zhukov's recommendation, the *Stavka* ordered the Northwestern, Leningrad, and Volkhov Fronts to conduct a truncated version of Operation Polar Star in early March against the same objectives designated in the original operation.[79] This time, the offensive was to begin in staggered fashion, with the Northwestern Front attacking on 4 March and the Leningrad and Volkhov Fronts on 14 March.[80] Zhukov subordinated the 34th, 53d, and 68th Armies and 1st Tank Army to Group Khozin and ordered the 27th and 1st Shock Armies to capture Staraia Russa and reach the Polist' River. If the latter two armies captured the town, Khozin's entire force was to exploit toward Pskov and Narva.

Once again, the *Stavka* ordered the Leningrad and Volkhov Fronts to conduct supporting attacks in the Leningrad region, this time a shallower encirclement of German forces north of Mga without a frontal assault on Siniavino. It did so based on intelligence information that the German Eighteenth Army was concentrating strong forces near Siniavino with the intention of conducting a flank attack against both the 55th Army from positions at Pushkin and the 67th and 2d Shock Armies to restore the blockade. The *Stavka* order, issued at 0400 hours on 7 March, sketched out the parameters of the shallow envelopment:

To conduct the operation to destroy the enemy Mga-Siniavino grouping, the *Stavka* of the Supreme High Command *orders:*

1. The commander of the Volkhov Front will penetrate the enemy's defenses along the Voronovo and Lodva front with a force of 10 rifle divisions and 4 rifle brigades and capture the Sologubovka and Mga region. After severing the enemy communications along the dirt roads in that region, [it] will subsequently develop the attack into the rear of the enemy Mga-Siniavino grouping. Link up with the Leningrad Front's forces in the Voitolovo region so as to move north into the Mga region, encircle the enemy Mga-Siniavino grouping, and destroy or capture it.

Temporarily go over to the defense along the 2d Shock Army's front.

2. The commander of the Leningrad Front will penetrate the enemy's defense in the Krasnyi Bor and Poselok Peschanka front with a force of eight rifle divisions and three rifle brigades. Attack in the direction of Ul'ianovka, and, after cutting the railroad and highway communications in the Ul'ianovka and Mga sector, subsequently develop the attack to Voitolovo in the rear of the enemy Mga-Siniavino grouping.

Link up with the Volkhov Front's forces in the Voitolovo region and, together with the Volkhov Front, encircle the enemy Mga-Siniavino grouping and destroy or capture it.

Temporarily go over to the defense along the 67th Army's front.

3. The operations by both *fronts* will commence on 14 March 1943. The operation to liquidate the enemy Mga-Siniavino grouping will be completed no later than 25 March 1943.

4. The *front* commander, Comrade Meretskov, is entrusted with directing the operation in the Volkhov Front, and the *Stavka* representative Comrade Voroshilov in the Leningrad Front.

5. The *Stavka* representative, Comrade Voroshilov, is entrusted with organizing cooperation between the Volkhov and Leningrad Fronts.

[signed] I. Stalin[81]

In the Leningrad region, the Leningrad Front's 55th Army and the Volkhov Front's 8th Army were to destroy German forces at Siniavino and Mga in conjunction with Zhukov's assault near Staraia Russa. At the same time, the Volkhov Front's 52d Army was to conduct a limited-objective offensive against Novgorod, both to assist the Northwestern Front's assault on Staraia Russa and to draw some of the Eighteenth Army's forces away from Leningrad. To facilitate more effective command and control, the *Stavka* had transferred the 2d Shock Army to the Leningrad Front a week before so that it could join the 67th Army in an advance along a single axis.[82]

According to the new offensive plan, Sviridov's 55th Army was to attack from its salient at Krasnyi Bor with 8 rifle divisions and 3 rifle brigades. After penetrating German defenses, it was to capture Ul'ianovka, sever the Ul'ianovka and Mga railroad and road, and link up with the 8th Army. Starikov's 8th Army was to attack in the Voronovo-Lodva sector east of Mga with 10 rifle divisions and 4 rifle brigades, penetrate German defenses, capture Sologubovka and Mga, and link up with the 55th Army at Voitolovo. This time, the exhausted 67th and 2d Shock Armies, which remained on the defense opposite Siniavino, were to join the attack only if it succeeded. Voroshilov supervised the operations in the Leningrad region, which were to achieve their objectives by 25 March.

The second attempt to activate Operation Polar Star faltered from the very start and, thereafter, developed piecemeal as a frustrated *Stavka* and Zhukov strained to milk some success from the effort. The Northwestern Front's 27th and 1st Shock Armies attacked on 5 March (after a one-day delay) but achieved virtually nothing. Then, in reaction to a successful German counteroffensive in the Khar'kov region, on 7 March, the *Stavka* ordered Zhukov and Timoshenko to transfer Katukov's 1st Tank Army southward to the Kursk region and limited Operation Polar Star to the capture of Staraia Russa and the elimination of the Mga salient.[83]

Despite the departure of the 1st Tank Army, Trofimenko's 27th Army assaulted German defenses east of Staraia Russa once again on 14 March, while Kurochkin's 11th, Lopatin's 34th, and Zhuravlev's 53d Armies attacked German defenses south of Ramushevo. While the latter managed to advance several kilometers to the Red'ia River before their assault failed with heavy losses, all other attacks in the region failed miserably. After further intense but futile fighting, on 17 March the *Stavka* ordered Zhukov to end the offensive and fly to Kursk to restore some order to the Red Army's deteriorating situation in that region. Many of the Northwestern Front's best forces soon followed Zhukov south.[84]

While these dramatic events were unfolding in the Northwestern Front's sector to the south, Govorov and Meretskov began their Mga offensive. Lieutenant General V. F. Iakovlev's 52d Army began diversionary operations in the Novgorod region on 14 March. His small army consisted of four rifle divisions, one ski brigade, two aerosleigh battalions, and one fortified region, but no tanks, and, just prior to the attack, Meretskov reinforced his army with two more rifle divisions.[85] Iakovlev's assault across the Volkhov River south of Novgorod struck the defenses of the XXXVIII Army Corps' 1st Luftwaffe Field Division but achieved only limited gains in fighting that lasted until 27 March. Nevertheless, the fighting achieved its ends, since Lindemann had no choice but to reinforce the Novgorod sector with the 217th and 58th Infantry Divisions from the Kirishi region and Demiansk.

Sviridov's 55th Army began its attack south of Krasnyi Bor on 19 March after a delay of two days to complete its offensive preparations. The assault struck the German LIV Army Corps' SS Police Infantry Division, which had been reinforced by the Flanders Legion, which was supported on the right by the 24th Infantry Division and on the left by the 250th Spanish Division. Borshchev's 268th Rifle Division and the 55th Rifle Brigade, in Sviridov's first echelon, penetrated the SS Police Division's defenses and advanced 3 kilometers (1.9 miles) to the outskirts of Sablino by day's end. The Leningrad diary tracked the futile operations:

> *Friday, 19 March.* The forces of the 55th Army have resumed the offensive southeast of Krasnyi Bor. Having penetrated the enemy's defense, our units encountered stiff enemy resistance.
>
> *Sunday, 21 March.* Attacking southeast of Krasnyi Bor toward Ul'ianovka, the 268th Rifle Division and 55th Rifle Brigade have penetrated the enemy's defense and advanced 3 kilometers (1.9 miles). Two battalions of the 952d Rifle Regiment, commanded by Lieutenant Colonel A. I. Kliukanov, have reached the northwestern outskirts of Sablino. However, the enemy halted their advance with strong counterattacks. Heavy combat is raging.
>
> *Thursday, 25 March.* Southeast of Krasnyi Bor the enemy is counterattacking time and again trying to recapture his lost positions.[86]

However, the Flanders Legion, supported by 88mm Flak (antiaircraft) guns and several Tiger tanks from the 502d Panzer Battalion counterattacked and drove Sviridov's forces back to their jumping-off positions. Sviridov tried in vain for eight days to rekindle his offensive but failed. The bitter but fruitless fighting continued until 2 April, when the *Stavka* ordered Govorov's *front* to abandon further offensive operations. By this time, both sides had suffered heavy losses. For example, the Flanders Legion counted only 45 survivors out of its initial strength of 500 men.[87]

Starikov's 8th Army began its assault on Mga from its sector south of Voronovo at the precise hour that the 55th Army attacked from Krasnyi Bor toward Mga. Starikov's army consisted of nine rifle divisions, two rifle and two separate tank brigades, and four separate tank regiments. He concentrated his 286th, 256th, 378th, 374th, and 265th Rifle Divisions in first echelon supported by the 35th, 25th, 33d, and 50th Tank Regiments. The 239th, 64th Guards, and 364th Rifle Divisions and the 122d and 185th Tank Brigades were in second echelon, and the 372d Rifle Division and 58th Rifle Brigade were in reserve. Meretskov supported Starikov's army with most of his *front*'s artillery. The 8th Army faced the 1st, 223d, and 69th Infantry Divisions of the Eighteenth Army's XXVI Army Corps, which occupied defenses extending from Gontovaia Lipka, north of the Mga railroad to Pogost'e, and were backed up only by the 285th Security Division.[88]

Starikov's army began its assault early on 19 March after a 135-minute artillery preparation. During the first three days of intense fighting, the army's first-echelon divisions penetrated 3–4 kilometers (1.9–2.5 miles) along a 7-kilometer (4.3-mile) front at the junction of the defending 1st and 223d Infantry Divisions. Starikov then committed a small mobile group, which consisted of the 64th Guards Rifle Division's 191st Guards Rifle Regiment and a battalion of the 122d Tank Brigade, whose orders were to cut the Mga-Kirishi rail line and wheel northwest toward Mga Station. Advancing in heavy rain, which prevented the 14th Air Army from providing any air support, the mobile group managed to reach the Mga-Kirishi rail line east of Turyshkino Station before being halted by German reinforcements. In haste and despite the bad weather, Lindemann managed to transfer combat groups from the 21st, 61st, and 121st Infantry Divisions to the threatened sector, where they were able to contain Starikov's thrust, but only barely.

Despite the initial failure, Zhukov insisted that Starikov continue his attacks throughout the remainder of March. On 1 April Zhukov ordered him to commit Colonel F. F. Korotkov's 14th Rifle Division and the 1st Separate Rifle Brigade from reserve to support yet another assault by Major General N. A. Poliakov's 64th Guards Rifle Division on German defenses around Karbusel', just east of the Mga-Kirishi railroad. The German 121st Infantry Division repelled the assault, inflicting heavy losses on the attackers. Finally, on 2 April, the *Stavka* permitted Starikov to halt his attacks and go over to the defense.[89] Relative calm then descended over the front in the Leningrad region on 3 April.

In part, the *Stavka* ordered the two *fronts* to end their Mga offensive because their forces failed even to dent German defenses south of Leningrad, and the spring thaw had begun. The Leningrad war diary summed up the reasons for the failure and pointed out the benefits of the operations:

> *Friday, 2 April.* The spring also affected combat operations: the thaw complicated the offensive by our forces along the Ul'ianovka axis, which had begun on 19 March. However, this was not the only reason why we ceased the offensive today. The operations of the Leningrad Front's 55th Army and the Volkhov Front's 8th Army ran into heavy enemy resistance. Having decided to weaken other sectors of the front, he concentrated considerable forces in this region. The thaw further hindered our offensive.
>
> Nevertheless, even though we did not complete the main mission (which was the destruction of the enemy Mga-Siniavino grouping and the widening of ground communications with Leningrad), it is hard to underestimate the importance of this operation and the Krasnyi Bor operation conducted in February. Forced to defend, the enemy could no longer contemplate any offensive against Leningrad. He also did not have the opportunity to transfer reserves from Leningrad to the south, where our forces were continuing to develop an offensive successfully.[90]

In reality, however, the *Stavka* halted the Mga operation because Operation Polar Star, which gave meaning and context to the offensive at Leningrad, had failed. In addition, even the *Stavka* could no longer permit the immense waste of manpower in continued futile offensives in the region. Despite its failure, however, the offensive contributed significantly to the *Stavka*'s overall efforts by ending, once and for all, any German thoughts about capturing Leningrad and by pinning down 30 German divisions, some of which could have helped the OKH stabilize the situation along the western and southwestern axes.[91]

The Red Army's victory in Operation Spark at Siniavino in January 1943 was far more significant than the Red Army's modest territorial gains indicated. Not since December 1941 at Tikhvin, when the Leningrad Front blunted Army Group North's bold attempt to encircle Leningrad from the east, did the *Stavka* have as much to celebrate. The Red Army's wresting of the narrow land corridor from the *Wehrmacht*'s grasp in January ended over 12 months of repeated, embarrassing, and often staggering defeats.

Operation Spark, however, was also frustratingly incomplete, and the *Stavka* knew it. The vital Siniavino strong point, town, and adjacent heights were still in German hands, and the *Stavka* knew that as long as they were, neither Leningrad's defenses nor its supply lines from the east would be entirely secure. This fact alone turned the January struggle for Siniavino into prelude rather than postscript. Pride as well as strategic imperatives compelled the *Stavka* to order its forces to seize Siniavino and Siniavino Heights as soon as possible and at any cost. It was, therefore, inevitable that Operation Polar Star would follow closely after Operation Spark.

Given the *Stavka*'s ambitious strategic aims in the winter of 1942–1943, Operation Polar Star and its counterpart offensives in the Leningrad region represented the logical culmination to the prolonged series of Red Army offensives that spread from south to north across the entire Soviet-German front. Given the Red Army's capabilities, however, like other offensives, Polar Star failed. It did so because the Red Army was not yet capable of winning such victories, certainly not in the difficult terrain of the Leningrad region, where large tank forces could not be brought to bear. Thereafter a more sober and realistic *Stavka* chose more carefully when and where to fight, attacking only if victory seemed achievable. Despite this greater prudence, Siniavino remained its nemesis, and, even in summer, the *Stavka* could not resist its fatal lure.

Like previous operations, both Operation Spark and Operation Polar Star proved costly to the many hundreds of thousands of Red Army soldiers who fought in them and tried to overcome the most trying of terrain and weather conditions. Although complete Soviet casualty figures for the first quarter of 1943 are not yet available, those that have been released and estimated figures vividly underscore how costly these operations actually were.

According to official Soviet count, the Leningrad and Volkhov Front's lost 115,082 men in Operation Spark, including 33,940 dead, captured, and missing, out of 302,800 troops initially committed to action.[92] The February and March operations added at least 150,000 casualties to this count, including 35,000 dead, out of a total of over 250,000 troops committed to battle in February and over 150,000 in March.[93] Nor did the Northwestern Front fare any better. It began Operation Polar Star with a force of 327,600 men facing roughly 100,000 German troops. During the period from 15 to 28 February, the *front* lost 33,663 men, including 10,016 killed, captured, or missing and 23,647 wounded or sick.[94] After assembling all of the forces designated to participate in Operation Polar Star, the Northwestern Front's strength rose to 401,190 men on 1 March 1943. It then lost another 103,108 men, including 31,789 killed, captured, or missing and 71,319 wounded or sick, during its March offensive.[95] This brought the gruesome toll to over 130,000 men, including over 40,000 irrecoverable losses, out of a force of just over 400,000 men. German sources verify the staggering toll, indicating that the Red Army lost about 270,000 men just in the fighting around Siniavino.[96]

Although German forces incurred far fewer casualties than the Red Army, they too suffered grievously in the hard-fought battles, and they could ill afford to lose troops they could not replace. By July 1943 Army Group North's strength had fallen to 760,000 men. Worse still, the fighting in early 1943 severely weakened virtually every division in Eighteenth Army because, as was the case in the French Army at Verdun in 1916, every division in the Eighteenth Army was bloodied at or around Siniavino. As Lindemann strained to find fresh forces to parry each Soviet blow, he was forced to transfer virtually every division in his army into and out of the active combat sectors. After January 1943 Army Group North possessed virtually no operational reserves and, as a result, had to rely on the swift maneuver of regimental- and battalion-size combat groups to contain the Red Army's attacks. All the while, the army group's divisions had to stand and fight and suffer the consequences in blood. Like the Spanish 250th Division, which lost 3,200 men or about 30 percent of its strength, in the February fighting, other divisions suffered equally heavy losses. Given this constant attrition and the dwindling supply of replacements, it was only a matter of time before Army Group North could no longer stem the tide.

Finally, Operations Spark and Polar Star clearly demonstrated the *Stavka*'s resolve to achieve victory at Leningrad, a resolve many histories of the war have since overlooked. At the same time, the two operations indicated how difficult this task would be. Armed with this awareness, it would take another 10 months for the *Stavka* to mount another credible strategic operation along the northwestern axis. When it finally did, the *Stavka* would place the liberation of Leningrad at the top of its list of strategic priorities for 1944.

Colonel General L. A. Govorov, Commander, Leningrad Front *(left)*, with his commissar, A. A. Zhdanov *(right)*

The Volkhov Front's Military Council, including *(left to right)*, T. F. Shtykov, Commissar; K. A. Meretskov, Commander; F. P. Ozerov, Chief of Staff; I. P. Zhuravlev, Commander, 14th Air Army

Lieutenant General I. I. Fediuninsky,
Deputy Commander, Volkhov Front

Major General N. P. Simoniak,
136th Rifle Division

Katiushas firing during the artillery preparation, January 1943

Red Army officers at a forward observation post before the January offensive

Soldiers of the 86th Rifle Division storm Preobrazhenskaia Hill

German field fortifications and obstacles, January 1943

Red Army soldiers and tanks in their jumping-off positions, January 1943

A German heavy gun captured by Red Army forces, January 1943

Leningrad Front troops assault a German pillbox, January 1943

Leningrad and Volkhov Front forces link up, January 1943 (artist's rendition)

A German fuel train blown up by partisans, January 1943

A Red Army armored train after the cracking of the Leningrad blockade, January 1943

A Red Army woman antiaircraft artillery observer at Leningrad

CHAPTER 10

Stalemate

May–November 1943

THE SITUATION IN THE SPRING AND SUMMER OF 1943

After the Red Army failed to achieve the objectives the *Stavka* had assigned to it in February and March, a period of relative calm descended over the Soviet-German front. The massive Soviet winter offensive and Army Group South's subsequent counteroffensive, which was orchestrated by Manstein, deprived the Red Army of some of its winter gains and restored some stability to the front but left both sides exhausted. As the spring thaw seized both forces in its watery grip, a three-month lull set in across the front as Hitler and Stalin planned feverishly to regain the strategic initiative in the summer.

Ultimately, Hitler and the OKH decided to conduct yet another summer offensive, this time more limited in scope and aim. They chose as their target the Kursk "bulge," a large salient jutting westward between German Army Groups Center and South, which, to the Soviets, symbolized the success its forces had achieved during the previous winter and, to the Germans, represented an inviting target. By striking the Kursk "bulge" and destroying the large Red Army forces in it, Hitler hoped to undo some of the damage done to the *Wehrmacht* during the past winter and restore German fortunes in the East.

In the Soviet camp, Stalin and the *Stavka* sought to exploit the Red Army's winter victories by conducting massive new offensives in the summer to achieve both the objectives that had eluded the Red Army during the previous winter and then more. Based on previous experience and conditioned by a new prudence born of past defeats, Stalin decided to blunt the *Wehrmacht*'s summer offensive before unleashing the Red Army on a major summer offensive of its own. Once the Red Army defeated the German offensive, which the *Stavka* correctly assumed would be at Kursk, it planned to launch multiple offensives of its own beginning against the flanks of German forces in the Kursk region and then expanding to encompass the entire front. Therefore, the *Stavka* decided to begin its summer offensive with a premeditated defense of the Kursk salient.

During its initial defense at Kursk and its counteroffensives thereafter, Soviet forces in the Leningrad region were to remain on the defense, conducting only limited-objective offensives in support of the Red Army's far

305

larger-scale offensive operations to the south. Thus, prior to the Battle for Kursk, the *Stavka* secretly transferred sizable forces, including the Northwestern Front's 11th, 27th, 53d, and 68th Armies and numerous smaller formations, southward into the Kursk region.[1] Deprived of much of their strength, the three Soviet *fronts* operating along the northwestern axis temporarily deferred any offensive operations and, in a sharp departure from previous practice, rested and refitted their forces throughout the spring and summer. Govorov withdrew the nine rifle divisions, one tank brigade, and two tank regiments of Dukhanov's 67th Army into *front* reserve for rest and refitting. At the same time, Meretskov withdrew four rifle divisions, three tank brigades, and one tank regiment into his *front* reserve and ordered his component armies to form reserves of one or two divisions each.[2]

After Red Army forces defeated German forces at Kursk in early July, the *Stavka* ordered offensive operations to resume along the northwestern axis. This time, however, the aims of these operations were limited to improving the operational situation around Leningrad and attracting German attention and forces away from more critical front sectors. By early July, Soviet intelligence assessed that the Leningrad Front outnumbered the opposing German forces by a factor of 2 to 1 and the Volkhov by a factor of 1.3 to 1.[3] German estimates confirmed this Soviet superiority. According to Foreign Armies East *(Fremde Heere Ost)* estimates, on 20 July 1943, Army Group North numbered 760,000 men organized into 43 infantry divisions and was opposed by 734,000 Soviet troops, backed up by 491,000 reserves. The same report indicated that Army Group North had 49 tanks and 2,407 guns and mortars facing an estimated 209 Soviet tanks and 2,793 guns and mortars, backed up by 843 tanks and 1,800 guns and mortars in Soviet reserves.[4] In the *Stavka*'s judgment, this was a sufficient force with which to conduct a new offensive.

THE RED ARMY'S FIFTH SINIAVINO OFFENSIVE, JULY–AUGUST

Immediately after the Red Army halted the German offensive at Kursk, the *Stavka* ordered the Leningrad and Volkhov Fronts to prepare to conduct a new offensive.[5] The *fronts'* missions were to end, once and for all, any German attempt to conduct offensive operations aimed at restoring the Leningrad blockade, crush the German Eighteenth Army, and create conditions necessary for its complete destruction (Map 16). While doing so, the two *fronts* were to tie down German forces and prevent them from reinforcing other front sectors. The Leningrad war dairy recounted the Leningrad Front's mission:

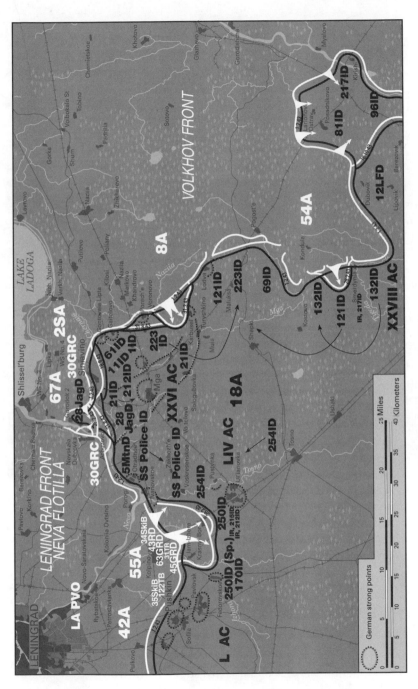

Map 16. Soviet Operations in the Leningrad Region, May–November 1943

Monday, 12 July. Our artillery has been concentrating along the Siniavino axis since 1 July. Today it began the planned destruction of enemy engineer works and the suppression of his artillery and mortar batteries. It is as if it were an overture to the forthcoming operation whose main mission is to spoil possible enemy attempts to restore the complete blockade of Leningrad. It is also important to widen the "corridor" that we punctured through the enemy's defense during the beginning of the year and protect the movement of trains which connect Leningrad with the "Great Land." The enemy's artillery is still firing on the new railroad branch line.[6]

The *Stavka* ordered Govorov and Meretskov's *fronts* to accomplish these missions by attacking German defenses in the Mga salient from three sides with the 55th, 67th, and 8th Armies. Sviridov's 55th Army was to attack eastward across the Neva River toward Mga in tandem with assaults conducted by Dukhanov's 67th Army between the Neva River and Siniavino, and Starikov's 8th Army was to attack westward from the Gaitolovo and Lodva sector toward Mga. If successful, the offensive would capture Mga and Siniavino, destroy the German XXVI Army Corps, and set up the Eighteenth Army for subsequent destruction. Dukhanov's army was to conduct Govorov's main attack in the narrow sector from the Neva River to Siniavino, and Sviridov's army was to conduct a secondary assault across the Neva River. To the east, Starikov's army of Meretskov's *front* was to attack from the Gaitolovo-Lodva sector, penetrate German defenses, sever the Mga-Kirishi railroad, and advance on Mga from the east. The entire operation was designed to capture Mga and, by extension, Siniavino by enveloping the German strong point from the northwest and east, and, by doing so, expand the corridor from Leningrad to the Soviet rear area and wear down the German Eighteenth Army.

Dukhanov's 67th Army was to conduct its assault from the Gorodok No. 2 region east of the Neva with the newly formed 30th Guards Rifle Corps, commanded by General Simoniak, the former 136th Rifle Division commander, who had recently been promoted to corps command. Simoniak's guards corps, which consisted of the 45th, 63d, and 64th Guards Rifle Divisions, supported by the 30th Guards and 220th Tank Brigades and the 31st and 29th Guards Tank Regiments, was to capture Arbuzovo and advance on Mga from the north. To the east, the 90th, 268th, 43d, and 123d Rifle Divisions of Dukhanov's army, deployed from west to east, were to attack in the Siniavino and Gontovaia Lipka sector east of Siniavino to tie down the German forces defending Siniavino. The German XXVI Army Corps' 121st, 23d, 11th, and 290th Infantry Divisions manned defenses between Arbuzovo and Gontovaia Lipka. This force of roughly 35,000 men faced a Soviet force of in excess of 75,000 men and 120 tanks.[7] Sviridov's 55th Army was to support

Dukhanov's advance with a smaller attack of its own south of the Neva River, but only if Dukhanov's assault succeeded.

East of Mga, Starikov's 8th Army's was to conduct its main attack from a 13.6-kilometer (8.5-mile) sector in the Voronovo region, penetrate the Germans' defenses, and exploit to link up near Mga with the 67th and 55th Armies attacking Mga from the north. The army's immediate mission was to reach the Tortolovo-Karbusel' line. Subsequently, it was to exploit the offensive to link up with the 67th Army's forces at Mga, while detaching at least two rifle divisions and one tank brigade to strike Siniavino from the south. Starikov's army was also ordered to conduct a supporting attack from the region north of Pogost'e on the Mga-Kirishi rail line toward Karbusel' and Turyshkino to protect the main shock group's left flank.[8]

To penetrate the strong German defenses successfully, Starikov organized his army into two shock groups, each formed in two echelons, to attack north and south of the Mga railroad. The first shock group consisted of the 18th and 378th Rifle Divisions in first echelon and the 379th and 239th Rifle Divisions in second and the southern shock group, the 256th and 364th Rifle Divisions in first echelon and the 165th and 374th Rifle Divisions in second. Starikov reinforced each first-echelon division with a tank regiment and assigned his 16th and 122d Tank Brigades to the second echelon with orders to exploit the offensive.[9] He ordered the 265th and 382d Rifle Divisions and the 1st and 22d Rifle Brigades to conduct the supporting attack on the left, while the 372d Rifle Division defended the army's right flank, and he retained the 286th Rifle Division and 58th Rifle Brigade in his reserve.

Starikov's northern shock group faced the bulk of the German 5th Mountain Division, which was deployed astride the Mga-Volkhov rail line, and his southern shock group the remainder of the 5th Mountain Division and the left-flank regiment of the 69th Infantry Division. His supporting attack force north of Pogost'e faced the full 132d Infantry Division. So configured, Starikov's reinforced army, which fielded about 80,000 men supported by over 250 tanks, had a two- to fivefold superiority over the defending Germans. In his main attack sector alone, Starikov's force of at least 50,000 men and over 150 tanks outnumbered the German defenders by a factor of almost five to one and far more in armor, but the ratio was considerably less favorable in the secondary attack sector.[10]

Dukhanov's 67th Army began its assault early on 22 July after a 150-minute artillery preparation. Colonels A. F. Sheglov's and S. M. Putilov's 63d and 45th Guards Rifle Divisions of Simoniak's 30th Guards Rifle Corps spearheaded the attack on the 121st and 23d Infantry Divisions' defenses at Arbuzovo. Major General Ia. P. Sinkevich's 43d Rifle Division assaulted the 11th Infantry Division's defenses west of Siniavino. The 13th Air Army and 2d Guards

Leningrad PVO Fighter Aviation Corps supported the assault by flying 540 air sorties on the first day of the operation.[11]

Although Sheglov's guards division managed to achieve its first day's objectives, the XXVI Army Corps quickly reinforced its defenses across the entire Siniavino front, converting the struggle into what one Soviet participant termed "an offensive on our bellies." The Leningrad war diary captured the furor of the fighting:

> *Thursday, 22 July.* Battle has once again burst out around Siniavino. The artillery preparation began at first light, 0430 hours. Then bombers and assault aircraft appeared over the battlefield. The infantry advanced at 0605 hours. They rose up from the reeking, swampy, and putrid foxholes located in the damp low ground in order to storm the enemy, who were dug in on Siniavino Heights.
>
> The combat was heavy and bloody. But it was inescapable. The forces had the mission of improving their positions and preventing possible enemy attempts to storm Leningrad. In addition, while tying down Hitlerite reserves, the defenders of Leningrad were preventing the transfer of enemy forces to the Kursk bulge, where the enemy situation was becoming more and more critical.
>
> One can judge the effectiveness of today's attack on the enemy, who are lodged on Siniavino Heights, based on the testimony of a prisoner. "On the 22d of July," said one of them, "I was in the divisional penal platoon, which was thrown forward into the forward edge. Only five or six of the platoon's men survived the first few minutes of the Russian artillery preparation. All of the others perished."
>
> A corporal from the 1st Company of the 11th Infantry Division's 23d Infantry Regiment provided a detailed account: "The Russian artillery destroyed and pulverized everything in the defensive sector of the 1st Battalion. Almost everything alive was destroyed. After the artillery preparation had ended, the trenches were leveled. The terrain was so mangled that it was difficult to identify where trenches had been. I could no longer see any personnel in my company. Some were buried in the earth or killed by the falling shells."
>
> In addition to the artillery, aircraft supported our forces. . . . Nevertheless, the enemy, who had constructed a powerful and deeply echeloned defense on Siniavino Heights, offered strong resistance to our attacking forces.
>
> *Friday, 23 July.* Heavy fighting is going on in the Siniavino region.
>
> *Saturday, 24 July.* The enemy is suffering heavy casualties around Siniavino but, as before, is offering heavy resistance to our forces. His superb positions on the heights are well fortified. Here every step involves heavy combat. Our artillery has destroyed many enemy pillboxes. However, ma-

chine gun fire suddenly emanates from hidden embrasures that no one knew existed. . . .

Yesterday the 63d Guards Division's 192d Regiment occupied the first enemy trenches in the Arbuzovo region. Today the second line of trenches was seized during the morning. Only the third line, which is located on the slope of the sandy heights, remains to be taken. The loss of that position will threaten the Germans with serious misfortune. They are unleashing counterattacks. . . .

Sunday, 25 July. Heavy battle is continuing at Siniavino Heights. . . .

Tuesday, 27 July. Several paragraphs appeared in today's news from the Soviet Informburo concerning the situation on the Leningrad Front: "Our forces have been conducting battles of local significance north and east of Mga, during the course of which they have improved their positions." [People] are speaking about combat of the Siniavino axis.

Saturday, 31 July. Today was a difficult day along the Siniavino axis. Striving at all cost to hold on to that region, the enemy threw yet another division into combat. Supported by tanks, he succeeded in pushing our forces back somewhat. Counterattacking against the enemy, Leningrad's defenders fought with exemplary bravery and selflessness. . . .

Sunday, 1 August. Having pressed our subunits at Siniavino back 500 meters last night, the enemy tried to exploit his success. Today he became active in the air, however, our fighters protected the battlefield. . . .

Wednesday, 4 August. Regarding the Leningrad Front [the Soviet Informburo bulletin] said only that an artillery and mortar exchange is going on north and east of Mga. Talk is going on about the battles around Siniavino. Although we have not achieved territorial success there, the battles have brought definite benefit. Having attracted several enemy reserve divisions [into the region], the Leningrad Front has undoubtedly helped our forces, which are struggling in the Kursk bulge. It certainly causes pain, that, as before, Siniavino remains a stumbling block for the defenders of Leningrad.[12]

Over the course of the several days after Dukhanov's initial assault, the Germans committed first the 58th and then the 28th Jager and 126th Infantry Divisions with supporting tanks into the combat near Siniavino. Consequently, Dukhanov's assault soon degenerated into a slugfest, with advances measured in tens of meters. The fierce fighting, which lasted until 22 August and ended with Siniavino still in German hands, caused heavy Soviet casualties and only minimal gains. Dukhanov's failure also prompted Govorov to cancel Sviridov's supporting attacks.

Starikov's two 8th Army shock groups launched their assault against the German 5th Mountain Division's defenses along the Mga-Volkhov railroad north and south of Voronovo at 0635 hours on 22 July. For six days prior to the assault, his artillery had pounded German defenses to destroy as many fortified positions as possible, while engineers constructed new trench lines from which to launch the assault in the 700–800 meters of no-man's-land that separated the two forces. Where new trenches could not be constructed, the assaulting infantry advanced slowly through the Germans' forward trench lines behind a creeping barrage.

Despite Starikov's careful preparations, the assaulting troops captured the forward German trenches but then encountered stiff resistance and heavy air strikes that slowed their forward progress to a snail's pace. Worse still, many of Starikov's supporting tanks bogged down in the marshy terrain or were blown up by enemy mines and antitank guns. With his offensive at a standstill, in late July, Starikov committed Colonel M. V. Simonov's 379th and Colonel V. I. Morozov's 165th Rifle Divisions to reinforce the two shock groups and withdrew Major General M. N. Ovchinnikov's 18th and Major General F. K. Fetisov's 256th Rifle Divisions for rest and refitting. However, the reinforcements did not improve the situation. By this time, Lindemann at Eighteenth Army had replaced the 132d Infantry Division, which had repelled all Soviet attacks in its sector, with the 121st Infantry Division from the Arbuzovo sector and sent the 132d to reinforce the beleaguered 5th Mountain Division. The 132d arrived in the nick of time to forestall disaster.

On 9 August Starikov's assault groups detected what they thought was a weak place in the German defenses around a small bridgehead on the eastern bank of the Naziia River. The bridgehead was defended by the 5th Mountain Division, which had suffered extremely high casualties in the previous weeks of fighting. Starikov quickly ordered fresh forces to concentrate opposite the bridgehead. Early on 11 August, he committed Fetisov's 256th and Colonel V. Ia. Popov's 374th Rifle Divisions and the 35th and 50th Guards Tank Regiments in support of the 378th, 364th, and 165th Rifle Divisions, which were already fighting in the region. Although his reinforced shock group almost enveloped the defending Germans and Fetisov's division captured the Porech'e strong point, the attack once again stalled with heavy German fire as the 132d Division joined the fight. A German participant described the scene:

> The days prior to the 132d Division's arrival on the line had remained relatively quiet; however, on 11 August the enemy launched a major attack. Attacking in regimental strength against the Poretschay bridgehead, the Soviets succeeded in breaking through the thinly held line but were later repulsed with heavy losses following our counterattack. A second assault launched in the evening was again beaten back with support from our heavy artillery. . . .

On 12 August at exactly 0900, the enemy launched an attack along the entire front in full strength. It consisted of numerous waves of brown-clad infantrymen heavily supported by artillery fire, tanks, and overwhelming airpower.

These attacks in company, battalion, and regimental strength, which lasted an entire day, were beaten back either in brutal hand-to-hand combat or with a combination of all available resources. Isolated penetrations were countered with assembled reserves. In the sector held by Grenadier Regiment 437, however, the enemy was successful in penetrating the forefront of the bridgehead and was able to enlarge the penetration to the south for a total of three hundred meters. The counterattack by the reserves remained mired and ineffective in the face of the massive fire support from enemy artillery and advancing tanks.[13]

On 13 August a frustrated Meretskov then threw his last reserves, Colonel B. A. Vladimirov's 311th Rifle Division and the 503d Separate Tank Battalion, into the bloody melee in one final desperate attempt to crack the German defenses. A German participant described the bloody struggle that ensued:

On 13 August at 0430 the Russians again struck the line and, following an initial success in pushing back the German defenders, were unable to further penetrate the line held by the surviving landsers. At 0600 we counterattacked against overwhelmingly superior enemy forces supported by heavy artillery blocking fire but were able to make little progress in restoring the line to our old positions. As our own attack ground to a halt, the enemy again struck with renewed strength, penetrating the defenses with concentrated armor under heavy-artillery support. As the battle pivoted back and forth through the shattered forests and swamps, the Soviets were able to break through to the south and occupy the area northeast of Poretschay.

Again our regiment was thrown into the attack. In vicious fighting that lasted throughout the day, we finally succeeded in bringing the Soviet advance to a halt at 1700 and recaptured the Poretschay sector. After suffering numerous casualties, the Russians were stopped along the ridge marked as 54.1, approximately two hundred meters south of Barskoya Lake. This effort required the use of the last reserves of men and material and was successful only after heavy fighting throughout the afternoon.[14]

After repeated attacks and counterattacks that decimated both the attacking and defending forces, Starikov's offensive collapsed in utter exhaustion. His army had captured the Porech'e bridgehead, which the Germans evacuated on the night of 14–15 August, but was still far from Mga.[15]

Early on 16 August, the fresh 1st and 254th Infantry Divisions relieved the battered 132d, which, in the words of one division soldier, was "reduced by casualties and exhausted to the point of incoherence."[16] The same German participant captured the ferocity of the battle:

> During the course of this battle, the enemy had thrust these divisions and armored units into the battle: 364th Rifle Division, with parts of three regiments; 374th Rifle Division, with two regiments; 165th Rifle Division, with two regiments; 378th Rifle Division, with two regiments; 311th Rifle Division, with one regiment; 256th Rifle Division, with one regiment; 503d Armored Battalion, with fourteen tanks; 35th Armored Regiment, with fifteen tanks; 50th Armored Regiment, with fifteen tanks; 77th Independent Engineer Battalion.
>
> Twelve to fourteen enemy battalions were reported as decimated. Twenty-four tanks were destroyed, ten of which were knocked out in close combat with light weapons. The Russians suffered extremely high casualties during the intensive attempts to break the defense line. With the withdrawal of our division, the battle south of Lake Ladoga came to an end.[17]

At 1440 hours on 22 August, the *Stavka* finally admitted that the offensive had indeed failed by issuing directives to the two *fronts* to cease offensive operations:

> Given the existing situation in the Leningrad and Volkhov Fronts and considering that, in the process of the operation, the *fronts'* forces attracted considerable enemy operational reserves, inflicted a severe defeat on his forces, and, at the same time, fulfilled a portion of the *fronts'* assigned mission, the *Stavka* of the Supreme High Command *orders:*
>
> 1. Cease further attacks after 22 August.
>
> 2. Go over to a stubborn defense in all *front* sectors with the mission of firmly holding on to all occupied positions. All force formations will refit at the expense of *front* resources, create reserves along main axes, and prepare forces for offensive operations. Simultaneously, conduct active reconnaissance and determine enemy intentions.
>
> [signed] I. Stalin, A. Antonov[18]

The Leningrad and Volkhov Fronts' fifth offensive at Siniavino certainly burnished Siniavino's reputation as a graveyard for Red Army soldiers. Of the 253,300 soldiers the two *fronts* committed to battle, 79,937 became casualties, including 20,890 dead, captured, or missing.[19] With losses that high one might have assumed the *Stavka* would desist from further offensives, at least for a time. That was not to be the case.

THE RED ARMY'S SIXTH SINIAVINO OFFENSIVE, SEPTEMBER

As if drawn to the Siniavino strong point by magnetic force, a gruesome post-script to the Red Army's July and August Siniavino offensive occurred in mid-September, when Govorov's and Meretskov's forces once again tried to expel German forces from Siniavino. Acting on *Stavka* orders, the two *front* commanders ordered their forces to attack and capture Siniavino and Siniavino Heights at the nose of the Mga salient to drive German forces southward out of artillery range from the critical supply artery that ran through the corridor south of Lake Ladoga. This time, Govorov's forces were to assault Siniavino and its adjacent heights directly from the north, while Meretskov's forces were to attack westward from the Gaitolovo and Voronovo sectors to envelop Siniavino from the southeast. Given the configuration and direction of the attacks and the composition of the attacking forces, it is likely that they sought to capture only the eastern half of the Mga salient.[20]

Govorov assigned the difficult task of storming Siniavino Heights to his most experienced force and his most illustrious commander, Simoniak's 30th Guards Rifle Corps. By 13 September Simoniak's guards corps consisted of Putilov's 45th, Sheglov's 63d, and Trubachev's 64th Guards Rifle Divisions, supported by at least three tank brigades or regiments.[21] On 13 and 14 September, Simoniak's corps regrouped from the region east of Leningrad, where it had been resting and refitting after the August offensive, into the sector south of Shlissel'burg, where it was temporarily assigned to Dukhanov's 67th Army, which was to support his assault.

At the time, Dukhanov's army consisted of Major General A. I. Andreev's 43d Rifle Corps (the 11th, 128th, and 314th Rifle Divisions), the 43d, 124th, 196th, and 268th Rifle Divisions, the 55th Rifle and 73d Naval Rifle Brigades, the 16th Fortified Region, the 98th and 264th Tank Regiments, and supporting artillery and engineers.[22] Dukhanov was to support Simoniak's assault by launching attacks with two additional shock groups on Simoniak's left and right flanks. The shock group attacking on Simoniak's left flank consisted of Sinkevich's 43d and Major General A. P. Ivanov's 123d Rifle Divisions and the shock group on Simoniak's right flank, Colonel A. V. Batluk's 120th, Colonel M. D. Papchenko's 124th, and Major General P. F. Ratov's 196th Rifle Divisions. In addition, Colonel V. I. Shkel"s 11th and Colonel N. D. Sokolov's 268th Rifle Divisions, through whose sectors the 30th Guards Rifle Corps was to attack, were to support the assault during the later stages of the operation.

By mid-September the Eighteenth Army was defending the sector from the Neva River eastward past Siniavino to Gaitolovo with the XXVI Army Corps. The corps' 58th, 126th, 11th, 290th, and 254th Infantry Divisions and the 5th Mountain Division defended from west to east backed up by the 28th Jager Division, which was situated in reserve south of Siniavino. The 11th and 290th Infantry Divisions' forces were dug in around Siniavino proper and along the adjacent heights.[23]

Govorov and Dukhanov ordered Simoniak's corps "to penetrate the strongly fortified and deeply echeloned enemy defenses and capture the Siniavino Heights."[24] To do so, in addition to the supporting infantry, both Dukhanov and Govorov supported Simoniak's assaulting forces with extensive armor and engineer support and the bulk of army and *front* artillery. Based on previous experience, the Soviets significantly altered the pattern of their artillery support to make it more effective:

> The battle that had occurred here previously demonstrated that, for success in the attack, it was insufficient to suppress and destroy the enemy firing points and achieve fire superiority. [Instead] it was necessary to destroy the trenches and communications trenches thoroughly to deprive the enemy of the capability for exploiting them for maneuver. One had to change the method of artillery preparation, which had become stereotypical. Usually the enemy soldiers waited through it [the preparation] in "foxes' lairs" and other shelters, and, when the fire shifted into the depth of the defense, they hurried back to the forward trenches in order to greet the attackers with organized fires.[25]

To correct this stereotypical pattern, Govorov and his chief of artillery ordered the employment of an entirely new form of artillery preparation in the September assault. Their goal was to ensure that the artillery fire on the forward German trenches did not cease as the infantry approached them. Essentially, the *front* artillery commander ordered the two hitherto distinct phases of the so-called artillery offensive—the artillery preparation and fires in support of the attack—be combined into a single phase. What resulted was fire that "crept" into the depth of the defense as the infantry advanced, thus preventing the enemy from detecting the interval between phases and shifting his forces between defense lines as the preparation proceeded.

While Simoniak's corps was assaulting Siniavino from the north, Starikov's 8th Army was to launch heavy assaults westward from the Gaitolovo and Voronovo sectors with a force of between four and eight rifle divisions. At the time, the nucleus of Starikov's army consisted of the 18th, 265th, 286th, 364th, 372d, 374th, and 379th Rifle Divisions, the 1st, 22d, and 58th Rifle Brigades, the 16th and 122d Tank Brigades, and the 50th Guards, 25th, and 185th Tank Regiments. The 1443d Self-propelled Artillery Regiment, five separate tank battalions, and assigned artillery and engineers supported this force.[26]

Starikov formed two shock groups to conduct his assault. The first, which consisted of Radygin's 372d, Simonov's 379th, and Colonel B. N. Ushinsky's 265th Rifle Divisions and the 58th Rifle Brigade, was to strike German defenses at the junction between the 290th and 254th Infantry Divisions near Gaitolovo, north of the Mga rail line. The second shock group, consisting of Major General M. Absaliamov's 18th, Colonel A. R. Belov's 378th, Colonel A. G. Koziev's 256th, and Vladimirov's 311th Rifle Divisions, was to attack the 5th Mountain Infantry Division's defenses between the rail line and Voronovo.

The new artillery firing procedure ordered by Govorov apparently worked as planned. Simoniak's three guards rifle divisions attacked early on 15 September, with Putilov's 45th and Sheglov's 63d Guards Rifle Divisions in first echelon and Trubachev's 64th Guards Rifle Division in second echelon. The vastly more effective artillery fire indeed prevented the Germans from meeting the assault with their normally devastating hail of infantry fire. In a vicious 30-minute assault, the three divisions seized the heights that they had attempted to capture on numerous other bloody occasions. The Leningrad war diary described the assault:

> *Wednesday, 15 September.* While the operation to destroy the German 18th Army is still being worked out in the headquarters, a small portion of the overall plan has already been carried out on the field of battle. On 15 September the 45th and 63d Guards Rifle Divisions, which are part of the newly formed 30th Guards Corps commanded by General N. P. Simoniak, once again attacked the enemy, who are dug in on Siniavino Heights. They attacked and dealt the enemy an irresistible blow. The Hitlerites' main strong point—the heights—which our forces unsuccessfully stormed in July and August, were captured in only 30 minutes.
>
> The success was achieved by newly organized cooperation between the infantry and artillery. . . .
>
> The seizure of these heights not only improves our positions, which in itself is important, but also deprives the enemy of the opportunity of correcting the fire of his batteries that are shelling the rail line that, since the winter of 1943, has linked Leningrad with the eastern parts of the country.
>
> Aviation facilitated the success, which the guardsmen achieved in storming Siniavino Heights. They flew 721 sorties in a single day and not only helped crush enemy resistance but also inflicted significant losses on his approaching reserves.[27]

Although supported on the left and right by an additional four to five rifle divisions, Dukhanov's assault bogged down after three days of heavy fighting, and the *Stavka* permitted Govorov to halt his offensive on 18 September: "Having driven the enemy from Siniavino Heights and dug in on them, our forces have ceased the offensive in order to prepare for a decisive blow."[28]

Quick reaction by German tactical reserves contained Dukhanov's and Simoniak's attacking forces on the heights before they could penetrate toward Mga in the lowlands to the south. The Germans prevented greater damage by committing the 28th Jager Division and the 215th and 61st Infantry Divisions from other Eighteenth Army sectors to contain Simoniak's attack. The short-lived but violent assaults cost the attackers another 10,000 casualties.

While Simoniak's forces were storming Siniavino Heights, Starikov's shock groups went into action to the east but achieved very little in three days of heavy fighting. While the northern shock group's attack failed outright, the southern group managed to penetrate German defenses slightly before being contained. While substantiating the very existence of the 8th Army's assault, an interesting fragmentary German account of the attack near Gaitolovo re-counts the Soviets' use of underground mining techniques to assist in the destruction of German defensive strong points:

In late August 1943, the 2d Battalion of the German 474th Infantry Regi-ment [the 254th Infantry Division] moved into the area of Gaytolovo. . . . The terrain around Gaytolovo is broken by many minor elevations and ridges which readily lent themselves to underground excavations. In this sector the Germans occupied a number of Russian bunkers and dugouts. One of the latter, known as Strong Point Olga, was situated on a little ridge about 20 feet above the level of a swamp in which the Russians had es-tablished their positions. The ridge sloped down so steeply toward the Russian lines that its base could not be observed by the troops occupying the strong point. The German and Russian positions were about 55 yards apart at this point. The intermediate terrain contained a number of trenches, which the Russians had vacated. Company E, which occupied Strong Point Olga, had frequently reconnoitered the intermediate terrain, but nothing unusual was ever noticed.

At 0515 on 15 September, the Russians directed heavy artillery fire on the strong point. The intermediate terrain was not visible to Company E because of a heavy ground fog which the Russians had supplemented with a smoke screen. At 0520 Russian infantry moved out from their jumping-off positions and stealthily crossed the intermediate terrain. The artillery fire continued until 0525. Then, just as the advancing Russian infantry was about to storm Strong Point Olga, a terrific explosion suddenly rocked the German troops in the area, pulverized Strong Point Olga, and all but wiped out Company E, leaving only 13 stunned and bleeding survivors. More than 100 Russians who had ventured too close to the German po-sition before the explosion were buried under the debris.

The commander of the adjoining sector quickly assembled his men and rushed toward the site of the former strong point just as another wave of Russian infantry came over the top. In the ensuing fighting, the Germans successfully repulsed three Russian attacks. The Russians, who had not expected such determined resistance after the blast, suffered heavy losses and were forced to withdraw to their jumping-off positions.[29]

A subsequent investigation by the Germans indicated that the blast was caused by a Russian mining operation, probably conducted by the 8th Guards Battalion of Miners, which had deposited the high explosives under the German positions.

At this point, and mercifully, a period of relative calm descended over the front south of Leningrad. Kuechler used the respite to prepare his defenses for what he was certain would be another Soviet onslaught. His most serious problem was his total lack of reserves necessary to counter any new Soviet thrust. To generate the requisite reserves to do so, it was vitally important that he shorten his front. However, the very mention of this necessity was anathema to Hitler. Nevertheless, after considerable heated discussions, in late September, Kuechler and Lindemann requested and received Hitler's permission to abandon the Kirishi salient, which jutted out to the northeast along the Volkhov River north of Chudovo.

The subsequent German withdrawal from the Kirishi salient released the 12th Luftwaffe Field, 81st, 132d, and 96th Infantry Divisions of the Eighteenth Army's XXVIII Army Corps, which occupied the salient, for use elsewhere along the front. The four German divisions began their withdrawal from the salient on 1–2 October, occupying prearranged successive defense lines during the withdrawal. Although Meretskov's 4th Army, which was now commanded by Lieutenant General N. I. Gusev, attempted to organize a hasty pursuit, the German forces were able to escape unharmed and erect new defenses along the Tigoda River.

An account of the withdrawal by a soldier in the 132d Infantry Division underscored the Germans' success in eluding effective Soviet pursuit:

> The evacuation order was set into motion during the night of 1–2 October with the withdrawal of the Second Company, Grenadier Regiment 437, which had been designated the bridgehead reserve. . . . The evacuation was flawlessly executed without interruption from enemy forces and with no losses in men and matériel. . . .
>
> No large-scale enemy movement was detected, however, until the afternoon of 5 October, when enemy-tracked vehicles piled high with infantry were observed moving into the area of Irssa-Dubrovo, and they were quickly taken under artillery fire. After the last battle-weary landsers

crossed the Volkhov River during the night of 2–3 October, preset demo-
lition charges were detonated, completely destroying the railroad bridge
and rendering it unusable to the enemy.

By midnight on 5 October the division was occupying new positions at
Kussinka and had completed defensive preparations. With the withdrawal
of the last rear guard from Grenadier Regiment 437 and Fusilier Regiment
132 on the morning of 6 October, Operation Hubertusjagt came to an end.[30]

Although it overstated its importance at this juncture, the Leningrad war
diary recorded the significance of the German loss of the Kirishi salient:

> *Sunday, 3 October.* The enemy is beginning to abandon the so-called
> Kirishi bulge. Although this territory formally belongs to the Volkhov
> Front, the events unfolding here have a direct relationship to Leningrad.
> For the Hitlerites, the Kirishi was a bridgehead from which they intended
> to strike toward Tikhvin and Volkhov. In the event such an offensive suc-
> ceeded, Leningrad could be completely encircled.
>
> The success of our forces on the southern flank of the Soviet-German
> front has forced the enemy to abandon any idea of an offensive at Lenin-
> grad. He is hurriedly smoothing out his front and freeing up forces, which
> are now clearly inadequate. Having detected the enemy withdrawal, our
> forces are quickly pursuing.[31]

As was their custom, Soviet propagandists quickly capitalized on this opportunity to undermine the morale of the withdrawing German forces. As
described by the veteran of the 132d Infantry Division, "We received more
propaganda leaflets from the Red Army that month," which read:

> For the soldiers of the 7th company, Infantry Regiment 437, 132 Infan-
> try Division!
>
> GERMAN SOLDIERS!
>
> Hitler has led you into a catastrophe. In attempts to conceal this fact,
> your high command speaks of a "flexible defense" and a "shortening of
> the front line." . . .
>
> The fascist dictators have earlier said that you must sacrifice yourselves
> for the victorious end of the "blitzkrieg." Now they say you must fight to
> the last man for the "flexible defense" to succeed. You can easily recog-
> nize the lies of the fascists. But what price must you continue to pay? Here
> are a few facts from the tragic history of your company: . . .
>
> In September 1942 the company was reorganized and its losses replaced
> on the Volchov Front, and it was then engaged in the fighting at Gaitolovo
> on the Mga. After this battle only 15 of 100 men remained.

11 October 1943. The 7th Company had already been withdrawn when it once again was hastily ordered to support the 12th *Luftwaffe* Field Division. Your commanders threw you into a counter-attack that needlessly cost you heavy losses in defeat. The 7th Company was beaten back and left a third of its soldiers lying upon the battlefield.

Soldiers!

You are spilling your blood for Hitler, a sacrifice that benefits neither yourselves nor the German people. Nothing can save you from this carnage. Break away from this army of Hitlerite oppressors, otherwise you will face destruction. . . .

Decide before it is too late.[32]

The course and outcome of the *Stavka*'s summer-fall campaign in the Leningrad region was indeed immensely frustrating. Although its operations made Leningrad more secure and ended any possibility of a future German offensive in the region, the repeated Red Army offensives failed spectacularly and did not appreciably widen the corridor north of Siniavino. However, while the Soviet casualty toll mounted to well over 150,000 men, German strength was also seriously eroding. Army Group North's strength fell from 760,000 in mid-July to 601,000 men on 14 October; during the same period, Soviet strength increased from 734,000 men with 491,000 in reserve to 893,000 with 66,000 in reserve.[33]

Worse still for Kuechler, beginning in early October, the situation to the south deteriorated, forcing him to transfer sizable forces from the Eighteenth Army at Leningrad to the Sixteenth Army in the Nevel' region. In its October Nevel' offensive, the Soviet Kalinin Front drove a wedge between Kuechler's Sixteenth Army and the adjacent Army Group Center. So perilous was Army Group North's situation that, in early September, the OKH ordered a new defense line, the Panther Line, be constructed from Narva through Pskov to Ostrov in Army Group North's deep rear. In addition, Kuechler's army group began building an elaborate system of intermediate positions forward of the Panther Line in case it needed to withdraw from the Leningrad region. German occupation forces levied thousands of the region's inhabitants to complete the construction work.

GERMAN PREPARATIONS TO WITHDRAW TO THE PANTHER LINE

The Germans began constructing their Panther Line, which extended along the Narva River, through Lakes Peipus and Pskov and Ostrov to south of Nevel', on 8 September 1943. The defense line was just one segment of the vaunted German "Eastern Wall," which, when completed, was to extend from Narva southward along the course of the Dnepr River to the Black Sea. The northern half of the Panther Line was anchored on natural obstacles such as the Narva River and Lakes Chud and Pskov. The southern half jutted eastward to protect the major road and rail centers at Pskov and Ostrov and tied in with Army Group Center's portion of the line south of Nevel'. When fully occupied, the line would shorten Army Group North's front by 25 percent.

In addition to the Panther Line itself, Army Group North also constructed a series of intermediate lines forward of the main defense line at varying distances from the front, whose phased occupation would make for an orderly withdrawal westward. Southwestward from the existing German front lines, the most important intermediate positions were the Mga, Kussinka, Rollbahn (railroad), 2d Wolchow (Volkhov), Oredesh (Oredezh), Ingermannland, and Luga positions. Integrated into these defense lines were major strong points at Gattschina (Krasnogvardeisk), Tschudowo (Chudovo), Nowgorod (Novgorod), Luga, Jamburg (Kingisepp), and Narwa (Narva). The Panther Line was actually well developed by late 1943. A 50,000-man construction force, including thousands of people levied from the civilian population, improved communications back to Riga and Dvinsk, built 6,000 bunkers, 800 of which were concrete, laid 125 miles of barbed wire, and dug 25 miles of trenches and antitank traps. Construction materials rolled in at a rate of 100 railcar loads per day during November and December.[34]

Army Group North began planning for a withdrawal to the Panther Line in September under the code name "Operation Blau." When implemented, the plan required the army group's forces to withdraw successively through the series of intermediate lines. The most serious dilemma faced by the army group planners as they implemented the withdrawal concerned the fate of the approximately 900,000 civilians living in the region, whom the Red Army would undoubtedly conscript when it reached the area. Attempts to move the population back to Germany in early October produced "so much confusion, misery, and hostility that Kuechler ordered the rear-area commands to adopt less onerous methods."[35] Thereafter, German forces forcibly moved the male population (some 250,000 souls) back into Lithuania and Latvia until accommodations were no longer available.

Initially, Army Group North planned to complete the withdrawal in stages from mid-January through the spring of 1944. On 22 December, however, the OKH informed army commanders that Hitler would not implement Operation Blau unless a new Soviet offensive forced him to do so. Hitler believed the Red Army had lost so many men in the Ukraine that it could ill afford a major offensive elsewhere.

Although Leningrad clearly remained a secondary theater of military operations throughout all of 1943, Red Army operations along the northwestern strategic axis during that period made significant contributions to Soviet offensive efforts elsewhere along the Soviet-German front. The January offensive partially cracked the blockade, and the February and March offensive operations seriously eroded German Army Group North's strength. The Leningrad Front strengthened the city's fortifications, and the Red Army's July and August offensives and the Germans' subsequent loss of the Kirishi salient eliminated any German threat to capture the city. The Red Army's capture of Siniavino Heights in September symbolized the futility of German attempts to maintain any semblance of its siege of the city.

The Leningrad and Volkhov Fronts' incessant offensive operations also materially assisted the Red Army's offensive efforts in other key front sectors by tying down German forces and even drawing some German reserves back to Leningrad in mid-summer. The Red Army's summer-fall offensive to the south drew major forces away from Army Group North, prompting the Germans to prepare plans to withdraw to the Panther Line and paving the way for a fresh and larger Soviet offensive in January. It was no coincidence that, as early as 6 October, the *Stavka* issued orders for Govorov and Meretskov to initiate their planning for a major offensive designed to drive German forces from the Leningrad region altogether.

Like previous operations, the Fifth and Sixth Siniavino offensives proved costly to both *fronts*. The Leningrad, Volkhov, and Northwestern Fronts suffered over 1 million casualties during 1943, including 255,447 men killed, captured, or missing. Of this total, the Leningrad Front suffered 390,794 casualties, including 88,745 killed, captured, or missing, and the Volkhov Front 321,404 casualties, including 77,904 killed, captured, or missing. As a result, however, the die was cast for Army Group North. As Kuechler, Lindemann, and a host of German corps and division commanders well knew, Army Group North would be sorely pressed to repel another determined Red Army offensive in the region.

PART III
VICTORY

CHAPTER 11

Liberation

January 1944

THE SITUATION ON 1 JANUARY 1944

By the end of 1943, the Red Army had seized the strategic initiative across the entire Soviet-German front. It had won the Battle of Kursk, and its forces had driven the *Wehrmacht* back to the Sozh and Dnepr rivers in central and southern Russia and were beginning operations into Belorussia and the Ukraine. By this time, the Red Army's forces had penetrated the Panther Line, the vaunted German Eastern Wall, at several locations in the central and southern sectors of the front. Worse still for the Germans, the Red Army Air Force had complete air superiority over the battlefield, the partisan movement was growing in the German rear, and Soviet industry was producing and equipping its forces with immense quantities of new tanks, artillery, and aircraft of all types.

As the year ended, the *Stavka* planned to conduct a series of major strategic offensives aimed at clearing enemy forces from all Soviet territory and beginning the liberation of Nazi-occupied Europe. These offensives, which had already begun in mid-fall against German forces in Belorussia and the Ukraine, would grow during the winter to encompass all three strategic axes. The Soviet's twofold military superiority over Axis forces seemed to guarantee success. According to Soviet estimates, the German Armed Forces numbered 10,680,000 men on 1 January 1944, of which 7 million were in the field forces and the remainder in the reserves. At this time, said the Soviets, German ground forces numbered 4,399,000, of which 2,740,000 (63 percent), organized into 198 divisions and 6 brigades, were deployed on the Soviet front.[1] On the other hand, German records indicate that the German Army fielded 2,498,000 men on its Eastern Front on 14 October 1943, which were organized into 151 infantry and 26 panzer divisions. In addition, the Finns, Hungarians, and Rumanians fielded another 500,000 men, bringing the total strength of Axis forces to 3,068,000 men. The same records indicate that these forces faced 6,165,000 Soviet men.[2] At the very least, Soviet numerical military superiority forced the Germans to go over to the strategic defense in virtually every sector.

Along the northwestern axis, by 1 January 1944, the Leningrad and Volkhov Fronts had restored communications to Leningrad, removed any chance of a future German offensive against the city, and created conditions suitable for the utter defeat of German Army Group North. Kuechler's army group still occupied defenses in close proximity to the city and was able to strike it and its communications lines with impunity with artillery and air strikes. However, the deteriorating situation elsewhere along its Eastern Front precluded the OKH from providing Kuechler any reinforcements. Thus, the *Stavka* decided to liberate the city and all of Leningrad region as its first order of business in 1944.

On 1 January 1944, the 7th Separate Army and the Leningrad and Volkhov Fronts, supported by the Baltic Fleet and Ladoga Flotilla, faced Finnish forces deployed north of Leningrad and German forces operating south of the city. Lieutenant General A. N. Krutikov's 7th Separate Army faced the Finnish Olonets Operational Group in the heavily wooded and lake-strewn region between Lakes Ladoga and Onega. The Leningrad Front, still commanded by Army General Govorov, faced Finnish forces on the Karelian Isthmus and German forces south and east of Leningrad proper. Lieutenant General A. I. Cherepanov's 23d Army of Govorov's *front* defended astride the Karelian Isthmus from the Gulf of Finland to Lake Onega less than 30 kilometers (18.6 miles) north of Leningrad, and the 2d Shock Army, once again under Fediuninsky's command, controlled all forces deployed in the Oranienbaum bridgehead west of the city. The 2d Shock Army had replaced the Coastal Operational Group in November, and on 15 December 1943 the *Stavka* disbanded the 67th Army, transforming the 55th Army headquarters into a new 67th Army, effective 30 December.[3]

The 42d Army and the new 67th Army, commanded by Colonel General I. I. Maslennikov and Lieutenant General Sviridov, respectively, since December 1943, defended the southern and southeastern approaches to Leningrad from the Gulf of Finland to east of Siniavino against the German Eighteenth Army's left wing. Admiral Tributs's Baltic Fleet, which was still subordinate to the Leningrad Front and was based at Leningrad and Kronshtadt, was defending sea communications between Leningrad and the Oranienbaum bridgehead.

Meretskov's Volkhov Front occupied defenses opposite the German Eighteenth Army's right wing from east of Siniavino to Lake Il'men' with Starikov's 8th, Roginsky's 54th, and Korovnikov's 59th Armies and occupied an 8-kilometer (5-mile) bridgehead on the western bank of the Volkhov River 50 kilometers (31.1 miles) north of Novgorod.[4] The *Stavka* had disbanded his 4th Army in November to improve *front* command and control and assigned its forces to adjacent armies. To the south, Army General M. M. Popov's 2d Baltic Front, which had been formed from the Baltic Front on 20 October 1943, defended the sector from Lake Il'men' southward to just north of Nevel' with its 22d, 1st and 3d Shock, 6th Guards, and 15th Air Armies. His *front* faced Army Group North's Sixteenth Army.[5] On Popov's left flank, Colonel Generals I. M. Chistiakov's 6th Guards and N. E. Chibisov's 3d Shock Armies were pursuing German forces, who were withdrawing northward from Nevel to new defenses west of Novosokol'niki.

So configured, as of 14 January 1944, the Leningrad Front's strength was 417,600 men, the Volkhov Front's 260,000, and the 2d Baltic Front's 1st Shock Army 54,900 men, which, with the Baltic Fleet's 89,600 men, meant a total of 822,000 men available to participate in the forthcoming offensive. In addition, about 35,000 partisans organized into 13 partisan brigades were operating in Army Group North's rear area.[6]

Army Group North's Eighteenth and Sixteenth Armies defended the front from the Gulf of Finland southward to the Nevel' region with 44 infantry divisions, including 1 panzer grenadier division, for a total of roughly 500,000 men.[7] North of Leningrad, 4 infantry divisions and 1 cavalry brigade of the Finnish Army's Karelian Isthmus Group occupied defenses opposite the Leningrad Front's 23d Army. South of the city, Colonel General Lindemann's Eighteenth Army manned defenses extending from the Gulf of Finland to Lake Il'men' facing the Leningrad and Volkhov Fronts. After losing 7 infantry divisions to other sectors from September through December, the Eighteenth Army received 1 division (the SS Panzer Grenadier Division "Nordland") and two brigades (the SS Panzer Grenadier Brigade "Nederland," and the 1,000-man Spanish Legion) as reinforcements.

By Soviet count, on 1 January Lindemann's army fielded 14 infantry, 5 *Luftwaffe* field, and 1 panzer grenadier division, 1 divisional combat group, and 3 infantry and 1 panzer grenadier brigade. In addition, it had formed two artillery groups, the first north of Krasnoe Selo, with which to bombard Leningrad, and the second north of Mga, with which to interdict Soviet communications routes into Leningrad. The Eighteenth Army possessed 2,950 guns and mortars, 200 tanks and assault guns, and 200 aircraft of the First Air Fleet to provide fire support to its infantry forces.[8] South of Lake Il'men', Colonel General Busch's Sixteenth Army, which consisted of 18 infantry divisions, 1 *Luftwaffe* field division, 1 infantry brigade, and composite Group Eicholm (with 17 battalions), faced Popov's 2d Baltic Front.

According to German records, on 14 October Army Group North's 44 divisions (including forces in Northern Finland), with a strength of 601,000 men, 146 tanks, and 2,389 guns and mortars, faced an estimated 959,000 Soviet troops, 650 tanks, and 3,680 guns and mortars. Discounting the forces in northern Finland, the Eighteenth and Sixteenth Armies fielded roughly 500,000 men from the Gulf of Finland to north of Nevel' against about 800,000 Soviet troops.[9] By concentrating its forces, the Red Army was able to improve its strategic superiority of less than two to one over opposing German forces to a more than fourfold superiority operationally and more than eightfold tactically. Worse still for Kuechler, his army group had few reserves. Army

Group North defended with all of its divisions arrayed in single echelon and with three security divisions and one training division in reserve. However, the threadbare reserves were constantly occupied in security operations against Soviet partisans. In addition, the Eighteenth Army had one infantry division in reserve and Sixteenth Army, three infantry divisions.

The Germans compensated for their numerical weakness in the Leningrad region by constructing strong defenses organized in great depth back to the Panther Line.[10] The weakest German defenses were in the sector opposite the Oranienbaum bridgehead and the strongest were south and east of Leningrad. The German defenses around the Soviets' Oranienbaum bridgehead consisted of a single defensive belt with two defensive positions and few fortified strong points, which were manned by one regiment of the SS Police Division, SS Panzer Grenadier Division "Nordland," and the 10th and 9th *Luftwaffe* Field Divisions. The strongest German defenses were opposite the Leningrad Front's 42d Army and the Volkhov Front's 59th Army, where the Germans' fortified main defensive belt was 4–6 kilometers (2.5–3.7 miles) deep, backed up by a second belt 8–12 kilometers (5–7.5 miles) to the rear.

The Germans fortified virtually every town and village along the forward edge and in the shallow depths of their defense and formed multiple strong points into larger centers of resistance. The strongest centers of resistance were at Uritsk, Staro-Panovo, Novo-Panovo, Bol'shoe Bittolovo, Aleksandrovka, Pushkin, Krasnoe Selo, Hill 172.3 (Voron'ia Hill), Mga, Podberez'ia, Khutini, Kirillovskoe Monastery, and Novgorod.[11] Weather conditions in winter 1944, which were mild and subject to frequent thaws, favored the defense. The ice cover on rivers and lakes could support trucks and regimental artillery but not heavy weaponry or tanks, and the swamps were only partially frozen and difficult to traverse.

Based on Foreign Armies East *(Fremde Heere Ost)* intelligence reports, in the fall of 1943 Kuechler initially concluded that the Red Army was planning to conduct a large-scale offensive around Leningrad and Novgorod to encircle and possibly destroy the Eighteenth Army. Therefore, he prudently decided to preempt the offensive and shorten his front by withdrawing his forces to the Panther Line in time-phased fashion. Hitler, however, would permit no such action.

By early January 1944 the threat of a major Soviet offensive seemed somewhat to diminish. Although the obvious Soviet force buildup in the Oranienbaum bridgehead disturbed Kuechler and his staff, they concluded that the Leningrad Front was relying on replacements obtained solely from Leningrad's population to replenish its forces. This, they assumed, was clearly not sufficient to mount or sustain a major offensive effort. Furthermore, the Red Army was conducting major offensives at Vitebsk and elsewhere to the south, and these offensives appeared to be drawing off reserves necessary for the

Leningrad and Volkhov Fronts to mount any full-scale offensive. Finally, Lindemann, his Eighteenth Army commander, boldly asserted that his forces could successfully fend off any Soviet offensive.[12] Accordingly, from 29 December to 4 January, the OKH transferred three divisions from Eighteenth to Sixteenth Army to help deal with the crisis west of Nevel' and at Vitebsk.

Based on Kuechler's and Lindemann's fairly optimistic assessments, Hitler ordered Army Group North to hold firmly to its defenses at all cost. Despite Lindemann's confidence and Hitler's order, throughout December Kuechler secretly prepared plans to withdraw the Eighteenth Army from the Leningrad region and established new supply bases in Estonia. In the meantime, his forward forces dug in ever deeper, convinced they could hold on. On 10 January Army Group North's intelligence department once again assessed that the Soviet buildups in the Oranienbaum bridgehead and east of Novgorod were still modest, particularly in reserves. Without reserves, it concluded, a prospective Red Army offensive could not go deep, and any Russian offensives from the Oranienbaum bridgehead and at Novgorod would "very likely" be staggered.

While the German command exuded confidence and the fighting at Siniavino was still smoldering, on 9 September Govorov forwarded his appreciation of the situation and proposals for a decisive new offensive by his and Meretskov's *fronts* to the *Stavka*. His initial plan required the Leningrad and Volkhov Fronts to conduct two successive offensive operations designed to capture Luga and encircle and destroy the Eighteenth Army. In the first offensive, his 42d Army and Coastal Operational Group were to attack southward toward Krasnoe Selo from Leningrad proper and the Oranienbaum bridgehead and link up to form a continuous front south of Leningrad. After the fall of Krasnoe Selo, the 67th Army would join the offensive and capture Krasnogvardeisk, and the 42d Army and COG would then advance toward Kingisepp. Together, the twin offensives were designed to expel German forces from the Leningrad region and cut off the Eighteenth Army's withdrawal routes to the west.[13] On 14 September Meretskov presented the *Stavka* with a similar plan in which he recommended that his Volkhov Front attack from the region north of Novgorod toward Luga to encircle and destroy the Eighteenth Army's main force and prevent it from withdrawing westward to the Luga or Panther Line.

The *Stavka*, however, was not convinced that the two *fronts* were yet capable of conducting so ambitious an offensive. On the other hand, both the *Stavka* and the two *fronts* were alarmed by the increasing number of intelligence reports indicating that the Germans might be planning for an orderly withdrawal from the Leningrad region. Early on 29 September, these fears prompted the General Staff to order the Leningrad, Volkhov, and Northwestern Fronts to take vigorous measures to forestall any German attempt to withdraw:

According to agent intelligence, which requires verification, the enemy is preparing to withdraw his forces, which are opposing the Leningrad, Volkhov, and Northwestern Fronts.

In connection with this eventuality:

1. Intensify all types of reconnaissance and determine the enemy's intentions.

2. Increase the vigilance and combat readiness of your forces.

3. Create shock groupings along the likely axes of enemy withdrawal so that they can pursue along his withdrawal routes.

4. Create mobile pursuit detachments in first-echelon units and begin an energetic pursuit in the event of an enemy withdrawal.

While conducting the pursuit, employ aviation extensively against the withdrawing enemy.

Report measures undertaken.

[signed] Antonov[14]

Less than two weeks later, on 12 October, the General Staff formally accepted Govorov's initial plans, stating, "We do not object to your plan of operations for the Leningrad Front. Put it into effect quickly in the event of an enemy withdrawal."[15]

After modestly reinforcing Govorov's and Meretskov's *fronts*, the *Stavka* ordered Govorov to transfer the 2d Shock Army to the Oranienbaum bridgehead and prepare to conduct two strong concentric assaults from Leningrad and the Oranienbaum bridgehead to encircle German forces in the Petergof and Strel'na regions.[16] The revised *Stavka* plan required the two *fronts'* forces to destroy the Eighteenth Army south of Leningrad, raise the Leningrad blockade, and liberate the entire Leningrad region. Initially, they were to smash the Eighteenth Army's flanks by simultaneous attacks southwest of Leningrad and in the Novgorod region and then destroy the entire army and reach the Luga River from Kingisepp to Luga. Subsequently, they were to advance toward Narva and Pskov to clear German forces from the southern portion of the Leningrad region and begin liberating the Baltic republics. Simultaneously, the 2d Baltic Front was to attack the Sixteenth Army's right flank north of Nevel' to tie down the army's forces and prevent it from reinforcing German forces in the Leningrad region.

Govorov began planning his forthcoming offensive on 6 October, even before he received the *Stavka's* permission. The Leningrad war diary described the operation's form and intent:

> *Wednesday, 6 October.* While working out a plan for liberating Leningrad from the blockade, the *front* commander did not exclude the possibility that the enemy might begin withdrawing his forces. To that end,

two variants were prepared, conditionally named Neva 1 and Neva 2. Since the first of these was based on the circumstance that the Hitlerite forces would begin a preemptive withdrawal in an attempt to escape an offensive, an operational directive of the Leningrad Front's Military Council, dated 6 October 1943, ordered its forces to feel out the enemy's defenses firmly and persistently and, if need be, prepare for an immediate offensive. Simultaneously, it was to prepare a general penetration of the enemy's front as envisioned by variant Neva 2.[17]

PLANNING THE LENINGRAD-NOVGOROD STRATEGIC OFFENSIVE

Govorov began planning his initial offensive, code-named Operation Neva 2, in early November, after he transferred the 2d Shock Army into the Oranienbaum bridgehead. His final offensive concept required the 2d Shock and 42d Armies to penetrate German defenses along the eastern flank of the Oranienbaum bridgehead and near Pulkovo southwest of Leningrad, link up at Ropsha, and encircle and destroy German forces in the Krasnoe Selo, Ropsha, and Strel'na regions. All the while, the 67th Army was to tie down German forces south and east of the city and prevent them from reinforcing their forces in the 2d Shock and 42d Armies' sectors. After capturing its initial objectives, the 2d Shock and 42d Armies were to advance southwest toward Kingisepp and south toward Krasnogvardeisk, while the 67th Army attacked through Mga and Ul'ianovka toward Krasnogvardeisk from the northeast.

Govorov assigned the three armies participating in the Ropsha offensive their specific missions between 6 November and 23 December. To confuse the Germans, the 2d Shock Army was to attack a day before the 42d Army. The 13th Air Army, the 2d Guards Fighter Aviation Corps (PVO), and part of the Baltic Fleet's air forces were to provide artillery and material support to Govorov's shock groups.[18]

The 2d Shock Army, once again under the command of the experienced Fediuninsky, formed Govorov's first shock group. It consisted of two rifle corps, seven rifle divisions, one rifle, two naval infantry, and one tank brigade, one fortified region, and three tank regiments.[19] Fediuninsky's mission was to attack eastward from the Oranienbaum bridgehead with Major Generals A. I. Andreev's 43d and P. A. Zaitsev's 122d Rifle Corps, capture Ropsha, link up with the 42d Army, and help destroy German forces in the Krasnoe Selo and Ropsha regions. If Fediuninsky's initial assault failed, Major General M. F. Tikhonov's 108th Rifle Corps and Colonel A. Z. Oskotsky's 152d Tank Brigade, which were in his second echelon, were to strengthen the offensive by attacking toward Krasnoe Selo and Dudergof. If, on the other hand, the army's first echelon managed to link with the 42d Army successfully, its second-echelon rifle corps was to initiate a pursuit to the south and capture the vital German withdrawal routes southwest of Leningrad. According to the plan, Fediuninsky's army was to advance 17–21 kilometers (7.5–13 miles) in a period of five to six days.[20]

Before Govorov could mount his offensive, however, he faced the complex and daunting task of transferring the entire 2d Shock Army from Leningrad into the Oranienbaum bridgehead. He did so by employing the Baltic Fleet's forces to transport the army via the ice roads over the Gulf of Finland. The entire process, which lasted from 5 November to 21 January, was still under way when the offensive began. By that time, the 2d Shock Army headquarters, 5 rifle divisions (the 11th, 43d, 90th, 131st, and 196th), 13 RVGK artillery regiments, 2 tank and 1 self-propelled artillery regiment, 1 tank brigade, and 700 wagons with ammunition and other cargoes had moved into the bridgehead. During the same period, the *front* regrouped most of its artillery from the Mga-Siniavino sector into the Oranienbaum bridgehead and the 42d Army's sector.[21]

Govorov's second shock force, 42d Army, commanded by the equally experienced former NKVD officer, Maslennikov, consisted of 3 rifle corps, 10 rifle divisions, 1 fortified region, 2 tank brigades, and 5 tank regiments. His army's 30th Guards and 109th and 110th Rifle Corps, commanded by Major Generals Simoniak, I. P. Alferov, and I. V. Khazov, respectively, were to penetrate German defenses in the 17-kilometer (10.6-mile) sector from Ligovo Station to Bol'shoe Kuz'mino southwest of Leningrad and capture Krasnoe Selo. Thereafter, attacking from second echelon, Major General G. I. Anisimov's 123d Rifle Corps was to link up with the 2d Shock Army at Ropsha and help destroy German forces in the region. At the same time, a mobile group consisting of Colonel V. I. Volkov's 1st and Lieutenant Colonel V. L. Protsenko's 220th Tank Brigades and two self-propelled artillery regiments was to envelop Krasnoe Selo from the south and spearhead the army's advance on Ropsha. Maslennikov retained two rifle divisions in his reserve. Although his plan required the 42d Army's forces to advance 20–25 kilometers (12.4–15.5 miles), it set no time limits on the advance.[22]

Govorov allocated 80 percent of his *front*'s artillery, the Baltic Fleet's naval guns, and the bulk of its supporting aviation to support the 42d and 2d Shock Armies' shock groups. While he planned to pulverize the Germans' defenses with a 160-minute artillery preparation before the assault, he also ordered the 67th Army to conduct its own artillery preparation to deceive the Germans regarding the location of his main attack. A total of 653 aircraft from the 13th Air Army were to provide air support and protection against the Eighteenth Army's estimated 140 aircraft.

As had been the case in previous operations, Govorov's armored force, which amounted to 550 tanks and self-propelled guns, was relatively light. The strong German defenses, the difficult terrain, and insurmountable movement problems forced Govorov to restrict most of his armored operations simply to providing support for his advancing infantry. On the other hand, Govorov relied heavily on engineer and sapper support to help the infantry overcome the powerful German defenses, the swampy-forested terrain, and obstacles created by the severe winter weather conditions.[23]

Meretskov ordered Korovnikov's 59th Army to conduct two attacks: a main attack from its bridgehead on the western bank of the Volkhov River 30 kilometers (18.6 miles) north of Novgorod, and a secondary attack across Lake Il'men' south of Novgorod. The attacks were to converge west of Novgorod, encircle and destroy the German XXXVIII Army Corps, and capture the city. Subsequently, the 59th Army was to exploit westward and southwestward, capture Luga, and cut off the withdrawal of German forces in the Tosno and Chudovo regions. Simultaneously, Starikov's 8th and Roginsky's 54th Armies were to attack toward Tosno, Liuban', and Chudovo to prevent the Germans from transferring forces to Novgorod and to encircle and destroy German forces in the Tosno and Chudovo regions. If German forces began withdrawing from the Tosno and Chudovo regions after the 59th Army's assault, initially the 8th and 54th Armies were to clear German forces from the rail line and fortifications between Tosno and Chudovo. After doing so, they were to attack toward Luga to assist both the Leningrad Front and the 59th Army in the destruction of the Eighteenth Army. Meretskov assigned his armies their specific missions between mid-October and 31 December.[24]

Meretskov's largest army and main attack force, Korovnikov's 59th Army, consisted of three rifle corps, nine rifle divisions, one rifle brigade, three tank brigades, and four tank regiments. Major General S. P. Mikul'sky's 6th and Major General P. A. Artiushenko's 14th Rifle Corps were to penetrate the XXXVIII Army Corps' defenses 50 kilometers (31.1 miles) north of Novgorod and sever German communications routes into Novgorod from the west. South of the city, the army's Southern (Il'men') Operational Group, whose nucleus consisted of a reinforced rifle brigade, was to cross Lake Il'men' (on the ice), link up with the main shock group west of Novgorod, and help capture Novgorod and destroy German forces in the city. Commanded by Korovnikov's deputy, Major General T. A. Sviklin, the Southern Operational Group consisted of the 58th Rifle Brigade, 299th Rifle Regiment, a 225th Rifle Division ski battalion, and the 34th and 44th Aerosleigh Battalions, all of which received special training to perform their particularly tricky mission. Subsequently, Korovnikov's army was to advance westward to Luga and assist in the destruction of the Eighteenth Army.[25]

Korovnikov's army was to advance to a depth of 30 kilometers (18.6 miles) in a period of from three to five days and liberate Novgorod. The depth of the *front*'s entire operation was an ambitious 110–120 kilometers (68.4–74.6 miles). Meretskov also assigned 80 percent of his artillery and most of his air assets to support the 59th Army and planned to precede his ground assault with a 170-minute artillery preparation. He planned to support his assault with 257 aircraft from the 13th Air Army and 330 additional night bombers from the four long-range aviation corps provided by the *Stavka*. This force vastly outnumbered the roughly 103 aircraft that the Germans could muster to operate in his sector. Meretskov's armor, which totaled 231 tanks and 25 self-propelled guns, performed the same infantry support function as Govorov's armor. While performing the same tasks as the Leningrad Front's engineers, those assigned to the Volkhov Front had to prepare numerous crossings over the Volkhov and other rivers and Lake Il'men'. For this reason, Meretskov assigned additional engineer forces to the 59th Army.[26]

Finally, both Govorov and Meretskov employed stringent operational security measures and deception plans to confuse the Germans regarding the timing and location of the offensive, Govorov by posturing for an offensive along the Kingisepp axis and Meretskov by conducting a demonstration near Mga and a false concentration near Chudovo. The Germans responded to the deception by transferring the Panzer Grenadier Brigade "Nederland" to the Leningrad region from Yugoslavia. So effective was the deception that even Red Army personnel believed the assault would occur in that region.

The Germans also regrouped their forces prior to the Soviet offensive, although the new force configuration was not conducive to an effective defense in the Leningrad region. The OKH transferred the 96th and 254th Infantry Divisions from the Eighteenth Army to Army Group South. The Eighteenth Army shifted the 61st Infantry Division from the Mga region to just north of Krasnogvardeisk beginning on 10 January, and the SS Panzer Grenadier Brigade "Nederland" to positions opposite the 2d Shock Army's right flank in response to the Soviet deception plan. To the south, Busch's Sixteenth Army moved its reserve, the 290th Infantry Division, to the Shimsk, Utorgosh, and Sol'tsy regions to back up German defenses at the junction of the Sixteenth and Eighteenth Armies.[27]

In addition, for the first time in the war, both Govorov and Meretskov fully integrated partisan operations in the offensive. In November, the Leningrad Headquarters of the Partisan Movement ordered its partisans to conduct major sabotage and diversionary operations in support of the offensive:

1. Broaden the centers of popular uprisings in the areas of operations of the 2d, 5th, 7th, and 9th Partisan Brigades. Foment popular uprisings in the Volosovo, Kingisepp, Os'mino, Krasnogvardeisk, Oredezh,

and Tosno regions in northern Leningrad region and in the Porkhov, Pozherivitsk, Slavkovichi, Soshikhin, and Ostrov regions in southern Leningrad region.

2. During the course of the developing uprisings, completely destroy the occupation authorities' local organs, such as *uyezd* [large town], regional [mid-size town], and *volost'* [small town] organs and create Soviet administrative organs under armed partisan protection. Save the population from destruction or transport to Germany and deny the enemy command the opportunity to use the population in the construction of defensive positions. Defend populated points from destruction and disrupt the transport to Germany of grain, livestock, clothing, and other materials.

3. Intensify combat operations by partisan brigades, detachments, and groups against enemy communications—roads and railroads—with all means at your disposal. Put the Krasnogvardeisk-Luga-Pskov, Krasnogvardeisk-Kingisepp-Narva, Pskov-Slantsy-Veimari, Staraia Russa-Dno-Porkhov-Pskov, and Pushkin-Dno-Chikhachevo rail lines out of commission for the longest period possible in order to paralyze completely the transport of personnel, equipment, and ammunition for the enemy's operating armies, particularly during the period of the Leningrad, Volkhov, and 2d Baltic Fronts' offensives.[28]

In accordance with this general directive, the Leningrad Headquarters of the Partisan Movement assigned specific missions to each partisan brigade, detachment, and group participating in the partisan operation.

By the time their offensive preparations were complete, both *front* commanders had created overwhelming numerical superiority over the opposing Germans by concentrating their forces. Govorov concentrated 72 percent of his infantry, 68 percent of his artillery, and all of his tanks and self-propelled guns in the 2d Shock and 42d Armies' sectors. Similarly, Meretskov concentrated 48 percent of his infantry, 55 percent of his artillery, almost all of his *Katiushas,* and 80 percent of his armor in the 59th Army's sector. Tactical concentration increased this superiority by factors of two to three in both *fronts*. Govorov's forces outnumbered the Germans threefold in infantry, fourfold in artillery, and sixfold in tanks and self-propelled guns, and Meretskov's well over threefold in infantry and artillery and elevenfold in tanks and self-propelled guns.[29]

With their preparations complete, Govorov's and Meretskov's assault forces occupied their final jumping-off positions for the attack two to three nights before the assault. The remaining forces and supporting arms phased into attack positions the day and night before the assault. Supporting tanks deployed forward during the artillery preparation.

THE LENINGRAD FRONT'S ROPSHA–KRASNOE SELO OFFENSIVE, 14–20 JANUARY

Despite the heavy snow that began falling across the front on the night of 13–14 January, 109 Soviet night bombers pounded German defenses overnight. At dawn Govorov's massed artillery rained 104,000 shells on the defenses of the III SS Panzer Corps' 9th and 10th *Luftwaffe* Field Divisions during a thundering 65-minute artillery preparation. As the hurricane of devastating artillery fire ended with a barrage of screaming *Katiusha* rockets, at 1000 hours, the massed infantry of the 48th, 90th, and 131st Rifle Divisions, leading the assault of Andreev's 43d and Zaitsev's 122d Rifle Corps, lunged forward into the German defensive positions. Fediuninsky and Govorov observed the assault from the 2d Shock Army command post on nearby Kolokol'nia Hill. The three attacking divisions quickly overcame the Germans' forward defenses and, by day's end, had wedged up to 3 kilometers (1.9 miles) deep into the shattered German forward defensives along a 10-kilometer (6.2-mile) front. Oskotsky's 152d Tank Brigade and the 22d and 204th Tank Regiments provided critical armor support for Fediuninsky's attacking infantry.

The Leningrad war diary captured the drama of the day:

> *Friday, 14 January.* The morning was hazy. Aviation had prepared a massive blow against the enemy, but fog covered the ground so densely that one could hardly make out anything. It was fortunate that long-range aviation had operated the night before. It subjected the greatest concentration areas of the enemy's heavy batteries, his untouched artillery grouping, to intense bombing.
>
> The first-echelon regiments occupied their jumping-off positions during the night. The sappers cut lanes through the minefields and exploded shells under the enemy barbed wire. . . .
>
> At 0935 hours the artillery began to rumble. Not only the 2d Shock Army's regiments' artillery struck the enemy but also the powerful guns at Kronshtadt, Forts Seraia Loshad' and Krasnaia Gorka, and ship artillery. . . .
>
> The enemy did not doubt that our forces would undertake an offensive to liberate Leningrad from the blockade. But he knew not when it would occur. Now, when the powerful artillery preparation began, the enemy was still estimating where and in what place he should expect the main attack.
>
> A powerful artillery preparation also began north of Novgorod in the Volkhov Front. Units of the 42d Army conducted intense fire from Pulkovo. The 67th Army's artillery destroyed enemy firing points south of Lake Ladoga.

The fascist command was disoriented. However, everything became clear 65 minutes after the beginning of the artillery preparation. The offensive began from the Oranienbaum bridgehead. At the same time, it also began along the Volkhov Front's Novgorod axis.

The avalanche of shells had hardly rolled into the depth of the enemy's defenses when three divisions of the 2d Shock Army, the 48th, 90th, and 131st, rose up in attack from Oranienbaum. It was 1040 hours. Soon red flags began appearing above the enemy's positions as if they were tongues of flame. . . .

Supported by the tanks, infantrymen seized the enemy's first trenches from the march. The artillery continued to pound the routes forward. In spite of the weather, aircraft began appearing over the field of battle. . . .

The troops advanced forward capturing Porozhki, Pereles'e, and Zrekino. . . .

By evening the width of the penetration in the enemy defense reached 10 kilometers. Especially heavy fighting raged for Gostilitsy, which the enemy had transformed into a strongly fortified center of resistance. Gathering his wits after the first stunning blows, the enemy began to commit his reserves into the battle. Hand-to-hand fighting occurred several times on the northwestern outskirts of Gostilitsy. After capturing that village, our forces wedged into the Hitlerites' second defensive position. . . .

In the meantime, no sort of official report concerning the commencement of the offensive was issued, but the city's inhabitants could only guess about it based on the peals of the unusual cannonade. Many Leningraders later said that they worked with special enthusiasm to that cannonade.[30]

Overnight on 14–15 January, Colonels N. G. Liashchenko's 90th and P. L. Romanenko's 131st Rifle Divisions, supported by the 2d and 204th Tank Regiments and Oskotsky's 152d Tank Brigade, advanced 4 kilometers (2.5 miles) deeper into the Germans' second defensive position. During the advance, the 130th Separate Artillery–Machine Gun Battalion swept forward and dug in to protect the shock group's right flank. Throughout the day and into the night, the 42d Army's artillery delivered devastating fires on German positions on Pulkovo Heights, and the 67th Army's artillery fired on German defenses north of Mga and Siniavino in an attempt to confuse the Germans as to when and where the next assault would come.[31] The Germans' doubts evaporated at 1100 hours the next morning, when the 2d Shock and 42d Armies struck simultaneously after fresh artillery preparations.

Attacking from the west early on 15 January, the forward divisions of Andreev's 43d and Zaitsev's 122d Rifle Corps, in the vanguard of Fediuninsky's army, lunged into the German defenses, shattering what remained of the III SS Panzer Corps' 10th *Luftwaffe* Division. As the *Luftwaffe* division began crumbling, the III SS Panzer Corps tried to halt the attack by throwing three construction battalions and a battalion from SS Panzer Grenadier Division "Nordland" into the battle, but with little positive effect. Fediuninsky's army advanced 6 kilometers (3.7 miles) on the first day of battle, committed its second-echelon divisions late in the day, and captured Sokuli after heavy fighting, but was halted by heavy German fire west of Ropsha.[32]

Less than 20 kilometers (12.4 miles) to the east, Maslennikov's 42d Army attacked the Germans' defenses near Pulkovo at 1100 hours, after its artillery had poured more than 220,000 shells into the German defenses. As the artillery barrage shifted into the depths, Simoniak's 30th Guards Rifle Corps swept forward into the German defenses.

> *Saturday, 15 January.* The new day of the offensive was commemorated with a cannonade even more powerful than the day before. . . . Today the 42d Army's formations are attacking. But before the infantry moved forward, more than 220,000 artillery and mortar shells, not counting rocket rounds, fell on the enemy's defense. 2,300 guns struck along a 17-kilometer front from Uritsk to Pushkin. . . .
>
> The unexpected squall raged for 1 hour and 40 minutes. The infantry attacked at precisely 1100 hours. The guardsmen of General N. P. Simoniak attacked in the center, from Pulkovo Heights. The hero of Hango and the hero of the penetration of the blockade is now predestined to become the hero of the complete liberation of Leningrad. But if a brigade fought under Simoniak's command in 1941 and a division in the winter of 1943, now he is leading a corps of three divisions into battle.
>
> The guardsmen advanced forward resolutely, crushing the enemy's defense. . . . The Germans called their defense lines at Leningrad the Northern Wall. It was genuinely powerful. Nevertheless, on the first day of the 42d Army's offensive, the depth of the penetration reached 4.5 kilometers in the center of the 30th Guards Rifle Corps' sector and about 1.5 kilometers on the flanks.
>
> Also beginning with an artillery preparation, the Volkhov Front's forces achieved considerable success. Today they cut the Novgorod-Chudovo railroad. . . .
>
> In Leningrad, no one doubts that what has begun at Pulkovo is the start of something very important.[33]

However, the divisions of Alferov's 109th and Khazov's 110th Rifle Corps, which were assaulting on Simoniak's flanks, soon encountered heavy German resistance. The ensuing fight with the L Army Corps' 126th, 170th, and

215th Infantry Divisions soon degenerated into a typical slugfest, with attacking Soviet infantry gnawing their way through the dense German defenses in costly successive assaults.[34]

Simoniak's corps penetrated up to 4 kilometers (2.5 miles) deep along a 5-kilometer (3.1-mile) front by day's end, but could do no more. Soviet after-action reports blamed the slow progress by both armies on poor reconnaissance and command and control, particularly in the 2d Shock Army. In addition, the armies' heavy weaponry could not keep up with the infantry, and an effective counter-barrage fired by the L Army Corps' artillery blunted the 42d Army's ground assault. In addition, the 2d Shock Army's 204th Tank Regiment lost 19 tanks in enemy minefields, 5 in enemy trenches, and 4 while crossing the Chernaia River. The 42d Army's 260th Tank Regiment became bogged down in an antitank ditch and subsequently lost 6 KV tanks to German mines.[35] Despite these problems, Govorov intensified his assaults the next day, when Fediuninsky's lead divisions penetrated the entire depth of the German's main defensive belt and Maslennikov's forces painfully advanced another 3–4 kilometers (1.9–2.5 miles), primarily in the sector of Simoniak's guards corps.

The assault continued with even greater fury on 16 January:

> *Sunday, 16 January.* On the night of 15–16 January, our forces attacking along the main attack axis, supported by tanks, decisively attacked and occupied Aleksandrovka, which is separated from Pushkin only by a depot.
>
> In the morning the attackers cut the Pushkin–Krasnoe Selo road.
>
> The enemy, who has to defend simultaneously along several directions, was subjected to yet another assault—the Volkhov Front's 54th Army went over to the attack. The direction of the attack is toward Liuban'. However, the enemy's resistance still has not been overcome. He is continuing to cling fiercely to every clump of ground and launching counterattacks. It is requiring considerable bravery and selflessness to overcome him.[36]

Fediuninsky's forces succeeded in penetrating the entire depth of the Germans' main defensive belt by day's end on 16 January, while Maslennikov's troops painfully advanced another 3–4 kilometers (1.9–2.5 miles), primarily in the sector of Simoniak's 30th Guards Rifle Corps. Dissatisfied with his forces' forward progress, Fediuninsky threw a small mobile group, consisting of Oskotsky's 152d Tank Brigade with a self-propelled artillery regiment, a truck-mounted rifle battalion, a light artillery battalion, and three sapper battalions on trucks attached, into combat early on 17 January. Oskotsky's orders were simple and clear—to capture and hold on to Ropsha at all cost.[37] However, German counterattacks halted his small armored task force only halfway to its objective:

Monday, 17 January. The 90th Rifle Division, which is attacking from the Oranienbaum bridgehead, penetrated into Diatlitsy. The tank troops of the 152d Tank Brigade are advancing farther east and captured the village of Gliadino by day's end. One can count the kilometers to Ropsha. The troops attacking from Leningrad are nearing Krasnoe Selo.

The threat of encirclement looms over the enemy grouping defending north of Ropsha and Krasnoe Selo. The enemy is constantly counterattacking in order to hold on to the road, which is necessary for the withdrawal of the combat weaponry and troops that may soon be encircled.

The enemy situation is worsening not only at Leningrad. This morning the forces of the Volkhov Front's 59th Army seized the enemy strong point at Podberez'e. The arrow of the offensive is aimed at Novgorod.

Strikes are also occurring against the enemy's rear area. On the night of 17 January, the 12th Partisan Brigade blew up several rails on the rail line between Kingisepp and Tikopis'. Beginning on 15 January, for the third day, the 5th Partisan Brigade put separate sections of the Vitebsk railroad out of commission. On 17 January they struck enemy communications in the Sol'tsy-Utorgosh' sector.[38]

While Fediuninsky was committing Oskotsky's mobile group to action, Maslennikov ordered Mikul'sky's 123d Rifle Corps, which was in second echelon, to join battle on the right flank of Simoniak's 30th Guards Rifle Corps and exploit its success. At midday he also committed his army's mobile tank group, whose nucleus was formed by Volkov's 1st Leningrad Red Banner and Protsenko's 220th Tank Brigades, into action with orders to envelop Dudergof and Krasnoe Selo from the west and capture the German strong points. However, the Germans detected its mobile group's forward deployment and engaged it with effective counterattacks the moment it attacked, forcing the tank group to withdraw to Pulkovo with heavy losses.[39] Despite the failure of the two mobile groups to reach their objectives, by day's end the forward elements of Fediuninsky's and Maslennikov's advancing infantry were only 18 kilometers (11.2 miles) apart. Faced with the prospect of imminent encirclement, the German 126th Infantry and 9th *Luftwaffe* Field Divisions clung grimly to their shrinking salient north of Krasnoe Selo and prepared to withdraw their forces to the south.

Despite the threatening situation, Lindemann still exuded confidence on 16 January. He informed his army commanders that the Russians had committed all of their forces, and he told Kuechler that he could win the battle by taking some risks in quiet sectors. However, by this time, Lindemann had already committed his last reserve, the 61st Infantry Division, in support of the shattered 10th *Luftwaffe* Division in an attempt to slow the 2d Shock Army's advance.[40]

The next day, an increasingly concerned Kuechler informed the OKH that the situation was deteriorating and requested Hitler's permission to withdraw forces from the Mga salient back to the Rollbahn Line so that he could free up two divisions to counter the Soviet assaults southwest of Leningrad. The Rollbahn Line was forward of and parallel to the vital railroad and road running from Leningrad to Chudovo. Saying neither yes nor no, Hitler instead suggested that Kuechler abandon the front between Oranienbaum and Leningrad. Kuechler protested that to do so would permit the Soviets to unite their forces and launch an even stronger assault. Ignoring Hitler's prohibitions, Lindemann reinforced his defenses north of Krasnoe Selo with portions of the 225th and 21st Infantry Divisions, which he withdrew from Mga and Chudovo, and with the SS "Nordland" and 11th Infantry Divisions, but to no avail.[41]

While Hitler, Kuechler, and Lindemann were debating the Eighteenth Army's fate, Fediuninsky and Maslennikov settled the issue for them by committing their second-echelon corps to combat, leaving the Germans no choice but to withdraw their forces back to Krasnoe Selo. Fediuninsky's entire army surged forward on 18 January. Alferov's 108th Rifle Corps went into action early in the day with its two divisions, and the army's tank reserves and Zaitsev's 122d Rifle Corps captured Ropsha the next day. Meanwhile, Andreev's 43d Rifle Corps captured Volosovo and dug in to protect the shock group's right flank. Only a matter of hours later, at 2100 hours on 19 January, the 462d Rifle Regiment of the 108th Rifle Corps' 168th Rifle Division linked up with the 54th Engineer Battalion of the 42d Army's mobile group just south of Ropsha. The next morning the two armies' main forces met all along the entire penetration front, slamming the door shut on German forces still locked in combat to the north.[42]

Farther east, Simoniak's guards corps resumed its assaults of 19 January and finally captured Krasnoe Selo late in the day, thus blocking the withdrawal routes of German forces from Strel'na though Krasnoe Selo to Krasnogvardeisk:

Tuesday, 18 January. The battle for Krasnoe Selo is beginning. The Strel'na-Krasnoe Selo-Gatchina [Krasnogvardeisk] road has been cut, and the fate of the Hitlerites who are still situated in Leningrad's immediate suburbs, including their untouched artillery grouping, has been decided.

Wednesday, 19 January. The ferocious battle of Krasnogvardeisk has resulted in victory! The occupiers have kept house here since 12 September 1941. They turned the town into a fortress, which they considered impregnable. But the 42d Army's forces took this fortress. In essence, the town itself no longer exists, but the important road junction is in our hands.

A little bit to the west, the 2d Shock Army has liberated yet another of Leningrad's suburbs, Ropsha.

Today in Moscow at 2100 hours, for the first time a 20-volley artillery salute occurred in honor of the Leningrad Front's forces.

At precisely the same time—a significant coincidence—the forward units of the 2d Shock and 42d Armies linked up in the vicinity of Russko-Vysotsky southwest of Krasnoe Selo and southeast of Ropsha. The first to make this brotherly embrace were scouts from the 168th Rifle Division's 462d Rifle Regiment, which were attacking from Oranienbaum, and sappers from the 54th Engineer Battalion, which were accompanying the 42d Army's mobile tank group.

Later the tank troops who were attacking from Pulkovo and Oranienbaum met up. The ring around the enemy's Petergof-Strel'na grouping has closed. However, today the Hitlerites still launched 23 heavy artillery shells on the city.

A direct road extends from Krasnoe Selo to Gatchina [Krasnogvardeisk]. Today, with an ulterior motive, the commander of the German 11th Infantry Division wrote in his order, "The enemy wants to penetrate through to Gatchina. We must thwart this intention. We must hold the existing lines at all costs."

Thus the order was to hold on to Voron'e Hill at all costs. Nevertheless, the submachine gunners of the 190th Guards Regiment, under Captain Vladimir Massal'sky, captured it. It was an intense battle. Although wounded several times, the captain continued to direct the assault on Voron'e Hill. He knew that, without the capture of that hill, there would be no advance on Krasnoe Selo. Voron'e Hill was seized by the morning of 19 January.[43]

Overnight on 19–20 January, Maslennikov's mobile tank group attacked westward from Krasnoe Selo with headlights blazing, demoralizing and defeating German forces that were withdrawing southward from Petergof, Strel'na, and Uritsk. The group linked up with the 2d Shock Army forces south of Ropsha, encircling the remnants of German forces that were still defending the Petergof and Strel'na regions to the north. However, at this point the linkup involved only reconnaissance and tank forces, and the two armies' main infantry forces were still lagging far behind. Consequently, on the night of 19–20 January, many German troops in the Strel'na and Uritsk regions infiltrated southward in small groups and made their way through the porous Soviet lines, thereby escaping destruction. Soviet forces liquidated those who failed to do so on 20 January. The Leningrad war diary that day recorded: "Early today the attacking forces of the 2d Shock and 42d Armies definitively linked up with one another in the Ropsha region. The enemy's fully encircled Petergof-Strel'na grouping was crushed. More than 1,000 soldiers and officers were taken prisoner. More than 265 enemy artillery pieces, including 85 heavy caliber (152–400mm) guns, were captured during the battle. These are the weapons that shelled Leningrad."[44]

Early on 18 January, Lindemann finally informed Kuechler that his front southwest of Leningrad and near Novgorod was collapsing. Once again, Kuechler sought permission from Hitler and the OKH to withdraw Lindemann's forces to the Mga River and the Rollbahn Line, but was denied permission to do so. When Krasnoe Selo fell in the afternoon, on his own volition, Kuechler decided to abandon the Mga position and so informed the OKH. Hitler finally approved Kuechler's decision at midnight, but only after Zeitzler told him that he had already given Kuechler the order to withdraw. In any event, the order was issued too late to save the divisions defending the Petergof and Strel'na salient, only small elements of which escaped destruction.[45]

In six days of nearly constant heavy combat, Fediuninsky's and Maslennikov's armies penetrated prepared German defenses, advanced 25 kilometers (15.5 miles), and linked up at Ropsha, restoring a contiguous front and communications between the Leningrad Front's disparate forces south and west of the city. The victory also improved the *front*'s command and control, logistical support, and maneuver capabilities. In the process, they destroyed two German divisions, damaged five others, and captured over 1,000 prisoners, seriously weakening the Eighteenth Army. The Leningrad Front also reported destroying or capturing 265 guns (85 heavy), 159 mortars, 30 tanks, and 18 warehouses with ammunition.[46] The successful Ropsha offensive paved the way for subsequent offensive operations toward both Krasnogvardeisk and Kingisepp.

THE VOLKHOV FRONT'S NOVGOROD OFFENSIVE, 14–20 JANUARY

While Fediuninsky's and Maslennikov's armies were demolishing German defenses southwest of Leningrad, despite deteriorating weather that made operations difficult at best, Korovnikov's 59th Army unleashed its assaults against the Eighteenth Army's right flank in the Novgorod region. After pulverizing German defenses by firing 133,000 artillery shells during its preparation, assault detachments from each of Korovnikov's first-echelon rifle battalions began the ground assault at 1050 hours. Mikul'sky's 6th Rifle Corps attacked from the bridgehead west of the Volkhov River on Korovnikov's right flank, protected on the right by Major General D. A. Luk'ianov's 2d Rifle Division. Colonel N. V. Rogov's 310th and Colonel A. Ia. Ordanovsky's 239th Rifle Divisions spearheaded Mikul'sky's advance, and Mikul'sky prepared to support their advance with Colonel K. O. Urvanov's 16th Tank Brigade. To the south, Artiushenko's 14th Rifle Corps attacked with Colonel A. R. Belov's

378th, Major General I. N. Burakovsky's 191st, and Colonel P. I. Ol'khovsky's 225th Rifle Divisions, deployed from north to south in the sector from Leliavino to Novgorod. Finally, Sviklin's Operational Group advanced across the northern portion of Lake Il'men', south of Novgorod. To the rear, Major General F. Ia. Solov'ev's 112th Rifle Corp remained in army second echelon with Lieutenant Colonel I. D. Bachakashvili's and Major D. M. Savochkin's 29th and 122d Tank Brigades. Major General R. I. Panin's 7th Rifle Corps constituted Korovnikov's reserve.

Despite the heavy artillery preparation, the assault by Mikul'sky's 6th Rifle Corps stalled after advancing only 1 kilometer (.6 miles) into the Germans' first defensive position. The assault failed largely because the infantry support tanks arrived too late and many fell victim to craters and swamps because of poor reconnaissance and engineer work. Nevertheless, during the night sappers erected a bridge over the Volkhov River capable of carrying tanks. Fortunately for Korovnikov, to the south a regiment of the 14th Rifle Corps' 378th Rifle Division attacked prematurely and without orders, taking advantage of the fact that German troops had abandoned their forward defenses during the artillery preparation, and seized a portion of the Germans' defenses. The neighboring 1254th Regiment then joined the attack and the two regiments overcame the first two German trenches and seized a small bridgehead over the Pit'ba River at Malovodskoe.[47]

South of Novgorod, Sviklin's Southern Operational Group crossed the ice on Lake Il'men' without an artillery preparation, surprised the German defenders, and captured a bridgehead 6 kilometers (3.7 miles) deep and 4 kilometers (2.5 miles) wide on the eastern shore of the lake. Fearing that its communications between Shimsk and Novgorod would be severed, the German XXXVIII Army Corps dispatched the 290th Infantry Division's 503d Infantry Regiment and the Cavalry Regiment "Nord" to block the Soviet advance south of Novgorod and the 24th Infantry Division from Mga to do likewise north of Novgorod.

Korovnikov, too, reinforced his advancing forces on 15 January. The reinforcements included one rifle division from second echelon and an armored car battalion from his reserve to develop his success south of Novgorod. To the north, he first committed Urvanov's 16th Tank Brigade and a self-propelled artillery regiment in support of the 6th Rifle Corps. Soon after, he reinforced Mikul'sky's corps with Colonel G. E. Kalinovsky's 65th Rifle Division and Bachakashvili's 29th Tank Brigade from Solov'ev's second-echelon 112th Rifle Corps.[48]

Once reinforced, Mikul'sky's rifle corps advanced 7 kilometers (4.3 miles) against heavy resistance, encircling and defeating elements of the 28th Jager Division. Later in the day, Urvanov's 16th and Bachakashvili's 29th Tank Brigades and Ordanovsky's 239th Rifle Division approached the Chudovo-

Novgorod road and engaged a regiment of the 24th Infantry Division, which had been sent by the XXXVIII Army Corps to hold on to the vital rail line. Despite the German reinforcements, Mikul'sky's forces cut the rail line the next day. Together with Artiushenko's 14th Rifle Corps, which had cut the Finev Lug–Novgorod road to the south, by late on 16 January the two attacking rifle corps had tore a gaping 20-kilometer (12.4-mile) hole in the Germans' main defense belt.

While penetrating the Germans' defenses north of Novgorod, Meretskov also increased the pressure on the sagging German front by ordering Roginsky's 54th Army to join the assault out of the Volkhov River bridgehead south of Kirishi and from south of Pogost'e. Roginsky's mission was to capture Liuban', prevent the Germans from reinforcing their defenses at Novgorod, and assist the 59th Army in the destruction of the German XXVIII and XXXVIII Army Corps, which defended the Liuban' and Chudovo regions. Initially, Roginsky attacked with his 80th Rifle Division and the 281st and 285th Rifle Divisions of Major General S. B. Kozachek's 115th Rifle Corps, but subsequently his army's 44th Rifle Division joined the assault early on 17 January by attacking south of the Tigoda River.[49] Although Roginsky's army had advanced only 5 kilometers (3.1 miles) by 20 January, his attack prevented the XXXVIII Army Corps from transferring any additional forces to relieve the unrelenting Soviet pressure on the Novgorod region.

South of Novgorod, Korovnikov reinforced Sviklin's Southern Operational Group with Ol'khovsky's 225th and Colonel P. I. Radygin's 372d Rifle Divisions, which broke out of their bridgehead and cut the Shimsk-Novgorod railroad west of Novgorod. Faced with the possible encirclement of his entire Novgorod force, initially Lindemann reinforced the forces with elements of the 24th and 21st Infantry Divisions from Mga, the 250th Infantry Division from Sol'tsy, and the 8th Jager Division. Later, the SS Cavalry Regiment "Nord" went into action south of Novgorod on 16 January and the 121st Infantry Division from Tosno north of Novgorod on 17 January.[50]

Nevertheless, Korovnikov's army continued its slow but inexorable advance, enveloping German forces in Novgorod from the north and south. According to Soviet after-action critiques, poor army and corps command and control, heavy German fortifications, the poor terrain, and a sudden thaw hindered the 59th Army's advance and permitted the Germans to bring up fresh reserves.[51] Korovnikov, however, remained confident that he could succeed despite the incessant problems his forces faced. Therefore, on 18 January he committed Solov'ev's 112th Rifle Corps and Savochkin's 122d Tank Brigade from second echelon to protect his army's right flank and to cooperate with 54th Army's forces in the destruction of the two German corps in the Liuban' and Chudovo regions. His commitment of fresh forces placed the entire German force defending Novgorod in jeopardy, a fact not lost on Lindemann:

On the morning of the 18th Lindemann reported that the fronts east of Oranienbaum and west of Leningrad were collapsing. The same thing was happening at Novgorod, where the encirclement was nearly complete, and the few extra battalions the army had been able to throw in would not even be enough to hold open an escape route much longer. After seeing for himself how near complete exhaustion the troops at the front were, Kuechler asked and was denied permission to withdraw to the Rollbahn.[52]

Lindemann quickly ordered his XXXVIII Army Corps to abandon Novgorod, withdrawing along the only remaining road to the west, and occupy new defenses at Batetskii to protect the approaches to Luga from the east.

However, bad weather, the swampy and heavily wooded terrain, and a lack of transport slowed the 59th Army's advance west of Novgorod. For example, the Volkhov Front's 52d Separate Automobile Regiment lacked 48 percent of its required trucks, and its 11th Regiment was short 82.3 percent of its rolling stock. Together, the two transport regiments were short 666 of their required vehicles.[53] Nevertheless, assisted by sappers, Mikul'sky's 6th Rifle Corps struggled through the frozen swamps, finally cutting the Novgorod-Batetskii railroad late on 19 January. Further south, Sviklin's Southern Operational Group had cut the Shimsk-Novgorod railroad the previous day, but Artiushenko's 14th Rifle Corps made little progress in its enveloping attack against Novgorod from the north, ostensibly because of poorly organized reconnaissance. While the latter was preparing to storm Novgorod the next morning, elements of the German 28th Jager and 1st *Luftwaffe* Field Divisions, two separate battalions, and units of the SS Cavalry Regiment "Nord," which had been defending the city, began evacuating their stronghold without serious interference. A German account described the harrowing escape:

On the night of 19 January, those troops of 28 Light [Jager] Division encircled in Novgorod received the order to break out. The seriously wounded had to be abandoned in the ruins, the medical staff volunteering to remain behind with them, and all who could carry weapons, including the walking wounded, tried to withdraw under cover of darkness. Elsewhere to the north-east, troops fell under heavy enemy artillery fire while the Red Air Force bombed and machine-gunned all movement. German formations and units became mixed and confused and fighting units included in their number stragglers and leave and baggage men. All suffered from the wet and lack of sleep and food, and unless supply column commanders took most energetic action to maintain contact, replenishment failed. *Luftwaffe* divisions disintegrated, and in some of the infantry divisions nearly all of the regimental and battalion commanders were killed or wounded. Divisional infantry strengths fell to only 500 men. Scaremonger rumours ran up and down the front and there were some cases of flight or panic.[54]

At 0930 hours on 20 January, the 191st and 225th Rifle Divisions of Artiu-shenko's 14th Rifle Corps and the 382d Rifle Division of Panin's 7th Rifle Corps captured Novgorod without a fight after the last Germans out destroyed the bridge over the Volkhov River.[55] The loss of Novgorod was not, however, bloodless for the Germans. The next day, Mikul'sky's 6th Rifle Corps and Radygin's 372d Rifle Division of the Southern Operational Group encircled and later destroyed elements of the 28th Jager and 1st *Luftwaffe* Field Divisions, two separate battalions, and elements of SS Cavalry Regiment "Nord" west of the city.[56]

After midnight on 19 January, Kuechler requested Hitler's permission to withdraw what he termed "the five German battalions" surrounded by "eight Soviet divisions" through the swamps west of Novgorod. Although he still stubbornly claimed that Novgorod was of "extraordinary symbolic significance," Hitler agreed to Kuechler's request, but insisted his forces hold east of the Rollbahn Line. Fifteen minutes later he gave permission for that withdrawal as well, but tried to gain Kuechler's guarantees that they would hold on to the Rollbahn Line itself. On 20 January, Kuechler assessed the situation and informed the OKW that the tactical setbacks at Novgorod and southwest of Leningrad had resulted from lack of reserves and an overextended front. Since the same conditions still existed, he requested that the withdrawal to the Rollbahn Line become the first step in a general withdrawal to the Panther Line because the three divisions released by the withdrawal would soon be consumed in the intense fighting.[57]

In seven days of combat, Korovnikov's army penetrated strong enemy defenses, liberated Novgorod, and advanced 20 kilometers (12.4 miles) westward, widening its penetration to 50 kilometers (31 miles). While doing so, they destroyed or seriously damaged two German divisions, one regiment, four separate battalions, and other smaller units and captured 3,000 prisoners. Soviet sources also claim Red Army forces destroyed or captured 182 guns, 120 mortars, 263 vehicles, 21 tractors, and 28 warehouses filled with supplies.[58] The Germans, however, left Novgorod a virtual wasteland, destroying 2,460 of 2,500 homes and most other installations and churches, and only 50 inhabitants were left in the city, the remainder having been shipped back to Germany.

Although Govorov's and Meretskov's *fronts* resoundingly smashed both flanks of the Eighteenth Army and threatened it with a general offensive from the Gulf of Finland to Lake Il'men', the *Stavka* was still not pleased with their progress. It duly noted a host of shortcomings in the 2d Shock, 42d, and 59th

Armies' operations and demanded they be corrected. Among the most serious of these deficiencies were poor exploitation of maneuver to bypass or envelop enemy strong points, lack of night combat, inadequate reconnaissance of German defenses, and ineffective command and control, particularly at army and corps levels.[59]

However dissatisfied it was, the *Stavka* took solace in the fact that, while the Leningrad and Volkhov Front were savaging the Eighteenth Army, Kuechler faced a new crisis on his southern flank. There a new Red Army offensive threatened to unhinge Army Group North's entire defense in the Leningrad region.[60] In late December Kuechler had ordered Busch's Sixteenth Army, then under attack north of Nevel', to begin withdrawing to new defenses west of Novosokol'niki. General M. M. Popov's 2d Baltic Front pursued, reached the new German defense line on 7 January, and launched a fresh offensive with Chibisov's 3d Shock Army and the 10th Guards Army, which was now commanded by Lieutenant General A. V. Sukhomlin, on 12 January. Two days later, he reinforced his assault with Lieutenant General V. A. Iushkevich's 22d Army. After Chibisov's 3d Shock Army failed in its assault toward Pustoshka, Popov regrouped his army westward to exploit the 10th Guards Army's success. After days of confused and heavy fighting and several regroupings, on 18 January, the 22d Army captured a narrow sector of the Leningrad-Nevel' rail line, where, on 20 January, it went on the defense.[61]

Although it was not dramatically successful, the 2d Baltic Front's offensive tied down the Sixteenth Army and prevented it from reinforcing the beleaguered Eighteenth Army at Leningrad and Novgorod. In fact, it forced Kuechler to send two security divisions and the bulk of the 290th Infantry Division to assist the Sixteenth Army.[62] Worse still, by seizing the Novosokol'niki-Dno rail line, the 22d Army severed the Germans' main lateral communications artery, endangering German forces in the Novosokol'niki and Staraia Russa regions. This would become an important factor in Kuechler's decision-making, as he soon faced new crises that threatened to unhinge both his Eighteenth and Sixteenth Armies' defenses.

THE LENINGRAD FRONT'S ADVANCE ON LUGA, 20–30 JANUARY

During the waning stages of Operation Neva (the Ropsha offensive), and the Novgorod operation, Govorov and Meretskov submitted revised plans to the *Stavka* for a continuation of the offensive. Their new objective was to destroy the bulk of the German Eighteenth Army and complete liberating the entire southern portion of the Leningrad region. The new plans required the Leningrad Front's armies to capture Krasnogvardeisk and Tosno, and the Volkhov

Front's armies to seize Chudovo and encircle and destroy the German XXVIII and XXXVIII Army Corps in the Mga, Tosno, and Liuban' regions. If successful, the joint operations would end the Leningrad blockade, defeat Eighteenth Army, and clear German forces from the southern half of Leningrad region.

Govorov ordered Maslennikov's 42d Army to capture Krasnogvardeisk, Pushkin, Slutsk, and Tosno to cut off German forces south and southeast of Leningrad and Fediuninsky's 2d Shock Army to attack southward to protect Maslennikov's right flank. Meretskov planned to continue his offensive toward Luga, cut the Pushkin-Dno and Krasnogvardeisk-Luga-Pskov railroads, and encircle and destroy German forces in the Mga, Liuban', and Chudovo regions in cooperation with Govorov's forces. He ordered Korovnikov's 59th Army to advance toward Luga and Oredezh against the German XXXVIII Army Corps while protecting the *front*'s left flank. At the same time, Roginsky's 54th Army would capture Liuban' and envelop the German XXVIII Army Corps from the north, and five partisan regiments would support his offensive and help capture Oredezh, Batetskii, Utorgosh, and Shimsk.

The two *fronts* resumed their offensives on 21 January with the Leningrad Front's 2d Shock and 42d Armies attacking toward Krasnogvardeisk and the Volkhov Front's 59th Army toward Luga. While the Eighteenth Army's L Army Corps desperately clung to its defenses around Krasnogvardeisk, late on 21 January, Kuechler flew to the Fuehrer's headquarters to demand some freedom of maneuver from Hitler. Early the next morning Kuechler informed Hitler that Krasnogvardeisk would fall unless Hitler permitted him to abandon Pushkin and Slutsk. Hitler categorically rejected Kuechler's pleas, stating, "I am against all withdrawals. We will have crises wherever we are. There is no guarantee we will not be broken through on the Panther line. If we go back voluntarily, he [the Russians] will not get there with only half of his forces. He must bleed himself white on the way. The battle must be fought as far as possible from the German border."[63] Kuechler countered that the army group would not even be able to hold on to the Panther Line if it were too weak to do so when it got there.

Hitler, however, was adamant. Blaming the gaps in the front on the egoism of his army group commanders and insisting every square yard of ground be sold at the highest possible price in Russian blood, he demanded the Rollbahn Line be held and sent Kuechler on his way. A resigned Kuechler withdrew his forces from Mga and Siniavino to the Rollbahn Line, sending the 227th Infantry Division and a portion of the 225th Infantry Division to shore up his defenses at Krasnogvardeisk. The OKH, which was apparently more concerned about the deteriorating situation than Hitler, sent Kuechler the 12th Panzer Division from Army Group Center and the 502d Heavy Tank Battalion from Sixteenth Army to employ in his defense of Krasnogvardeisk.[64]

While Hitler and Kuechler were meeting at the Fuehrer's headquarters, late on 21 January, the Leningrad Front's Intelligence Directorate detected the German partial withdrawal from Mga and Siniavino, and Govorov immediately ordered Sviridov's 67th Army to pursue and destroy German forces in the Mga region. Although Sviridov's forces failed to catch the withdrawing Germans, they occupied Mga at 1700 hours on 21 January. This occasioned a burst of enthusiasm among Leningraders:

> *Friday, 21 January.* Mga has fallen! Moscow saluted the Leningrad and Volkhov Fronts' forces, which liberated that hitherto little known station, in the name of the Motherland.
> How long have the Leningraders dreamed of its liberation! The last train to Leningrad passed through Mga on 27 August 1941. Two days later, on 29 August 1941, two Leningrad evacuation trains managed to pass through Mga to the east. Mga fell on 30 August, and Leningrad, which was deprived of its last railroad route, was in a serious situation. Repeated attempts to liberate Mga cost great loss of life but brought no success.
> And now Mga, which the Fascists had turned into a powerful defensive strong point, was free. The direct railroad line to the east was open![65]

Despite the success of Sviridov's army, Soviet after-action critiques faulted Major General V. K. Paramzin's 118th Rifle Corps for its slow reaction, stating that its forward detachment operated "slowly and indecisively" in its pursuit of the withdrawing Germans.[66] The following day, Govorov ordered Sviridov to capture Tosno and clear all enemy forces from their Rollbahn Line. On the morning of 23 January, Lindemann finally acknowledged the fact that the Rollbahn Line was, in fact, untenable by ordering his troops to begin evacuating Pushkin and Slutsk and reporting to OKH that "it could either accept his decision or send a general to replace him."[67] However, by the time the Eighteenth Army's forces had completed their withdrawal from Mga southward to the Rollbahn Line, Soviet forces had already penetrated the defense line in several places.

The German decision to withdraw to and beyond the Rollbahn Line forced Govorov and Meretskov to alter significantly their plans for a general offensive and pursuit along the entire front from the Gulf of Finland to Lake Il'men'. They did so in new plans they submitted to the *Stavka* early on 22 January.[68] Since it was no longer necessary for Maslennikov's 42d Army to capture Tosno, Govorov ordered Fediuninsky's 2d Shock Army and Maslennikov's army to attack toward Kingisepp and Bol'shoi Sabsk and reach the Luga River by 30 January. At the same time, Sviridov's 67th Army was to attack southward and westward to destroy German forces at Pushkin and Tosno, keeping pace with the two armies on its right flank. If successful,

Govorov's offensive would force the Germans to withdraw southward across the forested and swampy terrain north of Luga and walk straight into the arms of Meretskov's forces advancing on Luga from the east. Wasting no time, an impatient *Stavka* approved Govorov's plan with amendments later that same day.[69]

Meretskov's plan complemented the plan prepared by Govorov.[70] Meretskov ordered Korovnikov's 59th Army to capture Luga and Starikov's 8th Army, which up to now had been assigned only secondary missions, to capture Tosno and clear German forces from the remainder of the Rollbahn Line. Subsequently, Starikov was to transfer his forces to Roginsky's 54th Army and move his headquarters to the *front*'s left flank to take control of part of the 59th Army's forces attacking Luga. Finally, after capturing Liuban', Roginsky's 54th Army was to help capture Tosno and Ushaki and attack southwestward in support of Sviridov's 67th Army and southeastward toward Oredezh to strike the left flank of the German XXXVIII Army Corps as it withdrew westward from Chudovo. The *Stavka* approved Meretskov's plan on 22 January and ordered him to capture Liuban' no later than 23–24 January and Luga no later than 29 30 January.[71]

Meanwhile, Fediuninsky's 2d Shock Army began its pursuit on 21 January against skillful German rear guards' actions. Because Fediuninsky was unhappy with the pursuit, since his subordinate commanders often conducted frontal attacks on German strong points and utterly failed to employ maneuver, he issued a blistering series of rebukes to correct the errors and spur his forces on. For example, a 23 January barb read:

> You have not fulfilled your mission of the day on 23 January 1944. In spite of my orders, the army's formations continue to mark time in place in front of the severely damaged enemy forces, neither suffering casualties nor achieving decisive success. As has been the case before, the corps commanders are displaying slowness, are directing combat weakly, and not directing the corps to employ maneuver and decisive movement forward. Exploiting our slowness, the enemy, who is conducting cover force operations in small groups, is withdrawing his main forces south and southwest from Krasnogvardeisk and Elizavetino.[72]

Maslennikov's 42d Army was plagued by many of the same difficulties that dogged Fediuninsky. He too responded with similar exhortations for his commanders, including a scathing criticism he issued early on 22 February:

> 1. In essence, the rifle corps commanders are not influencing the course of battle either with fire or reserves. They are clearly organizing command and control of the corps formations in intolerable fashion. . . .

2. A significant portion of the artillery and mortars are not taking part in the battle and have not even been deployed but are instead sitting on the roads in march formation. Consequently, the rifle corps command-ers are fulfilling their missions only with infantry, which is intolerable.[73]

Despite the nagging problems, Maslennikov ordered his main shock group to assault German defenses around Krasnogvardeisk at 1300 hours on 22 Janu-ary, after a 15-minute artillery fire raid. At the time, the German L Army Corps was defending Krasnogvardeisk with its 11th and 170th Infantry Divisions and remnants of the 126th, 61st, 215th, and 225th Infantry Divisions, and Pushkin and Slutsk with the 215th Infantry Division and part of the 24th Infantry Division. German heavy artillery was positioned southeast of Kras-nogvardeisk, and the 12th Panzer Division and 502d Panzer Battalion were beginning to concentrate south and southwest of the town.[74]

Anisimov's 123d and Major General V. A. Trubachev's 117th Rifle Corps, the latter newly committed from *front* reserve, attacked Krasnogvardeisk proper, and Khazov's 110th Rifle Corps advanced southeast to envelop Push-kin and Slutsk from the west. Although Maslennikov's forces managed to encircle the German defenders at Pushkin and Slutsk from three sides by late on 23 January, they were unable to dislodge German forces from the Kras-nogvardeisk strong point. Nevertheless, the Leningrad war diary was ecstatic over the offensive's progress:

> *Sunday, 23 January.* The offensive toward Kingisepp is developing across a broad front. Our forces have enveloped the enemy grouping defending in the Pushkin and Pavlovka regions from three sides. The Volkhov Front's forces are advancing on Tosno, Liuban', and Chudovo. Kolpino has already ceased being a town on the front lines. However, one more enemy shell exploded on the grounds of the Izhorsk Factory, per-haps the last, the 8,942d by last count.
>
> *Monday, 24 January.* Aiming its attack at Pavlovka, Lieutenant Gen-eral I. V. Khazov's 110th Rifle Corps bypassed Pushkin. The enemy gar-rison in Pushkin is half encircled. The Hitlerites could not withstand the simultaneous attacks by our forces from the front and rear. Soon, Pushkin, Pavlovka, and more than 40 other populated points were liberated.
>
> Liberated. . . . What a joyous word! But how much incredible pain, how much blood, and how much bravery and selflessness did it take! . . .
>
> The front is moving farther and farther from Leningrad. The pealing thunder of the artillery cannonades no longer reaches Leningrad. The signs on the walls of buildings, which prohibited passage because "this side of the street is most dangerous during artillery shelling," have be-come history.[75]

Farther east, Sviridov's 67th Army captured Mga, but failed to capture Ul'ianovka, Tosno, and the sector of the Rollbahn Line between the two towns. A frustrated Govorov berated his army and corps commanders for operating too slowly and exercising poor command and control and unrealistic linear tactics.

Recriminations also resounded in German ranks as Kuechler accused Lindemann of submitting false estimates of Soviet reserves at the end of December, and Lindemann admitted that "mistakes" had been made.[76] Amid this exchange, bad news overwhelmed both senior German commanders as news reached them that Russian forces were on the outskirts of Krasnogvardeisk and had rammed through the bend of the Luga River southeast of Luga. Although Lindemann tried to patch up his front by throwing in rear-echelon troops, by day's end on 24 January, he grudgingly admitted that his right flank had lost contact with Sixteenth Army and that Krasnogvardeisk would fall within 24 hours. That night Kuechler once again asked Hitler for permission to withdraw at least to the Luga Defense Line, but Zeitzler at OKW informed Kuechler coldly that Hitler's orders were to hold the corner posts and make the troops fight to the last. Since there was nothing else to do for the time being, Zeitzler advised the army group command to be "a little ruthless" for a while.[77]

The forces of Fediuninsky's 2d Shock Army continued their advance along the Krasnogvardeisk-Kingisepp railroad on 24 January but recorded only modest progress against determined German resistance. On the same day, Govorov realigned his forces, reinforcing Maslennikov's 42d Army with Tikhonov's 108th Rifle Corps from Fediuninsky's 2d Shock Army and transferring Khazov's 110th Rifle Corps from Maslennikov's 42d to Sviridov's 67th Army. Over the next two days, Andreev's 43d and Alferov's 109th Rifle Corps, which were attacking on Fediuninsky's right flank, advanced up to 16 kilometers (9.9 miles), and Zaitsev's 122d and Tikhonov's 108th Rifle Corps, which were advancing on his left flank, captured Elizavetino and cut the Krasnogvardeisk-Kingisepp railroad. After reaching the railroad, on 27 January, Fediuninsky wheeled his army to the west and began pursuing the German XXVI Army Corps toward Kingisepp. Late that day he transferred Zaitsev's 122d Rifle Corps to Maslennikov's 42d Army.

While his defenses were crumbling all around him, at Hitler's direction Kuechler attended a National Socialist Leadership Conference at Konigsberg in East Prussia on 27 January. In between Hitler's speeches, which were exhorting faith in the cause as a guarantee of ultimate victory, Kuechler reiterated to Hitler the dire consequences should he not be permitted to conduct a general withdrawal. Hitler categorically prohibited all voluntary withdrawals and reserved the decision to withdraw for himself. The next day, Kuechler informed the conference attendees that his Eighteenth Army had lost 40,000 casualties, and that his troops had fought as hard as could be expected. Hitler replied caustically that Kuechler's statement was "not quite true."[78] Hitler added that he had heard that the army group was not fighting everywhere with as much determination as it might. Kuechler returned to his headquarters a broken man. While he knew that his forces had to retreat, all the thoroughly cowed commander could talk about was displaying more determination and attacking—with what, nobody knew.

Given Kuechler's apparent paralysis, Lieutenant General Eberhard Kinzel, his chief of staff, took matters into his own hands and notified Lindemann's chief of staff that the time had come. An order to retreat must be issued, but the army group was forbidden to do that. Therefore, the army would have to act as if it had been given, by issuing its own implementing orders orally rather than in writing. He, Kinzel, would see to it that the army was covered "in the General Staff channel."[79] Finally, on 29 January, Kinzel prevailed on Kuechler to at least report to Hitler that the Eighteenth Army was split into three parts and could not hold any kind of a front forward of the Luga River.

Acting on Kinzel's scheme, Lindemann began withdrawing his main forces on the night of 27–28 January, leaving rear guards to protect his retrograde movements. Regiments and battalions left behind battalion- and company-size rear guards reinforced by artillery and tanks, whose orders were to conduct delaying actions in villages and along the roads. The Germans destroyed or mined all bridges and roads in the region as they withdrew. The heaviest German rear-guard resistance was along the rail line toward Kingisepp on the Eighteenth Army's left flank.[80]

Capitalizing on the German withdrawal, Fediuninsky's forces accelerated their pursuit on 27 January, achieving an advance rate of 10–15 kilometers (6.2–9.3 miles) per day, and reached the Luga River on the 30th, where they seized small bridgeheads on the river's southern bank. At the same time, Anisimov's 123d and Trubachev's 117th Rifle Corps of Maslennikov's 42d Army pressed German forces back toward Krasnogvardeisk against noticeably dwindling resistance. On Maslennikov's left flank, Khazov's 110th Rifle Corps and the 79th Fortified Region captured Pushkin and Slutsk and a train carrying German tanks at Antropshino Station. Lindemann then began shifting his forces westward from Krasnogvardeisk in a desperate attempt to keep open his withdrawal routes to Kingisepp.

The Battle for Krasnogvardeisk proper began early on 25 January, when the assault forces of Maslennikov's 42d Army attacked German defenses after a 10-minute fire raid. Combat groups from the 126th Rifle, 225th Infantry, 9th *Luftwaffe* Field, and 11th and 215th Infantry Divisions defended the approaches to the German strong point.[81] Tikhonov's 108th Rifle Corps and Protsenko's 220th Tank Brigade had advanced 5 kilometers (3.1 miles) by day's end, cutting the rail line west of the town, but encountered a German infantry battalion with 15 antitank guns and a company of Tiger tanks, which brought their advance to an abrupt halt. The Leningrad war diary recorded the intense action:

> *Tuesday, 25 January.* Our forces are advancing on Gatchina [Krasnogvardeisk] in heavy fighting. The Hitlerites, who are defending there, have been enveloped from the west and east. Battle is raging on the outskirts of the town. . . .
>
> One can judge how the Germans in Gatchina feel from the words of a platoon commander in the 11th Infantry Division's 11th Sapper Battalion, who stated, "The Russians began a powerful attack against our flanks on the morning of 25 January. Attempts to organize a planned defense failed. The soldiers began to scatter. I tried to assemble my people but no one listened to me. They all ran away in a panic. I remained alone."[82]

After regrouping, Tikhonov's forces resumed their attacks and fought their way into the town's northwestern section just as Colonel A. V. Batluk's 120th Rifle Division of Trubachev's 117th Rifle Corps, which was advancing from the north, penetrated into the town's northeastern section. After an all-night battle, Batluk's forces captured Krasnogvardeisk at 1000 hours the following morning:

> *Wednesday, 26 January.* The battle for Gatchina did not cease throughout the night. The enemy 11th Infantry Division, which has been defending the city, has been destroyed. At 1100 hours Colonel A. V. Batluk's 120th Rifle Division, cooperating with Colonel F. A. Burmistrov's 224th Rifle Division and other units, completely cleared the occupiers from Gatchina.
>
> The liberation of Gatchina was not the only victory celebrated on this day. Our forces also expelled the enemy from Tosno and reached the Oktiabr' rail line northwest of Novgorod and the Leningrad-Dno rail line west of Novgorod.[83]

Maslennikov's army continued its advance over the next few days against dwindling resistance and captured the important German supply base at Volosovo, as German forces conducted a skillful delaying action. After advancing 50 kilometers (31 miles), Maslennikov's spearheads reached the Luga River on 30 January and captured several bridgeheads on the river's southern bank. Meanwhile Govorov once again shuffled his forces. At 1600 hours on 27 January, he transferred Zaitsev's 122d Rifle Corps from the 2d Shock Army to the 42d Army and Trubachev's 117th Rifle Corps from the 42d Army to the 67th Army.[84]

While Fediuninsky's and Maslennikov's armies were advancing toward the Luga River from the north, on the left flank of Govorov's Leningrad Front,

Sviridov's 67th Army advanced on Pushkin, Slutsk, and Tosno against stubborn German opposition. Paramzin's 118th Rifle Corps captured Ul'ianovka late on 24 January, and, after capturing Pushkin and Slutsk, Khazov's 110th Rifle Corps reached the Izhora River. However, here Sviridov halted his advance temporarily, wasting an excellent opportunity to encircle and destroy the German LIV Army Corps, which was still defending southeast of Slutsk. As the Germans accelerated their withdrawal southward, the 67th Army continued its advance, capturing Tosno and the western sector of the once formidable Rollbahn Line on 25–26 January.

Late on 26 January, Govorov once again scolded his army commanders for the slowness of their pursuit, regrouped his forces, and issued fresh orders. Govorov, personally, and other Soviet critiques note that Sviridov's army "failed to fulfill the *front* commander's demand to destroy the German forces in the Pushkin, Slutsk, Ul'ianovka, and Tosno regions and reach the Vyritsa-Lisino-Korpus line by 26 January because of weak command and control."[85] Late on 26 January, Govorov once again warned his army commanders, "Despite the absence of a continuous enemy front and the weak and fragmented enemy command and control, the armies' movement continues to be exceptionally slow. Rather than being encircled and destroyed, the enemy is being pushed back. The armies are repeating the same mistakes noted previously."[86] Having scolded Sviridov and transferred Trubachev's 117th Rifle Corps from the 42d to the 67th Army, Govorov then withdrew Lieutenant General A. N. Astanin's 116th Rifle Corps and Colonel P. S. Federov's 13th Rifle Division from Sviridov's army and placed them in *front* reserve.

Govorov's revised orders to Sviridov required his army to advance toward Siverskii and Luga, protect the 42d Army's right flank, and assist the Volkhov Front's forces in the destruction of the German XXVIII and XXXVIII Army Corps in the Liuban' and Chudovo region to the southeast. Sviridov's army resumed its pursuit on 27 January, but Trubachev's 117th Rifle Corps immediately encountered heavy resistance southeast of Krasnogvardeisk, where the L Army Corps and 12th Panzer Division were protecting the LIV, XXVI and XXVIII Army Corps' withdrawal from the Slutsk, Tosno, and Liuban' regions.

To the east, Khazov's 110th and Paramzin's 118th Rifle Corps captured their designated objectives, Vyritsa, Kaushta, and Lisino-Korpus, on 28 January and, after being relieved by the 14th Fortified Region on 29 January, Paramzin's corps reverted to *front* reserve in Pushkin. Khazov's and Trubachev's rifle corps finally overcame the stiff German resistance and captured Siverskii late on 30 January, albeit with considerable difficulty. Since both corps had only recently been assigned to the 67th Army, command and control of the corps' forces and coordination with army headquarters were poor at best. The experienced 12th Panzer Division and the remnants of the L and LIV Army

Corps' 212th, 126th, and 11th Infantry Divisions had dug into positions from southeast of Krasnogvardeisk to Siverskii, and it took three days of heavy fighting to expel them from the town.[87]

Despite the heavy fighting and slow Red Army advance, Govorov's three armies reached positions extending from along the Luga River in the west to south of Siverskii in the east by 30 January. By this time, the German Eighteenth Army's left flank and center were in full retreat, and the vital town of Luga was in Govorov's sights, only 80 kilometers (49.8 miles) to the south. However, his prospects for reaching the enticing target and trapping a significant portion of the Eighteenth Army in the process depended in large part on the progress of Meretskov's forces to the east. However, the advance by Meretskov's forces met neither Govorov's nor the *Stavka*'s high expectations.

THE VOLKHOV FRONT'S ADVANCE ON LUGA, 20–30 JANUARY

While Govorov's armies were advancing southwestward toward Kingisepp and southward toward Luga, Meretskov's three armies were advancing on Luga from the east and northeast. Starikov's 8th Army began its pursuit of the withdrawing German XXVI Army Corps early on 21 January, linked up with the 67th Army at Mga, and approached the Tosno and Ushaki sector of the Rollbahn Line late on 24 January. However, a single German infantry division delayed the advance by the army's main forces for several hours along the Mga River. Unbeknownst to Starikov's staff, the XXVI Corps' experienced 227th Infantry Division, which had been defending along the Mga River, had been transferred to Krasnogvardeisk, leaving only the 212th Infantry Division with 7,750 men to defend the corps' entire sector. Starikov's two rifle divisions and single rifle brigade, whose strength were only 13,167 men, were unable to overcome the German division in so formidable a defense.[88] After failing to exploit this opportunity, Starikov turned his forces and sector over to the 54th Army on the night of 24–25 January and moved with his headquarters to the *front*'s left wing, where he took control of forces operating on the 59th Army's left flank on 26 January.

On Starikov's left flank between Smerdynia and Spasskaia Polist', Roginsky's 54th Army had made only slight progress by 20 January, advancing only 3–5 kilometers (1.9–3.1 miles) against stiff enemy resistance. The 54th Army faced the German XXVIII Army Corps' 121st and 21st Infantry Divisions, the Spanish Legion, and combat groups from the SS Police and 12th and 13th *Luftwaffe* Field Divisions. The German corps had begun withdrawing its left flank on the night of 20–21 January, sending the SS Police Division southward to oppose the 59th Army, while the 21st Infantry and 13th *Luftwaffe*

Divisions continued defending along the Volkhov River near Chudovo opposite the 54th Army's left flank.[89] Over the next four days, the forces on Roginsky's right flank advanced 20 kilometers (12.4 miles) southward toward Liuban', but encountered stiffer German resistance along the Rollbahn Line.

In response to the increased German resistance, on 25 January Meretskov redesignated most of the forces of Starikov's 8th Army as the new 119th Rifle Corps, under Major General F. K. Fetisov's command, and assigned the corps to Roginsky's army. Roginsky's reinforced army resumed its advance overnight on 25–26 January, captured Tosno and Ushaki, and reached the railroad southeast of Liuban'. The next day, Lindemann withdrew the Spanish Legion from Liuban' to Luga and ordered the 121st Infantry Division, which was now enveloped from three sides, to abandoned Liuban'. When they captured Chudovo on 29 January, Roginsky's forces controlled the entire length of the Oktiabr' railroad, the main link between Moscow and Leningrad. Fearing encirclement after their loss of Liuban' and Chudovo, the XXVIII Army Corps accelerated its withdrawal toward Luga with the 54th Army in pursuit. This was a wise decision since a successful linkup by the 54th and 59th Armies would have encircled both the XXVIII and XXXVIII Army Corps northeast of Luga.

At this critical juncture, Korovnikov's 59th Army, which was still struggling west of the Volkhov River, posed the greatest threat to the XXVIII and XXXVIII Army Corps but only if the army could reach Luga and cut off the withdrawal routes of the two German corps. After capturing Novgorod and regrouping his army, Korovnikov resumed his offensive on 21 January through difficult terrain that required significant engineer support to surmount. The 59th Army's mission was to penetrate the Germans' second defensive belt before German reinforcements arrived, capture Batetskii, and advance to Luga from the east. To help overcome the treacherous terrain, Korovnikov provided significant engineer support to his 6th, 7th, and 112th Rifle Corps so that they could cross the roadless and heavily forested swampland spanning the entire region east of Luga.[90]

In accordance with Meretskov's new instructions to Korovnikov, Mikul'sky's 6th Rifle Corps was to attack westward through Batetskii to Luga, supported on the right by Solov'ev's 112th Rifle Corps. Artiushenko's 14th Rifle Corps, which was deployed on Korovnikov's left flank, was to attack southwestward toward Shimsk. Finally, Panin's 7th Rifle Corps, which had initially been in second echelon, was to fill the gaps between the 6th and 14th Rifle Corps and exploit to Peredol'skaia Station on the Leningrad-Dno rail line southeast of Luga. Meretskov reminded Korovnikov that his forces could cut off and destroy the two German corps withdrawing from the Tosno, Liuban', Chudovo, and Novgorod regions only if he advanced decisively. Despite Meretskov's orders, however, Korovnikov's advance quickly bogged down.

It did so because Kuechler understood the perils he faced and quickly reinforced the defenses at the junction of Busch's Sixteenth and Lindemann's Eighteenth Armies with combat groups drawn from other army group sectors. For example, by day's end on 21 January, Combat Group Schuldt defended the sector from Spasskaia Polist' to Tatino Station and protected the Finev Lug axis along which the XXVIII Army Corps was withdrawing from the Liuban'-Chudovo region. Group Schuldt consisted of the 2d SS Brigade, the 28th Jager Division, and the remnants of the 24th, 121st, and 21st Infantry Divisions. On Group Schuldt's right flank, Group Speth, made up of the 1st *Luftwaffe* Division and elements of Cavalry Regiment "Nord," defended the defile between the swamps from Zapol'e to Vashkovo. Finally, the 8th Jager Division defended from Izori to Lent'evo, and Group Feurguth, with the 290th Infantry Division and Cavalry Regiment "Nord's" main body, defended along the railroad from Novgorod to Shimsk.[91]

Since German reinforcements were likely to be weak and threadbare at best, Meretskov was convinced that, if he acted decisively, Korovnikov's 59th Army would be able to overcome the Germans' defenses rather easily. However, Mikul'sky's 6th Rifle Corps, which was still being supported by Bachakashvili's 29th Tank Brigade, failed to do so. Instead, the advance faltered badly on 24 January after only minimal gains. Soviet after-action reports noted that the 6th Rifle Corps was exhausted and woefully understrength from its earlier fighting, its accompanying 29th Tank Brigade had only eight of its tanks operational, and Mikul'sky's force was required to penetrate a prepared defense in thaw conditions.[92] Worse still, instead of committing Panin's fresh 7th Rifle Corps along the Batetskii axis, Korovnikov ordered it to advance southward toward Shimsk and Peredol'skaia Station, a decision that overextended his army and ultimately resulted in the agonizingly slow progress along the Luga axis.

Subsequently, Korovnikov's advance turned into a slugfest in difficult terrain as the troops waded forward in waist-deep water, with their supporting tanks and artillery lagging far behind. An increasingly distraught Meretskov demanded Korovnikov concentrate his forces and capture Luga no later than 29–30 January, but despite Meretskov's entreaties, Mikul'sky's 6th Rifle Corps made little progress in four days of heavy fighting along the Batetskii-Luga railroad. Meretskov bitterly criticized Korovnikov for his army's slow advance, noting, in particular, that the 112th and 6th Rifle Corps failed to maneuver properly, made little use of their ski battalions, paid scant attention to adequate reconnaissance, and, when they encountered German strong points, frequently resorted to frontal attacks. By late on 26 January, Mikul'sky's rifle corps had finally penetrated the Germans' second defensive line and reached the Luga River, but only by committing its second echelon.[93]

While Mikul'sky's rifle corps was advancing toward Luga at a snail's pace, the 7th and 14th Rifle Corps made appreciably greater progress on the 59th Army's left flank. Korovnikov had assigned Panin's 7th Rifle Corps the mission of attacking at the junction of the 6th and 14th Rifle Corps, penetrating German defenses, and capturing Peredol'skaia Station to sever German communications between Luga and Shimsk. Supported by Major General B. I. Shneider's 7th Guards Tank Brigade, which had just been committed from *front* reserve, Colonel A. G. Koziev's 256th Rifle Division of Panin's corps conducted a rapid dash through the swamps and reached the outskirts of Peredol'skaia Station late on 27 January. Throughout its advance, Koziev's force cooperated closely with the nearby 5th Partisan Brigade.

At the same time, on Koziev's left flank, Major General P. N. Chernyshev's 382d Rifle Division captured Medved' from the 8th Jager Division and cut the Luga-Shimsk road. Farther to the south, Artiushenko's 14th Rifle Corps and Urvanov's 16th Tank Brigade cleared German forces from the western shores of Lake Il'men', reaching the outskirts of Shimsk late on 26 January. By this time, Panin's corps had penetrated the Germans' entire second defensive belt, had advanced up to 35 kilometers (21.7 miles) to the west and southwest in five days, and threatened to cut the Leningrad-Dno railroad in the Peredol'skaia region.

Since Meretskov had not anticipated advancing this far south, he ordered his 150th Fortified Region to take over the defense of the Shimsk sector and Artiushenko's 14th Rifle Corps to wheel northeast and reinforce the 6th Rifle Corps attack on Luga by deploying on Mikul'sky's right flank. To resolve the increasingly perplexing command and control difficulties he faced, Meretskov ordered Starikov's 8th Army to take control of all of the forces on the 59th Army's left (and his *front's*) left flank.[94] In its new configuration, Starikov's army included the 7th and 14th Rifle Corps, the 7th Guards, 122d, and 16th Tank Brigades, and the 150th Fortified Region. Thus, when the 59th Army resumed its offensive toward Luga on 27 January, it included only the 6th and 112th Rifle Corps and the 29th Tank Brigade.

Govorov ordered Korovnikov to capture Batetskii and Oredezh to the north and then Luga no later than 29–30 January. He ordered a single rifle division, Luk'ianov's 2d Rifle Division, to provide protection on his right flank. At the same time, on Korovnikov's left flank, Starikov's 8th Army was to capture Peredol'skaia Station, Utorgosh, and Pliussa, envelop Luga from the south and southeast, and capture Luga in conjunction with the 59th Army's assault. Although the redeployment of Starikov's 8th Army was designed to shorten the 59th Army's front significantly and ease the problem of command and control, it did not do so.

When Korovnikov resumed his advance on 27 January, Mikul'sky's 6th Rifle Corps seized a small bridgehead over the Luga River but then utterly stalled east of Batetskii. Meanwhile, in three days of heavy fighting, Solov'ev's 112th Rifle Corps fought its way across the Luga River, reaching to within 18 kilometers (11.2 miles) of Oredezh on 30 January. However, Luk'ianov's 2d Rifle Division, which was advancing on Solov'ev's right flank, did not have sufficient strength to keep pace. Lacking reserves with which to reinforce the single division, Korovnikov permitted the XXVIII Army Corps to escape from the Chudovo region. It was still possible, however, for the 112th Rifle Corps to block the German withdrawal, but only if Solov'ev's corps could capture Oredezh in a timely fashion, because the XXVIII Army Corps had to use the Oredezh-Luga road for its withdrawal, partisans having blown up the nearby rail line.[95]

Korovnikov's failure to reach and capture Luga meant that a successful advance on Luga rested in the hands of Starikov's 8th Army. However, before fulfilling the missions assigned to him by Meretskov, Starikov had to capture Peredol'skaia Station, which was no mean task. Although Panin's 7th Rifle Corps and the 5th Partisan Brigade had captured Peredol'skaia Station early on 27 January, thereafter the station changed hands three times in heavy fighting as the Germans threw fresh reserves into the battle. The Germans committed, first, the 285th Security Division and, later, part of the 12th Panzer Division into the fighting at Peredol'skaia Station, forcing Starikov to commit all of his reserves.[96] Worse still, Mikul'sky's 6th Rifle Corps lagged far behind, forcing Panin's 7th Corps to defend its overextended right flank by weakening its forces attacking toward Peredol'skaia Station. Although Panin's corps managed to advance several more kilometers westward by 30 January and cut the Leningrad-Dno railroad, Starikov's army failed to accomplish its priority mission and Luga remained firmly in German hands.

Since the 59th and 8th Armies' slow advance toward Luga threatened to disrupt its overall plan of cutting off and destroying all German forces north and east of Luga, the *Stavka* demanded that Meretskov's forces cut the road and railroad south of Luga no later than 30–31 January. The *Stavka* sent a directive to that effect to Meretskov at 2400 hours on 29 January:

> The enemy's grouping, which is operating in front of the Leningrad Front's left wing and the Volkhov Front's right wing, is withdrawing toward Luga and Pskov. Meanwhile, the offensive by the Volkhov Front's main grouping along the Luga axis is developing slowly, and the *Stavka*'s demand to capture Luga no later than 29–30 January is not being fulfilled.
>
> The *Stavka* of the Supreme High Command *orders:*
>
> 1. Direct the *front*'s main forces to capture Luga as quickly as possible. Mobile units will cut the highway and railroad south of Luga no later than 30–31 January. The *front*'s left wing will dig in firmly along the Utorgosh

and Shimsk line in order to protect the main force's operations toward Luga.

2. After occupying Luga, anticipate conducting an offensive toward Pskov from the Luga and Shimsk regions.

3. Report all orders given.

[signed] I. Stalin, A. Antonov[97]

Within a matter of hours, the *Stavka* had sent another enjoinder to Meretskov: "Do not engage in battle for Shimsk and Sol'tsy. It is not the main effort. Cover along that axis. The main thing is to capture Luga as quickly as possible. Upon capturing Luga deploy for an advance on Pskov along two axes."[98] It then reinforced Meretskov's *front* with 15,000 replacements and 130 tanks. However, despite being reinforced, Meretskov's forces failed to accomplish the new mission. Subsequent General Staff critiques later attributed Meretskov's failure to the *front*'s lack of concentration, poor terrain and weather conditions, extended supply lines, lack of effective air support due to bad weather, the artillery's inability to keep up with the infantry, and excessive tank losses. For example, Meretskov's four supporting tank brigades and four self-propelled regiments had only 19 tanks and 4 guns operational on 2 February, and his seven separate tank regiments and five separate tank battalions were in the same state.[99]

While Govorov and Meretskov's forces were plodding forward toward Kingisepp and Luga, Popov's 2d Baltic Front was preparing to mount a new offensive against the Sixteenth Army, which was defending on Army Group North's right flank, to support Meretskov's offensive to the north. After halting his earlier offensive north and west of Novosokol'niki in mid-January, Popov regrouped his forces and prepared a new offensive. Popov shifted the 10th Guards Army to new positions southwest of Novosokol'niki and prepared to attack with the 6th and 10th Guards Armies and part of the 22d Army.[100] However, the Sixteenth Army detected the attack preparations, withdrew from Novosokol'niki on 30 January, and occupied new defenses to the northwest. The 22d and 10th Guards Armies pursued but halted before the new German defenses. The 2d Baltic Front's inactivity and feeble pursuit allowed the Sixteenth Army to dispatch reinforcements to the Eighteenth Army's right flank, which helped to halt the 8th and 59th Armies' advance on Luga. These transfers included the 8th Jager Division, part of the 21st *Luftwaffe* Field Division, two battalions of the 32d and 132d Infantry Divisions, the 303d Assault Gun Battalion, and the 58th Infantry Division, all of which deployed from the Sixteenth Army's right flank.[101]

The Leningrad war diary properly celebrated the complete liberation of the city on 27 January:

Thursday, 27 January. The liberation of Leningrad from the enemy blockade has been completed!

The enemy has been thrown back 65–100 kilometers along the entire front.

Moscow gave Leningrad the honor of saluting the great victory. The Leningrad Military Council rather than the Supreme High Command signed the order concerning the salute. . . .

At 2000 hours in the city, on whose streets enemy shells were exploding five days ago, 24 volleys resounded from 324 guns. Despite the still existing light discipline, the skies blazed with fireworks.

The volleys of the Leningrad salute summoned forth joy in the hearts of millions of people around the entire world.

The English newspaper *Star* noted, "All free peoples and all peoples enslaved by the Hitlerites understand what a role the destruction of German forces around Leningrad played in the weakening of Nazi power. For a long time, Leningrad has already won for itself a place among hero-cities of the present war. The battle for Leningrad has sown alarm among the Germans. It makes them feel that they are only the temporary owners of Paris, Brussels, Amsterdam, Warsaw, and Oslo."

The newspaper *New York Times* wrote, "One can hardly find in history such an example of such endurance, which the Leningraders have displayed for such a prolonged time. Their exploits will be recorded in the annals of history as their own sort of heroic myth. . . . Leningrad embodies the invincible spirit of the Russian people."[102]

In over two weeks of heavy combat, Govorov's and Meretskov's forces penetrated German defenses along the entire front from the Gulf of Finland to Lake Il'men', inflicting a major defeat on the Eighteenth Army. While doing so, their forces drove German forces 100 kilometers (62 miles) south and southwest of Leningrad and 80 kilometers (49.7 miles) west from Novgorod and cleared German forces from the main rail line between Moscow and Leningrad. However, Meretskov's forces failed to capture Luga by 30 January, and, because of that failure, Lindemann managed to withdraw his L, LIV, and XXVI Army Corps relatively intact from the Leningrad and Mga regions and safely extract his XXVIII and XXXVIII Army Corps from the Chudovo, Liuban', and Novgorod regions. While Kuechler succeeded in establishing a new defense line protecting Luga and his vital withdrawal route to Pskov, the Red Army had once and for all raised the blockade of Leningrad and placed the entire Eighteenth Army in jeopardy.

The Red Army performed several noteworthy feats during the Ropsha and Novgorod operations and the initial advance toward Luga. First, it secretly moved the 2d Shock Army into the Oranienbaum bridgehead without producing undo German concern. It then conducted simultaneous offensives 200 kilometers (124.2 miles) apart against the flanks of the Eighteenth Army, utterly smashing Lindemann's defenses south of Leningrad proper. During the initial stages of these operations, the twin offensives encompassed a front of 400 kilometers (248.5 miles) and Red Army forces advanced to a depth of 100 kilometers (62.1 miles) in a period of 16 days, for an average advance rate of 6.2 kilometers (3.9 miles) per day. Shock groups concentrated on 10–12 percent of the front conducted the penetration operations, and the two *fronts* employed second echelons and reserves and frequent regroupings to sustain the offensives into the operational depths.

While Govorov's and Meretskov's offensives achieved their initial aims, they did so with considerable difficulty, and they failed to achieve their ultimate objectives. Their forces were plagued by a variety of problems that had hindered earlier Red Army offensive operations in the region. While superb on the defense, neither Govorov's nor Meretskov's forces were accustomed to conducting deep offensive operations. They had learned enough from their previous failures to enable them to mount a successful penetration operation; however, once the penetration operations were complete, commanders at every level found it difficult to organize proper command and control, cooperation between the infantry, artillery, armor, and engineers, and adequate logistical support. In fairness, many of these difficulties resulted from the difficult terrain and terrible weather conditions in which Govorov and Meretskov consciously chose to operate.

When all was said and done, however, despite its slow development, the offensive put Army Group North's Eighteenth Army "on the ropes." German defenses had successfully resisted the rising Red Army tide for over two years, but in January 1944 the tide broke over them and literally swept them away. Given the scope of the ensuing damage to Army Group North, it was unlikely that the army group could stem the mounting Red tide. Nor did the *Stavka* grant Kuechler and Lindemann any time to ponder that prospect. Without any pause whatsoever, Govorov's and Meretskov's forces resumed their offensive on 31 January, driven on by a *Stavka* whose intent was nothing short of driving German forces out of the Leningrad region and into the Baltic republics.

K. A. Meretskov, Commander, Volkhov Front *(left)*; F. P. Ozerov, *Front* Chief of Staff; and G. E. Degtiarev, *Front* Chief of Artillery, work on the Volkhov Front's plan for the January 1944 offensive

A. I. Eremenko, Commander, 2d Baltic Front; L. M. Sandalov, *Front* Chief of Staff; A. P. Pigurov, Chief, *Front* Political Department; and V. N. Bogatkin, *Front* Commissar, at the *front's* command post *(right to left)*

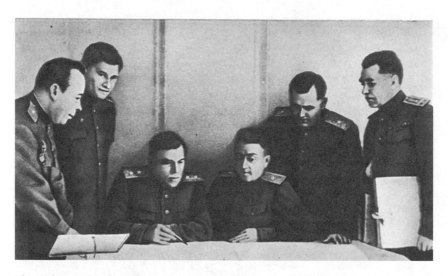

The 59th Army's Military Council: N. P. Koval'chuk, Chief of Staff; Ia. G. Poliakov, Commissar; I. T. Korovnikov, Army Commander; P. S. Lebedev, Commissar; and A. G. Korolev, Chief, Army Political Department *(left to right)*

The Leningrad Front's armor on the attack, January 1944

The 42d Army's 123d Rifle Corps assaults German defenses at Krasnoe Selo,
January 1944

Major General N. P. Simoniak, Commander, 30th Guards Rifle Corps, at his observation
post prior to the January 1944 offensive *(second from left)*

Troops of the 2d Shock and 42d Armies link up near Ropsha, January 1944

German destruction of the main hall in the Catherine Palace in Pushkin, January 1944

Leningrad Front submachine gunners entering the outskirts of Luga, February 1944

Leningrad Front soldiers burn a German road sign, January 1944

CHAPTER 12

To Narva, Luga, and the Panther Line

31 January–18 April 1944

THE SITUATION ON 31 JANUARY 1944

The Red Army's victory south of Leningrad and at Novgorod in January 1944 was an ominous portent for Adolf Hitler and his beleaguered *Wehrmacht*. It was by no means surprising that the Red Army would conduct yet another massive winter offensive, since, based on the experiences of 1941–1942 and 1942–1943, the Red Army had literally "owned" the winter. What was disconcerting to the Germans was the fact that the Soviet offensives were developing across so broad a front and were achieving such notable success.

Although it had attempted to accomplish more, during past winters the Red Army had achieved strategic success along only one strategic axis and forfeited many of its territorial gains to counterattacking German forces later in the spring. In the winter of 1941–1942 the Kalinin, Western, and Southwestern Fronts had driven German forces back from the approaches to Moscow, generating a genuine crisis in Army Group Center. However, the crisis had passed by late February, when the *Wehrmacht* was able to stabilize the front and even prepare a fresh strategic offensive for the summer. Worse still from the *Stavka*'s perspective, during late winter 1941–1942, defending German forces were able to parry the Soviets' blows along secondary axes and inflict serious damage on the attacking Soviet forces, particularly in the Leningrad region.

During the winter of 1942–1943, the Red Army prevailed along the southern axis, inflicting grievous losses on Axis forces, including the near-complete destruction, first, at Stalingrad, of three Axis armies, and, later, south of the Don River, two more. Despite the Red Army's initial signal successes, when the *Stavka* tried to convert its advance in southern Russia into a general offensive across the entire German Eastern Front in February and March 1943, the entire venture failed, largely due to Manstein's brilliant counteroffensive in the south.

Unlike the situation during the previous two winters, during the winter of 1943–1944, the *Stavka* planned and orchestrated strategic offensives that spanned the entire front. While the Leningrad and Volkhov Fronts savaged Army Group North's Eighteenth Army and raised the Leningrad blockade, the 1st Baltic, Western, and Belorussian Fronts pounded German defenses in Belorussia from west of Nevel' and Vitebsk in the north to east of Bobruisk in the south. At the same time, the 1st and 2d Ukrainian Fronts burst from their strategic-size bridgeheads across the Dnepr River, pressing German forces back through Zhitomir and Kirovograd to the approaches to Vinnitsa and Krivoi Rog. By 30 January the attacking Soviet *fronts* were enveloping and preparing to destroy German forces defending the last remaining sector of their vaunted Eastern Wall along the Dnepr River, the Korsun'-Shevchenkovskii salient. Simultaneously, the 3d and 4th Ukrainian Fronts repeatedly attacked over-extended German defenses north and south of Nikopol' at the tip of the great bend in the Dnepr River.

As January ended, the *Stavka* ordered its *fronts* to pursue their offensives relentlessly, in yet another attempt to collapse irrevocably German defenses in the East.[1] The 1st, 2d, and 3d Ukrainian Fronts, which were operating along the priority strategic axis, were to crush German defenses in the Ukraine and advance to the Polish and Rumanian borders, while the 4th Ukrainian and North Caucasus Fronts liberated the Crimea. To the north, the 1st Baltic and Belorussian Fronts were to liberate Minsk and complete the conquest of Belorussia. Finally, unlike previous winters, Soviet forces in the Leningrad region had every reason to believe that their offensive could complete the liberation of the Leningrad region and even pierce the Germans' Baltic defenses. For the first time in the war, the Germans lacked the confidence that they could prevent the Red Army from doing so. Nor would the Germans benefit from any operational pause between the disastrous events of January and Red Army actions in February.

CONTENDING PLANS AND MODEL'S SHIELD AND SWORD THEORY

At the end of January, the Leningrad Front's 2d Shock and 42d Armies were poised along the Luga River, prepared to advance on Narva, the gateway to the Baltic region, from the east, and the *front*'s 67th Army had advanced halfway from Leningrad toward Luga from the north and northwest. The Volkhov Front's 59th and 8th Armies were threatening Luga from the east, and its 54th Army was advancing on Oredezh and Luga from the northeast. A genuine opportunity existed for the two *fronts* to encircle and destroy the bulk of the Eighteenth Army north and northeast of Luga (Map 17).

Faced with impending disaster, Kuechler, who was still in command of Army Group North, once again visited with Hitler's headquarters in East Prussia on 30 January and finally received the Fuehrer's permission to withdraw Lindemann's Eighteenth Army to the Luga River Defense Line. However, with his customary obstinacy, Hitler ordered the nearly distraught

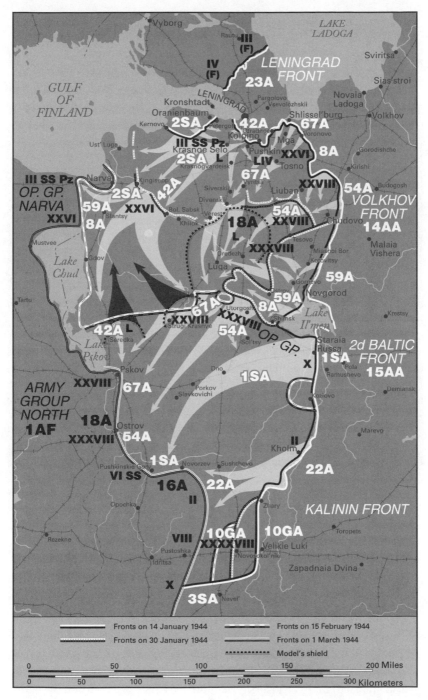

Map 17. The Soviet Leningrad-Novgorod Offensive, January–April 1944

Kuechler to hold the Luga Line, regain communications with his Sixteenth Army, which Meretskov's forces had disrupted, and close up all gaps in the front. When Kuechler passed this information to his operations officer (Ia), the latter protested to the OKH's Operations Branch that it was simply impossible to execute these orders. By this time, he said, one of the gaps in the army group's defenses was 50 kilometers (31.1 miles) wide, and the Russians were already across the Luga River at Staritsa northwest of Luga. Zeitzler later agreed to inform Hitler that the Eighteenth Army could not hold the Luga Line.

At noon the next day, Hitler relieved Kuechler of his command, replacing him with Field Marshal Walter Model. Model, a former panzer division, panzer corps, and army commander who had helped save German Army Group Center from encirclement in early 1942, had long served as Hitler's "fireman," handling crises in seemingly irreparable situations. Always the fighter, Model telegraphed ahead to his new headquarters, "Not a single step backward will be taken without my express permission. I am flying to Eighteenth Army this afternoon. Tell General Lindemann that I beg his trust in me. We have worked together before."[2]

What the compulsive Model did not realize was that the Eighteenth Army was a shell of its former self. After being driven back a significant distance during the last few days of January, its front was a shambles, and the attrition rate among its forces had risen alarmingly. The only relatively intact divisions at Model's disposal were the 12th Panzer, which had just returned to the region in late January, and the 58th Infantry, which was moving in from the south by train. On 29 January the army group reported that the Eighteenth Army had an infantry combat strength of 57,936 men as of 10 January. Since that time, it had lost 35,000 wounded and 14,000 killed and, including new arrivals, now had an infantry strength of 17,000 men.[3] As Earl Ziemke has noted:

> Model had never had a greater opportunity to display his talent as an improviser, and he took it with flamboyant zest which, though it did not change the tactical situation, quickly dispelled the sense of hopelessness and frustration that had been hanging over the army group. He also had the advantage of Hitler's tendency to give new appointees, particularly when they were also his favorites, greater latitude, at least temporarily, than he had allowed their predecessors.

Model's first moves were as much psychological as military. To dissipate what he called the PANTHER psychosis he forbade all references to the PANTHER position and abolished the designation. Past experience had shown that in times of adversity, named lines, particularly when the names suggested strength, had a powerful attraction for both troops and commands. On the other hand, the state of Eighteenth Army being what it was, Model could not attempt to enforce his original "no step backward" order.

Instead, he introduced something new, the *Schild und Schwert* [shield and sword] theory, the central idea of which was that withdrawals were tolerable if one intended to strike back in the same or a different direction in a kind of parry and thrust sequence. The theory was apparently Hitler's latest brainchild, a remedy for—as he viewed it—the disease of falling back to gain troops to build a new defense line which in a short time would itself prove too weak to be held.

That Model placed overly much faith in the theory may be doubted. He was enough of a realist to know that while the withdrawal was usually possible the counter-thrust was not. On the other hand, he was also well enough acquainted with Hitler to know that it was always advantageous to make a retreat look more like the first stage of an advance.[4]

The *Stavka* had no intention of giving Model the respite his army group so desperately required. Instead, on 29 January and 1 February, respectively, the *Stavka* ordered Govorov and Meretskov to smash German resistance on the Luga River and completely destroy the Eighteenth Army:

The enemy grouping, which is operating against the Leningrad Front's left wing and the Volkhov Front's right wing, is withdrawing toward Luga and Pskov. Meanwhile, the offensive by the Volkhov Front's main grouping toward Luga is developing slowly, and the *Stavka*'s demand that you capture Luga no later than 29–30 January is not being fulfilled..

The *Stavka* of the Supreme High Command *orders:*

1. Direct [the efforts] of the *front*'s main forces on the capture of Luga as rapidly as possible. Cut the highway and railroad south of Luga with mobile units no later than 30–31 January. The *front*'s left wing will dig in firmly along the Utorgosh' and Shimsk line and protect the main forces' operation toward Luga.

2. After capturing Luga, anticipate an offensive from the Luga and Shimsk regions toward Pskov.

3. Report orders given.

[signed] I. Stalin, A. Antonov[5]

The *Stavka* of the Supreme High Command *orders*

1. Establish the following boundary line between the Leningrad and Volkhov Fronts no later than 2400 hours 1 February: Chudovo, Chashcha Station, Mshinskaia, Volosovo, Zovka, the mouth of the Chernaia River, Pel'va, and Ainazhi (all points inclusive for the Leningrad Front).

2. Immediately transfer the 124th Rifle Corps, on the 54th Army's left flank, from the Volkhov Front to the Leningrad Front. Transfer the 124th Rifle Corps with the 18th, 80th, and 17th Rifle Divisions and all corps units and existing reserves. The Volkhov Front will supply the corps until 5 February.

3. The Leningrad Front's most immediate mission is to move rapidly into and capture the Mshinskaia Station region and capture Luga as quickly as possible to assist the Volkhov Front's right wing. After seizing the Mshinskaia Station region, withdraw the 67th Army into *front* reserve in the Volosovo and Kingisepp region.

4. Report on the corps' transfer and arrival.

[signed] I. Stalin, A. Antonov[6]

Simultaneously, the *Stavka* transferred Chibisov's 1st Shock Army, which was deployed in the Staraia Russa region on the 2d Baltic Front's right flank, to Meretskov's *front* in order to concentrate more power for his thrust toward Luga:

In connection with the advance of the Volkhov Front's left wing, the *Stavka* of the Supreme High Command *orders:*

1. Transfer the 1st Shock Army with four rifle divisions, one rifle brigade, and all of its existing reinforcing units, army rear service units and installations, and on-hand reserves from the 2d Baltic Front to the Volkhov Front, effective 2400 hours 2 February 1944.

2. From this time, establish the following boundary line between the Volkhov and 2d Baltic Front: Bologoe, Molvotitsy, Gubino, Dolgaia, Zhemchugova, Sokolovo, the mouth of the Sorot' River, Tilzha, and Pliavinas (on the Western Dvina). All points, besides Bologoe, are inclusive for the Volkhov Front.

3. Report the transfer and arrival of the army.

[signed] I. Stalin, A. Antonov[7]

Accordingly, on 29 January, Govorov ordered Fediuninsky's 2d Shock and Maslennikov's 42d Armies to force the Luga River, clear enemy forces from the southern coast of the Gulf of Finland, reach the Narva River, and capture bridgeheads on the river's western bank. Sviridov's 67th Army was to attack southward to cooperate with the Volkhov Front in the capture of Luga. Subsequently, Govorov's main forces were to concentrate north of Lake Chud and begin an advance into Estonia.

However, Meretskov's tardiness in capturing Luga and wheeling the Volkhov Front's forces westward toward Pskov forced Govorov to revise his *front*'s missions. On 1 February he ordered Maslennikov's 42d Army to advance southward west of Luga on the 67th Army's right flank to prevent the Germans from shifting forces from the Pskov and Luga axes to Narva. While protecting the left flank of Fediuninsky's army, Maslennikov's army was to advance southward east of Lake Chud to support the Volkhov Front's assault on Luga from the northeast and east. After the Volkhov Front's and 67th Army's forces captured Luga and wheeled westward toward Pskov, Maslennikov's forces were to complete clearing German forces east of Lake Chud and prepare to attack westward between Lakes Chud and Pskov.[8]

THE STRUGGLE FOR NARVA AND LUGA, 31 JANUARY–15 FEBRUARY

The First Battle for Narva

Initially at least, Fediuninsky's 2d Shock Army made rapid progress westward toward Narva. After conducting a 15-minute artillery preparation, Alferov's 109th Rifle Corps assaulted and captured Kingisepp on 1 February. Simultaneously, the army's 43d and 122d Rifle Corps advanced toward the Narva River, where they began forcing the river north and south of the key fortress-city of Narva, which dominated the narrow gateway to Estonia. Andreev's 43d Rifle Corps of Fediuninsky's army seized two bridgeheads across the river on the army's right flank north of Narva on 1 February, and two days later Zaitsev's 122d Rifle Corps seized two additional bridgeheads south of the city.

On 3 February, Govorov rewarded Fediuninsky for his capture of the Neva River bridgeheads by transferring Simoniak's 30th Guards Rifle Corps to his army.[9] At the same time, Govorov ordered Fediuninsky's army to widen and deepen the bridgeheads across the Narva River, penetrate German defenses west of the river, envelop Narva from the north and south and, subsequently, prepare to attack deeper into Estonia. Govorov then ordered Tributs's Baltic Fleet to support Fediuninsky's advance by conducting an amphibious landing with the 115th and 260th Naval Infantry Brigades northwest of Narva to capture and hold on to the railroad west of the city until relieved by the 2d Shock Army's forces.

Meanwhile, on 1 February, Model issued his first "shield and sword" directive to his Eighteenth Army. The directive ordered Lindemann to withdraw his main force back to a shorter defense line protecting Luga from the north and east and to close the gap between the Eighteenth and Sixteenth Armies with the 12th Panzer Division. After doing so, the 12th Panzer and 58th Infantry Divisions, and whatever other forces could be assembled, were to move to the west of Luga and attack northwestward along the Luga River to reestablish contact with the two German corps fighting in isolation at Narva. Model's order reduced the Eighteenth Army's frontage by two-thirds, released some forces to participate in the counterstroke, and, at least in theory, postulated use of the "sword" to counterattack and extend the front 80 kilometers (49.7 miles) to the west.[10]

However, in practice, it was next to impossible to apply the "shield and sword" on the Eighteenth Army's left flank because the LIV Army and III SS Panzer Corps, which were now commanded by General of Infantry Otto Sponheimer, the LIV Corps commander, had already fallen back from the Oranienbaum pocket to the Narva River line. They could fall back no farther without endangering the viability of the entire Panther Line.

Model inspected the III SS Panzer Corps' front on 2 February, just as Sponheimer's divisions were withdrawing to the river's western bank and a small bridgehead on the east bank of the river opposite Narva itself. Before day's end, the Russians had captured several small bridgeheads across the river. Elements of the Panzer Grenadier Division "Feldherrnhalle" from Army Group Center and a single regiment of the 58th Infantry Division were just arriving to strengthen the front south of Narva. Although everyone told Model the troops were worn out, he insisted they endure. In fact, as Ziemke has noted, "The near collapse of Eighteenth Army at the end of January had had the effect of a temporary disengagement, at least in places, as on the Narva River. Model's decision to close up to the front around Luga gave the army a chance to maneuver and to catch its breath."[11]

The Eighteenth Army's chance was, however, only temporary. Now reinforced to nearly twice its original size, Fediuninsky's 2d Shock Army struggled for a week to destroy the German forces protecting Narva and to widen its bridgeheads across the river. At the same time, Fediuninsky regrouped his forces for a general offensive into Estonia. In addition to outflanking the Panther Line from the north, a successful Soviet advance into Estonia would pose an immediate threat to vital shale oil refineries on the Estonian coast only 32 kilometers (20 miles) to the west.

After Govorov approved Fediuninsky's offensive plan with slight amendments, on 11 February his forces attacked with little success. Attacking northwest of the city, Andreev's 43d Rifle Corps advanced up to 2 kilometers (1.2 miles) along a 4-kilometer (2.5-mile) front but was halted by heavy resistance from the III SS Panzer Corps' 227th Infantry Division and the SS "Nederland" Brigade. Southwest of the city, Alferov's 109th and Zaitsev's 122d Rifle Corps advanced 12 kilometers (7.5 miles) to the west and northwest in five days of heavy fighting but were also halted by the SS "Nordland" Division, 170th Infantry Division, and Panzer Grenadier Division "Feldherrnhalle."

Simoniak's veteran 30th Guards Rifle Corps, however, achieved greater success when it cut the railroad and road running from Narva to Iykhvi on 15 February and captured Auvere on 17 February. However, it too then halted after Division "Feldherrnhalle" counterattacked. On the coast north of

Auvere, an ambitious amphibious landing by elements of the 115th and 260th Naval Infantry Brigades on the night of 13–14 February also failed when the 432 men who managed to land lost communications with the fleet and, hence, all of their fire support. German Combat Groups Berlin and Luczny subsequently destroyed the small amphibious force in four days of fighting.[12] However, during the struggle German "Stukas . . . bombed a German headquarters and knocked out several Tiger tanks." Model himself described the operation as "not pretty."[13] During the heavy but fruitless Soviet assaults, on 8 February, Govorov criticized the 2d Shock Army's staff for faulty reconnaissance, poor artillery fire planning, inadequate organization of combat formations at corps and division level, and poor organization of armor, engineer, antiaircraft, and logistical support. Subsequent combat in the region indicated that Fediuninsky's staff never really solved these shortcomings.[14]

At 2335 hours on 14 February, an obviously frustrated *Stavka* demanded that Govorov capture Narva at all cost no later than 17 February:

It is mandatory that our forces seize Narva no later than 17 February 1944. This is required both for military as well as political reasons. It is the most important thing right now.

I demand that you undertake all necessary measures to liberate Narva no later than the period indicated.

[signed] I. Stalin[15]

Fediuninsky dutifully regrouped Zaitsev's 122d Rifle Corps into the bridgehead south of Narva and reinforced his corps with Major General V. F. Damberg's 124th Rifle Corps, which Govorov had just dispatched to him from *front* reserve, and with additional armor. Although subsequent fighting was fierce and costly to both sides, this attack too failed. However, during the intense fighting on 13 February, the SS Estonian Brigade, whose morale was recognized as parlous, broke and ran as it approached the front.[16] That night Sponheimer told Model he could not hold on to Narva without reinforcements. Model reacted by ordering the 58th Infantry Division, now short one third of its personnel and all of its heavy equipment, to move to Narva after only a three-day rest. Early on 14 February, after Sponheimer reported he had no room to maneuver and no troops to close the gaps and the situation was therefore hopeless, Model asked OKH for permission "to evacuate the small bridgehead still being held east of Narva, to gain three battalions. Zeitzler approved and, in addition, offered to send him a fresh infantry division from Norway."[17]

The 2d Shock Army's offensive failed primarily because the Germans were able to reinforce their defenses at Narva quickly and significantly. Once fully assembled, the Germans named their force at Narva "Operational Group Sponheimer," after the III SS Panzer Corps commander. Group Sponheimer consisted of the SS Panzer Grenadier Divisions "Nordland" and "Feldherrn-halle," the Estonian SS Panzer Grenadier Brigade "Nederland," one infantry brigade, the remnants of the XXVI Army Corps' 61st, 225th, and 227th Divisions, now termed division groups, portions of the 170th Infantry Division, and other smaller units.[18] On 23 February, this group was renamed "Operational Group Narva." By exploiting the strongly prepared fortifications around Narva and along the Narva River and the severe climatic and terrain conditions, and by terrific exertions, this force was able to thwart this and subsequent Soviet attempts to capture Narva throughout the winter and ensuing spring. As was previously the case, Soviet after-action critiques of Fediuninsky's operations credited his army's poor performance to the strong German defenses, weak air support, and confused command and control.

Model's Counterstroke and the Fall of Luga

While Fediuninsky's army was struggling in vain to overcome the Germans' defenses at Narva, to the southeast Maslennikov's 42d Army crossed the ice-covered Luga River on 31 January and began pursuing the German L Army Corps' forces southward and southwestward along the Kingisepp-Narva and Siverskii-Luga roads. Since the Germans offered little resistance, Maslennikov's forces, which were spearheaded only by forward detachments, advanced 15–20 kilometers (9.3–12.4 miles) per day through 4 February. On 4 February Major General P. F. Ratov's 196th Rifle Division of Tikhonov's 108th Rifle Corps captured Gdov on the eastern shore of Lake Chud. To the east Colonel S. P. Demidov's 86th Rifle Division of Anisimov's 123d Rifle Corps' captured Liady on the Pliussa River, while Borshchev's 46th Rifle Division of the same corps liquidated a small German garrison encircled at Sara-Gora. There the army halted for two days to bring forward artillery and supplies.

Given the Volkhov Front's slow progress westward toward Luga, the *Stavka* decided to reinforce Meretskov's thrust by shifting the 42d Army's axis of advance eastward toward the northwestern approaches to Luga. Accordingly, on 1 February, it ordered Govorov to wheel Maslennikov's army southeastward and employ it to sever the Luga-Pskov railroad, capture Mshinskaia Station, and assist the Volkhov Front in the capture of Luga. At the same time, the *Stavka* transferred Damberg's 124th Rifle Corps from the Volkhov Front's 54th Army to the Leningrad Front's 67th Army to reinforce its advance on Luga from the north.[19]

After making these command adjustments, Govorov decided to capture Luga with the left flank formations of Maslennikov's 42d Army and Sviridov's reinforced 67th Army. He ordered Tikhonov's 108th and Anisimov's 123d Rifle Corps from Maslennikov's 42d Army to dig in east of Lake Chud on 6–7 February. Then Astanin's 116th Rifle Corps, in army second echelon, was to attack southeastward from Liady, capture Pliussa and Strugi Krasnye by 9 February, cut the Luga-Pskov railroad, and destroy German forces in the Luga region in cooperation with the 67th Army. Govorov assigned Paramzin's 118th Rifle Corps to Maslennikov's army on 6 February to reconstitute a new second echelon for his army.

The 42d Army's assault did indeed pose a deadly threat to the flank and rear of the German Luga force, which now consisted of the L, XXVIII, and XXXVIII Army Corps, and the Germans knew it. As early as 4 February, Army Group North headquarters informed the OKH that Meretskov had "massed one strong force and 200 tanks southwest of Novgorod, and Govorov was assembling another east of Lake Sambro, 30 miles (48.2 kilometers) from the Eighteenth Army's left flank."[20] It was obvious to the German command that the Russians were repositioning their forces to encircle the bulk of their Eighteenth Army in the Luga region.

Model, who still intended to strike back to the northwest, then proposed potential "large" and "small" solutions in the form of variants for a possible German counterstroke.[21] The "large" solution involved a counterstroke to extend the German defensive front the entire length of the Luga River westward to just east of Narva. The "small" solution included a weaker counterstroke to extend the front diagonally from the Luga River northwestward to the northern tip of Lake Peipus (Chud). At this juncture, however, it was clear that both solutions were highly problematic given Soviet force dispositions and superiority. Nevertheless, whichever solution the Germans adopted, at least they would be defending actively, and the movement alone would likely improve the coherence of their sagging defenses.

Hitler was uncharacteristically unenthusiastic about the counterstrokes Model proposed. Initially, he expressed severe reservations and even fear over the loss of Narva and the possibility of a Soviet advance westward between Lakes Chud and Pskov and finally instructed Model to request formal permission to withdraw to the Panther Line if any of these Soviet threats materialized.[22]

Taking Hitler's reaction as license to act, Model ordered Lindemann's Eighteenth Army to block any Russian advance west of Luga and keep open his communications routes with Pskov. Lindemann was to erect a solid front westward from Luga across the Pliussa River and southwest to the southern shore of Lake Chud by shifting divisions from the northern and eastern portion of his Luga defenses. While he left the XXXVIII Army Corps' 11th, 212th, and 215th Infantry Divisions to defend Luga proper, he ordered the 13th *Luftwaffe* Field Division to redeploy to the corps' left flank so as to fill in the gap in German defenses from just west of Luga to the Pliussa River.

At the same time, the L Army Corps' 24th, 58th, and 21st Infantry Divisions were to deploy west of the Pliussa River, and the XXVI Army Corps' 12th Panzer and 126th Infantry Divisions were to occupy positions east of

Lake Chud and prepare to counterattack to the north. All of these forces were to reach their designated positions between 4 and 11 February. Once in position, the XXXVIII and L Corps would form Model's "shield" by defending against a Soviet thrust against Luga from the west, and the XXVI Corps would serve as the "sword" by attacking northward along the eastern shore of Lake Chud.[23]

After issuing his final instructions for the first stage of his counterstroke on 7 February, Model took extraordinary measures to assemble the requisite forces. Lindemann withdrew his front north and east of Luga to free up nine divisions or, more properly, weak division groups. During the short regrouping, the army's strength began to rise as stragglers and returnees from leave and hospitals returned to their divisions. In addition, Model ordered 5 percent of his rear-echelon troops immediately transferred to line units.[24] Lindemann jockeyed his divisions into positions from 5 through 10 February under Model's watchful eye, but with considerable difficulty since partisan actions delayed the movement of several divisions.

Beginning on 7 February a classically chaotic meeting engagement began between Maslennikov's 42d Army, which was advancing southward toward the Luga-Pskov railroad, and the forces of Model's "sword and shield," which were moving into their assigned jumping-off positions southwest of Luga and east of Lake Chud. Maslennikov's army advanced southward with his 116th, 123d, and 108th Rifle Corps marching abreast from west of the Pliussa River to the eastern shore of Lake Chud.

Tikhonov's 108th Rifle Corps, on Maslennikov's right flank just east of Lake Chud, reached Iamm Station on the Zhel'ba River at midday on 7 February. There, his advance ground to a halt against the defenses of the newly arrived 207th Infantry Division. The 207th Division's mission was to contain any Soviet advance east of Lake Chud and protect the deployment into the region of the XXVI Army Corps headquarters, which was supposed to control Model's counterattack in the sector east of Lake Chud. The XXVI Army Corps counterattack force consisted of the 126th Infantry, 12th *Luftwaffe*, and 12th Panzer Divisions, which were to advance northward in the sector from Lake Chud northeastward to the Pliussa River. The XXVI Army Corps headquarters and the 126th Infantry, 12th *Luftwaffe*, and 12th Panzer Divisions began reaching the region on 9 February.

Farther to the east, Anisimov's 123d and Astanin's 116th Rifle Corps regrouped between 6 and 8 February and prepared to assault southeastward toward the Luga-Pskov railroad. However, when the two Soviet corps attacked at dawn on 9 February they ran straight into Model's "sword and shield" force, providentially well before most of the German divisions had reached their designated defense or attack positions. The 13th *Luftwaffe* Division managed to reach and occupy its assigned positions between Luga and the Pliussa River before the Soviet onslaught reached the region. However, the 58th Infantry Division, which was on the 13th *Luftwaffe*'s left flank, ran into Burmistrov's and Demidov's 224th and 86th Rifle Divisions, which were advancing at the junction of 116th and 123d Rifle Corps. The two rifle divisions attacked immediately and overwhelmed the unfortunate German division before it could occupy its defenses. The savage attack also turned the 13th *Luftwaffe* Division's left flank and forced its tired troops to occupy a hasty defense south of the Pliussa River with its left flank fully exposed.[25] The L Army Corps' 24th and 21st Infantry Divisions, which were supposed to protect the 58th Infantry Division's left and right flanks as it advanced, did not reach the region until the next day, leaving the 58th to fend for itself against overwhelmingly superior Soviet forces. By the time the two infantry divisions finally arrived, the 58th Infantry Division was being buffeted by heavy assaults from additional divisions of Astanin's rifle corps.

Meanwhile, the meeting engagement grew in ferocity west of Luga, south of the Pliussa River, and west of the Luga-Pskov rail line, as the counterattacking forces of Model's "sword" ran directly into the teeth of Maslennikov's attacking 42d Army. The first act of this violent drama began playing out early on 10 February, when the 12th Panzer Division began its planned counterattack on schedule. When it did so, it ran directly into the 196th and 128th Rifle Divisions of Tikhonov's 108th Rifle Corps and the 168th Rifle Division of Anisimov's 123d Rifle Corps, which were attempting to encircle German forces defending Iamm Station from the east. Although the 12th Panzer managed to halt Colonel P. K. Loskutov's 128th Rifle Division, which was trying to envelop its right flank, the sharp fight also halted the 12th Panzer Division's advance in its tracks.[26] Thus, Model's counterstroke faltered from the very start.

As if to add insult to injury, while engaging in the sharp fight with the XXVI Army Corps, the forces on Tikhonov's right flank continued their advance. Overcoming German resistance, they drove the German force southward, captured Podborov'e on 11 February, and assaulted westward across the narrow neck of land between Lakes Chud and Pskov on 12 February, capturing a small bridgehead on Lake Chud's western shore, as if by coincidence validating Hitler's worse fears.

On 10 February the situation worsened in the 58th Infantry Division's sector to the east. Already under attack by Demidov's 86th and Burmistrov's 224th Rifle Divisions from Anisimov's and Astanin's 123d and 116th Rifle Corps, Major General V. K. Zaionchkovsky's 291st Rifle Division joined Astanin's assault. The new attack struck the 58th Infantry Division's front and flanks south of the Pliussa River and collapsed the defenses of the 21st and 24th Infantry Divisions, which were trying to defend along the 58th Infantry Division's left and right flanks. After shattering all three divisions' defenses in the Zarudin'e,

Berezitsa, and Orekhovno sectors, the three attacking Soviet divisions encircled the 58th Infantry Division's 154th Infantry Regiment. Over the next
several days, the 116th and 123d Rifle Corps' three divisions strove desperately and simultaneously to destroy the encircled regiment and advance
southward and southwestward. A German account described the precarious situation in the L Corps sector:

> Russian forces filtered past [the 58th Infantry Division] on both sides, and
> the other divisions would have to attack to close up the front. That would
> not be easy since the divisions had only four understrength battalions each
> and the enemy strength was growing hourly as units moved in from the
> northeast. The swampy terrain also raised problems, but, on the other
> hand, it was probably the main reason why *Leningrad Front* could not
> bring its full force to bear more quickly.
>   By 10 February the 58th Infantry Division was split in two and one of
> its regiments was encircled. The 24th Infantry, trying to close the gap on
> the right of the 58th Division, got nowhere and for most of the day had
> trouble holding open the Luga-Pskov railroad. Although Eighteenth Army
> would try again the next day to regain contact with the 58th Division and
> close the gap, the prospects were worsening rapidly. Air reconnaissance
> had spotted convoys of 800 to 900 trucks moving southeast from Lake
> Sambro.[27]

Model reacted immediately to the setback west of the Pliussa River by ordering the 12th Panzer and 13th *Luftwaffe* Divisions to dispatch forces to rescue
the beleaguered 58th Infantry Division, whose 220th Infantry Regiment was
now also encircled in the Zovka region. The 12th Panzer did so by sending its
5th Panzer Grenadier Regiment northeastward to relieve the encircled 220th
Regiment, while the 13th *Luftwaffe* attempted to rescue the 154th Infantry
Regiment. However, no sooner was the German relief effort under way than
Anisimov ordered Major General A. A. Egorov's 168th Rifle Division to join
his assault in the gap between the 12th Panzer and 58th Infantry Divisions.
Simultaneously, Demidov's 224th Rifle Division of Astanin's 116th Rifle Corps
intercepted and defeated the 13th *Luftwaffe* Division's relief force.

Anisimov's and Astanin's forces continued their advance on 11 and 12 February, trying to destroy the fragmented and partially encircled German forces
and simultaneously fending off the German relief attempts. Demidov's and
Zaionchkovsky's 224th and 291st Rifle Divisions of Anisimov's rifle corps and
Burmistrov's 86th Rifle Division of Anisimov's rifle corps completed destroying the bulk of the 58th Infantry Division and the 12th Panzer Division's 5th
Panzer Grenadier Regiment in the Zarudin'e region on 12 February. A Soviet
account recorded the action:

On 13 February subunits of the 58th Infantry Division's 220th Infantry Regiment and the 12th Panzer Division's 5th Motorized Regiment attempted to penetrate from the region northwest of Lake Chernoe toward Strugi Krasnye. The attempt ended unsuccessfully. Throwing away its combat weaponry and supplies, the enemy began crossing Lake Chernoe on the ice on the night of 15 February.

During the fighting from 8 to 15 February, the 42d Army's left flank corps destroyed more than a regiment of the 58th Infantry Division and parts of the 12th Panzer Division's 5th Panzer Grenadier Regiment, which had been trying to halt our forces along the intermediate defense line on the Pliussa River. The enemy abandoned all of the division artillery regiment's equipment and that of two heavy reserve artillery battalions on the field of battle.[28]

A German account noted the far-reaching consequences of the bitter fighting:

The next afternoon [11 February] Eighteenth Army reported that the battle had taken a dangerous turn. The 24th Infantry Division was stopped. Soviet tanks had appeared. Both regiments of the 58th Infantry Division were surrounded and would have to fight their way back. That they could save their heavy weapons was doubtful. After nightfall, Lindemann told Model that the only way he could get enough troops to close the gaps on the left flank was to take the entire front back to the shortest line between the southern tip of Lake Peipus [Chud] and Lake Ilmen. Govorov had spread the right arm of the pincers out to the Peipus shore and was pushing south toward Pskov. He already had some units far enough south "to pinch the 12th Panzer Division in the backside." Reluctantly, Model agreed to let the army go back.[29]

At this point bad news piled on top of bad news:

The next day [12 February] brought more bad news. At Narva the Russians expanded their bridgehead and created another north of the city. Between Lakes Peipus and Pskov, Govorov poured in enough troops to threaten a crossing into the Panther position. If Model were to establish a front between Lake Peipus and Lake Ilmen he would have to fight for it. On the evening of the 12th Model informed the OKH that he still planned to take and hold that line and wanted to know whether Hitler approved. The OKH response indicated that nobody there, including Hitler, liked the idea. The opinion was—for once—unanimous that it was too late to set up a front between the lakes and that, in any event, it was more important to free one division for Narva and another for the Peipus-Pskov narrows. The operations chief in the OKH added that Hitler was repeating every day that he did not want to risk any encirclements forward of the Panther position. An hour before midnight Sponheimer reported breakthroughs north and south of Narva. On the north, III SS Panzer Corps had managed to close its front and even gain a little, but south of Narva the Feldherrnhalle Division did not have the strength even to offer effective resistance.[30]

Soon after, the Eighteenth Army reported that Soviet ski troops had appeared on the west shore of Lake Chud north of the narrows: "The security division [285th] reported that its Estonian troops were 'going home.' After that, Model told the OKH that he would begin the withdrawal to the Panther position on 17 February and complete it early on 1 March. He would mop up on the west shore of Lake Peipus in the next few days and use the two divisions freed to cover the lake shore."[31]

Since the counterstroke by Model's "sword" had failed, he was left no choice but to order Lindemann's Eighteenth Army to abandon Luga, which he did on 12 February. Soon after, Khazov's 110th and Trubachev's 117th Rifle Corps of Sviridov's 67th Army occupied the city on the heels of the departing Germans and began pursuing the defeated German forces southward. The pursuit accelerated after 17 February, when Model ordered the Eighteenth Army to commence a general withdrawal back to the Panther Line, a withdrawal which German forces were supposed to complete by 1 March.

After abandoning Luga, Lindemann's forces withdrew southeastward toward Pskov, all the while trying to hold fast to the critical Luga-Pskov railroad, which took heavy fighting to do so. All the while, Lindemann reinforced his army's left flank in the Strugi Krasnye and Pliussa sector and west of the Luga-Pskov railroad to contain the 42d Army's incessant attacks. To support Lindemann's withdrawal, Model assigned responsibility for defending the sector east of Lake Pskov to the XXIV Army Corps and reinforced the corps with the battered but still combat-capable 12th Panzer Division.

At the same time, after they mopped up the encircled German forces and regrouped their forces, Maslennikov ordered Anisimov's 123d and Astanin's 116th Rifle Corps to continue their attack to the south and southeast in an attempt to cut the Luga-Pskov railroad line. Although the two corps managed to capture Shchir and reach the outskirts of Pliussa, they were not able to overcome German resistance and capture Strugi Krasnye and Pliussa. The Luga-Pskov railroad remained open for Lindemann's Eighteenth Army to withdraw from Luga to Pskov in relative safety. Whether or not they could do so, however, depended on how effectively they could hold at bay the forces of the Leningrad Front's 67th and the Volkhov Front's 54th Armies, which were advancing on the Luga region from the north and east.

While Maslennikov's 42d Army was savaging Model's "sword" west and southwest of Luga, Sviridov's 67th Army was advancing on Luga proper from the north, and Roginsky's 54th, Korovnikov's 59th, and Starikov's 8th Armies of Meretskov's Volkhov Front were striking the Eighteenth Army from the east and southeast. The fighting in these sectors was equally fierce but far less decisive than the fighting west and southwest of Luga. Sviridov's forces gnawed their way southward against stubborn German resistance, and Meretskov's forces made greater headway only to encounter strong German counterattacks that damaged his forward forces and prevented them from making significant progress.

The Eighteenth Army's XXVIII and XXXVIII Army Corps defended the northern and eastern approaches to Luga city and the X Army Corps defended an extended front southeastward to Lake Il'men'. Because most of the defending German divisions had suffered heavy losses in previous fighting, most fought in combat group configuration and occupied a defense consisting of strong points protecting all likely Soviet axes of advance into the region. The three defending German corps included the 121st Infantry and 12th and 13th *Luftwaffe* Field Divisions, four division groups (the 215th, 212th, and Groups Speth and Pohl), the remnants of four infantry divisions (the 126th, 11th, 9th *Luftwaffe,* and Group Schuldt), two infantry brigades, and an OKH reserve panzer battalion.[32]

Govorov assigned Sviridov's 67th Army to defend the sector from Novinka to Liuban' on its left flank with the 14th Fortified Region and attack through Mshinskaia and Tolmachevo toward Luga with Khazov's 110th Rifle Corps on its left and Trubachev's 117th Rifle Corps on its right. The two rifle corps were to capture Luga by 5 February in conjunction with an assault by the Volkhov Front's forces from the east.[33] Sviridov's forces attacked on 2 February but made only minimal progress against skillful German resistance. After heavy fighting north and northeast of Luga, Khazov's 110th Rifle Corps, on Sviridov's left flank, linked up with Kozachek's 115th Rifle Corps from Roginsky's 54th Army north of Oredezh on 8 February. Sviridov then took over control of Kozachek's rifle corps for the final advance on Luga. To the west, Trubachev's 117th Rifle Corps reached and forced the Luga River north of Luga on 11 February.

That day the Germans began to evacuate Luga, leaving rear guards behind to delay the Soviet advance. Sviridov's forces completely enveloped and captured the city on 12 February, just as a forward detachment of the 112th Rifle Corps' 377th Rifle Division from Korovnikov's 59th Army was approaching the city from the southeast. After capturing Luga, the 67th Army's 110th and 115th Rifle Corps continued their pursuit, covering 30–45 kilometers

(18.6–28 miles) in three days. On 15 February the army's right flank reached the outskirts of Pliussa, leaving Trubachev's 117th Rifle Corps to regroup in Luga as a new second echelon for Sviridov's army.

The Volkhov and 2d Baltic Fronts' Advance

Meanwhile, the armies of Meretskov's Volkhov Front resumed their advance on Luga on 2 February after reaching the upper reaches of the Luga River east of Batetskii. Given the excellent progress made by Starikov's 8th Army on Meretskov's left flank, the day before, the *Stavka* had reinforced Meretskov's left wing with the 1st Shock Army so that Meretskov could expand his offensive against the Eighteenth Army's right flank. In accordance with the new instructions he had received from the *Stavka*, Meretskov decided to penetrate the German Sixteenth Army's defenses south of Staraia Russa with Lieutenant General G. P. Korotkov's 1st Shock Army, while the *front*'s main forces encircled and destroyed German forces defending Luga. Korotkov's army was to advance westward through Volot to Dno, link up with the forces on the 8th Army's left flank, and encircle and destroy the forces on the Sixteenth Army's left flank in the Staraia Russa region and southwest of Lake Il'men'.[34]

Meretskov ordered his 54th, 59th, and 8th Armies to converge on Luga from three sides. Roginsky's 54th Army, which consisted of just Kozachek's 115th Rifle Corps and Colonel I. A. Vorob'ev's 44th Rifle Division, was to advance toward Luga region from the northeast. At the same time, Korovnikov's 59th Army was to advance on Luga via Oredezh and Batetskii, and Starikov's 8th Army was to advance on Luga from the southeast. Meretskov assigned the latter the most difficult and ambitious mission. Starikov's army was to march westward, cut the Luga-Pskov road and railroad, and, at the same time, establish contact with partisan forces operating to the south. At this critical juncture, Roginsky's 54th Army was to castle its forces from the sector northeast of Luga to a new sector on the 8th Army's left flank and establish contact with the 1st Shock Army, which was attacking westward from south of Staraia Russa.

Meretskov's new offensive plan was all the more difficult since the 59th Army lagged significantly behind the adjacent forces, requiring Starikov to leave forces behind to protect his right flank during his westward advance. To assist Starikov in performing this delicate mission, Meretskov reinforced his 8th Army with Major General A. S. Griaznov's fresh 99th Rifle Corps, which had just arrived from the *Stavka* reserve. In addition, he assigned Starikov two tank regiments and one self-propelled artillery regiment and reinforced the 99th Rifle Corps with two additional tank regiments. The Central Partisan Headquarters also ordered eight partisan brigades (the 2d,

3d, 7th, 1st, 10th, 13th, 4th, and 8th), a total of 17,000 men, to cooperate with Meretskov's advancing forces.[35]

Roginsky's 54th Army began pursuing the German XXXVIII Army Corps' 121st, 12th, and 13th *Luftwaffe* Field Divisions on 31 January. Kozachek's 115th Rifle Corps advanced 75 kilometers (46.6 miles) in nine days and captured Oredezh on 8 February by attacks from the north and west. The next day the army transferred Kozachek's rifle corps to Sviridov's 67th Army, and Roginsky's army headquarters redeployed to Novgorod, on the *front*'s left flank, where it took over control of Major General B. A. Rozhdestvensky's 111th and Major General F. K. Fetisov's 119th Rifle Corps on 11 February. Once it completed its regrouping, Meretskov ordered Roginsky's army to penetrate German defense west of Shimsk and cooperate with Starikov's 8th and Korotkov's 1st Shock Armies in the destruction of the German Staraia Russa and Utorgosh groups. Thereafter, Roginsky's army was to advance southwestward toward Porkhov.

Korovnikov's 59th Army resumed its offensive westward toward Luga in early February but accomplished very little until 8 February, since Solov'ev's 112th and Mikul'sky's 6th Rifle Corps encountered heavy resistance from the German XXXVIII Army Corps. However, after the 54th Army captured Oredezh on 8 February, the Germans began withdrawing their forces to Batetskii to counter the growing threat to their left flank. Mikul'sky's rifle corps pursued but was again held up until 12 February by strong enemy defenses at Batetskii Station. Having advanced only 25 kilometers (15.5 miles) in five days, an increasingly frustrated Korovnikov wheeled his forces south to assist Starikov's 8th Army, whose overextended forces were now encircled by counterattacking German forces. The 59th Army's rescue force reached the beleaguered 8th Army forces on 15 February.[36]

The 8th Army's predicament that forced Korovnikov to halt his advance on Luga was a direct by-product of Meretskov's decision to send Starikov's army on its bold but risky thrust due west toward Pliussa. Starikov's forces began their westward march on 31 January with Panin's 7th Rifle Corps in the lead. The corps' 256th Rifle Division, under the command of Colonel A. G. Koziev, made spectacular initial progress, capturing several villages and successfully linking up with the partisans. On 1 February Koziev's division captured Okliuzh'e, only 10 kilometers (6.2 miles) from the Luga-Pskov road. However, the 59th Army's forces, which were supposed to protect the 8th Army's and 7th Rifle Corps' right flank, lagged well behind. Worse still, Artiushenko's 14th Rifle Corps, on the 7th Rifle Corps' left flank, was also not able to advance, leaving the southern flank of Panin's rifle corps wide open and vulnerable.

The Germans immediately capitalized on the situation. In fact, they had no choice in the matter. They had to act if they were to have any chance of halting the Volkhov Front's forces short of the Luga-Pskov road and saving the Eighteenth Army's main forces at Luga from destruction. On 1 February Group Karow, which consisted of two battalions of infantry and 15 tanks, struck Radygin's 372d Rifle Division, which was operating on the 7th Rifle Corps' right (northern) flank, and drove it back in disorder, thereby exposing the 256th Division's right flank. Simultaneously, attacking from the south, the 8th Jager Division forced Major General I. N. Burakovsky's 191st Rifle Division of the 14th Rifle Corps, which was operating on Koziev's left (southern) flank, to retreat to the north. Soon after, the 12th Panzer Division joined Group Karow's counterattack and successfully penetrated to within 8 kilometers (5 miles) of the 8th Jager Division's spearhead.[37]

Even though Panin's 7th Rifle Corps was in real danger of being encircled, Koziev's 256th Rifle Division ignored the threat and continued its attack westward. Two of Koziev's regiments crossed the Luga-Pskov road near Zaplius'e on 2 February. The following day combat groups of the 12th Panzer and 8th Jager Divisions linked up southwest of Melkovichi, cutting off the entire 256th Rifle Division and two of the 372d Rifle Division's regiments from the 7th Rifle Corps' main force. Initially, Meretskov demanded that Starikov destroy the encircling German forces with Colonel A. R. Belov's 378th Rifle Division, which had just repelled a German attack on the railroad south of Peredol'skaia Station. When that plan proved impossible, on 4 February, Meretskov approved a new plan proposed by Starikov.

Starikov's new plan required Griaznov's 99th Rifle Corps, then in army second echelon, to attack westward toward Utorgosh and Strugi Krasnye on the Luga-Pskov railroad to cut German withdrawal routes from Luga. At the same time, Artiushenko's 14th Rifle Corps, reinforced with one rifle division, was to protect the 99th Rifle Corps' left flank by attacking toward Sol'tsy. However, Starikov's "big solution," which did nothing to assist the 256th Rifle Division directly, failed. Griaznov's rifle corps attacked on 7 February and captured six German strong points but ran into stiff resistance from the 8th Jager Division, which had been reinforced by tanks and aircraft, and was forced to abandon four of the strong points on 8 February. Nor could the corps achieve any success the following few days.[38] Even though combat southwest of Luga forced Lindemann to transfer the 12th Panzer Division westward on 6 February (replacing it with the 121st Infantry Division), Starikov's attack continued to make no progress through 15 February.

German Groups Karow and Freissner tried to destroy Koziev's encircled force from 6 through 15 February.[39] Throughout the heated battle, Koziev flew around the encirclement in a Po-2 aircraft directing his beleaguered forces. From 2 to 8 February, Starikov flew 21,644 kilograms of supplies to the division, including 2,500 kilos of food and 19,000 kilos of ammunition. By 9 February Koziev's division had suffered 400 wounded, most of whom were treated at the 5th Partisan Brigade's hospital. The division maintained some communications with the outside, sending one officer out with the partisans on 7 February, and two groups of 25 men each entered the encirclement region on 8 February with ammunition and medicine. Meanwhile, German forces pushed Koziev's division back from the Luga-Pskov road but were not able to destroy it. Aircraft continued supplying the 256th Rifle Division with food and ammunition on the night of 13–14 February. Finally, on 15 February the 59th Army forces, which were attacking from the north, and the 8th Army's forces, which were attacking from the south, managed to relieve Koziev's encircled force.[40]

According to Soviet after-action critiques, Griaznov's 99th Rifle Corps failed to accomplish its mission because, having seen the carnage in German ranks during its approach march, it did not expect and could not cope with the heavy resistance it encountered. The corps' command and control, cooperation, and combat will simply broke down. In addition, the corps did not conduct proper reconnaissance and so failed to determine the real location of the forward edge and concentrate its artillery to support the relief attack.[41]

Despite the Eighteenth Army's temporary successes against Starikov's 8th Army, Model's difficulties continued to mount. Early on 1 February, the Volkhov Front's newly assigned 1st Shock Army and Popov's 2d Baltic Front joined the increasingly unequal struggle by attacking eastward on a broad front south of Staraia Russia. The assault by Korotkov's 1st Shock Army, which was designed to cut the Staraia Russa–Kholm road, made little progress, advancing only 4 kilometers (2.5 miles) against the 21st *Luftwaffe* Field Division. In fact, the 1st Shock Army lacked the strength necessary to develop the offensive since it had only four rifle divisions and one rifle brigade to operate in a 100-kilometer (62-mile) sector. In addition, on 2 February the Germans reinforced the 21st *Luftwaffe* Division with elements of the neighboring 30th Infantry Division, on 3 February with two batteries of assault guns, and on 8 and 9 February with the 15th Latvian SS Division.[42]

On Meretskov's orders, Korotkov resumed his assault on 5 February but advanced only 4 more kilometers (2.5 miles) by 25 February before his offensive collapsed in exhaustion. Popov's 2d Baltic Front also attacked north and west of Novosokol'niki with its 22d and 10th Guards Armies, but even after considerable regrouping, these attacks also faltered by 25 February after advancing only 10–20 kilometers (6.2–12.4 miles).

Thus, in near constant fighting during the first half of February, the Soviet Leningrad, Volkhov, and 2d Baltic Fronts defeated German forces in the Luga region and liberated the northern half of the Leningrad region. By 15 February, Fediuninsky's 2d Shock Army had reached the Narva River and managed to capture sizable bridgeheads on the river's left bank. However, it was unable to expel German forces from the fortress city of Narva. To the south, the Leningrad and Volkhov Fronts' 42d, 67th, 59th, 8th, and 54th Armies drove German forces to a line extending from the southeastern shore of Lake Chud through Pliussa to Shimsk at the western tip of Lake Il'men'. They did so without significant armor support in the most difficult weather and terrain conditions. The advance propelled Red Army forces 50 kilometers (31 miles) westward along the Narva axis, 120 kilometers (74.5 miles) south-westward along the Pskov axis, and 50–100 kilometers (31–62 miles) along the Luga axis at an average advance rate of 6–7.5 kilometers (3.7–4.7 miles) per day.

The Soviet advance to and beyond Luga was not an easy one. Largely due to Model's stout resistance and incessant counterattacks, Govorov and Merets-kov's forces advanced at near glacial pace. Nor was the *Stavka* pleased with their progress. In fact, the slow progress only prompted the *Stavka* to demand that the three *fronts* complete destroying Army Group North and penetrate the vaunted Panther Line before the onset of spring.

THE LIBERATION OF SOUTHERN LENINGRAD REGION, 16 FEBRUARY–1 MARCH

Soviet Plans

After liberating Luga on 12 February, the *Stavka* immediately reorganized its forces for a subsequent advance toward Pskov and Ostrov. At 2400 hours on 13 February it dissolved Meretskov's Volkhov Front, transferring the 59th, 8th, and 54th Armies and their offensive sectors, the 65th and 310th Rifle Divisions in the *front*'s reserve, and the 14th Air Army to the Leningrad Front, effective 15 February. At the same time, the 1st Shock Army reverted to 2d Baltic Front control.[43]

Govorov's Leningrad Front faced a particularly complicated command and control situation on 15 February, since its forces were operating along a broad front extending from Narva to Lake Il'men'. To complicate Govorov's problems, on 17 February Model began implementing his order to withdraw his forces back to the Panther Line by 1 March. Since the Soviet troops that had captured a small bridgehead at the western end of the narrow neck of land between Lakes Chud and Pskov did not attempt to expand their bridge-head, Model took immediate measures to contain the Soviet force. On 17 February, he assigned the L Army Corps headquarters responsibility for the lake sector and began shifting the 12th Panzer Division into the region.

Meanwhile, the situation in the Narva sector stabilized with neither side able to gain advantage. In response to the 14 February *Stavka* directive, Fediuninsky's 2d Shock Army had attempted to revive its offensive north and south of Narva but to no avail. Fediuninsky's forces were faced by Operational Group Sponheimer (the III SS Panzer and LIV Army Corps), which by now consisted of the SS Panzer Grenadier Division "Nordland," four divisional combat groups, two infantry brigades, and one panzer grenadier brigade. The force also contained the remnants of a panzer grenadier and *Luftwaffe* field division, a panzer battalion, and the remnants of a former infantry division.

To the east along the Pskov and Ostrov axes, the Leningrad Front's 42d, 67th, 8th, and 54th Armies continued their pursuit south of Luga opposed by the Eighteenth Army's XXVI, XXVIII, and XXXVIII Army Corps, which were now formed into Operational Group Freissner. By Soviet estimate, the German forces numbered eight infantry, two *Luftwaffe* field and two security divisions, one panzer division, one infantry brigade, three divisional combat groups, and the remnants of two *Luftwaffe* field divisions. Freissner's provisional group had been formed on 6 February from the headquarters of the VI SS Army Corps, and it included the Eighteenth Army's XXXVIII Army Corps and the X Army Corps from the Sixteenth Army. On 22 February the group was redesignated as Operational Group Herzog. After 17 February Freissner's force began slowly withdrawing along intermediate lines in an attempt to reach new defensive positions anchored on the Pskov-Ostrov Fortified Region of the Panther Line.[44]

In mid-February the *Stavka* had assigned Govorov's expanded *front* the overall missions of advancing along the Pskov and Ostrov axes, while continuing its efforts to capture Narva, preventing the Germans from establishing new defenses, and facilitating the 2d Baltic Front's offensive. On 17 February Govorov dispatched his proposed operational concept to the *Stavka* for its approval. His concept recommended that two mutually supporting columns conduct the offensive toward Pskov and Ostrov, the first consisting of the 42d and 67th Armies and the second of the 8th and 54th Armies. At the same time, Tikhonov's 108th Rifle Corps, on the 42d Army's right flank, was to conduct supporting attacks across the narrow neck of water between Lakes Chud and Pskov (Lake Teploe).

Govorov's plan required Fediuninsky' 2d Shock Army to capture Narva, penetrate German defenses between the Narva Bay and Lake Chud, and make its main attack southwest toward Parnu to destroy the newly reformed Eighteenth Army in Estonia and capture Tallin. Simultaneously, Maslennikov's 42d and Sviridov's 67th Armies were to attack along the Pskov axis, destroy the enemy, capture Pskov and Ostrov, and create favorable conditions for a subsequent advance to the lower reaches of the Western Dvina River by conducting their main attack toward Riga.

Maslennikov's and Sviridov's armies were to resume their attacks on the evening of 13 February, prevent the Germans from erecting defenses along intermediate lines, and reach the Seredka, Strugi Krasnye, Ludoni, and Bol'shoi

Zvad line no later than 17 February. Subsequently, while preventing German reserves from destroying their covering units, their forces were to capture the strong points at Pskov, Karamyshevo, and Porkhov no later than 25–28 February. At the same time, after reaching the Seredka, Strugi Krasnye, and Ludoni line, the forces on Maslennikov's right flank were to capture a bridgehead in the Mekhikorma region west of Lake Teploe and capture the Pskov center of resistance by 25 February. To the east, Starikov's 8th and Roginsky's 54th Armies were to encircle and destroy German forces in the Utorgosh, Sol'tsy, and Medved' region no later than 19 February. While they were doing so, Korovnikov's 59th Army and, later, Starikov's 8th Army were to regroup to the Narva axis to reinforce the 2d Shock Army.[45]

The Second Battle for Narva

Fediuninsky's 2d Shock Army resumed its assaults north and south of Narva after 15 February. Despite strong German resistance and frequent counterattacks, his army managed to expand the bridgehead across the Narva River to a width of 35 kilometers (21.7 miles) and a depth of 15 kilometers (9.3 miles) by the end of February. While Fediuninsky believed that his attacks had created favorable conditions for a subsequent advance into Estonia, the *Stavka* and Govorov considered the 2d Shock Army's progress inadequate at best. On 23 February Korovnikov's 59th Army joined Fediuninsky's 2d Shock Army at Narva, occupying positions in the Slantsy bridgehead sector south of the city. On Govorov's instructions, Fediuninsky assigned Korovnikov's army the sector from the mouth of the Mustaia River to the northern shore of Lake Chud and transferred Trubachev's 117th Rifle Corps and Zaitsev's 122d Rifle Corps to his control. Korovnikov's mission was to hold and broaden the bridgehead and prepare an offensive deeper into Estonia to cut off and destroy the German Narva grouping and exploit through Rakvere to Tallin. Soon the 43d, 109th and 6th Rifle Corps rejoined the 59th Army. However, as one critic noted, the new reinforcements did not appreciably improve the situation: "Unfortunately, the army's composition frequently changed . . . which complicated command and control; but the state of their [the corps'] combat readiness necessitated the withdrawal of the formations and units into *front* reserve for rest and replenishment."[46]

A German account offered a slightly different perspective of the intense fighting around Narva in February:

> In the north, along the Narva front, the Germans toward the end of the month had gained only enough strength to tip the scales slightly in their own favor. On 24 February, General der Infantrie Johannes Freissner, who had proved himself in the fighting on the Sixteenth–Eighteenth Army

boundary, took over Sponheimer's command which was then redesignated Armee-abteilung Narva. By then the troops of the 214th Infantry Division were beginning to arrive. They still needed seasoning, but could be used to relieve experienced troops from quiet parts of the line. Going over to what he called "mosaic work," Freissner cut into the extreme tip of the bridgehead south of Narva and pushed the enemy there into two small pockets. Although the Russians ignored the punishing artillery and small arms fire and kept pouring in troops through the open ends of the pockets, the danger of their reaching the coast was averted.[47]

The Leningrad Front's Advance to Pskov and Ostrov

After Maslennikov left a portion of his army's forces on the eastern bank of Lakes Chud and Pskov to provide security for his flanks, Tikhonov's 108th and Anisimov's 123d Rifle Corps attacked southward toward Pskov, and, to the east, Astanin's 116th Rifle Corps advanced toward Pliussa and Strugi Krasnye. As a result, a 40-kilometer (24.8-mile) gap formed between Maslennikov's advancing corps, forcing Astanin's corps to coordinate closely with forces on the right flank of Sviridov's 67th Army. The German XXVI Army Corp defended stubbornly along an intermediate line from the upper Lochkina River through Liubotezh to Gridino with its 126th Infantry and 12th Panzer Divisions and the shattered remnants of the 9th *Luftwaffe* Field Division.

Fortunately for Model's defense, the forces he had hastily assembled under L Army Corps control were able to defeat the threat posed by the forces on Maslennikov's right flank, which had occupied the bridgehead west of the gap between Lakes Chud and Pskov. After intense fighting, the 11th Infantry Division and Group von Krocher managed to drive the 42d Army's 128th and 90th Rifle Divisions and 5th Ski Brigade from their bridgehead on the western bank of Lake Chud on 16 February and from nearby Lake Pirissar on 24 February. Meanwhile, two divisions of Major General N. P. Iakunin's 98th Rifle Corps, which Govorov had assigned to Maslennikov to reconstitute his army's second echelon, went into action on his army's left flank on 20 February and, the next day, drove German forces back 7–8 kilometers (4.3–5 miles).

On 22 February a still impatient *Stavka* sent a new directive to Govorov that approved the plan he had submitted several days before and ordered him to accelerate his offensive:

The *Stavka* of the Supreme High Command approves your operational plan No. 126/sh and *orders:*

1. After penetrating enemy defenses on the isthmus north of Lake Chud, the *front*'s right wing, consisting of three armies (no fewer than

nine rifle corps not counting the Estonian rifle corps and one tank corps), will develop the attack toward Parnu with one army to cut off the withdrawal routes of the enemy's Tallin grouping and will attack southward toward Vil'iandi, Valga and Tartu, and Vyru with two armies.

2. The main forces of the *front*'s left wing, consisting of three armies (nine rifle corps), will be directed to capture the Ostrov region by enveloping Pskov from the north and forcing the Velikaia River. After which it will develop an offensive in the general direction of Riga. In connection with the withdrawal of the enemy's Staraia Russa grouping and the establishment of communications with the 2d Baltic Front's 1st Shock Army, it is not necessary to allocate a strong group to protect the main forces' left flank from the south.

[signed] I. Stalin, A. Antonov[48]

The *Stavka* also assigned Major General I. A. Vovchenko's 3d Guards Tank Corps to Govorov's *front* to facilitate his advance. However, the advance developed so slowly in light of Model's carefully planned withdrawal that Govorov was never able to commit Vovchenko's tank corps to combat. Golikov further refined Maslennikov's mission on 23 February by ordering his army to complete penetrating the Germans' intermediate defense line and reach the Razgovorovo-Dubniki-Toposhiino-Podborov'e line by the end of 25 February. Subsequently, Maslennikov's army was to capture the northern portion of the Pskov Fortified Region and the city of Pskov in cooperation with Sviridov's 67th Army.

Maslennikov's 42d Army resumed its offensive on 24 February, overcame German defenses, and captured Seredka, an important German strong point on the main axis of advance to Pskov. His army advanced 25 kilometers (15.5 miles) during the next three days and late on 28 February seized the line that Govorov had designated. By midday on 29 February, Maslennikov's forces had reached the northern face of the enemy's main defense belt, the Pskov-Ostrov Fortified Region, where increased German resistance halted Maslennikov's advance in its tracks.

To the east, after relinquishing control of Trubachev's 117th Rifle Corps to the Leningrad Front's reserve and gaining Astanin's 116th Rifle Corps in return, Sviridov's 67th Army resumed its offensive on 16 February. Its mission was "to capture the Strugi Krasnye, Ludoni, and Zvad line by 17 February, subsequently seize the Karamyshevo-Porkhov railroad sector, and reach the Volkova, Olisovo, Danilkina, and Zarech'e line no later than 25–28 February."[49] The 12th and 13th *Luftwaffe* Field and 24th Infantry Divisions of the XXVIII Army Corps stubbornly defended the approaches to the railroad south of Pliussa opposite the 67th Army as they conducted their planned withdrawal to Pskov. Sviridov's forces attacked German defenses at Pliussa for three days without appreciable results. Borshchev's 46th Rifle Division of Khazov's 110th Rifle Corps, together with the 6th and 7th Partisan Brigades, finally captured Pliussa from the 13th *Luftwaffe* Division on 18 February.

Assisting Sviridov's advance, Roginsky's 54th Army resumed its offensive on 17 February, and the 2d Baltic Front's 1st Shock Army captured Staraia Russa the next day. The relatively easy capture of Staraia Russa signaled the beginning of a wholesale, preplanned German withdrawal along successive lines to the southwest. Despite the Germans' deliberate decision to withdraw, Sviridov's offensive continued to develop at an exceedingly slow pace. Only on 19 February did the pace of his pursuit pick up after the XXVIII Army Corps began withdrawing its 13th *Luftwaffe* Division to new defenses east of Lake Pskov. Nevertheless, while the forces on the left flank and center of Sviridov's army advanced another 6–8 kilometers (3.7–5 miles), his right flank was unable to record any forward progress.

On 20 February Govorov caustically berated Sviridov for his army's lackluster performance, stating, "The enemy, who are opposing your army, are only employing covering forces in their fighting. The army is advancing slowly because, having dissipated its forces equally across the front, it has no shock 'fist' at all and has not exploited the enveloping position of the 116th Rifle Corps' right flank in relation to the enemy who is defending opposite the army."[50]

Accordingly, Govorov ordered Sviridov to transfer an additional rifle corps to his right flank and employ it in an attack along the Novosel'e, Tsapel'ka, and Iamkino axis to encircle and destroy the withdrawing enemy in cooperation with Roginsky's 54th Army. Sviridov's army was to capture the Novosel'e and Maiakovo line no later than 23 February and the Bol'shoe Zagor'e– Iamkino road no later than 25 February. If it did so in timely fashion, his army could cut off enemy forces withdrawing in front of its left wing.

However, Sviridov's army also failed to accomplish this mission, forcing Govorov to make further adjustments. On 23 February the *front* commander ordered Panin's 7th Rifle Corps transferred from Starikov's 8th Army to Sviridov's 67th Army, effective at 2400 hours 24 February, and withdrew the 67th Army's 115th Rifle Corps into *front* reserve. Further, he ordered Sviridov's army to envelop and capture the German strong point at Strugi Krasnye and reach the Novosel'e-Alekseevka military road on 24 February. Subsequently, the army was to develop an attack on its left flank and reach the Karmyshevo and Shishlova line no later than 29 February. Its distant mission was to capture the central portion of the Pskov-Ostrov Fortified Region in cooperation with the 42d and 54th Armies and force its way across the Velikaia River.[51]

Under unrelenting pressure, Lindemann's Eighteenth Army had no choice but to abandon its intermediate defense line on 23 February and continue its withdrawal toward Pskov. After capturing Strugi Krasnye, Sviridov's army resumed its pursuit. The XXVIII Army Corps attempted to halt the 67th Army's advance along the Novosel'e, Tsapel'ka, and Alekseevka line on 24 February but was forced to abandon the line after two days of heavy fighting and withdraw to defenses to the west. Sviridov's army advanced 65–90 kilometers (40.4–56 miles) during the six days from 23 through 29 February. Late during this period, Khazov's 110th and Panin's 7th Rifle Corps forced the Cherekha River from the march and then cut the Pskov-Opochka rail line. The 67th Army approached the northeastern and eastern edge of the Pskov-Ostrov Fortified Region in early March and immediately began preparations to penetrate the powerful German defense line.

While Maslennikov's and Sviridov's armies were driving the Eighteenth Army's XXVI and XXVIII Army Corps westward toward Pskov and Ostrov, the armies on the Leningrad Front's left wing resumed their attacks in a staggered sequence. Starikov's 8th Army began its pursuit to the southwest and south on 15 February after freeing Koziev's 256th Rifle Division from encirclement, although Roginsky's 54th Army did not join the attack, since it was in the midst of its offensive preparations.

Group Freissner's 28th Jager Division resisted the 8th Army's advance tenaciously and skillfully by taking advantage of the swampy terrain in the region, as it tried to prevent Starikov's forces from severing the critical Medved'-Nikolaevo military road southeast of Luga. Combat raged for five days in the Bol'shoi Utorgosh and Nikolaevo sector on the approaches to the road, as the 28th Jager launched counterattack after counterattack. On the evening of 20 February, Govorov issued new orders, this time directing Starikov to reach the Shimsk and Vidoni line no later than 23 February. Starikov's 8th Army did so by late on 27 February but only because German Group Herzog began deliberately withdrawing its forces rapidly to the southwest. Starikov's army pursued, advancing 20–25 kilometers (12.4–15.5 miles) in three days. Since the army's sector narrowed as it advanced, Govorov transferred Panin's 7th Rifle Corps to Sviridov's 67th Army and withdrew Starikov's 8th Army into *front* reserve, effective at 2400 hours 24 February. Govorov's intention was to transfer Starikov's army to the Narva region to reinforce Fediuninsky's 2d Shock Army.

Having finally completed its regrouping and offensive preparations, Roginsky's 54th Army resumed its offensive on the Leningrad Front's extreme left flank on 17 February. Roginsky's mission was to attack along the Veshki and Sol'tsy axis with his main force and capture the Utorgosh, Sol'tsy, and Shimsk line no later than 19 February, thereby protecting Starikov's right flank.[52] If successful, the 54th Army's advance would threaten the orderly withdrawal of the German X Army Corps from Staraia Russa, which had just begun that very day. Despite Roginsky's best efforts, however, the X Corps successfully held his forces at bay for three days along the Mshaga and Shelon' rivers while the corps withdrew its main forces in good order. During its withdrawal, however, the X Corps' troops had to run the gauntlet along the road from Staryi Medved' to Gorodishche through the 5th Partisan Brigade, whose forces harassed the Germans' every move and delayed the withdrawal by several hours.

Govorov issued new orders to Roginsky's army on 20 February, requiring it to advance in the general direction of Sol'tsy and Porkhov and capture the Bol'shie Pavy, Borovichi, and Dno line no later than 25 February. Thereafter, the 54th Army was to advance on its right flank and reach the Zaklin'e, Porkhov, and Dno line by 28 February. After pursuing German forces for four days, during which it traversed up to 60 kilometers (37.2 miles), Roginsky's forces captured Dno on the morning of 24 February in cooperation with the forces of Korotkov's 1st Shock Army.

Continuing their pursuit, Roginsky's forces then marched westward toward Porkhov, seeking to capture Ostrov and the southern portion of the Pskov-Ostrov Fortified Region in cooperation with Sviridov's 67th Army and, subsequently, force their way across the Velikaia River. After brushing aside German covering forces along the Shelon' River, the 54th Army captured Porkhov early on 26 February and, after three days of combat, advanced another 65 kilometers (40.1 miles) and reached the eastern edge of the German Panther Line.

The 13th Air Army provided significant air support throughout the Leningrad Front's slow advance during the second half of February. It flew more than 3,200 air sorties over the course of 15 days, while opposing German aircraft flew only 500. During the same period, frontal aviation claimed to have shot down 38 German aircraft and destroyed or damaged another 26 aircraft in air strikes against Tartu airfield on 26 February.[53]

During a period of 16 days, the Leningrad Front's 2d Shock, 42d, 67th, 8th, and 54th Armies overcame German resistance along prepared lines and in difficult terrain, advanced 50–160 kilometers (31–99 miles), and inflicted significant losses on the German Eighteenth Army. However, in the opinion of the *Stavka* and Govorov himself, the armies did so too slowly and without fulfilling their priority objectives. Specifically, Fediuninsky's 2d Shock Army failed to break cleanly through German defenses along the Narva River, capture Narva, and begin the liberation of Estonia. Nor were Maslennikov's 42d, Sviridov's 67th, and Starikov's 8th Armies able to rupture the Pskov and Ostrov Fortified Regions from the march. Finally, Roginsky's 54th Army failed to disrupt the X Army Corps' withdrawal westward from Staraia Russa.

Govorov's forces failed to accomplish their missions for a variety of reasons. Although terrain considerations played a significant role, so also did skillful and often desperate German resistance and a host of all too familiar problems, such as poor command and control, faulty force coordination, and inadequate fire and logistical support. However, during this phase of the operation, Soviet commanders did notably improve in all three respects. Above and beyond the familiar problems, the most important factor inhibiting Red Army success was the utter fatigue and exhaustion among the troops produced by 45 days of almost continuous combat in difficult terrain and harsh winter weather conditions. The combat strength of formations seriously eroded, unit tank strengths dwindled, ammunition was often in short supply, and commanders had to launch most attacks with only minimal preparation against prepared defenses whose penetration required far more careful preparation. By the end of February, many of Govorov's rifle divisions had decreased in strength by from 2,500 to 3,500 men each.[54]

German accounts of the operation accurately sum up Govorov's problems and achievements during the two-week period:

> In the swamps and forests east of Pskov Lake, Leningrad Front had trouble bringing its forces to bear, but on 24 February it began laying heavy pressure north of the city [Pskov] and launched probing attacks across the lake. According to intelligence reports, Stalin had called in Govorov and personally ordered him to take Pskov. By 26 February the threats to Pskov and on the Sixteenth Army right flank had made Hitler so nervous that he asked Model to try to speed up the withdrawal.[55]

The 2d Baltic Front's Advance on Idritsa

To make matters worse for Model, the Leningrad Front's successful advance from Luga to Pskov provided Popov's 2d Baltic Front with an opportunity to participate in the destruction of the Sixteenth Army, which, after 17 February, was caught in a salient between the two Soviet *fronts*. The *Stavka* certainly appreciated the opportunity at hand. Consequently, at 0400 hours on 17 February, it ordered the 2d and 1st Baltic Fronts to prepare an offensive operation adjacent to the Leningrad Front's left flank:

> The *Stavka* of the Supreme High Command *orders:*
> 1. The 2d Baltic Front will penetrate the enemy defense in the Lake Zhadro and Podrech'e sector (inclusive) with two armies (no fewer than 20 rifle divisions), and, by launching its main attack west of Velikaia River, capture the Opochka and Zilupe line and crossings over the Velikaia River north of Idritsa. Subsequently, occupy Rezekne and attack toward Karsava to destroy the German Ostrov grouping in cooperation with the Leningrad Front's left wing. . . .

3. After regrouping two armies (no fewer than 16–17 rifle divisions) to the Lake Sviblo and Lake Iazno regions, the 1st Baltic Front will penetrate the enemy's defense in the Podrech'e and Glukhovka sector and, by conducting its main attack in the general direction of Sebezh, will capture the Pasiene, Lake Lisno, and Kliastitsy line. Subsequently attack toward Dagdy to reach the Western Dvina River in the Dvinsk and Drissa sector. . . .

5. Begin the offensive on 28–29 February. . . .

[signed] I. Stalin, A. Antonov[56]

As of 17 February, Popov's forces faced the German Sixteenth Army's X, II, XXXXIIII, and VIII Army Corps, which were defending positions from the southern shore of Lake Il'men' southward to the western extremity of the Soviet-occupied salient west of Nevel'. Farther to the south, Army General I. Kh. Bagramian's 1st Baltic Front faced the Sixteenth Army's right flank (the I Army Corps) and the Third Panzer Army's left wing, which defended the sector from the western extremity of the Nevel' salient southeastward to Vitebsk. The Sixteenth Army fielded 12 infantry divisions and 2 infantry division combat groups, the bulk of which faced Popov's 2d Baltic Front.

Model at Army Group North, however, anticipated Popov's offensive and reacted accordingly:

On 19 February Army Group North became suddenly and acutely aware of an old danger that had been lurking in the background throughout the last month of crisis. On that day, for the first time in months, the attacks on the Third Panzer Army perimeter around Vitebsk stopped; and air reconnaissance detected truck convoys of 2,000 or 3,000 trucks moving out, most of them heading north and northwest. Army Group North intelligence estimated that two armies could be shifted to the Sixteenth Army's right flank in a few days. Model foresaw two possibilities. The first, and most likely, was that, after adding to its already strong concentration in the Nevel-Pustoshka area, Second Baltic Front would attempt to break into the Panther position below Pustoshka and roll it up to the north before the Sixteenth Army could establish themselves there. The second, the "big solution" as the Germans came to call it, was a thrust straight through to Dvinsk and on to Riga to cut off Army Group North in the Baltic States.[57]

In addition to divining the *Stavka*'s intentions, Model also speculated that the activity on the Sixteenth Army's right flank might be a sign that the *Stavka* was becoming discouraged with the attempts to encircle the Eighteenth Army.

Subsequent action to the north, however, quickly disabused Model of that thought. Prudently, Model took the only appropriate action he could. On 17 February he ordered the Sixteenth to begin withdrawing its forces, first of all those troops facing Soviet forces at Staraia Russa.

Soviet intelligence failed to detect the Germans' preparations to withdraw from Staraia Russa until it was too late to do anything about it. When the X Corps began to withdraw, Korotkov's 1st Shock Army began to pursue the following day, with its forward detachments fencing with withdrawing German rear guards. After occupying Staraia Russa on 18 February, Korotkov's army advanced toward Dno and Dedovichi. Then, on 19 February, Lieutenant General V. A. Iushkevich's 22d Army, which was deployed on Korotkov's left flank opposite the German II Army Corps, joined in Korotkov's pursuit. Major General M. N. Kleshnin's 44th Rifle Corps of Iushkevich's army advanced from the Avinovo and Ignatovo regions, 45–55 kilometers (28–34 miles) southwest of Kholm. On Iushkevich's right flank, Colonel K. G. Cherepanov's 26th Rifle Division, which had just been transferred from Korotkov's to Iushkevich's army, joined the advance at 0200 hours on 20 February by attacking west of Kholm. The mission of Kleshnin's rifle corps was to penetrate the enemy defense, advance northward, and cut the communications between German forces west of Kholm and those withdrawing from Staraia Russa.[58]

While the X Army Corps, which was still assigned to Group Freissner, was conducting its tricky withdrawal westward from the Staraia Russa region, the II Army Corps struggled to fend off the 22d Army's assaults and protect the X Corps' southern flank. Korotkov's 1st Shock Army, which was pursuing the X Corps' 30th Infantry, 15th Latvian SS, and 21st *Luftwaffe* Field Divisions, had advanced 25–45 kilometers (15.5–28 miles) by late on 20 February, finally establishing contact with Roginsky's 54th Army on the Leningrad Front's left flank. By that time, Kleshnin's 44th Rifle Corps of the 22d Army had overcome the defenses of the XXXXIII Army Corps' 218th and 331st Rifle Divisions and advanced 6–7 kilometers (3.7–4.3 miles). The Germans conducted the delaying action skillfully, employing battalion groups supported by tanks and aircraft, to parry Kleshnin's advance. Without ceasing its pursuit, Kleshnin's corps cut the Kholm-Loknia road early on 21 February. To the north, Cherepanov's 26th Rifle Division captured Kholm from a regiment of the II Army Corps' 218th Infantry Division.[59]

Over the next few days, the German withdrew westward rapidly, covering their withdrawal by temporary halts at strong points or along intermediate defense lines. According to a German-based account:

Meretskov tried for a breakthrough at Shimsk west of Lake Ilmen on 17 February [with Starikov's 8th Army]. For three days, while the flank of Sixteenth Army came back from Staraya Russa, the battle to maintain contact between the two armies swayed in the balance. On the 20th, when both armies [Eighteenth and Sixteenth] began pulling away from Lake Ilmen, that crisis [the splitting apart of the two armies] had passed.[60]

Model's principal intermediate defense line west of Staraia Russa extended along the north-south rail line from Dno to Nasvy. Appreciating the vital importance of Dno, Model concentrated the 8th Jager Division, a regiment of the 21st *Luftwaffe* Division, and two security regiments in the city and the 30th Infantry Division to the south. Major General P. A. Stepanenko's 14th Guards Rifle Corps of Korotkov's 1st Shock Army and Rozhdestvensky's 111th Rifle Corps of Roginsky's 54th Army launched converging assaults against German defenses around Dno late on 23 February, but were driven back by heavy counterattacks. The next day, however, the 14th Guards Rifle Corps' 182d Rifle Division, 137th Rifle Brigade, and 37th Tank Regiment and the 111th Rifle Corps' 288th and 44th Rifle Divisions and 16th Tank Brigade assaulted and captured the city. After capturing numerous other villages in the region on 24 February, Korotkov's army, now joined by elements from Iushkevich's 22d Army captured the important regional center at Dedovichi on the night of 24–25 February.[61]

Popov's 2d Baltic Front exploited its successes on 26 February. Stepanenko's 14th Guards Rifle Corps and Colonel V. K. Chesnokov's 208th Rifle Division from Korotkov's army forced the Shelon' River northwest of Dedovichi, crushed German resistance on the river's western bank, and advanced up to 12 kilometers (7.5 miles), capturing the Logovino–Novyi Krivets sector of the Porkhov-Chikhachevo road. The defending 30th Infantry and 21st *Luftwaffe* Divisions had no choice but to withdraw quickly to the west. At the same time, on Korotkov's left flank, Colonel A. D. Timoshenko's 391st Rifle Division attacked the 15th Latvian SS Division, forcing it to withdraw and destroying the small German garrison in Chikhachevo. On Korotkov's left flank, after a two-day battle with German rear guards, Iushkevich's 22d Army penetrated the XXXXIII Army Corps' intermediate defense line between Sushchevo and Loknia and advanced 10–20 kilometers (6.2–12.4 miles) along its entire front. The same day, Major General E. F. Bukshtynovich's 100th Rifle Corps, on the 22d Army's left flank in the Maevo Station region, also joined the assault along with Major General P. P. Bakhrameev's 93d Rifle Corps of Kazakov's adjacent 10th Guards Army. In short order, 22d Army forces captured Bezhanitsy, Loknia, Sushchevo Station, Maevo, and Zabel'e from the withdrawing XXXXIII Army Corps.[62]

If the expanding offensive against the Sixteenth Army was not problem enough for Model, on 26 February Major General F. A. Zuev's 79th Rifle Corps of Chibisov's 3d Shock Army entered the fray, attacking northward on the 10th Guards Army's left flank. However, Zuev's corps made little progress against stout resistance by the German 329th Infantry Division. Both the 10th Guards and 3d Shock Armies attacked, despite the fact that both armies were in the midst of a major regrouping. By day's end on 26 February, the incessant pressure by the 2d Baltic Front's 22d, 10th Guards, and 3d Shock Armies completely cleared German forces from the Dno-Novosokol'niki railroad and the Novosokol'niki-Maevo-Zabel'e railroad sector. The Sixteenth Army's XXXXIII Army Corps was left with no option other than to withdraw to new defensive positions to the west.

During the 2d Baltic Front's pursuit, the 1st Shock and 22d Armies advanced 10–22 kilometers (6.2–13.7 miles) on 27 February and the 10th Guards Army 5–18 kilometers (3.1–11.2 miles), and the key town Pustoshka and many adjacent towns and villages fell to Popov's advancing forces. Because of the steady German withdrawal, on 27 February the *Stavka* ordered the 2d Baltic Front to pursue the Germans without changing its axis of advance and without regrouping its forces. The *Stavka* ordered Popov to conduct artillery preparations only if and when his forces encountered fortified defense lines and protect the southern flank of his forces' advance toward Rezekne and Karsava.

However, Popov's forces were unable to fulfill the *Stavka's* order. Joined by the VIII Army Corps, the XXXXIII Army Corps' forces intensified their resistance along the front opposite the 1st Shock and 22d Armies and successfully withdrew their forces westward across the Velikaia River.[63] Although Korotkov's 1st Shock Army advanced 40 kilometers (24.8 miles) by day's end on 29 February and cut the Pskov-Opochka rail line, and Iushkevich's 22d Army advanced 12 kilometers (7.4 miles) and captured Novorzhev, the 3d Shock and 10th Guards Armies, on Popov's left flank, made no progress whatsoever. After it too encountered stiffening resistance, the 1st Shock Army also went over to the defense in early March.

One of many reasons the 2d Baltic Front was unable to fulfill its assigned missions during the second half of February was its lack of adequate air support during the pursuit. For example, during the 14-day period from 17 February through 1 March, the 15th Air Army conducted reconnaissance, transported supplies to the partisans, bombed and strafed enemy forces, and also provided air cover for the ground forces, flying a total of 1,200 aircraft sorties.[64] However, this support was not sufficient to support the sort of advance envisioned by the *Stavka*. Nevertheless, during its pursuit, the 2d Baltic Front's right flank advanced 180 kilometers (111.8 miles) from Staraia Russa to the Velikaia River, its center 125 kilometers (77.7 miles) from Kholm to Novorzhev, and its left flank 30 kilometers (18.6 miles) from Maevo to Pustoshka. While Popov's *front* inflicted some losses on the Germans, it failed to accomplish the mission assigned it by the *Stavka*. In the process, by official count, the 1st Shock Army suffered 5,012 casualties, including 1,283 killed, captured, or missing and 3,759 wounded or sick out of 54,900 men engaged from 14 January through 10 February. The 2d Baltic Front as a whole suffered 29,710 casualties from 10 February through 1 March, including 6,659 killed, captured, or missing and 23,051 wounded or sick.[65]

According to most Soviet histories and operational studies, the Leningrad and 2d Baltic Fronts went over to the defense in early March in front of the German Narva and Pskov-Ostrov Fortified Regions: "During the first few days of March, the forces of the Leningrad and 2d Baltic Fronts went over to the defense in the positions that they had seized and began to prepare for subsequent offensive operations to liberate the Soviet Baltic region."[66]

This simple statement, however, is misleading if not disingenuous. As was the case in many of its previous strategic offensive operations, the *Stavka* was not willing to admit that the forward momentum of the Red Army's offensive had ebbed. Therefore, throughout March and most of April, both *fronts* launched heavy assaults against German defenses along a broad front from Narva to Ostrov.

SOVIET ATTEMPTS TO PENETRATE THE GERMAN PANTHER LINE, 1 MARCH–18 APRIL

The Struggle for Narva

In late February, when Govorov's and Popov's forces were nearing the German Panther Line, the *Stavka* issued a series of directives ordering the Red Army to conduct offensives that it hoped would propel its forces through the vaunted German defense line before it fully gelled. When those offensives materialized, they did so along the entire front from Narva in the north to Ostrov in the south.

In a directive issued on 22 February, the *Stavka* had approved Govorov's overall plan to employ Fediuninsky's 2d Shock, Korovnikov's 59th, and, once it had arrived in the region, Starikov's 8th Army to smash, once and for all, the German defenses at Narva. However, the slow regrouping of forces and the necessity for refitting Fediuninsky's threadbare forces delayed the new offensive into early March. Govorov's offensive concept involved the use of all three armies to broaden the bridgehead, capture Narva, and extend the attack into Estonia:

> The further development of the bridgehead along the previous axis directly to the north to reach the Gulf of Narva has little prospect for success because the enemy has created a continuous defense employing two divisions (SS "Feldherrnhalle" Panzer Grenadier [should read "Nordland" and "Feldherrnhalle" Panzer Grenadier Divisions and the "Nederland"

Panzer Grenadier Brigade] and the 170th Infantry Divisions) and 50–60 tanks in this narrow 12-kilometer sector. In order to defeat the strong grouping of forces, which the enemy has created around Narva, it is necessary to conduct operations on a broad front from the occupied bridgeheads, which requires the commitment of additional forces and time to fill out and regroup the forces.

Therefore, I have decided:

1. To halt operations along the Narva axis temporarily and begin preparing future operations.

2. By exploiting the captured bridgehead, to develop further operations:

    a. From Auvere on the eastern face of the bridgehead toward Narva with the mission to widen the bridgehead to the northeast and reach the Narva-Vodava road.

    b. From the Sirgala-Krivaso line on the western face of the bridgehead with the mission of reaching the Iykhvi-Kurmiae-Kiula road and clearing the enemy from the Narva River from Krivaso to its upper reaches.

    c. To dig in temporarily along the northern face of the bridgehead in the sector of the railroad from Auvere Station to Kiriku-Kiula to protect the widening of the bridgehead to the east and west. After the operations along these axes have developed, reach the coast of the Gulf of Narva.

3. To launch the attack from the western face with the 59th Army with two rifle corps and the commitment of a third rifle corps to develop the penetration.

To conduct the attack from the eastern face with two rifle corps of the 2d Shock Army. When the 59th Army attack develops to the west, to exploit the attack toward Iykhvi with the 2d Shock Army from behind the 59th Army's right flank after smashing the remaining forces along that axis while liquidating the Narva salient.

The 8th Army, consisting of two rifle corps and the army headquarters, will regroup from the Pskov to the Narva axis from 24 to 25 February and, after the isthmus north of Lake Chud has been overcome, will be ready for commitment to exploit the attack to the southwest from behind the 59th Army's left flank.

As it arrives in the Kingisepp region, the 3d [Guards] Tank Corps will be concentrated to perform the same mission.

4. As the necessary preparations are made for the development of the bridgehead to the northeast, [I will] begin the 2d Shock Army's offensive two to three days earlier than the 59th Army's so as to protect the 59th Army's deployment and the concealment of the overall concept.

The readiness date to begin the offensive will be limited by the necessity of refitting the forces.

The 2d Shock Army's attack toward the east can begin on 25 February and the 59th Army's attack on 28 February.

[signed] Govorov, Zhdanov, Gusev[67]

As Govorov expected, these problems forced him to delay his assault until 1 March. The official history of the 59th Army describes the mission Govorov assigned Korovnikov's and Fediuninsky's forces during the operation:

The main strength of the army's formations [in late February] were directed at widening the bridgehead; however, separate attacks in a series of sectors had no success. Therefore, on order of the *front* commander, in early March, an attempt was made to make a concentrated attack to the north in the direction of Lastekolonin—an enemy strong point on the Finnish Gulf—with the 43d and 109th Rifle Corps. Their mission was to penetrate the enemy defense, cut the Narva-Tallin railroad, and reach the coast in the rear of the enemy grouping defending Narva. The 2d Shock Army's forces were to attack Narva simultaneously.[68]

Early on 1 March, Fediuninsky's and Korovnikov's armies struck according to plan. The 2d Shock Army's two attacking rifle corps achieved only limited success on the first day of its offensive, but on 2 March Govorov once again ordered Fediuninsky's army to "capture Narva and destroy the garrison of the Narva Fortified Region."[69] Nevertheless, Fediuninsky's assault faltered after three days of heavy fighting. Andreev's 43d and Alferov's 109th Rifle Corps of Korovnikov's 59th Army also attacked at dawn on 1 March after a 20-minute artillery preparation from positions 3 kilometers (1.9 miles) east of the Sirgala, Mitretskii, Razbegai, and Metsavakht line. Since the artillery preparation was apparently inadequate, the attacking forces encountered heavy resistance, particularly in the Sirgala and Putki sector, and made only limited progress. In the face of heavy German counterattacks, artillery fire, and air strikes, Korovnikov attempted to revive the offensive later on 1 March and, again, on 2 March, but to no avail. Thereafter, German forces launched heavy counterattacks against Korovnikov's forces from 4 to 6 March, and the fighting raged on in the 59th Army's sector until 8 April without any resolution.

Despite its earlier failures, Fediuninsky's 2d Shock Army resumed its offensive on 18 March with Mikul'sky's 6th Rifle Corps, which had just been transferred to his army from Starikov's 8th Army, spearheading his assault. The corps' 256th Rifle Division, which was still commanded by Koziev, attacked from the Auvere and Khindinurga line, managed to expand the bridgehead west of the Narva River, and seized a small section of the Tallin-Narva rail line west of Narva. After capturing the vital railroad sector, on 24 March Govorov requested permission from the *Stavka* to halt his offensive in the Narva sector for three to four weeks in order to prepare more thoroughly for a new offensive.[70] Although it is not clear whether the *Stavka* approved Govorov's request, a subsequent German counterstroke rendered Govorov's request irrelevant.

The 59th Army's history candidly assessed the outcome of the Leningrad Front's ill-fated Narva offensive, in doing so certainly overestimating German casualties without mentioning its own losses, which were probably quite heavy:

> The bloody battle continued throughout March and the beginning of April. The 59th Army's forces managed to broaden the front and depth of the occupied bridgehead somewhat. However, this had only tactical importance, and the forces were not able to reach the swampy region west of the Narva River.
>
> The 59th Army's forces inflicted great damage on the enemy in the fighting from 1 March through 8 April. The enemy lost more than 20,000 soldiers and officers, 82 aircraft, 63 tanks, 140 guns, 256 mortars, 630 machine guns, more than 5,000 rifles, and a great amount of other equipment.[71]

On 26 March, German Group Narva mounted a surprise counterstroke designed to restore its defenses along the Narva River. The group launched its assault with the 227th and 11th Infantry Divisions, attacking through the defenses of the 170th and 58th Infantry Divisions. As described by a Soviet source, the attack did little more than straighten the lines:

> The Hitlerite command decided to restore the rail line, and, to that end, launched a counterattack on 26 March. During the course of two weeks, the enemy launched attack after attack. At a cost of heavy losses, the enemy managed to wedge into the Soviet units' defenses, but part of their forces were encircled and destroyed, and the remainder withdrew to their jumping-off positions. Beginning on 12 April, the enemy began concentrating his forces to liquidate the Auvere bridgehead.[72]

After repelling the German counterstroke, on 10 April, in accordance with Govorov's orders, the 59th Army turned its sector over to Starikov's 8th Army and occupied new defenses from the source of the Narva River southward along the eastern shore of Lake Chud. Fediuninsky's 2d Shock Army also went over to the defense effective 12 April.

However, Model was not finished with his attempts to drive Soviet forces back across the Narva River. On 19 April, after a 30-minute artillery preparation, the German III SS Panzer and LIV Army Corps launched another major offensive, code-named Operation Narva, which was designed to clear Soviet forces from the Auvere bridgehead. By this time, Starikov's 8th Army defended the sizable bridgehead south of Narva.[73] Although Starikov's defending Soviet forces supposedly repelled 17 separate attacks on 19 April, in five days of subsequent heavy fighting the counterstroke forced his forces to abandon part of the sector between Auvere Station and Vanamyiza.

The audacious but futile German attacks made a definite impression on Govorov. Once the German offensive had ended, on 23 April Govorov began erecting a new reserve defensive line along the eastern bank of the Luga River east of Narva and assigned the newly arrived 8th Estonian Rifle Corps to occupy the new defenses.[74] By the end of April, the front lines in the Narva region stabilized until Govorov's Leningrad Front resumed offensive operations to capture Narva in July 1944.

The Battles for Pskov, Ostrov, and Idritsa

While Govorov's right-flank armies were trying to crush German defenses at Narva, the armies on his left flank and the armies of Popov's 2d Baltic Front struck hard and repeatedly at the Germans' Panther Line defenses between Pskov and Idritsa.

After his forces had failed to overcome German defenses from the march in late February, on 2 March Govorov ordered Maslennikov's 42d and Sviridov's 67th Armies to "liberate Pskov and Ostrov no later than 10 March and then force the Velikaia River."[75] Russian accounts of the subsequent fighting differ significantly. A recent account claims that the 42d and 67th Armies launched heavy assaults on German defenses from Pskov to Ostrov for two weeks between 2 and 17 March but failed even to dent the strong German defenses. Convinced of the utter futility of the assaults, this account claims that Govorov then ordered the two armies to go over to the defense on 17 March.[76] However, an earlier history provides an altogether different view:

> After concentrating its efforts on its left wing, on 9 March, the Leningrad Front began an offensive to capture Pskov and tie down German forces. From the very first day, heavy combat raged along the Pskov axis, which did not cease until early April. The *front*'s forces penetrated the enemy's strongly fortified defenses south of Pskov and, advancing up to 13 kilometers [8 miles], cut the highway and railroad running from Pskov to Ostrov. This offensive tied down Army Group North's reserves and prevented the German command from transferring forces from here to the south, where the position of German forces was catastrophic.[77]

Farther to the south, the 1st Shock, 22d, 10th Guards, and 3d Shock Armies of Popov's 2d Baltic Front also assaulted the Panther Line defenses between Ostrov and Idritsa. Once again, Russian accounts of the fighting vary from the grossly inaccurate to barely accurate. An account dating to the 1970s states:

> On the 2d Baltic Front's left wing, the 10th Guards and 3d Shock Armies resumed their offensive on 26 February and by 1 March reached a line east of Ostrov-Novorzhev-Pustoshka together with the forces of the Leningrad Front.
>
> On order of the *Stavka* of the Supreme High Command, on 1 March 1944, the forces went over to the defense in their existing positions to prepare for a new offensive operation.[78]

A more recent account simply states, "The 2d Baltic Front's attempts [after 29 February] to penetrate [the German defensive line east of Ostrov, Novorzhev, and Pustoshka] were not crowned with success. Thus, the offensive along the Northwestern axis came to an end."[79]

Thorough examination of admittedly fragmentary sources, including some newly released documents, now indicates that heavy fighting indeed raged across the entire sector from Ostrov to Idritsa throughout March and much of April 1944. In fact, on 3 March the *Stavka* and General Staff representatives to the 2d and 1st Baltic Front, Marshal S. K. Timoshenko and Colonel General S. M. Shtemenko, submitted a tentative plan to the *Stavka* for the destruction of German forces between Ostrov and Idritsa. The message contained their recommendations for the 2d Baltic Front's role in the offensive:

> 1. After careful study of the situation and an analysis of combat operations during the last two days, together with Comrades Markov and Khristoferov, we have concluded that operations in a narrow sector along the Idritsa axis will not produce the desired results in the immediate future, will lead to considerable personnel losses, and will require a significant expenditure of ammunition.
>
> The enemy has committed up to three infantry divisions and one panzer division along the axis of our main attack and is operating on favorable terrain.
>
> We think it necessary to broaden the offensive front to disperse enemy forces and select more favorable axes for both *fronts'* offensive operations in order to fulfill the mission assigned by the *Stavka*.
>
> Based on the above, we propose the following offensive missions:
>
> a. For the 2d Baltic Front:

Overall mission—to liquidate the enemy's Novorzhev-Idritsa grouping, capture his important communications center at Opochka, reach the Velikaia River, and, if possible, force it along its upper reaches.

The *front*'s left wing will cooperate with the 1st Baltic Front in the capture of Idritsa.

To fulfill this plan we will assign the following missions to the armies:

Korotkov's 1st Shock Army will attack along the Pskov-Idritsa railroad toward Pushkinskie Gory and Opochka with three rifle divisions and one rifle brigade.

Leave one rifle division and one rifle brigade to protect the Leningrad Front's left flank.

Iushkevich's 22d Army will penetrate enemy defenses south of Novorzhev with four rifle divisions and, by attacking along the Novorzhev-Opochka highway together with the 1st Shock Army, capture the Opochka region and assist the *front*'s left wing by reaching the rear of the enemy defending along the Novorzhev and Pustoshka line.

Kazakov's 10th Guards Army will attack in the Berezno and Tarasy sector with nine rifle divisions and conduct its main attack along the Krasnoe and Opochka axis.

Chibisov's 3d Shock Army will penetrate enemy defenses along the Tarasy (incl.) and Staraia Pustoshka front with nine rifle divisions and make its main attack to the west and southwest north of the Pustoshka-Idritsa railroad to assist the 1st Baltic Front in the capture of Idritsa.

Subsequently operate in the general direction of Ludzu.

b. For the 1st Baltic Front . . .

2. Boundary lines . . .

3. The *fronts'* mobile formations (the 3d Guards Cavalry Corps and the 5th Tank Corps) will be concentrated along the Idritsa axis and, depending on the situation, will be employed to exploit success wherever it is ordered to.

4. The regrouping will be conducted in secrecy, and units will be relieved only the day before the attack. . . .

It will require no fewer than four days to prepare the operation; therefore, movement can begin on 7–8 March 1944. . . .

[signed] Timoshenko, Shtemenko[80]

The *Stavka* approved Timoshenko's and Shtemenko's plan at 0200 hours the next morning but amended it to maintain pressure across a broad front:

The operational plan presented in your Enciphered Report No. 5 will lead to an excessive concentration of our forces and a weakening of the junction between the Leningrad and 2d Baltic Front, which to us seems disadvantageous.

The *Stavka* of the Supreme High Command *orders:*

1. The principal missions are the arrival of the 2d Baltic Front's main forces at the left bank of the Velikaia River north of Idritsa and the destruction of the enemy's Idritsa grouping by the combined efforts of the 2d and 1st Baltic Fronts. Under no circumstances weaken the junction with the Leningrad Front.

2. To fulfill this mission:

    a. Korotkov's 1st Shock Army will continue to attack along its present axis toward Shanino and Krasnogorodskoe while cooperating with the Leningrad Front's left wing.

    b. Iushkevich's 22d Army will attack in the general direction of Opochka, where it will force the Velikaia River, while, at the same time, exploiting the attack to the southwest and south.

    c. Kazakov's 10th Guards Army and Chibisov's 3d Shock Army will attack with the missions of reaching the Velikaia River in the Razriadino sector (17 kilometers [10.5 miles] south of Opochka) and to the south, force the Velikaia River there, and reach the rear of the enemy's Idritsa grouping. Part of the 3d Shock Army will attack toward Idritsa along the left bank of the Velikaia River and capture Idritsa in cooperation with Galitsky's 11th Guards Army. . . .

4. Begin movement no later than 7–8 March 1944. . . .

[signed] I. Stalin, A. Antonov[81]

The six armies under the Leningrad and 2d Baltic Fronts' control struggled almost continuously from early March to 18 April to overcome the strong German defenses manned by the Eighteenth and Sixteenth Armies' XXVIII, XXXVIII, VI SS, II, XXXXIII, VIII, and X Army Corps.[82] However, the meager results were in no way commensurate with the heavy casualties incurred by Govorov's and Popov's forces. The period was marked by frequent halts to regroup, repeated *Stavka* exhortations to accelerate the offensive, and separate major offensive impulses launched on 6 and 12 March and again on 7 April.[83] However, the *Stavka* did permit Govorov's 42d and 67th Armies to go over to the defense temporarily on 17 March, since they were utterly exhausted and totally incapable of even denting German defenses anchored on the Pskov and Ostrov fortified regions. Nevertheless, they once again participated in the 7 April offensive with similar negative results.

Despite the sketchy Soviet descriptions of the fierce fighting that took place during March and April along the broad front from Narva south to Ostrov, German sources vividly underscore the real intensity of the fighting, which Soviet histories have generally neglected:

On 1 March Army Group North took the last step back into the Panther position, and the Russians demonstrated that they were not going to let it come to a rest there. North of Pustoshka two armies hit the VIII Army Corps front. South of the town two armies threw their weight against X Corps. *Leningrad Front* massed two armies south of Pskov and poured more troops across the Narva River, attacking out of the bridgehead to the north, northwest, and west. For a week the battle rippled up and down the whole army group front. Except for small local losses, the German line held. On 9 March, *Second Baltic Front* stepped up its pressure against the Sixteenth Army right flank and began straining heavily for a breakthrough. . . .

At midmonth *Second Baltic Front* was still battering the Sixteenth Army flank while *Leningrad Front* probed for openings around Pskov and Narva. But the weather had turned against the Russians. After a warm winter— for Russia—the spring thaw set in early. A foot of water covered the ice on the lakes. Sixteenth Army reported that the Soviet tanks were sometimes sinking up to their turrets in mud. Against a weak front the Russians might have continued to advance, as they were doing in the Ukraine, but the Panther position, all that remained of the East Wall, was living up to German expectations.[84]

Finally admitting that the *fronts* on the threshold of the Baltic region were literally at the end of their leashes and could do no more, shortly after midnight on 18 April, Stalin ordered Govorov and Popov to cease all offensive operations:

The *Stavka* of the Supreme High Command *orders:*

1. In light of the unsuccessful offensive, upon receipt of this directive, the 2d Baltic Front will go over to a firm defense in all sectors of the front.

2. While organizing the defense, pay special attention to the Novorzhev and Pustoshka axes. Dig in strongly in the bridgeheads on the western bank of the Velikaia River.

3. Prepare a deeply echeloned defense. Prepare no fewer than three defensive lines in the front belt to a total depth of 30–40 kilometers.

4. Report all orders given.

[signed] I. Stalin, A. Antonov[85]

Although Stalin had hoped that the Leningrad and 2d Baltic Fronts could smash the Panther Line and advance on Riga, his hope was misplaced. Govorov's and Popov's forces simply lacked the strength to inflict terminal defeat on Model's Army Group North. Stalin, however, wasted no time in his search for a new opportunity to do so. The day after ordering his forces on the defense, he ordered the formation of a new 3d Baltic Front to better control Red Army forces operating along the Pskov and Ostrov axes. Stalin placed the new *front,* which was formed on the base of the 20th Army head-quarters and assumed control of Govorov's 42d, 67th, and 54th Armies, under Maslennikov's command. With virtually all of southern Leningrad region lib-erated, Stalin was already paving the way for future larger-scale offensive operations into the Baltic region and Finnish Karelia.[86]

The Leningrad, Volkhov, and 2d Baltic Fronts' Leningrad-Novgorod offen-sive operation was immensely significant. First and foremost, the liberation of Leningrad raised the morale of the Soviet population, inspired the Soviet Union's allies, and had a crushing effect on German morale. In addition, while representing only the first stage of the Red Army's winter offensive, it took place simultaneously with and supported major Red Army offensives along the western strategic axis into Belorussia and the southwestern strategic axes into the Ukraine.

During the course of 45 days, the three *fronts* smashed deeply echeloned defenses the enemy had erected over a period of two years, defeated Army Group North's Eighteenth and, to a lesser extent, Sixteenth Army, and raised the Leningrad blockade. By the end of February, Red Army forces had lib-erated all of southern Leningrad region and part of Kalinin region and en-tered Soviet Estonia, in the process saving millions of Soviet citizens from German enslavement or worse. The offensive opened the Moscow-Leningrad rail line, provided the Baltic Fleet freedom of action, and created prerequi-sites for driving Finland from the war.

The three Soviet *fronts* inflicted severe losses on the German Eighteenth and Sixteenth Armies during the operation, completely destroying 3 divisions and severely damaging 12 of Eighteenth Army's divisions and 5 of Sixteenth Army's. During the period from 14 January through 14 February, the Lenin-grad and Volkhov Fronts reported capturing 180 tanks, 1,800 guns, 4,660 machine guns, 22,000 rifles and submachine guns, 1,810,000 shells, 17 mil-lion cartridges, 2,648 vehicles, 615 railroad wagons, 353 warehouses, and 7,200 German soldiers.[87]

The Red Army performed several noteworthy feats during the second stage of the Leningrad-Novgorod operation. Although it failed to destroy the Eighteenth Army during the operation's first stage, during the second it drove the German army back to Narva and through Luga back to the Panther Line. By the time the Red Army forces reached Narva, Pskov, and Ostrov, its ad-vance had encompassed a 400-kilometer (248.5-mile) front to a depth of 300 kilometers (186.4 miles) in 47 days, with the forces advancing an average of 6.5 kilometers (4 miles) per day.

Considering the operation as a whole, armies designated to conduct main attacks formed for combat in two echelons of rifle corps and employed a wide array of artillery groups for fire support. The 2d Shock and 42d Armies formed antitank reserves, tank reserves, and mobile obstacle detachments, and the 42d Army formed a strong mobile tank group and a combined-arms reserve. The employment of such a reserve permitted the 30th Guard Rifle Corps to attack in single echelon. Within the armies, the rifle corps attacked in one, two, or three echelons depending on the situation, and, as a rule, rifle divisions formed in single echelon with a reserve to generate maximum offensive momentum.

However, some armies failed to commit their second echelons in timely or effective fashion, thus weakening the force of the main attack. For example, the 2d Shock Army committed its second-echelon 108th Rifle Corps over a period of two days (the 196th Rifle Division on 18–19 January and the 168th Rifle Division on 19 January). In another instance, the 42d Army committed its combined-arms reserve into combat one regiment at a time, and command and control failed. This error, combined with poor reconnaissance, inadequate artillery and engineer support, and weak command and control, negated the mobile tank group's effectiveness. Finally, the Volkhov Front's 59th Army committed its second-echelon 112th Rifle Corps into combat along a secondary axis, thereby dissipating the army's effectiveness and slowing its advance.

Often army commanders failed to capitalize on their artillery, tank, engineer, and aviation support and neglected to employ maneuver when attempting to capture German strong points and fortified regions. As a result, the infantry advance through swampy and forested regions degenerated into progressive "gnawing" through successive German defense lines. Often, too, the infantry had to advance without adequate artillery, armor, and engineer support. In these instances, it became quite difficult to conduct ammunition and food resupply and evacuate the wounded. While artillery was immensely valuable when supporting the penetration of strong German defenses and reducing strong points, it proved far less useful during operations across difficult terrain because it congenitally lagged 20–25 kilometers (12.4–15.5 miles) behind the infantry. Bad weather conditions and the shortage of bombers also limited aviation support, even though long-range aviation took up some of the slack.

The Red Army General Staff later identified major deficiencies in the offensives that hindered operations in the difficult terrain.[88] Poor engineer reconnaissance and a shortage of engineer forces made maneuver difficult for tanks and artillery and, at times, even for infantry. Since it was often easier to maneuver from the depth than laterally, the value of mobile detachments operating along the few existing roads increased sharply. The swampy and forested roads, even if frozen, also inhibited the establishment of effective communications. Bad terrain and the frequent dispersal of forces along separate axes made wire communications impossible and forced advancing units to rely on radios, which were in short supply.

Many other deficiencies identified by the General Staff mirrored those apparent in previous operations. For example, intelligence organs failed to reconnoiter the terrain and German defenses adequately, and this had an adverse impact on the effectiveness of artillery preparations and supporting fires. Commanders tended to disperse their forces in an apparent attempt to attack and win everywhere simultaneously and often neglected to concentrate sufficient forces to achieve decisive penetrations and advances along main attack axes. During the operations, commanders exercised weak command and control over their subordinate forces and either neglected night operations entirely or conducted them ineffectively. Worse still, both tanks and artillery often lagged far behind, depriving the infantry of critical artillery and tank support when they most needed it. Finally, when it did occur, supply was either late or inadequate, forcing units to operate without necessary ammunition, fuel, or foodstuffs. The foraging that inevitably resulted further reduced the units' combat effectiveness. All of these problems significantly reduced the rate of advance and prevented the encirclement and destruction of many otherwise vulnerable German forces. Most important, staffs at *front,* army, and corps level lacked experience in the conduct of large-scale offensive operations, and it showed.

One notable exception to this rule was the positive role partisans played in the operation. Partisan brigades, regiments, detachments, and small groups conducted extensive reconnaissance and diversionary work during the preparatory period. For example, the Leningrad Headquarters of the Partisan Movement reported that 22,000 partisans in Leningrad region killed 21,556 Germans and destroyed 58,563 rails, 51 railroad and 247 road bridges, 136 trains, 509 kilometers of telegraph lines, 1,620 vehicles, 811 carts, 28 warehouses, 33 tanks, and 4 aircraft from 14 January through 1 March 1944.[89]

Despite the many problems Soviet commanders experienced during the Leningrad-Novgorod offensive operation and the fact that the operation required far longer to complete than the *Stavka* had anticipated, the three Red Army *fronts* fulfilled their primary mission. By 1 March they had driven German Army Group North from the southern portion of Leningrad region. Nor was their failure to capture Narva, Ostrov, and Pskov and pierce the Panther Line a unique experience. As had been the case in previous strategic offensives, the *Stavka* routinely attempted to exploit offensive success whenever and wherever it could, regardless of the condition of its troops. While this practice failed in the Leningrad region in the winter of 1944, it proved expeditious in other front sectors. In addition, it also provided the

Stavka with a clearer understanding of how difficult it would be for Red Army forces to operate along the northwestern axis in future operations so that it could adjust its plans and forces accordingly.

While the Leningrad-Novgorod offensive achieved its strategic ends, it also proved costly for those who fought in it. From 14 January through 1 March 1944, the three Soviet *fronts* conducting the operation suffered 313,953 casualties out of an initial force of 822,100 men committed to action. This gruesome toll included 76,886 killed, captured, or missing and 237,267 men wounded or sick.[90] However, compared with earlier operations, by Soviet standards these losses were bearable. However, this official count does not include losses suffered in the bloody attempts to penetrate the Panther Line in March and April, which probably added in excess of another 200,000 men to this casualty toll.[91]

German Army Group North also suffered greatly. From late October 1943 through 1 May 1944, its personnel strength fell from 610,000 men supported by 146 tanks (108 serviceable) and 2,389 artillery pieces to 578,000 men (with 29,000 auxiliaries) supported by 432 tanks (203 serviceable) and 2,040 artillery pieces. During the same period, German Foreign Armies East estimated the strength of opposing Red Army forces had increased from 959,000 men, 650 tanks, and 3,680 guns and mortars to 1,318,000 men, 2,200 tanks, and 7,500 guns and mortars.[92] That amounted to an increase in Soviet superiority from 1.5 to 1 to almost 3 to 1 in troops, from 4.5 to 1 to over 5 to 1 in armor, and from over 3 to 1 to over 3.6 to 1 in artillery. Given these ratios, the total defeat of German Army Group North would only be a matter of time.

CHAPTER 13

The Liberation of
Northern Leningrad Region

June–August 1944

THE SITUATION IN JUNE 1944

The wave of offensives the *Stavka* ordered the Red Army to conduct in January 1944 served as prelude to an expanding torrent of Soviet offensive operations, which ultimately encompassed virtually the entire Soviet-German front. These operations included the Leningrad, Volkhov, and finally the 2d Baltic Fronts' offensive against Army Group North, the 1st Baltic and Belorussian Fronts' offensives against Army Group Center, and the 1st, 2d, 3d, and 4th Ukrainian Fronts' offensives against Army Group South.

Although Army Group Center stubbornly held much of its ground throughout the winter, the *Wehrmacht*'s strategic flanks sagged badly. Incessant Soviet offensives along the northwestern axis drove German forces back to the Panther Line and the borders of the Baltic republics. To the Germans' utter consternation, along the southwestern axis, the Red Army's four Ukrainian *fronts* continued their offensive operations without pause deep into the spring, liberating much of the Ukraine and the Crimea and reaching the Polish and Rumanian borders by early April 1944. This was the first time during the war that the Germans had been unable to halt Soviet offensive operations before the onset of spring.

By early 1944, also for the first time in the war, the Soviet Union's military-economic productive base was strong enough to sustain the Red Army's spectacular advance. Worse still for the Germans, coupled with their staggering losses in intense battles of attrition, the immense quantities of increasingly sophisticated weaponry produced by Soviet industry more than matched Germany's military productive capacity. While a seemingly endless flood of modern weaponry drowned the *Wehrmacht* on the field of battle, the Red Army continued to field or regroup strategic reserves at a pace sufficient to conduct successive and even simultaneous strategic offensives. Red Army field commanders at every level became increasingly proficient at planning and conducting complex offensive operations.

Hitler and his OKH struggled to parry the Red Army's multiple blows by conducting a strategic defense along all three strategic axes, anchoring their defenses on a series of heavily fortified defense lines and regions. This was particularly true along the northwestern axis. There, where German forces relied on the heavily fortified Panther Line to block future Red Army offensives, at least theoretically, Army Group North continue to pose a threat to Leningrad from the south and clung tenaciously to the Baltic States, East Prussia, and the southern shore of the Baltic Sea.

Given this strategic situation, Stalin's and his *Stavka*'s principal military-political aims in 1944 were to defeat and destroy German forces along the entire front from the Barents Sea to the Black Sea, complete the liberation of Soviet territory, and begin the liberation of Nazi-occupied territories in Eastern and Southeastern Europe. In so doing, Stalin also hoped to accelerate the breakup of the Nazi bloc by driving Finland, Rumania, Bulgaria, and Hungary from the war and gain postwar advantage in the vital region over his Western allies.

Stalin and the *Stavka* sought to achieve these strategic aims by conducting a series of large-scale offensive operations successively along the entire Soviet-German front.[1] The first of these offensives, the Leningrad-Novgorod offensive, succeeded in eliminating any German threat to Leningrad by pushing German Army Group North's forces back to Narva, Pskov, and Ostrov. However, despite this Red Army victory, Leningrad was still insecure, since a large Finnish force was still dug in across the Karelian Isthmus only 30 kilometers (18.6 miles) from the city's northern outskirts. The Finns also controlled southern Karelia and the Kirov railroad, the vital rail link that connected Leningrad with the Soviet Union's northern ports.

Therefore, in the summer of 1944, the Red Army's priority military mission in the northern theater of military operations was to defeat Finnish forces on the Karelian Isthmus and in southern Karelia, liberate Finnish-occupied territory, if possible, capture the Finnish capital at Helsinki, and drive Finland from the war. To do so, the *Stavka* ordered Govorov's Leningrad Front to defeat Finnish forces along the Vyborg axis and the Karelian Front, now commanded by Meretskov, to defeat Finnish forces along the Svir-Petrozavodsk axis in southern Karelia.

The situation on the Karelian Isthmus in summer 1944 was already tense. The Red Army's successes in early 1944 had prompted the Finnish government to approach Soviet officials in February 1944 to determine the conditions under which the Finnish government could leave the war with the least possible damage. The Finnish peace feelers were set against a backdrop of Soviet air raids on Finnish cities, including Helsinki, and increasing pressure by the Finnish press to sue for peace.[2] The Finnish government sent its prime minister, the former ambassador to the Soviet Union, Dr. Juho K. Paasikivi, to Stockholm to receive proposed peace terms from the Soviet ambassador to Sweden, A. M. Kollontai. Two weeks of secret talks ensued, while the Soviets continued their bombing raids, including a 300-plane raid on Helsinki on 27 February. The Soviets formally published their peace terms on 28 February.[3]

Although the Soviet government's conditions for a Finnish-Soviet peace were quite severe, they were dictated by the damage the Germans, with at least tacit Finnish assistance, had inflicted on the Soviet Union, and Leningrad and Leningraders in particular. Stalin required Finland to break off relations with Germany and intern German ground and naval forces (the Twentieth Mountain Army) in northern Finland. Finland was to restore the Soviet-Finnish Pact of 1940 and withdraw Finnish forces to the 1940 frontiers. It was to repatriate Soviet soldiers or civilians held in Finnish prisoner-of-war or labor camps to the Soviet Union immediately and thereafter return all property seized from the Soviet Union. Finally, the Finns were to restore the Petsamo (Pechenga) region to the Soviet Union, pay reparations whose amount was to be determined later, and, as determined by future negotiations, either partially or completely demobilize the Finnish Army.[4]

In response to Stalin's ultimatum, which it was in no position to accept, on 8 March the Finnish government rejected the proposed boundary changes and prisoner-of-war release as preconditions for an armistice. They also objected to interning the Twentieth Mountain Army, which, they maintained, was politically and militarily impossible, since Hitler was likely to refuse to do so. Perhaps heartened by the German successes in halting the Red Army's advance at the Panther Line, the Finns once again rejected the Soviet terms on 18 March but left the door open to future negotiations. Subsequent negotiations continued throughout March, but the Finns again categorically rejected the terms on 18 April. On 13 May the Soviet, U.S., and British governments appealed to the German satellite and warned it against continuing the war on Germany's side. Despite these appeals, the Finnish government instead decided to continue the war by defending its earlier gains and tying down Soviet forces in the Karelian and Baltic regions. The *Stavka* reacted accordingly by preparing offensive operations against the Finns.

When the *Stavka* began preparing for operations in Karelia in May 1944, two Red Army *fronts* faced Finnish forces on the Karelian Isthmus and along the vast sector of the front from Lake Ladoga northward to the Kola Peninsula and the coast of the Barents Sea west of Murmansk. The Karelian Front, which was commanded by Meretskov, who had been transferred from Volkhov to Karelian Front command in late February 1944, was deployed between the Barents Sea and Lake Ladoga. Within Meretskov's *front*, Lieutenant General F. D. Gorelenko's 32d and Major General A. N. Krutikov's 7th Armies were deployed in southern Karelia from Ukhty to Lake Ladoga facing eight Finnish divisions and three brigades of the Finnish Group Olonets's II and VI Army Corps.[5]

In the Leningrad Front's sector south of Lake Ladoga, Lieutenant General A. I. Cherepanov's 23d Army defended astride the Karelian Isthmus. Cherepanov's army consisted of the 108th Rifle Corps, commanded by

Tikhonov, who had been promoted to lieutenant general in late February, and Major General Kozachek's 115th Rifle Corps, each with three rifle divisions, the 142d Separate Rifle Brigade, and the 17th and 22d Fortified Regions. In addition, Cherepanov's army included one tank brigade, one tank regiment, four gun artillery regiments, seven mortar regiments, four antitank artillery regiments, and one antiaircraft artillery division. Both Tikhonov's and Kozachek's corps were experienced formations that had seen extensive action during the Leningrad-Novgorod offensive.

Cherepanov's army was deployed in a two-echelon defense, with Kozachek's 115th Rifle Corps and Colonel G. L. Sonnikov's 142d Rifle Division in first echelon and Tikhonov's 108th Rifle Corps in second echelon. Major General I. I. Iastrebov's 72d Rifle Division and Major General N. P. Iakunin's 98th Rifle Corps headquarters were in *front* reserve. The 115th Rifle Corps consisted of the 10th, 92d, and 314th Rifle Divisions, the 108th Rifle Corps, and the 46th, 90th, and 372d Rifle Divisions. The army's rifle divisions ranged in strength from 6,400 to 7,000 men each.[6]

The Finnish III and IV Army Corps, which included six infantry divisions, one armored division, and two coastal defense brigades, manned defenses opposite the 23d Army. The III Army Corps consisted of the 15th Infantry Division and 19th Infantry Brigade, and the IV Army Corps included the 2d and 10th Infantry Divisions. The Finnish 2d and 3d Coastal Defense Brigades defended the northern coast of the Baltic Sea and the western shore of Lake Ladoga, respectively. The 3d and 18th Infantry Divisions, the Lagus Armored Division, and the 1st Cavalry Brigade were in reserve.[7]

South of Leningrad, Starikov's 8th, Fediuninsky's 2d Shock, and Korovnikov's 59th Armies and Lieutenant General I. A. Pern's 8th Estonian Rifle Corps of Govorov's *front* occupied positions in and west of the Narva region. The crack 30th Guards Rifle Corps with three rifle divisions and the veteran 109th Rifle Corps with five rifle divisions, commanded, respectively, by Simoniak and Alferov, both now lieutenant generals, were in *front* reserve southwest of Leningrad. Lieutenant General of Aviation S. D. Rybal'chenko's 13th Air Army, which numbered 400 combat aircraft, had the mission of providing the Leningrad Front with air support.[8]

Finnish forces opposite the Karelian Front's left wing and the Leningrad Front's 23d Army totaled 15 divisions and 9 brigades, and each division numbered between 11,000 and 12,000 men. By Soviet count, this force numbered 268,000 men, 2,350 guns and mortars, 110 tanks, and about 250 aircraft (including roughly 70 aircraft sent by the Germans). However, according to Finnish accounts, although roughly half of Finland's total force of 500,000 soldiers were deployed on the Karelian Isthmus, Finnish Army equipment strength in that region was considerably less than Soviet estimates. The correlation of infantry forces was approximately equal in May 1944, but Soviet air forces were superior to Finnish forces, with 1,500 aircraft assigned to the two *fronts* and Baltic Fleet as opposed to 350 Finnish aircraft (by Soviet estimates). This Soviet superiority increased markedly by early June.[9]

Despite this clear Soviet numerical superiority, the difficult terrain and strong fortifications on the Karelian Peninsula favored the Finnish defense. Finnish forces defended the imposing Mannerheim Line, which lay along the former 1939 Soviet-Finnish border, and had constructed elaborate defenses forward of that line since 1941, particularly after the Soviet Stalingrad counteroffensive. These defenses consisted of three defensive belts south of Vyborg to a total depth of 120 kilometers (75.5 miles). The first belt, 35–40 kilometers (18.6–24.8 miles) from Leningrad's northern outskirts, was 3–5 kilometers (1.9–3.1 miles) deep and comprised of a series of strong points and centers of resistance connected by an intricate network of trenches and communications trenches. The second line, which was located 15–25 kilometers (9.3–15.5 miles) behind the first line and was 70–80 percent complete, was also 3–5 kilometers deep and far stronger than the first. A third but less complete line was located 60–65 kilometers (37.2–40.4 miles) from the front northwest of Leningrad.[10]

Vyborg's fortifications, which consisted of internal and external defensive rings, were tied into a fourth Finnish defense line, the VKT (Vyborg, Kuparsari, Taipale Line), which was located 70–90 kilometers (43.5–60 miles) from the forward edge. In addition, partially constructed defensive belts northwest of Vyborg, which the Finns began constructing in June 1944, protected the Vyborg-Helsinki axis. To varying degrees, all of these defensive lines consisted of extensive networks of trenches, fortified regions and centers of resistance, and well-prepared and often concrete fortifications and positions.

Ultimately, the *Stavka* ordered Meretskov's and Govorov's forces to defeat Finnish forces on the Karelian and Onega-Ladoga isthmuses decisively, eliminate the threat to Leningrad from the north, liberate the northern half of Leningrad region and southern Karelia, restore the 1940 border with Finland, and drive Finland from the war. It sought to do so by conducting successive offensives with the Leningrad Front and Karelian Front's left wing and the Baltic Fleet and Ladoga and Onega Flotillas, first along the Leningrad-Vyborg axis and, later, along the Svir-Sortavala axes. In addition to its forces' numerical superiority, the *Stavka* relied heavily on the element of surprise to overcome the strong Finnish defenses.

The Leningrad Front was to conduct the Vyborg operation in cooperation with Tributs's Baltic Fleet. Govorov was to conduct his main attack along the northern coast of the Gulf of Finland in the general direction of Staryi Beloostrov, Vyborg, and Lappenranta to destroy the bulk of the Finnish Army, reach positions west and northwest of Vyborg, and threaten the key population centers in southern Finland. Meretskov's Karelian Front was to conduct the Svir-Petrozavodsk operation with support from the Ladoga and Onega Flotillas. Meretskov was to launch his main attack along the shore of Lake Ladoga to destroy the Finnish Olonets grouping, clear Finnish forces from southern Karelia, and prepare to threaten central Finland.

To provide Govorov with sufficient forces to conduct his massive offensive, on 28 April the *Stavka* reinforced his *front* with the headquarters of Colonel General D. M. Gusev's 21st Army, which had just arrived in the Ropsha region from the *Stavka* reserve.[11] Soon after, Govorov regrouped Gusev's army to the Karelian Isthmus. Initially, the 21st Army consisted of the 124th and 97th Rifle Corps, commanded by Major Generals I. F. Nikitin and M. M. Busarov, respectively. The former consisted of the 281st, 286th, and 177th Rifle Divisions and the latter of the 178th, 358th, and 381st Rifle Divisions. The *Stavka* also transferred two artillery penetration divisions, one gun artillery brigade, two corps artillery regiments, five special-power artillery battalions (280mm and 305mm hoitzers), two tank and seven self-propelled artillery regiments, one assault engineer-sapper brigade, and one park of engineer vehicles to Govorov's *front* from its reserve.

In addition, on 1 June the *Stavka* assigned Khazov's veteran 110th Rifle Corps, with the 168th, 265th, and 268th Rifle Divisions and the 13th and 382d Separate Rifle Divisions, from the 3d Baltic Front to the Leningrad Front. Khazov, too, had recently been promoted to the rank of lieutenant general. Then the *Stavka* reinforced the 13th Air Army with the 334th and 113d Bomber and 281st Assault Aviation Divisions.[12]

By 10 June 1944, the Leningrad Front fielded 188,800 men on the Karelian Isthmus and the Karelian Front 202,300 men north of Lake Ladoga, for a total of 451,500 (including 60,400 in the fleet and flotillas) slated to be employed in the forthcoming operations. Roughly 10,000 guns and mortars, 800 tanks and self-propelled guns, and 1,547 combat aircraft backed up this infantry force. According to Soviet calculations, this produced Red Army numerical superiority of 1.7 to 1 in manpower, 5.2 to 1 in artillery, 7.3 to 1 in tanks, and 6.2 to 1 in aircraft.[13] However, considering normal force concentration prior to the assault, the actual Red Army superiority in main attack sectors was likely closer to 5 to 1 in infantry, 10–15 to 1 in tanks and artillery, and 15 to 1 in combat aircraft.

THE LENINGRAD FRONT'S PLANS

In accordance with the *Stavka*'s instructions, Govorov issued his own directive on 3 May 1944, articulating his concept for the offensive operation and established missions for his armies, the Baltic Fleet, and all supporting arms. Based on the configuration of Finnish troop dispositions, he decided to penetrate the Finnish defenses with the 21st and 23d Armies deployed in single echelon, with two rifle corps and four separate rifle divisions in reserve.

Gusev's 21st Army was to conduct the *front*'s main attack from the region northwest of Sestroretsk, with its three rifle corps reinforced by *front* reserves. This force was to penetrate Finnish defenses between Hill 107.4 and the Gulf of Finland, destroy the Finnish III and IV Army Corps, and exploit to capture Vyborg by the ninth to the eleventh day of the operation. After Gusev's three corps had penetrated the Finnish forward defenses and reached the Sestra River, two rifle corps of Cherepanov's 23d Army were to join Gusev's offensive and widen the breech. Together, the two armies would then penetrate the Finnish second and third defensive belts and advance to capture Vyborg. The planned depth of the operation as a whole was 110–120 kilometers (68.4–74.6 miles) at the intended advance rate of 12 kilometers (7.6 miles) per day.[14]

Gusev's 21st Army consisted of Simoniak's 30th Guards, Busarov's 97th and Alferov's 109th Rifle Corps, and the 22d Fortified Region. It was to attack in the general direction of Vyborg, penetrate the Finns' first and second defensive belts, defeat in succession the IV Army Corps and Finnish operational reserves, and prevent them from withdrawing to the third defensive belt. Subsequently, it was to exploit the attack toward Summa and, simultaneously, along the coastal railroad to Koivisto to reach the Finnish third defensive belt.

Gusev's immediate mission was to penetrate the Finns' first defensive belt by attacking in the *front*'s center along the Kallelovo and Vyborg roads and coastal railroad and destroying the defending 10th Infantry Division. His force would then force the Sestra River from the march and capture the Termolovo, Khirelia, Iappilia, and Kellomiaki line no later than the second day of the operation. If Finnish operational reserves managed to occupy the Sestra River line before Gusev's shock group reached it, his army was to halt and organize a deliberate forced crossing of the river. After it crossed the Sestra River, the army was to transfer Busarov's 97th Rifle Corps to the 23d Army, receive Tikhonov's 108th Rifle Corps from *front* reserve, and commit the fresh corps into combat along the coastal railroad. The entire army would then advance toward Raivola and Kivennapa with its main forces.

While Gusev was conducting his assault on the *front*'s left flank, Cherepanov's 23d Army was to defend its positions from Okhta to Lake Ladoga on the right flank with Kozachek's 115th Rifle Corps and the 17th Fortified Region. Tikhonov's 98th Rifle Corps was deployed in second echelon behind the army's left flank. When Cherepanov's forces reached the Sestra River, his 21st Army was to take over control of the 97th Rifle Corps and attack with it and the 98th Rifle Corps to widen the penetration and roll up Finnish defenses to the east. As his forces turned the Finnish flank, Cherepanov's army was to begin a general attack along its entire front and penetrate the Finnish second defensive belt with an attack toward Lake Valk-iarvi. Subsequently, the army was to destroy opposing Finnish forces, prevent them from withdrawing to their third defensive belt, and reach the Lakes Suvanto-iarvi, Vuoksi-iarvi, and Iaiuriapian-iarvi line.[15]

Tributs's Baltic Fleet was to support the offensive with all of its naval and coastal artillery concentrating their fires in the 21st Army's sector. For deceptive purposes, the fleet also planned to conduct real and demonstrative amphibious assaults to tie down Finnish forces. These included a real amphibious assault with the 224th Rifle Division in the Ino, Seiviaste, and Koivisto sectors and the transport of five rifle divisions from Oranienbaum to Lisii Nos (northwest of Leningrad) to reinforce Gusev's offensive. The fleet was to be prepared to conduct these operations by 3 June. In addition, the fleet was to prevent Finnish amphibious and naval action operations against the 21st and 23d Armies' flanks. Fleet aviation, which included the 1st Guards Fighter, 8th Torpedo, and 9th and 11th Assault Aviation Divisions, was to conduct reconnaissance at sea and provide air cover for the 21st Army. In addition, on 10 June it was to allocate two assault aviation regiments with 60 Il-2 aircraft to strike enemy defenses at Staryi Beloostrov and support the ground troops' advance.[16]

Combat and combat service support for the offensive was far more elaborate than had been the case in previous operations and was based largely on experiences derived from the Leningrad-Novgorod offensive. *Front* and army artillery had the mission of destroying enemy fortifications during the preparation, supporting the assault, and conducting counter-battery fires. The preparation in the 21st Army's sector, which was to last 140 minutes, involved 200–220 guns and mortars firing in support in each kilometer of the armies' front. Rybal'chenko's 13th Air Army was to destroy enemy strong points and artillery and mortar positions, prevent enemy troop movements forward of Vyborg, protect Soviet bases, support the 21st and 23d Armies' advance, and conduct reconnaissance to a depth of 150 kilometers (93.2 miles). Engineer forces were to facilitate the occupation of jumping-off positions, conduct reconnaissance, assist the infantry and tanks in overcoming the Finnish defenses and many river barriers, and assist the advancing forces in consolidating occupied positions. Antiaircraft (PVO) forces were to protect all Soviet ground and naval forces before and during the offensive and provide air cover for air and naval bases supporting the offensive.

Once formulated, Govorov's offensive plan incorporated some unique features based on previous combat experience. For example, the degree of force concentration was unprecedented. The 109th, 30th Guards, and 97th Rifle Corps were to conduct the main attack with nine rifle divisions in an 18-kilometer (11.2-mile) sector supported by the bulk of the *front*'s artillery and aircraft and then advance along the most direct axis toward Vyborg. The single-echelon configuration of the assault increased the shock effect of the attack, and the strong reserve, consisting of the 110th and 108th Rifle Corps, was positioned to reinforce the initial blow almost immediately. Thereafter, the bulk of the 23d Army (the 98th and 115th Rifle Corps) was to reinforce the 21st Army's assault and roll up the Finnish defenses.

In accordance with instructions that Govorov sent to the fleet on 23 May, prior to the offensive, the Baltic Fleet supported the extensive force regrouping by transporting the 21st Army from Oranienbaum to Lisii Nos on the fleet's ships. During the preparation for the offensive and the ground assault, Tributs was to organize four naval artillery groups to support the 21st Army's offensive. Collectively, the groups' missions were to destroy Finnish fortifications, support the ground offensive, interdict the movement of Finnish reserves, and destroy key objectives during the offensive.

The first naval artillery support group included railroad artillery (113mm to 180mm) and, the second, coastal artillery of the Kronshtadt and Izhora Fortified Region, the cruiser *Petropavlovsk,* four minesweepers, five cannon ships, and, in addition, one railroad artillery division, which reinforced the Izhora sector. The third group included artillery of the Naval Artillery Training Ground and the fourth group, the battleship *Oktiabr'skaia Revoliutsiia* and the cruisers *Kirov* and *Maksim Gor'kii.* In total, the Baltic Fleet supported the offensive with 175 guns, 90 percent of which were 130mm or greater caliber. In addition, throughout the offensive, naval aviation conducted reconnaissance and provided protection for sea transport and communications.[17]

The Ladoga Flotilla, which was subordinate to the Baltic Fleet, was to support the 23d Army with fires and demonstrative amphibious assaults in the Nikulaiasy and Lake Konevits sector. To do so, it organized its ships into two detachments, the first to support the 23d Army's right flank as it advanced and the second to conduct the demonstrative amphibious assaults.

Once Govorov's planning was complete, the armies prepared and refined their own offensive plans. In the 21st Army, Gusev decided to concentrate Alferov's 109th, Simoniak's 30th Guards, and Busarov's 97th Rifle Corps in single echelon from left to right in the center of his army's sector.[18] The three corps were to penetrate the Finnish 10th Infantry Division's defenses in the 18-kilometer (11.2-mile) sector from Hill 110.8 through Staryi Beloostrov to Khuvila, destroy the defending enemy, and force the Sestra River from the march. Once across the river, his three corps would capture the Termolovo, Iappilia, and Kellomiaki line no later than the second day of the offensive. Then his army would exploit to the northwest, destroy Finnish operational reserves, and reach and capture the Finnish second defensive belt. Subsequently, Gusev's army was to exploit to Summa and reach the Mannerheim Line.

Thus the 21st Army was to advance to a depth of 35 kilometers (21.7 miles) in three to four days in two distinct stages. During the first stage, the army was to fulfill its immediate mission within two days. During this period, Busarov's 97th Rifle Corps on the army's right would advance 10–12 kilometers (6.2–7.5 miles), and Simoniak's 30th Guards and Alferov's 109th Rifle Corps in the army's center and on the left flank were to advance 14–16 kilometers (8.7–9.9 miles). The corps' first-echelon rifle divisions were to advance 4 kilometers (9.9 miles) on the first day of the assault. During the second stage, the corps were to advance 15–20 kilometers (9.3–12.4 miles) in one to two days, overcome the Finnish second defensive belt, and reach the Vuotta, Kivennapa, Kutersel'ka, and Metsiakiulia line.[19]

While the 21st Army was penetrating the Finnish first defense belt, Cherepanov's 23d Army was to defend the remainder of the front eastward to Lake Ladoga. Cherepanov planned to defend the sector from the mouth of the Gannibalovka River to Kharvazi Swamp with Kozachek's 115th Rifle Corps, the 17th Fortified Region, the Osinovets Naval Base, the 48th Reserve Rifle Regiment, and one battalion of the 104th Border Guards Regiment.[20] Anisimov's 98th Rifle Corps was to remain in army second echelon concentrated in the Agalatovo, Serolovo, and Rappolovo regions behind the 21st Army's right flank.[21] Anisimov's corps was to attack as soon as Busarov's 97th Rifle Corps reached the Lainoia and Khirelia line and came under the 23d Army's control. Thereafter, Anisimov's corps was to advance along the Kekrola and Kakhala axis and Busarov's corps toward Mustalovo to envelop Termolovo from the west and encircle and destroy Finnish forces in the Termolovo and Mustalovo regions in cooperation with Kozachek's 115th Rifle Corps on their right flank. After destroying the Finnish 2d Infantry Division and any approaching Finnish operational reserves, Cherepanov's army was to capture the Rikhne, Kakhala, and Metsiakiulia line, reach the Finnish second defensive belt on the army's left flank, and capture it from the march.

If the Finns successfully occupied their second defensive belt before the 23d Army could capture it, two divisions and two artillery–machine gun battalions of Kozachek's corps were to halt and dig in. Cherepanov would then regroup the remainder of Kozachek's forces to his left flank, and the bulk of his army would penetrate Finnish defenses and advance toward Lake Valkiarvi.[22] Ultimately, Cherepanov deployed his army in two echelons, with five rifle divisions in the first echelon, two in second echelon, and one in reserve.

Given the heavy fortifications and difficult terrain facing the 21st and 23d Armies, artillery support was especially critical for the operation's success. Accordingly, the 21st Army planned to fire a 140-minute artillery preparation with 3,000 guns and mortars (including 284 45mm and 57mm guns) with a density of 120 tubes per kilometer of front. About 350 of these guns were to conduct direct fire on Finnish positions. Artillery density rose to 170–200 guns per kilometer in the 30th Guards Rifle Corps' main penetration sector.[23]

The *front*'s artillery employed creeping ("falling away") fire to support the advancing infantry and formed an extensive array of supporting artillery groups, each designated to perform a specific combat function. These groups included close combat groups (82mm and 120mm mortars) and direct fire groups in rifle regiments; infantry support groups in divisions; special designation groups in rifle corps, long-range artillery, destruction, multiple rocket launcher, counter-mortar, and antiaircraft groups at army level; and a Baltic Fleet naval group. Army artillery groups were further subdivided into half-groups to support each attacking rifle corps. The 3d Artillery Penetration Corps controlled the destruction and the counter-mortar artillery groups, and the 21st Army's artillery commander directed the long-range artillery groups. Govorov allocated the 21st and 23d Armies 2.5–3.0 combat loads of artillery, one load of which was to be expended in the preliminary destruction phase.[24]

The 13th Air Army and Baltic Fleet air forces supported the operation with 741 combat aircraft, including 158 fighters, 298 assault aircraft, 265 bombers, and 20 reconnaissance aircraft. The 13th Air Army and Baltic Fleet aviation planned preliminary strikes on Finnish defenses, a 30-minute aviation preparation, and 883 aircraft sorties on the first day of the offensive.[25]

The Leningrad Front's engineer forces concentrated their efforts on preparing troop jumping-off positions and repairing roads and bridges prior to the offensive. A total of 37 engineer-sapper battalions within the *front*'s engineer-sapper brigade and divisions, 7 pontoon-bridge battalions, and 2 mine-clearing battalions equipped with mine-detecting dogs performed this often tedious but essential work. On 8 June *front* engineers temporarily closed the gates in the dam over the Sestra River to lower the level of the Sestra Bay to 1.4 meters. This opened five more fords across the bay and eased the construction of bridges necessary to cross the river and bay. Finally, to deceive the Finns as to the date and precise location of the offensive, the *front* staff carefully camouflaged all troop movements and postured for an offensive at Narva.[26] The deception measures, coupled with the Soviet Union's diplomatic posturing, ensured that the offensive came as a surprise for the Finnish High Command.

The regrouping of forces necessary to launch the offensive was a large-scale and complex task. The most challenging aspect of it was the movement of Gusev's complete 21st Army 65–115 kilometers (40.1–71.2 miles) from the region southwest of Leningrad. To accomplish this move, the 97th Rifle Corps moved by rail and the 30th Guards and 109th Rifle Corps (five divisions) by sea through the Gulf of Finland, and other forces moved to their new assembly areas by a combination of rail, road, and sea transport. The Baltic Fleet employed 6 minesweepers, 2 mine layers, ferries, 10 assault tenders, and

5 barges under an air defense shield to transport the forces by sea along multiple routes. The scheduled movement took place between 7 May and 7 June. The army's rear service units and facilities regrouped between 7 and 23 May. Thereafter, the army's artillery, mortar, tank, and self-propelled artillery regiments and battalions moved from 22 May through 3 June, regimental and battalion artillery and regimental mortars from 1 through 4 June, tracked and wheeled transport from 4 through 6 June, and rifle regiments and divisions from 5 through 7 June.[27]

Once they completed their regrouping, the army's forces replaced defending forces and occupied their jumping-off positions for the attack from 8 through 10 June. One third of the direct fire guns occupied their firing positions on the night of 7–8 June. Then, on the night of 8–9 June, one rifle company per battalion, most of the infantry heavy weaponry, and the remaining direct fire guns moved into their attack positions, relieving all of the 10th and 92d Rifle Divisions' forces except their combat security elements. Finally, the remaining infantry units designated to replace combat security forces and conduct reconnaissances-in-force moved forward on the night of 9–10 June. All of Govorov's designated attack forces were in their required assault positions by early on 10 June.[28]

After deploying forward into their attack positions, the three attacking rifle corps of Gusev's 21st Army formed for their attack in the 22.5-kilometer (13.9-mile) sector from Hill 107.4 to the Gulf of Finland. Busarov's 97th Rifle Corps occupied a 9.5-kilometer (5.9-mile) sector on the army's right flank, with its 381st and 385th Rifle Divisions in first echelon and its 178th Rifle Division in second echelon. Simoniak's 30th Guards Rifle Corps deployed in a 6.5-kilometer (4-mile) sector in the army's center, with the 45th and 63d Guards Rifle Divisions in first echelon and the 64th Guards Rifle Division in second echelon. On the army's left flank, Alferov's 109th Rifle Corps manned a 6.5-kilometer (4-mile) sector, with its 109th and 72d Rifle Divisions in first echelon and the 286th Rifle Division in second echelon. This massive force of nine rifle divisions, backed up by six additional divisions from 98th and 108th Rifle Corps, was overwhelmingly superior to the defending Finnish force, which consisted of the 10th Infantry Division and the right-flank regiment of the 2d Infantry Division.

On the eve of the offensive, Cherepanov's 23d Army was deployed from Hill 107.4 to Lake Ladoga. Kozachek's 115th Rifle Corps was in army first echelon, with the 10th and 142d Rifle Divisions in its first echelon and the 92d in its second. Anisimov's 98th Rifle Corps' 177th, 281st, and 372d Rifle Divisions were in army second echelon, prepared to join battle in the 21st Army's sector. When fully assembled, Gusev's and Cherepanov's armies numbered 15 rifle divisions, 2 fortified regions, 10 tank and self-propelled artillery regiments, and more than 220 artillery and mortar battalions. Behind the formidable forces was Govorov's massive reserve. It consisted of the 46th, 90th, and 314th Rifle Divisions of Tikhonov's 108th Rifle Corps; the 168th, 265th, and 268th Rifle Divisions of Griaznov's 110th Rifle Corps; the 13th, 125th, and 382d Rifle Divisions; the 30th Guards and 220th Tank Brigades; and 4 tank and self-propelled artillery regiments.[29]

THE LENINGRAD FRONT'S VYBORG OFFENSIVE, 10–20 JUNE

The Penetration Phase and Forcing of the Sestra River, 10–12 June

In accordance with orders issued by Gusev on the evening of 7 June, at 0800 hours on 9 June, his corps commanders began 10 hours of destructive artillery and mortar fires against the Finnish 10th and 2d Infantry Divisions' defenses (Map 18). Simultaneously, Soviet aircraft struck the enemy defenses. To conceal the location of his main attack, Govorov had Cherepanov's artillery join in the preparation.[30] A letter from a young Soviet soldier to his mother recorded a Finnish prisoner of war's impression of the bombardment's effect:

> I will remember today for the rest of my life. I did not know whether my nerves would endure the artillery bombardment. Unending thunder began at 0630 hours. It seemed as if all of the forces of the world were put in motion and were brought down upon us. First the aircraft appeared. They were more numerous than I had ever before seen during the war. The Russian aircraft strafed and bombed. Everything shook all around us. Then the artillery shelling began with a force that we had never expected. The shelling lasted all day. Everything was in disorder, and no one grasped what was occurring.[31]

At 1745 hours on 9 June, Gusev's first-echelon rifle corps fired a 15-minute artillery preparation and then began a reconnaissance-in-force to determine the damage the artillery preparation had inflicted on the enemy's defenses. Cherepanov's army conducted similar reconnaissances-in-force across his front to deceive the Finns regarding the location of the Soviet main attack. Along 11 separate axes across the entire width of the front, platoon- to battalion-size forces, supported by from three to eight tanks each, conducted the reconnaissances-in-force. To the rear, in the ranks of their parent divisions, specially tailored forward detachments prepared to support the reconnaissance by exploiting success or pursuing the Finns should they have begun to withdraw.

Supported by sappers and tanks, the massed infantry of Gusev's 21st Army began their ground assault at 0820 hours on 10 June, after a 140-minute ar-

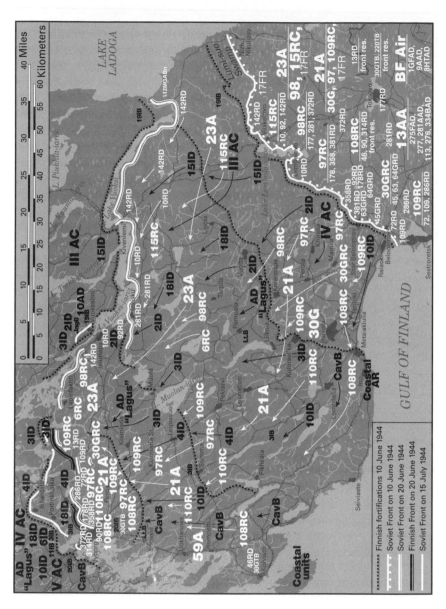

Map 18. The Soviet Vyborg Offensive, June–August 1944

tillery preparation. Busarov's 97th Rifle Corps attacked toward Kallelovo, Simoniak's 30th Guards Rifle Corps along the Vyborg road, and Alferov's 109th Rifle Corps along the coastal highway. By day's end their attacking forces had penetrated the Finnish forward defenses, crossed the Sestra River, and reached the Lake Lampi-iarvi, Kallelovo, Khapala, and Kuokkala line, tearing a breach 20 kilometers (12.4 miles) wide in the Finnish defenses. Although it should not have, the fierce assault caught the Finns totally by surprise and overran many forward Finnish defensive positions before they were fully manned. Throughout the first day of the assault, the 13th Air Army supported Gusev's forces with 900 aircraft sorties and claimed to have shot down 13 Finnish aircraft.

Simoniak's 30th Guards Rifle Corps achieved the most dramatic success on the first day of battle. Major Generals S. M. Putilov's and A. F. Sheglov's 45th and 63d Guards Rifle Divisions advanced 15 kilometers (9.3 miles) into the Finnish 10th Infantry Division's defenses and captured the Finnish strong points at Mainila and Staryi Beloostrov. However, on the army's right flank, Busarov's 97th Rifle Corps had considerably less success, advancing only 5 kilometers (3.1 miles) and reaching the southern bank of the Sestra River by day's end. Simoniak's assault nearly annihilated a full regiment of the Finnish 10th Infantry Division, and his seizure of a bridgehead across the Sestra River facilitated expanded operations.

The initial Soviet attack made it clear to the Finns that their forces could not hold anywhere in front of their second defensive belt. Therefore, on the morning of 10 June, Mannerheim transferred the 3d Infantry Division from his reserve and a regiment from the III Army Corps to the IV Corps and ordered these forces to conduct local counterattacks while they withdrew to the second defensive belt. At the same time, he also reinforced the IV Army Corps with the 1st Cavalry Brigade and deployed the Lagus Armored Division to the Muola-Kivennapa road to conduct a counterattack in the IV Army Corps' sector.

By midday on 10 June, the 21st Army's rapid penetration of the first defensive belt forced the Finns to order all of their forces still defending forward of the second defensive belt to retreat. The Finnish command judged that its forces had to hold firmly to the second defensive belt if they were to have any chance of counterattacking and restoring their initial defensive positions. With this aim in mind, the Finnish High Command ordered the 4th Infantry Division in southern Karelia and the 3d Infantry Brigade in northern Finland to deploy to the isthmus. Meanwhile, the IV Army Corps was to organize a defensive center of resistance at Kivennapa in the second defensive belt.[32]

Gusev issued new orders to his advancing forces at 2330 hours on 10 June, which contained new missions for the further development of the offensive.

Specifically, Gusev's army was to widen the flanks of its penetration and advance to the Termolovo, Iappilia, and Teriioki line by nightfall on 11 June and, by attacking toward the northwest, reach the Kivennapa and Raivola line with the army's main forces by day's end on 12 June. Cooperating with Simoniak's 30th Guards Rifle Corps, Busarov's 97th Rifle Corps was to exploit northward and capture Kallelovo on 11 June. Subsequently, Busarov's corps was to force the Sestra River, capture Termolovo and Khirelia, and dispatch forward detachments toward Kekrola.

At the same time, the forward elements of Simoniak's corps were to reach the Perola and Lake Pitkia-iarvi line, where they were to dig in. The corps' 64th Guards Rifle Division, now commanded by Major General I. D. Romantsov, was to deploy forward from the corps' second echelon, attack the flank and rear of Finnish forces defending Khirelia, which were blocking the 97th Rifle Corps' advance, and capture the Khirelia-Perola line by day's end on 11 June. Simoniak's corps as a whole was to capture Kivennapa, one of the most important strong points in the Finns' second defensive belt, by the end of 12 July.

On Gusev's left flank, Alferov's 109th Rifle Corps was to exploit to the northwest, capture Teriioki on 11 June and Raivola and Tiuriseva on 12 June, and reach the Finns' second defensive belt. A mobile group formed around the nucleus of Colonel V. I. Volkov's 1st Leningrad Tank Brigade was to lead Alferov's advance, capture Teriioki from the march on 11 June, and hold it until relieved by Alferov's main force. In addition to his tank brigade, Volkov's mobile group consisted of the 98th Tank and 1222d Self-propelled Artillery Regiments, an antitank battalion, and a sapper company. After capturing Teriioki, Volkov's mobile group was to join the 109th Rifle Corps and support its subsequent operations.

Gusev's army resumed its offensive at 0500 hours on 11 June, and, shortly thereafter, Anisimov's 98th Rifle Corps (from the 23d Army) joined the assault by attacking at the junction of Simoniak's 30th Guards and Busarov's 97th Rifle Corps. As Anisimov's rifle corps advanced, at 1500 hours, the 23d Army took control of Busarov's rifle corps and Tikhonov's 108th Rifle Corps reinforced the 21st Army. Gusev placed Tikhonov's corps in reserve behind Alferov's 109th Rifle Corps. Even though the weather deteriorated and heavy rains limited the 13th Air Army's air support to only 250 sorties, Gusev's 21st Army and the left flank of Cherepanov's 23d Army surged forward, inexorably pressing back the beleaguered 10th and 2d Infantry Divisions of the severely weakened Finnish IV Army Corps. All the while, the Ladoga Flotilla conducted a demonstrative assault and fired artillery at enemy positions at Metsiapirtti to tie down the forces on the Finns' left flank.[33]

By day's end on 11 July, the combined forces of Busarov's 97th and Anisimov's 98th Rifle Corps reached the Termolovo-Khirelia line and Cherepanov withdrew two of Anisimov's divisions into his army's reserve. To the west,

Putilov's 45th Guards Rifle Division of Simoniak's 30th Guards Rifle Corps, supported by the 31st Guards and 260th Tank and 1439th Self-propelled Artillery Regiments, captured Khirelia and Matilla and reached the outskirts of Ikola, 10 kilometers (6.2 miles) short of the Finnish second defensive belt. At the same time, Sheglov's 63d Guards Rifle Division stormed the Finnish strong point at Kivennapa and reached the forward edge of the second defensive belt. On Simoniak's left flank, the 109th Rifle Corps' 72d and 286th Rifle Divisions, supported by Volkov's 1st Tank Brigade and the 27th Guards Tank, 185th Tank, and 1222d Self-propelled Artillery Regiments, captured Kellomiaki Station, Raivola, and Teriioki. By this time, the 286th Rifle Division of Alferov's corps had also reached the Finnish second defensive belt.[34]

Thus, by the evening of 11 June, Gusev's and Cherepanov's armies had accomplished the missions assigned to them by Govorov. Their forces had expanded the penetration to a depth of 26 kilometers (16.2 miles) on the left flank and 23 kilometers (14.3 miles) in the center. The two armies had utterly collapsed the defenses of the Finnish 10th and 2d Infantry Divisions, crossed the Sestra River, and forced the Finns to begin a general withdrawal back to their second defensive belt. To this point, casualties were minimal for a penetration operation of this scale. However, Govorov's next challenge was to overcome the second defensive belt before the Finns could reinforce it.

In a directive to Govorov late on 11 June, the *Stavka* acknowledged Govorov's initial success but exhorted him to exploit his clear superiority over defending Finnish forces by quickly smashing their second defensive belt and capturing Vyborg by 18–20 June:

> The offensive by the Leningrad Front's forces on the Karelian Isthmus is developing successfully. The enemy is in disorder, he has suffered heavy losses, and his resistance has weakened. The *front*'s forces have a three-fold superiority over the enemy in infantry and a considerably greater superiority in artillery, tanks, and aircraft. This has created favorable conditions for further development of the offensive.
>
> 1. Continue the offensive by energetically pursuing the withdrawing enemy with the mission of capturing the Vyborg region by 18–20 June.
>
> 2. Take every measure for the rapid movement forward of heavy artillery following the infantry and for continuous material support of the forces.
>
> Report orders given.
>
> [signed] I. Stalin, A. Antonov[35]

When drafting orders to his army commanders, Govorov dutifully emphasized the necessity for bringing the heavy artillery forward and ensuring adequate resupply of his advancing forces.

The three rifle corps of Gusev's 21st Army resumed their offensive early on 12 June but, unlike the previous two days, achieved only limited success. Advancing along the Vyborg road, Simoniak's guards corps stormed the Finnish strong point at Kivennapa and reached the Metsiakiulia, Kivennapa, and Kontu line by day's end but was unable to penetrate the second defensive belt. This was due primarily to the resistance of the Lagus Armored Division, which had just reinforced Finnish defenses in this critical sector. At the same time, on Gusev's left flank, Alferov's 109th Rifle Corps overcame Finnish resistance in the coastal sector, advanced 7 kilometers (4.3 miles), and reached the Finn's second defensive belt. However, his corps was also not able to penetrate the defensive belt from Kutersel'ka to the Gulf of Finland, largely due to resistance from the Finnish 3d Infantry Division, which had just relieved the battered 10th Infantry Division on the IV Army Corps' right flank. In Gusev's rear, Tikhonov's 108th Rifle Corps, still in army reserve, concentrated in the Teriioki sector.

On 12 July Cherepanov's 23d Army continued its advance northward along the Siiranmiaki road with Anisimov's 98th Rifle Corps, while part of Busarov's 97th Rifle Corps enveloped Termolovo from the west to northeast. Throughout the day, the 13th Air Army supported the 23d Army's advance with about 300 aircraft sorties. However, due to skillful Finnish rear-guard actions, Cherepanov's forward progress continued to be rather slow; by day's end his forces had advanced only 2–6 kilometers (1.2–3.7 miles). At nightfall, Cherepanov withdrew Busarov's rifle corps into the *front*'s reserve for a brief rest and refitting.

During the initial three days of combat along the Vyborg axis, Gusev's and Cherepanov's armies had penetrated the Finnish first defensive belt, widened the penetration to 60 kilometers (37.2 miles), and advanced to the Finnish second defensive belt in the western third of the Karelian Isthmus. There, however, Govorov's advance ground to an abrupt halt in the face of heavy resistance and strong and repeated Finnish counterattacks. In clear testimony to the tenacity of the Finnish defense, Govorov decided that he would have to regroup his forces, plan, and conduct a formal penetration operation if his forces were to penetrate the Finnish second defensive belt successfully.

Govorov's decision to halt bore mute testimony to the resilience of the opposing Finnish forces. Although initially surprised and disorganized by the impetuous Soviet assault, thereafter the Finnish command worked frantically to shore up their defenses and deploy additional forces to the Karelian Isthmus from other less threatened sectors. Early on 13 June, Mannerheim requested additional assistance from General Dietl, the commander of the Twentieth Mountain Army:

Mannerheim's chief of staff told Dietl that if the second line was lost, the Finns would give up the Svir and Maaselka Fronts and pull back in East Karelia to a short line northeast of Lake Ladoga, thereby freeing two to three more divisions for the isthmus. . . .

Dietl urged the Finns to carry out the planned withdrawal but feared that out of reluctance to give up East Karelia they would hesitate too long. Later, he recommended to Hitler that the German policy be to tie the Finns to Germany by giving them as much support as possible and, at the same time, by requiring them to make the necessary tactical sacrifices, not allow them to dissipate their strength in an attempt to hang on to East Karelia.[36]

All the while, in addition to the 3d Infantry and Lagus Armored Divisions, which had reinforced Finnish defenses the day before, the Finnish Command moved fresh forces forward to bolster their second defensive belt. These included the 18th Infantry Division, which reinforced the III Army Corps' right flank east of Siiranmiaki; the cavalry brigade, which reinforced the IV Army Corps right flank along the coastal road; and several battalions on the Lagus Armored Division's right flank opposite the 21st Army's main attack axis.[37]

The Penetration of the Finnish Second Defensive Belt and the Exploitation toward Vyborg and Keksholm, 14–17 June

Late on 12 June, Govorov ordered the 21st and 23d Armies to penetrate the Finn's second defensive belt. Since the Finns had concentrated the bulk of their forces along the Vyborg road axis opposite the 21st Army's 30th Guards Rifle Corps, Govorov shifted his main attack to the coastal axis on the 21st Army's left flank. He then reinforced Gusev's army with Griaznov's 110th Rifle Corps and the 3d Heavy Howitzer Artillery Brigade transferred from Narva, which was to support Gusev's main attack.

According to Gusev's plan, Tikhonov's 108th and Alferov's 109th Rifle Corps were to conduct his army's main attack in the Kutersel'ka and Metsiakiulia sector. The two corps were to advance abreast toward Summa and reach the Liikola, Lake Vammel'-iarvi, Inonkiulia line by late on 14 June, an advance of 20 kilometers (12.4 miles). Subsequently, after Gusev committed Griaznov's 110th Rifle Corps, Alferov's and Griaznov's rifle corps were to advance toward Summa and Tikhonov's rifle corps toward Koivisto on the coast. The attack by all three corps was designed to prevent the Finnish IV Army Corps from successfully withdrawing to the third defensive belt, penetrate that belt, and capture Kiamiaria Station on the Leningrad-Vyborg railroad and Koivisto on the coast by late on 17 June. Having preempted Finnish defense along their final defensive belt east of Vyborg, Gusev's forces were to advance northwest and capture Vyborg by 18–20 June.[38]

On the right flank of Gusev's main attack, Simoniak's 30th Guards Rifle Corps was to dig in from Lake Sula-iarvi to north of Kivennapa to protect the shock group's flank. During the extensive regrouping required to concentrate forces necessary to launch the new offensive, Govorov had to shift Lieutenant General N. N. Zhdanov's full 3d Artillery Penetration Corps from the Kivennapa region across difficult terrain to the new offensive sector in only 24 hours. This involved moving about 110 artillery battalions a distance of 25–40 kilometers in relatively close proximity to the enemy.[39]

While Gusev's army was attacking directly toward Vyborg, Cherepanov's 23d Army was to penetrate the Finnish second defensive belt in the sector east of Siiranmiaki. Anisimov's 98th Rifle Corps was to advance northward toward Vuotta and Lake Valk-iarvi, protect its right flank toward Bol'shie Kirkiamiaki, and reach positions extending from the northern extremity of Lake Lembalovskoe through Bol'shie Kirkiamiaki and Lipola to Tarpila. Subsequently, the army was to exploit toward Lake Valk-iarvi and Kiviniemi and reach the third defensive belt in the sector from the Taipalen-ioki River to Muola, where it would halt to regroup its forces to the Vyborg axis. During Anisimov's advance, Kozachek's 115th Rifle Corps was to defend along the 23d Army's right flank from Lake Lembalovskoe to Lake Ladoga and join the advance once Anisimov's attack succeeded in dislodging the Finnish 15th Infantry Division defending opposite its left flank. The 13th Air Army was to support both Gusev's and Cherepanov's assaults, interdict all movement along roads between the second and third defensive belts, and strike Finnish operational reserves, in particular along the rail line from Vyborg.[40]

On 13 June both armies regrouped and prepared to conduct the new penetration operation, while the 23d Army's forces advanced right up to the Finn's second defensive belt on the heels of withdrawing Finnish forces. Anisimov's corps closed into positions from Vekhmainen to Kholttila, and the 10th Rifle Division of Kozachek's corps attacked Finnish defenses at Mustalovo. By the evening of 13–14 June, Gusev had concentrated 1,744 guns and mortars in his 21st Army's 20-kilometer (12.4-mile) penetration sector, creating an artillery density of 88 tubes per kilometer of front overall and up to 180–200 tubes in some sectors.[41]

While Gusev and Cherepanov were concentrating their forces to resume the offensive, the Finnish IV Army Corps withdrew its forces to the second defensive belt, where it dug in and was reinforced. The Finnish command also completed moving its 18th Infantry Division forward and attached it to the III Army Corps to fill in the gap between it and the IV Corps and ordered the III Army Corps to withdraw to the second defensive belt. Two days earlier, on 12 June, the Finnish command had already begun moving the 17th Infantry Division and the 20th Infantry Brigade from Group Olonets north of Lake Ladoga toward the Karelian Isthmus. On 13 June the 4th Infantry Division began concentrating south of Lake Sula-iarvi to the rear of the junction of the III and IV Army Corps, and the 3d Infantry Brigade from northern Finland was ordered to concentrate behind the IV Army Corps' center. In addition, Mannerheim asked the German OKW to release additional weaponry and grain (embargoed since March) to Finland, and Hitler agreed. By late on 13 June, the Finns were able to concentrate up to six divisions and two brigades opposite the 21st and 23d Armies' penetration sectors. In addition, one division and two brigades were on the march toward this region.[42]

Gusev's and Cherepanov's armies began operations to penetrate the Finnish second defensive belt on 14 June after a 90-minute preparation fired by army and fleet artillery in the 21st Army's sector and a 55-minute artillery preparation in the 23d Army's sector. The aviation preparation in the 21st Army's sector also lasted for 90 minutes. The 21st Army's 108th and 109th Rifle Corps began their ground assault at 0930 hours, and the 23d Army's forces joined the attack at 1000 hours. By 1800 hours, Major General I. I. Iastrebov's 72d and Major General N. A. Trushkin's 109th Rifle Divisions of Alferov's 109th Rifle Corps, supported by Volkov's 1st Tank Brigade, the 1222d Self-propelled Artillery Regiment, and the 98th Tank Regiment, captured the Finns' strong points at Kutersel'ka, Mustamiaki, and Sakha-Kiulia. The assault struck the junction of the 3d Infantry Division and 1st Cavalry Brigade and split the two forces apart. During the heavy fighting, Volkov's 1st Tank Brigade raced forward through Mustamiaki and Neuvola and reached the coastal road at Lempiialia, threatening to cut off the withdrawal of the forces facing Tikhonov's 108th Rifle Corps. The 13th Air Army flew more than 600 combat sorties in support of the Soviet advance on 13 June.[43]

Late on 14 June, the Finnish 3d Infantry Division struck back, launching heavy counterattacks against the 109th Rifle Corps' 72d Rifle Division, which had captured Kutersel'ka. Iastrebov's division repelled the counterattacks with the assistance of the 46th Antitank Artillery Brigade and the 119th Separate Antitank Artillery Battalion. However, the initial assault by Tikhonov's 108th Rifle Corps against the Finnish 1st Cavalry Brigade's defenses at Vankhasakha and Metsiakiulia failed.[44] The next day, however, Borshchev's 46th and Major General N. G. Liachshenko's 90th Rifle Divisions, supported by the 260th Tank and 1238th Self-propelled Artillery Regiments, finally captured the two Finnish strong points early on 15 June after firing a heavy artillery preparation to disrupt the Finnish defenses.

Tikhonov's belated success permitted the 109th Rifle Corps to resume its advance along the railroad to Perkiarvi. By late on 15 June, Alferov's corps fought their way to positions extending from Kutersel'ka south of Lake Sula-iarvi to the southern shore of Lake Kannel-iarvi. By this time, Colonel M. S.

Elshinov's 314th Rifle Division of Tikhonov's 108th Rifle Corps had reached the neck of land between Lakes Vammel'-iarvi and Riesk-iarvi, and Liash-chenko's 90th and Borshchev's 46th Rifle Divisions of the same corps were fighting along the rail line 3 kilometers (1.7 miles) west of Fort Ino. To support their advance, Gusev conducted a small amphibious assault in the bay near Fort Ino.

While the 21st Army was conducting its main attack toward Vyborg with two rifle corps, Simoniak's guards rifle corps defended the army's right flank east of Lake Sula-iarvi. However, when Cherepanov's 23d Army began its advance, late on 15 June, Simoniak turned his positions over to Major General S. N. Aleksandrov's 13th Rifle Division, which Govorov assigned to the 23d Army from *front* reserve, and Simoniak's corps itself reverted to *front* reserve to replenish and refit its forces. Thus, on 14 and 15 June, Gusev's 21st Army penetrated the Finnish second defensive belt along the Vyborg axis and advanced up to 15 kilometers (9.3 miles) along a 12-kilometer (7.5-mile) front.

During the later stages of Gusev's attacks, the Finnish IV Army Corps regrouped its forces and received additional reinforcements. On 14 June the 10th Infantry Division, which had earlier been withdrawn to rest and refit, occupied defenses between Lakes Vammel'-iarvi and Riesk-iarvi, and the next day the 4th Infantry Division and 3d Infantry Brigade took up positions to its rear. The 4th Division manned defenses along the Vyborg railroad to the rear of the 3d Infantry Division, and the 3d Brigade positions along the road south of Loistola.[45]

While Gusev's forces were breaking through the Finns' second defensive belt, Cherepanov's 23d Army successfully developed its offensive along the Keksholm axis on 14 and 15 June. On the army's left flank, early on 14 June, Anisimov's 98th Rifle Corps and the 10th and 92d Rifle Divisions of Koza-chek's 115th Rifle Corps attacked the Finnish 2d and 15th Infantry Divisions' defenses in the Lake Lembalovskoe and Kholttila sector. The attacking force captured Vekhmainen and Siiranmiaki, 500–600 meters into the Finns' second defensive belt by day's end. The next day, in the sector eastward to Lake Ladoga, the 142d Rifle Division of Kozachek's corps and the 17th Fortified Region, advanced 9 kilometers (5.6 miles) against the Finnish 19th Infantry Brigade, which had just received orders to withdraw, and finally completed penetrating the Finns' first defensive belt.

Thus, by early on 16 June, Govorov's two armies had penetrated to a depth of 40 kilometers (24.9 miles) along a 75-kilometer (46.6-mile) front in six days of heavier than anticipated fighting. Gusev's forces were just beginning their operation to penetrate the Finns' second defensive belt, while Cherepanov's army was just approaching it. During the two days of heavy fighting, the 13th Air Army flew 2,600 sorties in support of the advance.

Nor did the Finns' resistance slacken under this immense and unrelenting pressure. Govorov's two armies continued their attacks on 16–17 June without pause and against even heavier resistance, as the Finnish High Command committed fresh reserves into combat. Neither of Govorov's armies recorded spectacular progress. Advancing along the Vyborg axis, early on 16 June, Gusev committed Griaznov's 110th Rifle Corps into action from his second echelon to reinforce his main attack along the Usikirkko axis. Now attacking abreast, the 108th, 110th, and 109th Rifle Corps advanced 6–15 kilometers (3.7–9.3 miles) and reached positions extending from Perkiarvi Station through Usikirkko southeast of Lakes Khalolan-iarvi and Iulis-iarvi to Sortavala by day's end. However, adverse weather limited air support to only 182 sorties, and lacking air support, Gusev's advance was halted by the newly arrived Finnish 3d Infantry Brigade and 4th Infantry Division.[46]

On Govorov's right flank, Cherepanov's 23d Army advanced at a snail's pace through difficult terrain and against skillful Finnish rear-guard actions. On the left flank, Anisimov's 98th Rifle Corps failed to make any progress against the many strong points in the Finnish second defensive belt. However, on the right, Kozachek's 115th Rifle Corps advanced 5–12 kilometers (3.1–7.5 miles) along the Keksholm axis and finally reached the Finnish second defensive belt.

Given the limited progress, Govorov issued new orders to his two armies on the afternoon of 17 June:

The 21st Army will pursue the enemy energetically, prevent the enemy from transferring forces from the Keksholm to the Vyborg axis, capture the third defensive belt, and reach the Sintola, Kiamiaria Station, Khumola, and Iokhannes line no later than 17 June. Subsequently, attack toward Vyborg with no fewer than two rifle corps, capture that city, and reach positions 10–15 kilometers [6.2–9.1 miles] to its north and northeast no later than 18–20 June.

The 23d Army will pursue the Finns energetically along its entire front, prevent him from withdrawing to the Vuoksi water system, and seize positions along the southern shores of Lakes Suvanto-iarvi, Vuoksi-iarvi, and Iaiuriapian-iarvi to Muola no later than 18 June. Conduct your main attack along the Vuotta and Valk-iarvi axis on the left flank. Leave the 115th Rifle Corps and the 17th Fortified Region on the Suvanto-iarvi and Vuoksi-iarvi line, regroup the 98th Rifle Corps to the left flank, and prepare to attack northwest toward Repola to envelop Vyborg from the northeast.[47]

Govorov ordered both armies to lead their advance with strong advance guards reinforced with tanks and artillery. The 13th Air Army was to soften up Finnish defenses in the Vyborg and Summa regions, protect the advancing force, and block the movement of Finnish reserves.

In recognition of the immense pressure his forces faced and the utter futility of any continued defense along his second defensive belt, on 16 June Mannerheim ordered his beleaguered forces to withdraw to new defenses along the Vyborg-Vuoksi line.[48] Two days earlier, on 14 June, he had combined all of his forces on the isthmus into the Karelian Operational Group under the command of Lieutenant General Esh, the former commander of Group Olonets. On 15 June the Finnish High Command ordered Esh's force to withdraw to the VTK (Vyborg, Kuparsari, Taipale) line under the cover of rear guards and concentrate the bulk of its forces on the western bank of the Vuoksi water system.[49]

However, by the time General Esh arrived in the area on 15 June, the IV Army Corps had already lost the second defensive belt and had withdrawn to positions extending from Lakes Kuolem-iarvi to Kauk-iarvi and Perk-iarvi to Muolan-iarvi. At this time, units of the 10th Infantry Division and 3d Infantry Brigade were still operating forward of that line. That night the Finns ordered the III and IV Army Corps to withdraw to the VKT line and prepare an intermediate defense line from Rempetti through Iliakiulia, Summa, and Lake Muolan-iarvi to Lake Iaiuriapian-iarvi. The IV Army Corps ordered its forces to occupy this position. Pressure from the 21st and 23d Armies, however, forced the IV Army Corps to abandon the positions earlier than planned.

One Finnish soldier from the 3d Infantry Brigade recorded:

Yes [the 3d Brigade was transported by train to the Karelian Isthmus]. It was on the 15th of June as the transport was unloaded at Kuolemajarvi station when odd enemy movement was observed. Enemy soldiers were sneaking around the station house. The train left immediately, and we had to retreat 60 kilometers to Summa, where we stopped at the Mannerheim positions from the days of the Winter War. These positions were weak. They had been haphazardly repaired after their destruction in the Winter War, but it was too late and our only choice.[50]

Govorov's two armies resumed their offensive on 17 June. Gusev's 21st Army advanced 10–14 kilometers (6.2–8.7 miles) along the Vyborg axis against the Finnish IV Army Corps' withdrawing 4th and 10th Infantry Divisions and 3d Infantry Brigade. After being reinforced by the 13th Rifle Division, which protected the gap between the 21st and 23d Armies, Alferov's 109th Rifle Corps reached positions extending from Pampala through Taperi to the northern shores of Lake Sula-iarvi and Perkiarvi. On Alferov's left flank, Griaznov's 110th Rifle Corps reached Lake Mikkelin-iarvi, Loistola, Varpulila, and Pikhkala. Between Pikhkala and the coast, Tikhonov's 108th Rifle Corps captured the isthmus between Lakes Kuolem-iarvi and Kapinolan-iarvi. Thus, by day's end, the divisions on the 110th Rifle Corps' left flank and the entire 109th Rifle Corps had reached the Finnish third defensive belt. Meanwhile, Busarov's 97th Rifle Corps, which had just been transferred from Cherepanov's to Gusev's army, began concentrating southwest of Lounatioki Station in army second echelon behind the 109th Rifle Corps.[51]

To the east, on 17 June, Cherepanov's forces advanced 5–10 kilometers (3.1–6.2 miles) in the 30-kilometer (18.6-mile) sector along the Keksholm axis against heavy resistance by Finnish forces lodged in multiple strong points. Kozachek's 115th Corps fought its way to positions extending from the Taipalen-ioki River, 3 kilometers (1.9 miles) south of Rautu Station, to Suvenmiaki, and Anisimov's 98th Rifle Corps reached the Iulentelia, Kakhkala, and Tarpila line. The 13th Air Army flew 850 sorties in support of the two armies on 17 June.

During the four days from 14 through 17 June, Gusev's and Cherepanov's armies penetrated the Finns' second defensive belt and were in pursuit to the third defensive belt in the sector from the Vyborg road to the Gulf of Finland. However, both Govorov and the *Stavka* were dissatisfied, believing the advance to be far too slow. Thereafter, a flood of orders emanated from Moscow exhorting Govorov's forces on toward Vyborg.

The Penetration of the Finns' Third Defensive Belt and the Capture of Vyborg, 18–20 June

Gusev's 21st Army resumed its offensive early on 18 June. During the day, Alferov's 109th and Griaznov's 110th Rifle Corps, supported by Volkov's 1st and Colonel A. P. Koval'sky's 152d Tank Brigades, reached the Finnish third defensive belt south of Leipiasuo and Summa, which protected the Vyborg railroad. On Gusev's left flank, Borshchev's 46th and Elshinov's 314th Rifle Divisions of Tikhonov's 108th Rifle Corps, with Colonel S. A. Sokolov's 30th Guards Tank Brigade in support, penetrated the enemy's third defensive belt, advanced 25 kilometers (15.5 miles), and captured the port of Koivisto.[52]

On Govorov's right flank north of Lake Sula-iarvi, Cherepanov's 23d Army, now reinforced by Major General I. I. Fadeev's 6th Rifle Corps, which had just completed its movement from the Narva region, fought all day on 18 June to penetrate the Finns' third defensive belt. Cherepanov's forces advanced 15–20 kilometers (9.3–12.4 miles) by day's end and reached a line extending from the mouth of the Taipalen-ioki River, through Lakes Pet'-iarvi and Murmi-iarvi to Mar'ianiemi, and along the northern shores of Lakes Punnus-iarvi and Isk-iarvi to Kaurula. The 13th Air Army flew 750 air sorties to support the two armies' advance.[53]

At this point, Gusev decided to accelerate his advance on Vyborg by committing Busarov's 97th Rifle Corps, supported by the 1st and 152d Tank Brigades, from second echelon to penetrate the Finnish third defensive belt. Busarov's corps was to penetrate the third defensive belt between Summa and Markki at the boundary of the Finnish 4th Infantry Division and 3d Infantry Brigade, advance along the Summa-Vyborg road to Khumola, and capture the railroad junction in the Pero and Limatta stations sector south of Vyborg.

On Busarov's right flank, Alferov's 109th Rifle Corps was to defend the sector from Markki to Lake Muolan-iarvi with its main forces and deploy Iastrebov's 72d Rifle Division in second echelon behind his left flank. When Busarov's corps began its penetration operation, Iastrebov's division was to envelop Leipiasuo Station from the northwest and protect the 97th Rifle Corps' left flank. On Busarov's left flank, Griaznov's 110th Rifle Corps was to penetrate Finnish defensives near Summa, at the boundary of the 3d Infantry Brigade and 10th Infantry Division, attack northward along the Iokhannes road, and prevent Finnish forces from withdrawing to Vyborg along the coastal road. Subsequently, Griaznov's corps was to advance northward, capture Limatta Station and Khuvila, and then Vyborg. To the west Tikhonov's 108th Rifle Corps was to continue its northward advance along the coast.[54]

The 21st Army's planned assault encompassed the entire front from Lake Muolan-iarvi to Iliakiulia and, if successful, would tear a massive hole through the Finnish third defensive belt and open the road to Vyborg.

Gusev's forces struck early on 19 June and achieved almost immediate success. The attacking forces ripped a gaping 70-kilometer (43.5-mile) hole through the Finns' defenses from Muola to the Gulf of Finland and advanced 14 kilometers (8.7 miles) in 18 hours of heavy fighting against determined Finnish resistance. A 3d Infantry Brigade officer left a vivid description of the close-in and often confused fighting:

> We were in the trenches as the enemy fired a heavy artillery barrage on us and then tried to break through with a very massive charge along the [Summa] road. They had remarkably large numbers of infantry and tanks as well. We were expecting support from our own artillery, but we did not get one shell. The tanks kept charging, and the infantry followed. We had no antitank weapons, yet we held the line. Our company commander was killed, and I became his replacement. I promised Battalion Commander Ikonen that we would be able to hold the line until midnight (on 18 June) but no longer. We were relieved at midnight. The men were supposed to be relieved in their positions one at a time. I thought this was a bad idea considering that we were in direct combat contact with the enemy. The result was that the relievers and those being relieved were all mixed up, and everyone retreated.
>
> I was in a concrete bunker next to the road trying to sort things out with the captain of the relieving company. It turned out that the captain

did not have any combat experience; he was a rear-echelon man and had been posted as a rifle company commander unexpectedly. At that moment an enemy tank drove on top of the bunker and stopped. I went to the door with the company orderly, and, at the same moment, a 75mm anti-tank shell meant for the tank on top of the bunker hit the doorpost. The orderly was wounded in the left arm. I gave my submachine gun to the captain and said that he should see to it that no one came into the bunker, and then I began bandaging the wounded man. Soon the AT gun fired again, and the enemy tank was hit. Two survivors of its crew jumped in the trench and began approaching our bunker. As the tankers saw us they began to fumble for their side arms. The captain shouted, *"Ruki verkh!"* [Hands up!], and I shouted, "Shoot!" He did, but one of the enemy got away.

Then we agreed that we would retreat along the trench to the edge of a bog where a Maxim machine gun team, which was attached to our company, was firing a barrage in front of the trench. I ordered the machine gun to disengage. The men began proceeding downhill in the trench, with the enemy tanks and infantry 50 meters away. The trench ended in a bog, and we began to retreat along it. The swamp was so wet that the men were not able to carry the Maxim and its tripod. Therefore, we had to dump it. We proceeded northward toward our own troops in the dusk of the summer night. All the time, we heard noises made by the Russian as they advanced and talked. We did not talk, but instead kept moving among the Russians in the same direction as they did. Finally, we found our own troops at daybreak.[55]

The Finnish officer then offered a poignant account of the deteriorating situation:

It is very difficult for me to give an account of the happenings during the Russian offensive for one who has not been in a war and is not able to understand that anything can happen in a situation where your own and the enemy's troops are mixed up. . . . After the enemy breakthrough, the Finnish troops were dispersed and they strove to get back to our own side in small groups, while the Russians were advancing in the same direction. My platoon was fighting a kind of guerrilla war when we attempted to get back to our own troops. We were able to break out because we had to attack the advancing enemy in the rear—we were able to catch them by surprise. We tried to avoid the enemy, they were making quite a noise, but we engaged them when necessary. A few times, in the dusk of the night, we just walked through the enemy line in single file, with a couple of my men securing to the left and to the right. The Russians were no better informed than we were about the placement of their own troops because there were no battle lines. If we came across lost Finnish soldiers, I ordered them to join us until we got back to our troops.[56]

By day's end on 19 June, Alferov's 109th Rifle Corps swept forward along and east of the rail line and then wheeled eastward toward Kheikurila, north of Lake Muolan-iarvi. Major General M. D. Grishin's 286th Rifle Division captured Kiamiaria Station, and Trushkin's 109th Rifle Division captured Kiamiaria, swung to the east, and approached Kheikurila, where it encountered elements of the Lagus Armored Division, which the Finns had committed from their reserve. At the same time, Busarov's 97th Rifle Corps thrust northward along the Vyborg road, smashing the Finnish IV Army Corps' defenses. Radygin's 372d Rifle Division captured Summa, and by day's end its forward detachment, Koval'sky's 152d Tank Brigade, assaulted Autiokorpela. West of the Vyborg road, Griaznov's 110th Rifle Corps reached Kakinsari, Elshinov's 314th Rifle Division of Tikhonov's 108th Rifle Corps was fighting south of Kaislakhti Station on the Vyborg-Koivisto railroad, and the remainder of Tikhonov's corps completed clearing Finnish forces from the Koivisto region.[57]

East of Lake Sula-iarvi, Cherepanov's 23d Army finally caught up with Gusev's advancing forces and cleared forces from the Finns' III Army Corps from the region south of Lake Vuoksi-iarvi. Anisimov's 98th and Fadeev's 6th Rifle Corps penetrated the Finns' third defensive belt along the Iokisku and Lake Muolan-iarvi front, and Colonel P. F. Efimenko's 382d Rifle Division captured the strong point at Muola from the 3d Infantry Division. On Cherepanov's right flank, Kozachek's 115th Rifle Corps and the 17th Fortified Region forced the Finnish 15th Infantry Division to withdraw northward to a new defense line on the northern bank of the Vuoksi water system.

Just as Govorov's forces were about to complete smashing the Finns' defenses east and west of Summa and commence their final thrust toward Vyborg, the Finnish High Command ordered its two corps to withdraw to avoid utter destruction. On the night of 19–20 June, it ordered its IV Army Corps to withdraw to the third defensive belt by 0600 hours the next morning. The corps' 10th Infantry and Lagus Armored Divisions were to occupy reserve positions northwest of Vyborg, while the 3d and 4th Infantry Divisions and the 3d Infantry Brigade were to continue defending the corps' sector. However, Gusev's rapid penetration of the third defensive belt disrupted the full implementation of this planned withdrawal. While the IV Army Corps withdrew under fire as best it could, to the east the III Army Corps managed to withdraw its forces in orderly fashion and intact to the Vuoksi water system. The III Corps, which had received warning orders to this effect as early as 13 June, conducted its withdrawal in successive stages after 16 June and occupied its new defense line late on 19 June.[58]

Once the withdrawal was complete, Finnish forces occupied new defenses extending from the Vyborg Bay, south of Vyborg, eastward through Tammisuo and Repola to Kuparsari, along the Vuoksi River and Lakes Vuoksi, Suvanto-iarvi, and Taipalen-iarvi River to Lake Ladoga. When completely reassembled, the Finns managed to assemble a force of 10 divisions and 4 brigades, although some of these forces were woefully understrength due to the previous fighting. The Finns anchored their new defense system east of Vyborg on the region's river and many lakes, which improved the durability of their defense. Most important to the Finns, when Govorov's forces resumed their offensive, this time they would not benefit from the element of surprise.

Once in position, the V Army Corps, which had been transferred to Vyborg from the Onega-Ladoga sector, and the IV Army Corps defended the sector from Vyborg Bay to the Vuoksi River with four infantry divisions, one armored division, two infantry brigades, and one cavalry brigade. The 20th Infantry Brigade, which had just arrived from Group Olonets, defended positions from Cape Pallidaniemi, south of Vyborg, along Vyborg's southern and eastern outskirts to Kor'iala. The 3d Infantry Brigade, which had reassembled after its defeat at Summa, defended the sector from Kor'iala through Tammisuo to Lake Karetilian-iarvi. On the 3d Brigade's left flank, the 18th Infantry Division occupied the sector from Lake Karetilian-iarvi to Lake Repolan-iarvi. Finally, the 4th Infantry Division defended the Lake Noskuon-sel'kia sector, and the 3d Infantry Division defended eastward to the Vuoksi River. The 1st Cavalry Brigade occupied defensive positions to the rear and was responsible for assisting in defending the coast. West of Vyborg, the 2d Coastal Brigade defended the northwestern shores of the Gulf of Finland, with its main forces at Nisalakhti and on Melan-sari and Teikar-sari Islands.[59]

Although the defenses were strong and contiguous, many of the forces that occupied them had suffered considerably in previous battles. For example, an officer from the 3d Infantry Brigade recorded that his brigade occupied positions at Tammisuo, 3 kilometers (1.9 miles) east of Vyborg, for a "couple of days" after abandoning its positions at Summa, adding, "We did not get any rest during that time. There the brigade received new antitank weapons, Panzerfausts and Panzerschrecks. These were used by antitank-men, who destroyed 28 tanks in our front sector."[60]

To the east, the Finnish III Army Corps defended the sector from the Vuoksi River to Lake Ladoga with two infantry divisions and one infantry brigade. The 2d Infantry Division defended along the northern bank of the Vuoksi River to Ruissari but retained a bridgehead on the river's southern bank opposite Vuosaalmi. On its left flank, the 15th Infantry Division occupied the 50-kilometer (31-mile) sector eastward to Khaparainen, and the 19th Infantry Brigade defended the isthmus south of Taipale, adjacent to the western shore of Lake Ladoga. On the III Army Corps' lake flank, the 3d Coastal Brigade defended the western shore of Lake Ladoga to Cape Iarisevian-neime.[61]

The Finns also worked strenuously to form a reserve to back up their defenses at Vyborg. They placed the battered Lagus Armored Division and the reassembled 10th Infantry Division in reserve north of Vyborg with orders to support the V and IV Army Corps. The 17th Infantry Division, then en route to the Karelian Isthmus from the north, was to support Finnish forces in the Kilpenioki sector along with the 6th and 11th Infantry Divisions, which were also en route by rail from southern Karelia. In addition, on 18–19 June, the Germans reinforced the Finnish Air Forces with 20 Ju-87 and 10 Fw-190 aircraft.[62] By 20 June the strength of Finnish forces on the Karelian Isthmus totaled seven divisions and four brigades (less the coastal defense brigades), which were defending a 100-kilometer (62-mile) front, and three more divisions were en route to the region.

On 19 June Mannerheim issued a proclamation to his troops underscoring the importance of Vyborg's defenses:

> With our armies occupying defenses along the so-called VTK line, it is essential to close the enemy's penetration routes into the depth of our country. Therefore, I request that you defend this line stubbornly. Pay special attention to the fact that the penetration of this position can decisively weaken our defensive capabilities and thus will place our country and people in serious jeopardy. . . . I realize that defensive work either has not been conducted or is in its initial stages but believe that, if necessary, the Finnish soldier can exploit the terrain and his own tenacity to achieve an unshakable defense.[63]

During the night of 19–20 June, Govorov ordered the 21st and 23d Armies to "destroy the enemy Vyborg grouping and capture Vyborg no later than 20 June by developing the attack to the northwest. Reach the Antrea and Vyborg line with the [armies'] main forces no later than 21 June, while reliably protecting the shock grouping's flank and rear by a defense along the Vuoksi water system."[64]

Govorov's plan required Gusev's 21st Army to advance northwest from the Kamiarian-khovu and Somme Station line, capture Vyborg no later than 20 June, and reach the Kavantsari, Iuustila, and Tienkhara line no later than 21 June. Gusev planned to advance with three rifle corps abreast, with Tikhonov's 108th Rifle Corps assaulting northward along the coast, Busarov's 97th along the rail line, and Alferov's 109th toward Tali Station. Once they successfully breached the Finns' defenses, Busarov's and Alferov's corps were to envelop Vyborg's defenses from the northeast. The 13th Air Army was to support the ground assault, prevent the movement of enemy troop and equipment transport from Helsinki to Vyborg, and destroy withdrawing enemy forces.

To the east, Cherepanov's 23d Army was to make its main attack northwest from the Kiuliapakkola and Kheinioki line with Fadeev's 6th and Anisimov's 98th Rifle Corps, which were to reach the Kukauppi and Kavantsari Station line no later than 21 June. At the same time, Kozachek's 115th Rifle Corps was to protect the shock group's flank and rear by defending along the Vuoksi water system.[65]

Govorov's two armies began their assault early on 20 June, only to discover that the Finns had abandoned the city the night before: "On 21 June the Russians occupied Vyborg. The Finns had evacuated it the night before. Although the Army had not planned to defend the old city, its loss was a blow to Finnish morale."[66] The decision by the commander of the 20th Infantry Brigade, which was defending Vyborg, to abandon the city generated considerable controversy, which persists today.

Regardless of that decision, Gusev's three army corps adhered to their plan and pursued Finnish forces northward from the Vyborg defense line and the VTK line. After the Finnish forces began withdrawing northward and northwestward, the 314th and 90th Rifle Divisions of Tikhonov's 108th Rifle Corps and the 372d Rifle Division of Busarov's 97th Rifle Corps, supported by the 1st and 30th Guards Tank Brigades, captured Vyborg at 1900 hours on 20 June. By day's end, Gusev's forces reached and occupied new positions extending from Lukkiulia westward south of Tali and eastward through Tammisuo to the northern and western outskirts of Vyborg. The 13th Air Army supported Gusev's advance with 950 aircraft sorties, and the Baltic Fleet's aviation flew another 600 sorties. Farther east, Fadeev's 6th and Anisimov's 98th Rifle Corps of Cherepanov's 23d Army pursued Finnish forces northwestward and by nightfall reached positions extending from Lapinlakhti, on the western shore of Lake Vuoksi-iarvi, westward through Kiantiumia to Lukkiulia. He ordered his 115th Rifle Corps to defend along the southern shore of Lakes Suvanto-iarvi and Vuoksi-iarvi.[67]

During the final assault on Vyborg, the *Stavka* radioed a directive to the Leningrad Front promoting Govorov to the rank of Marshal of the Soviet Union and both Zhdanov and Gusev to the rank of Colonel General. Although the capture of Vyborg and the Red Army advance to the Vuoksi River line essentially ended the Vyborg operation, it did not satisfy the *Stavka's* strategic aims.

THE LENINGRAD FRONT'S OFFENSIVE INTO FINLAND, 21 JUNE–14 JULY

The Situation on 21 June and the Leningrad Front's Plans

The defeat of Finnish forces on the Karelian Isthmus and the capture of Vyborg posed a serious strategic dilemma to the Finnish government. Gusev's 21st

Army, which had captured Vyborg, now threatened other population centers in southern Finland, including Helsinki and central Finland. Worse still, the Karelian Front's offensive operations between Lakes Onega and Ladoga, which commenced on 21 June, only increased that threat. The Finnish government and High Command were by no means certain that their forces would be able to halt further Red Army incursions deeper into Finland. Therefore, on 19 June, they requested that Germany provide six divisions to take over the front in East Karelia so that Finnish forces could concentrate their forces on the Karelian Isthmus. They also requested additional weaponry for the Finnish Army.

Although he understood the Finns' dire needs, Hitler could not provide significant military support, primarily because the *Wehrmacht* was now under assault in Normandy. Nor did the situation improve thereafter, since the Red Army also struck a major blow against German Army Group Center in Belorussia on 23 June. Nevertheless, on 19 June the Germans delivered 9,000 *panzerfausts* (44mm recoilless antitank grenade launchers) to Finland by torpedo boats and three days later 5,000 *panzerschrecks* (88mm antitank rocket launchers) by emergency airlift. Although this and other assistance was helpful, it was far less so than the six divisions the Finns desired:

> On 20 June the OKW informed Mannerheim that it was ready to give Finland every kind of help if the Finnish Army was genuinely determined to hold the Vyborg-Vuoksi line. Aside from the weapons and supplies, the Germans offered the 122d Infantry Division [from Estonia], a self-propelled assault gun brigade [the 303d], and air units (a fighter group and a ground attack close support group *[Stukas]* plus one squadron). The ground troops were drawn from Army Group North and the planes from Fifth Air Force in northern Finland and First Air Force, attached to Army Group North. The aircraft were transferred immediately, and on 21 June flew 940 support missions for the Finnish Army.[68]

The 303d Assault Gun Brigade reached Finland on 23 June and the 122d Infantry Division on 28 June. In addition, on 22 June, German Foreign Minister Ribbentrop visited Helsinki and met with Finnish President Ryti. After several days of meetings, Ryti signed a pact affirming that Finland would not sign a separate peace with Russia and would continue the war in return for German support.

Given the Finns' apparent intransigence, at 0215 hours on 21 June, Stalin ordered Govorov to resume offensive operations:

> The *Stavka* of the Supreme High Command *orders:*
> 1. The Leningrad Front's forces operating on the Karelian Isthmus will continue their offensive with the mission of capturing the Imatra, Lap-

penranta, and Viroioki line by 26–28 June. Part of the force will attack toward Keksholm and Elisenvara to clear the Karelian Isthmus of enemy northeast of the Vuoksi River and Lake Vuoksi.

2. Subsequently, the main forces will exploit the offensive, with the mission of capturing the Kouvola and Kotka line and digging in along the eastern bank of the Kiumin-oiki River. Protect your main grouping [against attack] from the north. . . .

[signed] I. Stalin, A. Antonov[69]

To improve command and control within Govorov's *front*, the *Stavka* hastily transferred the headquarters of Korovnikov's 59th Army, but without its subordinate forces, from Narva to the Karelian Isthmus. By 21 June the right wing of Govorov's Leningrad Front consisted of the 21st and 23d Armies with 7 rifle corps and a total of 21 rifle divisions operating along a 200-kilometer (124-mile) front. One additional rifle corps was in Govorov's reserve. Worn down from weeks of continuous fighting, the rifle divisions in Gusev's army ranged in strength from 4,000 to 6,500 men and in Cherepanov's army from 4,200 to 6,600 men. The total strength of Govorov's two armies was now roughly 150,000 soldiers.

On the other hand, Finnish forces defending on the isthmus were stronger than they had been at the beginning of the operation on 10 June, and, unlike the case 20 days before, they expected the new Soviet attack. The total Finnish force now numbered 3 army corps totaling 14 divisions or brigades, including 7 infantry divisions, 1 armored division, and 1 cavalry, 3 infantry, and 2 coastal brigades.[70] The Finnish High Command combined these forces under the control of the Karelian Isthmus Group, which it had formed on 14 June.

In addition to these forces, the 6th and 11th Infantry Divisions were moving toward the isthmus from southern Karelia, and the German 122d Infantry Division and 303d Assault Gun Brigade were arriving from Estonia. The V and IV Army Corps defended numerous fortified points in the interlake defiles between the Vyborg Gulf and the Vuoksi River, and the III Army Corps occupied favorable defenses along the northern bank of the Vuoksi water system.[71]

On 21 June Govorov submitted his new offensive plan to the *Stavka* for approval. According to that plan, Gusev's 21st and Korovnikov's 59th Armies were to conduct his main attack toward Lappenranta and subsequently wheel to the west to reach the Lappenranta and Surpiala line. At the same time, Cherepanov's 23d Army was to force the Vuoksi River in the Antrea and Enso sector and attack toward Khitola to envelop Keksholm from the north.

The offensive was to develop in two stages, during which Govorov's forces were to advance westward to a depth of 50 kilometers (31 miles). During the first stage, which was to last from 22 to 24 June, the 21st and 23d Armies were to achieve the *front*'s immediate mission with a force of five rifle corps (three in the 21st Army and two in the 23d Army). Gusev's and Cherepanov's armies were to attack northwestward from the Kukauppi, Kavantsari Station, Iuustila, and Tienkhara sector and reach the Enso, Lake Nuiiama-iarvi, Lainela, and Nisalakhti (the former boundary with Finland) line no later than 24 June, while protecting their right flank along the Vuoksi River. Kozachek's 115th Rifle Corps, under direct *front* control, was to defend the sector from Lapinlakhti to Lake Ladoga.

During the offensive's second stage, which was to last from 24 to 25 June, all three armies were to attack westward and secure the Imatra, Lappenranta, and Surpiala line no later than 26 June. The armies' eight rifle corps were to seize the main Finnish strong points in the defensive belt along the 1940 and 1941 border and, simultaneously, prepare a powerful assault to penetrate that formidable belt. Korovnikov's 59th Army was to launch its attack from the Penttila and Lainela line with Alferov's 109th and Busarov's 97th Rifle Corps and subsequently advance along the Lappenranta axis. Gusev's 21st Army was to conduct its main attack along the coastal axis with Tikhonov's and Griaznov's 108th and 110th Rifle Corps and Simoniak's 30th Guards Rifle Corps, which was to be committed from the *front*'s reserve. The boundary line between the 59th and 21st Armies extended from Lainela to Mette.

To the east, Cherepanov's 23d Army was to force the Vuoksi River in the Antrea-Enso sector with Fadeev's 6th and Anisimov's 98th Rifle Corps and advance toward Khitola to protect the right flank of Gusev's assault. On Cherepanov's right flank, Kozachek's 115th Rifle Corps was to force the Vuoksi River in the Kiviniemi region and attack toward Keksholm in cooperation with the rest of the 23d Army.[72]

In order to carry out his ambitious plan, Govorov requested the *Stavka* provide him with two additional rifle corps, one engineer-sapper brigade, two motorized pontoon-bridge battalions, two special designation motorized battalions (amphibious vehicles), two NZP pontoon parks, and one dog minesweeper battalion. He also requested 30 T-34 tanks, 30 SU-76 guns, 100 *Studebeker* trucks for the pontoon and bridge units, and 17,000 multiple rocket launcher rockets. The *Stavka* approved Govorov's plan but refused him the two additional rifle corps, stating, "The *front* has sufficient forces to fulfill the assigned missions."[73]

The Leningrad Front began preparing for the offensive on 21–22 June. In the meantime, the Baltic Fleet began operations to capture the islands in the B'erk Archipelago, which were vital to the control of Vyborg Bay.

Baltic Fleet Operations against the B'erk Archipelago, 21–27 June

Although Gusev's 21st Army had cleared Finnish forces from the Koivisto Peninsula and the eastern shore of the Gulf of Finland by mid-June, Finnish forces still occupied the nearby B'erk Islands. The islands were vitally important for both sides. If they remained under Finnish control, they threatened the 21st Army's left flank and the temporary naval bases in Ollakhti and Khmalioki bays and also hindered Baltic Fleet operations in the Gulf of Vyborg. However, Red Army possession of the islands would deny German access to the Gulf of Vyborg and prevent the Germans from reinforcing the Finns by sea. Therefore, Govorov added the islands to his list of objectives during the Vyborg operation.

On 16 June Govorov ordered Tikhonov's 108th Rifle Corps to capture the islands and provided it with a brigade of skerry ships and one battalion of naval infantry with which to do so. These boats and one of Tikhonov's rifle regiments were to conduct the operation. However, his corps failed to carry out effective reconnaissance during the ensuing three days, even though it determined that Pii-sari Island was the most weakly defended, particularly on its coast side adjacent to B'erkezund Bay. Since Finnish defenses were too strong and Tikhonov's forces too unskilled to conduct an amphibious operation, Govorov canceled the 108th Rifle Corps' operation, and on 19 June he ordered the Baltic Fleet to conduct the operation independently and without the 108th Rifle Corps' forces. In turn, Admiral Tributs ordered the Kronshtadt Naval Defensive Region, commanded by Vice Admiral G. I. Levchenko, to conduct the operation and assigned him the skerry ship brigade and the 260th Naval Infantry Brigade to conduct it.[74]

At this time, by Soviet count, the Finns had concentrated more than 70 ships and 20 amphibious barges at its naval bases at Kotka and Vyborg in the eastern Gulf of Finland, which defended the islands and had mined the southern approaches to the B'erk Archipelago. The Finnish ships laid 60 mines during the period from 10 to 20 June. About 3,000 troops, divided into small garrisons, defended the islands, supported by about 40 coastal guns. Since the northeastern sector of the island defense was the weakest, this is where Levchenko planned to conduct his amphibious assault. He chose the northeastern coast of Pii-sari Island as his initial objective since, once they captured that region, his forces would be able to outflank the Finnish garrisons at Pii-sari and Tiurin-sari islands.

Levchenko's amphibious assault began overnight on 20–21 June, when a company-size reconnaissance detachment landed on the eastern coast of Pii-sari and captured a bridgehead 200 by 200 meters square. A second company of naval infantry landed early on 21 June. The Finns counterattacked with reinforcements that they had landed overnight, and, at the same time, a flotilla of eight enemy assault barges and four cutters entered the Koiviston-sari Bay from the north and began to shell the amphibious force and support ships. However, Soviet naval assault aircraft drove off the Finnish ships, damaging several in the process. Throughout 21 and 22 June, Levchenko's landing detachment repelled the Finns' attacks and drove their forces inland, and the remainder of the 260th Naval Infantry Brigade landed on Pii-sari Island at midday on 22 June. The brigade cleared the island of Finnish forces by late on 23 June and landed one battalion each on Tiurin-sari and Koivisto islands. On 26–27 June, the brigade also seized Ruonti and Tuppuran-sari islands.

Thus, by 27 June, Levchenko's forces had seized all of the islands in the B'erk Archipelago, the Baltic Fleet was able to operate freely in the Gulf of Vyborg, and Govorov could contemplate subsequent operations against Finnish defenses west of Vyborg from the sea.

The Leningrad Front's Continuation Offensive, 25 June–14 July

While the Baltic Fleet was completing its operations to seize the islands in the Gulf of Vyborg, Govorov's 21st and 23d Armies commenced their offensive operations to reach and restore the 1940–1941 Finnish-Soviet border north and west of Vyborg and drive Finland from the war. Gusev's 21st Army began its offensive against the Finnish IV and V Army Corps between Vyborg and Lake Vuoksi on 25 June, and, at the same time, Cherepanov's 23d Army attempted to force the Vuoksi River to outflank the III Army Corps and capture Keksholm. Although both Gusev's and Cherepanov's forces made some headway, their advance soon degenerated into a bloody slugfest against well-prepared Finnish forces, and Govorov's armies were not able to fulfill his ambitious plan.

According to Govorov's plan, Gusev's 21st Army was to penetrate Finnish defenses north and northeast of Vyborg, advance to the northwest, reach the Soviet-Finnish 1940–1941 border, and, subsequently, "advance into the depth of Finland." His army, which consisted of 12 rifle divisions of Tikhonov's 108th, Griaznov's 110th, Busarov's 97th, and Alferov's 109th Rifle Corps, was deployed from left to right in the 30-kilometer (18.6-mile) sector extending from the Gulf of Vyborg to south of Repola (east of Lake Noskuon-sel'ka). Govorov assigned Simoniak's 30th Guards Rifle Corps, which was then in *front* reserve, to Gusev's army on 25 June with orders to participate it the assault along Gusev's main attack axis. This brought Gusev's total strength to 15 rifle divisions with which he was to engage 4.5 divisions of the Finnish V and IV Army Corps.

When Gusev's forces attacked, the V and IV Army Corps defended the sector from Vyborg to the Vuoksi River with the 20th and 3d Infantry Brigades and the 18th, 4th, and 3d Infantry Divisions, a force of roughly 50,000 men as opposed to Gusev's roughly 150,000 attacking troops. In addition, the Finnish 3d Infantry Division faced the bulk of the 23d Army's 6th Rifle Corps, which was deployed from south of Repola to Kiuliapakkola on the western bank of the Vuoksi River.

On Gusev's right flank in the eastern sector of the Karelian Isthmus, Cherepanov's 23d Army had reached the southern shores of the Vuoksi water system by 20 June. By then his army consisted of Fadeev's 6th, Anisimov's 98th, and Kozachek's 115th Rifle Corps and the 17th Fortified Region, which were deployed from left to right along the 100-kilometer (62-mile) front from south of Repola through Iaiuriapia to the western shore of Lake Ladoga. The 17th Fortified Region defended from Lake Ladoga to the mouth of the Vuoksi River with six separate machine gun–artillery battalions. Cherepanov's main force, made up of Fadeev's 6th and Anisimov's 98th Rifle Corps with six rifle divisions, was concentrated on the army's left flank from south of Repola to Iaiuriapia on the western bank of the Vuoksi River.

The three divisions of the 6th Rifle Corps on Cherepanov's left flank faced the Finnish IV Army Corps' 3d Infantry Division west of the Vuoksi River. Cherepanov's 98th and 115th Rifle Corps and the 17th Fortified Region faced the Finnish III Army Corps, whose 2d and 15th Infantry Divisions and 19th Infantry Brigade defended along the northern bank of the Vuoksi water system. One regiment of the 2d Division held a small bridgehead southwest of Vuoksaalmi, on the river's southern bank. The well-fortified and heavily wooded bridgehead was anchored on heights south of the river and supported by a large artillery grouping. Cherepanov's force of roughly 100,000 men faced about 35,000 Finnish troops. On 21 June Govorov ordered Cherepanov's army to force the Vuoksi River near Vuoksaalmi, destroy the opposing enemy, and exploit the offensive toward Khitola and Keksholm.

The forces of Gusev's 21st Army began their assault early on 22 June as ordered. Attacking just south of Repola (east of Lake Karstilan-iarvi), the combined shock groups of Griaznov's 110th and Busarov's 97th Rifle Corps immediately penetrated about 2 kilometers (1.2 miles) into the Finnish defenses at the junction of the V and IV Army Corps.[75] Repeated assaults by the two corps and by Tikhonov's 108th Rifle Corps on the left flank and by Alferov's 109th Rifle Corps on the right forced the Finnish forces to pull back to new defensive lines anchored on the defensive strong point at Repola by day's end on 24 June. During the fighting, Busarov's and Alferov's troops also captured the Finnish strong points at Tammisuo and Tali. However, the assault by Fadeev's 6th Rifle Corps of Cherepanov's 23d Army against the Finnish 3d Infantry Division west of the Vuoksi River faltered almost immediately.

After failing to achieve a decisive penetration between 22 and 24 June, with the Stavka's approval, Govorov once again altered his plan. Instead of assigning the 97th and 109th Rifle Corps to the newly arrived 59th Army headquarters, he left the two corps under the 21st Army's control. He then ordered Korovnikov's headquarters to plan an amphibious assault across the Gulf of Vyborg to outflank Finnish defenses from the west. At the same time, he ordered Gusev to commit Simoniak's 30th Guards Rifle Corps in a new attempt to smash Finnish defenses and resume the advance toward the former Soviet-Finnish frontier. He chose the Repola sector as the penetration sector of Gusev's new offensive.[76]

Gusev's 21st Army attacked in the Repola sector on 25 June with an estimated force of 12 rifle divisions from Griaznov's, Alferov's, and Simoniak's rifle corps, backed up by heavy assault artillery, which fired a heavy preparation prior to the attack. In 24 hours of heavy fighting, the three attacking rifle corps penetrated 5 kilometers (3.1 miles) into the Finnish defenses against very heavy resistance.[77] During the fighting, the three corps captured the strong points at Mannikkola and Repola and approached the strong point at Portinkhaika late on 26 June.

A Finnish officer in the 3d Infantry Brigade, which was defending the sector opposite Gusev's main attack, described the action near Repola:

> *Question:* The [Finnish] official history states that, on the morning of 25 June 1944, the enemy fired an extremely heavy two-hour barrage on the front of the 3d Brigade, from the front line to the Saimaa Canal in the rear. Then heavy (JS-2) tanks broke through the line and the enemy infantry followed.
>
> *Answer:* At that hour the situation was quite unclear; there were skirmishes here and there. Once again, we had no contact with our troops, but we tried to retreat to the north. We had to cross Lake Karstilanjarvi by the narrow point; there we suffered a lot of casualties because the enemy concentrated their fire on the spot that we had to cross. We saw some Finnish tanks of the Lagus Division and German Stukas.[78]

Despite the tremendous force of Gusev's assault and the loss of considerable ground, the Finns were able to seal off and contain the penetration after four more days of heavy fighting. By 30 June, Gusev's forces had captured the Finnish strong points at Portinkhaika and Karisaalmi and reached the outskirts of Ikhantala, gaining access to better tank country north of Vyborg. During the operation, the 21st Army encountered strong resistance in very difficult terrain and was severely hindered by intensified air strikes at the end of the month. Thus, Gusev's army advanced a total of 8–10 kilometers (5–6.2 miles) in 10 days of heavy fighting and, by 30 June, was fighting along a line extending from west to east from the northeastern extremity of Suomsiveden-pokh'ia Bay through Karisaalmi, Ikhantala, and Portinkhaika to the southern shore of Lake Noskuon-sel'ka.

Further assaults by Gusev's army in early July produced no appreciable gains. His forces advanced 1–2 kilometers (.6–1.2 miles) against tenacious Finnish resistance but were halted in their tracks as the Finns committed their 6th and 11th Infantry Divisions from southern Karelia and the German 303d

Assault Gun Brigade from Estonia. The officer from the 3d Brigade once again summarized his unit's operations:

> After that [the withdrawal after the 25 June battle for Repola], we fought at Ventela until the 9th of July. (According to the official history, four enemy divisions, 40,000 men when at full strength, against our single almost decimated Finnish Brigade, whose initial strength was 5,000 men.) From Ventela our brigade was transferred to Viipurinlahti in July. First we were near Viipuri [Vyborg] and then at Keihasniemi.[79]

Given these failures, on 12 July Govorov ordered Gusev's 21st Army to go over to the defense effective 14 July. This ended the 21st Army's operations against Finland.

Meanwhile, to the east, despite heavy fighting, Cherepanov's army had even less success. After the assaults by Fadeev's 6th Rifle Corps west of Lake Vuoksi on 22 and 23 June achieved nothing, repeated assaults by Anisimov's 98th Rifle Corps in late June did not even dent the Finnish III Army Corps' river defenses and left the Finns' bridgehead at Iaiuriapia intact. Undeterred, Cherepanov's army repeated his assaults in early July, particularly from 4 to 11 July. During this period, Anisimov's 98th Rifle Corps reached the Vuoksi River and finally cleared Finnish forces from their bridgehead at Iaiuriapia on 7 July. Cherepanov then ordered Kozachek's 115th Rifle Corps to force a crossing over the river.

Major General I. M. Platov's 10th and Sonnikov's 142d Rifle Divisions of Kozachek's corps attempted to assault across the river on 9 July, during which Sonnikov's 946th and 461st Rifle Regiments managed to gain a tenuous foothold on the river's northern bank. Shortly after, the remainder of the divisions crossed the river and established a bridgehead 7 kilometers (4.3 miles) wide and 2 kilometers (1.2 miles) deep. However, the Finnish III Army Corps initially reinforced its 2d Infantry Division with portions of the 15th Infantry Division and the 19th Infantry Brigade, and on 10 July with elements of the 10th Armored Division's Jager Brigade, and still later with elements of the 3d Infantry Division.[80] These forces then began a prolonged series of counterattacks designed to crush the bridgehead:

> In the second week of July the Finns relinquished the right bank of the Vuoksi south of Vousalmi. The Russians followed up by taking a bridgehead on the north bank. Too weak to eliminate the bridgehead, the Finns tried to contain it. Despite this dangerous development and the continued heavy fighting, which brought the number of Finnish casualties to 32,000 by the 11th, the fronts on both sides of Lake Ladoga were beginning to stabilize. By 15 July the Finns had detected signs—confirmed

several days later—that, although the Soviet strength on the isthmus had risen to 26 rifle divisions and 12 to 14 tank brigades, the better units were being relieved and replaced with garrison troops. The tempo of the offensive could be expected to diminish.[81]

The ensuing struggle lasted from 9 through 11 July, and when it ended, Kozachek's exhausted rifle divisions still clung to their hard-won bridgehead. However, since the opportunity to expand the bridgehead had clearly evaporated, on 11 July Govorov ordered the 23d Army to go over to the defense.

The 59th Army's Amphibious Assault, 2–5 July

Given the 21st and 23d Armies' failure to smash Finnish defenses north and northeast of Vyborg and advance decisively to the former Soviet-Finnish border, Govorov decided to conduct a series of amphibious operations to outflank Vyborg from the southwest. Initially, he planned to attack the islands in the Gulf of Vyborg and, then, the northern shores of the Gulf of Vyborg to outflank Finnish forces defending southwest of the city and assist the 21st Army's advance.

Govorov assigned these missions to Korovnikov's 59th Army and Tributs's Baltic Fleet. At the time, the 59th Army consisted of only Colonel M. D. Papchenko's 124th and Colonel Burmistrov's 224th Rifle Divisions, which had just been assigned to the army from the *front*'s reserve. Papchenko's division was concentrated in the Niemelia and Kaislakhti region, and Burmistrov's division was moving by sea to Ollakhti Bay from Ust'-Lugi. On 2 July Govorov assigned Korovnikov the immediate mission of clearing Finnish forces from the islands in the Gulf of Finland in the sector from Vyborg and Khietala on the right to Cape Pulli-niemi and Cape Pitkianiemi on the left. Then Korovnikov's forces were to capture a bridgehead in the Tervoiki and Nisalakhti sector on the northern coast of the Gulf and, subsequently, capture Tienkhara northwest of Vyborg.

The Finns had already erected defenses along the northern coast of the Gulf of Vyborg in the expectation of a Russian assault and were in the process of reinforcing these defenses. The Finnish 2d Coastal Brigade defended the coast of the Gulf of Vyborg south of Nisalakhti, and the V Army Corps defended the coast to the northeast of Nisalakhti. The reinforced 1st Cavalry Brigade defended the islands, the 17th Infantry Division defended Capes Tienkhara and Kivasillansaalmi, and the 3d Infantry Brigade, just transferred from Ventela, defended the land sector between the Saimaa Canal and Lake Ventelian-sel'ka. The 10th Infantry Division was concentrated in reserve 6 kilometers (3.7 miles) southwest of Tienkhara, and the 11th Infantry Division and 20th Infantry Brigade were defending in the Khvinma region and west of Iuustila. The German 122d Infantry Division was also in reserve in the Siakkiiarvi region.

Given the Soviet seizure of the B'erk Islands and the growing threat to the islands in the Gulf of Vyborg, the Finns laid more mines, strengthened their anti-amphibious defenses on the coast, and concentrated 70 surface ships, 4 submarines, and 30 amphibious ships in the eastern gulf. They also assembled 80 aircraft for defense. According to Soviet intelligence, the 1st Cavalry and 2d Coastal Brigades had 31 artillery and mortar batteries with 130 guns and mortars (75–210mm).[82]

The 59th Army's initial amphibious assault echelon consisted of Burmistrov's 224th Rifle Division, one army gun artillery brigade, and one anti-aircraft artillery regiment. One mortar brigade, one howitzer and one antitank artillery brigade, one naval railroad artillery brigade, one guards-mortar regiment, one antiaircraft artillery division, one separate antiaircraft artillery battalion, and one separate correction-aviation squadron were to support the assault. Korovnikov commanded the amphibious operation, and the commander of the Kronshtadt Naval Defensive Region commanded the naval portion of the operation in subordination to Korovnikov. The joint command post was at Niemelia. The naval force consisted of 84 cutters and 30 amphibious tenders, supported by 18 85–130mm guns, 11 fleet railroad guns, 782 fleet aircraft, and a division of torpedo boats.[83]

On 2 July Korovnikov decided to begin his assault at first light on 4 July. Burmistrov's three rifle regiments were to land simultaneously on Teikar-sari, Suonion-Sari, and Ravan-sari Islands, and the 59th Army's forces as a whole were to concentrate at Tranzund at the northern end of Uransari Island by rail and sea. Admiral Levchenko, the commander of the Kronshtadt Naval Defensive Region, planned to concentrate his assault ships at Khannukkola and Iokhannes, load the 224th Division's regiments by late on 3 July, and land the force on Teikar-sari and Suonion-sari by 1000 hours on 4 July. Artillery (coastal and ship) and aircraft would support the passage, and a smoke screen would conceal the landing. The landing force was organized into two amphibious detachments of one regiment each, two naval artillery support detachments, and ship support and reserve detachments (an infantry battalion and nine KM cutters). Preparations for the assault lasted two days.

Artillery support included a 75-minute artillery preparation, beginning with a 5-minute fire raid on the islands, followed by methodical fire, and ending with another 5-minute fire raid. A total of 250 tubes under the 59th Army's control supported the operation. Aviation support included a 30–40-minute air preparation by 142 Pe-2 and Il-2 aircraft before the landing and continuous assaults after the landing by 700 13th Air Army and Baltic Fleet aircraft. A thousand sorties were planned for the first day. Concealed preliminary movements and smoke cutters assigned to each landing detachment protected the landing.

The amphibious operation began promptly at 0800 hours on 4 July, when the amphibious detachments left Iokhannes Bay escorted by 20 fighter aircraft. Simultaneously, the covering detachment of nine torpedo cutters and five hunter-cutters emerged from Cape Pulli-niemi. The artillery and aviation preparation began at 0845 hours. The amphibious detachments approached their landing sites and began landing at 1006 hours. The amphibious detachments completed landing at Suonion-sari Island at 1035 hours and occupied the entire island by 1400 hours. The Finnish defenders withdrew to Esi-sari Island. The second amphibious detachment, the 143d Rifle Regiment, occupied Esi-sari by 1700 hours. The 185th Rifle Regiment, which formed the third amphibious detachment, forced the Tranzund Straits by itself and occupied Ravan-sari Island and village by midday.

The first landing detachment, the 160th Rifle Regiment, encountered greater problems in its attack on Teikar-sari Island. Although it completed its landing operation successfully at 1100 hours, afterward it recorded only mixed success. After landing, it lost communications with the coast because a naval mine blew up the ship carrying the commander's radio. Once on the shore, the detachment encountered heavy resistance and, because of the lost communications, lacked any effective artillery or air support.[84] Nevertheless, the regiment secured the southern and central part of the island. As the Finns landed reinforcements, at 1645 and 1730 hours, Finnish ships tried to reach the island but were forced to withdraw, losing several craft.

Between 1900 and 2400 hours, the Finns managed to land a reinforced infantry battalion, which by day's end drove the 160th Rifle Regiment to the southern end of the island. The regiment then abandoned the island, leaving 200 men dug in on its southern tip. At midnight on 4–5 July Korovnikov ordered two infantry battalions and four tanks from Papchenko's reserve 124th Rifle Division to the island, and they landed successfully at 1100 hours on 5 July. Communication with the force was finally restored, and artillery and aircraft began to support the operation. The new Soviet reinforcements prompted the Finns to withdraw northward and begin evacuating the island. After failing once more to reinforce its garrison, the Finns abandoned the island at 2100 hours on 5 July to Papchenko's division.

At day's end on 5 July, the 59th Army's 224th Rifle Division was fighting for Turkin-sari and Musta-sari islands. By this time the 124th Rifle Division had captured Teikar-sari and Melan-sari islands, and the 43d Rifle Corps' 80th Rifle Division was in army reserve in the forests east of Kaislakhti Station.

While Korovnikov's amphibious operation managed to capture many of the islands in the Gulf of Vyborg, the Finnish command promptly took measures to shore up its coastal defenses southwest of Vyborg. It subordinated the coastal brigade southwest of Nisalakhti to the V Army Corps on 5 July to place all defensive forces under unified command. The 1st Cavalry Brigade, whose forces had been driven from the islands, defended the Maiapokhvia and Khankiulia sector, and part of the brigade and part of the 10th Infantry Division moved to the region southwest of Nisalakhti to reinforce coastal defenses. Finally, the command ordered the German 122d Infantry Division to move to the Nisalakhti and Pispansaari sector by late on 6 July.

That same day, Govorov ordered the Baltic Fleet to prepare to conduct yet another amphibious landing on 12 July on the western coast of the Gulf of Vyborg with two 59th Army divisions and, subsequently, reinforce it with one additional division. The fleet was to move the forces to the islands during the preparatory period and occupy the remaining smaller islands. However, after his offensive northeast of Vyborg failed, on 13 July, Govorov canceled the landing operation. He ordered Korovnikov's forces to cease all offensive operations and go over to the defense on 14 July and reinforced the army with two separate machine gun–artillery battalions.

By 14 July it was clear to Soviet and Finn alike that Govorov's offensive into southern Finland had failed. Nor did the Karelian Front's operation to the north materially assist Govorov's efforts on the Karelian Isthmus. There, between Lakes Ladoga and Onega, Meretskov's Karelian Front achieved some success. However, his 7th Separate Army, too, was unable to make any inroads into Finland proper, other than recapturing tracts of territory lost to the Finns in late 1941. By Soviet definition, the end of Meretskov's operation on 10 August also officially marked the end of the three-year Battle for Leningrad.

The most candid Soviet assessment of Govorov's final attempts to restore the 1940–1941 Soviet borders and invade southern Finland clearly acknowledged Govorov's failure to do so:

> Thus, as a result of more than three weeks of offensive operations—from 21 June through the middle of July—the forces on the Leningrad Front's right wing were not able to fulfill the missions assigned to them by the *Stavka* of the Supreme High Command's directive of 21 June 1944. The *front's* forces did not succeed in advancing to the state borders with Finland and completely clear the territory of the Karelian Isthmus of enemy. The Finnish command stopped the Soviet offensive into the depth of Finland by transferring additional forces from the flanks of the Karelian Isthmus.[85]

The Leningrad Front's offensive on the Karelian Isthmus lasted for more than a month. During this period, the *front* conducted the Vyborg offensive operation and amphibious operations in Vyborg Bay, and began offensive operations designed to penetrate into southern Finland. The Vyborg operation lasted 11 days, during which the forces on the Leningrad Front's right wing advanced 110–130 kilometers (68.3–80.7 miles) and liberated 5,000 square kilometers of the northern Leningrad region and the city of Vyborg. In doing so, Govorov's forces eliminated any threat to Leningrad from the north once and for all. By the time the offensive ended, the Soviet front lines extended more than 150 kilometers (93.2 miles) from the city, and Soviet forces were poised for a strike deep into southern Finland.

The success of the Vyborg operation facilitated subsequent Red Army operations in southern Karelia, the Baltic region, and northern Finland and provided the Baltic Fleet with vastly greater freedom of action. During the operation, the Leningrad Front penetrated four heavily fortified defensive belts and forced the Finns to transfer significant forces to the Karelian Isthmus, thus paving the way for the Svir-Petrozavodsk operation, which began on 21 July, and the advance by Meretskov's Karelian Front into central Karelia. While Govorov's three armies continued operations until mid-July with even more ambitious aims, these operations failed after achieving only minimal gains. Thereafter, the front on the Karelian Isthmus stabilized until war's end. Its successful defense against the Red Army's advance north and west from Vyborg permitted the Finnish government to continue the war until 19 September 1944.

The numerical superiority of Govorov's forces over the Finns contributed in a major way to his success in the Vyborg operation. However, his achievement of surprise, strategically, operationally, and tactically, was an even more important factor in his forces' initial success. Surprise deprived the Finns of the ability to exploit their strong defenses on the Karelian Isthmus and led to their relatively rapid withdrawal and loss of Vyborg. However, this situation changed during the later stages of Govorov's offensive. Once they were forewarned, the Finns were able to prepare more durable defenses northwest and north of Vyborg and along the Vuoksi water system. Deprived of the element of surprise, the offensives Govorov launched after 21 June failed and could not be revived. Given this failure and the Red Army's spectacular progress in Belorussia and the western Ukraine, by mid-July neither Stalin nor the *Stavka* was willing to waste precious manpower resources in what, by that time, had clearly become a secondary theater of military operations. Thus, Govorov's offensive ground to an abrupt halt, and his forces began flowing southward into the fight in the Baltic region.

The short but violent Karelian Isthmus operation inflicted heavy casualties on both sides. Finnish forces defending the region suffered 32,000 casualties in the June and July operations. By Soviet count, Govorov's armies suffered 30,029 casualties, including 6,018 killed, captured, or missing and 24,011 wounded or sick out of an initial force of 188,800 men committed into combat during the Vyborg operation.[86] However, this figure shows only those losses suffered from 10 to 20 June and does not include the heavy fighting from 21 June through 14 July, when Govorov's forces probably lost another 30,000 men.

Red Army heavy artillery pounding Finnish defensive positions

A captured Finnish strong point in the Mannerheim Line

Red Army infantry and artillery cross a river on the Karelian Isthmus

Red Army troops passing a destroyed Finnish artillery piece

Red Army aircraft on a bombing mission over the Karelian Isthmus

N. M. Shvernik, 1st Deputy Representative, USSR Supreme Soviet Presidium, awards L. A. Govorov, Commander, Leningrad Front, with his rank of Marshal of the Soviet Union

Soldiers of the Leningrad Front celebrate the capture of Vyborg

Red Army troops erect signs along the restored Soviet-Finnish border, June 1944

Conclusions

The Battle for Leningrad justifiably occupies a legendary place in the Red Army's struggle during its Great Patriotic War if only because the city, acknowledged as the birthplace of revolution, represented both a bastion of Socialism and Russian national identity and a massive example of heroism on an unprecedented scale. While the suffering and fate of Leningraders during the city's three-year siege had tremendous political importance for its military defenders and the Soviet people as a whole, its successful defense and ultimate liberation had an even greater impact on the country's morale.

The Red Army's defense of Leningrad, its numerous and often tragic attempts to raise the siege, and its liberation of the city in early 1944 both reflected and affected the Soviet Union's wartime military strategy. During the initial period of war in 1941, the Red Army's Northern (Leningrad) and Northwestern Fronts were the first Red Army forces able to halt the seemingly inexorable German Barbarossa tide. The Red Army conducted a tenacious though costly defense on the approaches to the city, contained German forces in the city's southern suburbs, and, though the city was nearly totally blockaded, thwarted German attempts to encircle the city completely from the east. In November 1941 the Red Army conducted its first successful counteroffensive of the war against the *Wehrmacht* at Tikhvin and Volkhov. In the process, they exhausted Army Group North, began bleeding it white, and forced the Germans to go on the defense in the entire Leningrad region. This feat challenged enduring German misconceptions about the morale, fighting spirit, and staying power of the Red Army and confounded Hitler's Plan Barbarossa.

The Germans' unexpected failure to capture Leningrad in September and October 1941 had far-reaching strategic consequences. First, at Leningrad the concept of blitzkrieg failed for the first time in the Second World War, reinforcing what had begun to occur in July and August at Smolensk and anticipating what would occur at Moscow in December. Second, Army Group North's failure to capture Leningrad forced Hitler to alter his Barbarossa strategy significantly. Instead of capturing Leningrad by a coup de main and then shifting forces to other axes, the desperate Soviet defense of Leningrad from July through December 1941 forced the *Wehrmacht* to reinforce Army Group North with 16 divisions and 2 brigades, including 7 divisions from Army

Group Center. This weakened the main German drive on Moscow, perhaps fatally. During this most critical period of the war, 32 percent of the *Wehrmacht*'s forces operating north of the Pripiat' Marshes, including almost two full panzer groups, were tied down in combat along or adjacent to the northwestern axis.

Leningrad figured significantly in the *Stavka*'s December 1941 counteroffensive and the Red Army's first strategic offensive in the winter of 1941–1942, during which the *Stavka* allocated its new Volkhov Front and four fresh armies, including the 2d Shock Army, to combat in the Leningrad region. It employed the bulk of these forces to conduct the Liuban' offensive, the first large-scale offensive designed to envelop German forces south of Leningrad and raise the blockade by an advance westward from the Volkhov River. While demonstrating *Stavka* resolve to raise the blockade, the dramatic but tragic and costly failure educated the *Stavka* on how difficult operations in this region were and would continue to be.

In the summer of 1942, the *Stavka* adopted a "smaller solution" to the problem of raising the Leningrad blockade by attacking to establish a corridor to Leningrad through Siniavino while distracting the Germans with offensive operations near Demiansk. Although smaller in scale than the Liuban' offensive, the Volkhov, Northwestern, and Leningrad Fronts' offensives at Siniavino and Demiansk in the summer and fall of 1942 demonstrated continued *Stavka* resolve to raise the Leningrad blockade. Although these offensives too failed, they affected the war in other more important theaters by attracting large German forces away from southern Russia and tying down German forces in the Leningrad region. The threat of renewed Red Army offensives and Hitler's fixation on seizing Lenin's city finally compelled the *Wehrmacht* to dispatch Manstein's Eleventh Army to the region in August and September at the critical moment when the Germans were trying but failing to achieve decisive victory at Stalingrad.

Once again, in early 1943 the *Stavka* demonstrated its concern for Leningrad by capitalizing on the German defeat at Stalingrad. In January its Leningrad and Volkhov Fronts partially raised the Leningrad blockade by conducting Operation Spark. Although the offensive fell far short of Soviet expectations, it put the lie to German claims that Leningrad was in their pocket for the taking at any time and ended all German hopes of starving Leningrad into submission. The partial penetration of the blockade and the establishment of ground communications with the city also dramatically improved the Leningrad Front's military capabilities and paved the way for a series of more powerful and ultimately more successful offensive operations along the northwestern axis.

The most ambitious of these offensives was Zhukov's Operation Polar Star, which, for the first time, sought to implement a "larger solution" to raising the Leningrad siege by enveloping and defeating all of Army Group North.

The failure of Operation Polar Star in February also symbolized the failure of the *Stavka*'s entire grand design for achieving victory in 1943. In a larger sense, it also signaled the birth of a new, more sober appreciation on the part of the *Stavka* of what would be required to achieve victory in the future.

In the summer and fall of 1943, while momentous events were unfolding at Kursk, Orel, Smolensk, and Khar'kov, along the Dnepr River, and, later, in eastern Belorussia and the Ukraine, the *Stavka* returned to "smaller solutions" to the problem of raising the Leningrad siege. During this period, it relied on a combination of major Red Army offensives elsewhere along the front and limited-objective offensives in the Leningrad region to raise the blockade of the city. While the Leningrad and Volkhov Fronts' attempts to envelop and destroy German forces in the Mga, Siniavino, and Tosno regions and significantly widen the Shlissel'burg corridor failed after only limited gains, they did tie down significant German forces and seriously weakened Army Group North. These fierce, costly, but largely ineffective offensives so weakened the German army group that by fall 1943 it was clearly no longer capable of withstanding another major Red Army offensive.

Because it understood how weak Army Group North was, and because raising the Leningrad blockade was still a high priority objective, the *Stavka* began its 1944 winter campaign in the Leningrad region before expanding it to the entire Soviet-German front. In January the Leningrad and Volkhov Fronts, joined later by the 2d Baltic Front, began large-scale offensive operations that ultimately endured through the summer. From mid-January through February, the Leningrad, Volkhov, and 2d Baltic Fronts defeated Army Group North, raised the Leningrad blockade, and liberated the southern half of the Leningrad region. By doing so, they paved the way for the liberation of the Baltic region and the defeat of Army Group Center in Belorussia in the summer of 1944. Despite its successful completion, the so-called Leningrad-Novgorod offensive was a difficult, time-consuming, and costly offensive that, once again, underscored the difficulties inherent in operating in so difficult a theater during the dead of winter.

During the summer campaign, the Leningrad and Karelian Fronts completed liberating the Leningrad region by mounting yet another major offensive, this time to liberate the northern Leningrad region on the Karelian Isthmus and in southern Karelia. While the Red Army was able to overcome the vaunted Mannerheim Line, capture Vyborg, and, ultimately, force Finland to leave the war, this offensive too fell far short of *Stavka* expectations. After exploiting its numerical superiority and the element of surprise to secure its initial objectives, the Red Army's offensive bogged down short of achieving rhe *Stavka*'s ultimate objectives.

Throughout the war Red Army operations in the Leningrad region tied down 15–20 percent of all Axis forces operating on the German Eastern Front.

At the same time, Red Army forces operating along the northwestern axis also suffered roughly 12–15 percent of the army's wartime casualties. Ultimately, the Red Army destroyed or seriously damaged 50 German and Finnish divisions in the region. However, despite the heavy fighting, for a variety of political, geographical, and military reasons, the *Stavka* did not consider the northwestern axis the most vital strategic axis in the war. That honor belonged to the vital western (Moscow-Minsk-Warsaw-Berlin) and, at times, the southwestern (Kiev-Khar'kov-Stalingrad) strategic axes, where, like the Germans, the *Stavka* well understood that it had to achieve victory if it were to prevail in the war. Therefore, both the *Wehrmacht* and the Red Army consistently concentrated their most important offensive and defensive efforts along these axes. However, this shared appreciation also made it impossible for either side to win along the western axis unless they won elsewhere. In short, the Germans could not capture Moscow in 1941, 1942, and 1943 unless and until they weakened Soviet defenses along the Moscow axis by operating successfully along other axes. Conversely, after defeating Army Group Center at Moscow in 1941 and 1942 and at Rzhev in late 1942, the Red Army appreciated that it could not win along the western axis unless it achieved victory elsewhere.

Within this context, the Red Army's victory at Tikhvin in November 1941 conditioned its victory at Moscow in December, and its partially successful and failed offensives in 1942 and 1943 marginally facilitated the Red Army's victories along the western and southwestern axes. Likewise, the Red Army's victory at Leningrad in early 1944 paved the way for Soviet victory in Belorussia and western Ukraine in the summer of 1944 by weakening the *Wehrmacht* overall and by releasing fresh large reserves for employment along other critical axes. Most important, however, throughout the war, Leningrad symbolized the Soviet Union's and Red Army's resilience, staying power, and will to ultimate victory.

The Battle for Leningrad made significant contributions, both positive and negative, to the evolution of what the Soviets and Russians term military art, which encompasses the realms of military strategy, operational art, and tactics. Despite defeats of catastrophic proportions, severe shortages of human and material resources, and appalling terrain and weather conditions, the *Stavka*, Red Army *fronts*, and Leningraders themselves organized the successful defense of the city in summer, fall, and winter 1941. While conducting a stubborn, costly, and often desperate defense along the approaches to Leningrad, the *Stavka* also incorporated a considerable degree of "offensiveness" in its defense that most histories of the war have since overlooked.

The short but exceedingly violent Red Army counterstrokes organized by Vatutin at Sol'tsy in July and Staraia Russa in August 1941 and by Zhukov at

Krasnoe Selo and Mga in August and September 1941 played an enormous role in the successful defense of Leningrad. These counterstrokes and other lesser counterattacks surprised the Germans and seriously disrupted their offensive plans. They forced the Germans to disperse their forces, weaken their shock groups, and alter their attack axes significantly. In turn, they slowed the German advance and won time necessary to erect stronger defenses along key operational axes. As a result, the closer the Germans advanced toward Leningrad, the fiercer the resistance became. Although German forces managed to reach the southern shore of Lake Ladoga and blockade the city from the land, they could not capture it. Given time to mobilize, Leningrad's defenders thwarted every German attempt to capture the city.

Leningrad's defenses set new standards of sophistication for the defense of a modern major city. Operating skillfully under the most trying of circumstances, the Northern and Leningrad Fronts erected complex and deeply echeloned defenses along the most critical southern and southwestern approaches to the city that incorporated the entire depth of the blockaded region and the city itself. For the first time during the war on the Soviet-German front, the defenses consisted of multiple fortified defensive lines, incorporating continuous trench lines, defensive regions, positions, and lines, and fortified regions, which while durable, also permitted forces to maneuver. The defense incorporated trenches, fortifications (pillboxes, bunkers, etc.), extensive obstacles, overhead cover for troops, and antiartillery, antitank, and antiaircraft defenses in the city itself.

Most important, for the first time in the twentieth century, the defense of a major city succeeded. Subsequently, the successful defense of Leningrad generated practical experiences that contributed to the defense of other cities (Stalingrad) and fodder for volumes of Red Army directives, regulations, and instructions on techniques for the defense of cities and defense in general. These experiences and techniques also proved invaluable to the Red Army as it prepared to conquer German-occupied cities such as Poznan, Breslau, Budapest, and Berlin.

For the first time in recent military history, the Leningrad and Volkhov Fronts confronted and ultimately solved the problem of defeating a large blockading force and raising a siege by conducting operations from within and without the besieged city. Despite the privations wrought by the siege and the often harsh weather conditions, the Leningrad Front organized its own attacks from within the city and successfully broke out, defeating a strong enemy grouping in the process. It accomplished this feat, however, only after repeated failures and with the vital assistance of the Volkhov Front attacking from the outside. This required close coordination between the two *fronts* attacking from within and from without, which the two *fronts* were not able to orchestrate until January 1943.

The Leningrad Front's Operation Spark in January 1943, which it conducted across the ice of the Neva River against well-prepared enemy defenses in harsh winter conditions that severely restricted force mobility and resupply, was also unique and unprecedented. Success in this operation depended directly on the skillful employment and coordination of artillery and engineers to cross the river successfully and extensive engineer support throughout the operation. Likewise, the Leningrad Front's Operation Neva (the Ropsha-Krasnoe Selo offensive) in January 1944 was also unique in that the two forces conducting the initial operation were attacking from positions only 10–15 kilometers (6.2–9.3 miles) apart. Success in this operation required the 2d Shock and 42d Armies to echelon their assault forces deeply so that they could penetrate the strong German defenses and parry the blows of German tactical and operational reserves. In addition, skillfully employed and extensive artillery support and multiple tailored assault groups were necessary to overcome the numerous German defensive strong points. In both cases, however, the Soviets depended on overwhelming numerical superiority to achieve their initial offensive successes. Thereafter, both offensives degenerated into brutal battles of attrition.

Juxtaposed against these successful offensive operations was a virtual catalogue of frequent embarrassing offensive failures, both large and small scale, all marred by the same characteristic mistakes and shortcomings and appallingly high Red Army casualty rates. The disaster at Liuban' in winter 1942 and the destruction of the 2d Shock Army in July 1942 headed this undistinguished list of spectacular defeats, followed closely by the Siniavino defeat of September 1942, when the new 2d Shock Army once again perished. These and other defeats at Siniavino in 1941 and at Krasnyi Bor, Mga, Tosno, and Siniavino in 1943 underscored how difficult it was for the Red Army to educate itself during wartime in the conduct of modern war. In these defeats and even in many other successful military operations, Red Army commanders often displayed ineptitude in reconnaissance, command and control, combined-arms coordination and support, and the intricacies of sound logistical support. When they overcame these deficiencies, they did so by a curiously Soviet combination of sheer force of will, callousness, and cold brutality.

Admittedly, both the Leningrad and Volkhov Fronts conducted their military operations in difficult terrain and under equally difficult weather conditions. As the German Army learned in 1941, even during the summer, usually the best season of the year to conduct military operations, the forested, swampy, and lake- and river-infested terrain severely inhibited these operations. In winter, when the temperature often plummeted to −23°C (−10°F) and periodic thaws punctuated periods of extreme frost, operations of any sort, and particularly offensive operations, became exceedingly difficult to conduct. This was particularly the case when inexperienced commanders and forces operated without sound communications and adequate artillery and armor support against well-prepared and deep defenses manned by the world's best-trained and most experienced soldiers. Even when adequately supported, the Red Army's offensive operations around Leningrad against strong German defenses required that infantry, artillery, and tanks maneuver constantly in often heavily restrictive terrain and conduct river crossings over numerous major and minor rivers and streams.

Unlike other theaters of war, the difficult terrain and harsh weather conditions in the Leningrad region inhibited easy maneuver by tanks and artillery and the movement of supporting forces and supplies of any sort, particularly when on the offense. This meant that Red Army infantry (rifle forces) had to perform the bulk of the defensive and offensive fighting. The broken terrain also meant that they had to do so by operating in small groups separated from one another.

In these conditions, artillery support was critical to defensive and offensive success. The Red Army's artillery techniques matured during and as a result of its operations in and around Leningrad. The Leningrad Front relied on its artillery to help defeat the German September 1941 assault on the city by conducting its first ever artillery and aviation counterpreparation. Although severe weaponry and ammunition shortages prevented artillery and aviation from defeating the German assault alone, the artillery fire disorganized and weakened the attacks so that the infantry and tanks could hold out. Artillery played a vital role in the defense but was also essential in penetrating heavy German defenses. While artillery preparations and, later, full "artillery offensives" softened up German defenses prior to infantry and tank assaults, the Leningrad and Volkhov Fronts employed artillery extensively in a direct fire mode to destroy specific German strong points and in a counterbattery role to counter German artillery. The Red Army also exploited these experiences in subsequent defensive and offensive operations.

Tank forces and, in particular, tank armies and tank and mechanized corps played a decisive role in the Red Army's achievement of victories in other sectors of the Soviet-German front throughout the entire war. By mid-1943 it was axiomatic that wherever the tank army and mobile corps went so also went the Red Army. Conversely, when tank forces failed to advance, the Red Army also failed to advance. However, this axiom did not apply to the Leningrad region. At Leningrad the Red Army had to operate and ultimately achieve victory without large-scale armor support because the poor terrain, harsh weather conditions, and limited road network restricted the employment of armor. Those small tank forces that were able to operate in the region did so at considerable cost.

The Leningrad and Volkhov Fronts employed tank brigades, separate tank regiments, and separate battalions, primarily in small groups to provide infantry support during penetration operations or to support specific groups, such as advanced guards or forward detachments during exploitation operations.[1] In a few isolated instances, tank forces formed the nucleus of mobile tank groups, which were designated to complete penetrations or lead exploitation operations. Additionally, for the first time in the war, the Leningrad Front employed amphibious tanks in river crossing operations, for example, to cross the Neva River in January 1943.

Given the restrictive terrain, the general absence of trafficable roads, and the strong German defenses, engineer and sapper forces played a vital role both in preparing defenses and supporting offensive operations. On the offensive, engineers prepared roads and jumping-off positions, cleared mines and obstacles prior to and during penetration operations, supported river crossings, helped overcome strong German defenses, and supported forces moving across difficult terrain. Often engineers were integrated into rifle regiments and divisions and special-purpose task forces such as mobile tank groups and forward detachments.

The defense of Leningrad was the first instance in the Soviet-German War when naval forces (the Baltic Fleet and Ladoga Flotilla), aviation, and air defense (PVO) forces were operationally subordinate to *front* control. This permitted the *front* commander to concentrate his forces more effectively to perform the most important defensive and offensive missions. For example, on 14 August 1941, the *Stavka* formed a special operational aviation group subordinate to the Northwestern Direction Command and, two months later, a similar group under Leningrad Front control. These groups, which centralized air forces under the *front* commander and permitted him to employ them more effectively, served as models for the air armies that the Red Army formed in 1942. Aviation in general, and long-range aviation in particular, played an equally vital role in both the defensive and the offensive operations, even when aircraft were in short supply.

Finally, as is the case in any offensive or defensive military operation in any war, logistics proved to be the single most important constraint on achieving success on both the defense and the offense. This was particularly true of the Leningrad Front, whose forces remained besieged and deprived of routine supplies in virtually every operation it conducted through January 1944. To a lesser extent, the Volkhov Front faced the same problem, given its overextended and often convoluted supply lines to Vologda, Moscow, and the Soviet rear area. Rear service forces also had to cope with the poor road network and the severe weather and terrain conditions.

The most impressive logistical feat performed by Soviet rear service forces during the Leningrad blockade was the construction and maintenance of the various ice roads across Lake Ladoga and between Leningrad, Kronshtadt, and the Oranienbaum bridgehead. No less impressive were the construction, maintenance, and defense, often while under fire, of the tenuous rail lines through the Shlissel'burg corridor in early 1943. At the same time, hundreds of logistical organizations at every level of command struggled to supply forces with the ammunition, fuel, and food necessary to sustain military operations. This was the case even after the blockade was lifted, since Red Army forces were advancing great distances across regions laid waste by the Germans.

Since war's end, historians have tended to treat military operations around Leningrad as a mere sideshow to more momentous operations occurring elsewhere along the Soviet-German front. They have focused primarily on the symbolic significance of the Leningrad defense and its population's brave and stoic resistance. While these factors were important, so also were the military operations that took place in the region, even if many failed and lacked the drama associated with more famous operations in other sectors of the front. The sad fact is that many military operations the Red Army conducted in the Leningrad region have remained obscure or even forgotten because they failed, often spectacularly, and, for a variety of reasons, Soviet historians have not dwelled on failed operations in any sector.

As was the case with the Soviet Union as a whole, the Communist Party ruled supreme in all matters political and military during the Leningrad blockade. Party leaders such as Zhdanov and Kuznetsov and Party executive committees at the regional, district, and city level played a vital role in mobilizing the city's population and resources for defense, in organizing the defense itself, and in enforcing discipline, order, and morale in the city and its defending forces. They did so while closely coordinating with, and in some instances dominating, military authorities. It is no coincidence that the militarily incompetent Voroshilov presided over so many operations in the region, and Stalin's caustic henchman, Mekhlis, attended Meretskov during the disastrous Liuban' offensive.

In a sense, strict and at times ruthless political control was necessary both to organize the city's defense so that it could survive and to counter natural panic, defeatism, and even instances of sabotage that characterized Leningrad's existence during the days when it was most imperiled. Militarily, it was also required to steel the backbone of Leningrad's defenders when they faced Germans at the city's gates from late 1941 through 1942. The crude and callous ruthlessness of Zhukov in September, so incomprehensible to Western observers in peace or in war, takes on far greater meaning when considering the results of his actions. The cold hard reality is that Leningrad was saved, in part by his actions, at a time when few, even including Stalin, retained any hopes for its salvation.

On the other hand, there was far less excuse for senior Soviet commanders to apply in 1942, 1943, and 1944 the same ruthless methods that had saved the city during the initial year of war. While the Liuban' and Siniavino disasters in 1942 could be attributed to inexperience, the failures of summer 1943 could not. Ultimately, senior commanders such as Govorov, Meretskov, and many army commanders learned how to operate effectively while on the offense. Interestingly enough, however, they did not learn how to do so in the summer months until their offensive against the Finns in June 1944, and, even then, their success was limited.

As many authors have vividly pointed out, Leningrad's population paid the highest price for the city's successful defense. They did so by defending the city as soldiers, air defenders, or auxiliaries, by manning the city's factories, or by simply surviving the rigors of the worst siege in recent history. Although they died by the hundreds of thousands, those who remained continued to serve at their posts until liberation was assured. By virtue of their work, Leningrad's industry continued to produce and support the city's defense throughout the blockade. Their intensive work in industry and the supply effort created the reserves necessary to conduct the January 1943 offensive and the subsequent offensive that liberated the city in 1944. After the blockade was raised, industrial production sharply increased.

However, in human, matériel, and cultural terms the price of victory was appalling. Although it will probably never be determined accurately, the cost in civilian dead probably reached 1 million souls. The Extraordinary Commission for the Investigation of Nazi War Crimes, which presented its findings at the Nuremberg war crimes trials after war's end, estimated the blockade produced 642,000 civilian dead, but this figure represents the low end of this gruesome spectrum. More recent estimates place the civilian death toll at between 800,000 and 1 million people. The figure of 800,000 dead juxtaposes Leningrad's prewar population of 2.5 million against its December 1943 population of 600,000 and takes into account the approximately 1 million people evacuated from the city and the 100,000 people conscripted into the Red Army. The figure of 1 million civilian dead incorporates the roughly 642,000 souls who died during the siege and another 400,000 who perished or otherwise disappeared during the evacuations.[2]

The military casualties the Red Army suffered in operations in and around Leningrad were equally staggering. During the two months of its existence, the Northern Front lost 85,459 soldiers killed, captured, or missing and 62,905 wounded or sick, for a total of 148,364 soldiers. Its successor, the Leningrad Front, lost 467,525 soldiers killed, captured, or missing and 1,287,373 wounded or sick, for a total of 1,755,898 throughout four years of war. Two thirds of these casualties occurred during the Battle for Leningrad. The Volkhov Front lost 298,623 soldiers killed, captured, or missing, and 667,234 wounded or sick, for a total of 965,857 casualties during its existence. In almost four years of war, the Karelian Front suffered 110,435 soldiers killed, captured, or missing and 309,825 wounded, for 420,260 total casualties. Finally, the 4th, 52d, and 7th Separate Armies lost roughly 56,000 soldiers killed, captured, or missing and 91,000 wounded or sick, for a total of 147,000 casualties over the course of their existence.

By war's end, by conservative official count, the fighting in the Leningrad region cost the Red Army 1,017,881 soldiers killed, captured, or missing, and 2,418,185 wounded or sick, for a total loss of 3,437,066 soldiers. This figure represented just over 10 percent of the Red Army's 10 million soldiers killed, captured, or missing during the war, over 13 percent of its 18.2 million wounded or sick, and 12 percent of its 28.2 million total military casualties.[3]

Considering the northwestern strategic axis as a whole, one must also add the Northwestern, Baltic, and 2d Baltic Fronts' casualties. The Northwestern Front lost 88,798 soldiers killed, captured, or missing, 246,653 wounded or sick, for a total of 335,451 casualties from 1941 through 1943. In addition, from its formation in late 1943 through 1945, the Baltic Front and its successor 2d Baltic Front lost 39,579 soldiers killed, captured, or missing and 152,097 wounded or sick, for a total of 525,127 casualties.[4] When added to the losses in the Battle for Leningrad, this results in 1,146,258 soldiers killed, captured, or missing and 2,816,925 wounded or sick, for a total of 3,964,193 casualties suffered in fighting along the northwestern strategic axis. This total represents 11.4 percent of the Red Army's total killed, captured, or missing during wartime, 15.4 percent of its total wounded and sick, and 14 percent of its total wartime casualties. These percentages reflect the importance of the northwestern axis relative to the western, southwestern, and southern axes.

Thus, the number of soldiers and civilians who perished during the Battle for Leningrad amounted to the awesome total of between 1.6 million and 2 million souls. These figures, which represent the cost of defending a single Soviet city, are six times greater than the United States' total death toll during the entire Second World War.

In matériel and cultural terms, the ultimate cost of the Red Army's victory at Leningrad was also staggering. German artillery and air power pummeled Leningrad relentlessly for much of the 900 days of siege, indiscriminately destroying military, economic, and civilian targets alike and ruining Leningrad's communications infrastructure. Despite the population's prodigious and often heroic efforts, most of Leningrad's factories, warehouses, power stations, and other like facilities went up in smoke and flame. The grisly toll encompassed about 1,000 industrial enterprises, 170 medical facilities, 500 schools, and 10,317 buildings, including such cultural and architectural treasures as the stately Admiralty Fortress, the magnificent Hermitage Palace, and the fabled Smol'ny Monastery.[5]

At the same time, German forces ravaged Leningrad's suburbs and adjacent regions, consuming, expropriating, or simply destroying all crops, woods, forests, buildings, rail lines and stations, and any other property or facilities of military, economic, or cultural value before retreating from the region in January 1944. Liberating Red Army troops were staggered by the wanton destruction:

On 26 January, after fierce street fighting, they [Red Army] troops entered Gatchina [Krasnogvardeisk]. A sad sight awaited the Soviet troops in these museum towns [Gatchina, Pushkin, and Pavlovsk]. The palaces had been plundered and burnt down and the monuments of the past destroyed. Magnificent parks had been cut down almost completely. All around were the scars of war and ruin. At this grim spectacle the troops gripped their submachine guns more firmly and hastened their step. They knew that only the destruction of the nazi vandals could save the Soviet land from profanation.[6]

In a final insult to Russian sensibilities, on the eve of and during the *Wehrmacht*'s retreat, German sappers systematically dynamited, bombed, or simply burned many of Russia's cherished imperial palaces in Leningrad's suburbs. Included in Hitler's final defiant insult to the Leningraders was the gutted Petergof Palace on the shores of the Baltic and the skeletal remains of the magnificent Catherine palace at Pushkin:

> The façade of the great Catherine Palace was intact. But inside the building was a ruin. The great hall was gone. So was the amber room. The amber had vanished, along with it the parquet floor of amaranth, rosewood and mahogany. The Zubovsky wing had been turned into a barracks for the Spanish Blue Division. Under the great Cameron Gallery a 500-pound bomb had been placed. Fortunately, it had not gone off.[7]

Like the Catherine Palace at Pushkin, Leningrad too was a shell of its former self. Its decimated but still defiant population, however, managed to raise the city from its ashes and ultimately prevail over its tormentors.

In the broadest sense, the course and outcome of the Battle for Leningrad represented the entire Great Patriotic War in microcosm. The fierce defense in 1941, the dramatic rebuff to the Germans in late 1941, the abortive attempts to penetrate the blockade in 1942, the cracking of the blockade in 1943, and the unambiguous victories of 1944 parallel the Red Army's feats elsewhere along the Soviet-German front. However, whereas the turning point in the Red Army's fortunes on the Soviet-German front as a whole occurred between Stalingrad in November 1942 and Kursk in July 1943, that turn in the north did not occur until January 1944. This was so because by 1943 both sides understood that the war would be won or lost along the western and southwestern axes.

In the final analysis, although the Battle for Leningrad played a significant role in the war's ultimate outcome, militarily its role was not decisive. In terms of drama, symbolism, and sheer human suffering, however, the Battle for Leningrad and its associated blockade has no peer either in the Great Patriotic War or modern war.

Top-Secret German
Planning Documents

Directive No. 21, Plan Barbarossa, 18 December 1940

The Fuehrer and Supreme Commander of the Armed Forces
OKW/WFSt./Abt.L (I)
Nr. 33 408/40 g.Kdos Chefsache

The armed forces of Germany must be prepared, even before the conclusion of the war with England, to defeat Soviet Russia in one rapid campaign.

In this case, the army must be prepared to commit all available formations, with the proviso that the occupied territories must be secured against surprise attacks. . . .

1. General Intentions

The mass of the [Red] army stationed in western Russia is to be destroyed in bold operations involving deep and rapid penetrations by panzer spearheads, and the withdrawal of combat-capable elements into the vast Russian interior is to be prevented.

By means of a rapid pursuit, a line is to be reached from beyond which the Russian Air Force will no longer be capable of attacking the territories of the German Reich. The operation's final objective is the establishment of a defensive barrier against Asiatic Russia running along the general line of the Volga to Arkhangel'sk. From such a barrier, the one remaining Russian industrial area in the Urals can be paralyzed by the *Luftwaffe* should the need arise.

During the course of this operation, the Russian Baltic Fleet will quickly lose its bases and, thus, will no longer be capable of continuing the struggle.

Effective intervention by the Russian Air Force is to be prevented from the very beginning of the operation by means of powerful strikes against it. . . .

3. The Conduct of the Operations

    a. The army (in accordance with my operational concept):

        The area of operations is divided into northern and southern halves by the Pripiat' Marshes. The point of the main effort will be made in the northern half. Here two army groups are to be committed.

        The southernmost of these two army groups—in the center of the whole front—will have the mission of breaking out of the area around and to the north of Warsaw with exceptionally strong panzer and motorized formations and destroying the enemy forces in Belorussia. This will create a situation that will enable strong formations of mobile troops to swing north; such formations will then cooperate with the northern army group—advancing from East Prussia in the general direction of Leningrad—in destroying enemy forces in the area of the Baltic states. Only after the accomplishment of offensive operations, which must be followed by the capture of Leningrad and Kronshtadt, are further offensive operations authorized, with the objective of occupying Moscow, the important communications and armaments manufacturing center.

Only a surprisingly rapid collapse of the Russian ability to resist can justify an attempt to achieve both objectives simultaneously.

[signed] Hitler

Directive No. 33, 19 July 1941

The Fuehrer and Supreme Commander of the Armed Forces
OKW/WFSt./Abt.L (I)
Nr. 441230/41 g.Kdos

The further conduct of the war in the East:

1. The second offensive to the east has been completed by the penetration of the "Stalin Line" along the entire front and by a further deep advance of the panzer groups to the east. Army Group Center requires considerable time to liquidate the strong enemy groups, which continue to remain between our mobile formations.

The Kiev fortifications and the operations of the Soviet 5th Army's forces in our rear have inhibited active operations and free maneuver on Army Group South's northern flank.

2. The objective of further operations should be to prevent the escape of large enemy forces into the depth of the Russian territory and to annihilate them. To do so, prepare [as follows] along the following axes:

a. *The southeastern sector of the Eastern Front.* The immediate mission is to destroy the enemy's 12th and 6th Armies by a concentrated offensive west of the Dnepr, while preventing them from withdrawing beyond the river.

The complete destruction of the enemy 5th Army can be carried out most rapidly by means of an offensive by the closely cooperating forces of Army Group Center's southern flank and Army Group South's northern flank.

Simultaneously with the turn by Army Group Center's infantry divisions southward, after they have fulfilled the missions assigned to them and have been resupplied and protected their flank along the Moscow axis, commit new and primarily mobile forces into combat. These forces will have the missions of preventing Russian forces that have crossed to the eastern bank of the Dnepr River from withdrawing farther to the east and destroying them.

b. *The central sector of the Eastern Front.* After destroying the numerous encircled enemy units and resolving supply problems, the mission of Army Group Center will be to cut the Moscow-Leningrad communications lines and, at the same time, protect the right flank of Army Group North advancing on Leningrad with mobile formations that will not participate in the advance to the southeast beyond the Dnepr line, while further advancing toward Moscow with infantry formations.

c. *The northern sector of the Eastern Front.* Resume the advance toward Leningrad only after the Eighteenth Army has restored contact with the Fourth Panzer Group and the Sixteenth Army's forces are protecting its eastern flank. When that is accomplished, Army Group North must strive to prevent Soviet forces that are continuing to operate in Estonia from withdrawing to Leningrad. It is desirable to capture as rapidly as possible the islands in the Baltic Sea, which can be Soviet fleet strong points.

d. *The Finnish Front.* As before, the mission of the Finnish main forces, reinforced by the German 163d Division, is to attack the enemy by delivering their main attack east of Lake Ladoga and, later, destroy him in cooperation with Army Group North's forces. The aims of the offensive operations that are being conducted under the command of the XXXVI Army and Mountain Infantry Corps remain unchanged. Since there is no possibility of providing strong support by air formations, one must expect the operation to be prolonged.

3. First and foremost, the *Luftwaffe*'s mission is to support the advance of forces along the principal axes in the southern sector of the front as soon as they are freed up in the central sector. Concentrate the required aircraft and antiaircraft artillery in their respective regions by bringing up additional forces quickly and also by regroupings.

It is necessary to begin air raids on Moscow as quickly as possible with forces of the Second Air Fleet, temporarily reinforced by bomber aircraft from the west, which must be "retribution" for Russian air raids on Bucharest and Helsinki.

4. The Naval Fleet's mission remains the defense of sea communications, particularly to protect ground operations insofar as the situation at sea and in the air affects them. To the degree possible, the fleet's efforts are to threaten the enemy's naval bases to prevent his fleet's combat forces from entering and being interned in Swedish ports.

As soon as naval forces (torpedo boats and minesweepers in groups of one flotilla each) are freed up from the Baltic Sea, they must be transferred to the Mediterranean Sea. It is necessary to dispatch some quantity of submarines to the Barents Sea to support German forces in Finland, whose operations are being hindered by the transport of reinforcements to the enemy by sea.

5. All three armed forces branches in the West and in the North must anticipate repelling possible English attacks against the islands in the English Channel and the Norwegian coast. It is necessary to prepare *Luftwaffe* forces for rapid transfer from the West to any region of Norway.

[signed] Hitler

Addendum to Directive No. 33, 23 July 1941

The Chief of Staff of OKW
The Chief of Staff of the Operations Department
Nr. 442254/41 g.Kdos

After the report of the OKW on 22 July 1941, I order [the following] as an addition to and broadening of Directive No. 33:

1. *The southern sector of the Eastern Front.* The enemy, which are still located west of the Dnepr, must be completely and fully annihilated. As soon as the operational situation and material-technical support permit, after capturing the Khar'kov

industrial region, the First and Second Panzer Groups, subordinate to Fourth Panzer Army headquarters, and the infantry and mountain infantry divisions that are following them are to undertake an offensive across the Don into the Caucasus.

The priority mission of the main mass of infantry divisions is the capture of the Ukraine, the Crimea, and the territory of the Russian Federation to the Don. When that is accomplished, Rumanian forces will be entrusted with occupation service in the regions southwest of the Bug River.

2. *The central sector of the Eastern Front.* After improving the situation in the Smolensk region and on its southern flank, Army Group Center is to defeat the enemy located between Smolensk and Moscow with sufficiently powerful infantry formations of both of its armies and advance with its left flank as far as possible to the east and capture Moscow.

The Third Panzer Group is temporarily assigned to Army Group North with the mission of supporting the latter's right flank and encircling the enemy in the Leningrad region.

To fulfill the subsequent missions—the advance to the Volga—the intention is to return the Third Panzer Group's mobile formations to their former subordination.

3. *The northern sector of the Eastern Front.* Having received control of the Third Panzer Group, Army Group North will be capable of allocating large infantry forces for the advance on Leningrad and thus avoid expending mobile formations on frontal attacks in difficult terrain.

Enemy forces still operating in Estonia must be destroyed. While doing so, it is necessary to prevent their transport by ship and passage through Narva toward Leningrad.

Upon fulfilling its mission, the Third Panzer Group must be once again transferred to Army Group Center's control.

4. Subsequently, as soon as conditions permit, the OKW will focus its attention on withdrawing part of Army Group North's forces, including the Fourth Panzer Group, and also part of Army Group South' s infantry force, to the Homeland.

While doing so, the combat readiness of the Third Panzer Group must be fully restored by transferring equipment and personnel from the Fourth Panzer Group to it. If necessary, the First and Second Panzer Groups must accomplish their missions by combining their formations.

5. The instructions contained in Directive No. 33 remain in force for the Fleet and Air Forces.

In addition, the Naval Fleet and Air Forces must ease the situation of the Mountain Infantry Corps. [They will do so] first, by decisive action of naval forces in the Barents Sea; and second, by transferring several groups of bomber aircraft into the region of combat operations in Finland, which will be carried out after the battle in the Smolensk region has ended. These measures will also deter England from attempts to join the struggle on the coast of the polar seas.

6. Forces allocated for the performance of security services in the occupied eastern regions will be sufficient to fulfill their missions only if the occupation authorities liquidate all resistance by employing extensive fear and terror rather than legal judgment of those found guilty to rid the population of any desire to resist.

Appropriate commands and the forces subordinate to them are entrusted with the responsibility for order in the occupied regions.

Commanders must determine means for ensuring order in the captured regions by employing appropriately Draconian measures and without requesting new security units.

[signed] Keitel

Directive No. 34, 30 July 1941

The Fuehrer and Supreme Commander of the Armed Forces
OKW/WFSt./Abt.L (I)
Nr. 441298/41 g.Kdos

The course of events in recent days, the appearance of large enemy forces before the front, the supply situation, and the necessity of giving the Second and Third Panzer Groups 10 days to restore and refill their formations have forced a temporary postponement of the fulfillment of aims and missions set forth in Directive No. 33 of 19 July and the addendum to it of 23 July.

Accordingly, I order:

I. ARMY FORCES

1. In the northern sector of the Eastern Front, continue the offensive toward Leningrad by making the main attack between Lake Il'men' and Narva to encircle Leningrad and establish contact with the Finnish Army.

North of Lake Il'men', this offensive must be limited by the Volkhov sector and, south of this lake, continue as deeply to the east as required to protect the right flank of forces attacking to the north of Lake Il'men'. In advance, restore the situation in the Velikie Luki region. All forces that are not being employed for the offensive south of Lake Il'men' must be transferred to the forces advancing on the northern flank.

Do not begin the anticipated offensive by the Third Panzer Group to the Valdai Hills until its combat readiness and the operational readiness of its panzer formations have been fully restored. Instead, the forces on Army Group Center's left flank must advance northeastward to such a depth as will be sufficient to protect Army Group North's right flank.

The priority missions of all of the Eighteenth Army's forces are the clearing of all enemy forces from Estonia. After this, its divisions can begin to advance toward Leningrad.

2. Army Group Center will go on the defense, while employing the most favorable terrain in its sector.

You should occupy favorable jumping-off positions for conducting subsequent offensive operations against the Russian 21st Army, and you can carry out limited objective offensive operations to this end.

As soon as the situation permits, the Second and Third Panzer Groups are to be withdrawn from battle and quickly refilled and reequipped.

3. For the time being, continue operations in the southern sector of the front only with Army Group South's forces. The objective of these operations is to destroy the

large enemy forces west of the Dnepr and create conditions for the subsequent crossing of the First Panzer Group to the eastern bank of the Dnepr by the seizure of bridgeheads at and south of Kiev.

The Russian 5th Army, which is operating in the swampy region northwest of Kiev, is to be drawn into combat west of the Dnepr River and destroyed. It is necessary to avert the danger of a possible penetration by that army's forces northward across the Pripiat' River.

4. The Finnish Front. Halt the offensive toward Kandalaska. Eliminate the threat of a flank attack from Motovskii Bay in the Mountain Infantry Corps' sector. Leave the commander of the XXXVI Army Corps only those forces necessary for defensive purposes and carry out preparations for a false offensive.

At the same time, attempt to cut the Murmansk railroad in the Finnish III Army Corps sector and, above all, along the Loukhi axis by transferring all forces necessary to fulfill that mission to that region. In the event the offensive in the III Army Corps' sector misfires due to the difficult terrain conditions, bring up German units and subordinate them to the Karelian Army. This particularly concerns motorized units, tanks, and heavy artillery.

Place the 6th Mountain Infantry Division and all types of transport at the Mountain Infantry Corps' disposal.

The Ministry of Foreign Affairs will determine the possibility for using the Narvik-Luleo railroad on Swedish territory.

II. AIR FORCES

1. *The northern sector of the front.* The *Luftwaffe* will shoulder the main effort of the air offensive in the northern sector of the front, and, to do so, the main forces of the VIII Air Corps are attached to the First Air Fleet. These forces must be transferred as quickly as possible so that they can support Army Group North's offensive along the main attack axis from the very beginning (the morning of 6 August).

2. *The central sector of the front.* The mission of *Luftwaffe* forces remaining with Army Group Center is to provide reliable antiaircraft defense along the Second and Ninth Armies' fronts and support their offensive. Continue the air offensive against Moscow.

3. *The southern sector of the Eastern Front.* Missions are unchanged. We do not anticipate a decrease in the air forces operating in Army Group South's area.

4. *Finland.* The primary mission of the Fifth Air Fleet is to support the Mountain Infantry Corps. In addition, it is necessary to support the Finnish III Army Corps' offensive along axes where the greatest success is achieved. It is necessary to conduct corresponding prepared measures in support of the Karelian Army.

[signed] Hitler

Addendum to Directive No. 34, 12 August 1941

OKW
The Staff of the Operations Department
Nr. 441376/41 g.Kdos

The Fuehrer has ordered the following on the further conduct of operations as an addition to Directive No. 34.

1. *The southern sector of the Eastern Front.* As a result of the decisive battle in the Uman' region, Army Group South has achieved complete superiority over the enemy and has secured freedom of maneuver for the conduct of further operations on that side of the Dnepr. As soon as its forces firmly dig in on the eastern bank of that river and secure rear-area communications, they will be able to achieve the large-scale operational aims assigned to them with their own forces with appropriate use of Allied forces and in cooperation with Rumanian ground forces.

Its missions are as follows:

    a. prevent the enemy from creating a defensive front along the Dnepr. To do so, it is necessary to destroy the largest enemy units located west of the Dnepr and capture bridgeheads on the eastern bank of that river as rapidly as possible;

    b. capture the Crimea, which, being an enemy air base, poses an especially great threat to the Rumanian oil fields; and

    c. seize the Donets Basin and the Khar'kov industrial region.

2. The battles to capture the Crimea may require mountain infantry forces. It is necessary to verify the possibility of their crossing the Kerch Straits for employment in a subsequent offensive toward Batumi.

Halt the offensive on Kiev. As soon as ammunition resupply permits, bombing from the air must destroy the city.

The entire range of missions depends on these actions being carried out sequentially rather than simultaneously by means of maximum massing of forces. In the first instance, achieve the greatest concentration of forces by committing additional groups of bomber aircraft to support combat operations in the region between Kanev and Boguslav and then to assist the creation of a bridgehead on the eastern bank of the Dnepr River.

3. *The central sector of the Eastern Front.* The priority mission in this sector is to eliminate the enemy flank positions wedging to the west, which are tying down large forces of Army Group Center's infantry. In the central sector of the front to the south, pay particular attention to the organization of the mixed flanks of Army Groups Center and South according to time and axis. Deprive the Russian 5th Army of any operational capabilities by seizing the communications leading to Ovrich and Mozyr' and, finally, destroy its forces.

North of the central sector of the front, defeat the enemy west of Toropets as rapidly as possible by committing mobile forces into combat. Advance Army Group Center's left flank far enough north that Army Group North will not fear for its right flank and will be capable of reinforcing its forces advancing on Leningrad with infantry divisions.

Regardless, undertake measures to transfer this or that division (for example, the 102d Infantry Division) to Army Group North as a reserve.

Only after the threatening situation on the flanks has been completely eliminated and the panzer groups have been refitted will conditions be conducive for an offensive by deeply echeloned flank groupings across a broad front against the large enemy forces concentrated for the defense of Moscow.

The aim of this offensive is to capture the enemy's entire complex of state economic and communications centers in the Moscow region before the onset of winter, thereby depriving him of the capability for restoring his destroyed armed forces and smashing the functioning of state control apparatus.

Complete the operation against Leningrad before the offensive along the Moscow axis begins and return the aircraft units transferred earlier by the Second Air Fleet to the First Air Fleet to their former subordination.

4. *The Northern sector of the Front.* The offensive being conducted here must lead to the encirclement of Leningrad and linkup with Finnish forces.

Insofar as the situation with airfields permits, in the interest of the effective employment of aviation, it is important that it be employed as far as possible massed along distinct axes.

As soon as the situation permits, you should liquidate enemy naval and air bases on Dago and Ezel' islands by the joint efforts of ground, naval, and air forces. While doing so it is particularly important to destroy enemy airfields from which air raids on Berlin are carried out.

The High Command of the Ground Forces (OKH) is entrusted with coordinating the conducted measures.

[signed] Chief of OKW, Keitel

Fuehrer Order, 15 August 1941

OKW
The Staff of the Operations Department
Nr. 441386/41 g.Kdos

After a report by the OKH, the Fuehrer orders:

1. *Army Group Center* will halt its further advance on Moscow. Organize a defense in sectors whose nature will prevent any possibility of the enemy conducting enveloping operations and will not require air support to repel his offensive operations.

2. The offensive by *Army Group North* must produce success in the immediate future. Only then can we think about resuming the offensive on Moscow. Danger has arisen because of the appearance of enemy cavalry in the Sixteenth Army's rear and the absence of mobile units in the I Army Corps' reserve, which, in spite of strong air support, has halted the promising offensive north of Lake Il'men'.

Without delay, allocate and transfer as great a quantity of mobile formations as possible from General Hoth's panzer group (for example, one panzer and two motorized divisions) to Army Group North.

[signed] OKW Chief of Staff, Jodl

OKW Order, 21 August 1941

The OKH's 18 August considerations regarding the further conduct of operations in the East do not agree with my intentions. I order:

1. The most important missions before the onset of winter are to seize the Crimea and the industrial and coal regions of the Don, deprive the Russians of the opportunity to obtain oil from the Caucasus, and, in the north, to encircle Leningrad and link up with the Finns rather than capture Moscow.

2. The favorable operational situation, which has resulted from reaching the Gomel' and Pochep line, must be exploited immediately by conducting an operation along concentric axes with the joined flanks of Army Groups South and Center. Our objective is not to push the Russian 5th Army back beyond the Dnepr by the Sixth Army's local attacks. Instead, [it is] to destroy the enemy before he can withdraw to the Desna River, Konotop, and Sula line.

Army Group South can do so only by digging in in the region east of the middle reaches of the Dnepr and continuing operations toward Khar'kov and Rostov with the forces operating in its center and on its left flank.

3. Army Group Center is to allocate sufficient forces to that offensive to ensure the destruction of the Russian 5th Army's forces, and, at the same time, it will be prepared to repel enemy counterattacks in the central sector of its front.

The decision to advance Army Group Center's left flank to the hills in the Toropets region and tie it in with Army Group North's right flank is unchanged.

4. The seizure of the Crimean Peninsula has colossal importance for the protection of oil supplies from Rumania. Therefore, it is necessary to employ all available means, including mobile formations, to force the lower reaches of the Dnepr rapidly before the enemy is able to reinforce its forces.

5. Only by encircling Leningrad, linking up with the Finns, and destroying the Russian 5th Army can we free up forces and create prerequisites for fulfilling the missions contained in the 12 August addendum to Directive No. 34, that is, a successful offensive and the destruction of Group Timoshenko.

[signed] Hitler

Directive No. 35, 6 September 1941

The Fuehrer and Supreme Commander of the Armed Forces
OKW/WFSt./Abt.L (I)
Nr. 441492/41 g.Kdos

The initial successes in operations against enemy forces located between the adjoining flanks of Army Groups South and Center, combined with further successes in the encirclement of enemy forces in the Leningrad region, have created prerequisites for the conduct of a decisive operation against Army Group Timoshenko, which is unsuccessfully conducting offensive operations in front of Army Group Center. It must be destroyed decisively before the onset of winter within the limited time indicated in existing orders.

To this end we must concentrate all of the efforts of ground and air forces ear-marked for the operation, including those that can be freed up from the flanks and transferred in timely fashion.

On the basis of the OKH's report, I am issuing the following orders for the prepa-ration and conduct of this operation:

1. *In the southern wing of the Eastern Front.* Destroy the enemy located in the Kremenchug, Kiev, and Konotop triangle with the forces of Army Group South, which have crossed the Dnepr to the north, in cooperation with the attacking forces of Army Group Center's southern flank. As soon as the situation permits, freed-up forma-tions of Second and Sixth Armies and also the Second Panzer Group should be re-grouped to carry out new operations.

No later than 10 September, mobile formations on Army Group South's front, reinforced with infantry and supported along the main axes by the Fourth Air Fleet, are to begin a surprise offensive northwestward through Lubna from the bridgehead created by the Seventeenth Army. At the same time, the Seventeenth Army will ad-vance along the Poltava and Khar'kov axis.

Continue the offensive along the lower course of the Dnepr toward the Crimea supported by the Fourth Air Fleet.

Movement of mobile forces southward from the lower course of the Dnepr to Melitopol' will considerably assist the Eleventh Army in fulfilling its missions.

2. *In the sector of Army Group Center.* Prepare an operation against Army Group Timoshenko as quickly as possible so that we can launch an offensive in the general direction of Viaz'ma and destroy the enemy located in the region east of Smolensk by a double envelopment by powerful panzer forces against his flanks.

To that end, form two shock groups:

- *The first* on the southern flank, presumably in the region southeast of Roslavl', with an attack axis to the northeast. The composition of the group [will include] forces subordinate to Army Group Center and the 5th and 2d Panzer Divisions, which will be freed up to fulfill that mission.
- *The second* in the Ninth Army's sector with its attack axis presumably through Belyi. Insofar as possible, this group will consist of large Army Group Center formations.

After destroying the main mass of Timoshenko's group of forces in this decisive encirclement and destruction operation, Army Group Center is to begin pursuing enemy forces along the Moscow axis while protecting its right flank on the Oka River and its left on the upper reaches of the Volga River. The Second Air Fleet, reinforced in timely fashion by transferred formations, especially from the north-ern sector of the front, will provide air support for the offensive. While doing so, it will concentrate its main forces on the flanks while employing the principal bomber formations (Eighth Air Corps) for support of the mobile formations in both attacking flank groupings.

3. *In the northern sector of the Eastern Front.* Encircle enemy forces operating in the Leningrad region (and capture Shlissel'burg) in cooperation with Finnish forces attacking on the Karelian Isthmus so that a considerable number of the mobile for-mations and the First Air Fleet's formations, particularly the VIII Air Corps, can be

transferred to Army Group Center no later than 15 September. First and foremost, however, it is necessary to strive to encircle Leningrad completely, at least from the east, and, if weather conditions permit, conduct a large-scale air offensive against Leningrad. It is especially important to destroy the water supply stations.

As soon as possible, Army Group North's forces must begin an offensive northward in the Neva River sector to help the Finns overcome the fortifications along the old Soviet-Finnish border, and also to shorten the front lines and deprive the enemy of the ability to use his air bases. In cooperation with the Finns, prevent enemy naval forces from exiting Kronshtadt into the Baltic Sea (Hango and the Moonzund islands) by using mine obstacles and artillery fire.

Also isolate the region of combat operations at Leningrad from the sector along the lower course of the Volkhov as soon as forces necessary to perform this mission become available. Link up with the Karelian Army on the Svir River only after enemy forces in the Leningrad region have been destroyed.

4. During the further conduct of operations, ensure that the southern flank of Army Group Center's offensive along the Moscow axis is protected by an advance to the northeast by a flank protection grouping in Army Group South's sector created from available mobile formations. [Also ensure] that Army Group North's forces are directed to protect Army Group Center's northern flank and also the advance along both sides of Lake Il'men' to link up with the Karelian Army.

5. Any curtailment of the period for preparing and acceleration of the operation's beginning will accompany the preparation and conduct of the entire operation.

[signed] Hitler

ADDENDUM: Inasmuch as the Fourth Air Fleet has not allocated forces to support the offensive from the Dnepropetrovsk bridgehead, the Fuehrer considers it desirable that all of the motorized divisions participate in the First Panzer Group's offensive from the Kremenchug bridgehead.

The 198th Infantry Division and also Italian or Hungarian forces are holding on to the bridgehead.

[signed] OKW Chief of Staff

Concerning the Blockade of Leningrad, 21 September 1941

Operations Department Ia
No. 002119/41
(Point paper)

Possibilities:

1. Occupy the city by the same methods that we employed while seizing other large Russian cities and, while doing so, do not accept responsibility for supplying the population with foodstuffs.

2. Encircle the city by means of an electrified barbed wire fence and fire machine guns through it. *Negative aspects:* Of the roughly 2 million inhabitants, the weakest will soon perish from hunger, but on the other hand, the strongest, who seize the food for themselves, will live. The danger of epidemic can also spread to our forces,

and, finally, it is doubtful whether our soldiers would fire on the fleeing women and children.

3. Evacuate the women, children, and old people from the city's limits; those remaining in the blockade will perish from hunger. *Negative aspects:* While a good decision in theory, the evacuation across the Volkhov River through the enemy rear is hardly possible in practice. Who can restrain and herd 100,000 people, and where will the Russian front then be?

- If we refuse to evacuate the Russians to the rear, this will affect the will of people dispersed through the entire country.
- In all instances, there will be the same shortcoming that the remaining starving population of Leningrad will be the seat of epidemics and that the strongest people will remain in the city for a long time.

4. When the Finns arrive and the blockade is complete, withdraw again back across the Neva and grant the northernmost sector to the Finns.

Finland has unofficially declared that is would like its state border to run along the Neva, excluding Leningrad. Such a decision is correct in a political respect. However, we, rather than the Finns, must resolve the matter of Leningrad's population. Results and proposals:

There is no satisfactory resolution. It is necessary for the Army Group North command to issue appropriate orders on this matter, which they should then carry out. Proposed:

We declare to the world that Stalin is defending Leningrad as if it were a fortress. Therefore, we are forced to view Leningrad and its entire population as a military objective. However, we will do otherwise. After the capitulation of Leningrad, we will allow the friend of humanity, Roosevelt, to accept the population of Leningrad, which does not include the prisoners of war, and, while supplying them with food, to transfer them to America carried on neutral ships under the guardianship of the Red Cross. To this end, the ships will be granted free exit from the port (certainly, such a proposal cannot be accepted, but it needs to be employed for propaganda aims).

Initially, we will blockade Leningrad (hermetically) and destroy the city, if possible, by artillery and air. (At first we have only small air forces available.)

When terror and hunger are doing their work in the city, we will open specific gates and permit the disarmed people through. If possible, we will evacuate them into the depths of Russia and then scatter the remainder in forced labor regimes at given localities.

The remnants of the "fortress garrison" will remain there in the winter. In the spring we will penetrate the city (do not object if the Finns do this before us), remove all who remain alive to the depths of Russia or take them prisoner, level Leningrad to the ground, and transfer the region north of the Neva to Finland.

[signed] [illegible]

Directive No. 39, 8 December 1941

The Fuehrer and Supreme Commander of the Armed Forces
OKW/WFSt./Abt.L (I)
Nr. 442090/41 g.Kdos

The early arrival of a cold winter on the Eastern Front and the resupply difficulties associated with it are forcing us to halt all offensive operations immediately and go on the defense. The way this defense will be conducted depends on the aims that it pursues, namely, hold on to those regions that have important operational and military-economic importance for the enemy; rest and replenish the forces; and by doing so, create conditions necessary to resume large-scale offensive operations in 1942.

Accordingly I order:

I. THE GROUND FORCES

4. c. Army Group North will shorten the front of its eastern and southeastern defense line north of Lake Il'men'. However, it is to do so while denying the enemy the road and railroad from Tikhvin to Volkhovstroi and Kolchanovo that support restoring, reinforcing, and improving his positions in the region south of Lake Ladoga. Only by doing so can we finally complete encircling Leningrad and establishing communications with the Finnish Karelian Army.

d. If we determine that the enemy has withdrawn his main forces from the coastal belt on the southern coast of the Gulf of Finland and does not intend to offer serious resistance there, we should occupy that sector of the coast to economize forces.

OKW Order, 16 December 1941

OKW
The Staff of Operations Department
Nr. 442182/41 g.Kdos

I order:

1. *Army Group North* is permitted to withdraw the internal flanks of its Sixteenth and Eighteenth Armies to the Volkhov River line and the rail line running northwest from Volkhov Station. Establish continuous communications with the XXVIII Army Corps' right flank along that rail line.

The army group's mission is to defend that line to the last soldier, do not withdraw a single step, and, at the same time, continue to blockade Leningrad.

I especially call your attention to reinforcing air defenses south and southeast of Leningrad.

Directive No. 41, 4 April 1942

The Fuehrer and Supreme Commander of the Armed Forces
OKW/WFSt./Abt.L (I)
Nr. 55616//42 g.Kdos

The winter battles in Russia have come to an end. Thanks to their distinguished bravery and selfless actions, the soldiers on the Eastern Front have managed to achieve a great success of German arms in the defense.

The enemy has suffered huge losses in personnel and weaponry. This winter he has squandered the majority of those reserves, which were earmarked to conduct subsequent operations, trying to develop imaginary successes.

As soon as the weather and terrain conditions become favorable, the German command and its forces must exploit their superiority once again, seize the initiative, and impose our will on the enemy.

The aim is to destroy conclusively the remaining forces under Soviet control and deprive the Russians of as great a number of important military-economic centers as possible.

All of the German Armed Forces' forces and those of her allies are to be employed to this end. While doing so, everything is to be done in all circumstances to ensure the security and defense of our occupied territory in Western and Central Europe, and especially the seacoast.

I. OVERALL CONCEPT

While Army Group Center conducts holding operations, capture Leningrad and link up with the Finns in the north and, on the southern flank, penetrate into the Caucasus region, adhering to the original main aim in the march to the east.

Rather than achieving these missions simultaneously along the entire front, instead we will achieve them in separate sectors depending on the situation that resulted from the consequences of the winter battles and also in accord with existing forces and weaponry and transport capabilities.

Initially, it is necessary to concentrate all existing forces in the southern sector of the front to conduct the main operation to destroy enemy forces west of the Don River and, subsequently, capture the Caucasus oil region and the passes across the Caucasus Mountains.

We will refrain from the final encirclement of Leningrad and the capture of Ingermanland [Oranienbaum] until such time as circumstances in the enveloped areas or the availability of otherwise sufficient forces permit.

II. THE CONDUCT OF THE OPERATION

(A description of the offensive in the south)

Operations Order No. 1, 14 October 1942

The Fuehrer and Supreme Commander of the Armed Forces, OKH
OKW/WFSt./Abt.L (I)
Nr. 420817/42 g.Kdos

With the exception of separate operations still under way and intended offensive operations of a local nature, this year's summer and fall campaign is at an end. Great results have been achieved. . . .

The conduct of a winter campaign stands before us. Excluding ongoing or projected offensive operations, the mission on the Eastern Front during its [the winter campaign's] course is to hold on to all captured positions at all costs, repel any enemy attempts to penetrate them, and, at the same time, create prerequisites for continuing the offensive in 1943 to complete the destruction of our most dangerous enemy. . . .

I. THE CHARACTERISTICS OF THE WINTER POSITIONS

The final winter positions run along the following lines:

   c. Army Group North and the Eleventh Army—the positions occupied at the present time (excluding the territory that will be occupied in combat in the Pustyn' region), [extended] to Lake Ladoga and the present Leningrad Front, independent of the operations in accordance with Operation *Nordlicht*.

Directive No. 50, 28 September 1943

Concerning preparations to withdraw the Twentieth Mountain Army to northern Finland and northern Norway:

The situation in Army Group North is completely consolidated, and a withdrawal of its forces from their occupied positions is not envisioned. In that regard, the Velikie Luki region, which is the most vulnerable sector in an operational sense, has been strengthened. Nevertheless, in the event that unfavorable military operations develop, especially in Finland itself, at present, a second defensive belt is being constructed behind Lake Chud and Narva.

Source: "Dokumenty nemetskogo komandovaniia po voprosam podgotovki voiny" [Documents of the German command on the matter of preparing for war] and "Dokumenty nemetskogo komandovaniia po voprosam vedeniia voiny" [Documents of the German command on the matter of the conduct of the war], in *Sbornik voenno-istoricheskikh materialov Velikoi Otechestvennoi voiny* [Collection of military-historical materials of the Great Patriotic War], issue 18 (Moscow: Voenizdat, 1960). Prepared by the Military-Historical Department of the General Staff's Military-Scientific Directorate and classified secret.

Soviet Planning Documents

The Northern Front's 1941 Defense Plan

TOP SECRET: Special Importance. Copy No. 1

NOTES ON THE PROTECTION [COVER] OF THE STATE BORDERS ON THE TERRITORY OF THE LENINGRAD MILITARY DISTRICT

To protect the mobilization and final deployment of the Leningrad Military District's forces, a plan has been developed on the basis of USSR People's Commissariat of Defense Directive No. 503913/ov/ss of 14 May 1941 for protecting [covering] the Leningrad Military District's borders.

DEFENSE MISSIONS

1. To prevent both enemy ground and air invasion of the district's territory.
2. A firm defense of fortified regions and field fortifications along the line of the state borders
   a. to provide for a reliable defense of Leningrad along the Vyborg and Keksholm axes, considering this to be the primary mission of the Leningrad Front's forces;
   b. to prevent the enemy from penetrating the defensive front and reaching Lake Ladoga;
   c. to protect the Kirov railroad's uninterrupted operation and, at all cost, prevent the enemy from reaching it;
   d. together with the Northern Fleet, to retain control of the Riabachii and Srednii peninsulas, to protect the port of Murmansk reliably, and to prevent enemy naval amphibious landings on the coast of the Kola Peninsula from Iokan'go to the state border with Finland.
3. Beginning on the ninth day of mobilization, accept transfer of the Estonian SSR coast from the Gulf of Narva to the Gulf of Matsalulakht [*sic*] from the Baltic Special Military District and defend it together with the Baltic Fleet, preventing enemy amphibious assault forces from landing on it.
4. Help the Red Banner Baltic Fleet to close the entrance into the Gulf of Finland for enemy naval forces by a defense of the northern coast of the Estonian SSR and the Hango Peninsula.
5. Determine in timely fashion the nature of enemy forces' concentrations and groupings by all types of intelligence means available to the district.
6. Secure air superiority by active air operations and destroy and disrupt the concentration and deployment of enemy forces by powerful strikes, primarily against railroad centers, bridges, staging areas, and force groupings.

7. Prevent enemy airborne assaults and diversionary activity on the district's territory.

8. All defending forces and army and district reserves will be prepared, if conditions are favorable, to deliver decisive blows against the enemy in accordance with the High Command's orders.

NEIGHBORS AND THEIR MISSIONS

On the right—the Arkhangel'sk Military District—is defending the southeastern part of the Kola Peninsula, the entrance and coast of the White Sea, and the city of Arkhangel'sk.

The boundary with it is from Cape Lenin (Sviatoi Nos), through Iokan'ga to Por'ia.

On the left—the Baltic Special Military District—is defending the coast of the Baltic Sea south from the Gulf of Matsalulakht to the border of the Lithuanian SSR to firmly cover [protect] the Riga and Dvina axes.

The boundary with it is from Ostashkov through Ostrov, Vyru (excl.), and Vil'iandi to the Gulf of Matsalulakht, excluding Ezel' and Dago Islands.

FORCE COMPOSITION AND WEAPONRY

The covering forces include 3 armies, 4 rifle corps, 2 mechanized corps, 17 rifle divisions, 4 tank divisions, 2 motorized divisions, 8 RGK artillery regiments, 8 aviation divisions, and, including fixed [units], 7 fortified regions and 1 fortified position, and 13 machine gun battalions. In addition, engineer units, signal units, and PVO units formed on the district's territories are fully subordinate. Only those VOSO units and rear service units that are necessary for the support of covering units are subordinate.

DECISION

Defend the Karelian Isthmus, the Petrozavodsk, Rebol-Ukhtinsk, Kandalaska, and Murmansk axes, the Rybachii Peninsula, the coast of the Kola Peninsula, and the Gulf of Finland in places favorable for naval assault landings reliably by relying on the fortified regions and field positions.

Conduct only observation with border troops and aviation in the intervals between the indicated axes.

THE COMPOSITION AND MISSIONS OF FORCES IN THE COVERING REGIONS

Covering Region No. 1—14th Army

Composition: the 14th Army's headquarters; the 42d Rifle Corps' headquarters; the 14th, 52d, 122d, and 104th Rifle Divisions; the 1st Tank Division; the 104th Gun Artillery Regiment RGK; the Murmansk Fortified Region; the 35th, 100th, 82d, 72d, and 101st Border Guards Detachments; and the Northern Fleet and its coastal defense.

In addition, engineer units, signal units, and rear-service units and installations according to the attached list (not included). The 14th Army commander is the chief of the covering region, and its headquarters is in Murmansk. Its left boundary is Staraia Kuzema (excl.), Regozero (excl.), and Pisto (excl.).

Missions:

a. Reliably protect Murmansk by defense of the Murmansk Fortified Region's permanent field fortifications on the Rybachii and Srednii peninsulas, in the Titovka region, and along the coast of the Kola Peninsula.

b. Prevent the enemy fleet from entering the Kola and Motovskii gulfs, close the entrances to Ura Bay, Apa Bay, Bol'shaia Bay, and the Western Litsa [Face], and prevent amphibious assault landings.

c. Reliably protect the Kirov railroad toward Kandalaska and Loukhi by a fortified defense in the Kor'ia, Kuoliarvi, and Vuoiarai regions and on the Lake Niasiarvi and Lekhtovara line.

Create five covering sectors in the region in accordance with the assigned missions. . . .

Missions of the aviation divisions:

a. Protect the port of Murmansk and the Northern Fleet base at Poliarnyi in cooperation with the Northern Fleet's aviation and the Murmansk and Poliarnyi PVOs' antiaircraft weapons.

b. Destroy enemy aircraft at the airfields at Salmiiarvi and Petsamo.

c. Prevent the landing of naval amphibious assaults by destroying them in the water in cooperation with units of the Murmansk Fortified Region and the Northern Fleet.

d. In the event of an enemy offensive from the Petsamo region, assist the 14th Rifle Division in repelling and destroying it with powerful strikes against enemy force concentrations.

e. Keep in mind supporting the 42d Rifle Corps in repelling the enemy if he attacks from the Miarkiaiarai region.

Covering Region No. 2—7th Army

Composition: the 7th Army headquarters; the 54th, 71st, 169th, and 237th Rifle Divisions; the 541st Howitzer Artillery Regiment RGK; the Sortavala Fortified Region, the 1st, 73d, 80th, and 3d Border Guards Detachments; the 55th Mixed Aviation Division; engineer, chemical, and signal units; and rear-service units and installations according to the attached list.

The 7th Army commander is the chief of the covering region, and its headquarters is in Suoiarvi. Its left boundary is Putsari, Ristalkhti, Keremiaki, and Kangasakhti islands.

Missions:

a. Reliably protect the state border along the Ukhta, Reboly, and Petrozavodsk axes by a defense of the field positions and the Sortavala Fortified Region and prevent the enemy from penetrating the front and reaching Lake Ladoga.

b. Ensure the uninterrupted operation of the Kirov railroad and under no circumstance permit the enemy to reach it.

c. Secure air superiority by active aviation operations, disrupt movement to concentration areas in the Ioensi, Kaliaani, and Kuopio regions by powerful strikes, and halt the concentration and deployment of enemy forces.

d. Prevent the jumping and landing of enemy air assaults and diversionary groups within the borders of the covering region.

Pay particular attention to antitank defenses along the Petrozavodsk and Sortavala axes. In the event of a tank penetration along these axes, isolate them from the infantry and liquidate them by combined operations of artillery, aviation, and infantry.

Envision employing all rear-service forces and NKVD garrison forces, which are protecting important government objectives, in the struggle with enemy air assaults and diversionary groups.

Consider in particular, the crucial axes: Iuntusranta, Ukhta; Kukhmo, Reboly; Ioensi, Petrozavodsk; and Ioensi, Sortavala.

Given its assigned mission, Covering Region No. 2 will have four covering sectors. . . .

COVERING REGION NO. 3—23d Army

Composition: the 23d Army's headquarters; the 19th and 50th Rifle Corps' headquarters; the 10th Mechanized Corps' headquarters; the 142d, 115th, 43d, and 123d Rifle Divisions; the 21st and 24th Tank and 198th Motorized Divisions; the 101st, 108th, and 519th Howitzer Artillery Regiment and the 573d Gun Artillery Regiment RGK; the Vyborg and Keksholm Fortified Regions; the 102d, 5th, and 33d Border Guards Detachments; the 5th Aviation Division; engineer, chemical, and signal units; and rear-service units and installations according to the attached list.

The 23d Army commander is the chief of the covering region, and its headquarters is in Kusa. Its left boundary is the coast line of the Gulf of Finland from Koivisto to Vyborg and from Vyborg to the state border.

Missions:

a. Prevent an enemy invasion of the Karelian Isthmus either by land or by air. Reliably protect the state border along the Keksholm and Vyborg axes by a defense of field fortifications and the Keksholm and Vyborg Fortified Region and prevent the enemy from penetrating the defensive front.

b. Prevent the landing of an amphibious assault on the northern coast of the Gulf of Finland from the state border to Vikhmiala together with the coastal defense of the Vyborg region.

c. Prevent the jumping and landing of enemy air assaults and diversionary groups within the borders of the covering region.

d. Reliably protect the city of Vyborg, the bridges over the Vuoksi River, and the combat formations of covering region units and supply stations from enemy air attack.

e. Secure air superiority by active aviation operations and subject to air attacks enemy airfields in the Savoklina, Mikkeli, Kouvela, and Khamina sector.

f. Disrupt and halt the concentration and deployment of enemy forces by powerful strikes against the Kouvola railroad center, the bridges over the Kiumin-Ioki River, and his force groupings.

g. Determine the nature of enemy troop concentrations and force groupings before the army's front in timely fashion by all types of reconnaissance.

h. Conduct an active defense. Immediately liquidate any enemy attempt to penetrate the defense by counterattacks with corps and army reserves.

i. Pay special attention to antitank defense along the Vyborg and Keksholm axes. In the event enemy tanks penetrate along the Vyborg and Keksholm axes, defeat them and liquidate the penetration by the combined operations of rifle forces, mechanized corps, and aviation.

j. Envision employing all rear service of the covering region and the troops of garrisons, which are securing and protecting important government objectives and installations (NKVD units), in the struggle with enemy air assaults and diversionary groups.

k. Consider in particular, the crucial axes: Vyborg, Leningrad; and Imatra, Keksholm.

In favorable conditions, all of the covering region's combat personnel will be prepared to deliver destructive blows against the enemy. To fulfill its assigned missions, Covering Region No. 2 will have two covering sectors. . . .

Missions of the 6th Mixed Aviation Division:

a. Destroy the enemy during his attempt to penetrate the defensive front in cooperation with the ground forces.

b. Protect the concentration areas of the 10th Mechanized Corps and 70th Rifle Division, successively, in the Muola, Kumiaria, and Leipiasuo regions.

c. Protect normal operations of the railroad sectors in the covering region's territory.

d. Prevent the landing of enemy amphibious assaults on the northern coast of the Gulf of Finland together with the Red Banner Baltic Fleet's coastal defense.

e. Prevent the jumping (landing) of enemy airborne assaults in the covering region.

COVERING REGION NO. 4—65th Rifle Corps

Composition: the 65th Rifle Corps (without corps artillery regiments), the 11th and 16th Rifle Divisions, and signal rear-service units according to the attached list. . . .

The 65th Rifle Corps commander is the chief of the covering region, and its headquarters is in Nymme (9 kilometers south of Talinn on a 1:100,0000 map). Its right boundary is from the small bay at Saka along the western shore of Lake Chud to Pskov. Its left boundary is Vormsi Island and the Gulf of Matsalulakht.

Mission: Prevent enemy naval and air assaults against the territory of the Estonian SSR and within the limits of the covering region. To fulfill its assigned missions, Covering Region No. 2 will have two covering sectors. . . .

COVERING REGION NO. 5—Hango Naval Base

Composition: the 8th Separate Rifle Brigade, the Hango Peninsula Fortified Region, the 13th Fighter Aviation Regiment, a separate reconnaissance aviation squadron, a submarine division, and a brigade of torpedo boats. The commander of the Hango Naval Base is the chief of the covering region, and its headquarters is in Hango.

Missions:

a. Prevent an enemy invasion and penetration from the mainland and an assault landing from the sea by a defense with the fortifications on the isthmus, the islands, and the coast of the peninsula.

b. Prevent the jumping or landing of airborne assaults on the Hango Peninsula and during the landing destroy them on the land and in the air.

c. Destroy the enemy fleet during its attempts to enter the Gulf of Finland with the coastal defense in cooperation with the Red Banner Baltic Fleet and naval and district aviation.

d. Reliably protect the most important forces on the Hango Peninsula against enemy air attack.

e. Conduct reconnaissance of the enemy in the Hango Peninsula region with aviation, ground forces, and coastal defenses to determine the enemy's grouping, his artillery positions, and his system of defensive installations and to discover enemy preparations for amphibious assaults in timely fashion.

To fulfill its assigned missions, Covering Region No. 2 will have two covering sectors. . . .

UNITS DIRECTLY SUBORDINATE TO THE LENINGRAD MILITARY DISTRICT
COMMANDER

The 1st Mechanized Corps (less the 1st Tank Division) is concentrated in Slutsk and Pushkin and will remain in that region until receipt of special instructions; and the 70th Rifle Division is concentrated in the Muola, Kheinuoki Station, Kiamiaria Station, and Leipasuo Station region on the Karelian Isthmus. The 191st and 177th Rifle Divisions will remain at their mobilization points until receipt of special instructions.

THE MISSIONS OF AVIATION DIRECTLY SUBORDINATE TO THE LENINGRAD
MILITARY DISTRICT COMMANDER

Composition: the 4th, 41st, 39th, 54th, and 3d Aviation Divisions (the latter two will be employed in the defense of Leningrad).

Missions:

a. Destroy enemy aviation at Kouvola, Kotka, Utti, Selianpia, Mikkeli, Porvo, Lakhti, Khololo, Khittuls, and Podosioki airfields.

b. Destroy the Kouvola railroad and the bridge at Koriia.

c. In cooperation with the Red Banner Baltic fleet, be prepared to deliver strikes against enemy ships and transport during their attempts to penetrate the Gulf of Finland or land amphibious assaults.

d. Cooperate with the 23d Army in repelling enemy attacks. The 4th and 41st Aviation Divisions will fulfill these missions. The 3d and 54th Aviation Divisions will protect Leningrad. . . .

THE SECURITY OF IMPORTANT GOVERNMENTAL OBJECTIVES

NKVD Troops for the Security of Especially Important Industrial Facilities and militia will secure objectives of special importance within the district's territory.

Forces of the 2d NKVD Division will protect operationally important road and railroad bridges in the territory of the district. A list of objectives to be protected by the 2d Division is attached. . . .

ANTIAIRCRAFT DEFENSE

The territory of the district, including the Arkhangel'sk region, constitutes the Northern PVO Zone. The Northern Zone (the territory of the district) includes five brigade PVO regions, two naval PVO regions, one corps PVO region, and the Arkhangel'sk PVO region. The allocation of weaponry per region and within regions by point and by objective is shown on the attached map and the list of personnel of the northern zones' antiaircraft artillery units. Antiaircraft defense of supply stations and force concentration regions will be performed by force PVO assets. . . .

[signed] Lieutenant General M. M. Popov, commander of
the Leningrad Military District

Corps Commissar [N. N.] Kliment'ev, Member of
the Leningrad Military District's Military Council

[Major General] D. [N.] Nikishev, Chief of Staff of
the Leningrad Military District

Prepared in 2 copies
Prepared by Major General Tikhomirov, Chief of the Leningrad Military District's Operations Department
Copy No. 1 to the Red Army General Staff
    No. 2 to the Leningrad Military District's Operations Department
    Archival citation: TsAMO RF [Central Archives of the Russian Federation's Ministry of Defense], f. 16, op. 2951, d. 242, ll. 46–70.

Source: Iu. A. Gor'kov and Iu. N. Semin, "Konets global'noi lzhi: Na sovetskom severo-zapade—Operativnye plany zapadnykh prigranichnykh okrugov 1941 goda svidetel'stvuiut: SSSR ne gotovilsia k napadeniiu na Germaniiu [The end of the global lie: In the Soviet north-west—The operational plans of the western border districts in 1941 bear witness that the USSR was not prepared for an attack on Germany], *Voenno-istoricheskii zhurnal* [Military-historical journal], no. 6 (November–December 1996): 2–7.

Red Army Order of Battle

22 June 1941

NORTHERN FRONT

7th Army: LTG F. D. Gorelenko
  54th Rifle Division: MG I. V. Panin
  71st Rifle Division: MG P. I. Abramidze
  168th Rifle Division: Col. A. R. Bondarev
  237th Rifle Division: MG D. F. Popov
  26th Fortified Region (Sortavalo)
  208th Separate Antiaircraft Artillery Battalion
  55th Mixed Aviation Division: Col. V. M. Filin
  184th Separate Sapper Battalion
14th Army: LTG V. A. Frolov
  42d Rifle Corps: MG G. I. Panin
    104th Rifle Division: MG S. I. Morozov
    122d Rifle Division: MG P. S. Shevchenko
  14th Rifle Division: MG A. A. Zhurba
  52d Rifle Division: MG N. N. Nikishin
  23d Fortified Region (Murmansk)
  104th High Command Reserve Gun Artillery Regiment
  1st Tank Division (1st MC): MG V. I. Baranov
  1st Mixed Aviation Division: Col. M. M. Golovnia
  42d Corrective-Aviation Squadron
  31st Separate Sapper Battalion
23d Army: LTG P. S. Pshennikov
  19th Rifle Corps: LTG M. N. Gerasomov
    115th Rifle Division: MG V. F. Kon'kov
    142d Rifle Division: Col. S. P. Mikul'sky
  50th Rifle Corps: MG V. I. Shcherbakov
    43d Rifle Division: MG V. V. Kirpichnikov
    70th Rifle Division: MG A. E. Fediunin
    123d Rifle Division: Col. E. E. Tsukanov
  27th Fortified Region (Keksholm)
  28th Fortified Region (Vyborg)
  24th Corps Artillery Regiment
  28th Corps Artillery Regiment
  43d Corps Artillery Regiment

573d Gun Artillery Regiment
101st Howitzer Artillery Regiment
108th High-power Howitzer Artillery Regiment (RGK)
519th High-power Howitzer Artillery Regiment (RGK)
20th Separate Mortar Battalion
27th Separate Antiaircraft Artillery Battalion
241st Separate Antiaircraft Artillery Battalion
10th Mechanized Corps: MG I. G. Lazarev
    21st Tank Division: Col. L. V. Bunin
    24th Tank Division: Col. M. I. Chesnokov
    198th Motorized Division: MG V. V. Kriukov
    7th Motorcycle Regiment
5th Mixed Aviation Division: Col. E. E. Erlykin
41st Bomber Aviation Division: Col. I. Ia. Novikov
15th Corrective-Aviation Squadron
19th Corrective-Aviation Squadron
109th Motorized Engineer Battalion
153d Separate Engineer Battalion
Front subordinate
177th Rifle Division: Col. A. F. Mashoshin
191st Rifle Division: Col. D. A. Luk'ianov
8th Separate Rifle Brigade: Col. N. P. Simoniak
21st Fortified Region
22d Fortified Region (Karelian)
25th Fortified Region (Pskov)
29th Fortified Region
541st Howitzer Artillery Regiment (RGK)
577th Howitzer Artillery Regiment (RGK)
2d Corps PVO: MG M. M. Protsvetkin
    115th Antiaircraft Artillery Regiment
    169th Antiaircraft Artillery Regiment
    189th Antiaircraft Artillery Regiment
    192d Antiaircraft Artillery Regiment
    194th Antiaircraft Artillery Regiment
    351st Antiaircraft Artillery Regiment
    Vyborg Brigade PVO Region
    Murmansk Brigade PVO Region
    Pskov Brigade PVO Region
    Luga Brigade PVO Region
    Petrozavodsk Brigade PVO Region
1st Mechanized Corps: MG M. L. Cherniavsky
    3d Tank Division: Col. K. U. Andreev
    163d Motorized Division: MG I. M. Kuznetsov
    5th Motorcycle Regiment

2d Mixed Aviation Division: Col. P. P. Arkhangel'sky
39th Fighter Aviation Division: Lt. Col. B. I. Litvinov
3d Fighter Aviation Division PVO: Col. S. P. Danilov
54th Fighter Aviation Division PVO: Col. S. Ia. Simonenko
311th Reconnaissance Aviation Regiment
103d Corrective-Aviation Squadron
12th Engineer Regiment
29th Engineer Regiment
6th Pontoon-Bridge Regiment

1 August 1941

NORTHERN FRONT

7th Army: LTG F. D. Gorelenko
    54th Rifle Division: MG I. V. Panin
    71st Rifle Division: Col. V. N. Fedorov
    3d DNO: Col. V. G. Netrebo
    3d Naval Infantry Brigade
    9th Motorized Rifle Regiment
    24th Motorized Rifle Regiment
    452d Motorized Rifle Regiment
    108th High-power Howitzer Artillery Regiment (RGK)
    47th Separate Mortar Battalion
    Petrozavodsk Brigade PVO Region
    2d Tank Regiment
    7th Motorcycle Regiment
    55th Mixed Aviation Division: Col. V. M. Filin
    18th Separate Engineer Battalion
8th Army: MG I. M. Liubovstev
    10th Rifle Corps: MG I. F. Nikolaev
        10th Rifle Division: MG I. I. Fadeev
        11th Rifle Division: MG N. A. Sokolov
    11th Rifle Corps: MG M. S. Shumilov
        16th Rifle Division: Col. N. G. Suturin
        48th Rifle Division: Lt. Col. I. D. Romantsev
        125th Rifle Division: MG P. P. Bogaichuk
    118th Rifle Division: MG N. M. Globatsky
    268th Rifle Division: MG M. A. Enshin
    22d NKVD Rifle Division: Col. Bun'kov
    47th Corps Artillery Regiment
    51st Corps Artillery Regiment
    73d Corps Artillery Regiment
    39th Separate Antiaircraft Artillery Battalion
    103d Separate Antiaircraft Artillery Battalion
    29th Separate Sapper Battalion
    80th Separate Sapper Battalion

14th Army: LTG V. A. Frolov
  42d Rifle Corps: MG G. I. Panin
    104th Rifle Division: MG S. I. Morozov
    122d Rifle Division: MG P. S. Shevchenko
  14th Rifle Division: MG N. N. Nikishin
  52d Rifle Division: Col. G. A. Veshchezersky
  23d Fortified Region
  1st Motorized Rifle Regiment (1st Tank Division)
  104th Howitzer Artillery Regiment (RGK)
  208th Separate Antiaircraft Artillery Battalion
  Murmansk Brigade PVO Region
  Separate tank battalion
  1st Mixed Aviation Division: Col. M. M. Golovnia
  31st Separate Sapper Battalion
23d Army: LTG P. S. Pshennikov
  19th Rifle Corps: LTG M. N. Gerasimov
    115th Rifle Division: MG V. F. Kon'kov
    142d Rifle Division: MG S. P. Mikul'sky
    168th Rifle Division: Col. A. L. Bondarev
  43d Rifle Division: MG V. V. Kirpichnikov
  123d Rifle Division: Col. E. E. Tsukanov
  367th Rifle Regiment (71st Rifle Division)
  27th Fortified Region
  28th Fortified Region
  24th Corps Artillery Regiment
  28th Corps Artillery Regiment
  101st Howitzer Artillery Regiment (RGK)
  577th Howitzer Artillery Regiment (RGK)
  20th Separate Mortar Battalion
  27th Separate Antiaircraft Artillery Battalion
  241st Separate Antiaircraft Artillery Battalion
  485th Separate Antiaircraft Artillery Battalion
  198th Motorized Division: MG V. V. Kriukov
  5th Mixed Aviation Division: Col. E. E. Erlykin
  53d Separate Engineer Battalion
  54th Separate Engineer Battalion
  40th Pontoon-Bridge Battalion
  41st Pontoon-Bridge Battalion
  234th Separate Sapper Battalion
Luga Operational Group: LTG K. P. Piadyshev
  41st Rifle Corps: MG I. S. Kosobutsky
    111th Rifle Division: Col. S. V. Roginsky
    177th Rifle Division: Col. A. F. Mashoshin
    235th Rifle Division: MG T. V. Lebedev
  1st Rifle Regiment (3d DNO)
  260th Separate Machine Gun–Artillery Battalion

262d Separate Machine Gun–Artillery Battalion
541st Howitzer Artillery Regiment (RGK)
Luga Brigade PVO Region
24th Tank Division: Col. M. I. Chesnokov
259th Separate Sapper Battalion
Kingisepp Defense Sector: MG. V. V. Semashko
  90th Rifle Division: Col. I. I. Plenkin
  191st Rifle Division: Col. D. K. Luk'ianov
  2d DNO: MG I. M. Liubovtsev
  4th DNO: Col. V. A. Lansky
  Leningrad Kirov Infantry School
  21st Fortified Region
  1st Tank Division: MG V. I. Baranov
  60th Separate Armored Train
Front subordinate
  265th Rifle Division: Maj. I. S. Prytkov
  272d Rifle Division: Col. M. I. Potapov
  281st Rifle Division: Col. S. A. Sherstov
  1st GDNO: Col. I. M. Frolov
  2d CDNO: Col. G. I. Sholev
  3d GDNO: Col. V. P. Kotel'nikov
  4th GDNO: Col. G. L. Sonnikov
  8th Rifle Brigade
  22d Fortified Region
  29th Fortified Region
  Krasnogvardeisk Fortified Region
  2d PVO Corps: MG M. M. Protsvetkin
  Svir Brigade PVO Region
  Vyborg Brigade PVO Region
  7th Fighter Aviation Corps PVO: Col. S. P. Danilov
  39th Fighter Aviation Division: Lt. Col. B. I. Livinov
  2d Bomber Aviation Division
  41st Bomber Aviation Division: Col. S. I. Nechiporenko
  1st Mixed Aviation Brigade

1 September 1941

LENINGRAD FRONT

8th Army: LTG P. S. Pshennikov
  11th Rifle Division: MG N. A. Sokolov
  48th Rifle Division: Lt. Col. I. D. Romantsev
  118th Rifle Division: Col. A. I. Safronov
  125th Rifle Division: MG P. P. Bogaichuk
  191st Rifle Division: Col. D. A. Lukianov
  268th Rifle Division: MG M. A. Enshin

76th Latvian Rifle Regiment
266th Separate Machine Gun–Artillery Battalion
47th Corps Artillery Regiment
73d Corps Artillery Regiment
1st/24th Corps Artillery Regiment
39th Separate Antiaircraft Artillery Battalion
103d Separate Antiaircraft Artillery Battalion
23d Army: LTG M. N. Gerasimov
 19th Rifle Corps: MG F. N. Starikov
  142d Rifle Division: Col. S. P. Mikul'sky
  265th Rifle Division: Maj. I. S. Prytkov
 43d Rifle Division: MG V. V. Kirpichnikov
 123d Rifle Division: Col. E. E. Tsukanov
 291st Rifle Division: Col. N. A. Trushkin
 708th Rifle Regiment (115th Rifle Division)
 577th Howitzer Artillery Regiment (RVGK)
 28th Corps Artillery Regiment
 241st Separate Antiaircraft Artillery Battalion
 485th Separate Antiaircraft Artillery Battalion
 Vyborg Brigade PVO Region
 198th Motorized Division (less artillery regiment): MG. V. V. Kriukov
 7th Fighter Aviation Regiment
 153d Fighter Aviation Regiment
 235th Assault Aviation Regiment
 41st Pontoon-Bridge Battalion
 234th Separate Sapper Battalion
42d Army: MG V. I. Shcherbakov
 2d GDNO: LTG F. S. Ivanov
 3d GDNO: Col. V. P. Kotel'nikov
 Krasnogvardeisk Fortified Region
 51st Corps Artillery Regiment
 690th Antitank Artillery Regiment
 Mixed Artillery Regiment
 704th Artillery Regiment (198th Motorized Division)
 42d Pontoon-Bridge Battalion
 106th Motorized Engineer Battalion
48th Army: LTG M. A. Antoniuk
 138th Mtn. Rifle Division: MG Ia. A. Ishchenko
 311th Rifle Division: Col. T. S. Orlenko
 1st Mountain Rifle Brigade
 170th Separate Cavalry Regiment
 541st Howitzer Artillery Regiment (RVGK)
 21st Tank Division: Col. G. G. Kuznetsov
 109th Motorized Engineer Battalion
 12th Separate Sapper Battalion

55th Army: MG I. D. Lazarev
   70th Rifle Division: Maj. V. P. Iakutovich
   90th Rifle Division: Col. I. F. Abramov
   168th Rifle Division: Col. A. L. Bondarev
   237th Rifle Division: Col. V. V. Noskov
   1st DNO: Kombrig V. A. Malininkov
   4th DNO: Col. P. I. Radygin
   2d Rifle Regiment (3d GDNO)
   Slutsk-Kolpino Fortified Region
   14th Antitank Artillery Brigade
   24th Corps Artillery Regiment
   47th Separate Mortar Battalion
   84th Separate Tank Battalion
   86th Separate Tank Battalion
Kopor Operational Group
   1st GDNO: Col. I. M. Frolov
   2d DNO: MG I. M. Liubovtsev
   522d Rifle Regiment (191st Rifle Division)
   519th Howitzer Regiment (RVGK)
   2d Tank Regiment (1st Tank Division)
   295th Separate Sapper Battalion
Southern Operational Group
   41st Rifle Corps: MG I. S. Kosobutsky
      111th Rifle Division: Col. S. V. Roginsky
      177th Rifle Division: Col. A. F. Mashoshin
      235th Rifle Division: MG T. V. Lebedev
   1st Rifle Regiment (3d DNO)
   260th Separate Machine Gun-Artillery Battalion
   262d Separate Machine Gun-Artillery Battalion
   274th Separate Machine Gun-Artillery Battalion
   Antitank Artillery Regiment (Major Bogdanov)
   Luga Brigade PVO Region
   24th Tank Division: Col. M. I. Chesnokov
   24th Pontoon-Bridge Battalion
   259th Separate Sapper Battalion
Front subordinate
   10th Rifle Division: MG I. I.Fadeev
   16th Rifle Division: Col. N. G. Suturin
   115th Rifle Division: MG V. F. Kon'kov
   281st Rifle Division: Col. G. I. Sholev
   4th Guards DNO: Col. F. P. Utkin
   1st Rifle Division NKVD: Col. S. I. Donskov
   8th Rifle Brigade
   3d Rifle Regiment (1st DNO)
   22d Fortified Region

29th Fortified Region
101st Howitzer Artillery Regiment
108th High-power Howitzer Artillery Regiment (RVGK)
16th Separate Mortar Battalion
20th Separate Mortar Battalion
27th Separate Antiaircraft Artillery Battalion
2d PVO Corps: MG M. M. Protsvetkin
Svir Brigade PVO Region
1st Tank Division (less 2d Tank Regiment): Col. A. I. Liziukov
48th Separate Tank Battalion
7th Fighter Aviation Corps PVO: Col. S. P. Danilov
8th Fighter Aviation Division: Col. N. S. Toropchin
39th Fighter Aviation Division: Lt. Col. B. I. Livinov
2d Mixed Aviation Division: Col. P. P. Arkhangel'sky
53d Separate Engineer Battalion
54th Separate Engineer Battalion
21st Pontoon-Bridge Battalion
52d Separate Army *(Stavka):* LTG N. K. Klykov
267th Rifle Division: Kombrig Ia. D. Zelenkov
285th Rifle Division: Col. P. I. Kiselev
288th Rifle Division: Col. G. P. Lilenkov
292d Rifle Division: Col. A. F. Popov
312th Rifle Division: Col. A. F. Naumov
314th Rifle Division: MG A. D. Shemenkov
316th Rifle Division: MG I. V. Panfilov
442d Corps Artillery Regiment
881st Antitank Artillery Regiment

1 January 1942

LENINGRAD FRONT

8th Army: MG A. L. Bondarev
10th Rifle Division: Col. I. V. Romantsov
86th Rifle Division: Col. A. M. Andreev
1st Rifle Division NKVD
11th Rifle Brigade
4th Naval Infantry Brigade
101st Howitzer Artillery Regiment
6th Antitank Artillery Regiment
7th Antitank Artillery Regiment
20th Separate Mortar Battalion
486th Separate Antiaircraft Artillery Battalion
28th Separate Armored Train
Separate armored car battalion
439th Fighter Aviation Regiment

2d Separate Sapper Battalion
112th Separate Sapper Battalion
23d Army: LTG A. I. Cherepanov
   123d Rifle Division: Col. Ia. A. Panichkin
   142d Rifle Division: Col. V. K. Paramzin
   291st Rifle Division: MG M. A. Enshin
   22d Fortified Region
   260th Howitzer Artillery Regiment
   577th Howitzer Artillery Regiment
   27th Separate Antiaircraft Artillery Battalion
   241st Separate Antiaircraft Artillery Battalion
   48th Separate Tank Battalion
   106th Separate Tank Battalion
   30th Separate Armored Train
   5th Mixed Aviation Regiment
   117th Reconnaissance Aviation Squadron
   234th Separate Sapper Battalion
42d Army: LTG I. F. Nikolaev
   13th Rifle Division: Col. V. P. Iakutovich
   189th Rifle Division: Col. A. D. Kornilov
   21st Rifle Division NKVD
   247th Separate Machine Gun–Artillery Battalion
   291st Separate Machine Gun–Artillery Battalion
   292d Separate Machine Gun–Artillery Battalion
   14th Artillery Brigade PVO
   47th Artillery Regiment
   73d Artillery Regiment
   541st Howitzer Artillery Regiment
   1st Antitank Artillery Regiment
   2d Antitank Artillery Regiment
   3d Antitank Artillery Regiment
   4th Antitank Artillery Regiment
   5th Antitank Artillery Regiment
   3d Special-power Artillery Battalion
   72d Separate Antiaircraft Artillery Battalion
   89th Separate Antiaircraft Artillery Battalion
   51st Separate Tank Battalion
   29th Separate Engineer Battalion
   54th Separate Engineer Battalion
   106th Separate Engineer Battalion
55th Army: LTG V. P. Sviridov
   11th Rifle Division: MG V. I. Shcherbakov
   43d Rifle Division: Col. K. A. Antonov
   56th Rifle Division: Col. I. S. Kuznetsov
   70th Rifle Division: Col. V. P. Iakutovich

72d Rifle Division: MG T. M. Parafillo
85th Rifle Division: MG I. M. Liubovtsev
90th Rifle Division: Col. A. I. Korolev
125th Rifle Division: MG I. I. Fadeev
177th Rifle Division: Col. A. G. Koziev
268th Rifle Division: MG E. V. Kozik
261st Separate Machine Gun–Artillery Battalion
267th Separate Machine Gun–Artillery Battalion
283d Separate Machine Gun–Artillery Battalion
289th Separate Machine Gun–Artillery Battalion
290th Separate Machine Gun–Artillery Battalion
24th Corps Artillery Regiment
28th Corps Artillery Regiment
690th Antitank Artillery Regiment
2d Special-power Artillery Battalion
47th Separate Mortar Battalion
198th Separate Antiaircraft Artillery Battalion
84th Separate Tank Battalion
86th Separate Tank Battalion
"People's Avenger" Separate Armored Train
2d Separate Engineer Battalion
53d Separate Engineer Battalion
325th Separate Sapper Battalion
367th Separate Sapper Battalion
54th Army: MG I. I. Fediuninsky
3d Guards Rifle Division: Col. A. A. Krasnov
80th Rifle Division: Col. B. F. Brygin
115th Rifle Division: Col. I. V. Gribov
128th Rifle Division: MG I. F. Nikitin
198th Rifle Division: Col. N.M. Martynchuk
281st Rifle Division: MG I. K. Kravtsov
285th Rifle Division: Col. T. A. Sviklin
286th Rifle Division: MG E. V. Kozik
294th Rifle Division: Col. A. A. Kichkailov
311th Rifle Division: Col. S. T. Biiakov
1st Mountain Rifle Brigade
6th Naval Infantry Brigade
2d Separate Ski Regiment
4th Separate Ski Battalion
5th Separate Ski Battalion
882d Artillery Regiment
883d Artillery Regiment
"Akkuks" Howitzer Artillery Regiment
2d/5th Guards-Mortar Regiment
4th/4th Guards-Mortar Regiment

21st Tank Division: Col. G. G. Kuznetsov
16th Tank Brigade: Col. I. N. Baryshnikov
122d Tank Brigade: Lt. Col. M. I. Rudoi
60th Separate Armored Train
18th Bomber Aviation Regiment
46th Fighter Aviation Regiment
563d Fighter Aviation Regiment
116th Reconnaissance Aviation Squadron
5th Separate Engineer Battalion
109th Separate Engineer Battalion
135th Separate Engineer Battalion
136th Separate Engineer Battalion
262d Separate Engineer Battalion
12th Separate Sapper Battalion
Coastal Operational Group
    48th Rifle Division: Col. A. I. Safronov
    2d Naval Infantry Brigade
    5th Naval Infantry Brigade
    3d Separate Rifle Regiment Baltic Fleet
    50th Separate Naval Infantry Battalion Baltic Fleet
    519th Howitzer Artillery Regiment
    Separate mortar battalion
    286th Separate Tank Battalion
    295th Separate Sapper Battalion
Front subordinate
    168th Rifle Division: MG P. A. Zaitsev
    265th Rifle Division: Col. Ia. S. Ermakov
    8th Rifle Brigade
    9th Rifle Brigade
    20th Rifle Division NKVD
    13th Motorized Rifle Regiment NKVD
    1st Separate Ski Battalion
    Separate Guards-Mortar Battalion
    123d Tank Brigade: MG V. I. Baranov
    124th Tank Brigade: Col. A. G. Rodin
    Battalion, separate tank brigade
    107th Separate Tank Battalion
    "Baltietz" Separate Armored Train
    "For the Fatherland" Separate Armored Train
    26th Separate Armored Train
    2d Mixed Aviation Division: Col. V. A. Sandalov
    39th Fighter Aviation Division: Lt. Col. B.I. Litvinov
    92d Fighter Aviation Division: Col. S. Ia. Simonenko
    127th Fighter Aviation Regiment
    286th Fighter Aviation Regiment

Headquarters, 90th Mixed Aviation Division:
Headquarters, 91st Mixed Aviation Division
21st Pontoon-Bridge Battalion
41st Pontoon-Bridge Battalion
42d Pontoon-Bridge Battalion

VOLKHOV FRONT

2d Shock Army: LTG G. G. Sokolov
    327th Rifle Division: Col. I. M. Antiufeev
    22d Rifle Brigade
    23d Rifle Brigade
    24th Rifle Brigade
    25th Rifle Brigade
    53d Rifle Brigade
    57th Rifle Brigade
    58th Rifle Brigade
    59th Rifle Brigade
    39th Separate Ski Battalion
    40th Separate Ski Battalion
    41st Separate Ski Battalion
    42d Separate Ski Battalion
    43d Separate Ski Battalion
    44th Separate Ski Battalion
    18th Artillery Regiment
    839th Howitzer Artillery Regiment
    160th Separate Tank Battalion
    162d Separate Tank Battalion
    121st Bomber Aviation Regiment
    522d Fighter Aviation Regiment
    704th Light Bomber Aviation Regiment
    1741st Separate Sapper Battalion
    1746th Separate Sapper Battalion
4th Army: MG P. A. Ivanov
    4th Guards Rifle Division: MG A. I. Andreev
    44th Rifle Division: Col. P. A. Artiushenko
    65th Rifle Division: Col. P. K. Koshevoi
    92d Rifle Division: Col. A. N. Larichev
    191st Rifle Division: MG T. V. Lebedev
    310th Rifle Division: MG A. T. Volchkov
    377th Rifle Division: Col. K. A. Tsalikov
    1st Grenadier Rifle Brigade
    27th Cavalry Division: MG G. T. Timofeev
    80th Cavalry Division: Col. L. A. Slanov
    84th Separate Ski Battalion
    85th Separate Ski Battalion

86th Separate Ski Battalion
88th Separate Ski Battalion
89th Separate Ski Battalion
90th Separate Ski Battalion
881st Artillery Regiment
6th Guards-Mortar Battalion
9th Guards-Mortar Battalion
46th Tank Brigade: MG V. A. Koptsov
119th Separate Tank Battalion
120th Separate Tank Battalion
128th Separate Tank Battalion
3d Reserve Aviation Group
   160th Fighter Aviation Regiment
   185th Fighter Aviation Regiment
   239th Fighter Aviation Regiment
   218th Assault Aviation Regiment
   225th Bomber Aviation Regiment
159th Pontoon-Bridge Battalion
248th Separate Sapper Battalion
52d Army: LTG N. K. Klykov
   46th Rifle Division: LTG A. K. Okulich
   111th Rifle Division: Col. S.V. Roginsky
   225th Rifle Division: Col. K. Iu. Andreev
   259th Rifle Division: Col. A. V. Lapshov
   267th Rifle Division: Kombrig Ia. D. Zelenkov
   288th Rifle Division: Col. I. M. Platov
   305th Rifle Division: Col. D. I. Barabanshchikov
   25th Cavalry Division: MG N. I. Gusev
   442d Artillery Regiment
   448th Artillery Regiment
   561st Artillery Regiment
   884th Antitank Artillery Regiment
   44th Guards-Mortar Battalion
   2d Guards Fighter Aviation Regiment
   513th Fighter Aviation Regiment
   313th Assault Aviation Regiment
   673d Light Bomber Aviation Regiment
   3d Separate Engineer Battalion
   4th Separate Engineer Battalion
   770th Separate Engineer Battalion
   771st Separate Sapper Battalion
   55th Pontoon-Bridge Battalion
59th Army: MG I. V. Galanin
   366th Rifle Division: Col. S. I. Bulanov
   372d Rifle Division: Col. N. P. Korkin

374th Rifle Division: Col. A. D. Vitoshkin
376th Rifle Division: Lt. Col. D. I. Ugorich
378th Rifle Division: Col. I. P. Dorofeev
382d Rifle Division: Col. G. P. Sokurov
45th Separate Ski Battalion
46th Separate Ski Battalion
47th Separate Ski Battalion
48th Separate Ski Battalion
49th Separate Ski Battalion
50th Separate Ski Battalion
104th Separate Guards-Mortar Battalion
105th Separate Guards-Mortar Battalion
203d Separate Guards-Mortar Battalion
163d Separate Tank Battalion
166th Separate Tank Battalion
Front subordinate
87th Cavalry Division: Col. V. F. Trantin
137th High-power Howitzer Artillery Regiment
430th High-power Howitzer Artillery Regiment
216th Separate Antiaircraft Artillery Battalion
2d Reserve Aviation Group
138th Bomber Aviation Regiment
283d Fighter Aviation Regiment
434th Fighter Aviation Regiment
515th Fighter Aviation Regiment
504th Assault Aviation Regiment
520th Fighter Aviation Regiment
539th Separate Motorized Engineer-Sapper Battalion

1 January 1943

LENINGRAD FRONT

23d Army: LTG A. I. Cherepanov
10th Rifle Division: Col. I. D. Romantsov
92d Rifle Division: Col. Ia. A. Panichkin
142d Rifle Division: Col. A. F. Mashoshin
291st Rifle Division: Col. V. K. Zaionchkovsky
27th Rifle Brigade
17th Fortified Region
22d Fortified Region
260th Army Artillery Regiment
336th Gun Artillery Regiment
91st Antitank Artillery Regiment
883d Antitank Artillery Regiment
104th Army Mortar Regiment

532d Mortar Regiment
73d Separate Antiaircraft Artillery Battalion
618th Separate Antiaircraft Artillery Battalion
152d Tank Brigade: Col. P. I. Pinchuk
30th Separate Armored Train
915th Mixed Aviation Regiment
234th Separate Engineer Battalion
42d Army: LTG I. F. Nikolaev
   85th Rifle Division: Col. K. V. Vvedensky
   109th Rifle Division: Col. N. A. Trushkin
   125th Rifle Division: MG I. I. Fadeeev
   189th Rifle Division: Col. A. D. Kornilov
   79th Fortified Region
   14th Guards Army Artillery Regiment
   73d Army Artillery Regiment
   289th Antitank Artillery Regiment
   304th Antitank Artillery Regiment
   384th Antitank Artillery Regiment
   509th Antitank Artillery Regiment
   705th Antitank Artillery Regiment
   760th Antitank Artillery Regiment
   533d Mortar Regiment
   631st Antiaircraft Artillery Regiment
   72d Separate Antiaircraft Artillery Battalion
   1st Tank Brigade: Lt. Col. A. S. Borodin
   31st Guards Tank Regiment
   1st Separate Armored Car Battalion
   2d Separate Armored Car Battalion
   914th Mixed Aviation Regiment
   54th Separate Engineer Battalion
   585th Separate Engineer Battalion
55th Army: LTG V. P. Sviridov
   43d Rifle Division: Col. Ia. P. Sinkevich
   56th Rifle Division: Col. S. N. Bun'kov
   72d Rifle Division: Col. I. I. Iastrebov
   90th Rifle Division: Col. N. N. Proskurin
   14th Fortified Region
   12th Guards Army Artillery Regiment
   126th Gun Artillery Regiment
   690th Antitank Artillery Regiment
   531st Mortar Regiment
   474th Antiaircraft Artillery Regiment
   71st Separate Antiaircraft Artillery Battalion
   220th Tank Brigade: Col. I. B. Shpiller
   71st Separate Armored Train

987th Mixed Aviation Regiment
325th Separate Engineer Battalion
367th Separate Engineer Battalion
67th Army: LTG M. P. Dukhanov
    45th Guards Rifle Division: MG A. A. Krasnov
    46th Rifle Division: MG E. V. Kozik
    86th Rifle Division: Col. V. A. Trubachev
    11th Rifle Brigade: Col. S. I. Kharitonov
    55th Rifle Brigade; Col. F. A. Burmistrov
    123d Rifle Brigade; Lt. Col. F. F. Shishov
    138th Rifle Brigade: Col. M. D. Bezperstov
    142d Naval Rifle Brigade: Col. N. A. Koshchienko
    35th Ski Brigade: Lt. Col. V. I. Volkov
    16th Fortified Region
    Artillery Division
        380th Light Artillery Regiment
        596th Light Artillery Regiment
        871st Light Artillery Regiment
        311th Gun Artillery Regiment
        1155th Gun Artillery Regiment
        56th Howitzer Artillery Regiment
        511th Howitzer Artillery Regiment
        577th Howitzer Artillery Regiment
    28th Light Artillery Regiment
    1106th Gun Artillery Regiment
    High-power artillery battalion
    882d Antitank Artillery Regiment
    127th Army Mortar Regiment
    134th Army Mortar Regiment
    144th Army Mortar Regiment
    174th Mortar Regiment
    175th Mortar Regiment
    5th Guards-Mortar Brigade
    523d Separate Guards-Mortar Battalion
    524th Separate Guards-Mortar Battalion
    525th Separate Guards-Mortar Battalion
    465th Antiaircraft Artillery Regiment
    632d Antiaircraft Artillery Regiment
    89th Separate Antiaircraft Artillery Battalion
    108th Separate Antiaircraft Artillery Battalion
    613th Separate Antiaircraft Artillery Battalion
    86th Separate Tank Battalion
    118th Separate Tank Battalion
    3d Separate Armored Car Battalion
    407th Mixed Aviation Regiment
    53d Separate Engineer Battalion

Coastal Operational Group
    48th Rifle Division: Col. A. I. Safronov
    168th Rifle Division: Col. A. A. Egorov
    50th Rifle Brigade
    56th Rifle Brigade
    48th Naval Rifle Brigade
    71st Naval Rifle Brigade
    338th Separate Machine Gun–Artillery Battalion
    519th Howitzer Artillery Regiment
    184th Mortar Regiment
    287th Separate Tank Battalion
    295th Separate Engineer Battalion
13th Air Army: CG S. D. Rybal'chenko
    273d Fighter Aviation Division: Col. N. D. Antonov
    275th Fighter Aviation Division: Lt. Col. F. M. Mishchenko
    276th Bomber Aviation Division: MG A. P. Andreev
    277th Assault Aviation Division: Col. F. S. Khatminsky
    5th Long-range Reconnaissance Aviation Squadron
    10th Fighter Aviation Squadron
    12th Corrective Aviation Squadron
Front subordinate
    13th Rifle Division: Col. V. P. Iakutovich
    123d Rifle Division: Col. A. P. Ivanov
    136th Rifle Division: MG N. P. Simoniak
    224th Rifle Division: Col. S. I. Gerasimenko
    268th Rifle Division: Col. S. N. Borshchev
    102d Rifle Brigade; Lt. Col. A. V. Batluk
    162d Rifle Brigade
    250th Rifle Brigade
    34th Ski Brigade: Lt. Col. Ia. F. Potekhin
    13th Fortified Region
    Internal Defense of Leningrad
        122d Separate Machine Gun–Artillery Battalion
        123d Separate Machine Gun–Artillery Battalion
        124th Separate Machine Gun–Artillery Battalion
        125th Separate Machine Gun–Artillery Battalion
        130th Separate Machine Gun–Artillery Battalion
        131st Separate Machine Gun–Artillery Battalion
    38th Guards-Mortar Regiment
    320th Guards-Mortar Regiment
    321st Guards-Mortar Regiment
    7th Antiaircraft Artillery Division: Col. G. I. Boichuk
        785th Antiaircraft Artillery Regiment
        803d Antiaircraft Artillery Regiment
        970th Antiaircraft Artillery Regiment
        988th Antiaircraft Artillery Regiment

92d Separate Antiaircraft Artillery Battalion
116th Separate Antiaircraft Artillery Battalion
61st Tank Brigade: LTC V. V. Khrustitsky
222d Tank Brigade: LTC A. Z. Oskotsky
Bn/Separate tank regiment
5th Separate Aerosleigh Battalion
17th Separate Aerosleigh Battalion
42d Separate Aerosleigh Battalion
72d Separate Armored Train
2d Special Designation (Spetsnaz) Engineer Brigade: Col. A. K. Akatov
52d Engineer-Sapper Brigade: Col. A. P. Shubin
7th Guards Battalion of Miners
8th Pontoon-Bridge Battalion
12th Pontoon-Bridge Battalion
14th Pontoon-Bridge Battalion
18th Pontoon-Bridge Battalion
21st Pontoon-Bridge Battalion
41st Pontoon-Bridge Battalion
42d Pontoon-Bridge Battalion
106th Separate Engineer Battalion
267th Separate Engineer Battalion
447th Separate Sapper Battalion

VOLKHOV FRONT

2d Shock Army: LTG V. G. Romanovsky
   11th Rifle Division: Col. E. I. Marchenko
   18th Rifle Division: MG M. N. Obchinnikov
   71st Rifle Division: Col. V. N. Fedorov
   128th Rifle Division: MG F. N. Parkhomenko
   147th Rifle Division: MG N. A. Moskvin
   191st Rifle Division: Col. P. A. Potapov
   256th Rifle Division: Col. F. K. Fetisov
   314th Rifle Division: Col. I. M. Aliev
   327th Rifle Division: Col. N. A. Poliakov
   372d Rifle Division: Col. P. I. Radygin
   376th Rifle Division: MG N. E. Argunov
   22d Rifle Brigade
   561st Army Artillery Regiment
   168th High-power Howitzer Artillery Regiment
   5th Mortar Brigade (2d Artillery Division)
   122d Army Mortar Regiment
   191st Army Mortar Regiment
   192d Army Mortar Regiment
   193d Army Mortar Regiment
   194th Army Mortar Regiment
   499th Army Mortar Regiment

502d Army Mortar Regiment
503d Army Mortar Regiment
504th Army Mortar Regiment
165th Mortar Regiment
20th Guards-Mortar Regiment (less 211th Battalion)
29th Guards-Mortar Regiment
43d Antiaircraft Artillery Division: Col. I. G. Burdaev
    464th Antiaircraft Artillery Regiment
    635th Antiaircraft Artillery Regiment
    1463d Antiaircraft Artillery Regiment
    1464th Antiaircraft Artillery Regiment
45th Antiaircraft Artillery Division: Col. F. D. Shkurikhin
    1st Antiaircraft Artillery Regiment
    2d Antiaircraft Artillery Regiment
    737th Antiaircraft Artillery Regiment
15th Separate Antiaircraft Artillery Battalion
213th Separate Antiaircraft Artillery Battalion
16th Tank Brigade: Col. K. I. Ivanov
98th Tank Brigade: Lt. Col. Z. G. Papkin
122d Tank Brigade: Col. Ia. A. Davydov
185th Tank Brigade: Col. E. A. Iurevich
32d Guards Tank Regiment
500th Separate Tank Battalion
501st Separate Tank Battalion
503d Separate Tank Battalion
507th Separate Tank Battalion
32d Separate Aerosleigh Battalion
44th Separate Aerosleigh Battalion
22d Separate Antiaircraft Armored Train
696th Mixed Aviation Regiment
136th Separate Engineer Battalion
770th Separate Engineer Battalion
4th Army: LTG N. I. Gusev
  44th Rifle Division: Lt. Col. I. A. Vorob'ev
  288th Rifle Division: Col. G. S. Kolchanov
  310th Rifle Division: Col. N. V. Rogov
  24th Rifle Brigade
  58th Rifle Brigade
  39th Ski Brigade
  206th Separate Machine Gun–Artillery Battalion
  8th Guards Army Artillery Regiment
  211th Guards-Mortar Battalion (20th GMD)
  7th Guards Tank Brigade: Col. B. I. Shneider
  32d Separate Armored Train
  689th Mixed Aviation Regiment
  365th Separate Engineer Battalion

8th Army: LTG F. N. Starikov
   80th Rifle Division: Col. N. V. Simonov
   265th Rifle Division: Col. B. N. Ushinsky
   286th Rifle Division: MG D. L. Abakumov
   364th Rifle Division: MG F. Ia. Solov'ev
   1st Rifle Brigade
   53d Rifle Brigade
   73d Naval Rifle Brigade
   71st Guards Army Artillery Regiment
   70th Army Artillery Regiment
   884th Antitank Artillery Regiment
   145th Mortar Regiment (5th Mortar Brigade)
   146th Army Mortar Regiment
   500th Army Mortar Regiment
   501st Army Mortar Regiment
   30th Guards-Mortar Regiment
   318th Guards-Mortar Regiment
   509th Separate Heavy Guards-Mortar Regiment
   512th Separate Heavy Guards-Mortar Regiment
   41st Antiaircraft Artillery Division: Col. P. V. Mamchemkov
      244th Antiaircraft Artillery Regiment
      245th Antiaircraft Artillery Regiment
      463d Antiaircraft Artillery Regiment
      634th Antiaircraft Artillery Regiment
   177th Separate Antiaircraft Artillery Battalion
   25th Separate Tank Regiment
   107th Separate Tank Battalion
   502d Separate Tank Battalion
   47th Separate Armored Car Battalion
   49th Separate Armored Car Battalion
   50th Separate Armored Train Battalion
   4th Separate Antiaircraft Armored Train
   123d Separate Antiaircraft Armored Train
   935th Mixed Aviation Regiment
   112th Separate Engineer Battalion
52d Army: LTG V. F. Iakovlev
   65th Rifle Division: Col. V. Ia. Nikolaevsky
   165th Rifle Division: Col. V. I. Morozov
   225th Rifle Division: Col. F. I. Gerasimenko
   38th Ski Brigade
   150th Fortified Region
   448th Army Artillery Regiment
   506th Army Mortar Regiment
   231st Guards-Mortar Battalion (28th GMR)
   34th Separate Aerosleigh Battalion
   53d Separate Aerosleigh Battalion

662d Mixed Aviation Regiment
109th Separate Engineer Battalion
366th Separate Engineer Battalion
54th Army: LTG A. V. Sukhomlin
   115th Rifle Division: Col. I. M. Belousov
   177th Rifle Division: Col. A. G. Koziev
   198th Rifle Division: Col. V. D. Daniliuk
   281st Rifle Division: MG I. K. Kravtsov
   285th Rifle Division: Col. A. R. Belov
   291st Rifle Division: Col. V. K. Zaionchkovsky
   311th Rifle Division: Col. T. A. Sviklin
   140th Rifle Brigade
   6th Naval Infantry Brigade
   319th Guards-Mortar Regiment
   461st Separate Antiaircraft Artillery Battalion
   124th Tank Brigade: Col. A. N. Vecherchuk
   48th Separate Armored Car Battalion
   691st Mixed Aviation Regiment
   364th Separate Engineer Battalion
59th Army: LTG I. T. Korovnikov
   2d Rifle Division: Col. D. A. Luk'ianov
   377th Rifle Division: Col. N. P. Koval'chuk
   378th Rifle Division: MG I. M. Platov
   382d Rifle Division: Col. A. D. Vitoshkin
   37th Ski Brigade
   42d Separate Machine Gun–Artillery Battalion
   47th Separate Machine Gun–Artillery Battalion
   215th Separate Machine Gun–Artillery Battalion
   367th Army Artillery Regiment
   505th Army Mortar Regiment
   28th Guards-Mortar Regiment (less 231st GMBn)
   29th Tank Brigade: Lt. Col. E. M. Kovalev
   48th Separate Armored Train
   660th Mixed Aviation Regiment
   539th Separate Motorized Engineer-Sapper Battalion
   771st Separate Engineer Battalion
14th Air Army: LTG I. P. Zhuravlev
   2d Fighter Aviation Corps: MG A. S. Blagoveshchensky
   209th Fighter Aviation Division: Col. V. M. Zabaluev
   215th Fighter Aviation Division: LTG G. P. Kravchenko
   279th Fighter Aviation Division: Col. F. N. Dement'ev
   280th Bomber Aviation Division: Col. N. N. Buiansky
   281st Assault Aviation Division: Lt. Col. S. E. Gres'kov
   844th Transport Aviation Regiment
   8th Long-range Reconnaissance Aviation Squadron
   28th Corrective Aviation Squadron

Front subordinate
    239th Rifle Division: MG P. N. Chernyshev
    379th Rifle Division: MG I. I. Popov
    11th Ski Brigade
    12th Ski Brigade: Lt. Col. N. A. Sebov
    13th Ski Brigade
    2d Artillery Division: Col. V. I. Sokolov
        20th Light Artillery Brigade
        7th Gun Artillery Brigade
        4th Howitzer Artillery Brigade
    13th Guards Army Artillery Regiment
    21st Army Artillery Regiment
    24th Army Artillery Regiment
    430th High-power Howitzer Artillery Regiment
    46th Antiaircraft Artillery Division: Col. P. N. Vedenichev
        21st Antiaircraft Artillery Regiment
        22d Antiaircraft Artillery Regiment
        23d Antiaircraft Artillery Regiment
        24th Antiaircraft Artillery Regiment
    707th Antiaircraft Artillery Regiment (45th AAD)
    168th Separate Antiaircraft Artillery Battalion
    216th Separate Antiaircraft Artillery Battalion
    23d Separate Armored Train
    1st Engineer-Miner Brigade
    39th Special Designation Engineer Brigade (Spetsnaz): Lt. Col. R. M. Soldatenko
    53d Engineer-Sapper Brigade
    8th Guards Battalion of Miners
    734th Separate Miner-Sapper Battalion
    32d Pontoon-Bridge Battalion
    34th Pontoon-Bridge Battalion
    36th Pontoon-Bridge Battalion
    38th Pontoon-Bridge Battalion
    55th Pontoon-Bridge Battalion
    40th Separate Engineer Battalion
    135th Separate Engineer Battalion

1 January 1944

LENINGRAD FRONT

    2d Shock Army: LTG V. Z. Romanovsky
        43d Rifle Corps: MG A. I. Andreev
            48th Rifle Division: MG A. I. Safronov
            90th Rifle Division: Col. N. G. Liashchenko
            98th Rifle Division: Col. N. S. Nikanorov

122d Rifle Corps: MG N. M. Martynchuk
   11th Rifle Division: Col. V. I. Shkel'
   131st Rifle Division: Col. P. L. Romanenko
   168th Rifle Division: MG A. A. Egorov
43d Rifle Division: MG Ia. P. Sinkevich
50th Rifle Brigade
48th Naval Rifle Brigade
71st Naval Rifle Brigade
16th Fortified Region
116th Corps Artillery Regiment
154th Corps Artillery Regiment
533d Separate Heavy Gun Artillery Battalion
535th Separate Heavy Gun Artillery Battalion
760th Antitank Artillery Regiment
230th Guards-Mortar Regiment
144th Mortar Regiment
184th Mortar Regiment
281st Mortar Regiment
30th Guards-Mortar Regiment
318th Guards-Mortar Regiment
322d Guards-Mortar Regiment
803d Antiaircraft Artillery Regiment
92d Separate Antiaircraft Artillery Battalion
116th Separate Antiaircraft Artillery Battalion
152d Tank Brigade: Col. A. Z. Oskotsky
98th Separate Tank Regiment
204th Separate Tank Regiment
222d Separate Tank Regiment
17th Separate Aerosleigh Battalion
42d Separate Aerosleigh Battalion
4th Separate Armored Car Battalion
295th Separate Engineer Battalion
447th Separate Engineer Battalion
734th Separate Engineer Battalion
23d Army: LTG A. I. Cherepanov
   10th Rifle Division: Col. A. F. Mashoshin
   92d Rifle Division: MG Ia. A. Panichkin
   142d Rifle Division: Col. G. L. Sonnikov
   17th Fortified Region
   22d Fortified Region
   8th Corps Artillery Regiment
   336th Gun Artillery Regiment
   94th Antitank Artillery Regiment
   883d Antitank Artillery Regiment
   276th Mortar Regiment

618th Separate Antiaircraft Artillery Battalion
5th Aerosleigh Battalion
1st Separate Armored Car Battalion
42d Army: LTG F. I. Nikolaev
  30th Guards Rifle Corps: MG. N. P. Simoniak
    45th Guards Rifle Division: MG S. M. Putilov
    63d Guards Rifle Division: Col. A. F. Sheglov
    64th Guards Rifle Division: MG I. D. Romantsov
  109th Rifle Corps: MG A. S. Griaznov
    72d Rifle Division: MG I. I. Iastrebov
    109th Rifle Division: MG N. A. Trushkin
    125th Rifle Division: MG I. I. Fadeev
  110th Rifle Corps: MG M. F. Bukshtynovich
    56th Rifle Division: MG S. M. Bun'kov
    85th Rifle Division: Col. K. V. Vvedensky
    86th Rifle Division: MG N. A. Poliakov
  189th Rifle Division: Col. P. K. Loskutov
  79th Fortified Region
  18th Artillery Penetration Division: MG B. I. Koznov
    65th Light Artillery Brigade
    58th Howitzer Artillery Brigade
    3d Heavy Howitzer Artillery Brigade
    80th Heavy Howitzer Artillery Brigade
    120th High-power Howitzer Artillery Brigade
    42d Mortar Brigade
  23d Artillery Penetration Division: MG N. K. Rogozin
    79th Light Artillery Brigade
    38th Howitzer Artillery Brigade
    2d Heavy Howitzer Artillery Brigade
    96th Heavy Howitzer Artillery Brigade
    21st Guards High-power Howitzer Artillery Brigade
    28th Mortar Brigade
  1157th Corps Artillery Regiment
  1106th Gun Artillery Regiment
  1486th Gun Artillery Regiment
  52d Guards Separate Heavy Gun Artillery Battalion
  304th Antitank Artillery Regiment
  384th Antitank Artillery Regiment
  509th Antitank Artillery Regiment
  705th Antitank Artillery Regiment
  1973d Antitank Artillery Regiment
  104th Mortar Regiment
  174th Mortar Regiment
  533d Mortar Regiment
  534th Mortar Regiment
  20th Guards-Mortar Regiment (less 211th GMBn)

38th Guards-Mortar Regiment
320th Guards-Mortar Regiment
321st Guards-Mortar Regiment
7th Antiaircraft Artillery Division: Col. G. I. Boichuk
    465th Antiaircraft Artillery Regiment
    474th Antiaircraft Artillery Regiment
    602d Antiaircraft Artillery Regiment
    632d Antiaircraft Artillery Regiment
32d Antiaircraft Artillery Division: Col. V. V. Snamensky
    1377th Antiaircraft Artillery Regiment
    1387th Antiaircraft Artillery Regiment
    1393d Antiaircraft Artillery Regiment
    1413th Antiaircraft Artillery Regiment
631st Antiaircraft Artillery Regiment
72d Separate Antiaircraft Artillery Battalion
1st Tank Brigade: Col. V. I. Volkov
220th Tank Brigade: Lt. Col. V. L. Protsenko
31st Guards Separate Tank Regiment
46th Guards Separate Tank Regiment
49th Guards Separate Tank Regiment
205th Separate Tank Regiment
260th Separate Tank Regiment
1439th Self-propelled Artillery Regiment
1902d Self-propelled Artillery Regiment
2d Separate Armored Car Battalion
71st Separate Armored Train Battalion
72d Separate Armored Train Battalion
54th Separate Engineer Battalion
585th Separate Engineer Battalion
67th Army: LTG V. P. Sviridov
    116th Rifle Corps: LTG A. N Astinin
        13th Rifle Division: Col. P. S. Fedorov
        46th Rifle Division: Col. S. M. Borshchev
        376th Rifle Division: MG M. D. Grishin
    118th Rifle Corps: MG V. K. Paramzin
        124th Rifle Division: Col. M. D. Papchenko
        128th Rifle Division: Col. P. A. Potapov
        268th Rifle Division: Col. N. D. Sokolov
    291st Rifle Division: MG V. K. Zaionchkovsky
    14th Fortified Region
    81st Gun Artillery Brigade
    267th Guards Gun Artillery Regiment
    21st Gun Artillery Regiment
    260th Gun Artillery Regiment
    564th Gun Artillery Regiment
    599th Howitzer Artillery Regiment

532d Separate Heavy Gun Artillery Battalion
289th Antitank Artillery Regiment
690th Antitank Artillery Regiment
882d Antitank Artillery Regiment
884th Antitank Artillery Regiment
122d Mortar Regiment
127th Mortar Regiment
134th Mortar Regiment
175th Mortar Regiment
193d Mortar Regiment
504th Mortar Regiment
567th Mortar Regiment
970th Antiaircraft Artillery Regiment
988th Antiaircraft Artillery Regiment
71st Separate Antiaircraft Artillery Battalion
73d Separate Antiaircraft Artillery Battalion
108th Separate Antiaircraft Artillery Battalion
613th Separate Antiaircraft Artillery Battalion
14th Separate Armored Train Battalion
53d Separate Engineer Battalion
234th Separate Engineer Battalion
325th Separate Engineer Battalion
367th Separate Engineer Battalion
8th Separate Flame-thrower Battalion
13th Air Army: CG S. D. Rybal'chenko
276th Bomber Aviation Division: MG A. P. Andreev
277th Assault Aviation Division: Col. F. S. Khatminsky
275th Fighter Aviation Division: Col. A. A. Matveev
283d Fighter Aviation Regiment
13th Reconnaissance Aviation Regiment
12th Corrective Aviation Squadron
49th Corrective Aviation Squadron
52d Corrective Aviation Squadron
Front subordinate
108th Rifle Corps: MG M. F. Tikhonov
196th Rifle Division: MG P. F. Ratov
224th Rifle Division: Col. F. A. Burmistrov
314th Rifle Division: MG I. M. Aliev
117th Rifle Corps: MG V. A. Trubachev
120th Rifle Division: Col. A. V. Batluk
123d Rifle Division: MG A. P. Ivanov
201st Rifle Division: MG V. P. Iakutovich
123d Rifle Corps (Headquarters): MG G. I. Anisimov
3d Artillery Corps (Headquarters)
51st Gun Artillery Brigade
12th Guards Gun Artillery Regiment

14th Guards Gun Artillery Regiment
73d Gun Artillery Regiment
126th Gun Artillery Regiment
129th Gun Artillery Regiment
409th Separate Heavy Gun Artillery Battalion
4th Guards-Mortar Division: Col. F. N. Zhukov
    2d Guards-Mortar Brigade
    5th Guards-Mortar Brigade
    6th Guards-Mortar Brigade
536th Separate Antitank Artillery Battalion
1st Separate Aerostatic Balloon Artillery
    Observation Battalion
8th Separate Aerostatic Balloon Artillery
    Observation Battalion
43d Antiaircraft Artillery Division: Col. I. G. Burdeev
    464th Antiaircraft Artillery Regiment
    635th Antiaircraft Artillery Regiment
    1463d Antiaircraft Artillery Regiment
    1464th Antiaircraft Artillery Regiment
785th Antiaircraft Artillery Regiment
758th Separate Antiaircraft Artillery Battalion
30th Guards Tank Brigade: Col. V. V. Khrustitsky
17th Guards Tank Regiment
261st Separate Tank Regiment
1344th Self-propelled Artillery Regiment
3d Separate Armored Car Battalion
2d Special Designation Engineer Brigade (Spetsnaz)
52d Engineer-Sapper Brigade
5th Heavy Pontoon-Bridge Regiment
7th Guards Battalion of Miners
34th Separate Engineer Battalion
106th Separate Engineer Battalion
1st Guards Pontoon-Bridge Battalion
21st Pontoon-Bridge Battalion
42d Pontoon-Bridge Battalion
175th Separate Backpack Flame-thrower Company

VOLKHOV FRONT

8th Army: LTG F. N. Starikov
    119th Rifle Corps: MG F. K. Fetisov
        286th Rifle Division: Col. F. Iu. Tsarev
        374th Rifle Division: Col. A. A. Volkov
    18th Rifle Division: MG M. Absaliamov
    364th Rifle Division: Col. V. A. Verzhbitsky
    1st Rifle Brigade
    22d Rifle Brigade

258th Light Artillery Regiment (20th LAB)
8th Guards Gun Artillery Regiment
71st Guards Gun Artillery Regiment
223d Guards Gun Artillery Regiment
500th Mortar Regiment
18th Guards-Mortar Regiment
41st Antiaircraft Artillery Division: Col. P. V. Mamchenkov
    245th Antiaircraft Artillery Regiment
    634th Antiaircraft Artillery Regiment
1468th Antiaircraft Artillery Regiment
177th Separate Antiaircraft Artillery Battalion
33d Guards Tank Regiment
185th Tank Regiment
32d Separate Aerosleigh Battalion
49th Separate Armored Car Battalion
50th Separate Armored Train Battalion
4th Separate Armored Train
112th Separate Engineer Battalion
54th Army: LTG S. V. Roginsky
   111th Rifle Corps: MG B. A. Rozhdestvensky
      44th Mountain Rifle Division: Col. I. A. Vorob'ev
      288th Rifle Division: MG G. S. Kolchanov
   115th Rifle Corps: MG S. B. Kozachek
      281st Rifle Division: Col. G. P. Isakov
      285th Rifle Division: Col. B. A. Gorodetsky
      14th Rifle Brigade
      53d Rifle Brigade
   80th Rifle Division: MG D. L. Abakumov
   177th Rifle Division: Col. A. Ia. Tsigankov
   198th Rifle Division: Col. V. D. Daniliuk
   2d Fortified Region
   1097th Gun Artillery Regiment
   194th Mortar Regiment
   499th Mortar Regiment
   29th Guards-Mortar Regiment
   244th Antiaircraft Artillery Regiment (41st AAD)
   463d Antiaircraft Artillery Regiment (41st AAD)
   1467th Antiaircraft Artillery Regiment
   1469th Antiaircraft Artillery Regiment
   15th Separate Antiaircraft Artillery Battalion
   124th Separate Tank Regiment
   107th Separate Tank Battalion
   501st Separate Tank Battalion
   48th Separate Armored Car Battalion
   32d Separate Armored Train Battalion
   48th Separate Armored Train Battalion

22d Separate Antiaircraft Armored Train
2d Guards Special Designation Engineer Brigade (Spetsnaz)
9th Assault Engineer-Sapper Brigade
8th Guards Battalion of Miners
364th Separate Engineer Battalion
539th Separate Engineer Battalion
59th Army: LTG I. T. Korovnikov
  6th Rifle Corps: MG S. P. Mikul'sky
    65th Rifle Division: Col. G. E. Kalinovsky
    239th Rifle Division: Col. A. Ia. Ordanovsky
    310th Rifle Division: Col. N. V. Rogov
  14th Rifle Corps: MG P. A. Artiushenko
    191st Rifle Division: MG I. N. Burakovsky
    225th Rifle Division: Col. P. I. Ol'khovsky
    378th Rifle Division: Col. A. R. Belov
  112th Rifle Corps: MG F. Ia. Solov'ev
    2d Rifle Division: MG D. A. Luk'ianov
    372d Rifle Division: Col. P. I. Radygin
    377th Rifle Division: Col. S. S. Safronov
    24th Rifle Brigade
  150th Fortified Region
  2d Artillery Division: Col. K. A. Sedash
    20th Light Artillery Brigade
    7th Gun Artillery Brigade
    10th Guards Howitzer Artillery Brigade
  121st High-power Howitzer Artillery Brigade
  13th Guards Gun Artillery Regiment
  70th Gun Artillery Regiment
  367th Gun Artillery Regiment
  448th Gun Artillery Regiment
  1096th Gun Artillery Regiment
  5th Mortar Brigade
  30th Mortar Brigade
  192d Mortar Regiment
  505th Mortar Regiment
  506th Mortar Regiment
  10th Guards-Mortar Brigade
  12th Guards-Mortar Brigade
  28th Guards-Mortar Regiment
  319th Guards-Mortar Regiment
  211th Guards-Mortar Battalion (20th GMR)
  3d Separate Aerostatic Balloon Artillery
    Observation Battalion
  45th Antiaircraft Artillery Division: Col. F. T. Shkurikhin
    707th Antiaircraft Artillery Regiment
    737th Antiaircraft Artillery Regiment

1465th Antiaircraft Artillery Regiment
1466th Antiaircraft Artillery Regiment
1470th Antiaircraft Artillery Regiment
213th Separate Antiaircraft Artillery Battalion
461st Separate Antiaircraft Artillery Battalion
16th Tank Brigade: Col. K. O. Urvanov
29th Tank Brigade: Lt. Col. I. D. Bachakashvili
122d Tank Brigade: Maj. D. M. Savochkin
32d Guards Separate Tank Regiment
35th Guards Separate Tank Regiment
50th Guards Separate Tank Regiment
25th Separate Tank Regiment
1433d Self-propelled Artillery Regiment
1434th Self-propelled Artillery Regiment
500th Separate Tank Battalion
502d Separate Tank Battalion
503d Separate Tank Battalion
34th Separate Aerosleigh Battalion
44th Separate Aerosleigh Battalion
47th Separate Armored Car Battalion
1st Engineer-Sapper Brigade
2d Guards Separate Engineer Battalion
35th Separate Engineer Battalion
40th Separate Engineer Battalion
109th Separate Engineer Battalion
135th Separate Engineer Battalion
365th Separate Engineer Battalion
34th Pontoon-Bridge Battalion
36th Pontoon-Bridge Battalion
55th Pontoon-Bridge Battalion
9th Separate Flame-thrower Battalion
14th Air Army: LTG I. P. Zhuravlev
280th Bomber Aviation Division: Lt. Col. P. M. Podmogil'nyi
281st Assault Aviation Division: Col. S. E. Gres'kov
269th Fighter Aviation Division: Col. A. P. Nikolaev
386th Fighter-Bomber Aviation Regiment
742d Reconnaissance Aviation Regiment
844th Transport Aviation Regiment
4th Aviation Regiment Civil Aviation Fleet
44th Corrective Aviation Squadron
59th Corrective Aviation Squadron
Front subordinate
7th Rifle Corps: MG R. I. Panin
256th Rifle Division: Col. A. G. Koziev
382d Rifle Division: MG P. N. Chernyshev

58th Rifle Brigade
11th Guards Separate Antiaircraft Artillery Battalion
168th Separate Antiaircraft Artillery Battalion
7th Guards Tank Brigade: MG B. I. Shneider
123d Separate Armored Train
12th Engineer-Sapper Brigade
38th Pontoon-Bridge Battalion

1 July 1944

LENINGRAD FRONT

2d Shock Army: LTG I. I. Fediuninsky
    48th Rifle Division: Col. Ia. I. Kozhevnikov
    131st Rifle Division: MG P. L. Romanenko
    191st Rifle Division: MG I. N. Burakovsky
    16th Fortified Region
    161st Gun Artillery Brigade
    760th Antitank Artillery Regiment
    328th Separate Special-power Artillery Battalion
    230th Guards-Mortar Regiment
    194th Mortar Regiment
    499th Mortar Regiment
    38th Guards-Mortar Regiment
    863d Antiaircraft Artillery Regiment
    116th Separate Antiaircraft Artillery Battalion
    432d Separate Antiaircraft Artillery Battalion
    4th Separate Armored Car Battalion
    72d Separate Armored Train Battalion
    175th Separate Flame-thrower Company
8th Army: LTG F. N. Starikov
    112th Rifle Corps: MG F. Ia. Solov'ev
        2d Rifle Division: Col. M. I. Perevoznikov
        11th Rifle Division: Col. V. I. Shkel'
    117th Rifle Corps: MG V. A. Trubachev
        43d Rifle Division: MG P. V. Borisov
        123d Rifle Division: MG A. P. Ivanov
        256th Rifle Division: MG A. Z. Koziev
    122d Rifle Corps: MG N. M. Martynchuk
        98th Rifle Division: Col. N. S. Nikanorov
        189th Rifle Division: MG P. A. Potapov
    124th Rifle Corps: MG I. F. Nikitin
        196th Rifle Division; MG P. F. Ratov
        374th Rifle Division: Col. B. A. Gorodetsky
        377th Rifle Division: Col. S. S. Safronov

120th Rifle Division: MG A. V. Batluk
201st Rifle Division: MG V. P. Iakutovich
9th Fortified Region
79th Fortified Region
81st Gun Artillery Brigade
154th Corps Gun Artillery Regiment
14th Guards Gun Artillery Regiment
70th Gun Artillery Regiment
126th Gun Artillery Regiment
367th Gun Artillery Regiment
882d Antitank Artillery Regiment
884th Antitank Artillery Regiment
409th Heavy Gun Artillery Battalion
104th Mortar Regiment
144th Mortar Regiment
174th Mortar Regiment
184th Mortar Regiment
192d Mortar Regiment
540th Mortar Regiment
505th Mortar Regiment
18th Guards-Mortar Regiment
30th Guards-Mortar Regiment
322d Guards-Mortar Regiment
7th Antiaircraft Artillery Division: Col. G. I. Boichuk
    465th Antiaircraft Artillery Regiment
    474th Antiaircraft Artillery Regiment
    602d Antiaircraft Artillery Regiment
    632d Antiaircraft Artillery Regiment
1468th Antiaircraft Artillery Regiment
73d Separate Antiaircraft Artillery Battalion
92d Separate Antiaircraft Artillery Battalion
108th Separate Antiaircraft Artillery Battalion
168th Separate Antiaircraft Artillery Battalion
82d Separate Tank Regiment
806th Self-propelled Artillery Regiment
1198th Self-propelled Artillery Regiment
1844th Self-propelled Artillery Regiment
1st Engineer-Sapper Brigade
34th Pontoon-Bridge Battalion
21st Army: ColG D. N. Guzev
   30th Guards Rifle Corps: LTG N. P. Simoniak
      45th Guards Rifle Division: MG S. M. Putilov
      63d Guards Rifle Division: MG A. F. Sheglov
      64th Guards Rifle Division: MG I. D. Romantsov
   97th Rifle Corps: MG M. M. Busarov
      178th Rifle Division: MG A. L. Kronik

358th Rifle Division: Col. P. F. Zaretsky
372d Rifle Division: MG P. I. Radygin
108th Rifle Corps: LTG M. F. Tikhonov
    46th Rifle Division: Col. S. N. Borshchev
    90th Rifle Division: MG N. G. Lashchenko
    314th Rifle Division: Col. M. S. Elshinov
109th Rifle Corps: LTG I. P. Alferov
    72d Rifle Division: MG I. I. Iastrebov
    109th Rifle Division: MG N. A. Trushkin
    286th Rifle Division: MG M. D. Grishin
110th Rifle Corps: MG A. S. Griaznov
    168th Rifle Division: MG A. A. Egorov
    265th Rifle Division: Col. F. I. Andreev
    268th Rifle Division: Col. F. I. Voitulevich
5th Guards Heavy Artillery Penetration Division: Col. V. N. Ivanov
    71st Light Artillery Brigade
    17th Guards Gun Artillery Brigade
    67th Howitzer Artillery Brigade
    95th Heavy Howitzer Artillery Brigade
    18th Guards High-power Howitzer Artillery Brigade
    27th Mortar Brigade
15th Artillery Penetration Division: MG A. A. Korochkin
    35th Howitzer Artillery Brigade
    85th Heavy Howitzer Artillery Brigade
    106th High-power Howitzer Artillery Brigade
51st Gun Artillery Brigade
127th Gun Artillery Brigade
8th Guards Gun Artillery Regiment
260th Gun Artillery Regiment
28th Corps Gun Artillery Regiment
138th Corps Gun Artillery Regiment
1157th Corps Artillery Regiment
94th Antitank Artillery Regiment
32d Separate Special-power Artillery Battalion
34th Separate Special-power Artillery Battalion
40th Separate Special-power Artillery Battalion
329th Separate Special-power Artillery Battalion
276th Mortar Regiment
534th Mortar Regiment
2d Guards-Mortar Brigade
19th Guards-Mortar Brigade
24th Guards-Mortar Regiment
40th Guards-Mortar Regiment
318th Guards-Mortar Regiment
32d Antiaircraft Artillery Division: Col. V. V. Snamensky
    1377th Antiaircraft Artillery Regiment

1387th Antiaircraft Artillery Regiment
1393d Antiaircraft Artillery Regiment
1413th Antiaircraft Artillery Regiment
716th Antiaircraft Artillery Regiment
177th Separate Antiaircraft Artillery Battalion
30th Guards Tank Brigade
27th Guards Separate Tank Regiment
260th Guards Separate Tank Regiment
27th Separate Tank Regiment
98th Separate Tank Regiment
124th Separate Tank Regiment
351st Guards Separate Self-propelled Artillery Regiment
394th Guards Separate Self-propelled Artillery Regiment
397th Guards Separate Self-propelled Artillery Regiment
1222d Separate Self-propelled Artillery Regiment
1238th Separate Self-propelled Artillery Regiment
49th Separate Armored Car Battalion
14th Separate Armored Train Battalion
23d Separate Armored Train Battalion
17th Assault Engineer-Sapper Brigade
21st Engineer-Sapper Brigade
52d Engineer-Sapper Brigade
1st Guards Pontoon-Bridge Battalion
29th Separate Flame-thrower Battalion
23d Army: LTG A. I. Cherepanov
6th Rifle Corps: MG I. I. Fadeev
13th Rifle Division: Col. V. A. Rodionov
177th Rifle Division: Col. V. M. Rzhanov
382d Rifle Division: Lt. Col. A. A. Zolotarev
98th Rifle Corps: LTG G. I. Anisimov
92d Rifle Division: MG Ia. A. Panichkin
281st Rifle Division: Col. G. I. Iaskov
381st Rifle Division: MG A. V. Iakushev
115th Rifle Corps: MG S. B. Kozachek
10th Rifle Division: MG I. M. Platov
142d Rifle Division: Col. G. L. Sonnikov
17th Fortified Region
47th Guards Gun Artillery Brigade
21st Gun Artillery Regiment
151st Gun Artillery Regiment
336th Gun Artillery Regiment
165th Antitank Artillery Regiment
641st Antitank Artillery Regiment
883d Antitank Artillery Regiment
1072d Antitank Artillery Regiment
175th Mortar Regiment

456th Mortar Regiment
506th Mortar Regiment
567th Mortar Regiment
70th Guards-Mortar Regiment
1469th Antiaircraft Artillery Regiment
71st Separate Antiaircraft Artillery Battalion
618th Separate Antiaircraft Artillery Battalion
46th Separate Guards Tank Regiment
226th Separate Tank Regiment
938th Self-propelled Artillery Regiment
952d Self-propelled Artillery Regiment
71st Separate Armored Train Battalion
20th Engineer-Sapper Brigade
59th Army: LTG I. T. Korovnikov
   224th Rifle Division: Col. F. A. Burmistrov
   34th Guards Gun Artillery Brigade
   46th Antitank Artillery Brigade
   18th Mortar Brigade (15th Artillery Penetration Division)
   29th Guards-Mortar Regiment
   43d Antiaircraft Artillery Division: Col. I. G. Burdaev
      464th Antiaircraft Artillery Regiment
      635th Antiaircraft Artillery Regiment
      1463d Antiaircraft Artillery Regiment
      1464th Antiaircraft Artillery Regiment
   1470th Antiaircraft Artillery Regiment
   22d Engineer-Sapper Brigade
13th Air Army: ColG S. D. Rybal'chenko
   113th Bomber Aviation Division: MG M. V. Shcherbakov
   276th Bomber Aviation Division: MG A. P. Andreev
   277th Assault Aviation Division: Col. F. S. Khatminsky
   281st Assault Aviation Division: Col. S. E. Gres'kov
   275th Fighter Aviation Division: Col. A. A. Matveev
   13th Reconnaissance Aviation Regiment
   203d Corrective-Reconnaissance Aviation Regiment
   283d Fighter Aviation Regiment
   212th Medical Aviation Regiment
   199th Separate Aviation Supply Regiment
Front subordinate
   8th Estonian Rifle Corps: LTG L. A. Pern
      7th Rifle Division: Col. K. A. Allikas
      249th Rifle Division: MG I. Ia. Lombak
   43d Rifle Corps: MG A. I. Andreev
      80th Rifle Division: Col. A. D. Kornilov
      124th Rifle Division: Col. M. D. Papchenko
   125th Rifle Division: Col. V. K. Zinov'ev
   22d Fortified Region

132d Separate Machine Gun–Artillery Battalion
3d Artillery Penetration Corps: MG N. N. Zhdanov
    18th Artillery Penetration Division: MG B. I. Koznov
        65th Light Artillery Brigade
        58th Howitzer Artillery Brigade
        3d Heavy Howitzer Artillery Brigade
        80th Heavy Howitzer Artillery Brigade
        120th High-power Howitzer Artillery Brigade
        42d Mortar Brigade
    23d Artillery Penetration Division: MG N. K. Rogozin
        79th Light Artillery Brigade
        38th Howitzer Artillery Brigade
        2d Heavy Howitzer Artillery Brigade
        96th Heavy Howitzer Artillery Brigade
        21st Guards High-power Howitzer Artillery Brigade
        28th Mortar Brigade
1st Guards-Mortar Division: MG V. G. Solov'ev
        2d Guards-Mortar Brigade
        5th Guards-Mortar Brigade
        6th Guards-Mortar Brigade
85th Corps Artillery Regiment
330th Separate Special-power Artillery Battalion
1st Separate Aerostatic Balloon Observation Battalion
8th Separate Aerostatic Balloon Observation Battalion
785th Antiaircraft Artillery Regiment
11th Guards Separate Antiaircraft Artillery Battalion
1st Tank Brigade: Col. V. I. Volkov
152d Tank Brigade: Col. A. P. Koval'sky
220th Tank Brigade: LTC M. I. Lampusov
26th Guards Separate Tank Regiment
31st Guards Separate Tank Regiment
45th Separate Tank Regiment
185th Separate Tank Regiment
221st Separate Tank Regiment
222d Separate Tank Regiment
1294th Self-propelled Artillery Regiment
1495th Self-propelled Artillery Regiment
283d Separate Special Designation Motorized Battalion
1st Separate Armored Car Battalion
3d Separate Armored Car Battalion
32d Separate Armored Train Battalion
48th Separate Armored Train Battalion
50th Separate Armored Train Battalion
4th Separate Armored Train Battalion
2d Motorized Engineer Brigade

5th Heavy Pontoon-Bridge Regiment
34th Separate Engineer Battalion
67th Separate Engineer Battalion
21st Pontoon-Bridge Battalion
36th Pontoon-Bridge Battalion
42d Pontoon-Bridge Battalion
62d Pontoon-Bridge Battalion
159th Pontoon-Bridge Battalion
9th Separate Flame-thrower Battalion

Sources: Boevoi sostav Sovetskoi armii, chast' 1 (iiun'–dekabr' 1941 goda) [The combat composition of the Soviet Army, part 1 (June–December 1941)] (Moscow: Voroshilov Academy of the General Staff, 1963), 7, 30, 39–40; *Boevoi sostav Sovetskoi armii, chast' 2 (ianvar'–dekabr' 1942 goda)* [The combat composition of the Soviet Army, part 2 (January–December 1942)] (Moscow: Voenizdat, 1966), 7–8; *Boevoi sostav Sovetskoi armii, chast' 3 (ianvar'–dekabr' 1943 goda)* [The combat composition of the Soviet Army, part 3 (January–December 1943)] (Moscow: Voenizdat, 1972), 8–10; *Boevoi sostav Sovetskoi armii, chast' 4 (ianvar'–dekabr' 1944 goda)* [The combat composition of the Soviet Army, part 4 (January–December 1944)] (Moscow: Voenizdat, 1988), 8–10, 186–187; and *Komandovanie korpusnogo i divizionnogo zvena Sovetskykh Vooruzhennykh Sil perioda Velikoi Otechestvennoi voiny 1941–1945* [Corps and division commanders of the Soviet Armed Forces during the Great Patriotic War 1941–1945] (Moscow: Frunze Academy, 1964).

German Order of Battle

22 June 1941

ARMY GROUP NORTH: Field Marshal Ritter von Leeb

  Eighteenth Army: ColG Georg von Kuechler
    XXVI Army Corps
      291st Infantry Division
      61st Infantry Division
      217th Infantry Division
    XXXVIII Army Corps
      58th Infantry Division
    I Army Corps
      11th Infantry Division
      1st Infantry Division
      21st Infantry Division
  Fourth Panzer Group: ColG Erich Hoepner
    XXXXI Motorized Corps
      1st Panzer Division
      269th Infantry Division
      6th Panzer Division
      36th Motorized Division
    LVI Motorized Corps
      290th Infantry Division
      8th Panzer Division
      3d Motorized Division
    SS "T" Motorized Division
  Sixteenth Army: ColG Ernst Busch
    X Army Corps
      30th Infantry Division
      126th Infantry Division
    XXVIII Army Corps
      122d Infantry Division
      123d Infantry Division
    II Army Corps
      121st Infantry Division
      12th Infantry Division
      32d Infantry Division
      253d Infantry Division

Army Group and OKH Reserves
  XXIII Army Corps (Army group)
    254th Infantry Division
    251st Infantry Division
    206th Infantry Division
  L Army Corps (OKH)
    86th Infantry Division
    SS Police Infantry Division
  207th Security Division
  285th Security Division
  281st Security Division

1 August 1941

ARMY GROUP NORTH: Field Marshal Ritter von Leeb

Eighteenth Army: ColG Georg von Kuechler
  XXXXII Army Corps
    291st Infantry Division
    217th Infantry Division
  XXVI Army Corps
    254th Infantry Division
    61st Infantry Division
    93d Infantry Division
Fourth Panzer Group: ColG Erich Hoepner
  XXXVIII Army Corps
    58th Infantry Division
  XXXXI Motorized Corps
    1st Infantry Division
    1st Panzer Division
    36th Motorized Division
  LVI Motorized Corps
    269th Infantry Division
    8th Panzer Division
    SS Police Infantry Division
    3d Motorized Division
Sixteenth Army: ColG Ernst Busch
  XXVIII Army Corps
    122d Infantry Division
    121st Infantry Division
    SS "T" Motorized Division
  I Army Corps
    11th Infantry Division
    21st Infantry Division
  X Army Corps
    126th Infantry Division

30th Infantry Division
290th Infantry Division
II Army Corps
  123d Infantry Division
  32d Infantry Division
  12th Infantry Division
L Army Corps (Ninth Army control)
  251st Infantry Division
  253d Infantry Division

1 September 1941

ARMY GROUP NORTH: Field Marshal Ritter von Leeb

Eighteenth Army: ColG Georg von Kuechler
  XXXXII Army Corps
    61st Infantry Division
    217th Infantry Division
    254th Infantry Division
Fourth Panzer Group: ColG Erich Hoepner
  XXVI Army Corps
    93d Infantry Division
  XXXVIII Army Corps
    1st Infantry Division
    291st Infantry Division
  XXXXI Motorized Corps
    6th Panzer Division
    36th Motorized Division
    1st Panzer Division
  L Army Corps
    269th Infantry Division
    SS Police Infantry Division
    8th Panzer Division
Sixteenth Army: ColG Ernst Busch
  XXXIX Motorized Corps
    12th Panzer Division
    20th Motorized Division
    18th Motorized Division
  XXVIII Army Corps
    96th Infantry Division
    121st Infantry Division
  I Army Corps
    21st Infantry Division
    11th Infantry Division
    122d Infantry Division
    126th Infantry Division

X Army Corps
   290th Infantry Division
   30th Infantry Division
LVI Motorized Corps
   SS "T" Motorized Division
   3d Motorized Division
II Army Corps
   123d Infantry Division
   32d Infantry Division
   12th Infantry Division

1 January 1942

ARMY GROUP NORTH: Field Marshal Ritter von Leeb

Eighteenth Army: ColG Georg von Kuechler
   XXVI Army Corps
      217th Infantry Division
      93d Infantry Division
      212th Infantry Division
   L Army Corps
      58th Infantry Division
      SS Police Infantry Division
      121st Infantry Division
      122d Infantry Division
   XXVIII Army Corps
      96th Infantry Division
      1st Infantry Division
      227th Infantry Division
      223d Infantry Division
      269th Infantry Division
      IR, 291st Infantry Division
      Part, 12th Panzer Division
   I Army Corps
      11th Infantry Division
      21st Infantry Division
      291st Infantry Division (-)
   XXXIX Motorized Corps
      12th Panzer Division
      20th Motorized Division
Sixteenth Army: ColG Ernst Busch
   XXXVIII Army Corps
      61st Infantry Division
      215th Infantry Division
      126th Infantry Division
      250th Spanish Infantry Division

X Army Corps
    290th Infantry Division
    30th Infantry Division
    SS "T" Motorized Division
    18th Motorized Division
II Army Corps
    12th Infantry Division
    32d Infantry Division
    123d Infantry Division
Army group reserves
    8th Panzer Division
    81st Infantry Division

1 January 1943

ARMY GROUP NORTH: ColG Georg von Kuechler

Eighteenth Army: General of Cavalry Georg Lindemann
    L Army Corps
        225th Infantry Division
        9th *Luftwaffe* Field Division
        215th Infantry Division
        2d SS Infantry Division
    LIV Army Corps
        250th Spanish Infantry Division
        2d SS Police Infantry Brigade
        5th Mountain Division
    XXVI Army Corps
        170th Infantry Division
        227th Infantry Division
        1st Infantry Division
        223d Infantry Division
    I Army Corps
        69th Infantry Division
        132d Infantry Division
        61st Infantry Division
        11th Infantry Division
        217th Infantry Division
        21st Infantry Division
    XXVIII Army Corps
        24th Infantry Division
        121st Infantry Division
        28th Jager Division
    XXXVIII Army Corps
        254th Infantry Division
        212th Infantry Division
        1st *Luftwaffe* Field Division

10th *Luftwaffe* Field Division
96th Infantry Division
285th Security Division
Sixteenth Army: ColG Ernst Busch
    X Army Corps
      18th Motorized Division
      5th Jager Division
      21st *Luftwaffe* Field Division
    Group Hohne
      8th Jager Division
      290th Infantry Division
      225th Infantry Division
      126th Infantry Division
    II Army Corps
      122d Infantry Division
      30th Infantry Division
      329th Infantry Division
      32d Infantry Division
      12th Infantry Division
      123d Infantry Division
    Group Tiemann
      218th Infantry Division
      93d Infantry Division

1 January 1944

ARMY GROUP NORTH: ColG Georg von Kuechler

Eighteenth Army: General of Cavalry Georg Lindemann
    III SS Panzer Corps
      IR, SS Police Infantry Division
      SS "Nordland" Panzer Grenadier Division
      10th *Luftwaffe* Field Division
      9th *Luftwaffe* Field Division
    L Army Corps
      126th Infantry Division
      170th Infantry Division
      215th Infantry Division
    LIV Army Corps
      11th Infantry Division
      24th Infantry Division
      225th Infantry Division
    XXVI Army Corps
      61st Infantry Division
      227th Infantry Division
      254th Infantry Division
      212th Infantry Division

XXVIII Army Corps
  Spanish Legion
  121st Infantry Division
  2d *Luftwaffe* Field Division
  96th Infantry Division
  21st Infantry Division
  13th *Luftwaffe* Field Division
XXXVIII Army Corps
  2d Latvian SS Brigade
  28th Jager Division
  1st *Luftwaffe* Field Division
Sixteenth Army
  X Army Corps
    30th Infantry Division
    8th Jager Division
    21st *Luftwaffe* Field Division
  II Army Corps
    218th Infantry Division
    93d Infantry Division
    331st Infantry Division
  XXXXIII and VI SS Army Corps
    205th Infantry Division
    15th Latvian SS Brigade
    83d Infantry Division
    263d Infantry Division
    69th Infantry Division
  I Army Corps
    58th Infantry Division
    122d Infantry Division
    290th Infantry Division
    23d Infantry Division
  VIII Army Corps
    329th Infantry Division
    81st Infantry Division
    Group Jackeln
    Group Wagner (132d ID)

Sources: Schematische Kriegsgliederung, Stand: B-Tag 1941 (22.6), "Barbarossa" (original), "Lagenkarten 8.7.41–1.8.41," *Heeresgruppe Nord* (original maps), and "Der Feldzug gegen die Sowjet-Union der Heeresgruppe Nord, Kriegsjahr 1942, 1943, and 1944," *H. Gr. Nord,* all in National Archives microfilm (NAM) series T-311.

A Rough Comparison of
Red Army and *Wehrmacht* Forces

Red Army	*Wehrmacht*
Front	Army Group
1941 June: 4–6 armies, 1–3 mechanized/ cavalry corps	1941 2–3 armies, 1–3 panzer groups
December: 4–6 armies, 1 cavalry corps	
1942 3–6 armies, 1 tank army, 1–2 tank, mechanized, or cavalry corps	1942 2–3 armies, 1–2 panzer armies
1943 3–6 armies, 1–2 tank armies, 1 air army, 3–5 tank, mechanized, or cavalry corps, 1–2 artillery divisions	1943 2–3 armies, 1–2 panzer armies
1944–1945 6–7 armies, 1–3 tank armies, 1 air army, 1–3 tank, mechanized, or cavalry corps, 1 artillery penetration division	1944–1945 2–3 armies, 1–2 panzer armies
Armies	Armies (panzer groups)
1941 June: Rifle—2–3 rifle corps (6–15 rifle divisions), 1 mechanized or cavalry corps (60–80,000 men, 400–700 tanks)	1941 Field army—2–4 army corps Panzer group—2–3 motorized corps, 1–2 army corps
December: Rifle—5–6 rifle divisions or brigades, 1–2 cavalry divisions, 1–2 tank brigades or battalions (70,000 men, 20–90 tanks)	
1942 Rifle—6–10 rifle divisions or brigades, 2–4 tank brigades, 1–2 tank corps (80–100,000 men, 250– 450 tanks)	1942 Field army—3–4 army corps, 1–2 motorized corps Panzer army—2–3 motorized corps, 1–2 army corps
Tank—2–3 tank corps, 1 cavalry corps, 1–3 rifle or cavalry divisions, 1 tank brigade (35,000 men, 350– 500 tanks)	
Air—4–12 fighter, bomber, assault, or mixed aviation divisions	

Red Army	*Wehrmacht*
Armies	**Armies (panzer groups)**
1943 Rifle—rifle corps (7–12 rifle divisions), 3–4 tank or self-propelled artillery brigades, 1–2 tank, mechanized, or cavalry corps (80–130,000 men, 250–450 tanks)	1943 Field army—3–6 army or panzer corps (corps groups)
	Panzer army—3–5 panzer or army corps
Tank—2 tank corps, 1 mechanized corps (46,000 men, 450–560 tanks)	
Air—2–3 fighter aviation divisions, 1–2 bomber aviation divisions, 1 assault aviation division (700–1,000 aircraft)	
1944–1945 Rifle—3 rifle corps (7–12 rifle divisions), 1–3 artillery brigades, 2–3 tank or self-propelled artillery regiments, 1 tank, mechanized, or cavalry corps (80,000–120,000 men, 300–460 tanks)	1944–1945 Field army—4–6 army or panzer corps (corps groups)
	Panzer army—3–6 panzer or army corps (corps groups)
Tank—2 tank corps, 1 mechanized corps (48,000–50,000 men, 450–700 tanks)	
Air—1–5 fighter, bomber, or assault aviation corps or 2–5 aviation divisions	
Corps	**Corps**
1941 June:	1941 Army—1–5 infantry divisions
Rifle—2 rifle divisions (50,000 men)	Motorized—2 panzer divisions, 1 motorized division, 1–2 infantry divisions
Mechanized—2 tank and 1 motorized division (36,080 men, 1,031 tanks)	
Cavalry—2 cavalry divisions (19,430 men, 128 tanks)	
December:	
Rifle—none	
Mechanized—none	
Cavalry—2 cavalry divisions, 1 light cavalry division (12,000 men)	
1942 Rifle—2–3 rifle divisions (25,000–37,000 men)	1942 Army—3–5 infantry divisions, 1 panzer or motorized division
Tank—3 tank brigades, 1 motorized rifle brigade (7,800 men, 168 tanks)	Motorized—1–2 panzer divisions, 1–2 motorized divisions, 1–2 infantry divisions
Cavalry—3 cavalry divisions (14,000 men)	1943 Army—3–5 infantry divisions,

Red Army	Wehrmacht

Corps

1943 Rifle—3 rifle divisions (37,000 men)

Tank—3 tank brigades, 1 motorized rifle brigade, 1 self-propelled artillery regiment (10,977 men, 220 tanks)

Mechanized—3 mechanized brigades, 1 tank brigade, 1 self-propelled artillery regiment (15,018 men, 229 tanks)

Cavalry—3 cavalry divisions, 1 self-propelled artillery regiment (21,000 men, 129 tanks)

1944–1945 Rifle—3 rifle divisions, 1 artillery brigade, 1 self-propelled artillery regiment (20,000–30,000 men, 21 tanks)

Tank—3 tank brigades, 1 motorized rifle brigade, 3 self-propelled artillery regiments (12,010 men, 270 tanks)

Mechanized—3 mechanized brigades, 1 tank brigade, 3 self-propelled artillery regiments (16,442 men, 246 tanks)

Cavalry—3 cavalry divisions, 1–2 self-propelled artillery regiments (22,000 men, 150 tanks)

Divisions

1941 June:

Rifle—3 rifle regiments, 2 artillery regiments, 1 tank battalion (14,483 men, 16 tanks)

Tank—2 tank regiments, 1 motorized rifle regiment (10,940 men, 375 tanks)

Motorized—3 motorized rifle regiments (10,000 men)

Cavalry—4 cavalry regiments, 1 tank regiment (9,240 men, 64 tanks)

December:

Rifle—3 rifle regiments, 1 artillery regiment (11,626 men)

Cavalry—3 cavalry regiments (light or regular) (3,447–4,200 men)

Corps

1 panzer or panzer grenadier division

Panzer—2–3 panzer or panzer grenadier divisions, 1–2 infantry divisions

1944–1945 Army—3–6 infantry, panzer, or panzer grenadier divisions

Panzer—3–6 panzer, panzer grenadier, or infantry divisions

Divisions

1941 Infantry—3 infantry regiments (9 infantry battalions) (17,000 men)

Mountain—3 infantry regiments (13,000 men)

Jager—2 infantry regiments (13,000 men)

Panzer—1 panzer regiment (2–3 panzer battalions), 2 motorized infantry regiments (5 motorized infantry battalions, 4 truck- and 1 motorcycle-mounted) (14,000 men, 150–202 tanks)

Motorized—2 motorized infantry regiments (6 motorized infantry battalions), 1 panzer battalion (16,000 men, 30–50 tanks)

Waffen SS Infantry—3 infantry regiments (6 infantry battalions) (14,000 men)

Security—2 security regiments (10,000 men)

1942 Infantry—3 infantry regiments

Red Army	*Wehrmacht*
Divisions	**Divisions**
1942 Rifle—3 rifle regiments, 1 artillery regiment (10,386 men)	(6–9 infantry battalions (15,500–17,000 men)
Cavalry—3 cavalry regiments (4,619 men)	Jager—2 infantry regiments (13,000 men)
Destroyer—2 destroyer brigades (4,000 men)	Panzer—1 panzer regiment (2–3 panzer battalions), 2 motorized infantry regiments (5 motorized infantry battalions, 4 truck- and 1 motorcycle-mounted) (14,000 men, 150–202 tanks)
Fortified region—4–6 machine gun–artillery battalions (4,100 men)	Motorized—2 motorized infantry regiments (6 motorized infantry battalions), 1 panzer battalion (16,000 men, 30–50 tanks)
	Waffen SS Infantry—3 infantry regiments (6 infantry battalions) (14,000 men)
	Waffen SS Motorized—same as motorized division (15,000)
	Luftwaffe field—2–3 infantry regiments (4–6 battalions) (10,000–12,500 men)
	Security—2 security regiments (10,000 men)
	1943–1945 Infantry—2–3 infantry regiments (6 infantry battalions) (10,000–12,500 men)
1943 Rifle—3 rifle regiments, 1 artillery regiment (9,380 men)	Jager—2 infantry regiments (13,000 men)
Cavalry—3 cavalry regiments, 1 tank regiment (6,000 men, 39 tanks)	Panzer—1 panzer regiment (2–3 panzer battalions), 2 motorized infantry regiments (5 motorized infantry battalions, 4 truck- and 1 motorcycle-mounted) (13,000–17,000 men, 100–130 tanks)
Destroyer—2 destroyer brigades (4,000 men)	
Fortified Region—4–6 machine-gun artillery battalions (4,100 men)	Panzer grenadier—2 motorized infantry regiments (6 motorized infantry battalions), 1 panzer battalion (16,000 men, 3–50 tanks)
1944–1945 Rifle—3 rifle regiments, 1 artillery regiment (9,380 men) Cavalry—3 cavalry regiments, 1 tank regiment (6,000 men, 39 tanks)	*Waffen* SS Panzer—same as panzer (17,000 men, 200–250 tanks)
Fortified Region—4–6 machine-gun artillery battalions (4,100 men)	*Luftwaffe* field—2–3 infantry regiments (4–6 battalions) (10,000–12,500 men)
	Security—2 security regiments (10,000 men)

Red Army	*Wehrmacht*

Brigades
  1941 June:
   Rifle—3 rifle battalions (4,500 men)

  1941 December:
   Rifle—3 rifle battalions (4,480 men)

   Naval rifle—3 battalions (4,334 men)

   Naval infantry—4–6 infantry
   battalions (4,480–6,000 men)

   Tank—2 tank battalions,
   1 motorized rifle battalion (1,471
   men, 46 tanks)

   Ski—3 ski battalions (3,800 men)

  1942 Rifle—4 rifle battalions (5,125 men)

   Naval rifle (infantry)—4 rifle
   battalions (5,125 men)

   Tank—2 tank battalions,
   1 motorized rifle battalion (1,038
   men, 53 tanks)

   Motorized rifle—3 motorized rifle
   battalions (3,151 men)

   Ski—3 ski battalions (3,800 men)

   Destroyer—1 artillery antitank
   regiment, 2 antitank rifle
   battalions, 1 mortar battalion,
   1 engineer-mine battalion, 1 tank
   battalion (1,791 men, 32 tanks)

  1943 Rifle—4 rifle battalions (5,125 men)

   Naval rifle—4 rifle battalions
   (5,125 men)

   Tank—3 tank battalions,
   1 motorized rifle battalion (1,354
   men, 65 tanks)

   Mechanized—3 motorized rifle
   battalions, 1 tank regiment (3,558
   men, 39 tanks)

   Motorized rifle—3 motorized rifle
   battalions (3,500 men)

   Ski—3 ski battalions (3,800 men)

  1944–1945 Rifle—4 rifle battalions
   (5,125 men)

   Tank—3 tank battalions,
   1 motorized rifle battalion (1,354
   men, 65 tanks)

   Mechanized—3 motorized rifle
   battalions, 1 tank regiment (3,354
   men, 39 tanks)

   Motorized rifle—3 motorized rifle
   battalions (3,500 men)

Red Army	*Wehrmacht*

Separate Regiments and Battalions
    1941–1945 Aerosleigh battalion—
                3 aerosleigh companies (100 men,
                45 aerosleighs)

                Tank battalion—4 tank companies
                (189 men, 36 tanks)

                Tank regiment—4 tank companies
                (572 men, 39 tanks)

                Tank penetration regiment
                (Hvy)—4 tank companies (215
                men, 21 tanks)

                Tank engineer regiments— 4 tank
                companies (374 men, 21 tanks)

                Machine gun–artillery—4 machine
                gun companies (667 men in 1942,
                669 men in 1943)

                Armored train battalion—1 armored
                train

NKVD Forces
    1941–1945 NKVD rifle (motorized rifle)
                division—3–5 regiments, 1–2
                battalions (8,000–14,000 men)

                NKVD rifle brigade—4–8 rifle
                battalion (4,500 men)

                NKVD regiment—3 rifle battalions
                (1,651 men)

Note: As of 22 June 1941, December 1941, July 1942, July 1943, and December 1944.

Soviet Military Casualties

Losses in Specific Operations

	Initial Strength	LOSSES		
		KIA, MIA, Captured	WIA, Sick	Total
Leningrad Strategic Defensive Operation, 10 July–30 September 1941				
Northern Front (10.7–23.8.41)	153,000	40,391	15,044	55,535
Northwestern Front (10.7–30.9.41)	272,000	96,953	47,835	144,788
Leningrad Front (23.8–30.9.41)	—	65,529	50,787	116,316
52d Separate Army (1.9–30.9.41)	—	1,721	2,389	4,110
Baltic Fleet (entire period)	92,000	9,384	14,793	24,177
Total	517,000	214,078	130,848	344,926
Staraia Russa Offensive Operation, 12–23 August 1941				
Northern Front (48th Army)	ca 100,000	—	—	ca 33,000
Northwestern Front (11th, 27th, 34th Armies)	327,099	—	—	128,550
Total	427,099	—	—	158,550
Siniavino Offensive Operation, 10 September–28 October 1941				
54th Army (Leningrad Front, 26.9), Neva Operational Group	71,270	22,211	32,768	54,979
Tikhvin Defensive Operation, 16 October–18 November 1941				
54th Army (Leningrad Front), 4th and 52d Separate Armies	135,700	22,743	17,846	40,589
Tikhvin Strategic Offensive Operation, 10 November–30 December 1941				
54th Army (Leningrad Front)	55,600	6,065	11,486	17,551
4th Separate Army	62,700	8,916	16,018	24,934
52d Separate Army	42,660	871	1,769	2,640
Novgorod Operational Group	31,900	2,072	1,704	3,776
Total	192,950	17,924	30,977	48,901
Liuban' Offensive Operation, 7 January–30 April 1942				
Volkhov Front, 54th Army (Leningrad Front)	325,700	95,064	213,303	308,367

		LOSSES		
	Initial Strength	KIA, MIA, Captured	WIA, Sick	Total
2d Shock Army Escape from Encirclement, 13 May–10 July 1942				
2d Shock, 52d, 59th Armies	231,900	54,774	39,977	94,751
Siniavino Offensive Operation, 19 August–20 October 1942				
Leningrad Front (Neva Operational Group, 67th Army, 13th Air Army), Volkhov Front (2d Shock, 8th Army, 14th Air Army), Baltic Fleet, Ladoga Flotilla	190,000	40,085	73,589	113,674
Operation to Penetrate the Leningrad Blockade (Spark), 12–30 January 1943				
Leningrad Front (67th Army, 13th Air Army)	133,300	12,320	28,944	41,264
Volkhov Front (2d Shock Army, 8th Army, 14th Air Army)	169,500	21,620	52,198	73,818
Total	302,800	33,940	81,142	115,082
Demiansk Offensive Operation (Polar Star), 15–28 February 1943				
Northwestern Front	327,600	10,016	23,647	33,663
Staraia Russa Offensive Operation, 4–19 February 1943				
Northwestern Front	401,190	31,789	71,319	103,108
Mga-Siniavino Offensive Operation, 22 June-22 August 1943				
Leningrad Front (67th Army, 13th Air Army), Volkhov Front (8th Army, 14th Air Army)	253,300	20,890	59,047	79,937
Leningrad-Novgorod Strategic Offensive Operation, 14 January–1 March 1944				
Leningrad Front (minus 23d Army)	417,600	56,564	170,876	227,440
Volkhov Front	260,000	12,011	38,289	50,300
1st Shock Army (2d Baltic Front) (14.1–10.2.44)	54,900	1,283	3,759	5,042
2d Baltic Front (10.2–1.3.44)	—	6,659	23,051	29,710
Baltic Fleet	86,600	169	1,292	1,461
Total	822,100	76,686	237,267	313,953
Vyborg-Petrozavodsk Strategic Offensive Operation, 10 June–9 August 1944				
Karelian Front (7th, 32d Armies, 7th Air Army) (21.6–9.8.44)	202,300	16,9241	46,679	63,603
Leningrad Front (21st, 23d Armies, 13th Air Army)	188,800	46,679	24,011	30,029
Baltic Fleet, Ladoga and Onega Flotillas	60,400	732	2,011	2,743
Total	451,500	23,674	72,701	96,375
Narva Offensive Operation, 24–30 July 1944				
Leningrad Front (2d Shock, 8th Armies, 13th Air Army)	136,830	4,685	18,602	23,287

Sources: G. F. Krivosheev, ed., *Grif sekretnosti sniat: Poteri Vooruzhennykh Sil SSSR v voinakh, boevykh deistviiakh i boevykh konfliktakh, Statisticheskoe issledovanie* [The secret classification has been removed: The losses of the Soviet Armed Forces in wars, combat operations, and military conflicts, a statistical study] (Moscow: Voenizdat, 1993); and V. V. Gurkin, "Liudskie poteri Sovetskikh Vooruzhennykh sil v 1941–1945: Novye aspekty" [Personnel losses of the Soviet Armed Forces 1941–1945: New aspects], *Voenno-istoricheskii zhurnal* [Military-historical journal], no. 2 (March–April 1999): 2–13.

Summary of Military Personnel Losses by *Front* and Period

	KIA	MIA and POW	Other Dead	Subtotal	WIA	Sick	Frostbite	Subtotal	Total
Northern Front (64 days)									
1941	22,334	61,537	1,588	85,459	60,271	2,634	—	62,905	148,364
Leningrad Front (1,353 days)									
1941	62,187	74,280	8,284	144,751	165,305	17,712	1,762	184,799	329,530
1942	62,747	14,560	6,371	83,678	153,661	80,184	1,861	235,706	319,384
1943	74,473	9,841	4,431	88,745	213,602	88,263	184	302,049	390,794
1944	128,999	12,231	3,872	145,102	406,153	114,094	478	520,725	665,827
1945	3,653	230	1,306	5,249	11,040	33,073	1	44,114	49,363
Total	332,059	111,142	24,324	467,525	949,761	333,326	4,286	1,287,373	1,754,898
Volkhov Front (746 days)									
1941	199	—	—	199	1,307	—	542	1,849	2,048
1942	117,237	82,337	8,935	208,509	326,477	53,081	4,034	383,592	592,101
1943	69,794	6,520	1,590	77,904	189,587	53,766	147	243,500	321,404
1944	11,479	466	66	12,011	33,343	4,939	11	38,293	50,304
Total	198,709	89,323	10,591	298,623	550,714	111,786	4,734	667,234	965,857
Northwestern Front (882 days)									
1941	31,511	142,190	8,563	182,264	83,816	3,741	266	87,823	270,087
1942	133,573	41,720	8,970	184,263	319,111	53,878	1,856	374,845	559,108
1943	77,763	8,531	8,531	88,798	188,234	58,230	189	246,653	335,451
Total	242,847	192,441	20,037	455,325	591,161	115,849	2,311	709,321	1,164,646

Summary of Military Personnel Losses by *Front* and Period, *continued*

	KIA	MIA and POW	Other Dead	Subtotal	WIA	Sick	Frostbite	Subtotal	Total
Baltic Front and 2d Baltic Front (539 days)									
1943	22,133	1,631	553	24,317	62,428	18,814	35	81,277	105,594
1944	110,710	7,831	2,823	121,364	91,302	91,302	208	445,794	567,158
1945	34,396	3,656	1,527	39,579	116,847	35,190	60	152,097	191,676
Total	167,239	13,118	4,903	185,260	533,559	145,306	303	679,168	864,428
4th Separate Army (80 days)									
1941	10,946	5,390	1,407	17,743	24,468	1,117	803	26,388	44,131
52d Separate Army (81 days)									
1941	3,557	9,638	564	13,759	7,435	489	111	8,035	21,794
Baltic Fleet (1,418 days)									
1941–1945	19,836	32,709	3,345	55,890	25,509	10,193	—	35,702	91,592

Source: G. F. Krivosheev, ed., *Grif sekretnosti sniat: Poteri Vooruzhennykh Sil SSSR v voinakh, boevykh deistviiakh i boevykh konfliktakh, Statisticheskoe issledovanie* [The secret classification has been removed: The losses of the Soviet Armed Forces in wars, combat operations, and military conflicts, a statistical study] (Moscow: Voenizdat, 1993), 233–234, 247–248, 253–254, 273–274, 289–290, 301.

Estimated Civilian Losses in the Siege of Leningrad

Date of Estimate	Estimated Losses	Source
Summer 1943	642,000	Extraordinary Commission to Investigate Nazi Crimes
1945	642,000	Nuremberg Trials
1952	632,253	V. M. Koval'chuk and G. P. Sobolev, "Leningradskii rekviem" [Leningrad requiem], *Voprosy istorii*, no. 12 (December 1965). Based on prewar population of 2.5 million and December 1943 population of 600,000 with 1 million evacuees and 100,000 conscripted into the Red Army.
1965	>800,000	
2000	641,000	(in the siege proper)
	1,000,000	(in the siege and during the evacuation) *Russian Military Encyclopedia*

1. The City of Peter and Lenin

1. For more details on the city's early history, see S. F. Platonov, *History of Russia,* trans. E. Aronsberg, ed. F. A. Golder (New York: Macmillan, 1929), 222; R. D. Charques, *A Short History of Russia* (New York: Dutton, 1956), 110–111; Bernard Pares, *A History of Russia* (New York: Knopf, 1960), 202–203; and L. Jay Oliva, *Russia in the Era of Peter the Great* (Englewood Cliffs, N.J.: Prentice-Hall, 1969), 153–155, and a host of more recent English- and Russian-language works.

2. "Leningrad," in N. V. Ogarkov, ed., *Sovetskaia voennaia entsiklopediia* [Soviet military encyclopedia], vol. 4 (Moscow: Voenizdat, 1977), 611. Hereafter cited as SVE.

3. See Sergei Pushkarev, *The Emergence of Modern Russia 1801–1917,* trans. Robert H. Neil and Tovas Yedlin (New York: Holt, Rinehart and Winston, 1963), 46, 227.

4. Charques, *A Short History of Russia,* 116.

5. Pushkarev, *The Emergence of Modern Russia,* 46, 227.

6. Ibid., 62–73.

7. The twin dates represent the old style calendar (without parentheses), which prevailed prior to the 1917 revolution, and the new style calendar (within parentheses), which the Bolshevik government adopted after the revolution. All subsequent dates accord with the new calendar.

8. See, for example, *Petrograd v dni Velikogo Oktiabria* [Petrograd during the Great October (Revolution)] (Leningrad: Lenizdat, 1967).

9. V. V. Brimov, *Rozhdenie Krasnoi Armii* [The birth of the Red Army] (Moscow: Voenizdat, 1961); and N. M. Iakupov, *Bor'ba za armiiu v 1917 godu* [The struggle for the army in 1917] (Moscow: 'Mysl', 1975).

10. Among many works on the Civil War, see N. N. Azovtsev, ed., *Grazhdanskaia voina v SSSR v dvukh tomakh* [The Civil War in the USSR in two volumes] (Moscow: Voenizdat, 1980); G. V. Kuz'min, *Razgrom interventov i belogvardeitsev v 1917–1922 gg.* [The defeat of the interventionists and White Guards in 1917–1922] (Moscow: Voenizdat, 1977); M. I. Svetachev, *Imperialisticheskaia interventsiia v Sibiri i na Dal'nem vostoke (1918–1922 gg.)* [The imperialist intervention in Siberia and the Far East (1918–1922)] (Novosibirsk: Nauka, 1983); and I. I. Denikin, *Pokhod na Moskvu* [The march on Moscow] (Moscow: Voenizdat, 1989).

11. See Robert Conquest, *The Great Terror: Stalin's Purge of the Thirties* (New York: Macmillan, 1968). Numerous other English- and Russian-language works now confirm the contents of Conquest's seminal work.

12. For further details, see A. I. Gribkov, ed., *Istoriia ordena Lenina Leningrad-skogo voennogo okruga* [A history of the Order of Lenin Leningrad Military District] (Moscow: Voenizdat, 1974), 168–183.

13. "Leningradskii voennyi okrug," in *SVE*, 4: 614–616; and "Leningradskii voennyi okrug," in I. D. Sergeev, ed., *Voennaia entsiklopediia v vos'mi tomakh* [Military encyclopedia in eight volumes], vol. 4 (Moscow: Voenizdat, 1999), 422–424, hereafter cited as *VE*.

14. The most thorough source on the Russo-Finnish War is Carl van Dyke, *The Soviet Invasion of Finland 1939–1940* (London: Frank Cass, 1997).

15. During the mid-1930s, Popov had also served as chief of staff of a mechanized brigade and the 5th Mechanized Corps.

16. See *Boevoi i chislennyi sostav vooruzhennykh sil SSSR v period Velikoi Otechestvennoi voiny (1941–1945 gg.): Statisticheskii sbornik no. 1 (22 iiunia 1941 g.)* [The combat and numerical composition of the USSR's Armed Forces in the Great Patriotic War (1941–1945): Statistical collection no. 1 (22 June 1941)] (Moscow: Institute of Military History, 1994). Hereafter cited as *BICS*.

17. Subsequently, the NKO reorganized the 2d PVO Corps into the Leningrad PVO Corps Region in November 1942 to improve command and control. Later still, it supplemented the Leningrad Corps Region with the Ladoga PVO Brigade Region and transformed it into the Leningrad PVO Army, commanded by Major General of the Coastal Service G. S. Zashikhin, in January 1942.

18. V. P. Ivanov, "Baltiiskii flot," in *VE*, 1: 361.

19. N. Iu. Berezovsky, "Kronshtadt" in *VE*, 4: 305.

20. "Hanko [Hango]," in *SVE*, 8: 355–356.

21. "Ladozhskaia voennaia flotiliia [The Ladoga Military Flotilla]," in *VE*, 4: 379–380.

22. Subsequently, the NKO reorganized the LMD's headquarters into the Northern Front on 24 June 1941, and, in turn, subdivided the Northern Front into the Karelian and Leningrad Fronts on 23 August 1941. The Northern and Leningrad Fronts continued to fulfill the responsibilities of the district military headquarters. The NKO reformed the Leningrad Military District on 15 July 1941 as the Northern Front's rear service organ, and the General Staff subordinated the new military district to the Northern Front on 25 July 1941. The NKO finally disbanded the LMD on 21 August 1941, to fill out the Leningrad Front's headquarters.

23. Iu. A. Gor'kov and Iu. N. Semin, "Konets global'noi lzhi: Na sovetskom severo-zapade—Operativnye plany zapadnykh prigranichnykh okrugov 1941 goda svidetel'-stvuiut: SSSR ne gotovilsia k napadeniiu na Germaniiu [The end of the global lie: In the Soviet northwest—The operational plans of the western border districts in 1941 bear witness that the USSR was not prepared for an attack on Germany], *Voenno-istoricheskii zhurnal* [Military-historical journal], 6 (November–December 1996): 2. Hereafter cited as *VIZh*.

24. For details on the General Staff planning process, see David M. Glantz, *Stumbling Colossus: The Red Army on the Eve of World War* (Lawrence: The University Press of Kansas, 1998), 90–101; *Nachal'nyi period Velikoi Otechestvennoi voiny* [The initial period of the Great Patriotic War] (Moscow: Voroshilov Academy of the General Staff, 1989); and M. V. Zakharov, *General'nyi shtab v predvoennye gody* [The General Staff in the prewar years] (Moscow: Voenizdat, 1989), 230–273.

25. "Konets global'noi lzhi," 3–4.

26. The Leningrad Military District's organization for battle on 25 May is contained in "Konets global'noi lzhi," 3–7, and its organization on 22 June in *Boevoi sostav Sovetskoi armii, chast' I* (iiun'–dekabr' 1941 goda) [The combat composition of the Soviet Army, part 1 (June–December 1941)] (Moscow: Voroshilov Academy of the General Staff, 1963), 7. Prepared by the General Staff's Military-Scientific Directorate and classified secret. Hereafter cited as *Boevoi sostav, chast' 1*.

27. In Soviet generic parlance, the term "formation" *(formirovanie)* is used to designate corps and divisions, "unit" *(chast')* means brigades and regiments, and "subunit" *(podrazdelenie)* means forces of battalion size or below. Above this level, the term *"soedinenie"* means a large formation or combination, that is, armies and *fronts*.

28. For a detailed description of the state of the Red Army in June 1941, see Glantz, *Stumbling Colossus*.

29. The tank division consisted of two tank regiments, one motorized infantry regiment, and reconnaissance, antitank, antiaircraft, engineer, and signal battalions. For details on the structure of the Red Army's mechanized forces, see O. A. Losik, ed., *Stroitel'stvo i boevoe primenenie sovetskikh tankovykh voisk v gody Velikoi Otechestvennoi voiny* [The formation and combat use of Soviet tank forces during the Great Patriotic War] (Moscow: Voenizdat, 1979); and, in English, David M. Glantz, *Soviet Military Operational Art: In Pursuit of Deep Battle* (London: Frank Cass, 1991), 74–121.

30. The actual strength of the mechanized corps varied widely. Some had considerable quantities of new weaponry. For example, the Baltic Front's 3d Mechanized Corps had 651 tanks, of which 110 were new KV-1 heavy and T-34 medium tanks. Other corps, especially those farther from the frontier, were much weaker. In the Western Front's 4th Army, for example, the 14th Mechanized Corps had only 518 aging T-26 light tanks instead of its authorized complement of 1,031 medium and heavy tanks. Draconian factory discipline could only do so much to make up for past neglect in weapons production. The Southwestern Front's 19th Mechanized Corps had only 453 of its authorized tanks, all but 11 of them obsolete models. Moreover, this corps was expected to use requisitioned civilian trucks for its wheeled transportation when the war actually began, the "motorized rifle" regiments in its two tank divisions had to march on foot 193 kilometers (120 miles) to battle, slowing the movement of the available tanks. As new equipment became available from the production lines, that equipment was distributed to select corps among those in the forward area. The paucity of new machines (1,861), however, was such that even full-strength mechanized corps included a hodgepodge of vehicles. All this complicated maintenance to an enormous extent. In addition, Soviet formations remained notoriously weak in radio communications and logistical support, making coordinated maneuver under the chaotic conditions of the surprise German invasion almost impossible. For details on Red Army strength on 22 June 1941, see *BICS*.

31. Most Soviet rifle divisions lacked the tank battalion, since all available tanks had been employed to fit out the new mechanized corps.

32. See *BICS*.

33. *BICS*, 11–17.

34. At least one designer was shot for "sabotage" when an experimental aircraft crashed, and many other engineers were put to work in prison design shops. To put it mildly, such sanctions did not encourage innovative design solutions.

35. On 12 April 1941, Timoshenko and Zhukov complained to Stalin that training accidents were destroying two or three aircraft each day and demanded the removal of several senior Air Force officers. For the best English coverage of the state of the Red Air Force in 1941, see Van Hardesty, *Red Phoenix: The Rise of Soviet Air Power, 1941–1945* (Washington, D.C.: Smithsonian Institution Press, 1982).

36. Throughout the disastrous summer of 1941, Soviet bombers stubbornly attacked at an altitude of 8,000 feet, too high to ensure accurate bombing but high enough for German fighters to locate and attack them. Despite the bravery of individual Soviet fighter pilots that repeatedly rammed German aircraft, their combat formations were too defensive to be effective against their dog-fighting opponents.

2. Target Leningrad

1. Gotthardt Heinrici, *The Campaign in Russia,* vol. 1 (Washington, D.C.: United States Army G-2, 1954), 85. Unpublished National Archives manuscript in German (unpublished translation by Joseph Welch).

2. Franz Halder, *The Halder War Diary 1939–1942,* ed. Charles Burdick and Hans-Adolf Jacobsen (Novato, Calif.: Presidio Press, 1988), 294.

3. The original Plan Marcks had called for a force of 147 divisions, including 24 panzer and 12 motorized divisions. The total force deployed for combat in the East included 138 divisions (104 infantry and 34 mobile) in the 3 forward army groups, 9 security divisions, 4 divisions in Finland, 2 divisions under OKH control, and a separate regiment and motorized training brigade. The most recent Soviet sources place German strength at 153 divisions and 3 brigades manned by 4.1 million men and equipped with 4,170 tanks, 40,500 guns and mortars, and 3,613 combat aircraft. See V. A. Zolotarev, ed., *Velikaia Otechestvennaia voina 1941–1945* [The Great Patriotic War 1941–1945], book 1 (Moscow: Nauka, 1998), 95; hereafter cited as VOV. See also, *Schematische Kriegsgliederung, Stand: B-Tag 1941 (22.6) "Barbarossa."* This document is the original German order of battle for Operation Barbarossa.

4. *Schematische Kriegsgliederung.* Army Group South's Eleventh Army controlled all forward-deployed Romanian forces, and the Romanian Third and Fourth Armies controlled the remaining Romanian forces.

5. "Dokumenty nemetskogo komandovaniia po voprosam podgotovki voiny" [Documents of the German command on issues in preparing for war], in *Sbornik voenno-istoricheskikh materialov Velikoi Otechestvennoi voiny* [Collection of military-historical materials of the Great Patriotic War], issue 18 (Moscow: Voenizdat, 1960), 236–238. Prepared by the Military-Historical Department of the General Staff's Military-Scientific Directorate and classified secret. Hereafter cited as *SVIMVOV.*

6. Earl F. Ziemke and Magna E. Bauer, *Moscow to Stalingrad: Decision in the East* (Washington, D.C.: Office of the Chief of Military History, United States Army, 1987), 15.

7. See *Schematische Kriegsgliederung.*

8. Ibid.

9. See Jonathan M. House, *Toward Combined Arms Warfare: A Survey of 20th Century Tactics, Doctrine, and Organization* (Fort Leavenworth, Kans.: Combat Studies Institute, 1984), 81–83, and 96–97; and F. W. von Senger und Etterlin, *Die Panzergrenadiere: Geschichte und Gestalt der mechanisierten infanterie 1930–1960* (Munich: J. F. Lehmanns, 1961), 72–77.

10. Timothy Wray, *Standing Fast: German Defensive Doctrine on the Russian Front during World War II: Prewar to March 1943* (Fort Leavenworth, Kans.: Combat Studies Institute, 1986), 1–21.

11. To avoid telegraphing German intentions, many of these aircraft had remained in the West, continuing the air attacks on Britain until a few weeks before the offensive.

12. Similarly, the May 1941 airborne invasion of Crete had devastated German parachute formations and air transport units; 146 Ju-52s had been shot down, and another 150 were seriously damaged. See Williamson Murray, *Luftwaffe* (Baltimore, Md.: Nautical and Aviation Publishing Co. of America, 1985), 79, 83.

13. For the best German assessment of the first six months of the war, see Klaus Reinhardt, *Moscow—The Turning Point: The Failure of Hitler's Military Strategy in the Winter of 1941–1942*, trans. Karl B. Keenan (Oxford: Berg, 1992), 26–28.

14. See *Boevoi i chislennyi sostav*, 16–17.

15. V. A. Zolotarev, ed., *Velikaia Otechestvennaia voina 1941–1945, kniga 1: Surovye ispytaniia* [The Great Patriotic War 1941–1945, book 1: A harsh education] (Moscow: Nauka, 1998), 148.

16. Ibid., 149.

17. The 12th Mechanized Corps also lost 11,832 of its 28,832 men during the first two weeks of combat. See Glantz, *Stumbling Colossus*, 156. See this book for the combat state of all Red Army forces on 22 June. For a detailed description of the fighting, see Zolotarev, *VOV*, 150–151; and "Boevye dokumenty po oboronitel'noi operatsii v Litve i Latvii, provodivsheisia s 22 iiunia po 9 iiulia 1941 g. voiskami Severo-zapadnogo fronta" [Combat documents on the defensive operation in Lithuania and Latvia conducted from 22 June through 9 July by Northwestern Front troops], in *Sbornik boevykh dokumentov Velikoi Otechestvennoi voiny* [Collection of combat documents of the Great Patriotic War], issue 34 (Moscow: Voenizdat, 1958). Prepared by the Directorate for the Exploitation of War Experience of the General Staff's Military-Scientific Directorate and classified secret; hereafter cited as *SBDVOV*. The 11th Mechanized Corps' 23d and 28th Tank Divisions were commanded by Colonels T. S. Orlenko and I. D. Cherniakhovsky, respectively. The latter later rose to command armies and a full *front*.

18. For a full description of this heated action, see Charles V. P. von Luttichau, *The Road to Moscow: The Campaign in Russia*, Unpublished Center for Military History Project 26-P (Washington D.C.: Office of the Chief of Military History, 1985).

19. Glantz, *Stumbling Colossus*, 126.

20. Zolotarev, *VOV*, 153.

21. Ibid.

22. For the appropriate orders, see V. A. Zolotarev, ed., "Stavka VGK: Dokumenty i materialy 1941 god" [*Stavka* VGK: Documents and materials 1941], in *Russkii arkhiv:*

Velikaia Otechestvennaia [voina] [The Great Patriotic (War)], vol. 16 (5-1) (Moscow: Terra, 1996).

23. Zolotarev, *VOV*, 154. According to G. F. Krivosheev, ed., *Grif sekretnosti sniat: Poteri vooruzhennykh sil SSSR v voinakh, boevykh deistviiakh i voennykh konfliktakh* [The secret classification has been removed: The losses of the Soviet Armed Forces in wars, military operations, and military conflicts] (Moscow: Voenizdat, 1993), 162. During the period from 22 June through 9 July 1941, the Northwestern Front lost 88,486 men (75,202 killed, captured, or missing) and 13,284 men wounded or sick out of its initial force of 498,000 men.

24. John Erickson, *The Road to Stalingrad* (New York: Harper & Row, 1975), 144–147.

25. Harrison E. Salisbury, *The 900 Days: The Siege of Leningrad* (New York: Harper & Row, 1969), 174.

26. For details on Leeb's mission and his army group's subsequent action during this period, see Luttichau, *The Road to Moscow*, ch. 28.

27. S. P. Platonov, ed., *Bitva za Leningrad 1941–1944* [The Battle for Leningrad 1941–1945] (Moscow: Voenizdat, 1964), 27–30, and Zolotarev, *VOV*, 154.

28. Zolotarev, "*Stavka* VGK 1941," 47.

29. Ibid., 70.

30. Platonov, *Bitva za Leningrad*, 28.

31. Erickson, *The Road to Stalingrad*, 144.

32. Platonov, *Bitva za Leningrad*, 29–30. For details on the raising and employment of people's militia forces, see A. D. Kolesnik, *Opolchenskie formirovaniia Rossiiskoi Federatsii v gody Velikoi Otechestvennoi voiny* [Militia formations of the Russian Federation in the Great Patriotic War] (Moscow: Nauka, 1988).

33. Erickson, *The Road to Stalingrad*, 149.

34. Later, on 8 August, Stalin assumed the title of Supreme High Commander, and thereafter, the organ was known as the *Stavka* of the Supreme High Command (SVGK). For details on the *Stavka*'s creation and evolution, see V. D. Danilov, "Stavka VGK, 1941–1945," in *Zashchita Otechestva* [Defense of the Fatherland] 12 (December 1991); 1–39; V. D. Danilov, "Razvitie sistemy organov strategicheskogo rukovodstva v nachale Velikoi Otechestvennoi voiny" [The development of a system of organs of strategic leadership in the beginning of the Great Patriotic War], *VIZh* 6 (June 1987): 25–30; A. M. Mairov, "Strategicheskoe rukovodstvo v Velikoi Otechestvennoi voine" [Strategic leadership in the Great Patriotic War], *VIZh* 5 (May 1985): 28–40, M. Zakharov, "Strategicheskoe rukovodstvo Vooruzhennymi Silami" [The strategic leadership of the Armed Forces], *VIZh* 5 (May 1970): 23–34; and V. Kulakov, "Strategicheskoe rukovodstvo Vooruzhennymi Silami" [The strategic leadership of the Armed Forces], *VIZh* 6 (June 1975): 12–24.

35. Zolotarev, "*Stavka* VGK 1941," 62–63.

36. On 10 July, the LOG consisted of the 191st and 177th Rifle Divisions, the 1st and 2d DNOs, the 1st Separate Mountain Rifle Brigade, and the 41st Rifle Corps (the 111th, 90th, 235th, and 118th Rifle Divisions), the latter refitting east of Luga.

37. Gribkov, *Istoriia ordena Lenina Leningradskogo voennogo okruga*, 207; and Platonov, *Bitva za Leningrad*, 32.

38. Luttichau, *The Road to Moscow*, ch. 28, pp. 26, 32.

39. For additional details on Reinhardt's battle, see ibid., 25–33.

40. "Direktiva Stavka GK komanduiushchemu voiskami Severo-zapadnogo Fronta o perekhode k aktivnym boevym deistviiam" [*Stavka* of the High Command Directive to the Northwestern Front commander concerning the conduct of active military operations], in Zolotarev, "*Stavka* VGK 1941," 62.

41. Colonel L. V. Bunin commanded the 21st Tank Division. Major General M. M. Ivanov commanded the 16th Rifle Corps, and Major Generals A. E. Fediunin and D. F. Popov, the 70th and 237th Rifle Divisions, respectively.

42. Erich von Manstein, *Lost Victories* (Chicago: Henry Regnery, 1958), 194–195.

43. Luttichau, *The Road to Moscow,* ch. 28, p. 27.

44. See "Lagenkarten 8.7.41–1.8.41," *Heeresgruppe Nord* (original maps), which graphically show the details of the complex struggle around Sol'tsy and west of Kholm.

45. For details on the 8th Army's defense of Estonia and Tallin, see Luttichau, *The Road to Moscow,* ch. 28, pp. 40–42 and ch. 29, pp. 17–27; and Platonov, *Bitva za Leningrad,* 38–43.

46. The XXVI and XXXXII Army Corps consisted of the 61st, 254th, and 217th Infantry Divisions and Task Force Friedrich. Tallin was defended by Major General I. F. Nikolaev's 10th Rifle Corps and Baltic Fleet forces under the combined command of Vice Admiral V. F. Tributs, the Baltic Fleet commander, who took command on 17 August. The besieged force included the 10th and 11th Rifle Divisions, the 16th Lithuanian Rifle Division's 165th Rifle Regiment, the 22d NKVD Motorized Rifle Division, the 25th, 31st, 42d, 44th, 45th, 47th, and 91st Baltic Fleet Construction Battalions, the 1st Separate Armored Car Regiment, and Estonian and Latvian Workers Regiments. The force's strength totaled 27,000 men and 85 aircraft. The Germans penetrated to the city's outskirts from 20 to 27 August, and the *Stavka* ordered the city's garrison evacuated to Leningrad on 26 August. The Baltic Fleet evacuated the Soviet forces to Leningrad and Moon Island and the fleet ships to Kronshtadt. The evacuation, which took place between 28 and 30 August, involving 100 ships, 67 transports, and 20,500 men, escorted by the cruiser *Kirov* and the destroyers *Minsk* and *Leningrad,* was harrowing because of constant German air attacks. During the evacuation, German aircraft sank one transport with 6,500 wounded. The evacuation convoy, which extended 25 kilometers (15.5 miles), ran through German minefields, in addition to the constant air attacks. Thirty-eight ships were sunk and 10,000 lives lost. The XXXXII Army Corps claimed taking 11,432 prisoners, and the *Luftwaffe* claimed it destroyed 717 aircraft and the Navy 70 ships. Soviet sources admit to the loss of 53 out of 197 ships during the evacuation. After the fall of Tallin, the German 254th Infantry Division turned east toward Narva and the XXXXII Army Corps and 61st Infantry Division moved to attack the Baltic Islands.

47. Soviet forces defending the Moon Islands included the 2d Separate Rifle Brigade and Baltic Fleet coastal defense forces, equipped with 19 coastal batteries and 7 motorized artillery and antiaircraft batteries, totaling 15,000 men occupying Muhu (Moon), Saaremaa (Oesel), and Hiimaa (Dagoe) islands. Attacking German forces included the 61st and 217th Infantry Divisions, the latter against Hiimaa Island, and the former against first Moon and then Saaremaa Island. The operations included attacks against Vormsi Island (8–11 September), Moon Island (14–19 September),

Saaremaa Island (17 September–3 October), and Hiimaa Island (12–22 October). By German count, the operation bagged 15,388 Russian prisoners, and another 750 Russians escaped. Soviet sources claim 500 men escaped. The German force suffered 2,154 men lost during the operation. The 8th Separate Rifle Brigade defending Hango held out from 1 July to 2 December before the Baltic Fleet evacuated an estimated 22,000 defenders and other Soviet personnel to Leningrad.

48. The order transferring the 1st Tank Division southward from Kandalaska is found in Zolotarev, "*Stavka* VGK 1941," 70.

49. Platonov, *Bitva za Leningrad*, 49.

50. Ibid.

51. Ibid., 49–50.

52. Ibid., 51–52.

53. Zolotarev, "*Stavka* VGK 1941," 107–108. The 34th Army consisted of the 254th, 245th, 59th, 262d, and 257th Rifle Divisions, the 25th and 54th Cavalry Divisions, the 264th and 644th Corps Artillery Regiments, the 171st and 759th Antitank Artillery Regiments, and the 16th and 59th Armored Trains.

54. Platonov, *Bitva za Leningrad*, 50. See also "Sorok vos'maia armiia" [The 48th Army], in M. M. Kozlov, ed., *Velikaia Otechestvennaia voina 1941–1945: Entsiklopediia* [The Great Patriotic War 1941–1945: An encyclopedia] (Moscow: Sovetskaia Entsiklopediia, 1985), 672. Hereafter cited as *VOVE*.

3. The Defense of Leningrad

1. "Dokumenty nemetskogo komandovaniia po voprosam vedeniia voiny" [Documents of the German command on matters of conducting the war], in *Sbornik voenno-istoricheskikh materialov Velikoi Otechestvennoi voiny* [Collection of military-historical materials of the Great Patriotic War], issue 18 (Moscow: Voenizdat, 1960), 231–232. Prepared by the Military-historical Department of the General Staff's Military-Scientific Directorate and classified secret. Hereafter cited as *SVIMVOV*.

2. Ibid., 233–234.

3. Ibid., 236–237.

4. Luttichau, *The Road to Moscow*, ch. 29, p. 1, quoting an Army Group North *Feldzug* (campaign study).

5. Ibid., 1–3; and Platonov, *Bitva za Leningrad*, 47–48.

6. For exact German dispositions prior to and during Army Group North's offensive on Leningrad, see "Feindlagenkarten 19 July–1 Sep 1941," *Abtlg. Ic H. Gr. Nord, 75131/47 Box 103,* National Archives Microfilm (NAM) series T-311, roll 92.

7. "Direktiva Stavki VGK No. 00824 komanduiushchemu voiskami Severo-zapadnogo fronta, glavnokomanduiushchemu voiskami severo-zapadnogo napravleniia o provedenii operatsii v raion Solt'sy, Staraia Russa, Dno" [*Stavka* VGK directive no. 00824 to the Northwestern Front commander and the High Commander of Forces on the Northwestern Direction concerning the conduct of an operation in the Solt'sy, Staraia Russa, and Dno regions], in Zolotarev, "*Stavka* VGK 1941," 111–112.

8. Kachanov had replaced Pronin as 34th Army commander after the Sol'tsy counterstroke failed.

9. Platonov, *Bitva za Leningrad*, 58–59. See also David M. Glantz, *Forgotten Battles of the German-Soviet War (1941–1945), volume 1: The Summer–Fall Campaign (22 June–4 December 1941)* (Carlisle, Penn.: Self-published, 1999), 51–71.

10. Manstein, *Lost Victories*, 200–201.

11. For details, see ibid., 201; and Luttichau, *The Road to Moscow*, ch. 29, pp. 7–13.

12 "Direktiva Stavki VGK no. 00937 komanduiushchemu voiskami Severo-zapadnogo fronta ob uluchshenii upravleniia voiskami" [*Stavka* VGK directive no. 00937 to the Northwestern Front commander concerning the improvement of troop command and control], in Zolotarev, "*Stavka* VGK 1941," 116–117.

13. Luttichau, *The Road to Moscow*, ch. 29, p. 17.

14. Ibid., 14–16. Although Luttichau and Army Group North records cover this operation in considerable detail, most Russian-language sources say little about it. A notable exception is P. A. Zhilin, ed., *Na severo-zapadnom fronte 1941–1943* [On the northwestern front 1941–1943] (Moscow: Nauka, 1969), which contains several chapters covering aspects of these operations.

15. Platonov, *Bitva za Leningrad*, 53–54; and Luttichau, *The Road to Moscow*, ch. 29, pp. 1–4.

16. Luttichau, *The Road to Moscow*, ch. 29, p. 4.

17. Platonov, *Bitva za Leningrad*, 53–54.

18. Erickson, *The Road to Stalingrad*, 189–190.

19. Platonov, *Bitva za Leningrad*, 54.

20. Luttichau, *The Road to Moscow*, ch. 29, p. 47.

21. Platonov, *Bitva za Leningrad*, 55.

22. Luttichau, *The Road to Moscow*, ch. 29, p. 47. The Soviet account of the action is found in Platonov, *Bitva za Leningrad*, 56–57.

23. Luttichau, *The Road to Moscow*, ch. 29, p. 6.

24. Erickson, *The Road to Stalingrad*, 187.

25. Platonov, *Bitva za Leningrad*, 58.

26. Zolotarev, "*Stavka* VGK 1941," 126. The conversation between Stalin and Popov, which led to the GKO's 27 August decision, is in Zolotarev, "*Stavka* VGK," 140–141.

27. Voroshilov's order is found in "Oborona Leningrada 1941 goda" [The defense of Leningrad 1941], *VIZh* 6–7 (June–July 1992): 15.

28. Platonov, *Bitva za Leningrad*, 60.

29. For the specific *Stavka* orders, see Zolotarev, "*Stavka* VGK 1941," 129–130, 156–157; and Platonov, *Bitva za Leningrad*, 60. The 54th Army was formed in late August and early September. Under *Stavka* control, the army formed on the base of the 44th Rifle Corps and consisted of the 285th, 286th, 310th and 314th Rifle Divisions, the 27th Cavalry Division, the 122d Tank Brigade, and the 119th Separate Tank Battalion. Its mission was to defend along the Volkhov River. The 4th Army was formed in late September under *Stavka* control. It consisted of the 285th, 292d, and 311th Rifle Divisions and the 285th Rifle and 27th Cavalry Divisions from the 54th Army. It deployed along the Volkhov River in early October. The 52d Army was formed in August 1941 on the base of 25th Rifle Corps as a separate army under *Stavka* control. It consisted of the 276th, 285th, 288th, 292d, 312th,

314th, and 316th Rifle Divisions and occupied defenses along the Volkhov River at the end of August.

30. For details on the German assault, see Luttichau, *The Road to Moscow*, ch. 29, pp. 48–60.

31. The NAG consisted of the remnants of the 16th Rifle Corps' 237th Rifle Division, the 1st Mountain Rifle Brigade, and the fresh 305th Rifle Division. See *Boevoi sostav, chast' 1*, 39.

32. Platonov, *Bitva za Leningrad*, 62. March battalions consisted of unassigned conscript reinforcements for the Leningrad Front.

33. Ibid.

34. Ibid., 63; *Boevoi sostav, chast' 1*, 39; and V. A. Zolotarev, ed., "General'nyi shtab v gody Velikoi Otechestvennoi voiny: Dokumenty i materialy 1941 god" [The General Staff in the Great Patriotic War: Documents and materials from 1941], in *Russkii arkhiv: Velikaia Otechestvennaia [voina]* [Russian archive, The Great Patriotic (War)], vol. 23 (12-1) (Moscow: Terra, 1997). 139.

35. The most thorough descriptions of the XXXIX Motorized Corps' advance to Shlissel'burg and the Soviet defense are found in Luttichau, *The Road to Moscow*, ch. 29, pp. 48–52; and Platonov, *Bitva za Leningrad*, 63–64.

36. Luttichau, *The Road to Moscow*, ch. 29, p. 51.

37. A. V. Burov, *Blokada den' za dnem* [The blockade day by day] (Leningrad: Lenizdat, 1979), 53. Burov's war diary poignantly records every day's action in the Leningrad region from a Leningrader's perspective with remarkable accuracy and candor.

38. *Boevoi sostav, chast' 1*, 30.

39. Luttichau, *The Road to Moscow*, ch. 29, p. 47; and Platonov, *Bitva za Leningrad*, 65–66. For a day-by-day account of the LOG's operations, see Iu. S. Krinov, *Luzhskii rubezh god 1941-i* [The Luga line 1941] (Leningrad: Lenizdat, 1987).

40. Halder, *The Halder War Diary*, 524.

41. The full order in found in *SVIMVOV*, issue 18, 242–243.

42. Ibid.

43. For details on the 7th and 23d Armies' battle against the Finns, see Platonov, *Bitva za Leningrad*, 79–89.

44. For the details of German planning, see Luttichau, *The Road to Moscow*, ch. 29, pp. 52–54.

45. See the complete Soviet dispositions in Platonov, *Bitva za Leningrad*, 66–67.

46. "State Defense Committee Decree of 11 September 1941," TsPA IML (Central Party Archives of the Institute of Marxism and Leninism) f. 644, op. 1, d. 9.

47. Burov, *Blokada den' za dnem*, 54.

48. See Dmitri Pavlov, *Leningrad 1941: The Blockade* (Chicago: University of Chicago Press, 1965), 24–25.

49. Luttichau, *The Road to Moscow*, ch. 29, pp. 57–58, describes Reinhardt's frustration.

50. Platonov, *Bitva za Leningrad*, 68.

51. The 8th Panzer Division had played a major role in the encirclement and destruction of the LOG south of Krasnogvardeisk, a process that took over a week. This, plus the damage to it in its previous battles, made the regrouping and replenishment essential.

52. Luttichau, *The Road to Moscow*, ch. 29, p. 55.

53. Ibid., 59. The report referred to the 27th Cavalry Division assigned to Iakovlev's 4th Army.

54. For the contents of the *Stavka* directive, see Zolotarev, "Stavka VGK 1941," 175. Zhukov's account of his reassignment is in G. K. Zhukov, *Reminiscences and Recollections,* vol. 1 (Moscow: Progress, 1985), 398–400. The *Stavka* order assigning Zhukov command of the Leningrad Front was issued at 1910 hours on 11 September. This ends the confusion that has reigned in various sources regarding precisely when Zhukov received command.

55. V. Karpov, *Marshal Zhukov: Ego soratniki i protivniki v dni voiny i mir* [Marshal Zhukov: His comrades-in-arms and enemies in war and peace] (Moscow: Voenizdat, 1992), 339–340. Variations of this quote also appear in Harrison E. Salisbury, *The Unknown War* (New York: Bantam, 1978), and numerous other Russian sources. Although perhaps apocryphal, this conversation certainly rings true.

56. Luttichau, *The Road to Moscow,* ch. 29, p. 45.

57. Zhukov's arrival date in Leningrad has long been in doubt. In his diary, Burov notes Zhukov's arrival on 11 September, but Platonov states he arrived on 13 September. Other sources are divided as to the exact date. The recently published chronicle of Zhukov's wartime career clears up the situation. It notes that Zhukov arrived in Leningrad's city airfield on the evening of 9 September after leaving Moscow in the morning. Although he immediately took command of the Leningrad Front from Voroshilov, the *Stavka* order assigning him command was not issued until 1910 hours on 11 September. See S. I. Isaev, "Vekhi frontovogo puti" [The landmarks of front service], *VIZh* 10 (October 1991), 23. In August 1939, Zhukov had commanded Soviet forces that defeated a Japanese incursion into Mongolia at Khalkhin Gol (Khalkhin River).

58. Burov, *Blokada den' za dnem,* 59.

59. Platonov, *Bitva za Leningrad,* 68.

60. Ibid., 69.

61. Ibid., 70.

62. Erickson, *The Road to Stalingrad,* 192.

63. Ibid.

64. Platonov. *Bitva za Leningrad,* 70.

65. Burov, *Blokada den' za dnem,* 58–59.

66. Platonov, *Bitva za Leningrad,* 69–75, describes this action. See also Luttichau, *The Road to Moscow,* ch. 29, pp. 61–62.

67. Ivanov was rehabilitated after war's end, released from prison on 8 January 1946, and returned to Red Army duty. For details, see A. A. Maslov, *Condemned Generals: Soviet Generals Repressed by Stalin during the Great Patriotic War* (London: Frank Cass, forthcoming).

68. Platonov, *Bitva za Leningrad,* 71–72.

69. Burov, *Blokada den' za dnem,* 59.

70. B. N. Petrov, "Oborona Leningrada 1941 god" [The defense of Leningrad, 1941], *VIZh* 6–7 (June–July 1992): 18.

71. Ibid., 19.

72. Halder, *The Halder War Diary,* 537.

73. Ibid.

74. See the many *Stavka* directives to Kulik for his army to attack and the ensuing caustic exchanges between the *Stavka* and Kulik in Zolotarev, "*Stavka* VGK 1941," 186–187, 193–194.

75. See the *Stavka* directive forming Kulik's army in Zolotarev, "*Stavka* VGK 1941," 156–157, and its order of battle on 1 October in *Boevoi sostav, chast' 1*, 49.

76. See Kulik's dismissal order in Zolotarev, "*Stavka* VGK 1941," 200. Kulik's after-action report on his army's struggle from 22 to 28 September 1941 is found in Zolotarev, *Stavka* VGK 1941," 380–381.

77. Luttichau, *The Road to Moscow*, ch. 29, p. 71; and Platonov, *Bitva za Leningrad*, 73.

78. Krivosheev, *Grif sekretnosti sniat*, 167–168.

79. Erickson, *The Road to Stalingrad*, 195; and Luttichau, *The Road to Moscow*, ch. 29, p. 71.

80. Platonov, *Bitva za Leningrad*, 77.

4. The Encirclement Struggle

1. "Dokumentov nemetskogo komandovaniia po voprosam vedeniia voiny" [Documents of the German command on the matter of the conduct of the war], *SVIMVOV* 242–244.

2. Luttichau, *The Road to Moscow*, ch. 29, pp. 71–72.

3. Halder, *The Halder War Diary*, 543.

4. Ibid., 547.

5. Zolotarev, "Stavka VGK 1941," 224.

6. Platonov, *Bitva za Leningrad*, 102.

7. Cherepanov was appointed army commander in September to replace Lieutenant General M. N. Gerasimov, who had replaced Pshennikov in August.

8. The 23d Army consisted of the 43d, 123d, 142d, 198th, 265th, and 291st Rifle Divisions, a special NKVD Rifle Brigade, the 22d Fortified Region, the 48th and 106th Separate Tank Battalions, and supporting artillery and engineers. See *Boevoi sostav, chast' 1*, 49.

9. Ibid. The 8th Army consisted of the 16th Rifle Corps' 10th, 11th, and 85th Rifle Divisions, the 48th, 80th, 191st, and 281st Rifle Divisions, the 2d Naval Infantry Brigade, the 76th Separate Latvian Rifle Regiment, the 2d Separate Tank Regiment, an armored car battalion, and supporting artillery and engineers.

10. Ibid. Fediuninsky's army consisted of the 13th, 44th, 56th, and 189th Rifle Divisions, the 21st NKVD Rifle Divisions, the 6th and 7th Naval Infantry Brigades, the 268th, 282d, and 291st Separate Machine Gun–Artillery Battalions, the 51st Separate Tank Battalion, and supporting artillery and engineers.

11. Ibid. Overall, Lazarov's army contained the 70th, 86th, 90th, 125th, 168th, and 268th Rifle Divisions, the 17th Rifle Division's 55th Rifle Regiment, the Slutsk-Kolpino Fortified Region, the 84th and 86th Separate Tank Battalions, and supporting artillery and engineers. The 247th, 292d, 267th, 289th, 261st, 283d, and 290th Machine Gun–Artillery Battalions were in second echelon.

12. Ibid. The NOG consisted of the 115th Rifle and 1st NKVD Rifle Divisions,

the 4th Naval Infantry Brigade, the 1st, 4th, and 5th Destroyer Battalions, the 107th Separate Tank Battalion, and supporting artillery and engineers. The destroyer battalions were rifle antitank subunits.

13. Ibid. The 54th Army consisted of the 3d and 4th Guards and 128th, 286th, 294th, and 310th Rifle Divisions, the 1st Mountain Rifle Brigade, the 21st Tank Division (without tanks), the 16th and 122d Tank Brigades, and supporting artillery and engineers. All of Khozin's divisions were woefully understrength and had the following strength: 128th Rifle Division, 2,145 men; 3d Guards Rifle Division, 5,594; 310th Rifle Division, 3,735; and the 286th Rifle Division, 6,019 men. The two tank brigades fielded a total of 52 operable tanks, including 20 KV and T-34 models. See I. P. Barbashin and A. D. Kharitonov, *Boevye deistviia Sovetskoi armii pod Tikhvinom v 1941 godu* [Combat operations of the Soviet Army at Tikhvin in 1941] (Moscow: Voenizdat, 1958), 18.

14. Ibid., 53. The 4th Army consisted of the 32d, 285th, 292d, and 311th Rifle and 27th Cavalry Divisions, the 9th Tank Brigade, the 119th Separate Tank Battalion, and supporting artillery and engineers. The 52d Army fielded the 267th, 288th, 312th, and 316th Rifle Divisions and supporting artillery and engineers.

15. Ibid., 50. The NAG consisted of the 180th, 185th, and 305th Rifle and 3d Tank Divisions and supporting artillery and engineers. The 3d Tank Division, which lacked any tanks, was in the process of converting to a rifle division.

16. Zolotarev, "*Stavka* VGK 1941," 240; and Platonov, *Bitva za Leningrad,* 103.

17. Gorodok No. 1 means "Small Village" No. 1.

18. "Workers Settlement" is "Rabochii Poselok" in Russian.

19. Soviet force deployment details are in Platonov, *Bitva za Leningrad,* 103–104.

20. Ibid., 104. V. V. Gurkin, "Liudskie poteri Sovetskikh Vooruzhennykh sil v 1941–1945: Novye aspekty" [Personnel losses of the Soviet Armed forces 1941–1945: New aspects], *VIZh* 2 (March–April 1999): 4, places Soviet strength at 71,270 troops, while Platonov claims that Soviet strength was 63,000 men.

21. Burov, *Blokada den' za dnem,* 76–79.

22. See *Stavka* directives in Zolotarev, "*Stavka* VGK 1941," 257–259, 260–261, and 262–263.

23. Ibid., 260.

24. Ibid., 264.

25. Actually, on the *Stavka's* order, Khozin resumed his assaults toward Siniavino on 2 November, this time with an even stronger force. However, this offensive too failed after several days of heavy fighting.

26. Luttichau, *The Road to Moscow,* ch. 29, pp. 71–72.

27. Platonov, *Bitva za Leningrad,* 106.

28. Barbashin and Kharitonov, *Boevye deistviia Sovetskoi Armii pod Tikhvinom,* 6–7. This early Khrushchev-era study is one of the most thorough and accurate Soviet campaign studies.

29. Zolotarev, "*Stavka* VGK 1941," 250.

30. Details on the assault and subsequent operations are found in Barbashin and Kharitonov, *Boevye deistviia Sovetskoi Armii pod Tikhvinom,* 23–79; Platonov, *Bitva*

za Leningrad, 106–116; and Luttichau, *The Road to Moscow,* ch. 29, pp. 71–78. See also relevant Army Group North daily operational maps.

31. Zolotarev, "*Stavka* VGK 1941," 262–263, 260–261.

32. Ibid., 264.

33. Luttichau, *The Road to Moscow,* ch. 29, p. 73.

34. Army Group Center's Third Panzer Group captured Kalinin on 17 October and seemed capable of mounting an advance northwestward along the Moscow-Leningrad rail line. However, the *Stavka* mounted a major counterstroke, planned and led by Vatutin, against the German forces defending Kalinin. The counterstroke, which was the first serious reversal suffered by German forces in Operation Typhoon, almost recaptured the city and certainly ended any German hope of advancing Army Group Center's forces northward to support Leeb at Tikhvin. For details, see A. A. Zabaluev and S. T. Goriachev, *Kalininskaia nastupatel'naia operatsiia* [The Kalinin offensive operation] (Moscow: Voroshilov Academy of the General Staff, 1942), formerly classified secret.

35. Luttichau, *The Road to Moscow,* ch. 29, p. 73.

36. The first group included the 44th Rifle Division's 25th Rifle Regiment and the 60th Tank Division's 121st Tank Regiment.

37. Zolotarev, "*Stavka* VGK 1941," 391. This attack was timed to coincide with the Leningrad Front's (54th Army's) failed attempt to revive its offensive at Siniavino. Zolotarev also includes the *Stavka*'s directives criticizing Iakovlev's performance.

38. Luttichau, *The Road to Moscow,* ch. 29, p. 74.

39. Ibid., 77.

40. Platonov, *Bitva za Leningrad,* 109. The 310th Rifle Division was commanded by Colonel M. N. Zamirovsky.

41. Zolotarev, "*Stavka* VGK 1941," 279–280. Meretskov had served as Chief of the General Staff prior to January 1941, when Zhukov replaced him.

42. Ibid., 286, contains the *Stavka* directive to Fediuninsky.

43. Platonov, *Bitva za Leningrad,* 108–109; Luttichau, *The Road to Moscow,* ch. 29, p. 77; and Barbashin and Kharitonov, *Boevye deistviia Sovetskoi Armii pod Tikhvinom,* 30–31.

44. Halder, *The Halder War Diary,* 556–557.

45. Platonov, *Bitva za Leningrad,* 110; and Krivosheev, *Grif sekretnosti sniat,* 172. According to the same source, Krivosheev, *Grif sekretnosti sniat,* 224, at the beginning of the Tikhvin defense, the 54th, 4th, and 52d Armies had numbered 135,700 men.

46. Platonov, *Bitva za Leningrad,* 110. See the General Staff's approval of the offensive plan in Zolotarev, "General'nyi shtab," 237.

47. On 1 December Meretskov's 4th Army consisted of the 4th Guards, 44th, 65th, 92d, and 191st Rifle Divisions, the 1st Grenadier Rifle Brigade, the 27th Cavalry Division, the 60th Tank Division, the 46th Tank Brigade, the 119th, 120th, and 128th Separate Tank Battalions, and supporting artillery and engineers. See *Boevoi sostav, chast' 1,* 77.

48. See Meretskov's precise dispositions in Barbashin and Kharitonov, *Boevye deistviia Sovetskoi Armii pod Tikhvinom,* 38–39.

49. On 1 December Fediuninsky's 54th Army consisted of the 3d Guards, 80th, 128th, 285th, 286th, 294th, 310th and 311th Rifle Divisions, the 1st Mountain Rifle and 6th Naval Infantry Brigades, the 21st Tank Division (without tanks), the 16th and 122d Tank Brigades, the 1st and 2d Ski Battalions, and supporting artillery and engineers. See *Boevoi sostav, chast' 1*, 72.

50. On 1 December Klykov's 52d Army consisted of the 111th, 259th, 267th and 288th Rifle Divisions and supporting artillery and aviation. See ibid., 77.

51. The 3d Tank Division, which had no tanks, was soon converted into the 225th Rifle Division.

52. Platonov, *Bitva za Leningrad*, 111.

53. Luttichau, *The Road to Moscow*, ch. 29, pp. 77–78.

54. Ibid. Paul Carell [Paul Karl Schmidt], *Hitler Moves East 1941–1943* (Boston: Little, Brown, 1963), 269–270, claims that the 18th Motorized Division lost 9,000 men during the Tikhvin operation and was down to a combat strength of 741 soldiers by the time the operation ended.

55. Halder, *The Halder War Diary*, 579.

56. Ibid., 582.

57. Ibid.

58. Ibid., 583.

59. Luttichau, *The Road to Moscow*, ch. 29, p. 78.

60. Carell, *Hitler Moves East*, 269–270.

61. Halder, *The Halder War Diary*, 570.

62. Platonov, *Bitva za Leningrad*, 13.

63. Erickson, *The Road to Stalingrad*, 278.

64. The directives forming the Volkhov Front and assigning Meretskov to command are in Zolotarev, "*Stavka* VGK 1941," 329–330. Implementing instructions appear in Zolotarev, "General'nyi shtab," 282–283.

65. For details, see Zolotarev, "*Stavka* VGK 1941," 339.

66. Ibid., 338.

67. Ibid., 340, contains the Northwestern Front's complete mission.

68. Ibid., 331–332, 334, 343–334, for a representative sample of these messages.

69. Ibid., 390–391.

70. Ibid., 268.

71. Ibid., 277.

72. Ibid.

73. Ibid., 278.

74. Ibid., 243.

75. The Coastal Operational Group, commanded by Major General A. N. Astinin, took over control of the forces operating in the Oranienbaum bridgehead. See Gribkov, *Istoriia ordena Lenina Leningradskogo voennogo okruga*, 255.

76. Details on these hitherto unreported battles are found in documents in Zolotarev, "*Stavka* VGK 1941," 288–289.

77. Halder, *The Halder War Diary*, 558, 582.

78. Ibid., 575.

79. Krivosheev, *Grif sekretnosti sniat*, 172, 224; and Gurkin, "Liudskie poteri," 4.

80. Luttichau, *The Road to Moscow*, ch. 29, p. 79.

5. Winter under Siege

1. See Gribkov, *Istoriia ordena Lenina Leningradskogo voennogo okruga,* 185; and Erickson, *The Road to Stalingrad,* 120–121.

2. Burov, *Blokada den' za dnem,* provides daily entries pertaining to every aspect of the city's defense and routine work life, in addition to references to German air and artillery strikes and personnel and material losses.

3. Zhdanov was, simultaneously, secretary of the Leningrad Regional and City Party committees, Communist Party Politburo member, *Stavka* advisor, member of the Soviet Fleet's Main Military Council (commissar), and, insofar as Stalin had any, a personal friend of the dictator.

4. Platonov, *Bitva za Leningrad,* 189–190.

5. See the *Stavka* directive mandating creation of the Luga Defense Line and other defense lines around Leningrad in Zolotarev, "*Stavka* VGK 1941," 50.

6. Platonov, *Bitva za Leningrad,* 191.

7. Ibid., 192.

8. See a report on the deficiencies in the defense in Dzeniskevich, *Leningrad v osade,* 37–40.

9. Platonov, *Bitva za Leningrad,* 99–100.

10. See the complete order in A. R. Dzeniskevich, ed., *Leningrad v osade: Sbornik dokumentov o geroicheskoi oborone Leningrada v gody Velikoi Otechestvennoi voiny* [Leningrad in the Siege: A collection of documents concerning the heroic defense of Leningrad during the Great Patriotic War] (St. Petersburg: Liki Rossii, 1995), 51–53.

11. Platonov, *Bitva za Leningrad,* 100.

12. Ibid.

13. Ibid. See the initial *Stavka* order (of 18 July) regarding the air defense of Leningrad in Zolotarev, "*Stavka* VGK 1941," 79–80.

14. *Boevoi sostav, chast' 1,* 22.

15. Platonov, *Bitva za Leningrad,* 101.

16. Ibid., 102.

17. B. N. Petrov, "Oborona Leningrada 1941 goda" [The defense of Leningrad 1941], *VIZh* 6–7 (June–July 1992): 17.

18. Kolesnik, *Opolchenskie formirovaniia,* 15. This work provides the greatest detail about the formation and employment of militia forces. See the 4 July order (No. 3) that established the LANO in Dzeniskevich, *Leningrad v osade,* 30–33.

19. Platonov, *Bitva za Leningrad,* 184.

20. Kolesnik, *Opolchenskie formirovaniia,* 15.

21. Ibid., 17. Also see a report on the 1st DNO's deficiencies in weaponry in Dzeniskevich, *Leningrad v osade,* 34–35.

22. Ibid., 19.

23. Ibid., 19–20. See also Dzeniskevich, *Leningrad v osade,* 47–48, which contains a Leningrad Military Defense Council order dated 25 August mandating the formation of an additional 150 people's militia battalions, 77 of which were to be formed by 27 August. This illustrated the hasty nature of this entire process.

24. Kolesnik, *Opolchenskie formirovaniia,* 283–286. The seven surviving DNOs

were renumbered in late September as follows: the 13th (5th DNO), 44th (3d Gds. DNO), 56th (7th DNO), 80th (1st Gds. DNO), 85th (2d DNO), 86th (4th DNO), and 189th (6th DNO) Rifle Divisions.

25. Platonov, *Bitva za Leningrad,* 186.

26. Ibid., 187.

27. Ibid.

28. Ibid., 188.

29. Ibid.

30. Erickson, *The Road to Stalingrad,* 194. A complete account of the Baltic Fleet's operations during this stage of the blockade is found in A. M. Samsonov, ed., *Krasnoznamennyi Baltiiskii Flot v Velikoi Otechestvennoi voine 1941–1945* [The Red Banner Baltic Fleet during the Great Patriotic War 1941–1945] (Moscow: Nauka, 1981).

31. Platonov, *Bitva za Leningrad,* 188–189.

32. Ibid., 189. Detailed reports on the date, nature, strength, and effects of the German air and artillery bombardment from July 1941 though February 1942 and the work of the MPVO appear in Dzeniskevich, *Leningrad v osade,* 369–383. Even more interesting reports on crime and supposed treason on the part of the city's inhabitants also appear in Dzeniskevich's volume.

33. Platonov, *Bitva za Leningrad,* 193.

34. Ibid., 194.

35. Ibid.

36. Ibid.

37. Ibid., 195. See orders pertaining to the protection and evacuation of Leningrad's industries in Dzeniskevich, *Leningrad v osade,* 143–146.

38. Platonov, *Bitva za Leningrad,* 195.

39. For further details, see Erickson, *The Road to Stalingrad,* 234–235. The order creating the Special Aviation Groups is found in V. A. Zolotarev, ed., "Prikazy Narodnogo komissara oborony SSR: 22 iiunia 1941 g.–1942 g." [The orders of the People's Commissar of Defense: 22 June 1941–1942], in *Russkii arkhiv: Velikaia Otechestvennaia [voina]* [The Great Patriotic (War)], vol. 13 (2–2) (Moscow: Terra, 1997), 20–21.

40. Platonov, *Bitva za Leningrad,* 196.

41. Ibid., 197.

42. Ibid, 199.

43. Ibid., 200.

44. Ibid., 201.

45. For details on Pavlov's experiences at Leningrad, see Pavlov, *Leningrad v blokade.* Further details on the rationing system are found in Iu. G. Cherniavsky, *Voina i prodovol'stvie: Snabzhenie gorodskogo naseleniia v Velikoi Otechestvennoi voiny 1941–1945 gg.* [War and production: The supply of the urban population in the Great Patriotic War] (Moscow: Nauka, 1964).

46. Dzeniskevich, *Leningrad v osade,* 187–188, provides details on the ration regime in accordance with a 10 September order. Additional food production and availability figures are found on pages 187–211.

47. Platonov, *Bitva za Leningrad,* 201.

48. Dzeniskevich, *Leningrad v osade*, 194–195, shows the bread ration figure.

49. Platonov, *Bitva za Leningrad*, 201.

50. Dzeniskevich, *Leningrad v osade*, 209.

51. See the order halting beer production in ibid., 190–191.

52. Platonov, *Bitva za Leningrad*, 201

53. Ibid., 202.

54. For documents concerning disease and loss of life, see Dzeniskevich, *Leningrad v osade*, 280–281, 289–290, 292–296.

55. Platonov, *Bitva za Leningrad*, 203. See a thorough account of the daily death toll in Burov, *Blokada den' za dnem*.

56. Platonov, *Bitva za Leningrad*, 203.

57. Ibid.

58. Ibid., 203–204.

59. Valentina Fedorovna Kozlova lived in Apartment 65, House No. 7, Soldat Korzun Street, Leningrad. She kindly shared these recollections in writing with the author and readers.

60. Based on a written exchange of questions and answers between Kozlova and the author dated 15 July 2000.

61. Ibid.

62. Gribkov, *Istoriia ordena Lenina Leningradskogo voennogo okruga*, 267.

63. Platonov, *Bitva za Leningrad*, 204. See also A. Khrulev, "V bor'be za Leningrad" [In the struggle for Leningrad], *VIZh* 11 (November 1962): 27–36.

64. Ibid.

65. Platonov, *Bitva za Leningrad*, 205, and Pavlov, *Leningrad v blokade*, 122.

66. Ibid.

67. Ibid., 205–206. See also Khrulev, "V bor'be za Leningrad," 30–32, and Pavlov, *Leningrad v blokade*, 130.

68. Platonov, *Bitva za Leningrad*, 206.

69. Ibid., and Pavlov, *Leningrad v blokade*, 130.

70. Platonov, *Bitva za Leningrad*, 206; and Pavlov, *Leningrad v blokade*, 144.

71. Platonov, *Bitva za Leningrad*, 207.

72. Ibid., 208.

73. Burov, *Blokada den' za dnem*, 173.

74. Ibid., 175.

75. Platonov, *Bitva za Leningrad*, 209.

76. Ibid., 209–210. Khrulev, "V bor'be za Leningrad," 30, states that the monthly shipments to Leningrad amounted to 16,499 tons in November and December 1941, 52,934 tons in January 1942, 86,041 tons in February, 118,332 tons in March, and 87,253 tons in the three weeks of April.

77. See evacuation orders issued before and after the creation of the ice road in Dzeniskevich, *Leningrad v osade*, 273–305, including the overall summary of evacuations from 29 June 1941 through 15 April 1942.

78. Platonov, *Bitva za Leningrad*, 210. See also V. M. Koval'chuk, "Evakuatsiia naseleniia Leningrada letom 1941 goda" [The evacuation of Leningrad's population in the summer of 1941], *Otechestvennaia istoriia* [Patriotic history] 3 (May–June 2000): 15–24; hereafter cited as *OI*.

79. Platonov, *Bitva za Leningrad,* 210–211.

80. Ibid., 211.

81. Ibid., 213.

82. Ibid., 116.

83. Ibid., 117.

84. Ibid.; and T. Lesniak, "Nekotorye voprosy organizatsii i vedeniia partizanskoi bor'by v pervye mesiatsy voiny" [Some questions regarding the organization and conduct of the partisan struggle in the initial months of the war], *VIZh* 9 (September 1963): 32.

85. Platonov, *Bitva za Leningrad,* 118.

86. Lesniak, "Nekotorye voprosy," 32.

87. Platonov, *Bitva za Leningrad,* 118.

88. Ibid., 119.

89. Ibid., 120.

90. For an excellent discussion of the conflicting casualty figures, see Salisbury, *The 900 Days,* 491–492, 514–515, and the specific sources from which he derives his figures. The most recent tally of the overall death toll is found in Iu. V. Rubstov and V. M. Lur'e, "Blokada Leningrada: Vse li zhertvy uchteny?" [The Leningrad blockade: Have all of the victims been counted?], *VIZh* 3 (May–June 2000): 30–33.

91. Krivosheev, *Grif sekretnosti sniat,* 167–168.

92. Gurkin, "Liudskie poteri," 4.

93. Krivosheev, *Grif sekretnosti sniat,* 224; and Gurkin, "Liudskie poteri," 4.

94. Ibid.

6. False Dawn

1. V. A. Zolotarev, ed., "Stavka VGK: Dokumenty i materialy 1942" [The *Stavka* VGK: Documents and materials 1942], in *Russkii arkhiv: Velikaia Otechestvennaia [voina]* [The Great Patriotic (War)], vol. 16 (5–2) (Moscow: "Terra," 1996), 33.

2. Zolotarev, "*Stavka* VGK 1941," 338–339. The two orders read:

Stavka VGK Directive No. 005826 to the Volkhov Front Commander
Concerning the Transition to a General Offensive
2000 hours 17 December 1941

The *Stavka* of the Supreme High Command *orders:*

1. The Volkhov Front's forces, consisting of the 4th, 59th, 2d Shock, and 52d Army, will launch a general offensive to defeat enemy forces defending along the western bank of the Volkhov River and by the end of ___ reach the Liuban' and Chudovo Station front with the armies' main forces.

Subsequently, attacking to the northwest, encircle the enemy defending around Leningrad, and encircle and capture or, in the event they refuse to be taken prisoner, destroy the enemy in cooperation with the forces of the Leningrad Front.

2. On the right, the Leningrad Front will assist the Volkhov Front's forces in the encirclement of the enemy blockading Leningrad by active operations.

The boundary lines are: a) with the 7th Separate Army—Borisovo-Sudskoe (60 km north of Babaevo), Biriuchevo, Tokarevo, and Volchii Nos; b) with the Leningrad Front—the Volkhov River from its mouth to Kholm (25 km south of Volkhov), Pogost' St., Sablino St., Pokrovskaia, and Krasnoe Selo.

On the left, the Northwestern Front will protect the Volkhov Front's left flank.

The boundary line with it is Bologoe (this point is for the Northwestern Front's general use), Kresttsy, Navolok, and Iur'evo.

3. The 4th Army, consisting of the 4th Guards Rifle Division, the 191st, 44th, 65th, 377th, 92d, and 310th Rifle Divisions, the 27th and 80th Cavalry Divisions, the 60th Tank Division, the 46th Tank Brigade, the 881st Artillery Regiment, the 119th, 120th, and 128th Separate Tank Battalions, and the 6th Guards-Mortar Battalion, will attack in the general direction of Kirishi and Tosno and encircle and destroy the enemy that are advancing north of Mga to Lake Ladoga in cooperation with the Leningrad Front's 54th Army.

Subsequently, attacking along the Krasnogvardeisk and Ropsha axis, cooperate with the Leningrad Front's armies in the destruction of the enemy who is holding on to these points. The left boundary line is Polodnoe (50 km southeast of Tikhvin), Budkovo, Lezno (on the Volkhov River), Malaia Kunest', Vyritsa, and Diatlitsy.

4. The 59th Army, consisting of the 382d, 372d, 378th, 374th, 376th, and 366th Rifle Divisions, the 78th and 87th Cavalry Divisions, two army artillery regiments, two tank battalions, six ski battalions, and three mortar battalions, will attack in the direction of Gruzino, Siverskaia, and Volosovo.

The left boundary line is Narotovo, Bakharikha, Efremovo (on the Volkhov River), Divenskaia St. (inclusive), Rabititsy, Il'eshi, and Kotly.

5. The 2d Shock Army, consisting of the 327th Rifle Division, the 22d, 24th, 25th, 3d, 57th, 53d, 58th, and 59th Separate Rifle Brigades, six ski battalions, two tank battalions, three guards-mortar battalions, and one army artillery regiment, will attack in the direction of Chasha and Nizovskii stations and subsequently attack Luga.

The left boundary line is Zasobol'e, Burga, St. Russa (on the Volkhov river), Cholovo St., and Tashino (12 km southeast of Luga).

6. The 52d Army, consisting of the 46th, 288th, 259th, 267th, and 111th Rifle Divisions, with the subordinate Novgorod Operational Group (less the 180th Rifle Division, the 442d and 561st RGK Artillery Regiments, and the 884th Antiaircraft Artillery Regiment) will capture Novgorod and subsequently develop the offensive toward Sol'tsy to protect the Volkhov Front's offensive to the northwest.

7. Instructions concerning the material support of the *front*'s operations will be provided separately.

8. Confirm receipt.

The *Stavka* of the Supreme High Command

I. Stalin

B. Shaposhnikov

Stavka VGK Directive No. 005822 to the Leningrad Front Commander
Concerning Assistance to the Volkhov Front's Offensive
2000 hours 17 December 1941

The Volkhov Front will launch a general offensive to the northwest to destroy the enemy defending along the Volkhov River and subsequently encircle and either capture or destroy him in cooperation with the Leningrad Front's forces.

The *Stavka* of the Supreme High Command *orders:*

1. The forces of the Leningrad Front will assist the Volkhov Front in destroying the enemy defending around Leningrad and in liberating Leningrad from the blockade by active operations by the 42d, 55th, 8th, and 54th Armies and the Coastal Operational Group

The boundary line with the Volkhov Front during the operation is established along the Volkhov River from its mouth to Kholm (25 km south of Volkhov), Pogost'e St., Sablino, St. Pokrovskaia, and Krasnoe Selo (all points inclusive for the Leningrad Front).

2. The 54th Army, consisting of the 128th, 294th, 286th, 285th, 311th, 80th, 115th, 281st, 198th, and 3d Gds. Rifle Divisions, the 6th Naval Brigade, the 21st Tank Division, and the 81st and 882d Howitzer Artillery Regiments will launch an attack simultaneously with the Volkhov Front's forces with the following missions: to encircle and destroy the enemy advancing

on Lake Ladoga and blockading Leningrad from the east and southeast in cooperation with an attack by the Volkhov Front's 4th Army, which will attack toward Tosno.

3. The 8th, 55th, and 42d Armies will assist the Volkhov Front's encirclement of the enemy by [their own] attacks.

4. The Coastal Operational Group will cover the fleet's base by defending their existing positions and, when the Volkhov Front's armies reach the Krasnoe Selo and Begunitsy line, will attack to the southwest with the mission of severing enemy communications lines to Narva. To this end the Leningrad Front commander will prepare to launch air assaults and ski detachments.

5. The 23d Army will protect Leningrad from the north by a firm defense of the Karelian Fortified region.

6. The Red Banner Baltic Fleet will support the operations of the *front*'s armies by artillery fire from ships and coastal artillery.

7. Confirm receipt.

The *Stavka* of the Supreme High Command
I. Stalin
B. Shaposhnikov

3. Ibid., 340. The *Stavka* issued the Northwestern Front's order on 18 December.

4. K. Meretskov, "Na volkhovskikh rubezhakh" [In the Volkhov positions], *VIZh* 1 (January 1965): 54–70.

5. *SVIMVOV*, 252–255.

6. *SVIMVOV*, 255–257.

7. "Der Feldzug gegen die Sowjet-Union der Heeresgruppe Nord, Kriegsjahr 1942," *H. Gr. Nord, No. 75884*, National Archives microfilm (NAM) series NAM T-312. Maps and reports dated early January 1942.

8. Sokolov's 2d Shock Army was assigned the mission to: "Penetrate the enemy defense along the western bank of the Volkhov River and reach the Kerest' River with your main forces by the close of 19 January. Subsequently, attack in the direction of Finev Lug, Chasha Station, and Nisovskii Station, while protecting the army's left flank against counterattacks from Batetskaia Station with part of your forces. When you reach the Leningrad-Cholovo station rail line, plan to turn the army's main forces for an attack on Luga." See M. Khozin, "Ob odnoi maloissledovannoi operatsii" [Concerning one neglected operation], *VIZh* 2 (February 1966): 36.

9. E. Klimchuk, "Vtoraia udarnaia i Vlasov ili pochemu odin predal, a v perdateli popala vsia armiia" [The 2d Shock and Vlasov, or Why because of one traitor the blame was laid on the whole army] *Sovetskii voin* [The Soviet soldier] 4 (April 1990): 77.

10. Ibid. The author of these lines admitted that some of the units were well trained, such as Colonel I. M. Antiufeev's 327th Rifle Division, which was manned primarily by workers from Voronezh.

11. Klimchuk, "Vtoraia udarnaia i Vlasov," 77.

12. I. T. Korovnikov, N. S. Lebedev, Ia. G. Poliakov, *Na trekh frontakh; Boevoi put' 59-i Armii* [On three fronts: The combat path of the 59th Army] (Moscow: Voenizdat, 1974),

13. "Galanin, Ivan Vasil'evich," in M. M. Kozlov, ed., *Velikaia Otechestvennaia voina 1941–1945: Entsiklopediia* [The Great Patriotic War 1941–1945: An encyclopedia] (Moscow: Sovetskaia entsiklopediia, 1985), 199.

14. Platonov, *Bitva za Leningrad*, 136–137.

15. Krivosheev, *Grif sekretnosti sniat,* 224–225.

16. Ibid., 224.

17. S. Ruban, "Tragediia podviga: Liuban', god 1942-i" [The tragedy of a feat: Liuban', 1942], *Voennye znaniia* [Military knowledge], 2 (February 1993), 1.

18. Halder, *The Halder War Diary,* 599.

19. Burov, *Blokada den' za dnem,* 119.

20. Korovnikov, Lebedev, and Poliakov, *Na trekh frontakh,* 17.

21. "Boevoe donesenie komanduiushchego voiskami Volkhovskogo fronta Verkhovnomu Glavnokomanduiushchemu o khode nastupleniia 59–i armii i podgotovke k nastupleniiu 2-i udarnoi armii" [Combat report of the Volkhov Front commander to the Supreme High Commander Concerning the 59th Army's offensive and preparations for the 2d Shock Army's offensive], in Zolotarev, "*Stavka* VGK 1942," 482–483.

22. Ruban, "Tragediia podviga," 1.

23. In his memoirs, Meretskov claims that he requested and received a three-day delay, citing an excerpt from a telephone conversation with Stalin and Vasilevsky that went as follows, "Stalin and Vasilevsky are speaking. According to all available information, you will not be ready to attack by January 11. If this is true, it should be postponed for a day or two." What Meretskov did not quote was the rest of the conversation, which continued, "The Russians have a saying: 'Haste makes waste.' With you it is happening exactly like this. Without properly preparing the offensive, you were in a haste to launch it and wasted time. If you remember, I proposed to postpone the offensive until Sokolov's army is ready. You refused and now are reaping the fruits of your haste." Despite Stalin's and Vasilevsky's rejoinder, the attack resumed as Meretskov intended. See Klimchik, "Vtoraia udarnaia i Vlasov," 78.

24. Halder, *The Halder War Diary,* 600.

25. Burov, *Blokada den' za dnem,* 121.

26. Ruban, "Tragediia podviga," 1.

27. Ibid.

28. For example, see Zolotarev, "*Stavka* VGK 1942," 484–485, 485–486, 500–501.

29. Ibid., 52–53.

30. Halder, *The Halder War Diary,* 601.

31. Burov, *Blokada den' za dnem,* 123.

32. Ibid., 128. The entry for 20 January notes, "General I. I. Fediuninsky's 54th Army is continuing to attack the enemy and, judging by the trophies [captured equipment], not without success. On this day 26 machine guns, rifles, and automatic weapons, 55,000 bullets, 2 antitank guns, 8 motorcycles, and 70 bicycles were captured from the enemy in one sector alone." Halder noted on 15 January, "Relatively serious penetrations on the Volkhov front," but stated on 19 January, "On the Volkhov River, very heavy battle in Sixteenth Army sector. We have succeeded in establishing a very effective defensive barrier." Over the next six days he simply mentioned, "In AGp. North. Hard fighting, " but "No important change." Halder, *The Halder War Diary,* 603–606.

33. Ziemke and Bauer, *Moscow to Stalingrad,* 148.

34. Ibid.

35. "Boevoe donesenie komanduiushchego voiskami Volkhovskogo Fronta No. 613 Verkhovnomu Glavnokomanduiushchemu o plane peregruppirovki voisk s tsel'iu razvitiia uspekha 2-i udarnoi armii" [Combat report No. 613 of the Volkhov Front commander to the Supreme High Commander about the plan for regrouping forces to develop the 2d Shock Army's success], in Zolotarev, "*Stavka* VGK 1942," 486–487.

36. "Directiva Stavki VGK no. 170037 komanduiushchemu voiskami Volkhovskogo fronta ob utverzhdenii plana operatsii po razvitiiu uspekha 2-i udarnoi armii" [*Stavka* VGK directive no. 170037 to the Volkhov Front commander about the approval of the operational plan to develop the 2d Shock Army's success], in ibid., 57.

37. "Operativnaia direktiva komanduiushchego voiskami Volkhovskogo Fronta no. 0023 na razvitie operatsii po razgromu protivnika v raione Leningradskogo shosse" [Volkhov Front operational directive No. 0023 on the development of the operation to destroy the enemy in the region of the Leningrad road], ibid., 500–501.

38. "Der Feldzug gegen die Sowjet-Union der Heeresgruppe Nord, Kriegsjahr 1942," *H. Gr. Nord, No. 75884,* National Archives microfilm (NAM) series NAM T-312. Maps and reports dated late January and February 1942.

39. Major General V. I. Shcherbakov commanded the 11th Rifle Division and Lieutenant Colonel I. P. Ermakov the 22d Tank Brigade.

40. Platonov, *Bitva za Leningrad,* 141–142; Burov, *Blokada den' za den',* 144. The daily entry for 19 February states, "After penetrating the enemy defense in the region of Liubino Pole and Mostki villages on 12 February, the Volkhov Front's forces captured the village of Krasnaia Gorka (15 kilometers from Liuban') on 19 February. A threat from the rear now hangs over Fascist forces besieging Leningrad."

41. Ibid., 142.

42. Ziemke and Bauer, *Moscow to Stalingrad,* 188–189. Burov, *Blokada den' za dnem,* 148–149, recorded on 27 February, "Intense battle is raging along the Liuban' axis. The enemy is offering fierce resistance. Throwing up fortifications, he is pressuring the Volkhov Front's forces everywhere. In the vicinity to Liuban', he has succeeded in recapturing Krasnaia Gorka, which our forces had already occupied on 19 February."

43. "Direktiva Stavki VGK no. 170126 komanduiushchemu voiskami Volkhovskogo fronta o razgrome liuban'-chudovskoi gruppirovki protivnika" [*Stavka* VGK directive no. 170126 to the Volkhov Front commander concerning the destruction of the enemy Liuban'-Chudovo grouping], in Zolotarev, "*Stavka* VGK 1942," 110.

44. Ibid., 110. The directive was entitled, "Direktiva Stavki VGK no. 170127 komanduiushchemu voiskami Leningradskogo Fronta o nanesenii 54-i armii udara na Liuban'" [*Stavka* VGK directive no. 170127 to the Leningrad Front commander concerning the delivery of an attack on Liuban'].

45. Ibid., 119. The directive was entitled, "Direktiva Stavki VGK no. 170136 komanduiushchim voiskami Volkhovskogo fronta i 20-i armii o kadrovykh perestanovkakh" [*Stavka* VGK directive no. 170136 to the Volkhov Front and 20th Army commanders about cadre rearrangements].

46. Ibid., 118. The directive was entitled, "Direktiva Stavki no. 170134 komanduiushchemu voiskami Volkhovskogo fronta o kadrovykh izmeneniiakh vo 2-i udarnoi armii" [*Stavka* directive no. 170134 to the Volkhov Front commander about cadre

changes in the 2d Shock Army]. The directive removed Major General Vizzhilin for "poor work as chief of staff" and replaced him with Colonel Rozhdestvensky, the former chief of staff of the 52d Army. The same order replaced the chief of the 2d Shock Army's operations department for "poor work and false information."

47. Ibid., 111. The directive was entitled, "Direktiva Stavki VGK no. 170128 komanduiushchemu voiskami Volkhovskogo fronta o merakh po uskoreniiu razgroma liuban'-chudovskoi gruppirovki protivnika" [Stavka VGK directive no. 170128 to the Volkhov Front commander concerning measures to accelerate the destruction of the enemy Liuban'-Chudovo grouping].

48. Ibid., 120. The directive was entitled, "Direktiva Stavki VGK no. 170137 komanduiushchim voiskami Volkhovskogo i Leningradskogo frontov, zamestiteliu komanduiushchego VVS Krasnoi Armii o nanesenii udarov aviatsiei" [Stavka VGK directive no. 170137 to the Volkhov and Leningrad Front commanders and the deputy commander of the Red Army Air Force about the delivery of air strikes].

49. Ibid., 506. The report was entitled, "Donesenie komanduiushchego voiskami Leningradskogo fronta no. 15852 Verkhovnomu Glavnokomanduiushchemu o plane razgroma liuban'-chudovskoi gruppirovki protivnika" [Report no. 15852 of the Leningrad Front commander to the Supreme High Commander concerning the plan for the destruction of the Liuban'-Chudovo enemy grouping].

50. Ibid., 126–127. The directive was entitled, "Direktiva Stavki VGK no. 170148 komanduiushchemu voiskami Leningradskogo fronta o razgrome liubanskoi gruppirovki protivnika" [Stavka VGK directive no. 170148 to the Leningrad Front commander about the destruction of the enemy Liuban' grouping].

51. Burov, Blokada den' za dnem, 155, 158. On 8 March, Burov (Blokada den' za dnem, 153) first mentioned Fediuninsky's successes and noted an Informburo report that his army had destroyed 800 enemy soldiers and officers.

52. Halder, The Halder War Diary, 610.

53. Ibid., 611.

54. Khozin, "Ob odnoi maloissledovannoi operatsii," 38.

55. Ziemke and Bauer, Moscow to Stalingrad, 188.

56. "Der Feldzug." Maps and reports dated in March describe the boundary changes and the new fighting to close the penetration.

57. Ziemke and Bauer, Moscow to Stalingrad, 190–191.

58. Halder, The Halder War Diary, 608.

59. During the January offensive, the forces of the Soviet Kalinin Front had encircled several divisions on the right flank of the Sixteenth Army's II Army Corps at Kholm, which was located south of Staraia Russa. In March Kuechler mounted an operation with his XXXIX Motorized Corps to relieve the beleaguered force.

60. "Direktiva Stavki VGK no. 170156 komanduiushchemu voiskami Volkhovskogo fronta na otrazhenie kontratak protivnika v raione Miasnogo Bora" [Stavka VGK directive no. 170156 to the Volkhov Front commander on the repelling of enemy counterattacks in the Miasnoi Bor region], in Zolotarev, "Stavka VGK 1942," 133.

61. For details on Operation Raubtier, see Ziemke and Bauer, Moscow to Stalingrad, 191–192; Carell, Hitler Moves East, 396–397; and "Der Feldzug."

62. Ziemke and Bauer, *Moscow to Stalingrad*, 194.

63. Zolotarev, "*Stavka* VGK 1942," 506–507. The report was entitled, "Doklad komanduiushchego voiskami Volkhovskogo fronta no. 00368/op Verkhovnomu Glavnokomanduiushchemu o podgotovke novgorodskoi operatsii" [Report no. 00368/op of the Volkhov Front commander to the Supreme High Commander concerning the preparation of the Novgorod operation].

64. Ibid., 139. The directive was entitled, "Direktiva Stavki VGK no. 170175 komanduiushchemu voiskami Volkhovskogo fronta o podgotovke novgorodskoi operatsii" [*Stavka* VGK directive no. 170175 to the Volkhov Front commander concerning the preparation of the Novgorod operation]. The units sent to Meretskov included the 114th and 117th Rifle Brigades and the 2d Rifle Division. A subsequent *Stavka* directive (no. 170187 dated 24 March) substituted the 170th Rifle Division for the two brigades.

65. Khozin, "Ob odnoi maloissledovannoi operatsii," 38.

66. Zolotarev, "*Stavka* VGK 1942," 506–507. The report was entitled, "Donesenie komanduiushchego voiskami Volkhovskogo fronta no. 00440/op Verkhovnomu Glavnokomanduiushchemu o merakh po obespecheniiu razvitiia novgorodskoi operatsii" [Report no. 00440/op of the Volkhov Front commander to the Supreme High Commander concerning measures for protecting the development of the Novgorod operation].

67. Ibid., 145. The *Stavka* directive was entitled, "Direktiva Stavki VGK no. 170202 komanduiushchemu voiskami Volkhovskogo fronta ob utverzhdenii plana novgorodskoi operatsii" [*Stavka* VGK directive no. 170202 to the Volkhov Front commander concerning the approval of the plan for the Novgorod operation].

68. Khozin, "Ob odnoi maloissledovannoi operatsii," 38.

69. Ziemke and Bauer, *Moscow to Stalingrad*, 196–197.

70. Zolotarev, "*Stavka* VGK 1942," 509. The report was entitled, "Boevoe donesenie komanduiushchego voiskami Volkhovskogo fronta no. 00514/op Verkhovnomu Glavnokomanduiushchemu o merakh po podgotovke k zaversheniiu liubanskoi operatsii" [Combat report no. 00514/op of the Volkhov Front commander to the Supreme High Commander concerning measures for preparing for the completion of the Liuban' operation].

71. Ziemke and Bauer, *Moscow to Stalingrad*, 197.

72. Khozin, "Ob odnoi maloissledovannoi operatsii," 40; and "Direktiva Stavki VGK no. 170301 komanduiushchim voiskami Leningradskogo i Volkhovskogo frontov ob ob'edinenii frontov" [*Stavka* VGK directive no. 170310 to the Leningrad and Volkhov Front commanders concerning the combining of the *fronts*], in Zolotarev, "*Stavka* VGK 1942," 174–175. The next day, *Stavka* directive no. 170299 relieved General Fediuninsky of command of the 54th Army and replaced him with General Sukhomlin, the former 8th Army commander. Fediuninsky became the 5th Army commander, and General Starikov was elevated from deputy commander to commander of the 8th Army. See Zolotarev, "*Stavka* VGK 1942," 176.

73. Zolotarev, "*Stavka* VGK 1942," 170. The directive was entitled, "Direktiva Stavki VGK no. 170282 komanduiushchemu i zamestiteliu komanduiushchego voiskami Volkhovskogo fronta o naznachenii komanduiushchego 2-i udarnoi armii" [*Stavka*

VGK directive no. 170282 to the Volkhov Front commander and deputy commander concerning the appointment of the 2d Shock Army commander]. B. Shaposhnikov signed the 20 April directive.

74. For details on Kurochkin's Demiansk operation, see Platonov, *Bitva za Leningrad*, 145–150, and many specific *Stavka* directives and *front* reports related to it in Zolotarev, "*Stavka* VGK 1942," 33–175, 488–514. For details from the German perspective, see Ziemke and Bauer, *Moscow to Stalingrad*, 144–155, 186–198.

75. Platonov, *Bitva za Leningrad*, 148–149.

76. For details on this forgotten operation, see David M. Glantz, *The Ghosts of Demiansk: Soviet Airborne Operations against the German Demiansk Pocket (6 March–8 April 1942)* (Carlisle, Penn.: Self-published, 1998).

77. Ziemke and Bauer, *Moscow to Stalingrad*, 192–194; and Platonov, *Bitva za Leningrad*, 150.

78. Platonov, *Bitva za Leningrad*, 150. Burov (*Blokada den' za dnem*, 175–179) describes the German attack on Nevskaia Dubrovka, which began with a heavy artillery bombardment on 26 April. The bridgehead, which was defended by 357 men of the 86th Rifle Division's 330th Rifle Regiment, collapsed after several heavy German ground assaults. Most of the men, including Major V. Ia. Kozlov, the division chief of staff, and Senior Battalion Commissar A. V. Shchurov, the division commissar, perished in the battle.

79. A. A. Izmailov and V. F. Kon'kov, "Nevskaia Dubrovka," *SVE*, 4: 565.

80. Platonov, *Bitva za Leningrad*, 150–151. For details of the air operation against the Baltic Fleet, which the Germans code-named *Eisstoss* (Ice strike), see N. Ia. Komarov, "Aisshtoss" [Eisstoss], in I. N. Rodionov, ed., *Voennaia entsiklopidiia v vos'mi tomakh* [Military encyclopedia in eight volumes], vol. 1 (Moscow: Voenizdat, 1997), 1–6. Three hundred German bombers took part in the multiple raids, which damaged the cruisers *Kirov, Maksim Gor'ki, Svirepyi, Sil'nyi,* and *Groziashchii* at a reported cost of 78 German aircraft shot down.

7. Frustrated Hopes

1. *SVIMVOV*, 18: 257–261.

2. Ibid.

3. Khozin, "Ob odnoi maloissledovannoi operatsii," 41.

4. "Doklad komanduiushchego voiskami Leningradskogo fronta no. 00695 Verkhovnomu Glavnokomanduiushchemu o plane operatsii na volkhovskom napravlenii" [Report no. 00695 of the Leningrad Front commander to the Supreme High Commander concerning the plan of operations on the Volkhov axis], in Zolotarev, "*Stavka* VGK 1942," 517–518.

5. "Direktiva Stavki VGK no. 170351 komanduiushchemu voiskami Leningradskogo fronta ob izmenenii sostavy i pereimenovanii grupp voisk" [*Stavka* VGK directive no. 170351 to the Leningrad Front commander concerning changes on the composition and names of the groups of forces], in Zolotarev, "*Stavka* VGK 1942," 190. The *Stavka* approved Khozin's recommendations on 9 May. The new appointments included General Stelmakh as Leningrad Front chief of staff. See "*Stavka* VGK directive no. 170370," in Zolotarev, "*Stavka* VGK 1942," 197.

6. See "*Stavka* VGK directive no. 170352," dated 2230 hours 3 May 1942, in Zolotarev, "*Stavka* VGK 1942," 190.

7. "Operativnaia direktiva komanduiushchego voiskami Leningradskogo fronta no. 00120/op komanduiushchemu 2-i udarnoi armiei ob otvode armii" [Operational directive no. 00120/op of the Leningrad Front commander to the 2d Shock Army commander concerning the army's withdrawal], in Zolotarev, "*Stavka* VGK 1942," 519–520.

8. "Direktiva Stavki VGK no. 170379 komanduiushchemu voiskami Leningradskogo fronta ob otvode 2-i udarnoi armii" [*Stavka* VGK directive no. 170379 of the Leningrad Front commander concerning the withdrawal of the 2d Shock Army], in Zolotarev, "*Stavka* VGK 1942," 202.

9. "Donesenie komanduiushchego voiskami Leningradskogo fronta no. 00111 Verkhovnomu Glavnokomanduiushchemu ob etapakh operatsii po otvodu 2-i udarnoi armii" [Report no. 0111 by the Leningrad Front commander to the Supreme High Commander about the stages of the operation to withdraw the 2d Shock Army], in Zolotarev, "*Stavka* VGK 1942," 520–521.

10. See "*Stavka* VGK directive no. 170390," in Zolotarev, "*Stavka* VGK 1942," 205.

11. "Direktiva Stavki VGK no. 170406 komanduiushchemu voiskami Leningradskogo fronta o zadachakh i reorganizatsii volkhovskoi gruppy voisk" [*Stavka* VGK directive no. 170406 to the Leningrad Front commander about the missions and reorganization of the Volkhov Group of Forces], in Zolotarev, "*Stavka* VGK 1942," 212–213.

12. Major General I. T. Korovnikov now commanded the 6th Guards Rifle Corps in recognition of his previous success in commanding the special operational group.

13. Khozin, "Ob odnoi maloissledovannoi operatsii," 42.

14. Ibid., 43.

15. Ibid.

16. Ziemke and Bauer, *Moscow to Stalingrad*, 257.

17. Ibid.

18. "Der Feldzug." Maps and reports dated May 1942.

19. Ziemke and Bauer, *Moscow to Stalingrad*, 257.

20. Khozin, "Ob odnoi maloissledovannoi operatsii," 43.

21. Ibid.

22. Ibid.

23. "Direktiva Stavki VGK no. 170450 voennym sovetam Leningradskogo fronta i leningradskoi gruppy voisk, komanduiushchim 33-i armiei, voiskami Zapadnogo fronta i Narodnomu Komissaru Voenno-morskogo Flota o razdelenii Leningradskogo fronta" [*Stavka* VGK directive no. 170450 to the Military Councils of the Leningrad Front and Leningrad Group of Forces, the commanders of the 33d Army and Western Front, and the People's Commissar of the Navy concerning the division of the Leningrad Front], in Zolotarev, "*Stavka* VGK 1942," 244.

24. Klimchuk, "Vtoraia udarnaia i Vlasov," 80.

25. Ibid.

26. Ibid.

27. Ibid.

28. Khozin, "Ob odnoi maloissledovannoi operatsii," 43.

29. Ibid., 44–45.

30. "Komanduiushchemu voiskami Volkhovskogo fronta o poriadke vyvoda 2-i udarnoi armii iz okruzheniia" [To the Volkhov Front commander concerning the order of withdrawing the 2d Shock Army from encirclement], in V. A. Zolotarev, ed., "General'nyi shtab v gody Velikoi Otechestvennoi voiny: Dokumenty i materialy 1942, god" [The General Staff in the Great Patriotic War: Documents and materials from 1942], in *Russkii arkhiv: Velikaia Otechestvennaia [voina]* [Russian archives: The Great Patriotic (War)], vol. 23, 12 (2) (Moscow: Terra, 1999), 191.

31. "Nachal'niku shtaba Volkhovskogo fronta o merakh po utochneniiu polozheniia voisk 2-i udarnoi armii" [To the Volkhov Front chief of staff about measures to determine the condition of the 2d Shock Army's forces], in Zolotarev, "General'nyi shtab 1942," 238.

32. "Direktiva Stavki VGK No. 170518 komanduiushchemu voiskami Volkhovskogo fronta o dostavke komanduiushchego, nachal'nikov shtaba i sviazi 2-oi udarnoi armii iz-za linii fronta" [*Stavka* VGK directive no. 170518 to the Volkhov Front commander concerning the delivery of the 2d Shock Army's commander, chief of staff, and chief of communications from behind the front lines], in Zolotarev, "Stavka VGK 1942," 314.

33. Klimchuk, "Vtoraia udarnaia i Vlasov," 80.

34. Ibid.

35. Ibid.

36. Ibid., 80–81.

37. Ibid., 45.

38. Ibid.

39. Ibid., 45–46.

40. Ibid., 46.

41. Ibid., 76.

42. Ibid.

43. Ibid., 81.

44. Ziemke and Bauer, *Moscow to Stalingrad*, 409–410.

45. Ibid., 411. In addition to the three siege batteries, Hitler also ordered additional batteries, ranging in caliber from 240mm to 400mm, to deploy to the Leningrad region.

46. *SVIMVOV*, 18: 265–267.

47. Ziemke and Bauer, *Moscow to Stalingrad*, 412.

48. Ibid., 415.

49. S. A. Gladysh, "Upredili protivnika i otstoiali Leningrad: Nastupatel'naia operatsiia voisk Volkhovskogo i Leningradskogo frontov v Iuzhnom Priladozh'e (avgust–sentiabr' 1942 g) [They withstood the enemy and defended Leningrad: The Volkhov and Leningrad Fronts' offensive in the region south of Ladoga (August–September 1942), *VIZh* 5 (September–October 1998): 12.

50. Zolotarev, "Stavka VGK 1942," 309.

51. Gribkov, *Istoriia ordena Lenina Leningradskogo voennogo okruga*, 302.

52. Burov, *Blokada den' za dnem*, 217–219.

53. Ibid., 219–221.

54. Halder, *The Halder War Diary*, 645.

55. For details on the largely forgotten Demiansk operations, see David M. Glantz, *Forgotten Battles of the German-Soviet War (1941–1945), Vol. III: The Summer Campaign (12 May–18 November 1942)* (Carlisle, Penn.: Self-published, 1999), 174–193.

56. For example, a General Staff report to Meretskov on 6 August stated:

After completing the operation on the Volkhov front, the enemy has begun preparing an offensive operation against the Leningrad front. To this end, by 3 August 1942 (according to the Leningrad Front headquarters), the enemy has transferred the 225th, 58th, 90th, 215th, 291st, and the 121st Infantry Divisions and part of the SS Police Division from the Volkhov to the Leningrad Front. According to prisoner-of-war reports, the enemy envisions transferring [to Leningrad] all divisions, which had previously been operating there, to carry out an operation at Leningrad.

On the basis of this information, we can presume that, besides these divisions, the enemy can transfer an additional four divisions (probably the 1st, 96th, 254th, and 269th Infantry Divisions) from the Volkhov Front. It is essential that you verify the veracity of this information from captured prisoners and report to the Red Army General Staff.

[signed] Ivanov, Bokov

See "Komanduiushchemu voiskami Volkhovskogo fronta o proverke dostovernosti svedenii po perebroske protivnikom voisk pod Leningrad" [To the Volkhov Front commander about verifying the veracity of reports about the enemy transfer of forces to Leningrad], in Zolotarev, "General'nyi shtab 1942," 276.

57. "Der Feldzug." Maps and reports dated July–September 1942.

58. Ziemke and Bauer, *Moscow to Stalingrad*, 418.

59. Halder, *The Halder War Diary*, 654.

60. Ibid., 659.

61. Find all Soviet planning details in Platonov, *Bitva za Leningrad*, 162–165.

62. Ibid., 165.

63. Ibid., 164.

64. Ibid.

65. For a very detailed account of this complex operation, see "Zakhvat platsdarma v raione Ust'-Tosno" [The capture of a bridgehead in the Ust'-Tosno region], in *Sbornik materialov po izucheniiu opyta voiny no. 9 (noiabr'–dekabr' 1943 g.)* [Collection of materials for the study of the war experience, no. 9 (November–December 1943)] (Moscow: Voenizdat, 1944), 103–115. See also Burov, *Blokada den' za dnem*, for daily entries tracking the progress of the offensive.

66. For details on the Soviet assault, see Gladysh, "Upredili protivnika," 13–61.

67. Halder noted on 26 August, "In North, signs are increasing that the Russians will soon strike south of Lake Ladoga." The next day he stated, "The anticipated attack south of Lake Ladoga has started," but was repelled with "only minor penetrations." The next day, he admitted to "a very distressing situation south of Lake Ladoga." On 31 August he declared, "In North, the enemy penetration in the bottleneck seems for the most part to have been checked. Counterattack is under preparation." See Halder, *The Halder War Diary*, 662–665.

68. Ziemke and Bauer, *Moscow to Stalingrad*, 418.

69. Platonov, *Bitva za Leningrad*, 167; and Gladysh, "Upredili protivniki," 14.

70. Ziemke and Bauer, *Moscow to Stalingrad,* 418.

71. Ibid., 419.

72. *Boevoi sostav Sovetskoi Armii, chast' 2 (ianvar'–dekabr' 1942 goda)* [The combat composition of the Soviet Army, part 2 (January–December 1942)] (Moscow: Voenizdat, 1966), 165.

73. For details on the German defenses and the constant regrouping of German reserves, see a special series of maps showing day-by-day dispositions from 27 August through 15 October, in "Der Feldzug." Maps and reports dated July–October 1942.

74. Gladysh, "Upredili protivniki," 14.

75. Platonov, *Bitva za Leningrad,* 165–166.

76. Ziemke and Bauer, *Moscow to Stalingrad,* 420.

77. Ibid.

78. Ibid.

79. "Doklad komanduiushchego voiskami Volkhovskogo fronta no. 073/22 Verkhovnomu Glavnokomanduiushchemu o plane operatsii po razgromu Sinaivinskoi gruppirovki protivnika i vykhodu na Nevu" [Report no. 073/22 of the Volkhov Front commander to the Supreme High Commander on an operational plan for the destruction of the enemy Siniavino grouping and reaching the Neva], in Zolotarev, "*Stavka* VGK 1942," 546–547.

80. See Ibid., 397, for the *Stavka*'s entire answer.

81. See this exchange of messages in Zolotarev, "*Stavka* VGK 1942," 401, 547.

82. Ibid., 422; and Platonov, *Bitva za Leningrad,* 166.

83. Gribkov, *Istoriia ordena Lenina Leningradskogo voennogo okruga,* 305–306.

84. Ziemke and Bauer, *Moscow to Stalingrad,* 423.

85. Platonov, *Bitva za Leningrad,* 169.

86. Ziemke and Bauer, *Moscow to Stalingrad,* 423.

87. "Direktiva Stavki VGK no. 170629 komanduiushchemu voiskami Volkhovskogo fronta o vyvode 2-i udarnoi armii iz okruzheniia" [*Stavka* VGK directive no. 170629 to the Volkhov Front commander concerning the withdrawal of the 2d Shock Army from encirclement], in Zolotarev, "*Stavka* VGK 1942," 405–406.

88. See Meretskov's recommendations and the *Stavka*'s caustic response in Zolotarev, "*Stavka* VGK 1942," 546, 547.

89. "Boevoe donesenie komanduiushchego voiskami Volkhovskogo fronta no. 032 Verkhovnomu Glavnokomanduiushchemu ob obstanovke i perekhod na Mginskom napravlenii k chastnym operatsiiam" [Combat report no. 032 of the Volkhov Front commander to the Supreme High Commander concerning the situation and a transition to local operations along the Mga axis], in Zolotarev, "*Stavka* VGK 1942," 547–548.

90. "Direktiva Stavki VGK no. 170632 komanduiushchemu voiskami Volkhovskogo fronta ob oborone zanimaemogo rubezha" [*Stavka* VGK directive no. 170632 to the Volkhov Front commander concerning the defense of existing positions], in ibid., 409.

91. See Gurkin, "Liudskie poteri," 4. The Germans estimated that Soviet losses included 36,000 dead, 12,370 prisoners, and 244 destroyed or captured tanks. See Paul Carell, *Scorched Earth: The Russian-German War, 1943–1944* (Boston: Little, Brown, 1966), 216.

92. "Nachal'niku shtaba Volkhovskogo fronta o neudovletvoritel'noi organizatsii boevykh deistvii v Siniavinskoi nastupatel'noi operatsii" [To the Volkhov Front chief of staff concerning the improper organization of combat operations in the Siniavino offensive operation], in Zolotarev, "General'nyi shtab 1942," 322.

93. "Nachal'niku shtaba Volkhovskogo fronta o nedostatkakh v ispol'zovanii tankovykh chastei" [To the Volkhov Front chief of staff concerning shortcomings in the employment of tank units], in Zolotarev, "General'nyi shtab 1942," 350.

94. Platonov, *Bitva za Leningrad*, 168–169.

95. For the full Operation Order No. 1, see *SVIMVOV*, 18: 269–273.

8. The Continuing Siege

1. Dzeniskevich, *Leningrad v osade*, 105–112. A report issued on 3 January 1943, describes the scale of defensive work completed in 1942 and the role the population played in that work. This book provides extensive documentation regarding all aspects of Leningrad's defenses and daily life in the city, including reports on industrial production, transport and supply, crime and public morale, and health and cultural issues.

2. Platonov, *Bitva za Leningrad*, 99.

3. Ibid., 192.

4. "Postanovlenie voennogo soveta Leningradskogo fronta o neobkhodimykh meropriiatiiakh po prevrashcheniiu Leningrada v voennyi gorod" [Instructions of the Leningrad Front's Military Council concerning the necessity of measures for turning Leningrad into a military city], in Dzeniskevich, *Leningrad v osade*, 84–85.

5. Ibid., 88–89.

6. Ibid., 95–96.

7. Platonov, *Bitva za Leningrad*, 186.

8. Ibid.

9. See both orders in V. A. Zolotarev, ed., "Stavka Verkhovnogo Glavnokomandovaiia: Dokumenty i materialy 1943 god" [The *Stavka* VGK; Documents and materials 1943], in *Russkii arkhiv: Velikaia Otechestvennaia [voina]* [The Great Patriotic (War)], vol. 16, 5 (3) (Moscow: Terra, 1999), 111–112.

10. Platonov, *Bitva za Leningrad*, 279.

11. Dzeniskevich, *Leningrad v osade*, 289–290.

12. Ibid., 297–298.

13. Ibid., 298.

14. Platonov, *Bitva za Leningrad*, 214–215.

15. Dzeniskevich, *Leningrad v osade*, 307–308.

16. Ibid., 316.

17. Ibid., 317–318

18. Ibid., 344–346.

19. Ibid., 346–348. The report also broke the population by age group, indicating that the percentage of those 60 years or older fell to 4 percent of the population.

20. Platonov, *Bitva za Leningrad*, 215.

21. Ibid. See also Dzeniskevich, *Leningrad v osade*, 152–153, 163–166, for detailed production figures.

22. "Iz otcheta otdela oboronnoi promyshlennosti GK VKP (B) o proizvodstve boevoi tekhniki i boepripasov v Leningrade za 1942 g." [From a report of the Defense Industry Department of the GK VKP (B) concerning the production of military equipment and ammunition in Leningrad during 1942], in Dzeniskevich, *Leningrad v osade,* 167–169.

23. Platonov, *Bitva za Leningrad,* 216.

24. Ibid.

25. Ibid., 217. For specific details on transport, see Dzeniskevich, *Leningrad v osade,* 230–237.

26. Platonov, *Bitva za Leningrad,* 217.

27. Ibid., 218.

28. Ibid.

29. Ibid., 219. See Dzeniskevich, *Leningrad v osade,* 363–373, for reports concerning the intensity and effects of the German bombardment, and Burov, *Blokada den' za dnem,* for daily entries for April and May 1942.

30. Platonov, *Bitva za Leningrad,* 219.

31. Ibid.

32. Ibid.

33. Burov, *Blokada den' za dnem,* 252–253. This book records all action accurately on a day-by-day basis.

34. Platonov, *Bitva za Leningrad,* 220–221.

35. Ibid., 222.

36. Ibid., 223.

37. Ibid.

38. Ibid., 286. See Dzeniskevich, *Leningrad v osade,* 246–248, for the initial proposal to construct the rail line.

39. Platonov, *Bitva za Leningrad,* 287.

40. Ibid.

41. Ibid.

42. Ibid., 28.

43. Ibid., 223.

44. Ibid., 224. See documents related to the volume of supplies in Dzeniskevich, *Leningrad v osade.*

45. Platonov, *Bitva za Leningrad,* 152.

46. Ibid.

47. Ibid., 153.

48. Ibid., 154.

49. Ibid., 155.

50. Ibid.

51. Ibid., 173.

52. "Podstanovlenie GKO No. 1837ss o sozdanii Tsentral'nogo Shtab Partizanskogo dvizheniia pri Stavke VGK" [GKO instruction no. 1837ss concerning the creation of the Central Headquarters of the Partisan Movement in the Stavka VGK], in V. A. Zolotarev, ed., "Partizanskoe dvizhenie v gody Velikoi Otechestvennoi voiny 1941–1945 gg.: Dokumenty i materialy" [The partisan movement in the Great Patriotic War 1941–1945: Documents and materials], in *Russkii arkhiv: Velikaia Otechestvennaia*

[voina] [Russian archive: The Great Patriotic (War)], vol. 20 (9) (Moscow: TERRA, 1999), 114–115. The NKO implementing order was issued on 16 June 1942.

53. "Prikaz nachal'nika TsShPD o sozdanii operativnykh grupp shtabov partizan-skogo dvizheniia pri voennykh sovetakh armii" [Order from the chief of the Central Headquarters of the Partisan Movement concerning the establishment of operational groups of the Partisan Movement Headquarters in army military councils], in Zolotarev, "Partizanskoe dvizhenie," 118.

54. Zolotarev, "Partizanskoe dvizhenie," 119.

55. Platonov, *Bitva za Leningrad,* 173.

56. Ibid., 174.

57. Ibid. For a detailed report of partisan operations in the Leningrad and Volkhov Front's sectors in August and September 1942, see Zolotarev, "Partizanskoe dvizhenie," 137–138.

58. Earl F. Ziemke, *Stalingrad to Berlin: The German Defeat in the East* (Washington, D.C.: Office of the Chief of Military History, United States Army, 1968), 105.

59. Platonov, *Bitva za Leningrad,* 175–176.

60. Ibid., 176.

61. Ibid.

62. "Doklad Tsentral'nogo shtaba partizanskogo dvizheniia v TsK VKP (B) o sostoianii partizanskogo dvizheniia na vremenno okkupirovannoi territorii SSR" [Report of the Central Headquarters of the Partisan Movement in the Communist Party Central Committee concerning the condition of the partisan movement in the temporarily occupied territories of the USSR], in Zolotarev, "Partizanskoe dvizhenie," 162–163.

63. Platonov, *Bitva za Leningrad,* 283–284. A 7 January 1943 report by the Central Headquarters of the Partisan Movement showed 60 detachments with 2,756 men operating in the Leningrad region, 17 of which had radio or courier contact with the Soviet rear area. See Zolotarev, "Partizanskoe dvizhenie," 263.

64. Platonov, *Bitva za Leningrad.*

65. Ibid.

66. Ibid.

67. See numerous documents associated with this major operation in Zolotarev, "Partizanskoe dvizhenie," 300–312, 402–420.

68. Soviet sources record that partisans destroyed or damaged 156 trains, 133 locomotives, and 2,452 rail cars, platforms, and water towers, 19 rail and 151 road bridges, 72,020 telephone and telegraph lines, 12 tanks and 26 guns, 50 warehouses, and 37 small garrisons or security posts. See Platonov, *Bitva za Leningrad,* 285.

69. Ibid., 286.

70. For details from the German perspective, see Ziemke, *Stalingrad to Berlin,* 203–204, 261, 264, 304–308.

9. Breaking the Blockade

1. For context, see David M. Glantz, *When Titans Clashed: How the Red Army Stopped Hitler* (Lawrence: University Press of Kansas, 1995); David M. Glantz, *Marshal Zhukov's Greatest Defeat: The Red Army's Epic Disaster in Operation Mars* (Lawrence: University Press of Kansas, 1999); and David M. Glantz, *Forgotten Battles*

of the German-Soviet War (1941–1945), volume. III: The Summer Campaign (12 May–18 November 1942), and *volume IV: The Winter Campaign (19 November 1942– 21 March 1943)* (Carlisle, Penn.: Self-published, 1999).

2. For a detailed order of battle of the Leningrad and Volkhov Fronts on 1 January, see *Boevoi sostav Sovetskoi armii, chast' 3 (ianvar'-dekabr' 1943 goda)* [The combat composition of the Soviet Army, part 3 (January–December 1943] (Moscow: Voenizdat, 1972), 8–10.

3. Platonov, *Bitva za Leningrad,* 230–231.

4. Ibid., 231.

5. Ibid.

6. Ibid., 131–132.

7. Ibid., 232.

8. For German dispositions in the Leningrad region, see Platonov, *Bitva za Leningrad,* 232–234, and "Der Feldzug," maps and reports dated 1 January–31 December 1943.

9. Platonov, *Bitva za Leningrad,* 233.

10. Ziemke, *Stalingrad to Berlin,* 111.

11. Platonov, *Bitva za Leningrad,* 234.

12. Ibid., 235–237.

13. See Govorov's full proposal in "Doklad komanduiushchego voiskami Leningradskogo fronta Verkhovnomu Glavnokomanduiushchemu planov Shlissel'burgskoi i Uritskoi operatsii" [Report by the Leningrad Front commander to the Supreme High Commander on plans for the Shlissel'burg and Uritsk operations], in Zolotarev, "*Stavka* VGK 1942," 560–563. Govorov's 22 November report is contained in "Doklad komanduiushchego voiskami Leningradskogo fronta no. 100/612 Verkhovnomu Glavnokomanduiushchemu o plane boevykh deistvii na zimu 1943 goda" [Report by the Leningrad Front commander to the Supreme High Commander on a plan for combat operations in the winter of 1943], in Zolotarev, "*Stavka* VGK 1942," 563–565.

14. Specifically, Govorov recommended the offensives be supported by a total of 2 ski and 2 tank brigades, 14 artillery regiments, 4 fleet artillery battalions, 4 antiaircraft artillery battalions, 2 PVO artillery regiments, 2 antiaircraft artillery batteries, 9 guards-mortar battalions, 1 engineer-sapper brigade, and 4 pontoon-bridge and 3 road battalions. See Platonov, *Bitva za Leningrad,* 236.

15. See the full *Stavka* response in "Direktiva Stavki VGK no. 170696 komanduiushchim voiskami Volkhovskogo i Leningradskogo frontov ob utverzhdenii plana operatsii 'Iskra'" [*Stavka* VGK directive no. 170696 to the Volkhov and Leningrad Front commanders concerning the approval of the plan for Operation Spark], in Zolotarev, "*Stavka* VGK 1942," 458.

16. See the complete *Stavka* directive in "Direktiva Stavki VGK no. 170703 komanduiushchim voiskami Volkhovskogo i Leningradskogo frontov o zadachakh po proryvu blokady Leningrada i podgotovke Mginskoi operatsii" [*Stavka* VGK directive no. 170703 to the Volkhov and Leningrad Front commanders concerning missions in the penetration of the Leningrad blockade and preparations for the Mga operation], in Zolotarev, "*Stavka* VGK 1942," 464.

17. Platonov, *Bitva za Leningrad,* 238.

18. Ibid., 238–239.

19. Ibid., 239.

20. For details of the coordination plan, see ibid., 240. More planning details are found in S. M. Boitsov and S. N. Borshchev, *Operatsiia "Iskra"* [Operation Spark] (Leningrad: Lenizdat, 1973).

21. Platonov, *Bitva za Leningrad*, 240–241.

22. Ibid., 241.

23. Artillery fire planning details are found in ibid., 241–242.

24. A single combat load of artillery was equivalent to the number of shells required to support a given number of days of operations.

25. Ibid., 242–243.

26. The 13th Army's 414 aircraft included 52 bombers, 85 assault planes, 242 fighters, and 35 others, most of which operated over the main attack axis. See Platonov, *Bitva za Leningrad*, 243.

27. Ibid., 243–244. The 395 aircraft included 35 bombers, 174 assault aircraft, 163 fighters, and 23 reconnaissance aircraft.

28. Ibid., 244. See also V. I. Baranov, ed., *Tankisti v srazhenii za Leningrad: Vospominaniia, ocherki, dokumenty* [Tank troops in the Battle for Leningrad: Recollections, essays, and documents] (Leningrad: Lenizdat, 1987), for details on all tank operations throughout the Leningrad blockade.

29. Ibid., 244.

30. The engineer battalions were slightly larger and, hence, more capable than the sapper battalions.

31. Ibid., 245–246.

32. Ibid., 246.

33. Ibid., 247.

34. Operation Mars was the third Rzhev-Sychevka operation. The first operation had taken place in February–March 1942 as part of the Red Army's winter campaign, and the second operation, which was a virtual dress rehearsal for Operation Mars, occurred in August and September 1942. All three operations sought to defeat Army Group Center and all three failed.

35. For Zhukov's wartime work schedule, see Isaev, "Vekhi frontovogo puti," 25.

36. Carell, *Scorched Earth*, 219.

37. For details on the day-by-day actions, see Platonov, *Bitva za Leningrad*, 252–255; Burov, *Blokada den' za dnem*, 297–308; and D. K. Zherebov, I. I. Solomakhin, *Sem' ianvarskikh dnei Proryv blokady Leningrada 12–18 iarvaria 1943g.* [Seven January days: The penetration of the Leningrad blockade, 12–18 January 1943] (Leningrad: Lenizdat, 1987).

38. Carell, *Scorched Earth*, 220–223.

39. Ibid., 226; and Platonov, *Bitva za Leningrad*, 255–256.

40. Platonov, *Bitva za Leningrad*, 258.

41. Ibid., 259.

42. Ibid., 260; and Carell, *Scorched Earth*, 229. See five detailed situation maps covering the development of the operation in "Der Feldzug."

43. Platonov, *Bitva za Leningrad*, 261; and Carell, *Scorched Earth*, 229.

44. Carell, *Scorched Earth*, 229.

45. Colonels N. V. Simonov and B. N. Ushinsky commanded the 80th and 265th Rifle Divisions, respectively.

46. Platonov, *Bitva za Leningrad,* 263–264.

47. Ibid., 265–266.

48. Ibid., 264.

49. Carell, *Scorched Earth,* 234.

50. Platonov, *Bitva za Leningrad,* 267–268.

51. Iu. P. Petrov, ed., *Istoriia Velikoi Otechestvennoi voiny Sovetskogo Soiuza 1941–1942 v shesti tomakh, tom tretii* [A History of the Great Patriotic War of the Soviet Union 1941–1945 in six volumes], vol. 3 (Moscow: Voenizdat, 1961), 137–138.

52. Carell, *Scorched Earth,* 238. See also Platonov, *Bitva za Leningrad,* 267–268.

53. Burev, *Blokada den' za dnem,* 303–308, provides some detail of the action after 20 January.

54. Gribkov, *Istoriia ordena Lenina Leningradskogo voennogo okruga,* 323.

55. Krivosheev, *Grif sekretnosti sniat,* 184–185.

56. Maslov, *Fallen Soviet Generals,* 82.

57. The Soviets claim to have killed and wounded 19,000 German soldiers, captured 1,275 prisoners, and destroyed 272 guns, 120 machine guns, and more than 300 mortars destroyed. See Gribkov, *Istoriia ordena Lenina Leningradskogo voennogo okruga,* 323.

58. Salisbury, *The 900 Days,* 548.

59. Platonov, *Bitva za Leningrad,* 273.

60. Ibid., 274.

61. See Timoshenko's plan in "Doklad komanduiushchego voiskami Severo-zapadnogo fronta no. 0080 Verkhovnomu Glavnokomanduiushchemu o plane operatsii po zaversheniiu okruzheniia i razgromu demianskoi gruppirovki protivnika" [Report no. 0089 of the Northwestern Front commander to the Supreme High Commander on an operational plan to complete the encirclement and destruction of the enemy Demiansk grouping], in Zolotarev, "*Stavka* VGK 1943," 268–270. The *Stavka* approved his plan on 17 January. Former *front* commander Kurochkin was assigned to command the 11th Army.

62. A. A. Grechko, ed., *Istoriia Vtoroi Mirovoi voiny 1939–1945 v dvenadtsati tomakh* [A history of the Second World War 1939–1945 in twelve volumes], vol. 6 (Moscow: Voenizdat, 1976), 142.

63. G. K. Zhukov, *Reminiscences and Reflections, vol. 2* (Moscow: Progress, 1985), 145.

64. See "Direktiva Stavki VGK no. 30042 komanduiushchemu voiskami Severo-zapadnogo fronta o poriadke razgroma demianskoi gruppirovki protivnika" [*Stavka* directive no. 30042 to the Northwestern Front commander concerning the sequencing of the enemy Demiansk grouping's destruction], in Zolotarev, "*Stavka* VGK, 1943," 72–73.

65. See "Direktiva *Stavki* VGK no. 30039 komanduiushchemu osoboi gruppoi voisk na razgrom leningradsko-volkhovskoi gruppirovki protivnika" [*Stavka* VGK directive no. 30039 to the commander of the Special Group on the destruction of the enemy Leningrad-Volkhov grouping], in Zolotarev, "*Stavka* VGK 1943," 70–71.

66. See "Direktiva Stavki VGK no. 30034 komanduiushchim voiskami Leningrad-skogo i Volkhovskogo frontov o nanesenii udarov po siniavinskoi gruppirovke protivnika" [*Stavka* VGK directive No. 30034 to the Leningrad and Volkhov Front commanders concerning the delivery of attacks on the enemy Siniavino grouping], in Zolotarev, "*Stavka* VGK 1943," 56–57.

67. Platonov, *Bitva za Leningrad*, 276.

68. The 55th Army consisted of the 45th and 63d Guards, 43d, 46th, 56th, 72d, 131st, and 268th Rifle Divisions, the 56th and 250th Rifle, 34th and 35th Ski, and 222d Tank Brigades, and the 31st Tank Regiment. See *Boevoi sostav, chast' 3*, 57.

69. Carell, *Scorched Earth*, 246.

70. The 54th Army consisted of the 115th, 166th, 177th, 198th, 281st, 285th, 294th, 311th, 374th, and 378th Rifle Divisions and the 14th and 140th Rifle, 6th Naval Infantry, and 122d and 124th Tank Brigades. See *Boevoi sostav, chast' 3*, 58.

71. On 1 February 1943, the 2d Shock Army consisted of the 64th Guards, 11th, 18th, 71st, 128th, 147th, 314th, 364th, 376th, and 379th Rifle Divisions, the 72d Rifle, 73d Naval Rifle, and 16th and 98th Tank Brigades, the 32d Guards Tank Regiment, and the 501st, 503d, and 507th Separate Tank Battalions. The 67th Army consisted of the 13th, 46th, 90th, 142d, 189th, and 224th Rifle Divisions, the 11th, 55th, 56th, 102d, 123d, 138th, 142d, and 250th Rifle and 1st, 61st, 152d, and 220th Tank Brigades, the 31st and 46th Guards Tank Regiments, the 86th and 118th Separate Tank Battalions, and the 16th Fortified Region. See *Boevoi sostav, chast' 3*, 32.

72. Burov, *Blokada den' za dnem*, 312.

73. Carell, *Scorched Earth*, 246–247.

74. Burov, *Blokada den' za dnem*, 314.

75. Ibid., 316–317.

76. See "Direktiva Stavki VGK no. 30057 komanduiushchim voiskami Leningrad-skogo i Volkhovskogo frontov o zakreplenii na dostignutykh rubezhakh i podgotovke nastupleniia" [*Stavka* VGK directive no. 30057 to the Leningrad and Volkhov Front commanders concerning the consolidation in achieved positions and preparations for an offensive], in Zolotarev, "*Stavka* VGK 1943," 82–83. The full directive, which was issued at 2240 hours 27 February, read:

The operations being conducted by the Leningrad and Volkhov Fronts are not producing the expected results. The main shortcoming in the *fronts'* offensive operations is the fact that the 67th and 2d Shock Armies are operating separately, and each has been required to penetrate a strongly fortified enemy defense in its sector. This has led to a dissipation of forces and weaponry and to pointlessly heavy casualties in personnel and equipment. It is necessary to put an end to these shortcomings.

The *Stavka* of the Supreme High Command *orders:*

1. Temporarily cease the offensive by the Leningrad Front's 55th and 67th Armies and the Volkhov Front's 2d Shock and 54th Armies.

2. The Leningrad and Volkhov Fronts' forces will consolidate in their present positions and conduct active reconnaissance to detect weak places in the enemy's defenses.

3. The complete 2d Shock Army will be transferred to the Leningrad Front together with a portion of its *front's* reinforcements effective 2400 hours 28 February 1943. The transfer of reinforcing weaponry will take place on Marshal Voroshilov's orders.

4. Effective 2400 hours 28 February 1943, establish [the following] boundary line between the Leningrad and Volkhov Fronts: the Naziia River, Apraksin Gorodok, Gaitolovo, Sigolovo, Sologubovka, and Nechepert' (all inclusive for the Leningrad Front).

5. The commander of the Leningrad Front will submit an offensive plan to the *Stavka* no later than 3 March 1943 that calculates weak places in the enemy defense so that, in the future, the 67th and 2d Shock Armies' forces and weaponry can be concentrated along a single axis.

6. The commander of the Volkhov Front will submit his views regarding the conduct of an offensive operation in cooperation with the Leningrad Front no later than 3 March 1943.

7. Marshal Voroshilov will prepare his conclusions regarding the plan for joint operations by both *fronts* and present them to the *Stavka*.

[signed] I. Stalin

77. For details on the German withdrawal, see Ziemke, *Stalingrad to Berlin*, 112–113, and Carell, *Scorched Earth*, 249–257.

78. Gurkin, "Liudskie poteri," 7.

79. Zhukov submitted his report to the *Stavka*, which included his recommendations for a new offensive, at 1557 hours on 28 February. It read:

1. Our plan to penetrate the enemy defense was designed to penetrate a weak defense and, by introducing Group Khozin into the affair, to reach the rear of his Leningrad-Volkhov grouping quickly. By doing so, we intended for the 1st Shock, 53d, and 34th Armies to encircle the Demiansk grouping.

The situation has now drastically changed.

Having detected the concentration of the 1st Shock and 27th Armies and Group Khozin, the enemy is withdrawing behind the Lovat' River, and has apparently decided to settle for a defense along the Lovat' River with his forward defensive positions along the Red'ia River and, possibly, along the Lovat' River.

2. The roads have become untrafficable during the last 15 days because of the rain and the thaw. The swamps where the forces are now operating are beginning to become clear of ice, have become a mess, and are covered by continuous water.

The [weather] forecast is for warm weather beginning on 15 March 1943.

3. Considering the rapidly changing situation and the weather, I am very afraid that we are sitting with our groupings in the local swamps and untrafficable places, having failed to achieve our aims in Polar Star.

I think that:

1. We now need to limit the Northwestern Front's advance to reaching the Polist' River, give up on [the idea] of committing Group Khozin into the affair, seize Staraia Russa, and prepare a jumping-off region for a spring offensive.

2. [We need] to prepare Group Khozin for the spring [offensive] by reinforcing it with the 34th and 53d Armies.

We can bring these two armies, which consist of approximately 10–12 divisions, forward by 15 March and take 3 airborne divisions away from Korotkov [1st Shock Army].

Group Khozin can consist of the 34th, 53d, 68th, and 1st Tank Armies for a total of up to 20 rifle divisions and up to 18 rifle brigades plus the tank army.

I think that such a grouping can play a very great role in the spring.

I am reporting my opinion on your decision.

[signed] Konstantinov [Zhukov]

See "Doklad predstavitelia Stavki no. 43 Verkhovnemu Glavnokomanduiushchemu o predlozhenii o perenose srokov nachala operatsii "Poliarnaia zvezda" [Report no. 43 of the representative of the *Stavka* to the Supreme High Commander on a proposal concerning a shift in the timing of the commencement of Operation Polar Star], in Zolotarev, "*Stavka* VGK 1943," 282–283.

80. Zhukov's recommendations, which he forwarded to the Stavka on 8 March, read:

1. Since we delivered the main attacks toward the Verevkino and Liakhnovo regions with Korotkov's [1st Shock] army from the south and with Lopatin's [11th] and Trofimenko's [27th] armies from the north, the enemy has withdrawn his grouping's main forces and is committing them against Korotkov and in Staraia Russa. The enemy is maintaining a considerably weaker grouping in the center, that is, in the sector on the 11th Army's right flank and in the Ramushevo, Cherenchitsy, and Onufrievo regions on the 53d Army's right flank. Apparently, that region is the junction between his northern and the southern groupings.

2. Considering the presence of dirt roads, the proximity of the railroad, and the difficulty of operating because of the nature of the terrain, I have decided to bring Tolbukhin's [68th] army quickly forward to the Vasil'evshina, Godilovo, and Koloma region in the north, and to launch in a wedge attack against the enemy in the Ramushevo and Cherenchitsy sector along the general axis through Onufrievo and Sokolovo to Rechnye Kotsy to cut off Staraia Russa from the west.

Four days are required to regroup and prepare the offensive. Consequently, we can attack on the morning of 13 March 1943.

3. During this period, Kurochkin's [34th] entire army will be regrouped to the Malye Gory and Borisovo regions west of the Lovat' River, from which it will attack to the west in the general direction of Ozhedovo and, subsequently, toward Ivanovskoe and Velikoe Selo.

The 27th Army will concentrate all of its forces and weapons in the Penno region for an attack to envelop Staraia Russa from the south and southwest in full cooperation with the 34th Army.

I am ordering the *front* commander to reinforce the 34th Army with two rifle divisions.

Korotkov and Zhuravlev [53d Army] will perform their assigned missions along their previous axes.

The 14th Guards Rifle Corps is entrusted with protecting the axes to Kholm and Poddor'e.

4. If you have no objections, I will now begin to prepare the offensive. Tolbukhin will begin to move to his new region today during the night. I have given him a preliminary order.

[signed] Konstantinov [Zhukov]

See "Doklad zamestitelia Verkhovnogo Glavnokomanduiushchego no. 1496 Verkhovnomu Glavnokomanduiushchemu ob izmeneniiakh v plane razgroma protivnika v raione Staroi Russy" [Report no. 1496 of the Deputy Supreme High Commander to the Supreme High Commander concerning changes in the plan for the destruction of the enemy in the Staraia Russa region], in Zolotarev, "*Stavka* VGK 1943," 283–284.

Stalin approved Zhukov's new plan without any hesitation and at 2150 hours on 8 March issued an implementing directive, which stated, "I approve your operational plan. Immediately proceed with the appropriate regrouping of your forces. Do not cease the 1st Shock and 27th Armies' artillery fire during the regrouping so as to mask your maneuver." See "Direktiva Stavki VGK predstaviteliu Stavki ob utverzhdenii plana razgroma protivnika v raione Staroi Russy" [*Stavka* VGK directive to the representative of the *Stavka* concerning approval of a plan for the destruction of the enemy in the Staraia Russa region], in Zolotarev, "*Stavka* VGK, 1943," 91.

81. "Direktiva Stavki VGK no. 30066 komanduiushchim voiskami Leningradskogo i Volkhovskogo frontov, predstaviteliu Stavki na razgrom nginsko-siniavinskoi gruppirovki protivnika" [*Stavka* VGK directive no. 30066 to the Leningrad and Volkhov Front commanders and the representative of the *Stavka* on the destruction of the Mga-Siniavino enemy grouping], in Zolotarev, "*Stavka* VGK 1943," 89–90.

82. See "Direktiva Stavki VGK no. 30056 komanduiushchim voiskami Leningradskogo i Volkhovskogo frontov, predstaviteliu Stavki o perepodchinenii 2-i udarnoi armii" [*Stavka* VGK directive no. 30065 to the Leningrad and Volkhov Front com-

588   The Battle for Leningrad

manders and the representative of the Stavka concerning the resubordination of the 2d Shock Army], in Zolotarev, "*Stavka* VGK 1943," 89.

83. The *Stavka* was reacting to the counteroffensive by Manstein's Army Group South against Soviet forces in the Donbas, Khar'kov, and Belgorod regions.

84. For details on Soviet operations at Demiansk and Staraia Russa and the *Stavka* directives transferring forces to the south, see Glantz, *Forgotten Battles of the German-Soviet War (1941–1945), volume IV*, 382–429.

85. The 52d Army consisted of the 65th, 225th, 229th, and 310th Rifle Divisions, the 38th Ski Brigade, the 34th, and 53d Aerosleigh Battalions, and the 150th Fortified Region. The 229th and 310th Rifle Divisions reinforced it just prior to the attack. See *Boevoi sostav, chast'* 3, 58.

86. Burov, *Blokada den' za dnem*, 327–329.

87. Carell, *Scorched Earth*, 247; and Platonov, *Bitva za Leningrad*, 278–279.

88. See German and estimated Soviet dispositions in "Der Feldzug," daily operational and intelligence maps for March 1943.

89. Platonov, *Bitva za Leningrad*, 278.

90. Burov, *Blokada den' za dnem*, 333.

91. Hitler actually harbored some hopes of conducting new offensives in the Leningrad region, if the *Wehrmacht* achieved victory at Kursk. The German defeat at Kursk ended any such hope.

92. Krivosheev, *Grif sekretnosti sniat*, 184–185.

93. Official figures indicate that the Leningrad Front suffered 390,794 casualties in 1943, including 88,745 killed, captured, or missing. It suffered well over one third of these (about 130,000 and 30,000 dead) during the first quarter of the year. During the same period, the Volkhov Front suffered 321,404 losses, including 77,904 dead, captured, or missing. Almost one half of these (160,000 with 38,000 dead) occurred in the first quarter of the year.

94. Krivosheev, *Grif sekretnosti sniat*, 226.

95. Gurkin, "Liudskie poteri," 7.

96. Carell, *Scorched Earth*, 247.

10. Stalemate

1. Zolotarev, "*Stavka* VGK 1943," 94–127.

2. Platonov, *Bitva za Leningrad*, 278.

3. Ibid., 280.

4. "Kraftegegenuberstellung, Stand: 20. 7. 43," *Fremde Heere Ost (IIc)*, National Archives microfilm (NAM) series T-78.

5. Platonov, *Bitva za Leningrad*, 280.

6. Burov, *Blokada den' za dnem*, 373–374.

7. Gribkov, *Istoriia ordena Lenina Leningradskogo voennogo okruga*, 329.

8. For additional details, see A. I. Babin, ed., *Na volkhovskom fronte 1941–1944 gg.* [At the Volkhov Front 1941–1944] (Moscow: Nauka, 1982), 221–222. For confirmation, see the operational and intelligence depiction in "Der Feldzug," maps and reports dated July and August 1943.

9. The 8th Army also included the 32d, 33d, 35th, and 50th Guards and 25th and

185th Separate Tank Regiments, but their subordination during the attack remains obscure.

10. These figures are an estimate compiled by the author based on the existing condition of opposing forces.

11. Gribkov, *Istoriia ordena Lenina Leningradskogo voennogo okruga*, 329.

12. Burov, *Blokada den' za dnem*, 377–384.

13. Gottlob Herbert Bidermann, *In Deadly Combat: A German Soldier's Memoir of the Eastern Front*, trans. and ed. Derek S. Zumbro (Lawrence: University Press of Kansas, 2000), 177–178.

14. Ibid., 178–179.

15. For a vivid description of the ensuing fighting and the evacuation of the bridgehead, see ibid., 179–180.

16. Ibid., 181.

17. Ibid.

18. "Direktiva Stavki VGK no. 30175 komanduiushchim voiskami volkhovskogo i leningradskogo frontov na perekhod k oborone" [*Stavka* VGK directive no. 30175 to the Volkhov and Leningrad Front commanders on a transition to the defenses], in Zolotarev, "*Stavka* VGK 1943," 195.

19. Krivosheev, *Grif sekretnosti sniat*, 226.

20. The Russians have yet to release the *Stavka* and *front* directives and orders associated with this offensive. Therefore, it must be reconstructed from German and fragmentary Russian sources.

21. Possible supporting armor included Colonel V. V. Khrustitsky's 30th Guards and Lieutenant Colonel V. L. Protsenko's 220th Tank Brigades and the 31st, 46th, and 49th Guards Tank Regiments. See *Boevoi sostav, chast' 3*, 213, 243.

22. Ibid.

23. See "Der Feldzug," maps and reports dated September 1943.

24. Gribkov, *Istoriia ordena Lenina Leningradskogo voennogo okruga*, 333.

25. Ibid.

26. *Boevoi sostav, chast' 3*, 213, 243.

27. Burov, *Blokada den' za dnem*, 400.

28. Ibid., 401.

29. *Small Units Actions during the German Campaign in Russia*, Department of the Army Pamphlet No. 20-269 (Washington, D.C.: Department of the Army, 1953), 165–167.

30. Bidermann, *In Deadly Combat*, 197–198.

31. Burov, *Blokada den' za dnem*, 407–408.

32. Bidermann, *In Deadly Combat*, 198–199.

33. "Kraftegegenuberstellung."

34. For further details, see Ziemke, *Stalingrad to Berlin*, 249.

35. Ibid.

11. Liberation

1. Platonov, *Bitva za Leningrad*, 291.

2. "Kraftegegenuberstellung."

3. See the appropriate directives in Zolotarev, "General'nyi shtab 1943," 414, 449–450.

4. Lieutenant General S. V. Roginsky had succeeded Sukhomlin in command of the 54th Army in March 1943.

5. When formed on the base of the former Briansk Front on 1 October, the 2d Baltic Front's predecessor, the Baltic Front, occupied the sector between the Northwestern and Kalinin Fronts. On 16 October 1943, the *Stavka* renamed the Baltic Front the 2d Baltic Front and the Kalinin Front the 1st Baltic Front, effective 20 October. Later, on 15 November, the *Stavka* disbanded the Northwestern Front, effective 26 November, and assigned its sector and the 1st Shock Army's sector to the 2d Baltic Front. See Zolotarev, "*Stavka* VGK 1943," 214, 225, 236–237.

6. Krivosheev, *Grif sekretnosti sniat,* 199.

7. See German dispositions in "Der Feldzug," maps and reports dated 31 December 1943. For changes after 1 January 1944, see "Lagenkarten of subordinate units of Heeresgruppe Nord, January–July 1944, K.T.B.," *H. Gr. Nord, 85540,* National Archives microfilm (NAM) series T-311.

8. Platonov, *Bitva za Leningrad,* 295.

9. "Kraftegegenuberstellung," considering troops withdrawal since 14 October 1943.

10. For a graphic display of German fortifications, strong points, centers of resistance, and defense lines, see "Ruckwarkige Stellung im Bereich der 18. Armee, Stand: 31. 12. 1943," in "Der Feldzug."

11. Platonov, *Bitva za Leningrad,* 296.

12. See details on German planning in Ziemke, *Stalingrad to Berlin,* 248–251.

13. Platonov, *Bitva za Leningrad,* 299–300.

14. "Komanduiushchim voiskami Leningradskogo,Volkhovskogo i Severo-zapadnogo frontov o poriadke presledovaniia protivnika v sluchae ego otkhoda" [To the Leningrad, Volkhov, and Northwestern Front commanders concerning the order of pursuing the enemy in the event of his withdrawal], in Zolotarev, "General'nyi shtab 1943," 348.

15. Ibid., 371.

16. Additional reinforcements were scarce since at that time the *Stavka* was conducting simultaneous offensives in Belorussia and the Ukraine. Nevertheless, it assigned the Volkhov Front additional long-range aviation forces and one self-propelled artillery regiment and the Leningrad Front four self-propelled artillery regiments, tank reserves, and one assault engineer-sapper brigade.

17. Burov, *Blokada den' za dnem,* 408–409.

18. For all planning details in the Leningrad Front, see Platonov, *Bitva za Leningrad,* 302–303.

19. By late 1943, to improve command and control, the Red Army had reintroduced the rifle corps headquarters as the premier command link between the army and its subordinate rifle divisions. By this time, most armies consisted of from two to four rifle corps. Since most rifle divisions ranged in strength from 3,000 to 6,000 men, the rifle corps, which contained an average of three rifle divisions, was equivalent in strength to a reinforced regulation rifle division or a standard full-strength German, U.S., or British infantry division.

20. Ibid., 305–306.

21. For details on the 2d Shock Army's regrouping and operations, see also V. A. Kuznetsov, ed., *Vtoraia udarnaia v bitva za Leningrad* [The 2d Shock in the Battle for Leningrad] (Leningrad: Lenizdat, 1983); and A. Rakitsky, "Udar pod Leningradom" [The attack at Leningrad], *VIZh* 1 (January 1974): 26–36.

22. Platonov, *Bitva za Leningrad*, 305–306.

23. Ibid., 306–317.

24. Ibid., 306.

25. For details on the 59th Army's operations, see the army commander's detailed account in I. T. Korovnikov, *Novgorodsko-luzhkaia operatsiia: Nastuplenie voisk 59-i armii (ianvar'–fevral' 1944 g.)* [The Novgorod-Luga operation: The 59th Army's offensive (January–February 1944)] (Moscow: Voenizdat, 1960), and the formerly classified and even more exquisitely detailed "Novgorodskaia operatsiia" [The Novgorod operation], in *Sbornik materialov po izucheniiu opyta voiny, no. 12 (mai-iiun' 1944 g.)* [A collection of materials for the study of the war experience, no. 12, (May–June 1944)] (Moscow: Voenizdat, 1944), 30–53. Hereafter cited as *SMPIOV*.

26. Platonov, *Bitva za Leningrad*, 306–317.

27. See changes in German dispositions in "Lagenkarten."

28. Platonov, *Bitva za Leningrad*, 304.

29. Ibid., 330.

30. Burov, *Blokada den' za dnem*, 450–451.

31. Ibid., 332; and Kuznetsov, *Vtoraia udarnaia*, 234–235.

32. Platonov, *Bitva za Leningrad*, 333.

33. Burov, *Blokada den' za dnem*, 452.

34. For changes in German dispositions, see "Lagenkarten," maps for January 1944.

35. Platonov, *Bitva za Leningrad*, 336.

36. Burov, *Blokada den' za dnem*, 453. Burov cites numerous examples to illustrate his point.

37. Ibid., 337.

38. Ibid., 454.

39. Ibid., 339.

40. Ziemke, *Stalingrad to Berlin*, 253.

41. "Lagenkarten," maps from 17–19 January 1944.

42. Platonov, *Bitva za Leningrad*, 338–339.

43. Burov, *Blokada den' za dnem*, 454–455.

44. Ibid., 455.

45. Ziemke, *Stalingrad to Berlin*, 253–254.

46. Platonov, *Bitva za Leningrad*, 344.

47. Ibid., 345. For details, see Korovnikov, *Novgorodkso-luzhskaia operatsiia*, 73–74. Only 11 of the 39 tanks supporting the 6th Rifle Corps made it to the German forward positions.

48. Platonov, *Bitva za Leningrad*, 346. Earlier, Korovnikov had planned to use Urvanov's 16th Tank Brigade as an exploitation force in his army's main attack sector.

49. Ibid., 346–347.

50. "Lagenkarten," maps from 17–19 January 1944.

51. Platonov, *Bitva za Leningrad*, 347. See also *SMPIOV*, no. 12.

52. Ziemke, *Stalingrad to Berlin*, 253.

53. Platonov, *Bitva za Leningrad*, 348.

54. Albert Seaton, *The Russo-German War 1941–1945* (New York: Praeger, 1971), 411.

55. Soviet after-action critiques criticized Artiushenko, the 14th Rifle Corps commander, for poor reconnaissance and timidity in his assault on the city.

56. Platonov, *Bitva za Leningrad*, 348.

57. Ziemke, *Stalingrad to Berlin*, 254–256.

58. Platonov, *Bitva za Leningrad*, 349.

59. For example, see the *Stavka* directive in V. A. Zolotarev, ed., "Stavka VGK: Dokumenty i materialy 1944–1945" [*Stavka* VGK: Documents and materials 1944–1945] in *Russkii arkhiv: Velikaia Otechestvennaia [voina]* [Russian archive: The Great Patriotic (War)], vol. 16, 5 (4) (Moscow: Terra, 1999), 37.

60. In many ways, the *Stavka* plan resembled Zhukov's earlier plan for Operation Polar Star.

61. Soon after, the *Stavka* assigned Lieutenant General M. I. Kazakov, Popov's deputy, to command the 10th Guards Army. Like Govorov, Kazakov was an artillery officer whose background the *Stavka* assumed would suit him to assault heavy German defenses.

62. See, "Lagenkarten," maps from January 1944.

63. Ziemke, *Stalingrad to Berlin*, 256.

64. Platonov, *Bitva za Leningrad*, 355–356.

65. Burov, *Blokada den' za dnem*, 456.

66. Platonov, *Bitva za Leningrad*, 356.

67. Ziemke, *Stalingrad to Berlin*, 256.

68. See "Doklad komanduiushchego voiskami Leningradskogo fronta no. 762 Verkhovnomu Glavnokomanduiuschemu o plane razvitiia operatsii v napravlenii Tosno, Luga" [Report no. 762 of the Leningrad Front commander on a plan for the development of the operation toward Tosno and Luga], in Zolotarev, "Stavka VGK 1944–1945," 262.

69. See "Direktiva Stavki VGK No. 220012 komanduiushchemu voiskami Leningradskogo fronta ob utverzhdenii plana nastupleniia v napravlenii Tosno, Luga" [*Stavka* VGK directive no. 220012 concerning the approval of a plan for an offensive toward Tosno and Luga], in Zolotarev, "Stavka VGK 1944–1945," 36.

70. See "Doklad komanduiushchego voiskami Volkhovskogo fronta No. 87 Verkhovnomu Glavnokomanduiushchemu o plane razvitiia novgorodsko-luzhskoi operatsii" [Report no. 87 of the Volkhov Front commander on a plan for the development of the Novgorod-Luga operation], in Zolotarev, "Stavka VGK 1944–1945," 263.

71. See "Direktiva Stavki VGK No. 220013 komanduiushchemu voiskami Volkhovskogo fronta ob utverzhdenii plana razvitiia novgorodsko-luzhskoi operatsii" [*Stavka* VGK directive no. 220013 to the Volkhov Front commander concerning the approval of a plan for the development of the Novgorod-Luga operation], in Zolotarev, "Stavka VGK 1944–1945," 37.

72. Platonov, *Bitva za Leningrad*, 359.

73. Ibid.

74. See "Lagenkarten," maps from January 1944.

75. Burov, *Blokada den' za dnem,* 456–457.
76. Ziemke, *Stalingrad to Berlin,* 256.
77. Ibid.
78. Ibid., 256–257.
79. Ibid., 257.
80. Platonov, *Bitva za Leningrad,* 361.
81. See "Lagenkarten," maps from January 1944.
82. Burov, *Blokada den' za dnem,* 458.
83. Ibid.
84. Platonov, *Bitva za Leningrad,* 362–363.
85. Ibid., 367.
86. Ibid.
87. Ibid., 367–368.
88. Ibid., 369.
89. See "Lagenkarten," maps from January 1944.
90. Korovnikov, *Novgorodsko-luzhskaia operatsiia,* 104–105. Korovnikov attached a full engineer-sapper brigade to each of his rifle corps and the 109th Motorized Engineer Battalion to Mikul'sky's 6th Rifle Corps.
91. See "Lagenkarten," maps from January 1944.
92. Platonov, *Bitva za Leningrad,* 373.
93. Ibid., 374.
94. Command and control were difficult since the entire Volkhov Front had only four cable companies.
95. Platonov, *Bitva za Leningrad,* 376.
96. See "Lagenkarten," maps from January 1944.
97. "Direktiva Stavki VGK no. 220015 komanduiushchemu voiskami Volkhovskogo fronta na osvobozhdenie g. Luga" [*Stavka* VGK directive no. 2200015 to the Volkhov Front commander on the liberation of Luga], in Zolotarev, "*Stavka* VGK 1944–1945," 38.
98. Platonov, *Bitva za Leningrad,* 379.
99. Ibid., 380.
100. Ibid., 380–381.
101. See "Lagenkarten," maps from January 1944.
102. Burov, *Blokada den' za dnem,* 459.

12. To Narva, Luga, and the Panther Line

1. See the appropriate *Stavka* directive in Zolotarev, "*Stavka* VGK 1944–1945," 27–38.
2. For details on these exchanges between Kuechler, Hitler, and the OKH, see Ziemke, *Stalingrad to Berlin,* 256–257.
3. Ibid., 258.
4. Ibid.
5. "Direktiva Stavki VGK no. 220015 komanduiushchemu voiskami Volkhovskogo fronta na osvobozhdenie g. Luga" [*Stavka* VGK directive no. 220015 to the Volkhov Front commander on the liberation of Luga], in Zolotarev, "*Stavka* VGK

1944–1945," 38. The *Stavka* dispatched this directive to Meretskov at 2400 hours on 29 January.

6. "Direktiva Stavki VGK no. 220016 komanduiushchim voiskami Leningrad-skogo i Volkhovskogo frontov na perepodchinenie 124-go strelkovogo korpusa i aktivizatsiiu boevykh deistvii po osvobozhdeniu Lugi" [*Stavka* VGK directive no. 220016 to the Leningrad and Volkhov Front commanders on the transfer of the 124th Rifle Corps and the activation of combat operations for the liberation of Luga], in Zolotarev, "*Stavka* VGK 1944–1945," 39. This transmission went out at 1715 hours on 1 February.

7. "Direktiva Stavki VGK no. 220017 komanduiushchim voiskami Volkhovskogo i 2–go Pribaltiiskogo frontov, predstaviuteliu Stavki na perepodchinenie 1-i udarnoi armii" [*Stavka* VGK directive no. 220017 to the Volkhov and 2d Baltic Front commanders and the *Stavka* representative on the resubordination of the 1st Shock Army], in Zolotarev, "*Stavka* VGK 1944–1945," 39. The transmission went out at 1735 on 1 February. The *Stavka* representative was N. N. Voronov.

8. Platonov, *Bitva za Leningrad,* 382.

9. Ibid., 383. For details, see Kuznetsov, *Vtoraia udarnaia,* 256.

10. Ziemke, *Stalingrad to Berlin,* 259.

11. Ibid.

12. Platonov, *Bitva za Leningrad,* 385.

13. Ziemke, *Stalingrad to Berlin,* 263.

14. Platonov, *Bitva za Leningrad,* 385.

15. "Direktiva Stavki VGK no. 220025 komanduiushchemu voiskami Leningrad-skogo fronta o srokakh osvobozhdeniia Narvy" [*Stavka* VGK directive no. 220025 to the Leningrad Front commander concerning the periods for the liberation of Narva], in Zolotarev, "*Stavka* VGK 1944–1945," 44.

16. Ziemke, *Stalingrad to Berlin,* 262.

17. Ibid.

18. For details on German dispositions and force composition, see "Lagenkarten," maps for February.

19. Platonov, *Bitva za Leningrad,* 386.

20. Ziemke, *Stalingrad to Berlin,* 259.

21. Ibid., 260.

22. Ibid.

23. Ibid., 261. See also "Lagenkarten," maps for February.

24. Ziemke, *Bitva za Leningrad,* 261.

25. See details of the Soviet deployments and subsequent action in Platonov, *Bitva za Leningrad,* 387.

26. Ibid.

27. Ziemke, *Stalingrad to Berlin,* 261.

28. Platonov, *Bitva za Leningrad,* 388.

29. Ziemke, *Stalingrad to Berlin,* 261.

30. Ibid., 261–262.

31. Ibid., 263.

32. For details on the composition and dispositions of German forces during February and March, see "Lagenkarten," and the associated "Feindlage-handskizzen, 22.

2.–15. 6. 44," in *K.T.B. Oberkommmando Heeresgruppe Nord, No. 75131/49*, National Archives microfilm (NAM) series T-311.

33. Platonov, *Bitva za Leningrad,* 389.

34. Ibid., 391–392.

35. Ibid., 392–292, provides the specific missions assigned to each partisan brigade.

36. Ibid., 393–394.

37. Ibid., 394–395; and "Feindlage-handskizzen."

38. Platonov, *Bitva za Leningrad,* 395.

39. For details on the 256th and 32d Rifle Divisions' battle in encirclement, see F. N. Utenkov, "Boevye deistviia chastei 256-i i 372-i strelkovykh divizii v okruzhenii" [The combat operations of the 256th and 372d Rifle Divisions in encirclement], *VIZh* 2 (February 1988): 76–80.

40. Platonov, *Bitva za Leningrad,* 396.

41. Ibid., 395.

42. See German redeployments in "Feindlage-handskizzen."

43. "Direktiva Stavki VGK no. 220023 komanduiushchim voiskami Leningradskogo i Volkhovskogo fronta ob uprazdnenii Volkhovskogo fronta" [*Stavka* VGK directive no. 220023 to the Leningrad and Volkhov Front commanders concerning the dissolution of the Volkhov Front], in Zolotarev, "*Stavka* VGK 1944–1945," 43, and the associated directive to the 2d Baltic Front in Zolotarev, "*Stavka* VGK 1944–1945," 43–44. The directive read:

The *Stavka* of the Supreme High Command *orders:*
1. Transfer from the Volkhov Front effective 2400 hours 15 February:
   a. To the Leningrad Front:
- the 59th Army consisting of the 112th Rifle Corps (the 2d and 277th Rifle Divisions), the 6th Rifle Corps (the 286th and 239th Rifle Divisions and the 24th Rifle Brigade);
- the 8th Army consisting of the 7th Rifle Corps (the 372d, 256th, 378th, and 191st Rifle Divisions and the 58th Rifle Brigade), the 99th Rifle Corps (the 311th, 229th, and 265th Rifle Divisions), the 14th Rifle Corps (the 382d, 225th, and 285th Rifle Divisions), and the 2d and 150th Fortified Regions; and
- the 54th Army consisting of the 111th Rifle Corps (the 44th and 28th Rifle Divisions and the 1st Rifle Brigade), the 119th Rifle Corps (the 198th and 364th Rifle Divisions), and the 65th and 310th Rifle Divisions of the *front's* reserve.
   b. To the 2d Baltic Front:
- the 1st Shock Army consisting of the 14th Guards Rifle Corps (the 23d Guards and 208th Rifle Divisions and the 137th Rifle Brigade), the 391st Rifle Division, and the 14th Rifle Brigade.

2. Transfer the armies with all their reinforcing units and rear service units, installations, and reserves.
3. Leave all Volkhov Front rear service headquarters and units and facilities in place and temporarily subordinate them to the Leningrad Front commander.
4. After the transfer of the Volkhov Front's armies consider the *front* dissolved and temporarily leave the *front* headquarters in Novgorod in *Stavka* reserve.
5. Effective 2400 hours 15 February 1944, establish the following boundary line between the Leningrad and 2d Baltic Front: the mouth of the Shelon' River, Dno, Ostrov, Pliavinas, and farther along the Western Dvina River to Riga (all points inclusive for the Leningrad Front).
6. Report fulfillment.

[signed] I. Stalin, A. Antonov

44. Platonov, *Bitva za Leningrad*, 398.

45. Ibid., 398–399.

46. Korovnikov, Lebedev, and Poliakov, *Na trekh frontak*, 149–150.

47. Ziemke, *Stalingrad to Berlin*, 264–265.

48. "Direktiva Stavki VGK no. 220035 komanduiushchemu voiskami Leningrad-skogo fronta o razvitii nastupleniia v raione Chudskogo ozera" [*Stavka* VGK directive no. 022035 to the Leningrad Front commander concerning the offensive in the Lake Chud region], in Zolotarev, "*Stavka* VGK 1944–1945," 50. See Govorov's original proposal in Zolotarev, "*Stavka* VGK 1944–1945," 267–268. In this directive, Govorov placed priority on the capture of Narva.

49. Platonov, *Bitva za Leningrad*, 401.

50. Ibid.

51. Ibid.

52. Ibid., 402.

53. Ibid., 403.

54. Ibid.

55. Ziemke, *Stalingrad to Berlin*, 264.

56. "Direktiva Stavki VGK no. 220026 komanduiushchim voiskami 1-go i 2-go Pribaltiiskikh frontov o razvitii nastupleniia na idritskom i sebezhkom napravleniiakh" [*Stavka* VGK directive no. 220026 to the 1st and 2d Baltic Front commander concerning the development of an offensive along the Idritsa and Sebezh axes], in Zolotarev, "*Stavka* VGK 1944–1945," 44–45.

57. Ziemke, *Stalingrad to Berlin*, 264.

58. Platonov, *Bitva za Leningrad*, 404.

59. Ibid. See also "Feindlage-handskizzen."

60. Ziemke, *Stalingrad to Berlin*, 264.

61. Platonov, *Bitva za Leningrad*, 405.

62. Ibid.; and "Feindlage-handskizzen."

63. Platonov, *Bitva za Leningrad*, 406; and "Feindlage-handskizzen."

64. Platonov, *Bitva za Leningrad*, 406.

65. Krivosheev, *Grif sekretnosti sniat*,199.

66. Platonov, *Bitva za Leningrad*, 406.

67. "Doklad komanduiushchego voiskami Leningradskogo fronta no. 126 Verkhovnomu Glavnokomanduiushchemu o plane nastupatel'noi operatsii na narvskom napravlenii" [Report no. 126 of the Leningrad Front commander on a plan for an offensive operation along the Narva axis], in Zolotarev, "*Stavka* VGK 1944–1945," 267–268.

68. Korovnikov, Lebedev, and Poliakov, *Na trekh frontakh*, 151–152. There are few if any accounts of the 2d Shock Army's role in the fighting around Narva in March and April.

69. Zolotarev, ed., *VOV*, 30.

70. Ibid., 31.

71. Ibid., 152.

72. K. A. Orlov, ed., *Bor'ba za Sovetskuiu Pribaltiku v Velikoi Otechestvennoi voine, 1941–1945 v trekh knigakh* [The struggle for the Soviet Baltic region in the Great Patriotic War, 1941–1945, in three books], book 1 (Riga: Diesma, 1966), 120.

73. For details on the 8th Army's defense, see Gladysh, "O maloizvestnoi oboronitel'noi operatsii," 28–36. At the time Starikov's army consisted of the 112th, 122d, 117th, and 6th Rifle Corps deployed from left to right in the bridgehead south of Narva. A total of 10 rifle divisions defended the bridgehead.

74. Ibid., 121.

75. Zolotarev, *VOV*, 30.

76. Ibid., 31.

77. D. F. Ustinov, ed., *Istoriia Vtoroi Mirovoi voiny 1939–1945 v dvenadtsaty tomakh* [A history of the Second World War in twelve volumes], vol. 8 (Moscow: Voenizdat, 1977), 129.

78. Orlov, *Bor'ba za Sovetskuiu Pribaltiku,* 31.

79. Zolotarev, *VOV,* 31.

80. "Doklad predstavitelei Stavki i General'nogo Shtaba no. 5 Verkhovnomu Glavnokomanduiushchemu o plane razgroma idritskoi gruppirovki protivnika" [Report no. 5 by the representatives of the *Stavka* and General Staff on a plan for the destruction of the enemy's Idritsa grouping], in Zolotarev, "*Stavka* VGK 1944–1945," 276–277. The message was sent at 1510 hours on 3 March.

81. "Direktiva Stavki VGK no. 220045 predstaviteliu Stavki, komanduiushchim voiskami 2-go i 1-go Pribaltiiskikh frontov na razgrom idritskoi gruppirovki protivnika" [*Stavka* VGK directive no. 22 to the *Stavka* representative and the 2d and 1st Baltic Front commanders on the destruction of the enemy Idritsa grouping], in Zolotarev, "*Stavka* VGK 1944–1945," 55–56.

82. For details on the Germans' daily dispositions and a graphic representation of the little progress the Red Army made, see "Feindlage-handskizzen."

83. For further details on the offensive, see G. I. Berdnikov, *Pervaia udarnaia: Boevoi put' 1-i udarnoi armii v Velikoi Otechestvennoi voine* [The 1st Shock: The combat path of the 1st Shock Army in the Great Patriotic War] (Moscow: Voenizdat, 1985), 158–163; P. K. Altukhov, ed., *Nezabyvaemye dorogi: Boevoi put' 10-i gvardeiskoi armii* [Unforgettable roads: The combat path of the 10th Guards Army] (Moscow: Voenizdat, 1974), 107–112; and V. K. Piatkov, ed., *Tret'ia udarnaia: Boevoi put' 3-i udarnoi armii* [The 3d Shock: The combat path of the 3d Shock Army] (Moscow: Voenizdat, 1976), 91–92. See the appropriate *Stavka* orders, dated 1 April, 4 April, 12 April, and 18 April, in Zolotarev, "*Stavka* VGK 1944–1945," 67–68, 71, 73, 75.

84. Ziemke, *Stalingrad to Berlin,* 265.

85. "Direktiva Stavki VGK no. 220081 komanduiushchemu voiskami 2-go Pribaltiiskogo fronta na perekhod k oborone" [*Stavka* VGK directive no. 220081 to the 2d Baltic Front commander on the transition to the defense], in Zolotarev, "*Stavka* VGK 1944–1945," 75.

86. See "Direktiva Stavki VGK no. 220082 komanduiushchemu i zamestiteliu komanduiushchego voiskami Leningradskogo fronta o formirovanii 3-ogo Pribaltiiskogo fronta" [*Stavka* VGK directive no. 220082 to the Leningrad Front commander and deputy commander concerning the formation of the 3d Baltic Front], in Zolotarev, "*Stavka* VGK 1944–1945," 75–76.

87. Platonov, *Bitva za Leningrad,* 408.

88. Ibid., 412–413. See also "Novgorodskaia operatsia," 30–53.

89. Platonov, *Bitva za Leningrad,* 416.

90. Krivosheev, *Grif sekretnosti sniat,* 199.

91. For example, the Leningrad Front lost 665,827 soldiers in all of 1944, including 227,440 in the Leningrad-Novgorod offensive, 30,029 in the Karelian offensive (July–August), and 28,776 in operations to clear Estonia of German forces (September–November), for a total of 286,245 troops. Many of the remaining 380,000 troops perished in other operations, including the operations to penetrate the Panther Line. A similar situation existed in the 2d Baltic Front. See Krivosheev, *Grif sekretnosti sniat.*

92. See "Kraftegegenuberstellung."

13. The Liberation of Northern Leningrad Region

1. In Stalin's day, these operations were known as the nine blows, which included: (1) the Leningrad-Novgorod offensive, January–February 1944; (2) the Right Bank of the Ukraine offensive, February–March 1944, (3) the Odessa and Crimean offensive, April–May 1944, (4) the Karelian offensive, June 1944, (5) the Belorussian offensive, June–August 1944, (6) the L'vov-Sandomiersz offensive, July–August 1944, (7) the Iassy-Kishinev offensive, August 1944, (8) the Baltic offensive, September–October 1944, and (9) the Hungarian offensive, September–December 1944. See, for example, S. Golikov, *Vydaiushchiesia pobedy Sovetskoi armii v Velikoi Otechestvennoi voine* [The Soviet Army's outstanding victories in the Great Patriotic War] (Moscow: Gosudarstvennoe izdatel'stvo politicheskoi literatury, 1954).

2. For details on these negotiations, see Ziemke, *Stalingrad to Berlin,* 268–269; and Platonov, *Bitva za Leningrad,* 418.

3. Ziemke, *Stalingrad to Berlin,* 269.

4. Ibid.

5. For the most detailed Soviet description of the situation on the Karelian Isthmus prior to June 1944 and Soviet planning and conduct of the Vyborg offensive operation, see "Vyborgskaia operatsiia (10–20 iiunia 1944 g.)" [The Vyborg operation [10–20 June 1944], in *Sbornik materialov po izucheniiu opyta voiny no. 16 (ianvar'-fevral' 1945 g.)* [A collection of materials for the study of the war experience no. 16 (January–February 1945)] (Moscow: Voenizdat, 1945), 3–28. Prepared by the Red Army General Staff's Directorate for the Exploitation of War Experience and classified secret. Hereafter cited as SMPIOV. Platonov's study, *Bitva za Leningrad,* is derived directly from this study but also provides details on Leningrad Front operations after 21 June 1944.

6. Platonov, *Bitva za Leningrad,* 420–421.

7. Ibid., 421.

8. Ibid.

9. See ibid.; "An Interview with Mr. Hyry,"in Pasi Kusppamaki, ed., *A Web History of Finland,* Edition 2.3 (2000), 1–13; The website's URL is http://ky.hkkk.fi/~k21206/finhist.html#war and the interview's URL is http://www.warlinks.com/memories/hyry.htm. See also Paul Sjoblom, "Finland Did Not Capitulate," in Kusppamaki, *A Web History of Finland.* According to Finnish sources, the army had roughly 40 tanks, including 25 German assault guns and about a dozen captured Soviet T-34 and KV tanks, and 268 guns on the Karelian Isthmus, supported by about 170 aircraft.

10. Platonov, *Bitva za Leningrad*, 420–421. For a detailed formerly classified description of the Finnish defenses, see "Inzhenernoe obespechenie proryva oborony finnov na Karel'skom peresheike" [Engineer support of the penetration of the Finnish defense on the Karelian Peninsula], in *SMPIOV, no. 14 (sentaibr'-oktiabr' 1944 g.)* [A collection of materials for the study of the war experience, no. 14 (September–October 1944)] (Moscow: Voenizdat, 1945), 180–194.

11. The 21st Army had participated in the Smolensk offensive operation under Western Front control in late summer 1943, and in late October 1943 it transferred its forces to the 33d Army and reverted to *Stavka* reserve.

12. Platonov, *Bitva za Leningrad*, 427.

13. Ibid., 428. See also Ustinov, *Istoriia Vtoroi Mirovoi voiny*, 27. In late March 1944, the Leningrad Front's overall ration strength was 765,000 troops, and the Karelian Front's strength was 335,000 personnel. See "Postanovlenie GKO 12 marta 1944 g." [GKO order dated 12 March 1944], TsPA IMA (Central Political Administration of the Institute of Marxism and Leninism), f. 644, op. 1g, l. 218. These strengths had certainly increased by July 1944.

14. Platonov, *Bitva za Leningrad*, 429.

15. Ibid., 429–430.

16. Ibid., 430.

17. For additional details on naval support, see V. A. Kasatonov, ed., *Krasnoznamennyi Baltiiskii flot v Velikoi Otechestvennoi voine Sovetskogo naroda 1941–1945 v chetyrekh knigaksh* [The Red Banner Baltic Fleet in the Great Patriotic War of the Soviet people 1941–1945 in four books] book 2 (Moscow: Nauka, 1991).

18. The 109th Rifle Corps consisted of the 72d, 109th, and 286th Rifle Divisions, the 30th Guards Rifle Corps included the 45th, 63d, and 64th Guards Rifle Divisions, and the 97th Rifle Corps consisted of the 78th, 358th, and 381st Rifle Divisions.

19. Platonov, *Bitva za Leningrad*, 434–435.

20. The 115th Rifle Corps consisted of the 142d, 10th, and 92d Rifle Divisions.

21. The 98th Rifle Corp included the 372d, 281st, and 177th Rifle Divisions.

22. The 115th Rifle Corps would leave the 92d and 142d Rifle Divisions along its center and right flank.

23. Platonov, *Bitva za Leningrad*, 436.

24. Ibid., 436–437.

25. Ibid., 437.

26. For details, see "Inzhenernoe obespechenie proryva oborony finnov na Karel'skom peresheike."

27. Platonov, *Bitva za Leningrad*, 442–443.

28. Ibid., 443.

29. Ibid., 443–444. See also Gribkov, *Istoriia ordena Lenina Leningradskogo voennogo okruga*, 376–377. Gribkov also provides considerable details on the ensuing operation.

30. See more details on the artillery preparation in Platonov, *Bitva za Leningrad*, 444–445.

31. Ibid., 448.

32. Ibid., 449–451; and Ziemke, *Stalingrad to Berlin*, 298–299.

33. Platonov, *Bitva za Leningrad*, 451.

34. Ibid.

35. "Direktiva Stavki VGK no. 220116 komanduiushchemu voiskami Leningrad-skogo fronta na razvitie nastupleniia i osvobozhdenie Vyborga" [Stavka VGK direc-tive no. 220116 to the Leningrad Front commander concerning the development of the offensive and the liberation of Vyborg], Zolotarev, "*Stavka VGK 1944–1945*," 96. See also Platonov, *Bitva za Leningrad*, 452.

36. Ziemke, *Stalingrad to Berlin*, 299.

37. Gribkov, *Istoriia ordena Lenina Leningradskogo voennogo okruga*, 376–377.

38. Platonov, *Bitva za Leningrad*, 454.

39. Ibid., 455–456.

40. Ibid., 456; and Gribkov, *Istoriia ordena Lenina Leningradskogo voennogo okruga*, 377.

41. Platonov, *Bitva za Leningrad*, 456.

42. Ibid, 458; and Ziemke, *Stalingrad to Berlin*, 299.

43. Platonov, *Bitva za Leningrad*, 459.

44. As is the case with many Karelian place names, Soviet sources offer a variety of transliterations into Russian, such as Metsiakiulia or Miatsiakiulia.

45. Gribkov, *Istoriia ordena Lenina Leningradskogo voennogo okruga*, map be-tween 376 and 377.

46. Platonov, *Bitva za Leningrad*, 462.

47. Ibid., 463.

48. Ziemke, *Stalingrad to Berlin*, 299.

49. Platonov, *Bitva za Leningrad*, 464.

50. "An Interview with Mr. Hyry," 9–10.

51. Platonov, *Bitva za Leningrad*, 465.

52. Ibid.

53. Ibid., 466.

54. Ibid.

55. "An Interview with Mr. Hyry," 10.

56. Ibid., 10–11.

57. Platonov, *Bitva za Leningrad*, 466; and Gribkov, *Istoriia ordena Lenina Lenin-gradskogo voennogo okruga*, map between 376 and 377.

58. Platonov, *Bitva za Leningrad*, 467.

59. Ibid.

60. "An Interview with Mr. Hyry," 11.

61. Platonov, *Bitva za Leningrad*, 468.

62. Ibid. See also "An Interview with Mr. Hyry," 11, which states that the Ger-mans dispatched "a task force of 35 Ju-87 Stuka dive bombers and about 35 WF-190 Jabo fighter-bombers." Ziemke, *Stalingrad to Berlin*, 300, states that the Germans provided "air units (a fighter group and a ground attack close support group [Stukas] plus one squadron)."

63. Platonov, *Bitva za Leningrad*, 468.

64. Ibid.

65. Ibid., 468–470.

66. Ziemke, *Stalingrad to Berlin*, 301.

67. Platonov, *Bitva za Leningrad*, 470.

68. Ziemke, *Stalingrad to Berlin*, 300.

69. "Direktiva Stavki VGK no. 220119 komanduiushchemu voiskami Leningradskogo fronta o prodolzhenii nastupleniia na Karel'skom peresheike" [*Stavka* VGK directive no. 220119 to the Leningrad Front commander concerning the continuation of the offensive along the Karelian Isthmus], in Zolotarev, "*Stavka* VGK 1944–1945," 97–98.

70. These included the IV and V Army Corps' 3d, 4th, and 18th Infantry Divisions and 20th and 3d Infantry Brigades and the III Army Corps' 2d and 15th Infantry Divisions and 19th Infantry Brigade. In addition, this Soviet count includes the 6th and 10th Infantry Divisions, the Lagus Armored Division, and the 1st Cavalry Brigade, which were still refitting after fighting for 10 days during the Vyborg operation.

71. Platonov, *Bitva za Leningrad*, 475.

72. Ibid., 474. See the full text of Govorov's plan in "Doklad komanduiushchego voiskami Leningradskogo fronta no. 8831 Verkhovnomu Glavnokomanduiushchemu o plane razvitiia nastupleniia na Karel'skom peresheike" [Leningrad Front commander's report no. 8831 to the Supreme High Commander on a plan for the development of the offensive on the Karelian Isthmus], in Zolotarev, "*Stavka* VGK 1944–1945," 286–287.

73. "Direktiva Stavki VGK no. 220121 komanduiushchemu voiskami Leningrad-skogo fronta ob utverzhdenii resheniia po razvitiiu nastupleniia na Karel'skom peresheike" [*Stavka* VGK directive no. 220121 to the Leningrad Front commander concerning the decision for developing the offensive on the Karelian Isthmus], in Zolotarev, "*Stavka* VGK 1944–1945," 98.

74. Platonov, *Bitva za Leningrad*, 475.

75. This Repola is distinct from the Repola east of Lake Noskuon-sel'ka.

76. It remains unclear exactly when Govorov decided to employ the 59th Army in an amphibious assault and when the *Stavka* approved Govorov's new plan. It is likely that he did so either after his 22–24 June assault failed or after his 25 June assault faltered short of its objective. In fact, for obvious reasons, Soviet sources have been reluctant to reveal many details of these unsuccessful operations.

77. Gribkov, *Istoriia ordena Lenina Leningradskogo voennogo okruga*, 395–396.

78. "An Interview with Mr. Hyry," 12.

79. Ibid. By this time, the four Soviet divisions probably totaled fewer than 20,000 men, with an average strength of well under 5,000 men each.

80. Gribkov, *Istoriia ordena Lenina Leningradskogo voennogo okruga*, 399–400; and Platonov, *Bitva za Leningrad*, 484–485.

81. Ziemke, *Stalingrad to Berlin*, 303.

82. Platonov, *Bitva za Leningrad*, 478.

83. Ibid., 479.

84. Ibid., 482.

85. Ibid., 486–487.

86. Krivosheev, *Grif sekretnosti sniat*, 201–202.

14. Conclusions

1. Advanced guards were primarily responsible for reconnoitering or protecting the main bodies of forces while on the march or in the attack. Instead of engaging

602   The Battle for Leningrad

the enemy, they were to facilitate the deployment of the main force. On the other hand, forward detachments were combat forces designated to disrupt enemy defenses or secure objectives to facilitate the advance of its parent force. Their business was to fight, preempt, and exploit.

2. For a discussion of the civilian death toll, see Rubtsov and Lur'e, "Blokada Leningrada," 30–33; and Salisbury, *900 Days,* 514–517.

3. See Krivosheev, *Grif sekretnosti sniat,* 232, 247–250, 253–254, 287–290.

4. Ibid., 233–234, 273–274.

5. Platonov, *Bitva za Leningrad,* 566.

6. K. Meretskov, *City Invincible* (Moscow: Progress, 1970), 87.

7. Salisbury, *The 900 Days,* 567–568.

Selected Bibliography

Primary Sources

Boevoi i chislennyi sostav vooruzhennykh sil SSSR v period Velikoi Otechestvennoi voiny (1941–1945 gg.): Statisticheskii sbornik no. 1 (22 iiunia 1941 g.) [The combat and numerical composition of the USSR's Armed Forces in the Great Patriotic War (1941–1945): Statistical collection no. 1 (22 June 1941)]. Moscow: Institute of Military History, 1994.

Boevoi sostav Sovetskoi armii, chast' 1 (iiun'–dekabr' 1941 goda) [The combat composition of the Soviet Army, part 1 (June–December 1941)]. Moscow: Voroshilov Academy of the General Staff, 1963.

Boevoi sostav Sovetskoi armii, chast' 2 (ianvar'–dekabr' 1942 goda) [The combat composition of the Soviet Army, part 2 (January–December 1941)]. Moscow: Voenizdat, 1966.

Boevoi sostav Sovetskoi armii, chast' 3 (ianvar'–dekabr' 1943 goda) [The combat composition of the Soviet Army, part 3 (January–December 1943)]. Moscow: Voenizdat, 1972.

Boevoi sostav Sovetskoi armii, chast' 4 (ianvar'–dekabr' 1944 goda) [The combat composition of the Soviet Army, part 4 (January–December 1944)]. Moscow: Voenizdat, 1988.

"Boevye dokumenty po oboronitel'noi operatsii v Litve i Latvii provodivshiesia s 22 iiunia do 9 iiulia 1941 g. voiskami Severo-Zapadnogo Fronta" [Combat documents on the defensive operations in Lithuania and Latvia, conducted from 22 June to 9 July 1941 by the Northwestern Front]. In *Sbornik boevykh dokumentov Velikoi Otechestvennoi voiny* [A collection of combat documents of the Great Patriotic War], issue 34. Moscow: Voenizdat, 1958. Classified secret.

"Der Feldzug gegen die Sowjet-Union der Heeresgruppe Nord, Kriegsjahr 1942, 1943, and 1944." *H. Gr. Nord.* National Archives Microfilm (NAM) series T-311.

"Dokumenty nemetskogo komandovaniia po voprosam podgotovki voiny" [Documents of the German command on issues in preparing for war], and "Dokumenty nemetskogo komandovaniia po voprosam vedeniia voiny" [Documents of the German command on the matter of the conduct of the war]. In *Sbornik voenno-istoricheskikh materialov Velikoi Otechestvennoi voiny* [Collection of military-historical materials of the Great Patriotic War], issue 18. Moscow: Voenizdat, 1960. Classified secret.

"Dokumenty po ispol'zovaniiu bronetankovykh i mekhanizirovannykh voisk Sovetskoi armii v period s 22 iiunia po sentiabr' 1941 g. vkliuchitel'no" [Documents on the use of armored and mechanized forces of the Soviet Army in the period from 22

604   The Battle for Leningrad

June to September 1941, inclusively]. In *Sbornik boevykh dokumentov Velikoi Otechestvennoi voiny* [A collection of combat documents of the Great Patriotic War], issue 33. Moscow: Voenizdat, 1957. Classified secret.

"Feindlage-handskizzen, 22. 2.—15. 6. 44." In *K.T.B. Oberkommmando Heeresgruppe Nord, No. 75131/49*. National Archives Microfilm (NAM) series T-311.

"Feindlagenkarten 19 July–1 Sep 1941." *Abtlg. Ic H. Gr. Nord, 75131/47 Box 103*. National Archives Microfilm (NAM) series T-311, roll 92.

Gor'kov Iu. A., and Iu. N. Semin. "Konets global'noi lzhi: Na sovetskom severo-zapade— Operativnye plany zapadnykh prigranichnykh okrugov 1941 goda svidetel'stvuiut: SSSR ne otovilsia k napadengiiu na Germaniiu [The end of a global lie: In the Soviet northwest—The operational plans of the western border districts in 1941 bear witness: the USSR had not prepared for an attack on Germany]. *Voenno-istoricheskii zhurnal* [Military-historical journal] 6 (November–December 1996): 2–7.

"Inzhenernoe obespechenie armeiskoi nastupatel'noi operatsii" [Engineer support of an army offensive operation]. In *Sbornik materialov po izucheniiu opyta voiny no. 9 (noiabr'–dekabr' 1943 g.)* [A collection of materials for the study of the war experience no. 9 (November–December 1943)]. Moscow: Voenizdat, 1944. Classified secret.

"Inzhernernoe obespechenie proryva oborony finnov na Karel'skom peresheike" [Engineer support of the penetration of the Finns' defenses on the Karelian Isthmus]. *Sbornik materialov po izucheniiu opyta voiny no. 14 (sentiabr'–oktiabr' 1944 g.)* [A collection of materials for the study of the war experience no. 14 (September–October 1944)]. Moscow: Voenizdat, 1945. Classified secret.

Komandovanie korpusnogo i divizionnogo zvena Sovetskykh Vooruzhennykh Sil perioda Velikoi Otechestvennoi voiny 1941–1945 [Corps and division commanders of the Soviet Armed Forces during the Great Patriotic War 1941–1945]. Moscow: Frunze Academy, 1964.

Kozlev, Valentina Fedorovna. Interview with the author.

"Kraftegegenuberstellung, Stand: 20. 7. 43." *Fremde Heere Ost (Ic)*. National Archives Microfilm (NAM) series T-78.

"Lagenkarten 8.7.41–1.8.41." *Heeresgruppe Nord* (original maps).

"Lagenkarten of subordinate units of Heeresgruppe Nord, January–July 1944, K.T.B." *H. Gr. Nord, 85540*. National Archives Microfilm (NAM) series T-311.

Lomagin, N. *V Tiskakh goloda: Blokada Leningrada v dokumentakh germanskikh spetssluzhb i NKVD* [In the wrench of hunger: The blockade of Leningrad in German and NKVD intelligence documents]. Saint Petersburg: Evropeiskii Dom, 2000.

"Nekotorye vyvody po zimnim deistviiam Volkhovskogo fronta" [Some conclusions on the Volkhov Front's winter operations]. In *Sbornik materialov po izucheniiu opyta voiny no. 3 (noiabr'–dekabr' 1942 g.)* [A collection of materials for the study of the war experience no. 3 (November–December 1942)]. Moscow: Voenizdat, 1943. Classified secret.

"Novgorodskaia operatsiia" [The Novgorod operation]. In *Sbornik materialov po izucheniiu opyta voiny no. 12 (mai-iiun' 1944 g.)* [A collection of materials for the study of the war experience no. 12 (May–June 1944)]. Moscow: Voenizdat, 1944. Classified secret.

"Oborona Leningrada" [The defense of Leningrad]. *Voenno-istoricheskii arkhiv* 4 (1999): 161–170.

"Organizatsiia perepravy chastei Nevskoi operativnoi gruppy Lenfronta 26.09. 41–08.10. 42 g. na levyi bereg r. Neva" [The organization of the crossings of the Neva Operational Group to the left bank of the Neva River 26 September 1941– 8 October 1942]. In *Sbornik materialov po opytu boevoi deiatel'nosti Voenno-Morskogo flota SSSR, no. 1* [A collection of materials on the experience of the combat activities of the USSR's fleet, no. 1]. Moscow: Voenmorizdat, 1943. Classified secret.

Petrov, B. N. "Oborona Leningrada, 1941 god (Dokumenty i kommentarii)" [The defense of Leningrad, 1941 (Documents and commentary)]. *Voenno-istoricheskii zhurnal* [Military-historical journal] 4–5 (May–June 1992): 14–18; 6–7 (June–July 1992): 14–19.

Schematische Kriegsgliederung, Stand: B-Tag 1941 (22.6) "Barbarossa." Original.

"State Defense Committee Decree of 11 September 1941." TsPA IML (Central Party Archives of the Institute of Marxism and Leninism), f. 644, op. 1, d. 9.

"Vyborgskaia operatsiia (10–20 iiunia 1944 g.)" [The Vyborg operation (10–20 June 1944)]. In *Sbornik materialov po izucheniiu opyta voiny no. 16 (ianvar'–fevral' 1945 g.)* [A collection of materials for the study of the war experience no. 16 (January–February 1945)]. Moscow: Voenizdat, 1945. Classified secret.

Zabaluev, A. A., and S. T. Goriachev. *Kalininskaia nastupatel'naia operatsiia* [The Kalinin offensive operation]. Moscow: Voroshilov Academy of the General Staff, 1942. Classified secret.

Zolotarev, V. A., ed. "General'nyi shtab v gody Velikoi Otechestvennoi voiny: Dokumenty i materialy 1941 god" [The General Staff in the Great Patriotic War: Documents and materials from 1941]. In *Russkii arkhiv: Velikaia Otechestvennaia [voina]* [Russian archive: The Great Patriotic (War)]. Vol. 23, no. 12 (1). Moscow: Terra, 1997.

————. "General'nyi shtab v gody Velikoi Otechestvennoi voiny: Dokumenty i materialy 1942 god" [The General Staff in the Great Patriotic War: Documents and materials from 1942]. In *Russkii arkhiv: Velikaia Otechestvennaia [voina]* [Russian archive: The Great Patriotic (War)]. Vol. 23, no. 12 (2). Moscow: Terra, 1999.

————. "General'nyi shtab v gody Velikoi Otechestvennoi voiny: Dokumenty i materialy 1943 god" [The General Staff in the Great Patriotic War: Documents and materials from 1943]. In *Russkii arkhiv: Velikaia Otechestvennaia [voina]* [Russian archive: The Great Patriotic (War)]. Vol. 23, no. 12 (3). Moscow: Terra, 1999.

————. "Partizanskoe dvizhenie v gody Velikoi Otechestvennoi voiny 1941–1945 gg.: Dokumenty i materialy" [The partisan movement in the Great Patriotic War 1941– 1945: Documents and materials]. In *Russkii arkhiv: Velikaia Otechestvennaia [voina]* [Russian archive: The Great Patriotic (War)]. Vol. 20 (9). Moscow: Terra, 1999.

————. "Stavka VGK: Dokumenty i materialy 1941 god" [The *Stavka* VGK: Documents and materials 1941]. In *Russkii arkhiv: Velikaia Otechestvennaia [voina]* [Russian archive: The Great Patriotic (War)]. Vol. 16, no. 5 (1). Moscow: Terra, 1996.

————. "Stavka VGK: Dokumenty i materialy 1942" [The *Stavka* VGK: Documents and materials 1942]. In *Russkii arkhiv: Velikaia Otechestvennaia [voina]* [Russian archive: The Great Patriotic (War)]. Vol. 16, no. 5 (2). Moscow: Terra, 1996.

————. "Stavka Verkhovnogo Glavnokomandovaniia: Dokumenty I materialy 1943 god" [The *Stavka* VGK: Documents and materials 1943]. In *Russkii arkhiv: Velikaia Otechestvennaia [voina]* [Russian archive: The Great Patriotic (War)]. Vol. 16, no. 5 (3). Moscow: Terra, 1999.

————. "Stavka VGK: Dokumenty i materialy 1944–1945" [The *Stavka* VGK: Documents and materials 1944–1945]. In *Russkii arkhiv: Velikaia Otechestvennaia [voina]* [Russian archive: The Great Patriotic (War)]. Vol. 16, no. 5 (4). Moscow: Terra, 1999.

Secondary Sources

BOOKS

Altukhov, P. K., ed. *Nezabyvaemye dorogi: Boevoi put' 10–i gvardeiskoi armii* [Unforgettable roads: The combat path of the 10th Guards Army]. Moscow: Voenizdat, 1974.

Anfilov, V. A. *Nezabyvaemyi sorok pervyi* [Unforgettable 1941]. Moscow: Sovetskaia Rossiia, 1989.

————. *Proval "Blitskriga"* [The defeat of blitzkreig]. Moscow: Nauka, 1974.

Babin, A. I., ed. *Na volkhovskom fronte 1941–1944 gg.* [At the Volkhov front 1941–1944]. Moscow: Nauka, 1982.

Baranov, V. I., ed., *Tankisti v srazhenii za Leningrad: Vospominaniia, ocherki, dokumenty* [Tank troops in the Battle for Leningrad: Recollections, essays, and documents]. Leningrad: Lenizdat, 1987.

Barbashin, I. P., and A. D. Kharitonov. *Boevye deistviia Sovetskoi armii pod Tikhvinom v 1941 godu* [Combat operations of the Soviet Army at Tikhvin in 1941]. Moscow: Voenizdat, 1958.

Berdnikov, G. I. *Pervaia udarnaia: Boevoi put' 1–i udarnoi armii v Velikoi Otechestvennoi voine* [The 1st Shock: The combat path of the 1st Shock Army in the Great Patriotic War]. Moscow: Voenizdat, 1985.

Berezovsky, N. Iu. "Kronshtadt." In *Voennaia entsiklopediia v vos'mi tomakh* [Military encyclopedia in eight volumes], ed. I. D. Sergeev, 4: 305. Moscow: Voenizdat, 1997.

Bidermann, Gottlob Herbert. *In Deadly Combat: A German Soldier's Memoir of the Eastern Front*. Trans. and ed. Derek S. Zumbro. Lawrence: University Press of Kansas, 2000.

Boevye deistviia 42–i armii i oborona putei soobshcheniia v bitve za Leningrad [The 42d Army's combat operation and defense of communications routes in the battle for Leningrad]. Moscow: Order of Lenin Red Banner Order of Suvorov, Frunze Military Academy, 1975.

Boitsov, S. M., and S. N. Borshchev. *Operatsiia "Iskra"* [Operation Spark]. Leningrad: Lenizdat, 1973.

Burdick, Charles, and Hans-Adolf Jacobsen. *The Halder War Diary, 1939–1942*. Novato, Calif.: Presidio, 1988.

Burov, A. V. *Blokada den' za dnem: 22 iiunia 1941 goda–27 ianvaria 1944 goda* [The blockade day by day, 22 June 1941–27 January 1944]. Leningrad: Lenizdat, 1979.

Bychevsky, B. V. *Gorod-front* [City-front]. Moscow: Voenizdat, 1963.

Carell, Paul [Paul Karl Schmidt]. *Hitler Moves East 1941–1943*. Boston: Little, Brown, 1963.

———. *Scorched Earth: The Russian-German War, 1943–1944*. Boston: Little, Brown, 1966.

Cherniavsky, Iu. G. *Voina i prodovol'stvie: Snabzhenie gorodskogo naseleniia v Velikoi Otechestvennoi voiny 1941–1945 gg.* [War and production: The supply of the urban population in the Great Patriotic War 1941–1945]. Moscow: Nauka, 1964.

Cherokov, V. S. *Dlia tebia, Leningrad!* [For you, Leningrad!]. Moscow: Voenizdat, 1978.

Dzeniskevich, A. R., ed. *Leningrad v osade: Sbornik dokumentov o geroicheskoi oborone Leningrada v gody Velikoi Otechestvennoi voiny* [Leningrad in the siege: A collection of documents concerning the heroic defense of Leningrad during the Great Patriotic War]. Saint Petersburg: Liki Rossii, 1995.

Egorov, P. Ia. *Marshal Meretskov*. Moscow: Voenizdat, 1974.

Erickson, John. *The Road to Berlin*. Boulder, Colo.: Westview Press, 1983.

———. *The Road to Stalingrad*. New York: Harper & Row, 1975.

Fediuninsky, I. I. *Podniatye po trevoge* [Raised by the alarm]. Moscow: Voenizdat, 1964.

Fedoruk, A. G., ed. *Na beregakh Volkhova* [On the banks of the Volkhov]. Leningrad: Lenizdat, 1967.

Frolov, V. V., ed. *Trudy gosudarstvennogo muzeia istorii Sankt-Peterburga, vypusk V: Materialy k istorii blokada Leningrada* [Works of the St. Petersburg State Museum of History, issue V: Materials toward a history of the Leningrad blockade]. Saint Petersburg: Gosudarstvennyi muzei istorii, 2000.

Glantz, David M. *Forgotten Battles of the German-Soviet War (1941–1945), volume I: The Summer–Fall Campaign (22 June–4 December 1941)*. Carlisle, Penn.: Self-published, 1999.

———. *Forgotten Battles of the German-Soviet War (1941–1945), volume II: The Winter Campaign (5 December 1941–April 1942)*. Carlisle, Penn: Self-published, 1999.

———. *Forgotten Battles of the German-Soviet War (1941–1945), volume III: The Summer Campaign (12 May–18 November 1942)*. Carlisle, Penn.: Self-published, 1999.

———. *Forgotten Battles of the German-Soviet War (1941–1945), volume IV: The Winter Campaign (19 November 1942–21 March 1943)*. Carlisle, Penn: Self-published, 1999.

———. *Forgotten Battles of the German-Soviet War (1941–1945), volume V, parts 1 and 2: The Summer–Fall Campaign (1 July–31 December 1943)*. Carlisle, Penn: Self-published, 2000.

———. *Atlas of the Battle of Leningrad: Soviet Defense and the Blockade, July 1941–December 1942*. Carlisle, Penn: Self-Published, 2001.

———. *Atlas of the Battle of Leningrad: Breaking the Blockade and Liberation, 1 January 1943–15 July 1944*. Carlisle, Penn: Self-Published, 2001.

Golikov, S. *Vydaiushchiesia pobedy Sovetskoi armii v Velikoi Otechestvennoi voine* [The Soviet Army's outstanding victories in the Great Patriotic War]. Moscow: Gosudarstvennoe izdatel'stvo politicheskoi literatury, 1954.

Goure, Leon. *The Siege of Leningrad*. Stanford, Calif.: Stanford University Press, 1962.

Grechko, A. A., ed. *Istoriia Vtoroi Mirovoi voiny 1939–1945 v dvenadtsati tomakh* [A history of the Second World War 1939–1945 in twelve volumes]. Moscow: Voenizdat, 1973–1982.

———. *Sovetskaia voennaia entsiklopediia v vos'mi tomakh* [Soviet military encyclopedia in eight volumes]. Moscow: Voenizdat, 1976–1980.

Gribkov, A. I., ed. *Istoriia Ordena Lenina Leningradskogo voennogo okruga* [A history of the Order of Lenin Leningrad Military District]. Moscow: Voenizdat, 1974.

"Hanko [Hango]." *Sovetskaia voennaia entsiklopediia* [Soviet military encyclopedia, ed. N. V. Ogarkov, 8: 355–356. Moscow: Voenizdat, 1980.

Heinrici, Gotthardt. *The Campaign in Russia*, Vol. 1. Washington, D.C.: United States Army G-2, 1954. Unpublished National Archives manuscript in German. Unpublished translation by Joseph Welch.

Iarukhov, V. M. *Cherez Nevu (67–ia armiia v boiakh po proryvu blokady Leningrada)* [Across the Neva: The 67th Army in the penetration of the Leningrad blockade]. Moscow: Voenizdat, 1960.

Ivanov, V. P. "Baltiiskii flot." In *Voennaia entsiklopediia v vos'mi tomakh* [Military encyclopedia in eight volumes], ed. I. D. Sergeev, 4: 361. Moscow: Voenizdat, 1997.

Izmailov, A. A., and V. F. Kon'kov. "Nevskaia Dubrovka" In *Sovetskaia voennaia entiklopediia* [Soviet military encyclopedia], ed. N. V. Ogarkov, 4: 565. Moscow: Voenizdat, 1977.

Karasev, A. V. *Leningradtsy v gody blokady 1941–1943* [Leningraders in the years of the blockade 1941–1943]. Moscow: Akademii Nauk SSSR, 1959.

Karpov, V. *Marshal Zhukov: Ego soratniki i protivniki v dni voiny i mir* [Marshal Zhukov: His comrades-in-arms and enemies in war and peace]. Moscow: Voenizdat, 1992.

Kasatonov, V. A., ed. *Krasnoznamennyi Baltiiskii flot v Velikoi Otechestvennoi voine sovetskogo naroda 1941–1945 gg. v chetyrekh knigakh, kniga pervaia: Oborona Pribaltiki i Leningrada 1941–1944 gg.*, [The Red Banner Baltic Fleet in the Great Patriotic War of the Soviet people 1941–1945 in four books, book one: The defense of the Baltic and Leningrad 1941–1944]. Moscow: Nauka, 1990.

———. *Krasnoznamennyi Baltiiskii flot v Velikoi Otechestvennoi voine Sovetskogo naroda 1941–1945 gg. v chetyrekh knigakh, kniga vtoraia: Sniatie blokady Leningrada i osvobozhdenie Pribaltiki 1944–1945 gg.* [The Red Banner Baltic Fleet in the Great Patriotic War of the Soviet people 1941–1945 in four books, book two: The lifting of the Leningrad blockade and the liberation of the Baltic 1944–1945]. Moscow: Nauka, 1991.

Kazakov, K. P. *Ognevoi val nastupleniia* [Offensive barrages]. Moscow: Voenizdat, 1986.

Khorobrykh, A. M. *Glavnyi marshal aviatsii A. A. Novikov* [Chief Marshal of Aviation A. A. Novikov]. Moscow: Voenizdat, 1989.

Kirsanov, N. A. *Po zovu Rodiny: Dobrovol'cheskie formirovaniia Krasnoi Armii v period Velikoi Otechestvennoi voiny* [At the call of the Homeland: Volunteer formations of the Red Army in the Great Patriotic War]. Moscow: Mysl', 1974.

Kolesnik, A. D. *Narodnoe opolchenie gorodov-geroev* [The people's militia of hero cities]. Moscow: Nauka, 1974.

―――. *Opolchenskie formirovaniia Rossiiskoi Federatsii v gody Velikoi Otechest-vennoi voiny* [Militia formations of the Russian Federation in the Great Patriotic War]. Moscow: Nauka, 1988.

Korovnikov, I. T. *Novgorodsko-luzhskaia operatsiia: Nastuplenie voisk 59-i armii (ianvar'-fevral' 1944 g.)* [The Novgorod-Luga operation: The 59th Army's offensive (January–February 1944]. Moscow: Voenizdat, 1960.

Korovnikov, I. T., N. S. Lebedev, and Ia. G. Poliakov. *Na trekh frontakh: Boevoi put' 59-i Armii* [On three fronts: The combat path of the 59th Army]. Moscow: Voenizdat, 1974.

Krinov, Iu. S. *Luzhskii rubezh god 1941-i* [The Luga line 1941]. Leningrad: Lenizdat, 1987.

Krivosheev, G. F., ed. *Grif sekretnosti sniat: Poteri Vooruzhennykh Sil SSSR v voinakh, boevykh deistviiakh i boevykh konfliktakh, Statisticheskoe issledovanie* [The secret classification has been removed: The losses of the Soviet Armed Forces in wars, combat operations, and military conflicts, a statistical study]. Moscow: Voenizdat, 1993.

Krupatkin, B. *Batal'ony idut na shturm: Vospominaniia uchastnika tikhvinskoi operatsii 1941 goda* [Battalions on the assault: The recollections of a participant in the Tikhvin operation 1941]. Leningrad: Lenizdat, 1983.

Kuznetsov, V. A., ed. *Vtoraia udarnaia v bitve za Leningrad* [The 2d Shock in the Battle for Leningrad]. Leningrad: Lenizdat, 1983.

"Ladozhskaia voennaia flotiliia" [The Ladoga Military Flotilla]. In *Voennaia entsiklo-pediia v vos'mi tomakh* [Military encyclopedia in eight volumes], ed. I. D. Sergeev, 4:379–380. Moscow: Voenizdat, 1999.

"Leningrad." In *Sovetskaia voennaia entsiklopediia, tom 4* [Soviet military encyclopedia], ed. N. V. Ogarkov, 4:611. Moscow: Voenizdat, 1977.

"Leningradskii voennyi okrug." In *Sovetskaia voennaia entsiklopediia* [Soviet military encyclopedia], ed. N. V. Ogarkov, 4: 614–616. Moscow: Voenizdat, 1977.

"Leningradskii voennyi okrug." In *Voennaia entsiklopediia v vos'mi tomakh* [Military encyclopedia in eight volumes], ed. I. D. Sergeev, 4: 422–424. Moscow: Voenizdat, 1999.

Luttichau, Charles V. P. von. *The Road to Moscow: The Campaign in Russia 1941.* Washington, D.C.: Office of the Chief of Military History, 1985. Unpublished Center for Military History Project 26-P.

Manstein, Erich von. *Lost Victories.* Chicago: Henry Regnery, 1958.

Maslov, A. A. *Condemned Generals: Soviet Generals Repressed by Stalin during the Great Patriotic War.* London: Frank Cass, forthcoming.

―――. *Fallen Soviet Generals: Soviet General Officers Killed in Battle 1941–1945.* London: Frank Cass, 1998.

Meretskov, K. A. *Na sluzhbe narodu* [Serving the people]. Moscow: Politizdat, 1988. Translated as *Serving the People.* Moscow: Progress, 1971.

Nachal'nyi period Velikoi Otechestvennoi voiny [The initial period of the Great Patriotic War]. Moscow: Voroshilov Academy of the General Staff, 1989.

Oborona Leningrada 1941–1944: Vospominaniia i dnevniki uchastnikov [The defense of Leningrad: Recollections and diaries of participants]. Leningrad: Nauka, 1968.

Orlov, K. A., ed. *Bor'ba za Sovetskuiu Pribaltiku v Velikoi Otechestvennoi voine 1941–1945 v trekh knigakh, kniga pervaia: Pervye gody* [The struggle for the Soviet Baltic region in the Great Patriotic War 1941–1945 in three books, book one: The first years]. Riga: Diesma, 1966.

————. *Bor'ba za Sovetskuiu pribaltiku v Velikoi Otechestvennoi voine 1941–1945 v trekh knigakh, kniga vtoraia: K Baltiiskomu moriu* [The struggle for the Soviet Baltic region in the Great Patriotic War 1941–1945 in three books, book two: To the Baltic Sea]. Riga: Diesma, 1967.

————. *Bor'ba za Sovetskuiu pribaltiku v Velikoi Otechestvennoi voine 1941–1945 v trekh knigakh, kniga tret'ia: Zavershaiushchii etap* [The Struggle for the Soviet Baltic region in the Great Patriotic War 1941–1945 in three books, book three: The final stage]. Riga: Diesma, 1969.

Pavlov, D. V. *Leningrad v blokade (1941)* [Leningrad in the blockade (1941)]. Moscow: Voenizdat, 1958. Translated and published as *Leningrad 1941: The Blockade*. Chicago: University of Chicago Press, 1965.

Petrograd v dni Velikogo Oktiabria [Petrograd during the Great October (revolution)]. Leningrad: Lenizdat, 1967.

Petrov, Iu. P., ed. *Istoriia Velikoi Otechestvennoi voiny Sovetskogo Soiuza 1941–1942 v shesti tomakh* [A History of the Great Patriotic War of the Soviet Union 1941–1945 in six volumes]. Vol. 3. Moscow: Voenizdat, 1961.

Piatkov, V. K., ed. *Tret'ia udarnaia: Boevoi put' 3-i udarnoi armii* [The 3d Shock: The combat path of the 3d Shock Army]. Moscow: Voenizdat, 1976.

Platonov, S. P., ed. *Bitva za Leningrada 1941–1944* [The Battle for Leningrad 1941–1944]. Moscow: Voenizdat, 1964.

Portugal'sky, R. M., and L. A. Zaitsev. *Voennoe iskusstvo sovetskikh voisk v bitve za Leningrad* [The military art of Soviet forces in the battle for Leningrad]. Moscow: Izdanie Akademii, 1989.

Pospelov, P. N., ed. *Istoriia Velikoi Otechestvennoi voiny Sovetskogo Soiuza 1941–1945 v shesti tomakh* [A history of the Great Patriotic War of the Soviet Union 1941–1945 in six volumes]. Moscow: Voenizdat, 1960–1965.

Rodionov, I. N., ed. *Voennaia entsiklopediia v vos'mi tomakh* [A military encyclopedia in eight volumes]. Moscow: Voenizdat, 1997–1999.

Salisbury, Harrison E. *The 900 Days: The Siege of Leningrad*. New York: Harper & Row, 1969.

Samsonov, A. M., ed. *Krasnoznamennyi Baltiiskii flot v Velikoi Otechestvennoi voine 1941–1945* [The Red Banner Baltic Fleet in the Great Patriotic War 1941–1945]. Moscow: Nauka, 1981.

————. *Oborona Leningrada 1941–1944: Vospominaniia i dnevniki uchastnikov* [The defense of Leningrad: Recollections and diaries of participants]. Leningrad: Nauka, 1962.

Seaton, Albert. *The Russo-German War 1941–1945*. New York: Praeger, 1971.

"Small Units Actions during the German Campaign in Russia," Department of the Army Pamphlet No. 20–269. Washington, D.C.: Department of the Army, 1953.

Stupnikov, N. A., ed. *Dvazhdy Krasnoznamennyi Baltiiskii flot* [The Twice Red Banner Baltic Fleet]. Moscow: Voenizdat, 1990.

Sviridov, V. P., V. P. Iakutovich, and V. E. Vasilenko. *Bitva za Leningrad 1941–1944* [The Battle for Leningrad]. Moscow: Lenizdat, 1962.

Tikhvin, god 1941-i: Vospominaniia uchastnikov boev na tikhvinskom i volkhovskom napravleniiakh v oktiabre–dekabre 1941 goda [Tikhvin, 1941: Recollections of participants in combat along the Tikhvin and Volkhov axes in October–December 1941]. Leningrad: Lenizdat, 1974.

Ustinov, D. F., ed. *Istoriia Vtoroi Mirovoi voiny 1939–1945 v dvenadtsaty tomakh* [A history of the Second World War 1939–1945 in twelve volumes]. Vol. 8. Moscow: Voenizdat, 1977.

Vinogradov, I. V. *Trevozhnye dni marta* [The troubled days of March]. Leningrad: Lenizdat,1984.

Volkov, A. A. *Kriticheskii prolog: Nezavershennye frontovye nastupatel'nye operatsii pervykh kampanii Velikoi Otechestvennoi voiny* [Critical prologue: Incomplete *front* offensive operations in the initial campaigns of the Great Patriotic War]. Moscow: Aviar, 1992.

Werth, Alexander. *Leningrad*. London: Hamish Hamilton, 1944.

Wykes, Alan. *The Siege of Leningrad: Epic of a Survival*. New York: Ballantine Books, 1968.

Zakharov, Iu. D. *General armii N. F. Vatutin* [Army General N. F. Vatutin]. Moscow: Voenizdat, 1985.

Zakharov, M. V. *General'nyi shtab v predvoennye gody* [The General Staff in the prewar years]. Moscow: Voenizdat, 1989.

Zherebov, D. K., and I. I. Solomakhin. *Sem' ianvarskikh dnei: Proryv blokady Leningrada 12–18 ianvaria 1943 g.* [Seven days in January: The penetration of the Leningrad blockade, 12–18 January 1943]. Leningrad: Lenizdat, 1987.

Zhilin, P. A., ed. *Na severo-zapadnom fronte 1941–1943* [On the Northwestern Front 1941–1944]. Moscow: Nauka, 1969.

Zhukov, G. K. *Reminiscences and Reflections*. Vol. 1. Moscow: Progress, 1985.

Ziemke, Earl F. *Stalingrad to Berlin: The German Defeat in the East*. Washington, D.C.: Office of the Chief of Military History, United States Army, 1968.

Ziemke, Earl F., and Magna E. Bauer. *Moscow to Stalingrad: Decision in the East*. Washington, D.C.: Office of the Chief of Military History, United States Army, 1987.

Zolotarev, V. A., ed. *Velikaia Otechestvennaia voina 1941–1945: Voenno-istoricheskie ocherki v chetyrekh tomakh* [The Great Patriotic War 1941–1945: Military-historical essays in four volumes]. Moscow: Nauka, 1998–1999.

Zubakov, V. E. *Nevskaia tverdynia: Bitva za Leningrad v gody Velikoi Otechestvennoi voiny (1941–1944)* [The Neva stronghold: The Battle for Leningrad in the Great Patriotic War (1941–1944)]. Moscow: Voenizdat, 1960.

ARTICLES

Aviatsiia i kosmonavtika [Aviation and space], abbreviated as *A&K*.

Kommunist Vooruzhennykh Sil [Communist of the Armed Forces], abbreviated as *KVS*.

Morskoi sbornik [Naval collection], abbreviated as *MS*.

Otechestvennaia istoriia [Patriotic history], abbreviated as *OI*.

Sovetskii voin [Soviet soldier], abbreviated as *SV*.
Voennyi vestnik [Military herald], abbreviated as *VV*.
Voenno-istoricheskii zhurnal [Military-historical journal], abbreviated as *VIZh*.
Voennye znaniia [Military knowledge], abbreviated as *VZ*.
Voprosy istorii [Questions of history], abbreviated as *VI*.

Achkasov, V. "Sryv planov nemetsko-fashistskogo komandovaniia po unichtozheniiu Krasnoznamennogo Baltiiskogo flota" [Disruption of German-fascist command's plans for the destruction of the Red Banner Baltic Fleet]. *VIZh* 1 (January 1964): 36–46.

Babkin, B. "Gladko bylo na bumage: Predvoennye vzgliady na primenenie aviatsii v nachal'nyi period voiny" [It was smooth on paper: Prewar views on the employment of aviation in the initial period of war]. *A&K* 7 (July 1991): 37–38.

Babkin, V. "V boiakh uchilis' pobezhdat'" [They learned to conquer in battle]. *A&K* 8 (August 1991), 40–41.

Bukin. G. "Leningradskaia epopeia v krivom zerkale amerikanskogo istorika" [The Leningrad epic in the distorted mirror of an American historian]. *VIZh* 1 (January 1964): 85–88.

Bychevsky, B. "Pod Leningradom dvadtsat' let nazad" [At Leningrad twenty years ago]. *VIZh* 1 (January 1964): 60–69.

———. "V nachale voiny pod Leningradom" [In the beginning of the war at Leningrad]. *VIZh* 1 (January 1963): 60–69.

———. "V nachale voiny pod Leningradom" [In the beginning of the war at Leningrad]. *VIZh* 2 (February 1963): 60–70.

Chernukhin, V. A. "Na liubanskom napravlenii" [Along the Liuban' axis]. *VIZh* 8 (August 1992): 43–45.

Egorov, P. "Na novgorodsko-luzhskom napravlenii" [Along the Novgorod-Luga axis]. *VIZh* 2 (February 1974): 66–73.

Ermilov, S. K. "Deistviia aviatsii po sryvu operatsii 'Brazil'" [Aviation actions for the disruption of Operation Brazil]. *VIZh* 8 (August 1988): 27–31.

Fedorov, A. G. "Ognennyi taran Mikhaila Krivtsova" [The fiery ram of Mikhail Krivtsov]. *VIZh* 8 (August 1988): 69–57.

Fomichenko, N., and P. Shuktomov. "Kommunisty Leningradskogo fronta v ianvarskoi nastupatel'noi operatsii 1944 goda" [Communists of the Leningrad Front in the January offensive operation of 1944]. *VIZh* 1 (January 1974): 82–86.

Gargarin, Stanislav. "Miasnoi Bor." *KVS* 17 (September 1989): 90–96.

———. "Miasnoi Bor." *KVS* 18 (September 1989): 88–94.

———. "Miasnoi Bor." *KVS* 19 (October 1989): 89–95.

———. "Miasnoi Bor." *KVS* 20 (October 1989): 81–88.

———. "Miasnoi Bor." *Armiia* 23 (December 1991): 73–85.

Gerasimov, P. "Dlia sovetskikh soldat ne bylo nepreodolimykh pregrad" [There were no insurmountable obstacles for Soviet soldiers]. *VIZh* 7 (July 1967): 62–65.

Gladysh, S. "O maloizvestnoi oboronitel'noi operatsii 8-i armii (aprel' 1944 goda)" [Concerning a little-known 8th Army defensive operation (April 1944)]. *VIZh* 8 (August 1977): 28–36.

———. "Upredili protivnika i otstoiali Leningrad: Nastupatel'naia operatsiia voisk Volkhovskogo i Leningradskogo frontov v Iuzhnom Priladozh'e (avgust–sentiabr'

1942 g.)" [They withstood the enemy and defended Leningrad: The Volkhov and Leningrad Fronts' offensive in the region south of Ladoga (August–September 1942)]. *VIZh* 5 (September–October 1998): 12–15.

Gurkin, V. V. "Liudskie poteri Sovetskikh Vooruzhennykh sil v 1941–1945: Novye aspekty" [Personnel losses of the Soviet Armed forces 1941–1945: New aspects]. *VIZh* 2 (March–April 1999): 2–13.

"An interview with Mr. Hyry." In Pasi Kusppamaki, ed., *A Web History of Finland.* Edition 2.3 (2000). Website URL: http://ky.hkkk.fi/~k21206/finhist.html war. Interview URL: http:www.warlinks.com/memories/hyry.htm.

Isaev, S. I. "Vekhi frontovogo puti" [The landmarks of front service]. *VIZh* 10 (October 1991): 23.

Kalutsky, N. "Pervyi boi" [First battle]. *VIZh* 1 (January 1984): 54–60.

Kalutsky, N. V. "Neizvestnaia stranitsa voiny" [An unknown page of the war]. *VIZh* 12 (December 1985): 49–54.

Karasev, A., and V. Koval'chuk. "Bitva za Leningrad" [The battle for Leningrad]. *VIZh* 1 (January 1964): 82–84.

Khoroshilov, G. "Ognem s fronta, atakoi vo flang . . ." [Fire from the front and an attack in the flank . . .]. *VV* 11 (November 1972), 95–97.

Khozin, M. "Ob odnoi maloissledovannoi operatsii" [Concerning one neglected operation]. *VIZh* 2 (February 1966): 35–46.

Khrulev, A. "V bor'be za Leningrad" [In the struggle for Leningrad]. *VIZh* 11 (November 1962): 27–36.

Klimchuk, E. "Vtoraia udarnaia i Vlasov ili pochemu odin predal, a v predateli popala vsia armiia" [The 2d Shock and Vlasov, or Why because of one traitor the blame was laid on the whole army]. *SV* 20 (October 1989): 76–81.

Kolpakov, A. "Tallinnskii perekhod: Uroki i vyvody [The Tallin passage: Lessons and conclusions]. *MS* 8 (August 1991): 42–48.

Komarov, N. "Pobeda pod Leningradom" [Victory at Leningrad]. *KVS* 2 (January 1984): 33–38.

———. "24-ia gvardeiskaia strelkovaia diviziia v siniavinskoi operatsii" [The 24th Guards Rifle Division in the Siniavino operation]. *VIZh* 3 (March 1977): 56–65.

Koshevoi, P. "24-ia gvardeiskaia strelkovaia diviziia v siniavinskoi operatsii" [The 24th Guards Rifle Division in the Siniavino operation]. *VIZh* 4 (April 1977): 50–57.

Kosogorsky, N. "V boiakh pod Tikhvinom" [In the battles at Tikhvin]. *VIZh* 11 (November 1965): 50–54.

Koval'chuk, V. M. "Evakuatsiia naseleniia Leningrada letom 1941 goda" [The evacuation of Leningrad's population in the summer of 1941]. *OI* 3 (May–June 2000): 15–24.

———. "O zhertvakh blokadnogo Leningrada" [Concerning the victims of blockaded Leningrad]. *Voenno-istoricheskii arkhiv* 6 (1999): 108–124.

Kozlov, L. "Sokrushitel'nyi udar po vragu" [A crippling blow against the enemy]. *VIZh* 1 (January 1969): 39–44.

Krikunov, V. P. "V krovavom vikhre" [In a bloody vortex]. *VIZh* 2 (February 1990): 84–86.

Kudriavtsev, G. G. "Krasnyi stiag nad Osmussaarom" [The red banner over Osmussaar]. *VI* 3 (March 1990): 154–162.

Ladesov, V. "O rabote kvartirno-ekspluatatsionnykh organov v usloviiakh blokady Leningrada" [Concerning the work of apartment exploitation organs in the conditions of the Leningrad blockade]. *VIZh* 9 (September 1983): 42–46.

Lesniak, T. "Nekotorye voprosy organizatsii i vedeniia partizanskoi bor'by v pervye mesiatsy voiny" [Some questions regarding the organization and conduct of the partisan struggle in the initial months of the war]. *VIZh* 9 (September 1963): 30–37.

Meretskov, K. "Na iugo-vostochnykh podstupakh k Leningradu" [On the southeastern approaches to Leningrad]. *VIZh* 1 (January 1962): 65–79.

———. "Na volkhovskikh rubezhakh" [In the Volkhov positions]. *VIZh* 1 (January 1965): 54–70.

Mil'chenko, N. "Proval operatsii 'Aisshtoss'" [The failure of Operation *Eisshtross* (Ice Strike)]. *VIZh* 5 (May 1982): 40–47.

Mironov, N. "Proryv ukreplennogo raiona na Karel'skom peresheike" [The penetration of a fortified region on the Karelian Isthmus]. VIZh 6 (June 1974): 10–17.

Novikov, A. "Na dal'nikh iugo-zapadnykh podstupakh k Leningradu" [On the far southwestern approaches to Leningrad]. *VIZh* 1 (January 1969): 61–74.

———. "Na dal'nikh iugo-zapadnykh podstupakh k Leningradu" [On the far southwestern approaches to Leningrad]. *VIZh* 3 (March 1970): 63–72.

———. "Na dal'nikh iugo-zapadnykh podstupakh k Leningradu" [On the far southwestern approaches to Leningrad]. *VIZh* 4 (April 1970): 67–80.

———. "Na Karel'skom peresheike" [On the Karelian Isthmus]. *VIZh* 7 (July 1969): 62–73.

Osadchy, D. I. "S marsha v boi" [From the march into battle]. *VIZh* 6 (June 1988): 52–57.

Pal'chikov, P. "Delo n: 1713" [Affair n. 1713]. VZ 1 (January 1990): 6–7.

Perechnev, Iu. "Operativnoe iskusstvo v operatsii 'Iskra'" [Operational art in Operation Spark]. *VIZh* 1 (January 1983): 13–19.

Petrov, B. N. "Kak byl ostavlen Pskov" [How Pskov was abandoned]. *VIZh* 6 (June 1993): 17–20.

Petrov, B. N. "Voennye deistviia na severo-zapadnom napravlenii v nachal'nyi period voiny" [Combat operations along the northwestern axis in the initial period of war]. *VIZh* 7 (July 1988): 43–51.

Rakitsky, A. "Udar pod Leningradom" [The attack at Leningrad]. *VIZh* 1 (January 1974): 26–36.

Ruban, S. "Tragediia podviga: Liuban', god 1942-i" [The tragedy of a feat: Liuban', 1942]. VZ 2 (February 1993): 12.

Rubtsov, Iu. V., and V. M. Lur'e. "Blokada Leningrada: Vse li zhertvy uchteny?" [The Leningrad blockade: Have all of the victims been counted?]. *VIZh* 3 (May–June 2000): 30–33.

Semenov, V. "Iz opyta organizatsii i vedeniia operatsii na severo-zapadnom napravlenii" [From the experience of organizing and conducting an operation along the northwestern axis]. *VIZh* 9 (September 1967), 40–50.

Shikin, I. "Podvigu zhit' v vekakh!" [May this feat live through the ages]. *VIZh* 12 (December 1971): 52–62.

Sjoblo, Paul. "Finland did not capitulate!" In Pasi Kusppamaki, ed., *A Web History of Finland*. Edition 2.3 (2000). Website URL: http://ky.hkkk.fi/~k21206/finhist.html war. Interview URL: http:www.warlinks.com/memories/hyry.htm.

Utenkov, F. N. "Boevye deistviia chastei 256-i i 372-i strelkovykh divizii v okruzhenii" [The combat operations of the 256th and 372d Rifle Divisions in encirclement]. *VIZh* 2 (February 1988): 76–80.

Vladimirov, B. "140-ia otdel'naia strelkovaia brigada v Liubanskoi operatsii" [The 140th Rifle Brigade in the Liuban' operation]. *VIZh* 12 (December 1968): 84–93.

Volkotrubenko, I. "Obespechenie osazhdennogo Leningrada vooruzheniem I boepripasami" [The provision of besieged Leningrad with weapons and ammunition]. *VIZh* 1 (January 1984): 91–93.

Zaitsev, L., and A. Borshchev, "Taktika nastupatel'nogo boia pri proryve blokady Leningrada" [The tactics of offensive combat during the penetration of the Leningrad blockade]. *VIZh* 1 (January 1983): 20–25.

Zubakov, V. "21-ia armiia v vyborgskoi nastupatel'noi operatsii (10–20 iiunia 1944 g.)" [The 21st Army in the Vyborg offensive operation (10–20 June 1944)]. *VIZh* 6 (June 1971): 23–33.

Index

Abakumov, Colonel D. L., 221–222
Absaliamov, Major General M., 317
Admiralty Fortress, 4, 469
Aerial bombardment of Leningrad,
    German, 128–129, 144–145, 186,
    244, 247–248
Agalatovo, 424
Ainazhi, 371
Air defense (PVO), Soviet
    frontal, 271, 552n.36
    general, 123–124
    Leningrad, 127, 129, 144–145, 155, 235
    Local (MPVO), 128–129, 138–139
    Soviet National (PVO *Strany*), 123
Air defense (PVO) division regions,
    Soviet
    Ladoga, 261
Air defense (PVO) zones, Soviet
    Northern, 14
Air fleets (forces), German
    First, 63, 68, 88, 263, 446
    Second, 88
    Fourth, 87
    Fifth, 446
Air Force, Finnish, 444
Air Force (*Luftwaffe*), German, 29, 73, 82,
    123, 128–129, 175, 244, 555n.46
Air Force (VVS), Red Army
    general, 23–24
Air support, Soviet offensive, 269–270,
    334, 336, 455
Akimov, Lieutenant General S. D., xvii,
    48, 55, 62, 65
Aleksandrov, Major General S. N., 436
Aleksandrovka, 81, 165, 341
Aleksandrovskaia Colony No. 1, 197
Aleksandrovskoe, 197

Alekseev, A. V., 255
Alekseevka, 393, 394
Alexander II, Tsar of Russia, 6
Alferov, Major General I. P., 334, 340,
    343, 355, 373–374, 403, 418, 421,
    423–424, 426, 429–433, 435, 438–
    440, 442, 444, 448, 450–452
All-Russian Congress of Soviets,
    2d, 7
    7th, 8
Andreev, Major General A. I., 99–100,
    104, 315, 333, 338–339, 343, 355,
    373–374, 403
Anisimov, Major General G. I., 334,
    354, 356, 376, 379–380, 382, 391,
    424, 426, 430, 432, 434, 436–437,
    439, 442, 445, 448, 451, 453
Anna, Tsar of Russia, 5
Annenskoe, 223, 225, 263–264, 266
Antitank defense, Soviet, 122–123
Antiufeev, Colonel I. M., 569n.10
Antoniuk, Lieutenant General M. A.,
    xvii, 71
Antonov, Army General A. I., 314, 332,
    364, 371–372, 392, 397, 408–409,
    431, 447, 595n.43
Antrea, 444, 447–448
Antropshino Station, 356
Apraksin Bor, 164
Arbuzovo, 225, 264, 266–267, 296–
    297, 308–309, 311–312
Arefino, 164
Argunov, Major General N. E., 279
Arkhangel'sk, 27, 75, 266
Armed Forces Staff, German (OKW),
    xxiii, 27, 52–53, 59, 66, 86, 349,
    435, 446

617